...And

THOMAS CAPANO:
THE DEADLY SEDUCER

Never Let Her Go

Ann Rule

SIMON & SCHUSTER

SIMON & SCHUSTER
Rockefeller Center
1230 Avenue of the Americas
New York, NY 10020

ISBN 0-684-81048-4

...And Never Let Her Go

Prologue

IT WAS AFTER MIDNIGHT on June 30, 1996, but even so there was a yellow glow behind the sheer curtains framing two small windows on the top floor of 1718 Washington Street in Wilmington, Delaware. That was unusual. The young woman who lived in the third-floor walk-up was known to be an early riser, the first one to arrive at her job, and was almost always in bed well before the eleven-o'clock news flashed on the little television that sat on the radiator near her bed. If the sixty-watt bulbs behind the lacy curtains were whirling red and blue lights, they could not have signaled more alarm to those who knew her patterns.

Silhouettes moved past the windows. There were people in the room, pacing, staring out at the dark street below and the little park beyond, drinking yet another cup of black coffee. Sleep was not an option for any of those who waited there for a knock, a call, anything that might reassure them that the burgeoning dread they felt was only the result of their overactive imaginations.

Fear often begins with the slightest niggle that something taken for granted can no longer be trusted. A slice of a shadow darkens a spot that only a moment before was sunny, and a chill draft destroys what was warm and cozy. What was solid becomes suddenly fragile. It started that way for the brothers, sister, boyfriend, friends, and coworkers of the young woman who lived in that apartment. There

---

* The names of some individuals have been changed. Such names are indicated by an asterisk (*) the first time each appears in the book.

was nothing dramatic to go on. She had failed to return a few phone calls, she wasn't home when her boyfriend had called with a last-minute date idea two nights earlier. But gradually they realized that no one had seen or heard from her for at least forty-eight hours.

Anne Marie Fahey was thirty years old; she wasn't a teenager who had to be checked on. Why, then, did her sister and her friends feel such a sense of urgency? They didn't live in one another's hip pockets, didn't always talk on the phone every day.

Anne Marie—Annie to those close to her—led a busy life, both professionally and socially. She was Delaware governor Thomas Carper's scheduling secretary, responsible for getting him to all manner of appointments and events on time and for providing him with enough security so that she knew he was safe. She was so efficient and dependable that she'd worked for Carper since the time he was a congressman.

Anne Marie had more than a dozen close friends, a devoted family, and after many disappointments, she believed she had finally found the love she had looked for so long. She lived a life so full and complicated that it was akin to constantly juggling myriad balls in the air. Somehow, she managed it.

The day before—Friday—had passed without any real concern, although even Mike Scanlan, the bank executive she told friends she hoped to marry, couldn't seem to catch up with Anne Marie. And he was puzzled and a little hurt when she stood him up for a dinner with her brother Robert's family on Saturday night. He searched his mind for something he might have said to offend her, and couldn't come up with anything. He called Robert to say he hadn't heard from Anne Marie.

Mike—and Robert and his wife, Susan—had tried hard to explain Annie's absence with cautious rationalizations. Maybe she had gotten the date mixed up. Perhaps she had been called away to work late; almost everyone else in the governor's office was working through the night on this last weekend in 1996 that the state legislature was in session.

Those who gathered to wait in the strange quiet of Anne Marie Fahey's little apartment thought of a dozen reasons that would mean she was all right and would be coming home soon. But they all knew better. Annie never stood anyone up. She hated to hurt anyone's feelings. If there was one true thing about her, it was that she tried never to worry or offend anyone. Even if it meant that she herself suffered, she thought always of the other person. If she could see how frightened her sister, her boyfriend, and her friends were now, she would have apologized over and over for scaring them.

ANNE MARIE'S older brother Robert Fahey lived a half hour out of Wilmington. He and Susan had expected Annie and Mike for an early dinner that all of them had looked forward to, but they never arrived, nor did they call. This was so unlike Anne Marie—or Mike for that matter—that Robert and Susan began to worry. When Susan Fahey called her sister-in-law, all she got was an answering machine.

Mike Scanlan was concerned, too. He had surmised that Anne Marie had been home earlier in the day because he'd driven by her apartment and her car was there. And yet she hadn't returned any of his calls. At 9 P.M. Mike called Annie's older sister, Kathleen Fahey-Hosey.

"Michael called me and asked me if I had heard from Anne. I responded no," Kathleen recalled. "As soon as Michael told me they had plans and that Anne Marie didn't show, I knew something was terribly wrong. . . . She was just so happy with Michael—Michael was her future. She would never break plans on her own."

Kathleen told Mike she would call him right back, and then she called her sister's friend Ginny Columbus—who was a coworker at the governor's office—to see if she knew of any plans Annie might have had. Ginny was instantly alarmed, too, and she called Jill Morrison. Ginny and Jill lived closer to Annie's apartment than Kathleen did, so they volunteered to go over and check on her.

When no one answered their knocks at Anne Marie's apartment, the two women asked her landlady, Theresa Oliver, if she had seen her. Theresa hadn't seen Anne Marie for a day or so, but that wasn't particularly unusual. Anne Marie's step was so light that she could come in through the front door and be up the closed-off stairs to her apartment without anyone hearing her. Now, on Saturday night, Theresa walked up to the third floor and found Anne Marie's door locked, with the dead bolt in place. She opened the door and called Anne Marie's name—but there was no answer. Fearing that she was intruding, she walked through the living room to the kitchen, peered in the bedroom, but didn't see Anne Marie.

Jill and Ginny immediately called Kathleen back. "The lights are off, Kathleen, and her door was locked," Ginny said. "Annie's not there—but her car is parked outside."

"OK," Kathleen said, "I'll be right over."

Kathleen then did something that might seem an overreaction; she called the Wilmington Police Department to report Anne Marie as a missing person. The detective on duty told her she would have to come down to the station or call from her sister's apartment. The moment she called Mike Scanlan back, he said he was on his way to pick her up. Both of them felt such a sense of urgency, although they had nothing tangible to go on.

WHEN Kathleen and Mike arrived at Annie's apartment and spoke with Ginny and Jill, they learned that Annie apparently wasn't with anyone they might expect her to be with. With a dull sense of acceptance, they realized that since Thursday night, June 27, Annie hadn't been in any of the places or with any of the people who made up her world as they knew it.

With Kathleen beside her, Theresa Oliver unlocked the dead bolt on the door of Annie's apartment. Kathleen called her name softly. There was no answer.

A gush of fetid air washed over them, and they involuntarily held their breaths against the foul, rancid odor. It was initially indefinable, but then they smelled garbage and something rotting.

Kathleen rushed first toward the bathroom; all she could think of was that Annie had fallen in the shower and hit her head on something. She flung the door open, clicked on the light, and pulled back the curtain. The shower was empty. Everything in the bathroom was spotless. For some reason, she looked for Annie's toothbrush. It was there, where it always was.

Kathleen moved next to the single bedroom. Annie's bed was all white, with a comforter of white-on-white puffed hearts and ruffly white pillow shams. But it wasn't made the way she usually made it. Maybe it was her imagination, but it looked to Kathleen as if two fists had yanked the comforter up and then pushed it flat, leaving two indentations.

The little television set that Kathleen's husband, Patrick Hosey, had given Annie one Christmas sat in its usual spot on the radiator underneath the bedroom window. There was a new air conditioner there, too, and it was turned on. That was why there was such a chill in the apartment on this hot summer night.

Annie's jewelry boxes were lined up on top of the radiator, as always. Her blouses and dresses hung in the closet from hangers that were all pointing the same direction. Most of her shoes were in their original boxes, where she always kept them, but some of the boxes were scattered on the floor now—as if she had been in a hurry to change her shoes and intended to put things back together when she got home.

Anne Marie was the first to admit she was a compulsive neat freak. Her friends teased her and called her Anal Annie when she went through her little rituals. She arranged her CDs alphabetically, stacked her pennies so that Lincoln's profile faced the same way, and made her bed even as she was crawling out of it. She actually folded her soiled laundry, rather than just tossing it in the hamper. Kathleen always smiled at that; her sister did her laundry at Kathleen's house every Wednesday night, and usually had dinner there, too.

The U.S. Open T-shirt Annie had worn when Kathleen saw her last on Wednesday night now lay on the top of the clothes hamper. And there was a long floral-patterned Laura Ashley summer dress folded on a small settee rather than being placed with the rest of the laundry. A small thing, but very unusual for Annie. Kathleen recognized the dress; it was new and one that Anne Marie had bought to wear to the Point-to-Point amateur steeplechase with Mike Scanlan on May 6.

The red oblong box on the floor looked familiar, too. It was from Talbot's, one of the Wilmington area's better women's shops. It hadn't been opened. Kathleen slid the ribbons free, opened the box, and saw that the Talbot's seal still held the layers of tissue inside together. But she knew what the taupe garment beneath was; it was an expensive pantsuit, the same suit she had talked Annie out of buying a week earlier because it cost far too much for her budget. They'd had a little argument about that. When had she gone back to buy it?

There were five people in Anne Marie's apartment: Kathleen, Mike, her friends Jill Morrison and Ginny Columbus, and Ginny's mother, Virginia. They respected Annie's privacy, but they had to look around for some clue to where she might have gone, even as they knew it was an intrusion.

Annie didn't own much, and the furniture she did have was secondhand or the kind of inexpensive stuff that had to be assembled after purchase, but the way she had decorated her place was her and it was charming. There were photographs: family pictures with her brothers and sister one Easter, a candid shot of Anne Marie and Mike taken at her surprise birthday party at Kathleen's in January, and on the wall a picture of their mother, also named Kathleen. There were Annie's scruffy old stuffed animals wearing women's rights buttons, a motley collection of knickknacks that pleased her.

Anne Marie always kept her kitchen almost antiseptically clean. But this was the source of the miasma in her apartment; the whole room smelled of rotting food. The counter was littered with fruit and vegetables long since grown overripe and mushy. The strawberries were brown and had a sickly sweet odor; mushrooms dank as a swamp added to the stench. A garbage can with its plastic liner pulled up was next to the kitchen table, and it, too, was full of decaying food.

Mike shook his head. He knew that Anne Marie hated to keep any garbage in her apartment; when he picked her up for a date, she invariably carried a neat bag of garbage to put in the cans outside. There was no way she would have left her kitchen in this condition.

Looking into the refrigerator, Kathleen found two doggie bags of leftovers from a Philadelphia restaurant, Panorama. The food inside wasn't spoiled, but it looked dry, as if it had been there for a few days at least. Anne Marie wouldn't have left all this food out on the counter. She wouldn't even have kept restaurant food in her refrigerator so long. Kathleen looked at Mike questioningly. Had he and Anne Marie been to this restaurant? He read her mind and shook his head slightly.

Oddly, there were other things on the kitchen counter: prescription medications, sample size, arranged like a row of dominoes; pouches of Rice-A-Roni; pretzels. They hadn't been opened, but they hadn't been put neatly in the cupboards, either.

Perhaps most frightening of all, Anne Marie's purse was there in the kitchen, along with her wallet and all of her credit cards. There was about $40 in bills in the wallet. The day-runner that she used to keep track of all her appointments was also there, but her keys weren't. She kept her house and car keys on a ring attached to a leather pouch that held a little canister of Mace.

There was some unknown component in this puzzle that they couldn't grasp, some missing piece. They questioned one another and themselves, looking for some clue that would reveal Anne Marie's whereabouts. As time went on, their theories grew more outlandish and improbable, anything to make it seem that she was safe. It didn't matter if she had decided to step out of her everyday life without telling them. It didn't even matter if she had run away with no plan to come home again. The only thing that mattered was that they needed to hear from her, because the most terrible emotional anguish known to humans is not knowing.

Surrounded by her things, all the funky, sentimental, humorous, silly possessions that made this apartment so special to Anne Marie, this first real home of her own, it seemed to the people who waited there that at any moment the door downstairs would open and they would hear her voice calling up to them. Their Annie had a lovely pansy-eyed face, but her voice could carry a mile when she chose to shout. She could make people laugh with that voice, a beautiful woman who could bellow like a fishwife and then giggle.

Every creak of the old semidetached house made them hope it was her hand opening the door, her feet on the steps. They felt her essence around them wherever they turned. Annie was the most alive person they knew. And still, the more they willed her to come home, the farther away she seemed to be.

For everything they found that seemed normal and safe, they discovered something else that was totally atypical of Anne Marie. The disorder alone would be anathema to her. Above all else, this told them she was gone. The fact that Anne Marie's green 1995 Volkswagen Jetta was parked in its usual spot across the street frightened them, too. That meant she wasn't off on some errand of her own; she had to be with someone else. But who?

As if there might be some clue there, Kathleen looked to see what CD was in Annie's player. It was one of her sister's favorite singers—Shawn Colvin. Annie loved Shawn's strong, sweet Irish voice and the songs she wrote and performed. She had programmed the CD to play the track with the song "Get Out of the House."

Many of Shawn Colvin's songs spoke to Anne Marie; her lyrics were poems full of longing, lost love, the fear of danger and a need to be at home and safe again. But Anne Marie wasn't home.

At the moment when time becomes important it is relentless and unforgiving, and with each passing moment the fear and apprehension of Anne Marie's family and friends grew more palpable. It was not possible that Annie should have left of her own volition, that she could have gone away without telling any of these people who loved her.

Anne Marie and Mike should have been with Robert and Susan right now, maybe having coffee after dinner, maybe saying good-bye and getting ready to drive back to Wilmington. But instead, Mike was here, as worried as the rest of them. Kathleen knew that Annie was in love with Mike; she would have returned his calls. She would have called all of them back. Annie hadn't returned any of her calls since Thursday afternoon.

KATHLEEN couldn't wait any longer to take action. On Sunday, June 30, 1996, at approximately 12:15 A.M., with the full support of her brother Robert and of Michael Scanlan, the man Anne Marie had only just begun to love, she called again to report to the Wilmington Police Department that Anne Marie Fahey was missing. "I called the police," she said. "The Wilmington city police. I waited for what felt like an eternity, and they didn't come, so I called Ed Freel."

The Freels were almost like family to the Faheys. Ed Freel was the Secretary of State for Governor Carper. Kathleen called him at O'Friel's Pub, an Irish tavern owned and operated by the family. "I told him what was going on, and within a couple of minutes, there were two state policemen here."

Once it was official it seemed all the more terrible.

WHILE they had waited for Anne Marie, for the police, for some word, five of the people who meant the most to Anne Marie forced themselves to believe that she was OK, or even if she wasn't completely OK, that she was alive somewhere. And then they caught their breaths and took back even the thought that she wasn't alive. Annie was too vibrant and beautiful not to be somewhere out there. It was just that they had somehow lost touch with her.

Only those who have suddenly lost their connection to someone they love—not lost to death, simply lost—can begin to understand the agony of this vigil. Anne Marie Fahey was a young woman blessed with fair beauty as natural as a rose. She was the survivor of adversities that would have beaten a lesser woman, and yet still full of hope and, most of all, love. And now, in the first week of the summer that promised to be her happiest, she was inexplicably missing. This was the emptiest and most agonizing conclusion that her family and friends could come to.

And for Kathleen, one of two sisters among the six Fahey siblings, there were questions that returned to haunt her. She had spent the time as she waited for the police looking around the apartment to see if there was a note, maybe something Annie had jotted down in her day-runner, some clue to where she might be. The little blocks in her sister's calendar were mostly filled, but with prosaic notations—birthdays Annie wanted to remember, monthly notations of the anniversary of the day she'd met Mike, baby showers, lunches, some dinner dates. There was nothing there that looked even slightly ominous.

But Kathleen was soon almost as shocked as she was worried. She had found a number of notes and cards in Anne Marie's drawers, and they weren't all from Mike Scanlan. Annie was a sentimental pack rat, and she had saved all manner of sentimental mementos from Mike—ticket stubs from *Tosca* at the Grand Opera House, the

Russian ballet, the Luther Vandross concert—and even souvenirs from the pope's visit to Baltimore. Those were all in the top drawer of her bedroom dresser.

But in the top drawer of a hutch in Annie's living room, Kathleen had found an envelope that read *Anne Marie Fahey,* and beneath that, *Personal and Confidential.* Kathleen opened the envelope and inside was a long and complicated letter from a man who clearly knew her sister very well indeed, a man who appeared to know all of them and seemed intimately acquainted with their family relationships and plans. Scanning the pages was almost like reading a foreign language; this person knew about them and yet he was someone Kathleen barely knew, and not someone she could ever picture in her younger sister's life.

And yet he must be. The first letter ended, "All I want to do is make you happy and be with you. I love you."

That letter wasn't signed, but it didn't really have to be; all the letters and notes in the envelope were written on the letterhead of the law firm of Saul, Ewing, Remick and Saul—FROM THE DESK OF THOMAS J. CAPANO.

Thomas Capano. Kathleen's thoughts flashed back to the previous fall; her friend Bud Freel, who was a Wilmington city councilman, had mentioned something to her about Tom Capano and Anne Marie. He'd heard a rumor that they were dating. It was so preposterous then—and now—that Kathleen had looked at Bud dumbfounded. She had dismissed it from her mind so quickly that there was no time for a solid memory to form. Anne Marie had never talked about Capano to her family. How could she be involved with him and not mention it, when they were all so close? They had banded together when they were only children, the six of them against the world. It was impossible to believe that Annie might have held back such an important secret from her sister and her brothers.

Kathleen had casually asked Annie about Tom Capano, and she had laughed and said they were just friends—that he sometimes stopped by the governor's office on business. That had been enough for Kathleen; she had almost forgotten about their conversation. No, Capano was the last person in the world anyone would have connected to her sister in any significant way.

Kathleen didn't really know Tom Capano well, but she knew him. Everyone in Wilmington, probably everyone in Delaware, did. The whole Capano family was legendary, and Tom was a political power-hitter, wealthy, older, and married. Kathleen had met him sometime in the early eighties when she worked as a waitress and bartender at O'Friel's, through Bud Freel, whom she used to date. Kathleen hadn't seen Tom Capano for a year, and that was at the closing of Bud's other place: Buddy's Bar.

She stared at the letters in her hand. They seemed to suggest that Annie hadn't told her the whole truth about a hidden place in her life. Kathleen knew she had to tell Mike about the letters and notes from Tom Capano. But, first, they had to talk to the police. They had to do everything they could to try to find Annie. Perhaps then, they could sort out the secrets of her life.

IT was sometime after midnight that first night when Colonel Alan Ellingsworth, the superintendent of the Delaware State Police, was notified that one of Governor Carper's secretaries had apparently vanished. Ellingsworth phoned Lieutenant Mark Daniels at home and asked him to respond to 1718 Washington Street to assist the Wilmington Police Department in whatever capacity might be needed.

Daniels was a nineteen-year veteran of the Delaware State Police and was currently the administrative lieutenant in their Criminal Investigative Division in New Castle County. He and DSP officer Steven Montague joined Wilmington detective Robert Donovan at Anne Marie Fahey's apartment.

It was apparent that the missing woman's sister and her friends were terribly worried. Some people vanish on a whim, but this didn't sound like that kind of a disappearance. The investigators listened carefully as Kathleen Fahey-Hosey, Mike Scanlan, Jill Morrison, and the Columbuses reviewed their last contact with Anne Marie. What it came down to was that no one had actually seen or talked to her since Thursday afternoon.

Jill and Ginny said that Anne Marie had worked in the governor's office from 7:30 A.M. to 4:30 P.M. "She had an appointment with her psychiatrist at five," Jill explained. "And she was going to take Friday off."

Jill recalled that Anne Marie had been in good spirits, and was looking forward to Friday. She was going to have a day all to herself, be babied with a pedicure and a manicure, and then take a book to Valley Garden Park and just relax.

If Anne Marie had special plans for Thursday night, none of the witnesses knew about them. Lieutenant Daniels asked if anyone had listened to the messages on Anne Marie's phone.

Jill told him that she and Anne Marie both had Bell Atlantic's

"Answer Call" on their phones that recorded incoming messages. When Kathleen had picked up Annie's phone, she heard a steady beep-beep-beep, and Jill said that meant there were waiting messages.

"I know her code," Jill said. Daniels nodded, and Jill punched in Anne Marie's code so the detectives could listen to incoming messages. Maybe the answer lay there, although it seemed an intrusion, once more, into her privacy—the privacy that meant so much to her.

The outgoing message was so familiar to most of the people in the room. Now, hearing Anne Marie's voice with her lilting greeting made their hearts skip a beat. They listened, wanting to find answers but afraid of what they might hear.

The first four messages had come in before they lost touch with her. The others only confirmed how long she had been gone. They had begun on Thursday night, June 27, 1996.

RECORDER: Fifth saved message.

MICHAEL SCANLAN: Hey, Annie, remember me? I'm going to a little cookout thing for our interns. I'll be home around nine. Give me a holler. I'll talk to you when I get home. Thanks. Bye.

RECORDER: Sixth saved message.

MICHAEL SCANLAN: Hey, Annie, it's almost nine-thirty and a couple of us are headed out to Kid Shelleen's on the way home. I wanted to know if you wanted to step over and join us. I will call you before we head over there and see if you are back.

RECORDER: Seventh saved message.

MICHAEL SCANLAN: Hey, Annie, we're headed over to Kid Shelleen's right now and it's about a quarter to ten, so if you could stop by, that would be awesome. If not, I'll talk to you later. Bye.

RECORDER: Eighth saved message.

MICHAEL SCANLAN: Hi, Annie, this is Mike calling. It's around two-fifteen *[Friday]*. Give me a call. . . . Let me know what you're up to? See ya.

RECORDER: Ninth saved message.

EILEEN WILLIAMS: Hi, Annie. It's Ei. I was just calling. It's Friday around three-thirty. I was calling to see what you were doing tonight. I thought maybe we could get together. Give me a call? Bye.

RECORDER: Tenth saved message.

JILL MORRISON: Hey, girl, give me a call when you get in? I'm at work right now at three after eleven *[Saturday morning]*. I'll probably be here until one, and then I'll be home afterward. I need to ask you a question. Thanks. Bye.

RECORDER: Eleventh saved message.

MICHAEL SCANLAN: Hey, Annie. It's Mike. It's Saturday morning. Give me a call. Bye.

RECORDER: Twelfth saved message.

KATHLEEN FAHEY-HOSEY: Hi, Anne. It's Kathleen. Four o'clock on Saturday. When you come back from Robert and Susan's tonight, please bring the boys' sneakers? I forgot to bring them home today and poor Brendan has no shoes. But hold on. Kevin wants to say Hi. Say Hi—

KEVIN HOSEY *[small voice]*: Bye. Love you.

RECORDER: Thirteenth saved message.

SUSAN FAHEY: Annie, it's me. Calling to talk to you about tonight, but if I missed you, I will just talk to you when you guys come up. It's five o'clock. Five after five. Bye.

RECORDER: Fourteenth saved message.

Click [hang up].

RECORDER: Fifteenth saved message.

GINNY COLUMBUS: Hey, Annie. It's me. I need to talk to you. Please call me as soon as you get this message. *[Gives her number]* Thanks. Bye.

RECORDER: Sixteenth saved message.

SUSAN FAHEY: Annie, it's Saturday at eleven P.M. Give us a call. Bye.

The last call had been only two-and-a-half hours ago. And none of the messages needed explaining to the group listening. "Anne Marie would have called back," Jill said. "She always listened to her messages immediately, and she always called you back."

PART ONE

Pain has an element of blank—
It cannot recollect
When it began—or if there were
A day when it was not.

It has no future but itself—
Its infinite realms contain
Its past—enlightened to perceive
New periods of pain.

EMILY DICKINSON

PART ONE

_____ *Chapter One* _____

WILMINGTON RESIDENTS like to say that everyone who lives there is connected by only *three* degrees of separation, and it's true. If everyone in town doesn't actually know everyone else, they are at least related by marriage, employment, or coincidence. It would seem that keeping a secret in Wilmington would be akin to whispering it to a tabloid reporter, and yet deep and complicated clandestine relationships *have* survived Wilmington's sharpest eyes.

Perhaps because they know one another so well, Wilmingtonians can be initially standoffish to strangers, who don't fit into their grapevine of interconnected relationships. To truly belong, one has to be born and bred in Delaware and stay there until, as the natives say, "Mealey's carries you out." For many neighborhoods, Mealey's is the funeral parlor of choice.

The city's motto is carved into a sign on Delaware Avenue: WEL-COME TO WILMINGTON, A PLACE TO BE SOMEBODY, a slogan that is either wildly ambiguous or optimistic. Wilmington is burnished with its patina of history, rife with somebodies who have made names for themselves.

Wilmington is almost as old as America itself, the largest city in a state so small that it has only three counties, a state 110 miles long and not much more than thirty-five miles across at its widest point. Delaware's land area is 1,982 square miles (compared to Montana's

145,556). But Delaware was the very *first* state to enter the Union—on December 7, 1787—and it was a well-established region by then. It is an insular and even provincial state, fiercely proud. It always has been.

Delaware is a melting pot of cultures and origins, which is fitting for the first state. Sailing under the Dutch flag, Henry Hudson discovered Delaware in 1609, but the Swedes took over, at least temporarily, in 1638. England laid claim to Delaware three decades later and transferred its three counties to William Penn in 1682. Delaware fought as a separate state in the Revolutionary War, and although it was a slave state, it never seceded from the Union in the Civil War. There is, of course, a powerful French influence that permeates the state. In 1802, Eleuthère Irénée du Pont built a little gunpowder mill close by the shores of the Brandywine Creek, planting the first seed of a chemical industrial empire that would define Delaware ever after, bringing it prosperity and security.

Wilmington is a beautiful city, suspended between early-day history and the year 2000. It has block after block of row houses, most of them painted brick, with colorfully contrasting doors. Large private homes are built of brick or stone and wood, with wide porches, and the somewhat narrow streets are shadowy tunnels between grand old trees. The trees and bushes and houses—and even some mammoth rocks—have all been there so long that a feeling of permanence pervades everything.

Situated on Interstate 95 between the metropolises of Philadelphia and Baltimore, Wilmington has the sense of a city far larger than it really is; its population never topped a hundred thousand, and the race riots in 1968 blunted its growth when the national guard occupied the city for nine months. Since then, the population has steadily but inexorably dropped, to under seventy thousand today. The land in Wilmington is divided into both neighborhoods and areas that are almost towns in themselves. There is Brandywine Hundred, Mill Creek Hundred, Christiana Hundred; some say the names come from Revolutionary War days and signify that the regions could be counted on to muster a hundred men to fight. Other natives say it is only a geographical boundary.

Although Dover is the state's capital, Wilmington is its heart and blood supply, laced with waterways—the Delaware River, the Brandywine Creek, the Christina River, and the Red Clay Creek—and dotted with swaths of parkland. Brandywine Creek even divides the strata of society in Wilmington, with everything *west* of the creek north of Wilmington considered far more desirable. This is the Chateau Country where the du Ponts have their estates.

Cemeteries older than memory, with antiquated tombstones, rest where the city has grown around them. Professional offices are located in skyscrapers and in two-hundred-year-old one-story buildings, juxtaposed in the same block.

Wilmington *looks* like a major city. The magnificent Hotel du Pont, called simply "the hotel" by natives, takes up an entire block and challenges any hotel in America for elegance. The wind roars between narrow canyons created by the soaring downtown buildings that have sprung up in the last quarter century, and patriot Caesar Rodney rides forever atop his faithful horse in the square named for him in front of the grand hotel, while horseless and carless residents wait for buses beneath Rodney Square's flowering trees. Across another street, the Daniel Herrmann Courthouse fills its own block. In the late nineties, three major criminal proceedings would draw so many spectators, reporters, and photographers that even that huge courthouse would be crammed to its marble walls.

DESPITE the early Dutch, Swedish, and English settlers, Delaware today has as much Irish and Italian ethnicity as anything else. The tremendous success of the du Ponts opened doors to immigrants looking for a better life, and boom followed boom. The du Ponts (who have since capitalized the *D:* DuPont for the company) kept their workers from feeling the recessions that hit other parts of America. None of their employees had to worry about health care. Until the late 1970s they also owned both of the state's daily newspapers— the *Evening Journal* and the *Morning News.* They founded the Delaware Trust Company and the Wilmington Trust Company, and they controlled high society. It was a cradle-to-grave security blanket. E. I. du Pont de Nemours & Co. was known as "the company," and few Delawareans minded that almost everything stemmed from that source or that the du Ponts controlled where they stood on the economic or social ladder. Membership in the Wilmington Country Club came only with a tap on the shoulder from the company. It remains the most exclusive club in Delaware, and members are held to certain uncompromising standards. One commercial enterprise that came close to DuPont was Bancroft Mills.

Downtown Wilmington was the center of the world for business and shopping, before shopping malls and suburban sprawl took over and left even the grand old Wanamaker's department store an empty shell. After the Second World War, Wilmington changed, along with the rest of the country; cities all over America did. And some families would bloom while others faded.

THE Irish and the Italians contributed greatly to the abundant traditions that make Wilmington such a remarkably alive city, full of celebration and mourning, passion and rumor. The annual St. Anthony's festival in June attracts almost everyone in the city; there they eat meatball sandwiches, sausage and greens, drink beer and wine, listen to music, and catch up with old friends. It is a festival where they can go every year and know they will find people they have lost touch with.

The Friends of Ireland St. Patrick's Day dinner is another big draw, although it's considerably more sedate. In the fifties, Lucy and Walter Brady and their friends wanted to change the stereotyped image of the Irish as mill hands and blue-collar workers who spent St. Patrick's Day sitting in bars and getting drunk. The Bradys initiated the grand St. Patrick's Day dinner, an opulent feast in the Gold Ballroom of the Hotel du Pont. The local Catholic and Episcopal bishops, along with the governor of Delaware, the mayor of Wilmington, and every other important political figure, were present. Dancers from the McAleer School of Irish Dance entertained a crowd dressed in their finest.

One of the couples who faithfully attended the St. Patrick's Day dinner was Robert Fahey and his wife, Kathleen. Ex-mayor Bill McLaughlin, over eighty now, recalled how the Faheys met and fell in love. Sitting on his favorite stool at O'Friel's Pub, McLaughlin smiled as he remembered. "Anne Marie used to say to me, 'If it weren't for you, *I* wouldn't be here now,' and I guess that's true—I introduced her parents.

"Robert Sr. was a handsome young man, a salesman for IBM, as I recall, and he came calling to the DuPont plant in the early fifties," McLaughlin said. "Kathleen was working as a secretary in the chemical division, and he saw her there, and he thought she was the most beautiful girl he'd ever seen. She *was* a very pretty girl. He asked me to introduce him, and I did."

Kathleen's parents were both born in Ireland, and she had a soft brogue herself. It only made her more attractive. She was eight years younger than Robert, who was thirty.

"They got married in about 1953, and they had good years," McLaughlin recalled. "Really good years . . ."

For a while there *were* abundant and happy years. The Faheys bought a new house in McDaniel Crest, a neighborhood close by

State Road 202—the Concord Pike—in north Wilmington. In the postwar building boom, whole streets of houses were sprouting up overnight there on acreage that had long been farmland owned by the Weldin and Talley families. The Faheys' first house was small, a little over sixteen hundred square feet. It was more than adequate at first, but it soon seemed to shrink, as their children came along.

Robert switched to selling insurance. With his natural charm, he could sell anything. Kathleen stayed at home as most young wives did in the fifties. They had six children in a dozen years: Kevin first, in 1954, Mark in 1956, Robert Jr. in 1958, Kathleen in 1960, Brian in 1961, and the baby, Anne Marie Sinead Fahey, in 1966.

"Most of us kids were two years apart," Robert Jr. would remember. "Our house wasn't that big, and it seemed like there was never enough money."

Lucy and Walter Brady, strong proponents of preserving Irish heritage, met the young Fahey family through their friends the Whalens; all of them were interested in honoring their Irish roots, and Robert and Kathleen were enthusiastic about a program Lucy and Walter helped organize to bring Irish schoolteachers to America for a summer's visit. During the hot and humid Delaware summers, Robert and Kathleen opened their home to a number of the teachers from Ireland.

The Faheys had a good time together. They attended church faithfully for twelve years at St. Mary Magdalen Church on Concord Pike, and Kathleen tried to plan picnics and outings, always with a bunch of kids with curly heads bobbing in the backseat. If there was any precursor of trouble, it was Robert's problem with alcohol; if he was not an alcoholic yet, he had most of the danger signs. Kathleen tried to cope with it. At first his drinking didn't interfere with his job or with the family. They loved each other still, and their children were all exceptionally bright and attractive.

The five or more years between her siblings and little Anne Marie—or Annie, as they called her—put them virtually in different generations when they were children. Annie was a beautiful baby with huge blue eyes and a rollicking laugh that seemed too big for such a tiny girl, and her siblings and their friends made a fuss over her because she was the baby, probably the last Fahey baby.

When Anne Marie was born, on January 27, 1966, her mother, Kathleen, was almost thirty-six. The two of them were very close, partly because Kathleen's older five went off to school every day, and she and her baby girl were home together. It was natural that Anne Marie would form a special bond with her mother, even after she too started at Alfred I. du Pont elementary school. They were very much alike, both pretty and full of life and humor, both with a laugh you could hear a block away.

Kathleen was very protective of Annie, maybe because she *was* the baby. She was an exceptionally pretty little girl with her beautiful eyes, a spattering of freckles, and dark golden hair. Brian and Kathleen were ten and eleven, and their mother made them promise to hold Annie's hand on the way home from school—not only across the busy Concord Pike but all the way home. They hated that, but they did it. For extra protection, their mother always let their dog, Butch, out so he could be waiting on the corner to see them home safely.

Rather than say all six of their names when she referred to them, Kathleen had long since divided her children into two groups: Kevin, Robert, and Mark were "the three boys," and Brian, Kathleen, and Annie were "the little ones." Theirs was a safe, warm circle, with their mother the center of their lives; and then everything changed for the Faheys in 1974. Kathleen Fahey became ill with symptoms that seemed innocuous enough at first—but which got steadily worse. Unbelievably, tragically, she was diagnosed with lung cancer. She was just in her early forties, and she still had five children at home to raise. Only Kevin, who was twenty, had left.

Anne Marie was eight, and too young to understand how sick her mother was. She knew that she went to the doctor a lot and sometimes was confined in the hospital for a day or two, but her mother always came home, each time a little thinner and paler. Family and friends helped with meals and took care of the children when Kathleen was too weak to do it. Anne Marie was still cosseted in the bosom of the family she had always known, and she was a happy little girl.

Toward the end, Kathleen Fahey was in the hospital for almost two weeks before she was allowed to come home. And then she lay in bed all day, forcing a smile when her children tiptoed into her room. Of all of them, only Anne Marie seemed unaware that her mother had come home to die. No one realized that their little sister was worrying in silence. She asked her best friend, Beth Barnes, if her mother was going to die, and the two little girls tried to reassure each other that, of course, mothers didn't die and leave their children.

But on the gray day of March 16, 1975, Kathleen Fahey *did* die. Her older daughter and namesake, Kathleen, was fourteen, and would remember that day twenty-four years later: "The day that my mother died, our universe fell out from [under] us."

Anne Marie was two months past her ninth birthday when she lost her mother. Her father didn't want her to see her mother's body being carried from the house, so her uncle James, a Catholic priest, hurriedly took Anne Marie aside and tried to distract her long enough for the hearse from Mealey's to carry her mother away. As a priest, he had spent most of his life comforting the bereaved, but it was a terrible thing for him to accept that his sister, so young, was dead, leaving the little girl behind.

Ann Marie's brother Brian, who was thirteen when their mother died, has always believed that for a long time Anne Marie didn't realize their mother wasn't coming back. As her funeral arrangements were being made, the older children huddled upstairs. "The next day, none of us went to school," Brian said. "But you know, she was outside playing with her friends like it was just a normal day. So I don't think she understood."

Whether she grasped it or not, Anne Marie had just suffered a loss so profound that it would change the course of her life, casting a shadow over a future that had held so much promise. The changes would be subtle at first, at least for a nine-year-old girl, but the pain was already deeply ingrained. When she went back to school, the teacher made an announcement to the class that mortified her: "Anne Marie's lost her mother. Be nice to her."

Beth Barnes, who would remain Anne Marie's best friend for many years, recalled that she didn't want anyone to talk to her about her mother or ask her questions. "I remember how scared she was that we would look at her weird."

Jennifer Bartels was in Anne Marie's class, too, and she and Beth tried to make things better for her. Like Beth, Jennifer would always be in Anne Marie's life and always be her friend.

All of the Fahey children grieved for their mother, then watched their lives metamorphose from a secure middle-class existence to desperate circumstances, in which they would often go hungry. For as long as they could, her sister and brothers tried to keep Anne Marie safe from the bleak realities of their situation. They loved her as siblings, but as time went on, they became almost parent figures, too.

Robert Sr. was bereft without Kathleen. He had lost his anchor, the one person in the world who might have been able to keep him from drinking. The hold alcohol had always had over him grew more tenacious, and he was bitter, sure that life had been so unfair to him that no one could blame him for finding solace in a bottle. He worked less and less; he didn't have the heart to convince other families that they needed to prepare for illness, death, and loss of wages with the judicious choice of life insurance policies, when his own family had been shattered.

The older Fahey children ranged in age from Kevin at twenty-one to Brian at thirteen and they could take care of themselves, although they all were coping with not only the loss of their mother but also the end of their family as they had known it. But Anne Marie was only nine; in a sense, she had lost the most.

With their mother gone, *her* mother, their grandmother Katherine McGettigan, did her best to help. If only she could have, she would have taken them to live with her, but she had been a widow for over twenty years and had to work hard for her own living. She always had. Along with her brothers, James and Jack, Katherine grew up on a hardscrabble farm in Ireland—a place with five horses, a cow, and an acre of land that gave of itself grudgingly. In America, she had gone to work as a maid and a cook.

Katherine lived in Media, Pennsylvania, and she came down to Wilmington once a week to clean and cook for her grandchildren. The Fahey children called her Nan, and less often, Kate. She had worked for some very wealthy families and learned a lot about the niceties of life. She taught Kathleen and Anne Marie how to survive the humid summer nights without air-conditioning by powdering their sheets. Anne Marie faithfully poured talcum powder in her bed, convinced that she really did feel cooler. She would also remember how Nan told her it was important to have a pretty bed, and she dreamed that one day she would have flowered bedspreads and ruffled pillows.

Nan wasn't the cuddly kind of grandmother, and it was just as well. She taught her six grandchildren how to survive in a world where they were virtually on their own. She taught them to be doers who would get out there and make a place for themselves in the world, whatever fate or luck handed them.

"She had great internal strength," Robert Jr. recalled. "She was very shy and very stern, a little like the nuns who were our teachers, but we always knew what to expect from her. We had other adults in our lives who were variable, but Nan was predictable and we could count on her. She taught us a strong work ethic."

In her later years, Katherine McGettigan's job was as a meat wrapper at the A&P supermarket. She was on her feet all day, but the pay was better than she had ever known. Even though she couldn't move the Fahey children into her house in Media, they always knew she was available to them. She had Robert over for dinner every Wednesday night, and Kevin came on Sundays. For lonely boys at college, it meant a lot. Nan made special times for all of her grandchildren, and worried the most about little Annie.

To fill the gaps of what Nan could not do, young Kathleen tried her best to take her mother's place. "I think the tragic loss of our mother brought us closer in a lot of ways, but it was a very turbulent time," she said. "I was fourteen, and I assumed some of the mothering role, and I was ill equipped to handle the responsibility. And there were times that I'm not proud of, but it was just a very difficult time, and I think that anger with the situation we were in— we took it out on each other, because there was no one else around."

Anne Marie would remember that in one tussle with Kathleen, her sister stuck the vacuum cleaner so close to her long wavy hair that the suction drew strands of it painfully into the metal tube and they had a hard time untangling it. It was the kind of thing that happens when siblings get on each other's nerves—only there was nobody there to step in and play referee. There was no one to look after them.

Most of the time, Anne Marie and Kathleen got along as well as any sisters six years apart would; Kathleen called Anne Annie, and Anne Marie called Kathleen Cass or Kate. Sometimes names in the Fahey family could be confusing because so many of their first names had come down from prior generations.

There always seemed to be someone who tried to help the young Faheys, although their new existence was a pale imitation of the home that their mother had made for them. The Irish community included them in many activities. Along with all of her siblings, Anne Marie took Irish dancing lessons, and one of the other families who took lessons, the Mulherns, had seven children. The first summer after her mother died, Anne Marie visited often with the Mulherns.

"She would go over there for maybe five or six days in a row," Brian recalled, "and then come back for a couple, and that went on all summer."

With seven children already running through the house, one lonely little girl didn't make that much difference, and the family's hospitality was a godsend. Even so, Anne Marie must have begun to see the difference between those who had a *real* home and children like herself and her siblings, who lived on the edges of other people's lives.

Things at the Fahey house continued to crumble, despite the efforts of the older children to help out. The McDaniel Crest house was among the first things to go, but with help from friends they moved to a bigger house on Nichols Avenue shortly after their mother died.

There were so many things that a family with six children needed, and they all were determined to get an education. But Robert Sr. had come to a point where he wasn't working at all. Their only real income came from insurance payments and pension plans he had purchased in better days. Those would not last forever.

The mortgage payments were still due every month, and so were other bills, for utilities and groceries and clothing. Robert Fahey seemed simply to have given up. Concerned friends and family members continued to help out, thinking that surely he would get himself together before he lost everything.

_____ *Chapter Two* _____

THE IRISH MIDDLE-CLASS community in Wilmington had burgeoned in the fifties and sixties—as had the Italian. It was a splendid time, with opportunities for everyone willing to grasp them. Robert Fahey Sr. had done well until he was too overwhelmed with grief and the responsibility of six children to reach out. Louis J. Capano Sr. was a few years older than Robert Fahey, a family man too, but fortune had been kinder to him. As the Faheys faltered, the Capanos were thriving.

Louis Capano Sr. was born in a tiny mountain village in Calabria, Italy, in 1923. After his parents emigrated to Delaware in 1930, Louis and his brothers, Frank and Vincent, grew up in a whole new world. Joseph Capano, their father, was a bricklayer, and there was plenty of work for a man with his skills, even in the depths of the Depression. The young Capano family settled in New Castle, a few miles south of Wilmington on the Delaware River. Their relatives the Rizzos had a little construction business there and welcomed them. New Castle is the oldest town in America, where even today the cobbled streets and old houses that seem to lean together for support give the impression of stepping back in time hundreds of years. The Capanos lived, however, in a working-class part of town.

Immigrants from Calabria were sometimes looked down upon by other Italians who had come to America. When they heard that someone was *calabrese,* first-generation Italians from other regions often raised their eyebrows and made the deprecating gesture of a knife across their necks. Calabrese were said to be a hardheaded and stubborn bunch, and some said they were cutthroats. The Capanos, like most Calabrese, were stolid, hardworking, and clannish with family: they ignored the prejudice and set their minds to succeeding in America. Each Capano son chose a trade; Frank became a bricklayer like his father, Vincent a plumber, and Louis a carpenter. Louis was required to serve as an apprentice for four years before he could join the union, and then was hired by the Canterra Construction Company, working long hours summer and winter.

Family lore has it that Louis's first job was to build an outhouse, and that he was proud to do it. He was a short, solidly built man who took great pride in his workmanship. Early on, he was known for his honesty and his desire to do a job to the satisfaction of his foreman—and later, for his own customers. He didn't have a particularly good head for business; he was, instead, an artisan, who loved to see the perfect curve of a banister, the seamless appearance of dovetailed boards.

Louis Capano was still an apprentice carpenter when he met Marguerite Moglioni, the girl who would become his wife. Marguerite's mother, Assunta, had been married to a man named Pacelli first, and divorced—shocking for an Italian Catholic in the twenties—before she married Thomas Moglioni, a stonemason. Thomas accepted Assunta's son, Antony, and they had three children together: Mary, Marguerite, and Renaldo. They lived on Seventh Street near Rodney in Wilmington's Little Italy neighborhood. Thomas Moglioni did a lot of the stonework on St. Anthony's Church, the church that for decades would be central to the Italians who lived in Wilmington.

In the early days, Wilmington's Italian community was almost a city unto itself, and everyone in the neighborhood knew everyone else. A woman who grew up there recalled, "In nice weather, we wandered around the streets—we all did. I lived up on Rodney, and the Moglionis lived down the street. My friend's mother was a nurse and she gave shots to Assunta, so we would go, too. Of course, they spoke mostly Italian, so I never understood what they were saying— but the food was wonderful!"

In those days, children had to be Italian to get into St. Anthony's grade school and St. Anthony of Padua, the high school. And no matter *where* you lived in the city, if you were Italian, you went to Padua.

This was the background that Marguerite and Louis came from, and their values were similar. Their lives were wrapped around St. Anthony's Church, and they expected that they would have to work hard to get anywhere in the world. Marguerite was slender and very pretty, with dark-fringed blue eyes and soft hair that she wore short and feathered around her face. The couple was barely twenty, and poor, when they married. Deeply devout Catholics, they looked forward to having as many children as God sent them.

Their first child was a girl: Marian, born July 29, 1944. She was a pretty little thing with curly dark hair. Five years later came Thomas Joseph—named for his two grandfathers—born October 11, 1949. Louis Jr. was born two years after that, on October 24, 1951, and a year to the day later, Joseph. Although all of the Capano boys had October birthdays, they looked nothing alike, nor were their personalities similar. They were, however, very close to one another.

In the forties, Louis and Marguerite lived on the Du Pont Highway—Route 13. It wasn't a very good neighborhood, but it was what they could afford at the time. When Marian was three, Louis Sr. went into business with Emilio Capaldi. They formed the Consolidated Construction Company and specialized in store and office remodeling and renovations. The men would remain friends for life, a friendship forged working side by side for long hours. Lou Capano was an excellent finish carpenter.

Lou and Marguerite raised their family in the modest little house out on Route 13, and Lou's first office was a small place, but that all changed with the tremendous demand for housing after World War II. Consolidated Construction became Capaldi and Capano, and they began to build homes for the influx of young professionals who flocked to Wilmington to work for the DuPont company. Emilio did the architectural drawings and planned the subdivisions, and Lou oversaw the jobs.

Capaldi and Capano built good, solid houses, and almost overnight new neighborhoods sprang up in the north end of Wilmington. They were all built by the two Italian contractors, but they had English-sounding names like Galewood, Boulder Brook, Canterbury Hills, and Westminster.

Lou had the callused hands and thick forearms of a real builder. There were many who told him he could show a lot more profit if he wasn't so determined to deliver top quality. But at heart he was still a custom builder, an artist with wood and stone. He could not bring himself to cut corners even if he was the only one who would know that the floor joists were close enough together to meet the highest standard or that the studs behind the walls were the best grade.

"I remember seeing Louis Sr. when I was thirteen," a longtime Wilmington resident recalled. "My dad hired him to build our house, and my dad wasn't that easy to please. He'd gone to meet Mr. Capano and the architect. He came home and he said—talking about Mr. Capano—'He's very disarming, isn't he?' and that was my father's way of saying that he was going to hire him.

"Mr. Capano built us this big white house, but there was something my father wanted him to fix—the curve of our stairway wasn't quite right. He came back a couple of times—himself—to be sure it was exactly what my father wanted. I remember Mr. Capano standing in our yard, and he wore a trench coat. And he did have something—this *presence* about him. That house is still in good shape."

Lou continued to strengthen his reputation as a builder to be trusted. The "DuPonters" poured into Wilmington, and they needed more and more houses. Lou's banker summed up why he was so respected: "He was the kind of a builder who didn't play games—he told bankers the truth. If he was having troubles he would tell you. That was a nice thing for a banker, since so many builders tried to hide things and hoped they'd go away. But Lou Capano built the houses too good—and the building business is too cyclical."

Lou made deals worth hundreds of thousands of dollars on a handshake—and he was never known to go back on his word. Any house with his name on it as the builder automatically jumped a few thousand dollars in value. He drove himself, chain-smoking all the time. He expected his boys to work just as hard, and he was a strong patriarch in a typical Italian family. All three sons did their turn with a shovel and pickax working summers for their father. They dug ditches, moved bricks, and drove trucks. Their father wanted them to understand the construction business from the bottom up. Even so, they never knew the hard times that he had. The Capano children grew up in the magnificent gray-stone Colonial mansion Lou built for them on Weldin Road in Brandywine Hundred. It had gabled windows and bay windows, sunrooms, breezeways, and a huge garage. A circular driveway cut a swath through holly, fir, and maple trees, and it was landscaped with shrubs and flowers.

Marguerite moved with seeming ease from the little house to the mansion, although the change was akin to going from a furnished room to a penthouse. She never worked outside the home, and she knew nothing at all about business affairs or keeping books. She was a wife and a mother. But she was a strong woman who felt her husband and children could do no wrong. "She was one tough cookie," a woman who knew her then remarked.

When the boys were elementary school age, Joey Capano once made an anti-Semitic remark to a Jewish boy, and his mother called Marguerite to complain, asking her to intervene and reprimand Joey. Marguerite refused, saying, "Well, my kids get called wops and guineas. He should toughen up."

Lou and Marguerite's boys didn't resemble one another in looks or personality, but Tommy, Louie, and Joey all had dark hair and their father's charisma. Tommy was clearly the most scholastically adept. His sister, Marian, remembered fondly, "I can still picture him reading books at his little desk in his little room." Tommy was also the son who did the dishes and washed the pots and pans without complaint. Louie was charming and funny, and Joey was arguably the best looking and the rowdiest.

The Capanos loved kids, including the neighborhood kids. Whether in the old neighborhood or on Weldin Road, their home was open to children. When the sultry summer months suffused Wilmington with a blanket of heat and even the tomatoes and peppers growing in front yards drooped, anyone who could afford to headed for the ocean beaches on the Delaware coast, or to the little offshore islands of southern New Jersey, which rested in the Atlantic Ocean as if some giant chef had spattered bits of pancake batter on a hot griddle. In Delaware, vacationers called it "going to the beach"; in Jersey, it was "going down the shore."

Marguerite and Lou chose the Jersey shore. It was a two-and-a-half-hour drive from Wilmington across the Delaware River and then through a series of little towns in New Jersey. Lou bought a duplex in Wildwood. They rented out the lower floor and kept the upstairs for family vacations. They took their children, their relatives, and any neighbor child who wanted to go.

"It was a madhouse," a onetime tagalong remembered. "Kids and dogs, sleeping on mattresses, running in and out. It was like the old days on Seventh Street. Marguerite was cooking lots of Italian food, and she waited on everyone. Lou was just sitting there reading the paper as if everybody wasn't running around him. He was very calm, and very kind to all of us."

Marguerite and Lou were almost forty in the summer of 1962, Marian was in college, Tommy was in the eighth grade, Louie in the sixth, and their youngest son, Joey, was ten, when Marguerite found she was pregnant. This baby was a surprise, and somewhat worrisome because she had never had easy pregnancies and she was a decade past her last baby. She was confined to bed throughout this pregnancy, and her boys, especially Tommy, waited on her and did the chores she could not.

But Gerard was born healthy on May 25, 1963, and Marguerite recovered to full health. Still, it was to be a bad year for the family. Lou, only forty, had a serious heart attack and had to stay in bed for weeks. Gerard—Gerry—was taken care of as much by his older brothers, and his sister when she was home, as he was by his parents. Not surprisingly, he was soon spoiled rotten.

"Gerry had these long golden curls," a neighbor remembered, "and no one in his family could bring themselves to cut his hair for years. He really was a beautiful baby and he was hard to resist. Down at the shore the summer he was three, he went around saying to everyone, 'You're a pain in the ass!' and the family all just laughed at him. Nobody scolded him."

Before he went to school, they cut Gerard's long yellow curls, but he would always have a soft, baby face—even as a grown man.

LOU CAPANO recovered from his heart attack and went back to chain-smoking and working long hours as a builder. He and Emilio Capaldi dissolved their partnership, but they remained friends for life. High on Lou's agenda was the education of his sons. His own education had been rudimentary at best, and even when he became a financial success, he was intimidated by men with college degrees. He vowed that his children would go to the best schools, although it was sometimes a financial crunch for him as the real estate market rose and fell.

They all attended Catholic schools, just as the family attended St. Anthony's Church. It was the same church and the same priest, Father Robert Balducelli—Father Roberto—as it had been when Marguerite and Lou were first married; but the Capano sons went to St. Edmond's Academy for Boys during their elementary school years, and from the ninth grade on, Tommy and Louie attended Archmere Academy, a Catholic prep school in Claymont, Delaware, a dozen miles north of Wilmington.

The forty-eight-acre estate that would become Archmere was once home to John J. Raskob, at various times chairman of the board of General Motors, secretary to Pierre S. du Pont, and vice president in charge of finances for the DuPont company. He also built the Empire State Building. He lived at Archmere with his wife, Helen Springer Green, and their twelve children from 1910 until 1931. Not much removed by distance from Seventh Street and Rodney, where the Capanos, Rizzos, Moglionis, and their friends lived, it was like another planet in ambiance. Archmere was plush and private and absolutely perfect.

The twenties were an untroubled decade along the Delaware River; it was *the* place to reside—Scott and Zelda Fitzgerald lived just down the river from the Raskobs, and between one estate or the other, there was a constant flood of famous visitors. But as John Raskob became more well known and word of his wealth spread, he worried. The rest of the nation was caught in the Great Depression and feelings ran high. In 1931, Raskob was gravely concerned when a kidnapping threat to one of his children was conveyed to him. His children meant more to him than his great wealth, and he moved away from Archmere, leaving behind its Italianate Renaissance mansion—the Patio—and Manor Hall, where the servants lived. The Raskobs had their memories of parties, meetings with the Democratic National Committee, and visits from presidential nominee Governor Al Smith, for whom Raskob was campaign manager. When the Lindberghs' baby *was* kidnapped the next March, the Raskobs knew they had done the right thing in moving to a less accessible home.

A year later, the abbot of the Norbertine order of Catholic priests purchased Archmere for $300,000 and opened a boys' prep school with an enrollment of twenty-two students. Archmere expanded its student body and built more and more buildings, always adhering to its motto, *Pietate et Scientia* (By Holiness and Knowledge).

And so in the sixties the sons of a once-poor carpenter attended Archmere. Tommy was not only a superior student, he was student council president and a star on Archmere's football team. He was undeniably his parents' favorite child, quiet and conservative like his father, hardworking, and disciplined. Father Thomas A. Hagendorf, one of his teachers at Archmere Academy, recalled that "Thomas was a shining star."

Tommy always seemed to do everything first—and best—but Louie, two years younger, didn't resent his big brother. Rather, he idolized him. Tommy was good to him, someone he could always go to for advice. They each had distinctive personalities and a different circle of friends. Louie was the charmer who could work a roomful of strangers and leave with a bunch of new friends. He already had the attributes that would one day give him the Midas touch.

The priests at Archmere were nervous about the effect the sixties would have on the adolescent boys they supervised. One head-master wrote with relief, "Through the anxious, emotional, and in-tellectual years of the sixties, Archmere kept to a sane course, adhering to its philosophy of teaching religious, academic, and moral fundamentals, while at the same time improving the quality of its course offerings."

The Capanos had always invited their parish priests, especially their beloved Father Roberto Balducelli, who had been pastor at St. Anthony's for twenty-five years, home for dinner or for weekends at the shore, and the Archmere priests were brought into the family, too.

As always, the boys' friends were welcome in the Capano home. Blair Mahoney, whose father was Dave Mahoney of the Four Aces, the top-ten vocal group whose records swept America in the early to mid-fifties, was one of Tom's best friends. While the Four Aces were traveling the country singing "Tell Me Why" and "Stranger in Par-adise," Blair virtually lived with the Capanos during summers at Wildwood, and in Wilmington, too, when he and Tommy went to Archmere. "Mrs. Capano was like a mother to me," Mahoney re-called. "I wasn't the easiest young man to manage. She did great keeping me in line."

Although Archmere was then strictly a school for young men, coeducational dances were held there, and an invitation to attend was much to be desired by teenage girls in Delaware and New Jer-sey. Tommy was especially close to his cousin Donna, his aunt Mary Rizzo's daughter, and he often invited her and her girlfriends to the Archmere dances. The hall where the dances were held was fairly prosaic and it was the cachet of Archmere that drew them. That, and Tommy Capano.

"He was so handsome then," Donna's friend Emily Hensel re-membered. "He was just about anything a teenaged girl could want—good looking, popular, and a football star. I can close my eyes even today and see Tommy dancing on the floor. For some rea-son, the song I hear in my head when I think of Tommy is 'Time Won't Let Me,' by the Outsiders. It was *his* song—at least in my own memory."

Tommy was always known as the good brother, the dependable brother. Marguerite and Lou were proud of all of their boys, but Tommy was the one they could count on. Marian was in college, studying to be a psychologist, but she was only a girl, after all, and it was to his sons that Lou looked for his immortality.

For some reason, perhaps by their own private agreement, Tommy always drove a black sports car and Louie had a white one.

Everyone who lived in Brandywine Hundred hung out at the Charcoal Pit on the Concord Pike. It was a hamburger joint not unlike any other teenage hangout in America, but the charcoal-grilled burgers and the fancy ice cream floats, and most of all the ambiance, packed it every night and especially on weekends. When the Capano boys drove up in their new cars, young hearts beat a little faster. The Capano brothers cruised the boardwalk and the strip at the shore when the family summered in Wildwood, so tanned and good looking and sure of themselves.

In prep school, Tommy seemed unattainable for most girls. He was polite and friendly enough, but it seemed a given that he would choose a girl that everyone wanted. "I remember him in his black convertible," a Wilmington woman recalled. "He was dating this really rich girl—beautiful, of course—but I can't even remember her name. She lived in a house that was basically Tara, with the white pillars and all. Tommy's car would be parked out in front. I knew then that he was kind of—well, when you were around Tommy, you thought you were in the presence of a god. None of the rest of us could ever hope to actually *date* him."

Tommy Capano was just under six feet tall, not as handsome as Joey or as dynamic as Louie, but he *did* have the full lips and classic nose of an Italian statue. More than that, he was such a nice guy with a wonderful soft voice. "When Tommy talked to you," a woman who met him at a party said, "you had the feeling that you were the only person in the room. He focused *entirely* on you—no eyes darting around the room or over your shoulder."

Even the guys his own age who were jealous of Tommy because of his wealth and popularity, and because his father had bought him a sports car, admitted that he had earned his popularity. No one ever said he was less than kind to everyone. He was the leader, the one who would keep them together for reunions for decades to come. One of Tommy's classmates was a diabetic who sometimes went into a coma. It was Tommy who kept the syringe of insulin just in case, and Tommy who didn't hesitate to use it to bring his friend around.

"You could literally trust him with your life," a man who graduated from Archmere with Tom said. "He was always more mature than we were."

Joey, three years younger than Tommy and a year younger than Louie, attended Brandywine High School rather than Archmere. He was the huskiest of the brothers and the least academically inclined, but he was an outstanding wrestler in high school, competing in the 185-pound class.

During the time that his big brothers were at Archmere and Brandywine High, Gerry Capano was still a little kid, in kindergarten when Tommy was about to graduate from Archmere in 1967. Tommy, Louie, and Joey were like three extra fathers to him, and he adored them. He still got pretty much everything he asked for. Nobody saw any reason not to spoil Gerry.

Tom graduated from Archmere in 1967 and was accepted at Boston College. Louie, graduating in 1970, went to the University of Delaware in Newark. Joey went a year after that. Tom would remember his little brother, Gerry, sitting on his chest and begging him not to go away to college. It was a wrench for him, too; he considered himself as much Gerry's father as Lou was.

_____ *Chapter Three* _____

ROBERT FAHEY SR. failed to get himself together when he was widowed. "After my mom died," Brian remembered, "the family situation deteriorated—slowly at first, but completely after a while. My father eventually stopped working, and he had been a heavy drinker beforehand, but became an even more intense alcoholic."

Fahey's own insurance and pension plans ran out. And the commissions due on policies he had written in the past slowed to a trickle, then stopped completely. The Faheys had done so much to help others before their world collapsed, and now, without asking questions or pointing a finger of blame, friends stepped in and quietly paid their electric and phone bills.

While her five siblings were old enough to work, Anne Marie was not. Providing her with clothing and food was "haphazard," according to Brian. "We tried to look out for each other as best we could. It was complicated. We couldn't go and ask the neighbors for food or money, so we just tried to get by as best we could. We all just sort of hung in there together."

Most teenagers responsible for a nine-year-old could not have managed as well, but all of the Faheys were bright and resourceful, and devoted to family. In time the older brothers and Kathleen moved out, managing to attend college on grants and scholarships, until finally just Brian and Anne Marie were still living with their father. And when he was drunk, they stayed away from him. Anne Marie lost herself in books when she was sick and home from school. Sometimes she wasn't sick but didn't want to go to school, so she hid in the closet.

As young as she was, Anne Marie had a fierce pride. She never wanted anyone to feel sorry for her because she didn't have a mother, or a nice house or new clothes. She developed a persona that hid her insecurities and her sorrows; her laugh boomed louder than ever, and she was clever and full of mischief when she was with her friends. But she always went to *their* homes, because the Fahey children had long understood they couldn't bring friends home.

Anne Marie's home life was unpredictable, to say the least. And like all children of alcoholics, she and her siblings had come to fear their father's sudden outbursts of temper. They learned to absorb his words without really listening or simply to block out his rages, but they didn't want to have their friends know how bad things were.

Sometimes their house was cold because the electricity had been turned off again when the bill wasn't paid. Their father had used the social security checks to buy liquor instead. When there were no lights at home, they would study at friends' homes or at the library. There was often no hot water, and sometimes no water at all, a situation that would last for many months at a time. Once, the Faheys' telephone was cut off for an entire year. Anne Marie took her hot showers at school after gym class, and never told her friends that it was the only way she *could* take a shower. She went to tremendous lengths to appear to be just like the other girls her age. She could not bear to be pitied.

Anne Marie had love—from her siblings, her grandmother Nan, and a few other relatives—but she had little else. Her clothes came through hand-me-downs and a few Christmas presents. Even putting food on their table was problematic for the Fahey children, but somehow they managed. After they were grown, they sometimes wondered how they had done it—but something or someone always came through with clothes or food or a little money.

And they were all workers, just as their grandmother had taught them to be. Everybody but Annie worked at one time or another in the Freel's tavern, O'Friel's Irish Pub. On a busy Saturday night, Robert might be tending bar upstairs, and Brian was the bartender downstairs. Kathleen worked at O'Friel's for nine years. Kevin, the tall redheaded Freel brother, used to tease Anne

Marie, "We'll get you one day, too, Annie. Don't think you'll get away from us!"

She would laugh and say, "I don't work for you, Kevvy." She loved Kevin, and Bud and Ed and Beatrice. And they loved little Annie. She was too young to work then, only in school at Springer Junior High. Even so, she wanted a more exciting job than as a waitress. She had wonderful dreams for her future, and her dreams helped her make it through the present.

When Anne Marie was in the seventh grade, Robert Fahey married again. His new wife, Sylvia Bachmurski, had a son and a daughter by an earlier marriage. And so, in 1980, Anne Marie had a stepmother, and far from resenting her, she was delighted. It was comforting to have a grown woman in the house looking after things, and Anne Marie was so happy when she saw their dining room table covered with a white tablecloth and set with nice dishes and candles. It had been so long since they had eaten at a pleasant table the way other people did.

But her father's second marriage lasted only a few months. Sylvia had believed that Robert Fahey was working, and it was a terrible jolt when she found out he had lied. Too late, she realized that he was a practicing alcoholic and that she had walked all unaware into the chaos and deprivation his children had known for the last few years. She really cared about Brian and Annie, but Sylvia knew she couldn't stay once she found out how things really were. She pulled Annie and Brian aside one day and said, "I'm so sorry—but we're leaving. We just can't stay."

Anne Marie was so sad. Sylvia had assured her she could call to talk, and she did a few times. But she knew Sylvia wouldn't be coming back. The house quickly reverted to the way it had been, with everyone eating wherever they felt like eating, and no more pretty tables or flowers or candles.

In a vain attempt to change her father's downward spiral, Anne Marie hid his bottles and poured his drinks down the drain. She dreaded the sight of him sitting on a chair in the kitchen, drinking the evenings away. She would hide in her room until she heard him stumble off to bed. Her friend Beth Barnes later summed up Anne Marie's ordeal. "Annie's had the shittiest life," she said. "A lot of people who had what she had would fold, but she was strong."

ANNE MARIE could talk to her grandmother and drew a great deal of comfort from that relationship. Later she would write, "She was the most reliable, stable, sober adult person in my life."

She had needed someone like that desperately. She had lost her mother, and her father underwent a complete personality change when he was drunk. Anne Marie was the one who bore the brunt of the rage that swept over him, although both she and Kathleen had come to loathe and fear the man their father became when he was drinking. There was no explaining why he chose Annie to be his verbal punching bag. She was, perhaps, a reminder that he still had responsibilities and he could not simply abandon his life. She was the most vulnerable of his children, and yet she was feisty, too. Although she told herself that the man who shouted insults and obscenities at her wasn't her *real* father, his words did more damage than a physical blow could. He told her she was fat, that her legs were fat, that she was ugly, that no one would ever want such a fat, ugly girl for a wife. Sometimes he called her a slut. Terrible words that evoked terrible feelings.

Sometimes, caught unaware when she heard the front door open and the heavy steps that meant her father was drunk, Anne Marie escaped his vitriol by scrambling under the dining room table to hide. She made herself as small as possible, repeating Hail Marys in her head, praying he wouldn't find her. But he usually did, leaning over and shouting cruel words at her. Her fear as she hid under the furniture may have been the cause of her lifelong claustrophobia. For whatever reason, Ann Marie would grow up with an almost pathological fear of the dark and of closed-in places.

As she grew older and more able to fight back, Anne Marie fended her father off with her hockey stick. She poked it at him, keeping him at bay, threatening to strike him if he didn't go away. Occasionally she got so frustrated and angry with her father that she erupted, totally beyond fear. "If I remember correctly," Kathleen said later, "my father used to take Anne Marie's change, and she got tired of it and chased him around the house with a field hockey stick."

Why Robert Fahey told Annie she was fat and ugly is part of the mystery of the human brain on alcohol. She was neither fat nor ugly. She was growing into a tall, willowy, and transcendentally beautiful young woman. Despite living in an almost Oliver Twistian situation, she was a talented and bright girl, lovely as a flower, with friends, good grades, and hopes for the future. She wore that happy mask when she was at school. All the hurts and pain were hidden behind her laughing facade. She never spoke of the mother she had lost or of how she still grieved for her. She certainly never talked about the father who was as lost to her as her mother was. But at times she saw glimpses of the man her father had been, and in a way, that was even more painful.

At Brandywine High School, Anne Marie turned in her homework promptly, excelled at sports, and went home to a house that continued to disintegrate. Her sister and all of her brothers except Brian had moved out. Separated physically, they grew closer emotionally, while Annie, still living with her father on Nichols Avenue, used up a great deal of energy being afraid and looking for safe niches where she could hide. But even so, at the very center of her, there was a little kernel of self-esteem that would not die. Blighted as it was, the essence of Anne Marie Fahey would not give up. When Brian was home or whenever her other siblings came over, they stood between their Annie and her father's fury. When they weren't there, she managed to survive on her own.

Brian was a freshman in college when the inevitable happened and there *was* no house for them to live in. It had been in the process of foreclosure for a long time and went up for a sheriff's sale in 1980. Their father had long since stopped paying the mortgage, and their home sold for far less than its actual value. Over the years and now in this final eviction, they had lost almost everything of sentimental value. "There are some pictures," Robert Fahey recalled, "but our house was so torn up, there was such chaos, that things that mattered were lost—even my birth certificate."

Anne Marie was almost fifteen and a sophomore at Brandywine when she literally had no home at all. She had done a lot of babysitting for the cousin of one of her girlfriends, and when the woman, whose name was Carol Creighton, found out that the Faheys had lost their house, she told Anne Marie that she could come and live with her. Their father and Brian were moving into a small rental in a city west of Wilmington—Newark, Delaware. She had lost everything else, and Anne Marie wanted desperately to stay in her high school. She talked it over with Nan, who thought that it would be best for Annie to accept Carol's offer, but she cautioned her not to cause Carol any trouble.

As grateful as she was to have someplace to live in Brandywine Hundred, underneath, Anne Marie would always feel that she didn't belong in Carol's home, that she was only an interloper who was living on somebody else's charity. Carol certainly didn't feel that way, and the rest of her extended family considered Anne Marie to be one of them. But Anne Marie herself felt especially guilty about eating Carol's food because she was in no position to buy any groceries herself. She began to worry excessively about leaving her room—or any place in the house—messy. While most teenagers clomp around and leave a path of destruction through a house, Anne Marie tiptoed, figuratively wiping her footprints clean behind her.

She had never been obsessive about neatness or about food before, but now she was. She kept her room spotless so that Carol would never have to clean up after her. And she often left the table while she was still hungry because she didn't want to eat too much of her benefactress's food.

Anne Marie was still playing field hockey and basketball at Brandywine, and Brian often drove from Newark to give her a ride home afterward. He knew how she felt about accepting so much from Carol, and he always made a point of taking his younger sister out to a restaurant so she wouldn't have to eat supper at Carol's house. Although no one picked up on it then, Anne Marie was actually eating less and less, figuring the cost of every bite of food she put into her mouth and trying not to impose on anyone.

She was at the peak of adolescence, at the most vulnerable age a girl can be, and yet Anne Marie was trying to make herself inconspicuous rather than bloom as she deserved. There was no place where she felt she really belonged. She was grateful for everything people did for her, but inside, she must have raged sometimes that she *had* to be grateful. She had no mother, no real father. To make herself less and less of a burden, she ate less and became compulsive about being neat. It was the beginning of a lifelong pattern of behavior.

AROUND Thanksgiving of the year that Anne Marie was a junior at Brandywine, Carol told her that she could no longer put her up. There was no place for her to go but Newark, with her father and her brother Brian. She begged to be allowed to graduate with her class at Brandywine, and they figured out a way. Brian was twenty-one by then and had a car, so he drove her to school in the morning when he could. If he had to be somewhere else, he lent his car to their father and *he* drove Anne Marie to school. Brian was coaching hockey and basketball at the Friends School in Alapocas, and he would pick his sister up when he was through for the day.

Anne Marie got a job waitressing at the Charcoal Pit to help pay expenses. She could not even begin to afford the clothes that most of the girls in Brandywine Hundred wore, but she took scrupulous care of the clothes she had. With her salary and tips, she paid her own way as much as she could.

The logistics of seeing that his sister got safely to school, to work, and back home were difficult for Brian—but it was worth it. Anne Marie stayed with him and their father until June of her junior year at Brandywine. She had only one year to go when her brothers Kevin and Robert told her she could have a home with them. They'd bought a house together near Salesianum School, and they had a bedroom for Anne Marie. Best of all, it was close to Brandywine High. For her senior year in high school, she had someplace she could count on. She still played field hockey, and her coach was a friend of Brian's. Brian came out to most of Anne Marie's games.

The love that Anne Marie's siblings demonstrated for her was a testimony to how well Robert and Kathleen had parented the older children. When Kathleen died, their world evaporated, but the family they had created stayed remarkably cohesive. By sheer force of will, Anne Marie's brothers and sister would see her through to adulthood.

Anne Marie herself was determined to go to college. During this time, her father rallied and helped her find financial aid and college loans. Brian was pleased to see his father filling out the complicated financial aid forms so Anne Marie would get her wish.

When she graduated from Brandywine High School in 1984, Anne Marie was headed for Wesley College in Dover. Even with student loans, though, she would have to work. She quickly found a job as a waitress. All the Fahey kids were making it. By giving each other hands up, they had climbed out of the bad times on Nichols Avenue. Getting Anne Marie through high school and into college was a major accomplishment—not only for her, but also for her siblings.

Chapter Four

WHILE THE FAHEYS gritted their teeth and made it through a tough decade, everything the Capanos touched turned to gold, although it was dicey from time to time.

In 1970, with a great deal of trepidation, Louis Sr. decided to diversify his company; he had been building luxury homes, but the bottom was falling out of that market. People were looking for apartments within easy commuting distance of Wilmington. Lou bought land along I-95 and planned to build a large apartment complex there. He wanted to have a steady cash flow that he could count on when he retired, but the project meant borrowing more money than he had ever imagined.

The Cavalier Country Club complex was the biggest construction venture ever attempted by a builder in Delaware. There would be nine hundred units, apartments first and then ninety-six town houses to be sold outright. Louis Jr. was all for diving into real estate in a big way; he had a gift for it. He was attending the University of Delaware when his father got involved with Cavalier. Tom was far away at college in Boston and wasn't interested in the construction business, anyway.

The Cavalier project got under way, but when Lou Capano had to borrow money from his friends to make his first payment on the huge loan, he had visions of everything he'd worked for going down the drain. A project full of houses was one thing; nine hundred apartment units was a concept almost too big for him to grasp. "We really struggled," young Lou recalled. "We scraped for every last dime."

In 1972, when Louie was a senior in college, he realized that his father couldn't afford to pay real estate commissions. He needed an agent who would work for free. Louie quit college, got a real estate license so he could start selling the town houses, and jumped in to help his father. Lou Capano had invested in sons as well as real estate, and Louie had come through for him.

Slowly, the Cavalier project began to generate cash, and then, with Louie's natural gift for real estate, their fortunes grew exponentially. They had pulled off an almost impossible venture, son and father standing shoulder to shoulder. Joey dropped out of college, too, and Louis Capano & Sons, Inc., was in full swing.

They bought the Branmar Plaza, a big moneymaker in Brandywine Hundred, and the Midway Shopping Center in Milltown. It both impressed and alarmed Lou to watch his son seek out property. "My father was the kind of guy who said, 'OK, fine. Take over the whole thing,' " Louie recalled. "He really didn't like the financial end of things. He let me do whatever I wanted. I was buying and selling land—my father *never* bought land he didn't develop."

Lou still believed that a real builder turned his hand to fine houses. He bought a chunk of oceanfront property from the Catholic church in Stone Harbor, New Jersey, on the south end of Seven Mile Beach. Stone Harbor had a lot more cachet than Wildwood and was slated to be decidedly upscale. Villa Maria by the Sea, a nuns' retreat, abutted Lou's Stone Harbor lot. Villa Maria was a big white barn of a place with wide lawns.

Development in Stone Harbor hadn't even begun until 1970, and it was carefully planned, with wide streets and ordinances that would control future construction. Lou built a beach house in Stone Harbor for his family, and it demonstrated his vision. It was far more than a beach house; it dwarfed even the Weldin Road house. It rose majestically from the white sand and sea grasses and was over five thousand square feet, its oblique angles stained a rich brown, with skylights and walls of windows that faced only the sea beyond. The Stone Harbor place was more than a decade ahead of its time. When Lou built it, it sat alone on the beach, with an unobstructed view across the dunes to the endless expanse of the Atlantic Ocean.

There would be no more sleeping on mattresses on the floor. The Capanos all had their own rooms, and so did visitors, and their own access to a private beach. They swam and turned mahogany in the sun while Marguerite cooked pots of spaghetti or *pasta e fagioli* in her modern yellow-and-white kitchen. They still drank the strong red wine that Lou and the boys made: *dago red*. They called it that, too.

Lou Capano had come such a long way from the seven-year-old Calabrese immigrant in New Castle. Almost single-handedly he had built most of north Wilmington. He could drive down street after street and see the fine houses with his stamp on them. He had honored his family with short streets named for them. There were streets named Thomas, Louis, and Joseph, but there were also streets in Weldin Farms surely meant to commemorate the birth of his youngest son: one cul-de-sac called Gerard Circle, and the next, Capano Court. It was a small vanity for a man so down-to-earth.

Lou had given his family a mansion in the city and a paradise on the Atlantic Ocean, but still he always felt humble next to someone who had a formal education. And he had dreams for his children; he had meant for them all to go to college, and he would be the proudest man in Wilmington. Louie had proven that he didn't need a degree to carve the Capano name in Delaware real estate history. And Joey was in the business, too. But Thomas—Thomas was the scholar.

Someday his boys would take over Louis Capano & Sons, Inc., and maybe he and Marguerite would retire and live on the beach, welcoming grandchildren and watching the sea roll in.

Tom had graduated from Archmere in 1967 and been accepted at Boston College. There he met Kay Ryan, a pretty, half-Irish, half-

Italian nursing student who was a year younger. She was a sweet-tempered, capable girl from Connecticut, who would graduate in 1973. Kay came from a family of five children, and she had a twin sister. Her dad was a classic Irishman, ruddy and hearty, and Tom was so different, quietly brilliant, capable, and thoughtful so much of the time. Even though he spoke in a gentle voice, there was something compelling about him. Kay was a good foil to Tom. While he was sometimes moody, she was steady and a natural caretaker. They dated all through college. "I decided to go to law school at Boston College because of Kay," Tom remembered. "I had graduated, but she had another year to go."

Kay and Tom were married in Fairfield, Connecticut, at high noon on June 17, 1972. Tom always said it was easy to remember his wedding day because it was the same day as the Watergate burglary. When she graduated, Kay found a job as a public health nurse. Her work took her to some of the shabbier and more dangerous streets in Boston, but she enjoyed it. Kay didn't have to work—Lou and Marguerite supported the young couple and paid Tom's tuition—but she *wanted* to work and she loved her job.

When Tom graduated from law school in 1974, his father was so proud that he cried. His oldest son was a lawyer! It was the realization of all of his dreams.

Kay and Tom Capano moved back to Wilmington after he graduated, but he didn't look for a job right away. He studied that summer of 1974 for the Delaware bar exam. The young couple lived in a town house near Newark, Delaware, one of the ninety-six similar units in the huge Cavalier Country Club complex that Louie, Joey, and their father had built while Tom was in college in Boston.

Kay went to work immediately as a public health nurse, although Tom complained that he worried about her in the meaner neighborhoods of Philadelphia. He told people that he would have actually preferred that she not work at all. There was no need—his parents would take care of them until he was established.

In the fall, Kay enrolled at the University of Pennsylvania to work toward her master's degree. She was a natural caregiver and saw no point in studying so long to be a nurse and then never practicing her profession. Kay hadn't become pregnant in their more than two years of marriage and they were both a little disappointed about that, but not truly worried.

Marguerite approved of Kay as a daughter-in-law. She had seen how all of her sons had their eyes out for women, and there were any number of females she would not have chosen to join the Capano family. Kay Ryan Capano was pretty, smart, and strong—but not at all pushy. She adored Tom and waited on him hand and foot, just as Marguerite had always done.

July 4 was the official day for the Capanos to start the summer season at the shore. They always had a big party with fireworks. This year was no different, but now Tom and Kay were back in Wilmington with the family again. Tom studied for the bar exam all summer and he passed, but in Delaware, that didn't mean he was officially an attorney; he still had to serve six months as a clerk. After his apprenticeship in a law firm, Tom's first job as a lawyer was with the Public Defender's Office. He enjoyed it; he had always been more interested in public service than in high-powered business. There, he and Louie—and even Joey—seemed to differ. For a year, Tom defended the indigent. It didn't matter to his father where he worked; it was enough that his oldest son was officially a lawyer. He was very, very proud to be able to say, "My son the lawyer."

Tom moved from working as a defense attorney to being a prosecutor. For the next two years he was a prosecuting attorney for the Delaware Attorney General's Office, assigned to New Castle County and working in Wilmington. He hadn't made much money as a public defender, and he made exactly the same as a prosecutor, but he was excellent in his prosecutorial role and he was very popular around the courthouse.

One of the cases Tom successfully prosecuted was a murder charge against a man named Squeaky Saunders, convicted in the shooting death of an associate. Squeaky, a habitual offender, had shot one of his cohorts in the head, and then ordered the two men with him to fire into the body, too—so that they wouldn't be inclined to tell. They attempted to dump the body in the Delaware River, where it would eventually drift to the Delaware Bay and then into the seemingly bottomless depths of the Atlantic Ocean. Squeaky's plan went awry early on when the body was caught in some sluice gates and was recovered with an obvious bullet wound in the skull that made authorities dismiss the possibility of accidental drowning.

Tom studied autopsy reports that showed the path of the fatal bullet, the entrance and exit wounds. Although he had no plans to choose criminal law as his ultimate goal, he was, for the moment, caught up in the intricacies of his first murder case. With his coprosecutor, George "Butch" Seitz, Tom presented a case that sent Squeaky to Gander Hill Prison for a long time. Squeaky always claimed misconduct on the part of the investigating officers, but that was a common complaint among convicted felons.

Tom still had the natural ease with everyone he met that made them all feel special, that he was truly focusing on them. "He had a God-given *knack* for friendship," one court reporter recalled. "It seemed to come so easily to him to treat people kindly, and everyone really liked him." He was friendly with everyone and it didn't matter if it was a judge, a court reporter, or a janitor. Women around the courthouse were captivated by his sex appeal and by his voice. "He was *not* soft-spoken," one woman who'd worked two decades in the courthouse said. "Tom was gentle voiced, and there's a difference. Some people call it charisma, but he had something more than that."

Tom remained the "good" son, and Marguerite and Lou sometimes compared his steady dependability with Louie and Joey's more flamboyant style. Even so, all three of their older boys were considered the good Capanos, as opposed to the "bad" Capanos—some of Lou's brothers' boys had gotten into scrapes with the law, and that made Lou and Marguerite just a little smug about their sons. They never looked down on their nephews, but they were aware that people around Wilmington made a distinction between the various family units.

Family was family, however, and they all stuck together against outsiders who might snipe at any of the Capanos who had come from Calabria almost fifty years earlier to settle in New Castle. Lou always found jobs in his construction business for his relatives.

By bringing Louie into the Cavalier project, Lou Capano had assured not only his fortune, but a fortune for all of them. When that enterprise boomed the way it did, he knew he would never have to worry about having an income in his old age; with apartment houses and malls and whatever Louie visualized next, the Capanos were unbeatable. But even though Louie had brought that about, Tom was still the golden son. It was a fact that they all appeared to accept; there was no overt jealousy among the brothers, and probably no jealousy at all. There was so much to go around, so much of everything: money, love, social standing, and wonderful houses.

In addition to the place he built at the shore in Stone Harbor, New Jersey, Lou decided they needed another vacation spot. Delaware could be bitterly cold in the winter, so he bought a place in Boca Raton, Florida, that they could all share. Boca Raton, which means "the mouth of the rat" in Spanish despite its exotic soft sound, drew some of the richest tourists in America.

Marguerite and Lou had always been supportive of St. Anthony's Catholic Church and they helped Father Roberto Balducelli as much as they could. Father Roberto had always been tremendously impressed that their young son would be so concerned with the less fortunate. The priest felt that the church needed a center for its social work, and he approached church members to serve on the board of St. Anthony's Community Center. Tom joined the board of directors and often stayed after the meetings to talk with Father Roberto. He was very much interested in the welfare of children, and supported Father Roberto's project to provide a summer camp for children of the inner city. The camp, located close to the Delaware-Pennsylvania border, was called St. Anthony's of the Hills and was built against the better judgment of many parishioners, who believed it meant too much debt for the church to take on. But Tom welcomed the controversy, and he donated his time and his money generously to the church.

AFTER two years as a deputy attorney general, Tom decided to take a job in the private sector. Although he figured he could never hope to equal his brothers' income, he needed more money. "I really liked those jobs," he recalled. "I liked being in the courthouse . . . but I knew I couldn't do it for a career. I was recruited by a law firm here in Wilmington."

Tom's new position with Morris, James, Hitchens & Williams didn't pay appreciably more than his state job at first—but there was great opportunity for advancement. After a year and a half, his salary would increase. It was a general law firm—nothing exciting or particularly challenging—but a good solid spot for a young family man. Now, with his new prospects, he could afford to buy a house.

Tom and Kay Capano wanted very much to have children, but after five years of marriage, Kay still had not become pregnant. All around them, other couples were having children so easily, but they weren't. They talked with Father Roberto and decided to apply to adopt a baby through Catholic Children's Services.

Knowing that they *would* have children—one way or another—Tom and Kay went house hunting. They finally settled on a home that would have enough room for a dozen children; the Catholic diocese was selling the place that had been a residence for a succession of local bishops. The huge white stucco house on the corner of Seventeenth and Greenhill covered over half a city block with all its additions and annexes. Built in 1920, it had many large formal rooms and reception areas. Although the bishops had not served liquor, there was a grand bar area. The basement recreation room was all done in the finest woods, fitted out by a cabinetmaker.

The lot was 18,740 square feet, and it would only go up in value because it was in a good neighborhood near parks and schools. Although almost everyone else in the family was living in a Capano-built home, Kay and Tom decided to buy the house in August of 1978. It *was* a good investment; ten years later, it would have an assessed value many times what they had paid. Their contemporaries had homes with three bedrooms, a bath and a half, and a recreation room with a vinyl floor and plywood-paneled walls. Tom and Kay had a house that could easily have held two or three of their friends' places.

Tom moved steadily up through the ranks at Morris, James, Hitchens & Williams, his salary now far more than he had ever made as a prosecutor. He and Kay had a circle of friends—other young lawyers and their wives at Morris, James. He kept his friends from the courthouse. They went to the shore in the summer and to Boca Raton in the winter.

Although Tom was invariably friendly, one young attorney would recall that he could be a little stodgy and more than a little stubborn if he didn't get his own way. Several couples had driven down to Boca Raton during spring break week, and everyone thought it would be fun to go for dinner at one of the spots where the college kids were welcome. Not Tom. He suggested that they go to one of the most expensive restaurants in Boca, which was very formal and had many-course gourmet meals.

"We all wanted to wear shorts and T-shirts, and Tom got all dressed up," the attorney said. "We asked Kay what she wanted to do, and she just looked down at the ground—it was clear that Tom made the decisions."

At length, the vote among the group was to go to the casual hangout. "Tom wouldn't get out of the car. He just sat there. When we finally got him to come in, he stood at the end of the bar with a poker face and brought everybody down."

It was only one night, but it was a look into another side of Tom Capano. When he got his way, he was absolutely wonderful to be around. When he didn't, he could be coldly furious.

At Christmas 1979, Kay and Tom had exciting news to share with the family. There would be no need now to arrange for an adoption through Catholic Children's Services; Kay was pregnant, due in August.

Maybe life was too good. In 1980, Marian was thirty-five. Tom, Louie, and Joey were thirty, twenty-eight, and twenty-seven, respectively. Gerry was going on seventeen. Aside from some broken marriages, the "good" Capanos had had a remarkably smooth life. But on the bright edge of spring, they suffered a loss from which they would never recover. It was February 28, 1980, and Louie and his father were working together when Lou suffered a massive heart attack and died. He was fifty-seven years old.

Thousands of people came to pay their last respects to Louis J. Capano Sr. as his funeral services were held at McCrery's Funeral Home on Concord Pike. They were people who lived in the homes he'd built, worked for him, went to church with him, or just had heard of his reputation as a humble, hardworking Italian immigrant who had made his fortune in America—while still keeping his humanity and honesty. It was the end of an era, more than anyone could realize then. Tom asked that in lieu of flowers, donations be made in his father's memory to St. Anthony's of the Hills summer camp. And the money poured in.

Marguerite Capano was totally unprepared to lose her husband and hadn't the slightest idea how to manage her life without him. She was certainly too devastated even to begin to cope with a teenage son, and Gerry wasn't nearly as easy to raise as his three older brothers.

Tom stepped in and took over all of her bookkeeping and household worries; he was there every day for his mother, paying her bills, explaining the will, handling everything that his father once did. Marguerite didn't know what she would ever have done without him. She was fifty-seven, rattling around in a house that was suddenly far too big, and trying to raise Gerry without his father.

Louie and Joey were there to run the business, and Tom was there for his mother. Among them, they rode herd on their baby brother. Somehow they would all have to find a way to go on without the driving force in their lives.

Kay never resented all the time Tom spent with his mother. She was a strong woman who could take care of herself even though she was pregnant, keep on with her job as a nurse-practitioner, and comfort Marguerite, too. If Kay had any weaknesses, there was only one.

And that was her husband. Her world turned around Tom.

In August 1980, Kay gave Tom his first child, a little girl they named Christy. The baby made up for a lot of pain that everyone in the Capano family had felt that year.

_____ *Chapter Five* _____

THE CAPANOS were nouveaux riches in Wilmington, and they had ridden high on the wave of postwar building for the DuPonters. Although they were shattered by losing their patriarch, there was little chance they would ever be poor again.

The MacIntyres were old money, entrenched in Wilmington society for fifty years through their association with an industrial giant almost as old and important as DuPont. Bancroft Mills, more formally known as Joseph Bancroft and Sons, was established in 1831—108 years before Joseph Capano emigrated to Delaware with his wife and three sons. Bancroft Mills was American history, a fledgling cotton mill on the banks of Brandywine Creek, with Joseph Bancroft working his crew and his family seventy hours a week, enduring floods and hardship while still building a business that would survive more than a century.

In 1931, a hundred years after Bancroft started his mill, William Ralph MacIntyre became the first non-Bancroft to serve as president of the company, and he ran the company during its boom years, when it had trademarked a miracle formula known as Ban-Lon. Highly thought of in the company and in Wilmington, MacIntyre would work for Bancroft for forty-seven years, and his son, Bill, would join him in the upper echelons of Bancroft management.

Bill and his bride, Sheila, had a wonderful future ahead when they married in St. Ann's in Wilmington, just after World War II; they had each come from prominent families. Sheila Miller's father was an attorney who worked for the DuPont company, and an uncle, Don Miller, was one of the Four Horsemen, the legendary backfield that played football under Knute Rockne at Notre Dame in 1924. Sheila's brothers, Tom and Creighton, also played for Notre Dame. Both Bill MacIntyre and Sheila Miller were well placed in Delaware society, and they married for love.

But despite their high hopes going into it, this was to be a blighted marriage. Sheila was so fragile emotionally that she was incapable of being either a wife or a mother. Despite the wealth and privilege the MacIntyres enjoyed, her illness cast a pall over many generations of the family.

Deborah MacIntyre, Sheila and Bill's second daughter, always longed for a secure family life—and never found it. She would fill the walls of her homes with photographs of Millers and MacIntyres.

One particularly poignant picture shows Sheila at the age of eight in the early thirties, posing with what appears to be her perfect family. Harry and Mary Cecilia Duffy Miller and their children sat self-consciously on lawn chairs on a sweep of manicured grass. Within a year, the young woman with the marcelled bob would be dead, and Sheila left without a mother, a loss magnified by the fact that she was never allowed to grieve for her mother: child psychology of the era dictated that children must simply go on and not dwell on sadness. Indeed, Sheila did bottle up her tears and her questions, and it well nigh destroyed any hope that she would ever be able to cope with the world.

Catholic, Sheila and Bill MacIntyre had three children in just a little over two years; she was twenty-four and hadn't been able to care for even *one* baby confidently. In the winter of 1953, Mary Louise was three and a half, Debby was two and a half, and their little brother, Ralph, was barely one when Sheila had a complete nervous breakdown.

"That was the end of my having a mother," Debby MacIntyre recalled forty-five years later, the loss still caught somewhere in her voice. "I was abandoned. We were all abandoned. There was money—that's what saved us—but money doesn't make up for not having a mother. We lived with my father's parents for a year. My mother was in the Pennsylvania Psychiatric Hospital for six months."

When Sheila was released from the hospital, Bill bought a little white house on Woodlawn Avenue, four doors down from his parents' much larger home just off the Bancroft Parkway. The children stayed with their grandparents, while Bill and Sheila lived together for six months. They could *visit* their mother, but Debby and her brother and sister made Sheila too nervous for them all to live together. The elder MacIntyres were there to give them some semblance of a serene home. Eventually, the children did move back in with their parents, but it was never to be a normal home. Sheila never spoke of her own mother to her children. "I didn't even know my grandmother's name," Debby said, "not until one of my cousins told me it was Mary Cecilia."

Debby was Bill and Sheila's second child, but she was right in the middle of the birth order for many years. "My sister was the first grandchild on my father's side, and she could do no wrong," Debby recalled. "And my brother was the first son, the namesake, William Ralph MacIntyre III, and I was the one in the middle—the classic middle child. I needed to be noticed. I would do *anything* to be noticed. The way I grew up, I would do anything to please. I became the placater; I did everything to please my grandparents and my parents to get their love and attention.

"Sometimes I just had to keep doing it and doing it. I became very persistent because they just didn't notice me most of the time. I had to compromise—but to be strong about that—even as a little person."

Bill MacIntyre was the parent who looked after his children; Sheila couldn't—but Debby was too young to understand why. All she knew was that she had no mother in the sense that her friends did. Her mother was a vague, temperamental woman who withdrew to her room when her children got too close or too insistent.

"I wanted her to love me," Debby said later, "and I couldn't understand that she couldn't. It was a sad way to grow up." But her father was there, and pleasing him meant everything to Debby. "I learned to do what I was told. Always. That way, I would make whoever it was happy. I couldn't take anyone being mad at me, because that meant that I had failed."

Barely three, Debby formed behavior patterns that were natural to her. She never questioned her own reactions—not even as a grown woman. She made a little place for herself in the world and clung to it. She adored her father, and kept hoping that her mother might come to love her. She, of course, couldn't begin to understand what alcoholism or drug addiction meant.

Sheila MacIntyre not only was mentally ill, but also used both alcohol and drugs to assuage the depression that gripped her. The success of lithium in treating bipolar disorders was not yet proven, but even when it was, Sheila would continue in her addictions.

There was to be yet another child, another son, Michael, born in 1958, when Debby was six. But nothing really changed. Sheila couldn't care for three children—and now she couldn't care for four.

The MacIntyre children all attended the best private schools in Wilmington, and Tatnall was right up there in prestige. Debby would attend Tatnall for fifteen years. She was especially adept at athletics and would be nationally ranked in swimming—both in the butterfly and in the backstroke. As a young girl she was a pretty blond little tomboy. In high school she would still be athletic but hardly a tomboy. Her success in swimming competitions gave her her first glimmerings of self-esteem.

Unlike the Fahey family, the MacIntyres never lacked for food or clothing or a nice house, but they also lived in a home where things happened that they tried to keep secret. With Sheila abusing both drugs and alcohol, she was often very irrational, sometimes almost comatose. "I'm amazed she didn't *die*," Debby said later, "with what she was taking. She was unpredictable. Sometimes she would lash out. Sometimes she was incoherent. We didn't know what she was going to do. It was embarrassing to us, and it was a very stressful way to live. We never wanted anyone in the house because of what our mother might do."

The MacIntyre grandparents were appalled by Sheila's behavior. "My grandparents hated her because of what she did to our family," Debby said. "So I was torn. I didn't know what to think or who to side with—and I was still trying to be sure *everyone* was happy, because although I didn't realize it then, I felt that was still my *job*."

In December of 1966, when Debby was sixteen, Sheila MacIntyre moved out of the family home. Actually, she left because she needed to be hospitalized at the Pennsylvania Psychiatric Hospital once again. Bill committed his wife, and when she was released this time, he found her an apartment in Media, Pennsylvania. He had accepted the truth that she could never come home again, not with the children there. Her psychiatrist recommended that she have a quiet place of her own.

As a good Catholic, Bill had married for life. As a man, he still loved Sheila with a devotion that few could understand. He was terribly conflicted—but he stayed with the children.

"My mother just couldn't manage us as teenagers," Debby said. "It was ruining her, ruining the family—so she moved away. My brother Ralph, who's eleven months younger than I am, had been in boarding school since the seventh grade. My sister was invisible—that's the way she dealt with the situation. I have no idea where she went, but she was never there. I was left to care for my younger brother. I was sixteen and Michael ten."

Scrambling as they all were for a small place in the sun, there was little cohesiveness among Bill and Sheila MacIntyre's children. Debby was fully responsible for her youngest brother. "I was given the responsibility for raising him and running the house when I was sixteen."

A long time later, Bill MacIntyre admitted to his younger daughter that what he did was wrong—that he had compromised his children in his efforts to save his wife. "He loved my mother," Debby said, "but he never dealt with the fact that she had all these problems. And all the time he still loved her, and he put us [in line] behind her at a very critical time of our lives. And so we were really left to fend for ourselves. We all reacted differently. I continued to placate."

But sixteen-year-old Debby was finally angry at her mother. She had bailed out on the family, and Debby refused to talk to her for a year. "Then I came around to realizing she couldn't help it; she was sick."

DEBBY MACINTYRE met Dave Williams when she was a junior at Tatnall. She had broken up with her boyfriend the week before the prom, and a friend set her up with Dave. He was quite short but handsome, with wavy dark hair. He was an escape from all that was going on at home.

"No one guided me about choosing a husband—or anything else," Debby remembered. "My home life was terrible. Dave came into my life, and he was my savior. And all the time it was a match that never should have happened. But my dad always said I was impressionable. Later, he said, 'I knew it wouldn't work—but you were so impressionable that nothing I said would have made a darn bit of difference. You were so stubborn, so determined that you were going to make it work.' "

Debby and Dave dated all through high school, and continued to go together when she went off to Mt. Vernon College for Girls in Washington, D.C. She dated other boys casually, but she always planned to marry Dave.

Mt. Vernon was a two-year college, and Debby MacIntyre graduated salutatorian in her class, with honors. She earned a Phi Beta Kappa key, but she burned out and decided she didn't want to go back to college. She took a year of business courses, where the pressure to excel academically wasn't nearly so strong. After that she still didn't feel like going back to college, so she got a job as a receptionist in a brokerage firm.

Debby loved Dave and she was emotionally dependent upon him. She would always feel safer with men than with women. Even though her father had often chosen his wife over his children, she had come to understand that her mother was more helpless than she was, and that her father loved her; it was just that he loved her mother more. Dave would love *her* more, and she visualized marrying him and being the most important person in someone else's life for the first time.

"I do think that I loved Dave," Debby said later. "I told him that I loved him. I'm not sure how capable I was of understanding what that meant. I thought that I was going to have a wonderful, happy life with Prince Charming."

Dave graduated from college in 1972 and had been accepted at law school. He and Debby were married at St. Anthony's Church in Wilmington at noon on June 17, 1972. Father Roberto Balducelli performed the Catholic ceremony. Coincidentally, Debby and Dave were married at the very moment that Kay and Tom Capano were having their wedding ceremony in Connecticut.

Debby was twenty-one when she married Dave. They lived their first summer with his parents. It was a "terrible, *terrible* summer," according to Debby. "His father was an alcoholic, but of course, I didn't know anything else." She felt as if she had been plunged back into the situation she had tried so hard to escape.

In the fall, the young Williamses moved to Carlisle, Pennsylvania, where Dave went to law school at Dickinson College. Now Debby wanted so much to go back to college, but that opportunity was gone; she had to work to put her husband through school. She worked for a year in Harrisburg as a secretary to a man who had a government grant. When that funding was phased out, she got a job in a bank as a teller. She couldn't look for a career job because they had to move back to Wilmington each summer so Dave could do his law clerk internship.

Debby's marriage was not what she had hoped it would be. It's quite possible that no marriage could have been. Starved so long for attention and love, she still longed for a Prince Charming who would put her first in his life, sweep her off her feet, pay *attention* to her. But Dave had never had that kind of personality, and he wasn't naturally demonstrative. They never fought, never had an argument. Their relationship was very quiet and controlled. It always had been, but Debby thought that would change.

She was stunned when she finally realized that Dave wasn't the man she thought she was marrying. And of course, he wasn't. He immersed himself in his law studies, and she found herself alone in a strange town. "He had no friends—*we* had no friends, other than a few people I'd met at work," Debby said. "We had a very lonely existence. I was very lonely." But still anxious to please and to make everyone around her happy, she did all the wifely things as well as working. She kept the house clean and even took up needlepoint to make the time pass.

After Dave finished his first year at Dickinson, they bought a little house in Deerhurst, just east of the Concord Pike, in the area where Lou Capano had built dozens of homes. They bought it for an investment; they would rent it out while they were in Carlisle, and then hoped to move into it when Dave got his law degree. Debby's money paid for the house—she used some of a trust fund that had been established for her. Although money would never really be a problem for her now, she always preferred working to being alone at home.

In 1975, they *did* move into the Deerhurst house, and Dave studied for the bar exam. He passed and was accepted to the Delaware bar that October. He was, in Debby's words, "a workaholic, very, very focused. He was very thorough and he worked very hard."

Debby had to face reality. She had believed she was lonely when her husband was in law school because they were so far from home. But now they *were* home, and nothing had changed. "I remember sitting in our den, alone, one night, and I was *miserable*. I still remember that moment. But I was so out of touch with my feelings that I didn't know why. I was twenty-six then. I was trying to get pregnant and I couldn't. I thought if I had a baby, that would make me happy—and I couldn't even do that."

Debby went back to college and she felt better. She was doing something for herself and had a modicum of control over her own life. She got involved in Junior League and all manner of volunteer activities. "I tried to fill my time," she said. "And that worked for a little while, and then, finally, my daughter was born. I was so happy, and Dave became the most affectionate father in the world—to *her*. He showered her with so much love. I saw a side to him that I never knew existed."

Although she was thrilled that Dave was a wonderful father, Debby felt a certain bleakness, too. She had never been the recipient of any of the kind of affection and outpouring of love her husband was apparently capable of. Inside, although she didn't understand it then, she was still the little girl who had done everything she could to please, to make people happy, so they would love her and notice her. And she was still alone. She was a good mother and she loved caring for her daughter, Victoria.* Dave was a great father, a hard worker, but she was "just there."

Debby and Dave were moving in divergent paths that took them further and further away from each other. She sought out pursuits that made her happy. She studied art, became remarkably adept with a camera, and doted on her baby. When they did anything social together, it was usually with other couples from Dave's law firm: Morris, James, Hitchens & Williams. The "Williams" was Dave's father, but Dave's job was anything but nepotistic; he would become a very skilled labor attorney.

Debby enjoyed the get-togethers with their peers from the law firm. The wives were all attractive, well educated, and fun. Although she no longer believed that she was particularly attractive, in her late twenties Debby was *very* pretty. She was slim and blond, with her hair styled in the blunt short cut that skater Dorothy Hamill made famous.

But she was definitely not a femme fatale. She almost always had a baby on her hip and a diaper bag on the other arm. But most of all, her attitude was not that of a woman who was sending out signals. She believed she had failed at marriage, failed to please her husband enough so that he would love her.

DEBBY was twenty-seven when she met Tom Capano in 1977 at one of the law firm's functions. When Debby was pregnant with Victoria in the fall of 1978, she and Dave went to a lunch that Kay and Tom had at their Seventeenth Street house. "We all became friendly—we all had similar interests and young children," Debby said. "There was a group of us that became more and more involved socially."

By that time, the Williamses had moved into a little Cape Cod house near the house Debby had grown up in, near the Bancroft Parkway and Rockford Park. Her mother, despite all her excesses and mental problems, was still alive and living in her own apartment in Pennsylvania, and her father still took care of her—but Sheila wasn't available to Debby any more than she had ever been. Debby and her sister were not close, her brothers were far away, and she had no one but her father to talk to about the things that worried her.

Debby wouldn't recall having felt any special attraction to Tom Capano when she first met him. He seemed to be a nice person, and a very friendly person. He did not, however, impress her any more than the other men who worked with her husband. But later on, when he began to take a special interest in her, that mattered a lot. "I wasn't happy in my marriage," she said. "I didn't know how unhappy I was for a long time. My relationship with Tom wasn't the reason for my divorce, but he fulfilled something in my life that I wasn't getting in my marriage. He actually paid *attention* to me. He appeared to genuinely care for me—to like me, to be interested in me as a friend. And I was very flattered because my husband didn't seem to be any of those things."

The group of friends from the law firm grew much closer together in the late seventies and early eighties. "We were all affectionate with each other," Debby said. "And flirtatious, I guess. We hugged each other and kissed good-bye. Tom wasn't any more or less flirtatious than anyone. None of it meant anything."

Debby really liked Tom because he was so much fun and so charming, and because he seemed like such a good husband. He was openly affectionate to Kay in a way she had never known in her own marriage. It was New Year's Eve of 1980, at a party for the firm's younger set, when everything changed. Debby was headed down a hallway when Tom grabbed her and pulled her into a bathroom. "He leaned me up against the sink," she remembered, "and said, 'I cannot control myself anymore—I am madly in love with you.' "

"You couldn't be," she stammered.

"Of course I could. You are the most natural . . . the most loving . . . the most *giving* woman I've ever known."

Tom had just told Debby exactly the things she had longed to hear for most of her life. "I hadn't heard things like that from any man—*ever*. I was literally starving for affection, my marriage was empty, but I wasn't dealing with it."

She looked at Tom and laughed and said, "You're crazy," even as she wanted to believe what he was saying. "I was so guilt ridden the next morning," she said, "even though nothing happened. It was my own response that made me feel guilty."

Tom called Debby later in the week and apologized, but he was also opening the door a little wider. And he continued to call her. He knew what to say and he knew how to flatter her. "He hooked me," she would remember. "I think he looked for a person like me. I think he was such a good reader of vulnerable women."

DEBBY did not begin a physical affair with Tom right away, but she might as well have. She thought about him all the time, and if she forgot for an hour or so, he was on the phone, complimenting, persuading, cajoling in his soft, deep, and ultimately compelling voice. She knew her marriage was in serious danger. Up until the stolen kiss on New Year's Eve and Tom's declaration of his love for her, she had coasted in her marriage and looked for appropriate ways to fill her time. She had never allowed herself to think of divorce. Certainly, she had never considered having an affair.

Now with Tom importuning her constantly, she could think of little else. Debby had married with the full intention of being married forever, seeing Dave Williams not only as the love of her life but as a haven and a protector. Nine years later, she knew the marriage wasn't working, although it would be a long time after that before she understood her own unrealistic expectations and see why it never *could* have succeeded.

And nine years later, she was as desperate to be loved as she had ever been. That made her a sitting duck for Tom Capano's blandishments and protestations of utter devotion. It never occurred to Debby that she was probably not the first woman Tom had focused on. "He made me feel that I was so exclusive—that I was the woman he had never had and always yearned for."

Debby's feelings for Tom were all mixed up with the fact that she and Kay Capano had become friends; they exercised together, talked about babies, and formed play groups for their toddlers with the other young mothers in the group. She had no idea how Kay and Tom got along, however. Debby was chatty and Kay was not; she never spoke of her marriage in any intimate way. In the end, her fondness for Kay made Debby feel a great deal of guilt, but she didn't seem able, nonetheless, to stop what was happening. "I felt terrible about what I was doing. I had a conscience enough to know that it would be wrong, but I was just so compelled by his persistence."

It took almost five months, but Tom was finally able to convince Debby that it was all right for them to be together, and they made love for the first time in late May 1981. He suggested that it would be kindest to everyone for them to keep their relationship secret, and that was, of course, the only thing they could do. The place Tom selected for a regular sexual rendezvous was as trite and predictable as a B movie: the Motel 6 on Route 9 near the Delaware Memorial Bridge. "I told my husband that I was taking a course once a week at the University of Delaware, but I was really meeting Tom in a motel," Debby recalled. "Looking back on it, it was very demeaning, but I did it. I don't even like to talk about it now."

Once the affair began, Debby felt even greater guilt and regret for what she was doing to people who trusted her. It never occurred to her how much she might be harming herself and her already poor self-image. When she was with Tom, he said all the words and phrases that soothed her conscience and made her feel like a valuable and beloved woman. But as soon as he was gone, the terrible doubts and yawning emptiness came back—worse than ever.

Debby finally realized she couldn't go on with the affair and she told Tom that she had to try to salvage her marriage. Kay was pregnant for the second time, and there certainly was no real future for Debby with Tom Capano. At first she wasn't upset to learn that Kay and Tom were still sexually intimate; she had never really expected him to stay with her long. For as far back as she could remember, people had moved in and out of Debby's life. She vowed to try harder in her marriage, and it seemed to her that giving Dave another child might bring them closer.

She became pregnant almost at once, and her pregnancy was a welcome release. She didn't have to worry about Tom's persuasive arguments that they were meant to be together when she was heavily pregnant with her husband's child. She and Kay continued their easy friendship—much easier now for Debby. They walked together, talked about babies, and she tried to forget that she had betrayed both Kay and her own husband. It was over.

In February of 1982, Kay Capano gave birth to a second daughter—Katie. Tom was ecstatic with his olive-skinned baby girl. A few months later, Debby and Dave Williams had a chunky blond son they named Steven.* Although Dave was thrilled to have a son, a new baby wasn't the answer to a failing marriage. Nothing between Debby and Dave had changed. And it wasn't long before Tom was back in her life.

And then, as if in punishment for her unfaithfulness, Debby's family plunged into eighteen months of one crisis after another. Her mother-in-law had a stroke, there were deaths in her extended family, and worst of all, her four-year-old daughter, Victoria, was diagnosed with a severe kidney disorder. In April of 1983, to save her life, it was necessary to remove one of her kidneys.

"It sounds awful," Debby would recall, "but I was almost thankful that there were so many things that I had to deal with—because then I didn't have to face the issue of my marriage, which was looming over me."

In June of that same year, she confronted her feelings and knew that she didn't love her husband. They no longer spoke, and they lived separate lives. A man she could never have was telling her constantly how much *he* loved her and needed her, while the man she lived with apparently found nothing valuable about being with her. When Debby tried to discuss her feelings with her husband, he told her that she was obviously disturbed and needed help. He suggested that she go to a psychiatrist.

"I thought about it for a while," she said. "And then I did." She went to a therapist she had seen in high school after her mother left the family, and for the first time, she told her father that she was miserable in her marriage—and that she was having an affair. "I didn't tell him that it was Tom Capano. I never told anyone."

The therapist suggested that her marriage might have deteriorated to a point where a trial separation was needed. Sometimes a separation can show people they really do care for each other. And sometimes it shows them that they do not. "I looked at it all as a

temporary situation," Debby said. "I really didn't think that this relationship I was having with Tom Capano was impacting my marriage. That was so foolish of me." And when she suggested the trial
separation to her husband, he agreed at once. "Only, he said that it
was over. No trial separation. It would be a divorce. Just like that."

And it was.

Debby's marriage was irrevocably broken in October of 1983.
She and the children remained in the little white Cape Cod home on
Dickinson Lane where they had lived since May of 1979. Victoria
was almost five, and Steven was eighteen months old.

Tom had been very supportive of Debby's decision to confront
her husband. He had listened to her worries and fears and reassured
her that things would be fine. "It was a shock to me when it ended
so quickly," Debby recalled. "But it did. I wasn't scared, because I
could support myself and the children financially. Emotionally, I had
support from my family. I had Tom Capano and I thought I actually
had someone in him who cared for me quite a bit and whom I could
talk to. . . . But I knew he would never marry me. I never even considered that he would. I knew I would be fine."

But how she needed her talks with Tom. She felt like a complete
failure, full of regret and sure that the impending divorce was all her
fault. "I was so full of Catholic guilt, and I still felt that there was
something wrong with me because I couldn't seem to make people
happy."

Shortly after their divorce, Debby's ex-husband married his secretary, whose name was also Debbie. To avoid confusion, Debby
took back her maiden name and started to look for a place for her
and her two children to live. She would have to find something to do
with the rest of her life. She would never blame Tom for the failure
of her marriage; she was simply grateful that she had someone as
kind as he, as passionate in her defense—someone who made her
feel special and cherished.

_____ *Chapter Six* _____

AFTER ANNE MARIE FAHEY graduated from Brandywine
High School in 1984, she and her friend Beth Barnes spent the summer at Bethany Beach on the Delaware coast. They found jobs and
were young enough to survive on little sleep. "We would stay up all

night partying," Beth recalled, "and go to work the next morning. I think that was the happiest time of Annie's life."

It may well have been. Anne Marie was legally an adult and she had made it through a tumultuous childhood. She was enthusiastic about going to college, and for the first time in a very long time, she had a place to live that was just like other girls' her age. She was free to have fun. Their partying was innocent and hilarious. They all loved the beach, being tanned, and having little responsibility.

In the autumn, Anne Marie moved down to Dover to go to Wesley College, where she planned to major in international relations. It was more difficult now for her siblings to stay in close touch—but she was mature enough so they didn't have to keep tabs on her. The littlest of the "little ones" had flown the nest and her wings seemed strong. They phoned as often as they could. Dover was only fifty miles from Wilmington, but it was far enough that they couldn't just jump in the car on a whim to visit.

And that was all right; Dover was not nearly as large as Wilmington, and the college itself was small and welcoming. "It was like being in high school," one graduate remembered. "Very safe. During that era, Wesley College wasn't like going off to a big university."

Anne Marie had an athletic scholarship for the hockey team and some student loans, but she would still have to work. She had always been able to find a job, and sometimes she worked at a couple of jobs at once on a part-time basis, selling the trendy clothes at the Limited in the Dover mall, or waiting tables at W. T. Smithers, a wildly popular bar. She also worked for a dentist for a while.

Anne Marie lived in one of the two dorms at Wesley College. "I remember her well," another former student recalled. "I remember being so shy, and Anne Marie seemed to be so popular. I can picture her running in the hall on the second floor of our dorm, shouting and laughing. She was very athletic, and she was always on the go. She had lots of friends—she was very social and vivacious. I remember that she was always smiling."

And Anne Marie *was* happy at Wesley; but during the times when she felt discouraged or anxious, no one but her very close friends ever knew it. She had long since mastered the art of keeping an ebullient facade, no matter what was churning beneath the surface. With her scholarships and loans, and by working whenever she could, she managed to complete the two-year program at Wesley.

Robert Fahey Sr. had continued to live with Brian at the apartment in Newark for a while, but then he'd moved to live with Kevin and Robert at their house. His health wasn't good; years of drinking had aged him before his time, and his heart was in bad shape. He had also been diagnosed with leukemia. Once she no longer had to live with her father or depend upon him for the necessities of life, Anne Marie had made a tentative peace with him, although neither she nor her sister, Kathleen, could forget the bad years.

Robert Fahey Jr. came home on the evening of March 24, 1986, and found his father dead on the floor; he had succumbed to a heart attack. He was sixty-four. It was eleven years to the month since Kathleen Fahey had died. Now, with both her parents gone, Anne Marie was bedeviled by ugly memories that brought back the pain and the emotional chaos of living in a family dominated by alcoholism. She had repressed the recollections for so long that she had almost forgotten them, but they were there in her psyche, curled up and waiting to spring out. It was the beginning of a very difficult time for her.

At the end of October 1986, Anne Marie transferred to the University of Delaware in Newark so that she could get a four-year degree. She was twenty now, and while she had been happy at Wesley, the university, with an enrollment ten times that of Wesley, overwhelmed her. It may have been that the bigger college intimidated her, or it may have been that all the difficult experiences of her young life had worn away at her for so long that her carefully constructed defenses finally crumbled.

That semester at the university was a bad time; Anne Marie felt alone and isolated and fell into a depression. It grew harder and harder to paste on her perpetually happy mask. She stopped going to class, and the darkness of winter and the holiday season, fraught with remembrances of better—and worse—times, found her almost immobilized.

She didn't return to the University of Delaware for a second semester; she dropped out and moved in with her brother Brian in the house he'd bought on Van Buren Street. Her depression lasted about six months, and she sought professional therapy to help her out of the black hole that trapped her.

Still, there was always a core of strength in Anne Marie that began to surface when hopelessness gripped her. She thanked her grandmother Katherine McGettigan for that. Nan was still there for Annie, showing her as she always had that people didn't quit just because things got a little tough.

Gradually, Anne Marie worked her way up out of her despondency. She realized that she really missed Wesley College and Dover, and she decided to move in with friends there. Her decision worried her brothers and sister because she didn't have any firm plans about finishing school or getting a job. "It was hard right after she left," Brian recalled. "But after we got over that, we stayed in touch the same way we had before. I went down to visit a few times. She came up on weekends once in a while."

It took Anne Marie a little time to pull things together, but she did it, and they were all relieved when she found a job as a waitress.

Wesley had become a four-year college, and that worked out perfectly. Anne Marie re-enrolled and it proved to be a good decision for her, even though she would have to work to pay her way and it would take her longer than the average student to get enough credits to graduate.

Anne Marie had a gift for friendship; she had friends that she had known since she was a girl, and she made more in college. Her best friends from grade school, Beth Barnes and Jennifer Bartels, were still close to her. Another really good friend was Jackie Binnersley, whom Anne Marie had met in the seventh grade when Jackie moved in four or five houses up the street from the Faheys; and from that point on Jackie considered Anne Marie her best friend. During one period when things were rough at home, Anne Marie had lived with the Binnersleys for several months.

AFTER she graduated from college in Rhode Island, Jackie persuaded Anne Marie to come up to Hyannis Port, on Cape Cod. It was another wonderful summer. They called each other silly nicknames and talked about their hopes and their problems. Anne Marie's name was Annie Bananie, and sometimes Anal Annie because of her compulsive neatness.

When Anne Marie returned to Delaware, that long, good summer of 1991 was not yet over. She visited a girlfriend who was sharing a house on the Jersey shore at Sea Isle City. She also made another friend who would be very important to her: Kim Horstman. Kim, along with Jackie, Beth, and a young woman named Ginny Columbus—whose brother, Paul, Annie was dating, the first serious boyfriend she had ever had—would remain part of the inner circle of Annie's friends.

Still, even though Anne Marie had numerous close friends, there were perhaps only three or four in whom she confided, and those who felt they knew her intimately would have been surprised to discover how impenetrable the invisible wall she hid behind really was.

∎

ONE of Anne Marie's professors had been particularly helpful in getting her back into Wesley. She was most adept at languages and was fluent in Spanish. The professor was married, but his wife was European and lived abroad. When Anne Marie expressed an interest in an internship in Spain, her mentor helped her facilitate that and found a Spanish family she could live with.

Brian was her closest sibling in age, and perhaps in terms of bonding. She called him Seymour. It was an inside joke and he didn't mind. He was a man of great sensitivity who could connect without words with people he loved, and now he was concerned that Annie's teacher might have more than a professorlike interest in her. As it turned out, he was right. Brian warned his sister about the dangers of married men, and she just grinned. Didn't he think she had good sense? After all the waitress jobs she had had, she was perfectly capable of spotting a come-on, and also of turning it away. She told Brian that the professor *had* approached the subject, but he had graciously accepted her answer when she told him she would not even consider such a relationship.

"He turned out to be a nice guy," Brian recalled.

Her time in Spain was a good experience for Anne Marie, and she longed to go back one day. It had been like a vacation from her life. Afterward, she delighted in finding people who could converse with her in Spanish, and she sprinkled Spanish phrases through her conversation when she spoke English.

Back in Dover, refreshed and feeling much more serene, Anne Marie got her degree in political science from Wesley College on May 9, 1992. She had broken up with Paul Columbus in the summer of 1991 after a three-year relationship, but they were still good friends. Although she had dated lots of men, Paul was her first serious boyfriend. He was an aeronautical engineer and a pilot now, and he had found a job in Denver. Their breakup was so benign that Anne Marie moved in with his family for a while after she graduated. She and Ginny Columbus had become dear friends, and Ginny and Paul's mother thought of Annie as another daughter.

ANNE MARIE got another waitress job—at T.G.I. Friday's on the Concord Pike in Wilmington—to see her through while she looked for employment that would enable her to use her degree. A friend from Wesley encouraged her to apply for an internship with the OAS—Organization of American States—in Washington, D.C., and she was accepted. She would use her fluent Spanish to translate documents.

Washington was an exciting and somewhat intimidating spot for a young woman. Anne Marie's internship was funded for only four months, but it would give her an up-close look at national government. Because she didn't know anyone in D.C., she went through the "Housemate Wanted" ads in the Washington papers and found a place to share with other women her age. She worked at the OAS on weekdays and commuted back to her job at Friday's on the weekends, a two-hour drive. As frightened as she was of change and being away from the people who made her feel safe, no one in Washington ever knew it. Anne Marie had guts. Most young women in their early twenties would have been hesitant to start a new job in a new city without having a friend along, but she lived with perfect strangers and they got along well. She had learned to acclimate to whatever living situation she found herself in, but inside she longed for a permanent home.

With her degree in political science, Anne Marie was a natural on the political scene and she did well in Washington. But being able to return to Wilmington on weekends helped to keep her grounded. Her brothers, particularly Brian, phoned her during the week and she saw some of her family on most weekends.

When the OAS job ended, she was torn about what career move to make next. She had some political connections—Ed and Bud Freel were heavy hitters in Delaware politics—and Anne Marie learned that one of the representatives from Delaware, Congressman Tom Carper, had a job opening in his office. She arranged for an interview and was hired as a receptionist for Carper.

Anne Marie was the perfect employee for a congressman; she was intelligent, meticulous about details, and always smiling. She was also beautiful and hardworking. Carper was very impressed with her capabilities. Her job with him, however, looked as if it might be short-lived. After three or four months, he announced to his staff that he had decided to run for governor of Delaware and would be leaving Washington.

Things worked out, however, when Carper returned to Wilmington and Anne Marie was hired to work on his campaign. It was late fall of 1992 and she was twenty-six years old. She worked enthusiastically to help get Carper elected governor—doorbelling, mailing, answering phones. It was what old Delaware hands called "making your bones." Anne Marie had to earn the respect of her peers by doing the more onerous chores of a political campaign.

Another way to make your bones and earn respect in Delaware politics was to know things. If someone was up on the latest rumors, strategies, and other inside information, and if he knew *whom* to share that information with, he could move up rapidly. But it took longer to penetrate the inner circles than it did to do the scut work, particularly for a female. The young women—and the younger men, too—were welcomed into the political bastions for their sweat equity factor, but nobody trusted them with anything *really* important.

Nevertheless, it was a good time; Anne Marie was back in her home territory, and she had an exciting job. She was young and lovely and was at the center of a whirlwind of activity. And she hoped that if Tom Carper was elected, she might have a job on his staff.

Her childhood friend Jackie Binnersley had bought a house on North Clayton Street and invited Anne Marie to move in with her and her roommate, Bronwyn Puller. Annie and Jackie were, of course, old friends since seventh grade, and Annie and Bronwyn hit it off immediately. Instead of sharing a house with young women she'd met through the want ads, Anne Marie was *home*. She moved in right before Christmas 1992.

Anne Marie "was not shy," Jackie remembered. "She was a funny, funny person. She always talked about her problems and we were very, very close. I mean, we slept in the same bed together several times just as friends when we were growing up. She was very particular, very neat, very organized. She wasn't like that in high school, but when she moved in, I was a bit surprised—just some funny things she did. I'm sure we've all stayed at hotels; they pull a bed down and they put a mint on your pillow. *She* would do that and powder her sheets. When she got up in the morning, the first thing she would do was make her bed. She dusted her *baseboards*."

Anne Marie had learned to clean house from her grandmother, but a month before she moved in with Jackie and Bronwyn, Nan had died. It was anguishing for her to lose the grandmother who had taken her mother's place. A long time later, she noted Katherine McGettigan's death in her diary: "Nan died on November 2, 1992— the most tragic part of my life! I always believed Nan's life would be eternal. She was the most reliable, stable, sober adult person in my life. A part of me died with Katie. I still feel numb. The world is a less fortunate place, but Heaven is dancing with her arrival."

Anne Marie missed her grandmother more than anyone realized; she would catch herself dialing Nan's phone number, and then realize that it was too late. There was no one on the other end of the line any longer.

■

TOM CARPER *was* elected to the Delaware governorship in 1992 and was inaugurated in January of 1993. Anne Marie went with him to the governor's offices in Wilmington, in the Carvel State Building, where she became his scheduling secretary. It was a fascinating and challenging job, meant for a young woman who could keep track of dozens of details at once and still greet visitors with her wonderful smile.

The world should have been Anne Marie's oyster, but the ghosts of her past had come back to haunt her. She felt vulnerable and sad, especially since Nan was gone. A part of her was still the little girl whose mother was dead and whose father raged at her that she wasn't good enough, that she was ugly and fat. It didn't seem to matter what was reflected in the mirror; Anne Marie's self-image was so distorted that she saw only the picture in her mind. She began to clean her surroundings obsessively, even more than she had when she lived with Carol Creighton while she was in high school. It was a way she could control the world around her and, perhaps, feel in charge of her own life.

She tried to control her appetite too, because she believed that she was much too heavy, even though, at five foot ten inches, she weighed around 140 pounds, a perfect weight. When she could maintain rigid order in her surroundings and not give in to her hunger pangs, she was better able to quell the flurries of panic that sometimes washed over her.

No one else knew how difficult life could be for her. But Anne Marie recognized that she needed help. Fortunately, her health insurance had provisions for therapy, and she had to pay only $17 an hour, while the insurance made a copayment of $68. Otherwise, she wouldn't have been able to afford it. She found a psychologist named Bob Conner, who listened to her, accepted her, and understood her pain. And she gradually began to make progress. After five months of counseling, she sometimes laughed with Bob, because *he* was a little chubby and he was encouraging her to eat more—but only in a very gentle way.

Anne Marie, who had grown up poor and desperate in Wilmington, was now the governor's scheduling secretary. It was a great job. And she had, at last, all the circumstances for a wonderful life. Her only real enemy was the portrait she carried of herself inside her head, and she was learning to accept the knowledge that it was distorted, and to change that image. If only she could accept herself as other people accepted her, she was going to be fine.

Chapter Seven

TOM CAPANO'S PLACE in the hierarchy of Delaware business and politics would become more and more entrenched during the eighties. Despite his affair with the ex-daughter-in-law of one of his firm's founders, he stayed at Morris, James, Hitchens & Williams for eight years. There was no reason not to; he and Debby Mac-Intyre had agreed that it would hurt too many people if anyone got even the slightest hint of their true relationship. He was confident that no one knew about Debby.

At first, Debby had no expectation that they would be together in any long-term way. The affair that began with a brief encounter in mid-1982 and resumed in late 1983 continued on a regular basis. She and Tom spoke on the phone every day, often several times a day, and they met once a week on Wednesday nights because that was the night that her children were with their father. If anyone had asked her at that point if she loved Tom, Debby would probably have found it difficult to come up with an answer. She tried not to think about it, but she admitted to herself that she was growing emotionally dependent upon him. Any woman in her situation probably would have; Tom was there for her as no one else had ever been, with the possible exception of her father. But her father had always had one ear cocked for a call for help from her mother.

Although she wasn't planning a future with Tom, Debby was stunned when he told her that Kay was pregnant again. "I was very upset. I wasn't planning to ever have more children," she said, "and I guess I just assumed that he wouldn't either."

Debby had occasionally asked Tom if he was still sexually intimate with Kay, because she could not understand how he could be as close as he was with her and maintain a sex life within his marriage. "I felt if you were having sexual relations with someone, you were expressing your love for someone through intercourse—or rather, intimacy. He didn't believe that; he told me that sex could be, sometimes, *sport.*"

Debby thought he was simply arguing a point. And as so many women involved in affairs do, she told herself that Tom's marriage wasn't based on a sexual relationship—until she learned that Kay was pregnant so soon again.

Tom told everyone he was thrilled about his wife's pregnancy, and bragged to Father Balducelli at St. Anthony's when his third daughter, Jenny, was born in November of 1983, only one month after Debby's marriage ended. Less than two years later, in August of 1985, Kay would give birth to their fourth daughter, Alexandra. Tom never seemed to mind that he hadn't had a son, and he characterized his daughters as "the most important part of my life. Nothing else comes close."

If Tom's third child came as a shock to Debby, Kay's fourth pregnancy hurt her deeply. "Tom told me that he couldn't stop with an uneven number—so he had to have *four* children. He couldn't understand why I was upset."

Tom rarely had his picture taken at family gatherings without a tiny girl in his arms. All of his and Kay's daughters were extremely pretty, with high, rounded foreheads, heart-shaped faces, and huge brown eyes.

Even though her divorce meant she was no longer one of the wives who came to parties thrown by her ex-husband's—and Tom's—law firm, Debby and Kay Capano maintained their friendship, walking together, setting up play groups for their children. Debby genuinely liked Kay and admired her. They never discussed Tom. Kay never talked about her personal life, anyway, although Debby always had. Now, of course, she could not. Her personal life was Tom. But in her mind, he was somehow a *different* Tom than the man who was Kay's husband. By this time he was such a necessary part of Debby's world that she could not walk away from him. As it was, when he was with her, it was for such a small percentage of his time. Whenever she felt guilty—and she did—she was able to tell herself that she wasn't really hurting his wife. Kay had his name, his children, and shared Tom's life. Debby was someone no one was ever going to know about.

Debby, who was an excellent photographer, took dozens of pictures of her children and Kay's, at home and on the beach at Stone Harbor. Debby's family had a beach house there, too, and they all still met at the shore. Sometimes it was a bittersweet thing for her to watch her toddlers—and Tom's—riding in a toy car together or hugging one another. Their lives had become so convoluted.

There were moments when Debby looked up to see Marguerite Capano studying her, her face empty of expression. As off-putting as that was, Debby was sure that no one but she and Tom *knew*. He himself assured her over and over that everything was fine and they had nothing whatsoever to regret. For the moment, they were there for each other.

And how on earth could that hurt anyone?

■

In late 1984, Tom accepted an offer to work for the city of Wilmington as city solicitor. It meant a substantial salary reduction; his salary at Morris, James had risen a great deal in the nearly eight years he spent with the firm. "I did it exactly backwards," he would say somewhat ruefully. "Most people try to get these types of public-service jobs. And the tradition is you step from a job like that into a partnership with one of the law firms. I was *already* a partner at Morris, James, Hitchens & Williams. I left the law firm to become city solicitor."

His new job in the public sector wasn't particularly exciting. He ran the law department for the city and supervised a dozen attorneys and an equal number of support staff. His office was responsible for prosecutions in Wilmington Municipal Court, and for defending any claims that might be made against the city. Most of the cases his department prosecuted were only misdemeanors, but Tom tried to appear in court every few weeks, taking an active role, "just to have fun."

He planned to stay on as city solicitor for only two years, and then return to his law firm. As the good son, Tom had always leaned toward public service jobs, and he was intrigued by the political scene in Wilmington—and in all of Delaware, for that matter. He had gotten his feet wet, although he didn't expect to stay with city government. After two years, however, Mayor Dan Frawley, for whom Tom had campaigned in 1984, offered him another city job—one with considerable cachet. He accepted it and became chief of staff of the mayor of Wilmington.

In effect, Tom would be running the inner workings of the city. While Frawley set policy and did the public things that all mayors do, Tom was in charge of every department: public works, zoning, fire, police. "Every morning the chief of police had to call me," he said, "and report on what incidents had occurred the night before."

Even though his position as chief of staff meant that he had tremendous power and respect in Wilmington and that his name appeared regularly in the media, Tom got less pay than he had received as a partner in a law firm. Still, he committed himself to Mayor Frawley and promised to stay two years as his chief of staff. Tom was more than just the man who saw that everything ran smoothly; Frawley had a tendency to shoot from the hip when he was riled or in his cups, and Tom was the soul of tact and control. In the calm, soft voice that reminded a number of women of Clint Eastwood's, he could be counted on to defuse explosive situations.

It was a time of two-fisted politics, when the good old boys met to debate how to run Wilmington amid clouds of cigar smoke and the smell of draft beer and Irish whiskey in the most popular bars in town. Buddy's Bar was in, and there were Kid Shelleen's and the Columbus Inn. Tom was at home in that world too. He seemed to have everyting—a wife, four daughters, a beautiful home in the Rockford Park section, a church where he was considered one of the staunchest supporters of the young, the elderly, and the poor, *and* arguably the most influential position in city government. During the St. Anthony's festival, he could scarcely make his way through the crowd with his adorable daughters without being stopped every few feet by someone who admired him or who needed a favor. He had grown a modest beard that made him look almost professorial, and he wore glasses now.

Kay worked as a nurse-practitioner for a group of pediatricians, and Tom frowned on that. Their house wasn't as organized as he would have liked, and he hated the clutter of their busy lives. His mother had always stayed home and confined herself to taking care of her family, and that was the way it should be, at least in Tom's opinion.

As the girls grew older and were enrolled in Catholic school, there was always so much to do and so many places to go. The younger three were natural athletes, and Tom made a point of dropping in on their games, if only briefly. He had so many demands on his time, and yet as the pressures grew, he seemed only to become more adept at his personal balancing act. Marguerite still counted on him for all of her business affairs, and there had been innumerable problems with his youngest brother, Gerry.

Gerry Capano might as well have been born twenty years after his brothers; he was in a different generation, starting junior high in the seventies. Where his brothers had drunk beer as they cruised in Brandywine Hundred and at the shore, Gerry and his friends were experimenting with marijuana and numerous other drugs. His father had died when Gerry was at the height of adolescence, and his mother hadn't the faintest idea of how to deal with a teenage boy on her own.

Looking back, Tom figured that Gerry had begun using marijuana when he was attending St. Edmond's Academy, the private school for boys. He was only in the seventh or eighth grade then; Gerry himself admitted to drug use in high school, but none of the family really knew that his consumption of illegal and bizarre substances included everything from cocaine to methamphetamines and

LSD. Gerry was also an excitement junkie. The little kid with the long blond curls who everyone thought was so adorable was on the verge of running wild.

Gerry was no student, but his brothers pulled strings and persuaded the priests at Archmere Academy to admit him. It was a bad idea, according to Tom; the curriculum was too tough for him. "He was expelled for a drug-related matter," Tom said, "before the end of his sophomore year, and I remember it was like a wake at our house—the priests who delivered the news actually came to the house to deliver it personally."

Gerry transferred to Brandywine High but he was expelled from there, too, allegedly for dealing drugs. "And so I had to step in and handle it," Tom said. "I hired who I thought was the best criminal defense attorney in town . . . and we went to Family Court expecting it to be a first offense . . . but they didn't fool around with it. And much to everybody's shock, we had a very strange judge. He was sentenced to Ferris School."

Tom had hired Jack O'Donnell, an old friend, but it hadn't done much good in saving Gerry from being locked up. Marguerite was horrified at the thought of her baby going to such a place and she begged Tom to intervene. He managed to get his brother out of what was basically a reform school by agreeing to intensive psychological counseling for Gerry. Tom himself would have to drive his little brother to the appointments, although it "took a big chunk out of my days."

They all pulled together. Louie went to New England to check out boarding schools for problem adolescents, but Gerry refused to go to any he recommended. Finally, with Tom, Louie, and Joey putting their heads together, they found a college near Boca Raton that had remarkably low entrance requirements. Gerry went there for almost two years, but he actually had minimal interest in studying.

Despite frequent visits from Joey, whose sheer physical strength awed Gerry into paying attention, he dropped out of college. Louie and Joey made a place for him in Capano & Sons, hoping that he would mature and show some interest in the business their father had begun. It was an iffy experiment at best. They soon saw that it probably wasn't going to work, but they hung in there, anyway. Gerry was family.

TOM'S plate got fuller and fuller through the eighties. His career was demanding, his family was growing, and he was on so many boards and steering committees. And of course, there was Debby. Aside from their intense physical bond, he felt that she needed him to advise her on her problems at work and with her family. He always got along with women, and he prided himself on understanding their vulnerabilities and their frailties. First his mother had needed him, and then his wife and daughters. And he liked to think that he was unfailingly considerate to the young women he met through his work, giving them an ear or a shoulder when they had problems. Tom had an unerring instinct about him: he could see beyond the bright smiles that some pretty women affected, looking deep into the sorrows and lonely places of their hearts.

He worked the same magic with Debby. She and her sister both lived in the Wilmington area, but they had a poor relationship and Tom tried to bolster her about that, loyally telling her that *she* was the one who was in the right. She got along fine with her brothers, but they lived far away. Gradually, Tom had made himself indispensable to Debby's well-being, although she might have been startled to realize that.

In September of 1985, Debby found a wonderful old house on Delaware Avenue, a three-story white stucco that had once been the farmhouse on considerable acreage in the early days of Wilmington. It was known as the Little White House, even though it was anything but small. Debby bought it and moved in with her daughter and son, one six and the other only two and a half. She had always had a real talent for decorating, and now she worked with the fine old things her grandparents had left her. Her new house was cozy and tasteful. The children slept on the third floor high up under the eaves, and she took the second floor for her bedroom.

Her house was within a few blocks of Tom and Kay's house, as well as those of several of their mutual friends, but it was surrounded by high bushes and tall trees. As outrageously dangerous as it seemed, Tom was able to visit her without being observed. Debby's house was a haven for him, he told her, amid the many voices that needed something from him, the many hands tugging on his sleeve.

In this first home that was totally hers, Debby set about making a life for herself. Her trust fund meant that she didn't have to work, but she couldn't picture herself sitting around the house or filling up her days with empty activities. She plunged into volunteer work for the moment. She wasn't sure where she could actually find a real job; it had been several years since her days as a secretary, and she had never completed the work for a four-year degree.

When her son, Steve, was three and a half years old, a friend of Debby's asked her if she would like to work at Tatnall, the private school where she had spent most of her own school years. Her friend was developing an extended day care program there, and she thought Debby had the skills to help her do it.

"I said, 'Sure!' " Debby recalled. "I could take my children with me because they would be in school there, and the job was for school days only. It was a really easy job going in, and I got paid $5 an hour, but it was a *job,* and it worked for me."

Even so, Debby was going through a very difficult time. She was always aware of being a single parent when she was surrounded by couples who shared the responsibility of raising their children. If time conflicts came up, she always compromised herself in favor of her children. "I think most mothers do," she commented. "And I was very guilt ridden because I continued to have this relationship with Tom Capano, whom I had fallen in love with."

She hadn't expected that to happen, but she had never had an affair before, and she had fallen into the same emotional trap as legions of women before her. She had gone into one of the most intense transactions a woman can have, without any protection. And she was too unschooled in the art of the affair to know how total her commitment might become.

Even though her marriage had ended, Debby and Tom continued to be very discreet; she lived alone with her children, but she had never allowed him to come to her home when they were there—only on Wednesday nights. She spent most of her evenings alone. Still, their daily phone calls made her feel part of Tom's life. It seemed to her that they shared confidences about all the important parts of their lives. He knew all of her secrets, and she believed she knew all of his.

"And we saw each other at parties," she said. "We couldn't be together, of course, but it was OK. We had a secret. I knew that, other than Kay, I was the only one he cared about. That meant a lot."

Tom was a moody man, Debby had discovered, and she had always tried to be accommodating to him—to avoid upsetting him in any way. That was how she had dealt with every man who had ever been important to her. "I never rocked the boat," she said. "I wanted to please him, because I wanted his praise and I wanted him to love me. I thought that was the way it was. I was so afraid if I angered him, he would leave."

His pleading and persuasive courtship were far behind them now. And once Debby had capitulated, Tom was very sure that she would always be there waiting for him. He could be very judgmental, and when Debby said something that displeased him, he would shoot her a withering look and say, "That's a stupid statement. Why would you say something like that?"

"When that happened," she said, "I would make a mental note of what I shouldn't say, tell myself: God, don't talk about that—or don't talk like that *anymore,* at least in front of him."

There were so many things, it seemed, that annoyed Tom or upset him, so many forbidden subjects.

Tom and Debby had some common interests, but they were very different in other ways. She was old money and accepted by society; he was the son of an immigrant who had made good. He aspired to what had come so easily to the MacIntyres, which she knew didn't necessarily bring happiness.

Debby had always been athletic, and Tom was basically sedentary. She tried to get him to swim with her, and he grudgingly agreed to try it. "He actually went out and got goggles and earplugs and everything, and he went two laps when his earplugs fell out and his goggles fogged up, and he quit."

Debby loved working in the yard, and he "absolutely abhorred it."

She bought him presents that were not particularly expensive, but she had spent time picking them out because they just suited him, a music tape or a book. He bought her household gadgets like pasta makers and mixers, claiming that she had *everything,* and what could he really give her that she didn't already have?

But however they differed in tastes, hobbies, and recreation, they had a tremendously powerful sex life. In this, too, Debby always tried to please Tom. If she didn't, she was terrified that he would go away. She agreed to install a massive mirror opposite her bed and found a secure hiding place for the sex toys and gadgets, and the videos, that seemed to stimulate him. And she managed to repress his depiction of lovemaking as mere sport. He was too tender and too kind for her ever to believe that she meant nothing to him but a game won once again.

THERE were times when Tom was there for Debby when she truly needed someone. Gradually, she lost the people she counted on. Both of her grandparents died in 1984. It was more like losing parents than grandparents—she and her brothers and sister had found refuge with the elder MacIntyres many times.

It was Debby's greatest fear that her mother would survive her father. Sheila Miller MacIntyre, for all her neuroses and addictions, was in her sixties and still dependent upon her husband. With his children grown, Bill MacIntyre was able to focus most of his attention on Sheila, and she needed a great deal of care.

But as so often happens, it was the strong spouse who died first. Bill MacIntyre succumbed to a heart attack on September 7, 1987. He was only sixty-four. He had been a wonderful grandfather to Victoria and Steve, and he and Debby had long ago come to an understanding about his sense of duty toward the wife he loved but could not live with. Now, with their brothers living several states away, it was up to Debby and her sister to care for their mother.

They moved her into an apartment in Wilmington and arranged to have nurses stay with her most of the time. It was difficult sometimes for them to care for a mother who had never cared for them. But Debby, at least, made her peace with her mother, accepting finally that Sheila had never been capable of loving her children or even of living in the same house with them. Ironically, Sheila seemed to enjoy her grandchildren, and Victoria and Steve looked forward to visits at her apartment.

On the Saturday night before Mother's Day 1988, Debby called her mother several times; she knew that the nurse-companion who usually stayed evenings with Sheila had taken the night off so she could visit *her* mother. When she didn't get an answer, she assumed her mother had gone to bed early and couldn't hear the phone.

The next day, she bought a bouquet of flowers and headed to Sheila's apartment with Victoria and Steve. It was Debby's sister's birthday and she wouldn't be going over to Sheila's. "The kids were so excited," Debby said. "They ran in ahead of me and pounded up the stairs. They were too young to know why she wouldn't talk to them."

Debby found her mother, fully clothed, lying across her bed. Her eyes were open, but there was something so ineffably still about her body that she knew her mother was dead. And she had never felt so alone.

Debby called Tom at home, grateful that he answered the phone. She had no idea what excuse he gave for leaving in the midst of Mother's Day celebrations, but he did. "He came over as soon as he could," she said. "He went upstairs and checked my mother and he came back down and told me she was gone. And he closed my mother's eyes."

Tom made arrangements for someone from the police to come and verify that Sheila MacIntyre was dead, and then he called for a funeral director to take her body away. It took hours but he stayed with Debby. And for her it was a tremendously bonding experience, sitting there together in the silent house while her poor, lost mother lay upstairs. She had no idea what she would have done without Tom.

Sometimes, after that day, he would remind her, "Remember, I closed your mother's eyes."

It was hard to grieve for a mother who had never been there, but Debby did—more for what might have been than for what was.

_____ Chapter Eight _____

TOM WAS THERE for so many people when they were in crisis. His quiet voice, his calm manner, and his ability to make people understand what they needed to understand made him a natural mediator. Everybody who met him just seemed to like him.

But while Marguerite's favorite son rose in stature in Wilmington, her younger three were having their problems—and not just Gerry, who seemed to care for nothing but guns, shark fishing, big game hunting, and girls with big hair and clothes that fit like a second skin.

Louie had built his father's business into a major construction company, with both commercial and private projects worth many millions. When Louis Sr. died in 1980, his estate had been worth $1.2 million, and it included the Cavalier Apartments, part of a Holiday Inn in New Jersey, several housing developments, investment funds, and even a portion of a Pennsylvania coal mine. Tom, Louie, and Joey were designated as the trustees of the estate, and as such they were given the power to invest the money, open new businesses, and continue whatever current businesses they deemed proper.

That was only a jumping-off point for Louie and, of course, Joey, who had joined him in the business. Tom had never been interested in Capano & Sons, and his lack of interest continued. Lou's will stipulated that his three older sons were to pay Marguerite, Marian, and Gerry a monthly stipend, and give Gerry shares of the estate when he reached twenty-one, and again at thirty-five. Marian was given no share.

Eventually it had become apparent that Gerry didn't have the slightest aptitude for construction, and even less patience in dealing with clients. It was agreed that he should operate his own business, one that would complement Capano & Sons' many real estate holdings. Gerry started a landscaping and lawn care business. Among other contracts, his work crews took care of the grounds at Cavalier.

Since Gerry eschewed Wilmington in the summer in favor of the shore, he rarely took a hands-on approach during the peak months of his business. Indeed, he would one day hire a gardening service in Stone Harbor to take care of the house he bought there. His brothers feared that Gerry was still involved with drugs, but they tried to keep that from Marguerite.

Marian had two early marriages that were short-lived, but she finally made a match that seemed to make her happy. In the early seventies, she married L. Lee Ramunno, an attorney who practiced in one of the historic, one-story brick buildings on French Street near the courthouse in downtown Wilmington. They had three children together.

Lee, who obviously doted on his attractive wife, did not feel as kindly toward her brothers, particularly Louie. He may have resented the fact that Marian, the oldest child and for five years the *only* child of Lou and Marguerite, had been omitted from her father's will, except for a monthly dole at the pleasure of her brothers. It may have been some other dispute over money, but beginning in 1982, there was very bad blood between Lee Ramunno and Louie Capano.

Lee initiated a lawsuit against Louie, and Louie was served with it as he was having a good time acting as a guest bartender at a Wilmington restaurant. Outraged and embarrassed, Louie stormed out to the Ramunnos' home in Forest Hills Park. He hadn't come to visit and he didn't use the front door; he smashed a wooden chair through a sliding glass door and stepped in through the broken glass.

Louie grabbed Lee by the throat and began choking him, as Marian, nearly hysterical, tried to pull him off. The brothers-in-law fell to the floor and continued to struggle, while Marian tried to separate them. When she couldn't, she called the police. Louis, twenty-nine at the time, eventually entered an Alford Plea (no contest) to charges of second-degree reckless endangerment.

Family celebrations that included Louie and Lee were sparse after that, and the incident put a big strain on their espoused belief that family was family, no matter what. Tom got along well enough with his only sister's husband, but then, Tom got along with almost everyone.

■

DAN FRAWLEY ran for mayor again in 1988 and Tom worked hard to get him reelected. He had a great deal of positive impact on Frawley's campaign, and it was assumed that Tom would continue as chief of staff. But it didn't work out that way. In mid-January, Tom resigned from his city position. Everyone who knew him well was surprised to hear that he was leaving to join Capano & Sons.

Louie needed him. The family business needed him, and as much as he dreaded the thought of working in the construction business, Tom had acquiesced to his mother's pleas. He had a knack not only for getting along with everyone, but also for dealing with the sometimes onerous details that kept a company going. In 1989, the details were not onerous; they were scandalous, and his mother had begged him to help his brothers, to help the family.

Tom had promised her 365 days, and 365 days only.

Louie had the genius and the vision to make Capano & Sons boom, but along the way he had taken some shortcuts to grease the wheels of county government on a rezoning issue that he needed badly. County council members were the ones who voted on rezoning bills, and Louie had given Councilman Ronald J. Aiello $10,000 in 1987, in what was essentially an illegal campaign contribution. A year later, Louie went further over the line and gave Aiello $9,000 in an outright payment for a rezoning vote favorable to one of his developments.

Federal agents had heard rumors of Aiello's unlawful side income and they were watching him closely, but they needed evidence to trap him in a corruption scandal. Tom stepped in to handle the delicate negotiations between the U.S. Justice Department and his brother. It was Tom who played the pivotal role in extricating Louie from the threat of charges against him. The FBI needed someone who could set Aiello up in a sting operation so he could actually be witnessed taking a bribe. Once they had him, they could move in to seize physical evidence that would link him to dirty money.

On Tom's advice, Louie agreed to cooperate with the sting and set it up in his own office. The FBI special agents witnessed Ron Aiello accepting $25,000 in marked bills from Louie Capano. That was enough.

Louie was never charged with any crimes in connection with the situation. "I think he [Tom] straightened out Louis, who was in kind of a jam," former Wilmington mayor Thomas Maloney remarked. "Tom worked carefully with the Justice Department to solve a problem and alleviate a situation."

Everyone but the man arrested seemed content with the outcome of something that could have been really sticky. Louie moved easily back into doing what he did best, but Tom was chafing at Capano & Sons, waiting eagerly for the year he'd promised his mother to pass. "It wasn't the work," he explained later. "I had a different way of looking at things than my brothers. [They] had been in business together for a long time. . . . They had both started working when they were in college, and it was tough—even though I was the older brother—to impose the order that needed to be imposed."

In plain terms, neither Louie nor Joey would take orders from Tom, not about the business. The last months of Tom's year of servitude to his mother were tense.

Louie Capano's reputation was scarcely tarnished by the unpleasantness of 1989; he was a dashing figure, far more than his soft-spoken brother. Over the next decade, the family interests burgeoned exponentially. With Louie at the helm, the Capanos would soon own hundreds of prime acres around Wilmington and several more shopping centers. They continued to build high-end housing developments. "I don't think we've seen half of what he's going to do," the banker who funded Louie's father said. "It's almost as though he was born for it."

Many builders faced ruin when the real estate market took another dive in the early nineties, but the Capanos flourished. Other developers were poleaxed by Louie's cliff-hanger deals. Harry Levin, whose chain of Happy Harry's Drug Stores was ubiquitous on the Eastern seaboard, marveled at Louie. "Louie does so many things wrong," he laughed in the 1980s, "and they all turn out right."

Louie was by far the richest of Lou's sons. He and his first wife, Deborah, who had borne him a son, divorced amid rumors of Louie's roving eye. Deborah Capano went on with her life and became a state senator. All four Capano brothers had an appreciation for beautiful women, and they were not known for their faithfulness to their marriage vows—although even his own brothers didn't know about Tom's affair with Debby MacIntyre.

Louie's second wife was a nationally known athlete. Lauri Merton was a leading contender in the Ladies' Professional Golfing Association, winner of the national trophy in the early nineties, and a pretty blonde with light blue eyes and a deep tan. Louie got a big kick out of being Lauri's caddy in championship rounds; he was probably the wealthiest caddy ever to shoulder a golf bag, but he was more than self-confident enough to follow Lauri around the links. He enjoyed the pictures in the papers of himself and Lauri.

Louie and Lauri moved into a huge mansion in the Greenville

section that had once belonged to one of the du Ponts. Greenville was *the* address to have in the Wilmington area, and the gray-stone house with its garden paths, swimming pool, and parklike grounds was an estate any millionaire could be proud of.

IN January 1990, Tom heaved a sigh of relief as he finished out the 365th day of his servitude at Capano & Sons. It had taken a toll on him, but he had kept his promise to his mother, and he was more than ready to go back into government service. And what heady service it would be. Delaware governor Michael Castle had made Tom an offer that rather surprised him because he was a lifelong Democrat and Castle was a Republican. It was the position as Castle's chief counsel. The job paid about half of what Tom could have made at the law firms that had tendered job offers, but it was an honor to be asked to advise a governor on complicated legal issues. And it was an excellent way for him to move back into public service.

Tom Capano, not yet forty, now had an enviable reputation not only in Wilmington but in the whole state of Delaware. The Attorney General's Office was responsible for defending the state in all matters, but as Castle's chief counsel, Tom would be called upon to advise the governor on the constitutionality of all pending legislation. The prestige factor alone was more than enough to make up for any diminution of his salary. And of course, Tom shared in the legacy his father had left for his sons; he would never hurt for money. He could well afford to accept Castle's offer.

For some reason, Tom always played down his wealth, although he was probably worth $4 million or more by the early nineties. He and Kay still lived in their sprawling bishop's residence, but they didn't have a beach house as his brothers and sister did. "When I go to the shore," he said, "I mooch off my mother." He and Kay drove utilitarian vehicles rather than high-priced trophy cars, but of course, their daughters all went to private schools and money was not a problem.

While Tom was advising Governor Castle on legal issues, another of his brothers embarrassed the family. It seemed that Tom was always having to put out little fires set by his siblings. Joey was a handsome devil, and he had a beautiful wife, Joanne, and four children. But he also had a woman he had been seeing on the side for at least nine years. She had once been the baby-sitter for Joey's children, and she was a decade younger than he was. When they began as lovers, the girl was so young that Joey often had to dash out the back door of her house just as her parents were coming in the front entrance. Infatuated with him when she was a teenager, the girl had grown up and come to understand that there was no future in their relationship, as passionate and volatile as it was, and she broke off with Joey.

Joey couldn't stand the idea of her being with anyone else. He had finally separated from his long-suffering wife in an attempt to win back his paramour. Then on Halloween night 1991, Joey was in the grip of a sexual obsession that took him way across the line, both in terms of rekindling his affair and with regard to the law.

While her horrified sister looked on, he crashed into the young woman's home, literally carried her away, and held her captive while he forced her to have sex with him. When she was finally able to escape, she went to the police and Joey was charged with kidnapping and rape. Once more, Tom had to walk a fragile tightrope between the authorities and a brother. In the end, with Tom's coaching, Joey pleaded guilty to misdemeanor charges of assault, unlawful sexual contact, and criminal mischief. His ex-lover had relented and asked that the felony charges be dropped. It was a plea bargain that let Joey walk away from prison time for the very serious charges *and* gave him a promise from the state that he would not be charged with assaulting his girlfriend in two earlier incidents.

Eventually, Joey and his wife reconciled, and the rest of the family could sigh with relief. It was just one more thing for Tom to deal with in 1991, which had already been a difficult year. His job was very demanding and he was quickly in the middle of a crushing deadline to complete the construction of a women's prison and an addition to Gander Hill, the prison in Wilmington. He helped bring the projects in on time, giving credit to his connections with the city. But it was probably predictable that he would develop some physical manifestation of the stress he lived under. He was diagnosed with ulcerative colitis. His gut bled.

And yet there was no doubt at all that Tom relished his role as the governor's adviser, his family's cleanup man and shining example, the father of four lovely girls, and husband to Kay—and lover-adviser to Debby—just as he appeared almost to enjoy being the put-upon martyr, the man who had every right in the world to occasionally demonstrate a mercurial temperament with his women. People expected too goddamned much of him, often treated him badly—at least in his eyes—and didn't give him the allowances he deserved with the heavy load he carried.

Tom stayed with Governor Castle until 1992. He had always wanted to run for political office himself; he thought he would make a good attorney general for the state of Delaware. But he talked it over with some of the stronger Democrats, among them the Freels. Kevin Freel, who always said what he thought, while his brother Bud tended to be more enigmatic, told Tom to forget it. He was carrying too much family baggage on his back. His brothers' shenanigans would surely come back to haunt him if he ran for the highest law enforcement office in Delaware. Between his three brothers, the Republicans could dredge up everything from graft to drugs to rape and kidnapping, and he shouldn't think they wouldn't. Kevin warned him he would just be inviting a smear campaign. A Republican wag told Tom his campaign slogan would have to be "Tom Capano: The OTHER Capano."

Moreover, despite his success in public office, Tom was not a natural politician. He had little talent for glad-handing and working a crowd. The thought of shaking hands with strangers and kissing babies actually scared him a little. Rather, his forte was in quiet behind-the-scenes mediation. People loved Tom in private; he seemed to lose color and verve in the spotlight. He was just a little too plodding, a little prissy on details and regulations.

Tom decided not to run for office after all, and then he accepted a partnership at the law firm of Saul, Ewing, Remick and Saul, the bond counsel for the state of Delaware and the city of Wilmington. He would run the public finance department. It was a plum job, but he hastened to point out to anyone who raised eyebrows that he wasn't hired because he would bring government bond clients to Saul, Ewing. "They already had it all," he said. Both the city and the state did business with Saul, Ewing.

There were only two firms in the Delaware Valley that had large public finance departments, and Saul, Ewing (with principal offices in Philadelphia) was one of them. Tom would work in the Wilmington office, and as managing partner, he doubled the office staff, bringing in six partner-level attorneys. He was back in the private sector and in a position to make a very substantial salary. Setting the city and state bonds was very detailed work, but they were mostly multimillion-dollar deals, and the meticulous work paid well.

Tom's community service now filled many pages of his curriculum vitae. He was on the board of trustees at St. Mark's High School and Ursuline, Padua, and Archmere academies. He was a board member of the National Conference of Christians and Jews, chairman of the Wilmington Parking Authority, in charge of the Bench and Bar Committee and the Delaware Supreme Court's Long Range Planning Committee, and of course, still a stalwart at St. Anthony's.

His devotion to Catholic education and good works in no way slowed his affair with Debby MacIntyre or, seemingly, caused him any conflict of interests. He felt he gave so much to everyone that he deserved the—for him—*un*guilty pleasures of adultery. He was, he believed, a very special man, a man who shouldn't be fettered by the rules that governed lesser men.

Tom Capano had over the years polished his knack for friendship and for drawing people to him. He was a highly skilled negotiator and mediator; he *knew* people so well, knew what they wanted and what they needed. He knew the law and the law's weaknesses. He had used his charm and his intelligence—buoyed by his political connections—to get all three of his brothers out of tight spots. And he had boundless confidence in his own ability to make things happen the way he wanted them to happen.

_____ *Chapter Nine* _____

ANNE MARIE FAHEY started her new job with Governor Tom Carper right after he was inaugurated in January of 1993. Her desk would be on the twelfth floor of the Carvel state building, just past the elevators. She and Sue Campbell Mast, Carper's executive assistant, would be the lions at the gate that all visitors would have to pass before they reached the inner sanctum of Carper's private offices. The two women had desks five feet apart. Sue would answer the governor's direct phone line, and Anne Marie would field all the other calls. She was now at the very center of what was happening in Delaware, an essential part of the government of her state.

Anne Marie would make a number of women friends in this new job, including Sue, Jill Morrison, and Siobhan Sullivan. Jill worked in Constituent Services, directing Delawareans with problems to the proper agencies, and Siobhan was a Delaware State Police officer who worked in the Executive Security Unit, which protected Governor Carper and his family. She had come on board in a transfer from Troop 9 in Odessa, Delaware, and started guarding Governor Carper in December of 1992. Anne Marie and Jill began work at the same time, in January.

The Wilmington staff wasn't that big and they all knew one another well. When the legislature was in session, most of Carper's staff of around twenty-five was in Dover, leaving only four or five people in Wilmington. They were young and exuberant, although they contained their hilarity and kept their voices down on the twelfth floor, where the governor's office demanded respect. They tended to be a little loud and boisterous on the eleventh floor, where the interns' and Constituent Services offices were located. And Anne Marie's voice, speaking rapid and fluent Spanish to a Hispanic woman, became a familiar counterpoint to activities on the eleventh floor. She loved the language and practiced it often, against the day she would return to Spain.

Anne Marie and Jill rapidly became particularly good friends; they were both in their mid-twenties, and Jill had moved to an apartment a block from the house Anne Marie shared with Jackie and Bronwyn, so it was easy for them all to get together. Anne Marie introduced Jill to Ginny Columbus and her other close friends, and helped Ginny get a job in the governor's office.

Anne Marie and Jill got in the habit of having lunch together almost every day, and they went shopping together at the malls, walked when the weather was good, and often worked out on the machines at the Y. They also shared some of the perks that came with working in the governor's office—lots of free tickets to events or fund-raisers. While some of the functions turned out to be deadly boring, they weren't put off, and they were game to try almost anything they had tickets for. Neither was seriously involved romantically, and they never knew whom they might meet.

Jill was with Anne Marie on April 26, 1993, the night she first met Tom Capano. It was at Jim and Mary Alice Thomas's house on Red Oak Road in the Rockford Park section of Wilmington. The Thomases had a lovely home, which they opened up for a fundraiser for the Women's Democratic Club. Kathy Jamison, who was the scheduler for Lieutenant Governor Ruth Ann Minner, had arranged for the guest speakers—Lynn Yakel and Governor Jim Florio. The turnout wasn't as good as Kathy had hoped, but there were about 150 people there, many of them attorneys. Kay Capano had bought a ticket in her own name, but she wasn't able to attend, so she sent Tom to represent their family. He moved easily through the crowd, chatting with old friends and others he had worked with in city and state government. He was forty-three, handsome in a subdued way with his expressive eyes and perfectly trimmed beard. As a younger man, when his hair was very dark, he had had a smoldering look about him, but now he looked much more benevolent, even though he didn't smile much.

Jill and Anne Marie didn't know a lot of people there, but it was a good party with interesting speakers and a great buffet. They chatted with each other and tried to mingle with the crowd in as un-self-conscious a way as possible. "It was at the end of the evening," Jill remembered. "She spotted Mr. Capano and recognized him and Anne Marie approached him and introduced herself and said she thought that he might know her sister, Kathleen. Then she introduced me, and we had a little chitchat, a friendly first-time-meeting-someone conversation."

Tom was clearly a lot older than the two young women, at least fifteen years older. But he was very pleasant as he and Anne Marie found that they knew many of the same people. Of course, they had both been close to the Freel family for more than twenty years— Tom through politics and Anne Marie because the Freels had always been good to her family. And they were both staunch Democrats. Tom talked to Anne Marie and Jill as if they were the only people there, giving them his full attention, and that was flattering because he was an important figure in the Democratic Party in Wilmington and they were virtual newcomers.

Tom's position at Saul, Ewing brought him to the governor's office in the Carvel state building occasionally, and after that night he often paused at Anne Marie's desk to exchange a few words. Jill Morrison was aware that Anne Marie had lunch with him once in a while over the late spring and summer of 1993. Since Jill and Anne Marie usually had lunch together, when Ann Marie begged off and said she had other plans, Jill would ask, "Who with?" and sometimes it was Tom Capano. Jill didn't think anything of it.

"Anne Marie was just a very friendly person, and she explained that she was friends with him," Jill recalled, "and [said] they would have good conversations, and he relied on her advice. That's the way she was, so I found nothing odd at that point."

Sometime in the autumn of that year, Anne Marie told Jill that she was going out to dinner with Tom. She mentioned it offhandedly, as if it was a last-minute invitation. She asked to borrow a raincoat since the night had turned chilly, the wind was whipping fallen leaves around, and she hadn't worn a coat to work that day.

Somehow, going out to dinner with a man seemed more like a date than just having lunch during a workday. The next day, Jill's curiosity got the better of her and she asked Anne Marie how her dinner date had gone. "She told me about the restaurant, and that it was a nice evening—that Mr. Capano had ordered the food for her. I asked her, 'Did he kiss you?' and she said, 'Yes.'"

Women who are close friends ask each other things like that, although Jill was a little surprised at Anne Marie's answer. She didn't question her, but she wondered what kind of a relationship Anne Marie had, or contemplated having, with a married man so much older. Anne Marie had confided that Tom was about to have his forty-fourth birthday. She and Jill were only twenty-seven. Even so, she referred to him as Tommy, a name he apparently preferred. She always called him that.

Jill knew her friend well enough to know that she wouldn't find out any more than Annie wanted to tell. "She was always saying about herself," Jill quoted, " 'The more you push me in one direction, the more I go in the other direction.' And I did not want to push her. I figured if people want to tell me something, or confide in me, they will do it in their own time."

And apparently, Anne Marie had nothing she wanted to talk about with Jill, at least nothing about Tom Capano. She certainly had no exclusive arrangement with him; she had other dates, with men closer to her own age. She could be dramatic sometimes, and impossibly romantic, but it was clear to anyone who knew Annie well that she yearned to be in love, to be married, to have children of her own.

Men so often disappointed Anne Marie—or maybe it was that she shot herself in the foot because of the way she seemed to fear rejection. As beautiful as she was, she didn't see herself that way. If a man promised to call and didn't, she was convinced he would never call again—certain that *she* had said or done something to scare him off. And all the time she was absolutely lovely, with a figure both lush and angular with her full breasts and long arms and legs. Her eyes were wide and blue under heavy brows, and she had such thick, curly hair that it tumbled heavily down around her face unless she swept it up on her head and let tendrils escape. Her complexion was pure Irish, freckled skin that was suffused with pink washes when she felt emotion or embarrassment.

And Anne Marie was often caught unaware by both, although her defense system was locked in place so firmly that someone had to know her really well to see it. She seemed so happy and so confident, but she was as vulnerable as a wildflower growing on a freeway.

ONE night in the fall of 1993, Jackie Binnersley came home about eight after working out at the gym. She was startled to see Anne Marie sitting on the couch in their living room with a man. Jackie recognized him but would never have expected to find him in her own living room. He was well known around Wilmington. What surprised Jackie the most was the intimate way Annie was sitting with him on the couch. They were drinking wine, and a bottle of Rosemont merlot—Anne Marie's favorite—sat on the coffee table.

"They were facing each other," Jackie said. "As soon as I walked in, I detected *something*. I just felt uneasy. Body language tells a lot—you could just tell by the way they were sitting that there was some contact there."

Anne Marie was leaning toward her visitor, apparently entranced, her cheeks flushed. Jackie knew who Tom Capano was, and she knew he was married and had children. It seemed totally out of character for Anne Marie to be sitting there with him, drinking red wine. "She wasn't promiscuous at all," Jackie would recall. "She was very reserved, conservative, never had guys over to the house . . . but that night she had her cleavage showing."

Anne Marie usually wore tailored shirts or blouses with high, rounded necks. But now the top three buttons of her blouse were definitely undone. It was an awkward moment and Jackie apologized for intruding. Anne Marie quickly recovered her composure and introduced Jackie to Tom.

After he left, Jackie confronted Anne Marie. "What's going on?" she asked bluntly. "Why is this guy here? He's a married man. Why is he over here drinking a bottle of wine?"

"Oh, Jackie," Anne Marie said. "We're just friends."

Jackie never totally bought that explanation, although Anne Marie tried to convince her that there was nothing the least romantic about her being with Tom Capano. They had a work relationship and she couldn't *not* talk to him.

Tom continued to drop over to their house, although neither Jackie nor Bronwyn wanted to encourage that. He made them uneasy. He was so smooth and relaxed. Too smooth. Something made them want to protect Annie. "I didn't like him at first," Jackie said. "I didn't like him at *all*. I usually give people a chance, but I just got a bad impression. Why was he hanging out at the house? Why was he drinking wine with Annie?"

Both Jackie and Bronwyn found Tom's attempts to ingratiate himself to them unctuous. "He just went over a little bit too much," Jackie said. "I thought it was false the way he kind of gave me compliments on the house. He would bend over backwards to be nice . . . and say, 'This house looks great—you did this—you did that. Annie tells me you stained the floors?' or whatever."

His lavish compliments sounded false. It was too much; Jackie's house was only average, and she had heard that Tom was very wealthy and lived in a great big house. Why would he bother to gush about her house?

Jackie's suspicions went beyond her distrust of Tom's compliments. She had known Annie since they were both twelve, and she wanted something better for her than a married man who came calling with presents but who never seemed to take her out.

For a while, Tom was a regular visitor at their house, and he called Annie often, too. And when Jackie and Bronwyn went away for a weekend, they knew that Tom visited Annie in their absence. Once Jackie came home to see them leaving Anne Marie's bedroom, but Tom just looked her in the eyes with a slight smile. She didn't care what Anne Marie did in her private life, but she didn't want her to get hurt.

Abruptly, Tom's visits stopped, and Jackie and Bronwyn were relieved when they didn't see him for several weeks. But he was back again around Christmas 1993. Anne Marie still talked about him a lot and spoke of seeing him at work. It was obvious she was intrigued by him. Still, that didn't seem to be enough for Tom; her roommates sensed that he wanted all of her friends to like him too. It was as if he wanted them to shout for joy when he showed up, and neither Jackie nor Bronwyn was inclined to do that.

The main trouble with Tom Capano was that while he seemed to be what Annie wanted, in reality he wasn't available. He had a whole family out there on Seventeenth and Greenhill, and that was where he was going to be on Christmas Eve and Christmas Day and New Year's Eve. Anne Marie deserved better than that. Jackie knew that she had always been drawn to men with a little edge to them, and Tom had that. But her friends hoped devoutly that he was only a fleeting fancy.

ANNE MARIE was working extremely hard on her job. She charted every hour of Governor Carper's official days and nights and gave him file folders well in advance of every event, telling him where he would be, what the dress was, and which security staff would accompany him. No matter what might be going on in her personal life, she never missed a beat on the job. Tom Carper liked Anne Marie, and appreciated her personality as well as her cheerful efficiency. She didn't appear to have any special man in her life, and Carper kept his eye out for someone he felt was deserving of such a good woman.

■

ALTHOUGH she kept it to herself, there was a lot going on in Anne Marie's life away from the office—some good things and some frightening to her. More than ever, she needed to have a sense of control over her world. But there were some elements that she couldn't regulate. Her brother Mark had been in and out of rehab in a vain attempt to free himself of his addiction to alcohol. "He is worse now than he ever was," she wrote in her diary. "I no longer have a brother Mark, because that person inflicts too much pain in my life. It's much easier (emotionally) to leave him out. I spent too much of my life living with an alcoholic—that part of my life is over! Not forgotten—*over.*"

She didn't mean the part about shutting Mark out; she loved him too much. But she was so afraid for him and for the rest of her family. She could not bear to see the dread cycle play out again.

But far worse than her worries about her brother was Anne Marie's own conscience when it nattered at her about the secrets she was keeping from her family. She was involved with a totally unacceptable and unavailable man. She wasn't sure whether she would be—by definition—an adulteress or a fornicator, but both were forbidden by the Catholic Church, and her religion was as important to her as her family was.

On her twenty-eighth birthday—January 27, 1994—Anne Marie gave her heart away to the man she trusted to take care of it. "I have fallen in love with a very special person," she told her diary (but no one else),

> whose name I choose to leave anonymous. We know who each other are. It happened the night of my 28th Birthday. We have built an everlasting friendship. I feel free around him, and like he says, he "makes my heart smile"! He deserves some happiness in his life, and it makes me feel good to know that I can provide him with such happiness. Who knows if anything serious will ever happen between the two of us. (I only know what I dream.) Ciao, AMF.

TOM CAPANO insinuated himself into Anne Marie's life like a bindweed, whose heart-shaped leaves look so innocuous at first but which wraps its runners around whatever it selects until it nearly strangles its host. Tom wanted to know every detail of what went on in Anne Marie's life. Few women experience the kind of rapt attention he paid her, encouraging her to share her problems and her triumphs with him. And he wanted to meet all of her girlfriends.

Sometime in the spring of 1994, Tom suggested that Anne Marie pick two of her best friends, saying that he would take them all out to lunch at Tiffin, a very fancy restaurant where they would never have gone on their own. Anne Marie invited Jill Morrison and Ginny Columbus. When Jill asked suspiciously why Tom was taking them out to lunch, Anne Marie replied, "Tommy likes to do nice things for people that they might not normally be able to do on their own."

The four of them did have a nice time. Tom was a charming host and he told them to order whatever they wanted. He was very warm and pleasant to all of them, but it was clear that his eyes darted continually toward Anne Marie to see *her* reaction to the splendid lunch and the ambiance of Tiffin. She just smiled, happy to see him with two of her dearest friends.

But for all of her apparent happiness, Anne Marie was struggling with her life on many levels that spring of 1994. She was very grateful to her sister and brothers. As adults, they were determined to maintain solid family traditions and to create for *their* children the kind of childhood they had never known. Except for Mark, who was struggling with his own demons, they all had good jobs and nice houses. Good lives. Brian was a teacher and coach at the Friends School, Kathleen was the clinical coordinator of education at the Bryn Mawr Rehab Hospital, Robert was in commercial mortgage banking, and Kevin was a financial planner for Allstate Insurance. Anne Marie was part of everything they did, and they were all working hard to erase memories of the unhappy years. Robert, Kathleen, and Brian were happily married, and starting families. Mark's marriage to Debbie Gioffre had ended in divorce, but Anne Marie had a very special relationship with their son, Brian, born in 1991. For the three years before she disappeared, she made it an unbreakable habit to have dinner with her nephew Brian every Monday night. She wanted him to feel that he was a very important part of a large family.

Even for her diary, Anne Marie always seemed to put on a bright face, and she used exclamation points often. "Kathleen, Patrick, 'Seymour' [Brian], and I went to Robert's last Thursday for his birthday," she wrote in March 1994. "What fun! It's great having such a close beautiful family. Robert looks beautiful with Liam Michael. He will be such a great dad. He was a great substitute for me."

However, another entry on the same date revealed that Anne Marie was tremendously conflicted over her infatuation with Tom Capano. She told her diary that she and "Tomas" had had lunch on Friday, but that "we have problems because he has a wife and children, also. I don't want to be in love, but I can't help it. My God, please don't judge me!"

She continued to see Bob Conner, who had sensed Anne Marie's inner struggles and started her on a low dose of Prozac in an attempt to counteract her tremendous sense of social isolation, her hypersensitivity, and her obsession about her weight. But rather than easing her internal stress, Prozac only gave her headaches.

She might well have headaches; she wasn't eating enough to keep a bird alive. "No news on weight loss," she wrote in her diary.

> I am stuck at 135 pounds, and it's pissing me off! I can't starve myself any more than I already am. I suppose I should be thankful that I have not gained any weight either. I still avoid situations where there is food involved. G.R. was making mussels marinara and linguine with shrimp and chicken tonight, but I was afraid if I went over, I would eat, and when I got on the scales in the morning, I would have gained a pound or two. So I declined the invitation. When I lose my last five pounds, I will treat myself.

There were other worries. That March, Kathleen's three-month-old baby, Kevin—Anne Marie's godson—was very ill, Mark continued to slide down into the hell of alcoholism, Anne Marie was in love with a man with whom she knew she could have no future, and she had said good-bye to Paul Columbus, her first serious boyfriend, when he went off to the service. She wondered a little sadly in her diary why their romance hadn't worked out. All around her, people were pairing off, but she was still basically alone.

March was a hard month. Anne Marie's mother had died on March 16 nineteen years earlier, and March 24 was the eighth anniversary of her father's death. On the twenty-fourth, she wrote,

> Today is the day my father died! How sad. My father was a bad father, but he was the only father I ever had, so therefore I loved him. I do not think that he consciously meant to be a bad father—he just had no clue! He really made my life very sad and lonely. I will never forget the pain he caused me. He forced me to lie to protect my identity.

It was on that bleak anniversary that Tom Capano made an offer to Anne Marie. He, too, asked her to lie, but this time it was more to protect *his* identity. The words scrawled across the page of her diary sound almost childlike: "My boyfriend (Tomas) asked me today if I wanted to be a girlfriend and live alone and he would pay rent for my room. I need to think. I love him, but . . . he has four children (girls) and a wife. I will be a silent girlfriend. Oh my God."

Tom Capano may have sensed that he had not won over Anne Marie's housemates and felt their coolness when he dropped in. Or perhaps he liked the idea of having a mistress who would be alone somewhere in a room that he paid for, a young woman waiting for him to visit. But Anne Marie refused his offer. She wanted to stay with Jackie and Bronwyn.

And then there were the summers at the shore. For years, she and a number of compatible girlfriends had pooled their funds to rent a house on the New Jersey shore during the hot Delaware summer months. On weekends, they joined up either in Sea Isle City or in Avalon, both just north of Stone Harbor. If she had agreed to live in a room that Tommy paid for, Anne Marie knew that everything would change. She was afraid of being cut off from the friends who were such an integral part of her life.

Kim Horstman, the pretty blonde from Philadelphia who had met Anne Marie during one of the summers at the shore, remained one of her best friends. Kim was *always* a partner in the shared summer houses, although others came and went. And Kim was one of the few people who was privy to every aspect of Anne Marie's life. They were already planning to rent a house for the summer of 1994 in Sea Isle City with Eileen Duffy; Anne Marie felt she couldn't back out on that. She explained all of her concerns to Tom as she gently refused his offer of support.

Tom seemed to understand. He was so nice about *everything*. If something made her happy, he wanted her to have it. He told her again and again that he got a great deal of pleasure in seeing someone else happy. The money that was for him only a drop in the bucket was *supposed* to be used to make others happy. For instance, hadn't she and Jill and Ginny enjoyed the lunch at Tiffin? That was the kind of thing he meant. He cared about *her* and was concerned only about *her*.

Anne Marie and most of her friends lived from paycheck to paycheck, with the end of the month often looking pretty lean. She made around $31,000 a year as Tom Carper's scheduling secretary, less than $2,000 a month after taxes, and she tried to stay away from credit cards. Still, there always seemed to be something unexpected she needed to pay for. And she loved clothes. Anne Marie had gone through school wearing hand-me-downs, cheap imitations, and making do with what she could afford on a waitress's salary. Now she attended so many functions where women wore wonderful clothes, and she longed for them herself.

The first spring she was secretly seeing Tom, Anne Marie went shopping with Jill Morrison to find a dress to wear to a family wedding. They went to Talbot's and Anne Marie tried on a pale peach linen dress that suited her perfectly. But when she and Jill looked at the price tag, they gasped. It was way beyond Anne Marie's means. Nothing else she looked at could compete with the peach linen, so they left Talbot's without buying anything.

"About a week after the wedding," Jill recalled, "I asked Anne Marie, 'What did you end up wearing?' and she said, 'The peach linen dress.' She explained that Mr. Capano purchased it for her."

ANNE MARIE had begun an emotional roller-coaster ride. On April 22, Tom invited her to his house "to eat." She did not tell her diary if they were alone or if he had somehow managed to make her appear a casual business acquaintance. She only wrote, "My friend and I went to his house to eat. What a house! He enchants me. During the weekend, my thoughts are devoted to Tomas. I am afraid because I am in love with a man who has a family. I need to realize that our relationship will never be anything other than a secret."

On April 26, Tom came to Anne Marie's house to have dinner, and afterward, he told her gently that she deserved to have a man without children, a man who had a lot of time to spend with her, because she was "very special and deserved much more." She was bereft when he said that they could not go on seeing each other. And she watched from her window as he got into his car and drove away, probably, she thought, for the last time. She blamed herself, as she always blamed herself when someone left her behind. "I know it is my problem and my fault, because from the very beginning, I knew what I was getting myself into. After he left, I was so empty, sad, lonely. I [had] told him things that were hidden inside me. I feel so comfortable with him—I can say anything. I went to bed and cried myself to sleep."

Anne Marie grieved for two days and then Tom was back, calling to tell her that he loved her and could not stay away from her. They agreed to keep seeing each other, and her world seemed temporarily brighter, although she felt sorry for him because he told her he had to go to some stupid law seminar that he dreaded. "He is going to Canada from Wednesday to Friday for law school," she wrote in her diary. "Poor thing. Ciao Tomas, I love you."

■

BOB CONNER had known about Anne Marie's eating disorder for some time, but she had never really admitted it to him, and he was waiting for her to bring it up. On this Thursday, the same day she and Tom had agreed to continue their affair, she confessed her obsession with food to Conner.

> I cried a lot as well as informed him of my eating disorder. I realize how poor of an eater I've become, and that it's not healthy. However, it feels great every time I get on the scale if the needle has decreased from before! My ideal weight is 125. I can do it. I now weigh 133. Eight more pounds. I could easily do that in a week! I also feel that my world is so out of control, and the only thing I can control is my food intake. I know one thing, Prozac is not for me. Bob is aware, so I suppose we'll take it from here. Cheers—AMF

Anne Marie did not expect to see Tom the next week, since he would be in Canada for the law seminar. It may have been a relief for her not to listen for the phone, wondering if he was going to start the come-here, go-away, come-here discussions again. She *knew* he had gone away, at least for a time.

_____ Chapter Ten _____

THAT APRIL OF 1994, when Tom told Anne Marie that he wanted to continue seeing her, he was hardly a man alone. Not only did he have a wife, but Debby MacIntyre had been his mistress for almost twelve years. Tom had made Debby understand that his marriage was unhappy, but divorce wasn't even a consideration. "I'm miserable in my marriage," he told her in a soft, hopeless voice, "but I can't leave my kids. You know that, Deb."

Of course she did. From the way Tom described his situation, she pictured him living a life of quiet desperation. Kay was a truly nice person, but she and Tom were so different, and Debby had seen for herself how he doted on his girls. It would break Tom's heart to have to walk away from his four daughters.

Debby had been caught in an unhappy marriage and she had escaped—but then, *she* had her children with her. She couldn't even imagine what it would have been like to live away from them. She made sure their father saw them as often as he liked. Victoria and Steve needed their father, too, and she and her ex-husband had worked it out. They saw him every other weekend and stayed with him every Wednesday night.

"Tom loved his girls," Debby recalled. "I thought he would do *anything* for them." She could empathize with that; she would do anything for her children.

Tom was a highly organized man and he liked things to move smoothly, with chores and events fitting neatly into the time slots assigned to them. From his comments to Debby, it sounded as though his home wasn't run as efficiently as he would have liked, although she knew that it was *Kay* who saw that the girls got to school, to their games, to doctors' appointments, to birthday parties. She couldn't have been doing that bad a job, but how could anyone know what went on behind the walls of someone else's home? Tom made an appearance at the girls' games and meets, but his career rarely allowed him to attend an entire event, while Kay was always there.

Debby's own life revolved around her children—who were now in junior high and high school at Tatnall—her job, and Tom. He needed her to be his friend and confidante as well as his lover; and she tried to always be there for him, to listen to whatever was on his mind and provide a safe haven from the pressures of his world. She had been with him through his years with the city, through the time he advised Governor Castle, and now when he was back in private practice. He was so pressed for time and usually late for the times they had arranged to be together, sometimes *hours* late. But Debby always waited for him and never chided him, even though she was often terribly disappointed.

In all the years of their relationship, Debby had never once given Tom an ultimatum or told him she wanted to end their affair. She was so afraid that he would leave her, and she could not imagine her life without him.

Two or three times, Tom had alluded to some woman—a secretary at his office, she believed—who had taken too much for granted, pushed too hard. Debby thought that relationship had gone on a year or two before she came into Tom's life; she recalled her ex-husband saying something about Tom's having trouble over a woman. It hadn't mattered to her then, and she hadn't listened closely. But she knew Tom was like quicksilver; if anyone tried to trap him, he would be gone.

"I never rocked the boat," she remembered. "I always wanted

to please him, because I wanted his praise. I wanted him to love me. I thought that was the way I had to be for him to keep loving me. There were a number of times in our relationship over the years when I knew that it was wrong, I knew it was going nowhere, and that I had to *try* and break it off, and I *couldn't* do it. I didn't have the strength to do it. I never threatened to leave him. I never, ever could say that. I was always afraid that *he* would leave me."

And she could not have borne that. One bleak October, he *had* left her for several weeks, but he had come back. Debby had made her peace with the way her life had turned out. "I finally came to some level of happiness," she said, "thinking, Look at the good he's brought me. Look at how he's made me feel about myself. He's always there for me." If she and Tom were not meant to be together as a couple free to walk in the bright sunlight of public awareness, at least she knew she was *special* to him. And from the time she was a very little girl, all Debby had ever longed for was to be special to someone.

One of the topics that raised Tom's ire was Tatnall School. Debby had long since moved up into an administrative job. She ran the before- and after-school programs, and for five years the entire summer program. She was very efficient, worked long hours, and took pride in her work at Tatnall. But Tom often pointed out that she worked too much overtime and got too little pay and respect. He told her that she was always letting people walk all over her. "You are everybody's doormat," he said.

"You're right," Debby would agree. "I *do* let people walk on me."

It became a self-fulfilling prophecy for her. Every time he told her she was too wishy-washy, she felt weaker and her achievements seemed less important. "And *he* treated me like a doormat," Debby recalled. "He admitted it. He said, 'Sometimes, I treat you like a doormat. I don't mean to, Debby. You know that—but every once in a while, I do.' "

In truth, he almost always treated her that way. As much as she loved him and depended on him, Debby often had the feeling she wasn't smart enough, attractive enough, or worldly enough. Even though she did her best to anticipate his moods, she often irritated Tom because she had guessed wrong about what her response should be.

Twelve years should have made her a little confident in their relationship—but she never was. Tom told Debby often that she shouldn't be waiting around for him. She needed to have a life of her own and she should be seeing other men. He suggested that she go to bars and pick up men, and he seemed to have no jealousy about any physical relationship that might ensue. Rather, he told her he would love to hear about what she did with other men. When he talked like that, Debby felt sick. It was the ultimate rejection. He didn't want her and was ready to palm her off on other men. Worse, he wanted the details. She tried to tell herself that he didn't really mean it.

But he did. There had been incidents that she tried never to think of. Sometime in the late eighties, after they had been together for several years, Tom encouraged Debby to accept a date with a former classmate who was in town from New England. "I would do what he wanted to compromise what was best for me lots of times," she said ruefully.

This was one of those times. At Tom's instigation, Debby invited the man home and there was a sexual encounter, again following Tom's instructions. Indeed, he was watching from the window. She didn't understand why he would want to watch her with another man, or her own acquiescence in his voyeuristic fantasy. She tried to forget it had ever happened.

About five years later, Tom set up another situation designed to end in a ménage à trois. Debby had been surprised when Tom showed up at her house with Keith Brady in tow one evening. Keith was the attorney who had replaced him as adviser to Governor Castle, four years younger than Tom and a tall, handsome man, with black hair. Tom had confided in Keith about his own extramarital affairs, telling him in particular about Debby and describing her as "a wonderful person I care very much about."

Tom and Keith had been golfing. They had had some drinks at the country club, and Tom poured several more at Debby's house. It was an encounter orchestrated by Tom. At some point, he signaled to Debby and they moved to another room, where they made love. And then Tom asked her to approach Keith and do what was necessary to draw him into a sexual encounter. She didn't want to do it, but like an automaton, Debby did as Tom asked. "I was afraid if I didn't do it," she said later, "he'd get angry and leave. Leave *me.*"

At Tom's insistence, Debby performed oral sex on his friend, but Keith was as embarrassed as she was and failed to get an erection. It was a humiliating incident that would come back to haunt both of them. They tried to pretend nothing had ever happened between them. But Tom knew. It gave him a little more power over both of them.

On another occasion, Tom urged Debby to have lunch with Keith and then bring him back to her house and seduce him so that he could watch. She did have lunch with Keith, but neither of them wanted to take it any further than that, although Keith went on being Tom's friend—at least nominally.

Tom's sexual appetites had always been, at the least, unusual, and Debby had always tried to accommodate him. She had had little sexual experience before her years with Tom and wasn't sure if he was asking for more than most men would. They were very open with each other, and she felt somewhat secure in believing that, for him, she was the female in his life, and that she pleased him.

Both Debby and Keith Brady were mortified by their one intimate encounter, but there was no reason to think anyone would ever know about it. Keith went on to become the second in command in the Delaware Attorney General's Office. He was married and had children. Debby wondered sometimes why Tom urged people out of their safe worlds and put them into positions where they were caught in horrible, unforgettable acts. Maybe it made him feel stronger. He often told Debby that she had no self-esteem, railed at her for being so deficient, and then set about tearing her down. When she protested, Tom backed off and insisted he was only trying to help her.

After so many years, Tom and Debby still spoke on the phone a couple of times a day, and they were together on Wednesday nights. They had a favorite song, "Sailing," by Christopher Cross. Maybe they liked it because it made love sound so easy, without any of the complications that it had in the real world. They couldn't be seen together in Wilmington, but Tom took Debby to dinner in restaurants in Little Italy in Philadelphia. His favorite was a place called Villa d' Roma. "We never ran into anyone we knew," she recalled. "It was 'our spot.' It was very small, but the food was good, and I loved going there."

Tom was obsessed with hiding their relationship, and Debby thought it was because of his prominence in city government and because he wanted to protect Kay and his girls. Of course, it was unthinkable that they could go out to dinner in Wilmington. Every time they met accidentally in Wilmington, they had to pretend. As far as Debby knew, even Tom's brothers had no idea that he was involved with her.

Tom had never taken Debby on a real trip. When she traveled, she was alone with her children. She was surprised and delighted when he asked her if she would like to go to Montreal with him in April 1994. There was a law seminar he had to attend, but he assured her he would have a lot of free time, too. Tom explained that she couldn't actually go *with* him, of course, on the flight; they would have to travel separately. "He went up first," Debby recalled, "and then I came up. I lied to my family as to where I was going, which I'm not proud of. But it was wonderful. I loved Montreal. We walked all over—we had a really good time."

In all of their years together, Debby had never been with Tom for two days in a row. Now they were in another country, another world, and she knew he wasn't going to go away in a few hours. "It was so wonderful," she said.

Coming home, there was a reservations mix-up, which meant they had to fly back to Philadelphia on the same plane. But Tom was very concerned that they might be seen together on the flight. "He told me there was a woman lawyer there whom he knew," Debby said, "and he didn't want to chance her seeing us together, so I had to sit in another seat, far away from him. It made me feel like, *What am I doing here, anyway?*"

The flight from Montreal was so lonely that Debby had trouble hanging on to the blissful memories of their time together in Montreal. But when they got to Philadelphia, Tom asked her if she wanted to go out to dinner before they drove to Wilmington, and that made her feel better. He took her to a new place—the Panorama. It was an upscale Italian restaurant, very intimate, with the ceiling and walls draped in swaths of cloth so that it seemed as if patrons were dining in an elegant and sensuous boudoir. The maître d' said there was just one table for two left, right near the kitchen, and led them ceremoniously to be seated.

The food was delicious and their meal was very pleasant. Debby felt so much better about the trip; Tom wasn't brushing her off as if she was only some woman he'd spent a couple of nights in bed with and couldn't wait to be rid of. They smiled and talked, and it was OK again.

And then it was all ruined when they started the half-hour drive to Wilmington and Debby realized that she had left her purse on the floor beneath the table. They were on the south side of the Philadelphia airport before she reached for her purse and couldn't find it. She froze, certain that Tom would be absolutely furious with her when she told him.

And he was. "I can't believe you could do something so stupid!" he snarled. "So unbelievably dumb."

She begged him to let her call the Panorama on the cell phone and he nodded, his jaw set.

"And they had my pocketbook," Debby said. "So we turned around and went back. And I apologized profusely. By that point in our relationship, I was constantly apologizing to him about something. I was sorry . . . sorry . . . sorry. I was sorry for things that I didn't even need to be sorry for, and I was probably getting on his nerves. He made me feel like such an idiot. He was so verbally abusive that night."

It was not a propitious ending for their trip, and Debby got home feeling horrible. "He was obsessed with keeping our relationship secret," she said, "and I had left my purse with all my ID in it for anyone to see."

She would have felt far worse if she had known that Tom was in the first stages of an affair with a woman seventeen years younger than she was. But it had never even occurred to her that there might be any other woman in his life besides Kay. Debby believed that she and Tom had achieved such a degree of intimacy that they were almost *closer* than a married couple. However cruel he might be when he was in a mood, she could always take comfort in the knowledge that Tom had chosen her to have an affair with out of all the women he encountered. He might get angry with her, but he always came back.

ANNE MARIE was seeing Bob Conner for psychological counseling every week that spring of 1994, although she didn't want anyone to know. For that matter, few who knew her would have ever believed that she needed any therapy. She was consummately professional at her job, fun to be around, and she looked great. Her laughter often bounced off the walls of the governor's outer office; it sounded like the laughter of a woman without a trouble in the world. She had a ribald sense of humor and could scatter profanity through her conversation and still look like an angel.

Sometimes she dropped into O'Friel's Irish Pub. She would stand near the bar and bellow *"Keveyyy!!!"* at the top of her lungs, and then laugh when the handsome redheaded proprietor popped his head out of the back room. With its brick walls and wooden floors, O'Friel's might as well have been located in Dublin as in Wilmington; it was the headquarters for so many people in Wilmington, Irish and Italian alike. Many major political decisions had been hammered out at O'Friel's. For the Faheys, though, it was more like home. Anne Marie felt completely at ease there, and she should have because they all loved her.

Ed Freel liked to tease Anne Marie because she was working for the governor. "We got you after all, Annie!" he said. "You said you'd never work for us—but we got you."

"I said I wouldn't work *here*, Ed," she replied with a grin. "And I'm not serving beer, now am I?"

But for Ed Freel, the governor's office was like the family business, too, and he was pleased that Anne Marie was doing so well. She was like a little sister to him and Kevin and Bud. They had known her since she was such a little girl, and now she was five feet ten, all grown up and beautiful.

None of them knew how unhappy and anxious Anne Marie was behind her wide smile. She hid it so well; she had been hiding her true feelings for most of her life. She had constructed a facade that made her seem comfortable with bawdy comments, an earthy young woman who wasn't easily shocked. Nothing could have been further from the truth. She was not nearly as worldly-wise as she liked to pretend, but she never batted an eye in public. Despite her belief that she was overweight at 133 pounds, she had a lovely figure. And yet she worried about every ounce she put in her mouth.

Bob Conner summed up his sessions with Anne Marie in scribbled notes that were typically hard to decipher. But the same themes popped up again and again: "Codependency issues." "Turns to conflict to avoid depression." "Emotionally fragile—feels powerless." "Self-esteem issues." "Struggling with deeply held fear of abandonment, sense of aloneness, but with a core of 'unlovedness.' " "So frightened of hurting others." "Fear of rejection."

The Anne Marie she showed to the world was the envy of a lot of young women, who viewed her as having a wonderfully exciting life. Inside, she was fighting to rid herself of the self-image imprinted by her father's drunken taunts. But she had had the guts to seek out help and to peel the scabs away from her blocked memories and deal with her problems. She had a great deal of inner strength and she was making progress. With Bob Conner, whom she trusted completely, Anne Marie was learning ways to assert herself, beginning to believe that she was a good person, a smart person, and that she deserved to be happy.

And to be loved. She wanted so much to be loved.

JILL MORRISON and Anne Marie went to the Tour Du Pont bicycle races at Rodney Square in May of 1994 and watched the cyclists who had gathered from all over the world compete. Afterward, they attended a party in the old Holiday Inn. One floor of the garage was closed off so the riders could bring their bicycles, and band music bounced off the low ceilings. It was a chance to meet the cyclists, and Anne Marie looked for some of the Spanish-speaking competitors. She tried to make them feel comfortable in a country where they didn't speak the language, surprising them with her fluent Spanish. She loved showing off her Spanish.

Jill was unabashedly flirting with one of the coaches of the bicycling team from Spain. As she and Anne Marie walked out, Jill laughed and said, "He was pretty flirty, Annie. Maybe I should have kissed him. I've never kissed an older man before."

Anne Marie stopped, turned around, and said slowly, "Well, *I* have."

From the look on her face, Jill knew whom she meant. It had to be Tom Capano, and it sounded like more than the good-night kiss Anne Marie had described after she'd been to dinner with him six months earlier. She was apparently still seeing him, and that gave Jill a kind of sinking feeling. Annie could seem so together, but her good friends knew she wasn't.

THERE were a lot of changes in store for Anne Marie that spring. Bronwyn was going back to New Zealand, and Jackie was getting married in July, so that meant the end of their sharing Jackie's house. But it was more than that for Anne Marie; she was losing another home. She had no choice but to look for an apartment that she could afford on her own. She was saving her money, putting a little aside each month, for another reason, too. She and her brother Brian had decided that the best way to use their share of the inheritance from their grandmother's estate would be to visit Ireland and walk through the places where Katherine McGettigan had lived when she was a girl. There was just enough for plane fare, but they needed to save so they could rent a car and pay for lodgings.

Annie and Seymour in Ireland—they both liked the concept and looked forward to the trip that summer of 1994. It was a positive goal for Anne Marie. She and Brian were so much alike and such good friends. If they could trace their roots in Ireland, they would not only honor Nan's memory but also establish some continuity in their own lives. The two of them, who had been the last to leave the childhood home that had been sacrificed to debt and drink, would make new memories.

In the spring of 1994, Anne Marie was already trying to keep from being too dependent upon Tom Capano. He was offering her so many of the things she needed: a listening ear, the protectiveness of an older man—something she had never known—and the things that money could buy, also something she had never known. It was so tempting and so easy for her to love him. But she knew he could never offer her what she *really* wanted. He couldn't give her marriage or babies or self-respect. She couldn't take him to her family's holiday celebrations; he had a whole other life that would always keep him away from her when she needed him.

It was very difficult for Anne Marie to turn away from *anyone*, so fearful was she that she might hurt their feelings. Tom was being very reasonable and very nice, but she felt the pull of invisible strings. He knew that she desperately wanted to make a side trip from Ireland while she was in Europe. She had always hoped to return for a visit to the family she had lived with in Spain, but that was financially impossible, even with Nan's bequest. She couldn't dream of going to Spain, too.

One night, when Jill went with her to look at an apartment, Anne Marie blurted, "I just have to tell you something. I got a card from Tom—and it had five hundred-dollar bills in it."

Jill looked at her. "Why—?"

"The note said, 'Use this to go to Spain.' "

The two of them discussed whether Anne Marie should accept it. How could she explain how she had suddenly come up with that much money and just go off to Spain? What would Brian think? They agreed that $500 was probably nothing to Tom, but it was so much money to them—too much for Anne Marie to accept.

As the summer approached, it would become clear that Anne Marie was seriously questioning her relationship with Tom. Her Catholic faith was very important to her, her family's approval meant everything, and being with Tom went against those things. Still, she wasn't confident to be just herself, alone. Her diary was full of entries about other men—men who were free to date her. Although she was twenty-seven, she sounded more like a teenager when she wrote about the men in her life. She had begun dating late and she needed approval more than most women. Mature in her career, Anne Marie was sixteen in her heart.

On June 11, 1994, her brother Robert arranged a double date: he and his wife, Susan, along with Anne Marie and Mike Hines, a man Robert worked with. Anne Marie felt the blind date had worked out very well; in a little over a week, she wrote, "I think I'm falling for him real fast! I see myself marrying him."

Of course, it was much too soon. And the P.S. revealed more

about how frightened she really was of not being good enough, of being alone, of being unloved: "P.S. My weight is 129. I have a serious problem, but right now I am not able to confront it."

A week later, Anne Marie wrote of a wonderful evening with Mike at the beach, a Saturday night with a romantic stroll home. But—

> He said he would talk to me tomorrow, and I never heard from him. . . . He never called me Sunday nor Monday. So of course I now think he's blowing me off, and does not want to see me anymore. God, it is great to be young and insecure. I hope that's not the case, but if it is, I better learn to deal with it quick. Actually, I am good at dealing with rejection, much better than dealing with compliments.

Almost every woman who ever went on a date knew that feeling. Men rarely called when they said they would, and they *always* said they would. But Anne Marie's fear went deeper. She leapt to embrace rejection before it could sneak up and catch her unaware.

Mike Hines eventually called her and they went out again, but she questioned every comment, every phone call that didn't come or came too late. She was sure he wanted to dump her but was afraid to because he worked with her brother. She set arbitrary time limits; if he didn't call by Wednesday, that meant he was dumping her. Or by Friday. When he didn't accept her invitation to a Fourth of July celebration, that meant "I am not pretty, smart, fun, exciting, enough."

But she *was*. Only, she didn't believe it. When Anne Marie forced a premature confrontation on what Mike's feelings and intentions were after only a month of fairly casual dating, he was polite and sincere, and probably spooked. She did not mention another date with him in her diary.

ON July 20, 1994, Anne Marie and Brian arrived in Ireland. It was to be a respite from a frenetic eight months in which she had judged herself so very harshly. With the brother who loved her so dearly, folded into the country of her origins, Anne Marie blossomed. From Shannon to Limerick to Dublin to Ballinor to Cape Clear, her diary entries were full of joy and excitement about the trip, full of her tremendous appreciation for life.

> As I sit on this rock elevated at a few hundred feet, below a sky blue ocean, I do not know that I have ever been to a more beautiful

place (or ever will for that matter). As I look out all I can see is water, cliffs, and, last but not least, green pasture. There are a few homes scattered around the island. . . . I lay down for a bit, listening to the waves crash against the cliff with a fair hint of seagulls in the background. . . . I have never seen so many different shades of green, all representing this beautiful country. Everywhere I look (north, south, east, west) I am surrounded by the ocean. . . . I have my grandmother to thank for the relaxation I am experiencing right now. Without her this trip would not have been possible. Of course I would rather have her with me, but we all must die. I hope she knows I am here.

Their two weeks in Ireland closed an invisible circle for Anne Marie and Brian. Although they often stayed at hostels with few amenities and sometimes argued when they were tired or hungry or just sick of too much time together, they were connecting to the people who had gone before them.

Anne Marie fretted more than Brian did about the primitive or bizarre accommodations they were forced to choose because they had little money. And her journal entries were not all as poetic as her thoughts on the ocean. When they reached Dingle, she showed her well-developed irreverent side:

We dropped our belongings [at the hostel] in #10. I don't *think* so, "Doggie!" It was another ten-person, five-bunk-bed room from the 1960's. I realize I don't recall the sixties due to the fact that I was born in 1966; however that room was bullshit. Black walls with fluorescent psychedelic paint splatted all over. There was one side of the wall that had a big-ass toothbrush painted on it. How attractive! I told Seymour, "No way—get me the fuck out of this room!"

And in Dingle, the happy campers' patience was wearing a little thin. "I think Seymour is bored with me," Anne Marie wrote.

We had a "fight" at the bar because he said that my self-esteem is very low, and if he did not know me, he would think I was incapable of doing absolutely *nothing*. I was very sad and *furious!* I think that when two people go on a trip together for two weeks, one is bound to get on one another's nerves. I don't regret taking a trip with him, but *sometimes* I hope he likes a party and also would enjoy eating in a restaurant which is a little bit more expensive! Oh my God, shut your mouth, Ana Maria.

In close quarters for too long, Anne Marie began to think that Brian was ridiculously parsimonious, and he found her constant need to be doing something unreasonably hyper. But they pushed on, their verbal tangles typical of siblings. Anne Marie was so secure with Brian that she was actually asserting herself and speaking up, which, for her, was a significant accomplishment. They found the little hamlet on the way to Sligo that the Faheys were supposed to have come from and took a picture of Fahy Hardware. They were enjoying the very real sense of being in the place where they had roots.

And then they were in Kilmecrennan, the village where Nan and Grand Daddy had once lived. It was high summer and their time there could not have been more serendipitous. Brian and Anne Marie found the pub in Milford that Nan had owned; it was still called the White Heather Inn. And they met a cousin who looked just like Nan. Surrounded by relatives, Anne Marie felt totally at home, and it was like balm to her soul.

When she returned to Bob Conner's office on August 9, Anne Marie was happier than he had ever known her to be. She was living in her own cozy little apartment on Washington Street, where she could afford the rent all by herself. Her trip to Ireland had allowed her to step out of her life for two weeks, and he could see that her image of herself was much more positive. She confided that she had been able to speak her mind and nothing terrible happened. Her fingers crossed, it looked as if Annie was beginning to emerge from a long lonely tunnel.

_____ Chapter Eleven _____

WHEN NOTHING WORKED OUT with Mike Hines, Anne Marie had begun seeing Tom again. He often dropped by her desk in the governor's office, and she remembered how nice it was to be with him. He was supportive and kind, and he challenged her to a continuing game of trivia. It was light, at first, and fun.

Anne Marie told some of her friends part of the truth about her relationship with Tom, others very little, but she confided completely in Kim Horstman. They lived together at the shore every summer, and they spoke on the phone at least twice a week during the rest of the year. Kim knew about Annie's problem with eating, and she knew about the men in her life. That summer of 1994 in Sea Isle

City, Annie told Kim she was involved with Tom Capano—not just for lunches and an occasional dinner date, but in a romantic affair. She had referred to him often before, and he had gone out of her life for a while, it seemed, when Annie dated Mike Hines. But now Kim realized that she and Tom were involved in a far more intense relationship than before.

Anne Marie told Kim that Tom treated her "like a princess," that she could tell him all of her secrets, and that he bought her gifts and took her out to wonderful places. "I think she kind of thought of him maybe as a father figure," Kim recalled; "that she could share a lot with him."

If anyone needed a father figure, it was Anne Marie. But she was so torn. She told Kim about the guilt that was eating her up. "It was a very difficult situation for her because he was married with four children," Kim said, "and Annie is a Catholic and committing adultery is something that is against our religion. It was a very difficult struggle for her."

One day that summer, it became painfully clear to Anne Marie that Tom had another life totally separate from hers. She was shopping in Stone Harbor with her sister-in-law Linda when she bumped into him in front of one of the stores. He was waiting for one of his daughters to decide what she wanted to buy, and the three were chatting a little awkwardly when a coltishly pretty young girl came out of the store. It was Jenny, who was almost eleven.

"You look just like Natalie Wood," Anne Marie finally said, noting the resemblance that so many people did. Inside, she was checking her own emotions upon seeing Tom with one of his children. After some small talk, she and Linda went one way and Tom and Jenny another.

Anne Marie told Kim that Tom Capano wanted to meet her, because he knew that she had confided in Kim. Kim was the only one who knew about their affair at that point, or at least Anne Marie thought so. "It was Capano's idea," Kim recalled, "because we were very close and he knew that Annie was telling me about their relationship—so he said he wanted to meet me."

Kim was surprised and a little uncomfortable that Anne Marie's lover wanted to meet her, but she finally agreed. The three of them went to DiLullo's Restaurant in the center of Philadelphia, and Kim studied this man whom her friend was so taken with. He *was* a lot older than she and Annie were, but he seemed very nice and Annie was clearly nuts about the guy. "They acted very much like a couple," Kim recalled. "They were holding hands and they kissed across the table."

Anne Marie seemed so happy, but Kim knew how guilty she felt. Tom went out of his way to charm Kim. Why did he bother? It was Annie he wanted, and he certainly seemed to have her.

JILL MORRISON wouldn't have been happy to hear that. She had hoped that Anne Marie was over her fascination with Tom, but she had her doubts. When Annie came back from Ireland, she barely mentioned Mike Hines any longer. She and Jill were shopping at Macy's one day, and Anne Marie bought a phone for her new apartment. Jill saw her pay for it with a $100 bill. She had never known Annie to have a $100 bill, except for the time Tom sent her the five $100 bills to use for a trip to Spain. She hadn't gone to Spain, but now Jill wondered if he had convinced Annie to keep the money. Anne Marie didn't say anything about it, and Jill didn't ask.

Like her other good friends, Jill was worried about Anne Marie. She didn't look well. She hadn't been at all heavy when Jill first met her, and by the autumn of 1994, she was distressingly thin. When they went out to lunch now, Jill would order a good-sized sandwich, while Anne Marie said she wasn't hungry and nibbled on a pretzel and sipped ice water. In December, they were grocery shopping together in the Acme supermarket and Jill glanced from her cart to Anne Marie's with a sinking feeling. "I had a big basket full of food and all she had was fruit. And I told her I was very worried about her weight."

Anne Marie had deep smudgy circles under her eyes, and her arms and legs were so thin that her elbows and knees stuck out. "I told her I actually thought about calling Bob [Conner]," Jill recalled, "because I can't understand how you can be seeing a psychologist and they don't realize that you are as thin as you are, and that there is a problem here."

(Of course, Bob Conner knew all about Anne Marie's anorexia, although he was very careful about confronting her before *she* was ready. He knew she worked out too much, used laxatives to rid her body of food, and he was grateful that she was not bulimic.)

For once, when Jill brought it up, Anne Marie didn't try to avoid a discussion about her weight. Jill couldn't hold back her tears when she looked at Anne Marie in the bright store lights, and she touched her arm and said, "I can't watch you kill yourself like this."

Anne Marie had tears in her eyes, too, and promised, "Don't worry about me. I'll stick around for a long time."

Once again, the fall had been a difficult time for Anne Marie. Her glorious weeks in Ireland seemed remote now, but it was more than the end of summer that made her feel so down. There was always the anniversary of Nan's death to deal with, and then the holidays that evoked so many memories. She had put forth some ideas at work and felt they weren't taken seriously. She had asked for a raise, which was unbelievably difficult for her, and she was mortified when she didn't get it, even though it was because of the state's budget allocations and not because she wasn't doing a good job.

In her next session she told Bob Conner, "Annie's not going anywhere." She was characteristically angry at herself as always, feeling it was *her* fault that she didn't have enough confidence to explore other options.

Most of all, Anne Marie was still gripped by such a pervasive sense of loneliness. It was as if her whole life was spent on the outside looking in, and at any moment everyone she counted on could abandon her. When Conner asked her *who* might desert her, Anne Marie finally talked a little bit about a lawyer she was seeing, but she was very cautious about revealing much. She didn't tell him the man was married. She was too ashamed.

Just being in the affair with Tom was destructive and frightening for Anne Marie. She was so afraid of disappointing her brothers, and of offending God. And then there was Christmas coming up. She told Bob Conner she was afraid of Christmas and what might go wrong if there was alcohol and her brother Mark was there. And she was afraid she couldn't deal with Christmas dinner, so much food to resist, to push around her plate so no one would notice that she wasn't eating if she *did* resist.

Anne Marie clung to Conner emotionally because she trusted him completely, and that was fine. He was a man she *could* trust, a kind soul as well as a skilled therapist. Conner saw that she needed to believe in someone enough so that she could pour her heart out. It was important that anyone she chose to confide in understood that this beautiful and vibrant woman was often only a child without defenses. When she *did* trust, she was like a turtle without a shell, so pervious to hurt. Still, Anne Marie and Conner were making progress. For every step back she took, she leapt ahead three. Yes, she was still afraid of losing control of her life, but she was finally able to voice her fears and confront them.

Despite her feelings of inadequacy on the job, Tom Carper was very happy with Anne Marie's work. Her sister and brothers were proud of her, and she was always there to baby-sit when they needed her. The only real thing she could not control about her life was that Tom Capano had made himself indispensable. It was almost as if he had some radar that picked up the places where he could insinuate himself into her psyche. He ferreted out every vulnerability in her careful armor and seemed to play on that, drawing her a little closer with each move. She had come to need him, but she knew that it was a mortal sin to want him, and an impossibility to have him. The more she cared about Tom, the less she was able to eat. And since he was so very good to her, she could not pull away from him; he reminded her often that she hurt his feelings when she rejected him. Causing anyone else pain was anathema to Anne Marie.

DURING December of 1994, Anne Marie accepted intellectually that she could not have Tom, but emotionally she feared she could not leave him, either. She visited her sister's and brothers' homes with their Christmas decorations, their rosy babies, and she wanted that for herself; and then, of course, she felt guilty for her envy.

But Anne Marie knew she could sand off the hurtful edges of her Christmas feelings—and the old memories that came rushing back—when she saw Bob Conner during their January sessions. Finally, she had come to understand that most people had their areas of anxiety and were frightened sometimes; she wasn't a freak and she wasn't a hopeless case. She believed she could find a way to be free and healthy and deserving of happiness.

Bob Conner used role-playing and cognitive therapy with Anne Marie. They could not change the past; there was no gain in harping on old hurts, and she understood that. But she could learn to shut off the thoughts that led back inevitably to her childhood and her feelings of helplessness. Going into 1995, Anne Marie was fighting as hard as she could.

UNFORTUNATELY Anne Marie and Bob Conner would have only two more sessions. On January 5, 1995, they talked about Christmas dinner and the rage (over her father's alcoholism) and sadness (about Nan and her mother) that Anne Marie felt. Twelve days later, on January 17, 1995, Conner's last scribbled entry in Anne Marie's case file read: " 'Road Less Traveled' issues with self love." Only he knew exactly what that meant to him—and to her—and he would not be able to explain it.

They planned to meet again at 5 P.M. on January 24, but Conner called Anne Marie earlier that afternoon and asked if he could reschedule for the next day. He had a patient who was in crisis and he wanted to give him Anne Marie's time slot. Of course, she said yes. There had been times when *she* was panicked and needed to talk.

At 6 A.M. on January 25, Brian Fahey's phone rang and he fumbled sleepily to grab it. He recognized Anne Marie's voice, but she was crying so hard that he could barely make out what she was saying. And then he understood. Bob Conner was dead. His office had called Anne Marie to cancel her appointment. He had been coming home from his appointment the night before when a drunk driver crossed the center line and hit his car head-on.

A very real force for good in Anne Marie's life—and many others' lives—was gone. She had counted on Conner since 1992 to help her work her way out of her anxiety and depression. She loved him like a father or a big brother, and had trusted him completely. She was grieving for him, and because she was Anne Marie, she blamed herself for his death. "If I hadn't said it was OK to postpone my session," she sobbed, "he wouldn't have been out on that road so late. He would have been in his office at five with me, as always, and he would have just gone home like always."

Of course, that was her own circuitous reasoning, her leap to feel guilt over someone else's pain. And she knew it, too, but it was so hard to accept that Bob Conner was gone. So hard for *her* to accept that nothing she had done had killed him and nothing she might have done could have saved him.

As she often did, Anne Marie postponed writing about Conner's death until she was able to deal with it. She had noted her appointment with him, the session that was never to be, on her calendar for January 25—"5:00 Bob C."—and then gone back and filled in the last space on January 24: "Bob killed 6:50 p.m."

It would be a full month before she could truly put her feelings down:

> I loved Bob, and he has helped me grow so much, but we had a lot more work to do until I got to where I need to be at this point in my life. He was the only person who knew everything (even a little bit about Tommy [not much]) about me, and it felt great to get all this shit inside of me OUT. Bob was funny, intelligent, had a great smile, voice and sense of humor. He believed in me, and actually liked me for me. Not many people know the real Annie.

And that was true. Few people did.

ONCE more, Anne Marie struggled to cope with the death of someone she had loved and depended upon. She was two days away from her twenty-ninth birthday, and it was supposed to have been such a happy day. Jill Morrison, Ginny Columbus, and Jackie Binnersley were going to take her out to dinner at Toscana to celebrate. When Jill asked her if she still wanted to go, Annie said she did. She needed to be with her friends. She agreed to meet them all at Ginny's house.

Jackie, Ginny, and Jill waited for Anne Marie to get there for half an hour, worried. When she finally showed up, she explained that she was delayed because she'd had a surprise visitor. Tom Capano had dropped by her apartment to give her a birthday present—a twenty-seven-inch color television set. He had totally floored her with his gift.

Tom liked television and had told her that he had a set in his home in almost every room. Anne Marie was a little shamefaced when she told her friends that Tom said he'd brought her the big set because he thought the small TV Kathleen and Patrick Hosey had given her for Christmas was "cheap and chintzy."

None of them knew what to say. A twenty-seven-inch TV was a pretty big present for a married man to give a single girl on her birthday. But Anne Marie's friends knew she already felt bereft over Bob Conner's death, and they weren't about to make her feel worse by lecturing her on the evils of accepting lavish presents from a married man. Anyway, she *knew*; she berated herself more than they ever could.

It was all too obvious that Tom was back in Anne Marie's life, stronger than he had ever been. At first he had gone out of his way to charm her girlfriends, but in the early spring of 1995, he seemed intent on driving a wedge between her and her friends. Either he didn't realize how much they all meant to one another or he didn't care. Her friends knew how rough things had been for Annie. Jackie had seen firsthand the poverty and deprivation she had struggled with in school. Ginny knew how hard she had worked to get through college. They understood that if anyone was impressed with nice clothes and beautiful homes, it was Annie. They all knew that Tom Capano had the money and the sophistication to play into that. But they hoped that Anne Marie was savvy enough to know that some presents came with pretty ribbons that could entangle her.

_____ Chapter Twelve _____

AFTER BOB CONNER DIED, Anne Marie was left floating without a net. She tried to find another counselor, but it wasn't like changing mechanics or even dentists. It had taken her so long to feel absolutely safe with a therapist, and she could not simply switch her allegiance and her secrets to someone else. But while she was trying to find another therapist, she needed *someone* to confide in, and she had someone: Tom Capano.

Tom had told her so often about how miserable *he* was, and she worried about him. The sacrifices that he made so that his family would be happy and the lonely life he told her he led touched her heart. As Anne Marie often told her diary, he deserved to have some happiness in his life. Now, he was listening to her sorrows and fears and seemed so concerned about her.

Over the past year, Anne Marie had managed to distance herself from Tom for short periods, but when she was alone, he always seemed to be there, waiting. It would have been difficult for any man her own age to compete with the mystique of Tom Capano; he was a huge fish in a small pond, wealthy, charming, and well liked. And he had about him a kind of secret sorrow that drew Anne Marie to him. Despite her intelligence, she was far younger than her years in terms of sophistication, a truly hopeless romantic in an era when the term was a cliché. When Tom looked sad and hopeless, her heart wept for him.

Anne Marie knew no more about Debby MacIntyre than Debby knew about her—and that was nothing at all. And she didn't know what Kay Capano was really like; she knew only about Tom's life as it was channeled through his brain, spun, and pronounced.

Four days after St. Valentine's Day, Anne Marie received a phone call from Tom. It was a Saturday, and he mentioned that he was having a party for Buddy Freel at a friend's house and they were going to Buddy's Bar afterward. He didn't invite her, but he didn't tell her to stay away, either.

Anne Marie went to Buddy's Bar that night at midnight, taking Jill and Jackie along. Tom was there, but he was with Kay, something she hadn't expected. Anne Marie was shocked when Tom shot her a look full of anger; he had never been angry with her, but then she had never surprised him when he was sitting with his wife. Tom had always orchestrated their meetings, and he had not suggested that she go to Buddy's party or his bar.

Feeling his rage, Anne Marie left with her friends. Naively, she had thought she could sit across the room from Tom without making him uncomfortable. But obviously, she had. Worse, she had seen him with Kay and been forced to recognize that this was a man who was definitely not free. He had a very pretty wife who didn't look at all like the cold woman he had described. There was a familiarity between Kay and Tom that made them seem *married*. Tom had appeared to be having a good time with the people he was with, and the memory of the expression of absolute disgust on his face when he looked at her haunted Anne Marie.

All unaware, she had broken one of his rules—a rule that had never been explained to her. Anne Marie was experiencing what Debby MacIntyre had lived with for years. Tom was in charge of his affairs, and he would not abide women who interfered with his carefully orchestrated schedule.

Now that he had Anne Marie emotionally tethered to him, Tom had the power to hurt her. And he did. After her faux pas at Buddy's Bar, he didn't call her on either Sunday or Monday. When she called him late Monday afternoon, he was cold, and eager to get off the phone. "I have a very busy week," he said abruptly, "and everything in my life is wrong and my life sucks."

Anne Marie had told Tom *everything* about her life, and he had instantly perceived her insecurities, her fear of rejection, her sure knowledge that she would be abandoned. Her openness had been akin to giving an enemy a map of your gun deployment. He was clearly demonstrating to her what would happen if she ever again encroached on his real life. He may even have enjoyed the panic he created in Anne Marie when he suddenly stopped calling her and as he spoke to her in a cold, annoyed voice when she called him.

And of course, she did. She kept calling. She left a message for him on Tuesday and he didn't return the call. He had told Anne Marie over and over again how much he loved her and needed her to fill all the dark places in his wretched life. She had come to love him and, more important, to depend upon his approval and kindness—and now he was suddenly gone.

Tom allowed Anne Marie to twist in the wind for a week, ignoring her calls. She berated herself for all manner of inconsiderate things she must have done. "Why did I allow myself to fall in love with a married man?" she asked her diary.

I know exactly why: Tomas is kind, caring, responsive, loving, has a beautiful heart, is extremely handsome and was kind and gentle with me. If he loves me like he used to say (which I still believe he does) then why is he treating me like this?

The most difficult part of this relationship is the fact that I cannot talk to anyone about us . . . the only person that knows is T. And he is not talking to me. . . . Hopefully, soon the phone will ring.

When Tom finally did call Anne Marie, he spoke to her in a voice so heavy with depression that she was stricken. He hinted that something was wrong, and she was terrified that he might be sick with some terminal disease. He would neither confirm nor deny that. She was so convinced that he was either suicidal or fatally ill that she went to St. Anthony's to pray "to help and provide T. with the strength that he needs."

The game went on. Tom was unreachable, inscrutable, and spoke in such a bleak way that Anne Marie was sure she was going to lose him, just as she had lost Bob Conner only a month before. After ten days that were agonizing for Anne Marie, Tom finally called her and told her that he needed to speak with her. His message gave her hope.

Tom grudgingly agreed to meet with Anne Marie to talk about why he felt they had no future. It was a scene that would have qualified him to write soap opera scripts, but he knew that Anne Marie was easy prey. He told her that the problem was that his feelings for her were so strong that he was jealous whenever other men said anything about her. He kissed her, held her, and shed a tear or two before he said that he needed to let her go for her own sake, for her future.

When he made a show of forcing himself to walk away, he must have known that his scenario had worked. It always had.

"My life doesn't exist without Tomas," Anne Marie wrote in her diary. "He deserves happiness—he does not deserve to be miserable! I'll wait forever. He's a wonderful, kind, caring, generous, sensitive man who deserves to be showered with the same kind of generosity he gives. I want to be that person!"

She had no glimmer of what that would mean.

ANNE MARIE'S friends saw a change in their get-togethers that spring of 1995. It was subtle at first, but they could not help but notice how nearly impossible it was to make plans with Annie.

Jill Morrison and Anne Marie had decided to spend the evening of St. Patrick's Day together. It was one of *the* major holidays in Wilmington and they were both looking forward to it. Jill was supposed to pick Annie up and then they were going to O'Friel's.

"I was inside the apartment, and she was finishing getting ready when the phone rang," Jill recalled. "So I was sitting on the couch reading a magazine, and she got off the phone and said, 'I'm really sorry I have to ask you to do this—but I need to ask you to leave.' And I couldn't believe I was being asked to leave, and I said, 'Why?'

and she said Mr. Capano had called and he was very upset and needed someone to talk to, and that she would give me a call in thirty to forty minutes and we would head on over [to O'Friel's] at that point."

Jill reached for her purse and stood up to leave. There was nothing else to do. Tom's problems evidently came first.

Jill had been back home for about forty-five minutes when Anne Marie called and said she was ready to go. When Jill asked what Tom's pressing problem had been, Anne Marie said, "He was very upset. He was having difficulties in his marriage, and he needed to talk to someone."

They went to O'Friel's and had a good time, but from that point on, it seemed that Tom was always getting in the way of any plans Anne Marie made with her girlfriends. It was almost as if he didn't want them to have a good time together.

When the Tour DuPont bicycle races came round again in 1995, Jill and Anne Marie planned to go to several of the functions. The first night, Jill and a friend that Anne Marie had met at the Y were to meet at her apartment. "I was really excited," Jill said, "telling Annie how much fun we were going to have, when she said, 'I can't go.' And I said, 'What do you mean you can't go?' and she said she had a job interview."

Jill just stared at Anne Marie in confusion; she had no idea that Annie was even *looking* for a job, and she was curious about how it happened that she would suddenly have a job interview on the very night they had been looking forward to for months. Anne Marie was hesitant about giving details about her job search.

"She told me that it was for a personal assistant for someone in north Wilmington," Jill said, "where she would make the same salary [as at the governor's office] and there also would be an apartment provided to her—which would have been a good thing financially."

But Jill smelled a rat and kept asking questions. Finally, Anne Marie said that she was supposed to have an interview with Louie Capano—an interview set up by Tom. She was adamant that she really *had* to go because Tom had gone to so much trouble to set up the interview with his brother.

Jill shrugged her shoulders, and Anne Marie told them to go ahead to the races and the party afterward without her. She promised to meet them after her interview with Louie Capano. But she didn't show up for five hours, and when she did she was wearing old jeans and Jill could see she had been crying. By that time, the bi-cycle races were long over and her friends were at a party at the Hol-iday Inn. Anne Marie didn't want to talk about her interview with Louie. And she went into an elaborate explanation about her puffy eyes, explaining that she had been crying about Bob Conner's death. "Things keep reminding me that he's gone."

Jill looked closely at Anne Marie. Something wasn't right, but she didn't want to pressure her. That was the worst thing to do to Anne Marie. They didn't work in the same office anymore; Jill had been moved to the campaign office, and that meant she saw Tom Capano fairly often, because he was on the Democratic fund-raising committee. He still struck her as a very inappropriate person for Anne Marie to be seeing—and she worried about it.

The next night Jill and Anne Marie met for a drink at the Holi-day Inn, and Jill asked again how the interview had gone. Anne Marie didn't seem at all excited about it. Rather, she sipped at her drink with a bleak look on her face. Jill tried to phrase her questions tactfully, but Anne Marie was so discouraged that she barely knew where to start. Finally, she looked up at Jill and said quietly, "I think he wants to control me."

"Who? Louie?"

"No. Tom. If I took the job, it would be Tom who was control-ling where I worked, and where I lived. Everything."

Jill would always remember how many times the word "con-trol" came up in Anne Marie's conversation. Thirty-one thousand dollars a year wasn't a lot of money, and they did have to pay for their own apartments—but they were free. Once they walked out of the Carvel building, they could do what they wanted and go where they wanted. The way Anne Marie talked about the job with Louie Capano—a job Tom had obviously arranged—made it seem like she would be a prisoner.

Jill had said so many times over the last few months, "I think Tom's in love with you." And Anne Marie had always shaken her head and smiled. Now Jill figured love had nothing to do with it. Annie was always doing things that other people wanted her to do, giving up little pieces of herself to make other people happy. But there was something almost scary about Tom Capano.

After their drink, they split up so they could go home and change for a dressy affair that was part of the continuing bike race festivities. Jill was supposed to pick Anne Marie up, but when she called to say she was on her way, Anne Marie didn't answer the phone. "I kept calling," Jill said, "and it got to the point where I was angry—like, we had plans—but I was concerned, too, and I called every fifteen minutes."

And then, despite Anne Marie's protestations that she would not let Tom Capano run her life, Jill knew what had happened. She knew that Annie was with him. She didn't return any of her calls that night.

Deliberately playing detective, Jill called Tom the next morning on some pretext of campaign business, and then casually asked if he had seen Anne Marie that morning. He said, "She left for the beach very early this morning."

Well, that was clear enough. Jill had been right. And she didn't want to be right.

_____Chapter Thirteen_____

DESPITE HER CHAFING AT the invisible bonds that went with seeing Tom, Anne Marie stayed with him. In her view, she was the only thing that kept him from falling into a pit of despair, and she couldn't desert him. If he was sometimes possessive and unreasonable, she blamed it on the burdens he carried. She had made a pledge to be there for him, and she honored it. While the world saw Tom as powerful and capable, _she_ knew that he was a lonely man full of pain. He conveyed that to her often enough, whenever she did something he disapproved of.

There were many things that Tom didn't like. He hated her stuffy little apartment and reminded her often that she could have had a lovely apartment for free in north Wilmington if she had only accepted Louie's job offer. He told her how to dress. Tom didn't like to have her wear clothing that was too red, too bright, too tight, too short.

"You look like a whore when you dress like that," he said frequently. As if a woman whose face was like a blossoming rose with a thick, clean-smelling halo of hair could look like a prostitute. If he hadn't said it with such venom, it might have been funny. But Tom was never funny when he criticized Anne Marie.

Too late, she realized she had told him too much about herself. He knew she thought her legs were too big, and that she hated having large breasts. He knew she starved herself when she was frightened, and he knew all about her brother Mark, her searing memories of her childhood, her work at the governor's office, and all the secret things she worried about. He could use them against her if he wanted.

Tom particularly disapproved of Anne Marie's friends and failed to see why she felt it necessary to spend so much time with them. Didn't he take her to wonderful places that made evenings out with the girls pale by comparison? And of course, he did; they went to Philadelphia for meals at Le Bec-fin, Victor's, the Saloon, Pamploma, and Panorama. As always, he selected the wine and the entrée. Claiming he was hopeless at figuring percentages (an odd deficiency in a bond lawyer), he routinely slid the check across the table to Anne Marie so that she could calculate the tip. He let her sign his name to the credit card slip.

Anne Marie's overwhelming concern about her weight continued; it was impossible for her to enjoy food, no matter how much it cost. Going out to eat was stressful for her, but Tom enjoyed dining out in fine restaurants, so, of course, that was what they did.

THE summer of 1995 was almost upon them, and Kim Horstman and Anne Marie were planning to rent a communal house once again. There had never been any question that they would. But it would take at least a half dozen partners to swing a place at the shore; rents were going up. Anne Marie talked with a man in the governor's office who had located a house to rent, and he figured they would need five other men and maybe three or four women besides Kim and Anne Marie.

That was fine with Kim; it was a big place, and not everyone went down to the shore every weekend. But Anne Marie was very worried. She said Tom wouldn't want her to stay in a house at the ocean where there would be other men present. "I think he would be very much against that," she told Kim.

Kim stared at her. They *always* met men at the shore; that didn't mean they were going to sleep with them, or even date them. Anne Marie admitted then that Tom had "flat out" said that he didn't want her in *any* house at the shore.

The two old friends arranged to join in the rental in New Jersey anyway, but the summer was basically ruined. They rarely went. And Kim took to calling Tom "Capano," refusing to add the "Mr."

"We were not that comfortable in that house," she recalled, "because we didn't know any of the other people. But also there were fights about it between Capano and Annie. They would fight because she was going to this house at the shore, and we didn't know where we would be sleeping—or if we would be sleeping on the floor. And there were five or six single guys at the house, so it was always a problem for her because she was given a hard time from Capano."

They had originally met at the shore and all their other summers had been wonderful, but Kim and Anne Marie found that nothing seemed to be working out in the summer of 1995. It was because of Tom, of course; he was effectively caging Anne Marie. Even so, the two old friends made a valiant effort to spend the first weekend of June at the ocean. They agreed to meet at a mutual friend's house on the way down, and Anne Marie promised she would be there at noon on Saturday.

Kim remembered that day. "She wasn't there at one, and she wasn't there at two. And I kept calling her and I would get her answering machine. And finally, at maybe four or five, she called me at the Fords' house to say that Capano had just left, and they had had a huge fight because he did not want her going to the shore. And he brought over wine and salmon, and things for her apartment, and then this fight ensued and she was too exhausted to make the trip."

Kim tried to understand what Anne Marie was going through. Anyone on the outside looking in would have told her to flee, but it wasn't that easy. "She was in love with him," Kim said, "but she was confused. Because he was married with four children, she didn't think the relationship could really go anywhere."

That wasn't the only reason Anne Marie vacillated about Tom; she had seen how he felt about his four daughters, and she knew she would always come in a distant second to them in Tom's mind. And there was their age difference. It might have seemed romantic at first to be courted so passionately by an older man, but now that he had crowded her into a tiny world where she could scarcely breathe, she saw how little they really had in common. He wasn't interested in socializing with her friends, and she had trouble visualizing him with them, anyway. Tom tried very hard to be in sync with music, fashion, and the patois of people in their twenties, but he often came off only as trying too hard. He belonged to a different generation and it showed. But most of all, Anne Marie knew that her family would be extremely upset at the idea of their little sister and Tom Capano.

On the other hand, Tom was still pressing her with his arguments about why she should forget everyone but him. He "was buying her," Kim said. "He was explaining to her what he could offer her in this life. He could offer her anything she wanted, so that confused her—about the social status, and whether this was something she really wanted, having the comfort level of not having to worry about money anymore."

And that was a far bigger thing for Anne Marie than it would be for most young women. She had *always* worried about money, about where she would live, and even about what she would eat. She was still the little girl who had been afraid that her classmates would look down on her if they knew she lived in a house without lights and hot water.

Tom kept Anne Marie continually off balance. When he was pleased with her, he listened sympathetically as she spoke of her fears and insecurities, and he told her how wonderful she was. He offered her a world without any anxieties. But when she displeased him, he could be as cold as death.

Then again, he could be so nice. Jackie Binnersley Steinhoff, recently married, was hoping to open a coffee shop in Wilmington in the late summer of 1995, a place where she could serve breakfast and lunch five days a week to the business community, and do a lot of catering, too. Jackie told Anne Marie that she wasn't too comfortable dealing with the legal aspects and wasn't sure how to incorporate. Anne Marie mentioned Jackie's problems to Tom and he immediately offered to help her. He and Anne Marie met with Jackie over lunch and Tom gave Jackie advice on everything from her menu to leasing versus purchasing equipment. He told her the risks inherent in running a small business and did all the paperwork for incorporation without charge. He even promised to send catering business her way since his law firm was right next door to where Java Jack's would be. Jackie realized he had given her thousands of dollars' worth of legal help for free.

She was grateful for Tom's advice, but a little put off by the way he seemed to take over. "When I opened in August, he was adamant about it—he wanted to be the first customer," Jackie said. "He wanted to come down and set up a time to go over my books, which I felt was a little odd—a little invasion of my privacy."

But then she remembered that he had been so nice about giving her legal help for nothing, and Jackie wasn't as annoyed. He was being Tom; he didn't seem to have the same sense of personal boundaries that most people had—especially with young women. One habit of Tom's really bothered Jackie; he always kissed her on the mouth when he walked into Java Jack's every morning at nine, and she hated that. She tried to be in the kitchen or wearing gloves to avoid the contact. But that was just the way he was; he was one of those people who seemed unaware that they were invading others' personal space.

In July 1995, as Tom put more and more pressure on Anne Marie, she started seeing another counselor. Bob Conner had been dead for six months and she knew she needed help—although it wouldn't be easy trying to bond with another therapist. She began seeing Gary Johnson every other Tuesday afternoon. She was starting all over, but it would be a long time before she would feel safe enough to discuss the married man who had taken over her life.

Tom continued to maintain his links to Anne Marie's girl-friends. If he couldn't locate her or was worried about some aspect of their relationship, he was quick to call Jackie, Kim, Ginny, Jill, or any other of her friends to glean information. She was such a private person that it sometimes set Anne Marie's teeth on edge to know that he was doing that.

In July, Tom discovered a new way to keep in touch with Anne Marie. He began to send E-mail through the computer system at Saul, Ewing, Remick and Saul to her desk at the governor's office. His first try took six days to draw a response, but finally Anne Marie sent back a short reply. It was another connection, one that would have been impossible a decade before. He sent her trivia questions and she answered, usually correctly. It was all very light on the surface, unless she failed to respond as quickly as he liked. Along with his calls, his surprise drop-ins at her apartment, and their dates, his E-mail helped Tom to keep track of Anne Marie. Tom had no idea that E-mail had any life beyond the immediate time it was sent and retrieved; he knew virtually nothing about computers.

At first, Anne Marie hadn't realized that Tom was manipulating her emotions as if she were a puppet—but as much of a romantic as she was, she was also very bright. She had begun to see a frightening pattern. Tom had done so many nice things for her, but there always seemed to be a payback. The biggest payback was her loss of freedom and being aware that she could not make even a simple plan to do something with her friends without Tom's entering into it. In the summer of 1995, she pondered more and more often about what her life would be like without Tom. But even as she did, she felt disloyal—torn between gratitude for all he had done for her and her own need not to be controlled.

Even so, when Tom told Anne Marie he was taking her on a vacation in August of 1995, she tentatively agreed to go. He had chosen a luxury resort in Virginia called the Homestead. "The Homestead is the kind of place I always wanted to go to," Tom recalled. "But my kids are beach people. It's in the mountains; therefore it's cooler. It's something I had wanted to do, but also to be with her alone and away from everything, for . . . four days . . . we went [there] to work on our relationship."

Tom repeated a pattern that Anne Marie had seen many times before. He had been insistent that she should go to Virginia with him, but a night or two before they were supposed to leave, he abruptly took back the invitation. He was very solemn when he told her why he had decided against going. And once more he said that he thought it was time for her to move on without him. "Therefore, I told her we should not be going to the Homestead," he recalled. "We had a major discussion and she was very tearful, and she cried and cried and cried on my shoulder, [and said] that she wanted us to go and wanted us to work on our relationship."

His perceptions may have been skewed; Anne Marie was already thinking that it was time to move on. It's questionable whether she really cried. She *was* an emotional woman, who might well have wept over the end of an affair. But as it turned out, it was not the end. Tom changed his mind again and they went to the Homestead after all.

Tom remembered that they had had an idyllic time during their four days there. He said he had taught Anne Marie to play golf, and that they had massages every day and strolled around the grounds. He had prevailed upon her to dance with him, because he loved to dance, although she hated it. She didn't think she was graceful enough and she felt foolish, but he got his way as he usually did.

On the drive back from Virginia, Tom took the long way home—even though she hated car trips. "She said herself she wasn't very good company in a car," he said. "She liked to look at the scenery . . . and on the way down, we really didn't talk much. We just played tapes."

On the way back to Delaware, they *did* talk. Anne Marie carefully pointed out how many things they differed on. It began with something as prosaic as the fact that she liked Pepsi and Tom drank Coca-Cola. She began to write down their differences, calling it the "Coke/Pepsi list." He thought it was all in good fun, and it may have been. It may also have been a very subtle and safe way for Anne Marie to show Tom how ill suited they were for each other.

In retrospect, she was probably trying to ease out of the hold Tom had on her. The list covered everything from food preferences and sleep habits to his being Italian and her being Irish. She was a Gen-Xer and he was a baby boomer; money bored him, and she was very conscious of every penny. For three pages, Anne Marie wrote down their differences in her distinctive hand with round letters and fancy capitals. And somewhere, hidden within the dozens of unimportant things, she noted *very* important things.

"She wrote down that I'm academic," Tom said, reading from the list a long time later as he was questioned by a friendly inquisitor. "She was nonacademic. . . . I was observant, and she described herself as 'spacey.' She wrote that I had a double standard and that she did not have two standards. I *do* have a double standard. I think there are things men should do and women shouldn't. It's that simple."

Anne Marie put down the thing about Tom that bothered her the most, sheltering it between the silly things. "She wrote down quite correctly that I'm a homebody," Tom said. "I don't like to travel and she loves to travel. She wrote down that I'm a control freak. She was in control of the *pen,* so she wrote that," he said with a laugh.

Tom was asked: "She didn't write down anything opposite, under her name?"

"No, she didn't, which is interesting. . . . I remember getting into sort of a jocular argument about [that]. 'How can you say I'm a control freak when you usually do everything you want?' And she never wrote anything—I might have made some suggestions, you know, to complement that—but she never wrote anything down, and that's odd, so to speak."

Anne Marie bent her head over the pages as Tom drove his Jeep Grand Cherokee toward Wilmington. She noted the things they *did* have in common: "Bread (from DiFonzo's), Sinatra, music in general, National Public Radio, pasta, Italian food, movies on the VCR, reading, restaurants, finer things, children, wine, people . . ."

It wasn't nearly enough.

And Tom's memory of their trip as being idyllic warred with what Anne Marie told Kim Horstman. "She said it was a disaster," Kim recalled. They had fought for most of the trip, and Anne Marie said she had just wanted to have it over with and get home.

It wasn't too long after that trip when Tom told Anne Marie that he was thinking seriously about leaving Kay. She was horrified. She knew she could not live with the responsibility of taking a man away from his wife. She was having enough trouble with her Catholic guilt about being involved with a married man. But mostly, she didn't want to be with him any longer. He would put so many walls around her that she could never get out.

In one of her moments of strength, Anne Marie told Tom that he had to make up his mind whether or not to divorce his wife based purely on what *he* wanted. He was not to consider her as part of the equation. If he left Kay, she warned, it couldn't be because of her. He always nodded, but she wondered if he really heard what she was saying.

Tom was now living in Louie's mansion in Greenville—he *had* left Kay. He asked Anne Marie to stay with him for a few days while Louie was away. Why she agreed, only she knew. She may have viewed it as a way to talk with him and to somehow extricate herself gently from their relationship. Anne Marie was enchanted with Louie's house, the grounds and pool, but she was sorry she had come. Tom didn't want to talk about detaching. And he most definitely did not want to change their relationship.

She was trying to separate herself from him, but she didn't know how to do it. Anne Marie felt sorry for Tom because he seemed so unhappy, and she'd been there to listen to him complain about his life—but she realized now that she had been led into something she could never have imagined. Everything had happened much too fast and it seemed to Anne Marie that in whatever direction she turned, Tom was there blocking her path, hemming her in. She began to be a little frightened of him, although she might have been hard put to give a name to her fear.

Anne Marie had had relationships with men before, and many men had left her bereft because they weren't ready to make a commitment. But now she was caught in something that she couldn't understand. Being with Tom was like being in a carnival house of mirrors. Things kept changing. Just when she thought she was perceiving something one way, the light shifted and it became something else. And what seemed to be an exit or an open space was really only a cramped hallway with no way out.

ONE of the friends Anne Marie had made in Governor Carper's office was Siobhan Sullivan, the young state trooper who helped to provide security for the governor. Attractive, tall, and slender, with sun-streaked hair, Siobhan had been a basketball star before she joined the Delaware State Police. Anne Marie had introduced her to Tom at a function at Woodburn, the governor's mansion, and Siobhan noticed then that the two of them seemed to be very good friends. Anne Marie often had tickets to concerts or sports events and Siobhan would tease her, saying, "Tell me where you got those," and it was usually Tom who had bought the tickets.

Tom was such a familiar figure in Delaware political circles that no one noticed how often he called or dropped by the governor's suite on the twelfth floor of the Carvel building. Siobhan's position made her a little more curious than most people and she asked Anne Marie about him more than once. "She always said he was one of her best friends—and that they talked occasionally."

By September of 1995, Siobhan became aware that Anne Marie's friendship with Tom had frayed somewhat. He had begun to leave calls on Siobhan's pager, which surprised her a little since she didn't know him very well. "He would ask me if I wanted to go out for a beer, always when I got done work that night with the governor. He knew I coached basketball and wanted me to help his kids, coach them.

"One night, he was quite insistent. He wanted to know if I wanted to go get a beer and talk about basketball. I said I'd had a long day and needed to get home."

Tom asked Siobhan if she had spoken to Anne Marie during the day, and then said, "She's really mad at me."

"You have to just let her be, Tom," Siobhan answered.

"You know I left my wife and I'm just really lonely right now."

Siobhan tried to avoid a discussion about Anne Marie's personal business by pointing out that working in the governor's office sometimes left people stressed out. He would not be sidetracked. "Siobhan, that isn't *my* fault. I tried to get Annie to take the job I set up with my brother, but she wouldn't do it."

Siobhan knew about the job offer from Louie Capano, with the free apartment. Anne Marie told her that she had considered it—mostly because working in the governor's office *was* very stressful, part of the job that Siobhan understood. "We had a lot of stress," she said. "We probably had the most stress of anybody in the office. My stress would be safetywise, and Anne Marie's stress level would be she had to make sure the schedule flowed correctly for the governor."

It was clear to Siobhan that Tom was checking up on Anne Marie, trying to find out where she was and who she was with. As it happened, Siobhan didn't know. When she saw Anne Marie after the weekend, she mentioned that Tom had called her and paged her. "He was looking for you."

This was obviously not welcome news and Anne Marie's cheeks flushed. Her usually cheerful voice was angry as she looked at Siobhan. "He is a possessive, controlling maniac. I'm just getting tired of him!"

Before Siobhan could say anything else, Anne Marie stormed out of her office and went back to her own desk.

Anne Marie was the sunshine in the governor's office, her laugh rising distinctively above all others. It was out of character for her to show her true feelings to anyone other than Siobhan, Ginny, or Jill, but occasionally others saw behind her mask.

"I sometimes rode the elevator down with her," a woman who knew her only by sight recalled. "There were times when she looked so forlorn, like a different woman. She didn't know me, so maybe she let down her guard. I wondered what *she* could possibly have in her life to make her that sad."

_____ Chapter Fourteen _____

TOM HAD, INDEED, left his wife. Kay and their four daughters had been living alone in the bishop's residence on Seventeenth since September 1995. After twenty-three years of marriage, he had walked out. Since Kay *never* discussed problems in her marriage, friends could only speculate about why she and Tom had separated. Their split was shocking to a number of people in Wilmington. Tom had always been the steady, dependable Capano brother, and there were precious few people who knew about his affair with Anne Marie or even his fourteen-year relationship with Debby MacIntyre. Anne Marie and Debby still did not know about each other, and Kay appeared to be unaware of Tom's infidelities. He was so meticulous about his secret lives that, even in a town where gossip spread like wildfire, Tom had maintained his reputation as a man who always smoothed things over for *other* people when they made mistakes.

While he looked for a house to rent, Tom lived for a month in a wing of Louie's mansion in Greenville. He still visited his daughters, and if Tom and Kay had any angry discussions, they had them in private. Tom's world went on as it always had, only he had more freedom to come and go. He still saw Anne Marie, and he still saw Debby.

It had been many years since Debby had any hope that she and Tom might be together as man and wife. He hadn't told her that he was leaving Kay—not until a few days before he actually left—and she was amazed and happy when he did. Their relationship had continued since 1982 with daily phone calls and physical intimacy at least one night a week and sometimes more often. Debby loved Tom; she had loved him for a very long time. She was in her mid-forties in 1995, although she hardly looked it. She was still trim and athletic and very attractive. She and Anne Marie—and Kay, too, for that matter—were physically three completely different types. Debby had short blond hair and was tiny, Anne Marie had long brown hair and stood close to six feet tall, and Kay was somewhere in between them in height, with olive skin and dark eyes and hair.

All three were pretty, intelligent, and had good figures. They were all Catholic. But though they looked nothing alike, they all had something very important in common. Each was principally concerned with making other people happy before she thought of herself. The three women whom Tom encircled had all grown up in homes where alcohol caused problems that made children walk softly and try, at great lengths, to please and to appease.

Had Tom known that, or had he just accidentally homed in on women who would sacrifice themselves to make him happy?

DEBBY had never remarried. How could she when she was in love with Tom? Virtually the only dates she had with other men were those that he urged her to go on, and she hadn't enjoyed herself. It wouldn't be too long before both of her children were out of the house. She had devoted her life to Tom, her children, and Tatnall School. And now it was going to be all right, after all. "When he left Kay," Debby said, "he told me that he needed eighteen months to be a bachelor, so he wouldn't embarrass Kay by marrying again right away. But then we would get married. That was one of the happiest times of my life."

As well it should have been. While they still didn't date much in Wilmington—in deference to Kay—Tom was much more available to Debby. She could call him at any time, and he called her more often. They saw each other several times a week. After being alone for a dozen years, waiting in the shadows of Tom's life, Debby felt secure now in the knowledge that they were going to be together forever. She had waited for him this long; another year and a half would be a cakewalk.

SEPTEMBER 1995 was a watershed point for a number of people in Wilmington. Governor Tom Carper, who had no idea that Anne

Marie was involved with one of the lights of the Democratic Party, was about to play Cupid. Carper, who was a contemporary of Tom Capano, had met a young man in the spring who seemed the perfect match for Anne Marie. The governor went up to Mike Scanlan and asked him if he was single. When he said yes, Carper asked him if he was "interested in meeting a nice young lady."

They both forgot about the discussion for a few months, until Carper had occasion to send a business letter to Scanlan. On the bottom of the letter, he jotted down Anne Marie's name and phone number. Tom Carper cared a great deal for Anne Marie, and he approved of Mike Scanlan as a person. He had checked Mike out before he broached the subject with Anne Marie. Mike, thirty, was a senior executive vice president of the MBNA America Bank, the massive Delaware-based credit card company. He was in charge of community relations and responsible for MBNA's grants to charitable organizations. In fact, his life since graduation from Georgetown University had been devoted to philanthropy of one sort or another. He had worked with troubled kids in Maryland and Florida, combining training and discipline in programs that used the sea as a teacher: aquatics, marine biology, oceanography. He was like a fish himself, a champion swimmer in the backstroke on the Georgetown swim team.

Mike was Irish and Catholic, one of seven children, and grew up in Bristol, Rhode Island. His father worked for General Mills and his mother was a librarian. But Carper knew that all those attributes weren't what really mattered on a blind date. Mike was six feet, two inches tall, and handsome, with a wide smile. He was a nice guy who owned his own home in Sharpley off the Concord Pike, he made more than $100,000 a year, and he was still single.

After Governor Carper told Mike about Anne Marie, and even though he wasn't any more enthusiastic about blind dates than she was, he considered calling her. "I kept it [her phone number] and thought about it for a while, and finally got up the guts and called her." It was arranged that they would meet on Friday, September 15. The likely spot was O'Friel's Irish Pub.

Mike asked around a little bit about Anne Marie, but he really knew only about her family and where she'd grown up. He got to O'Friel's first, and he was teased unmercifully by the regulars. Former mayor Bill McLaughlin chuckled as he sipped beer at the bar, enjoying the suspense. Mike was asking, "Is she a dog? Tell me, you guys," and Kevin Freel was making faces. Someone fed Mike the dread line "She has a *really* nice personality," and he looked a little pale.

And then Anne Marie walked in, dragging Jill Morrison along for moral support, just as Mike had brought along his friend Dan Simons. And of course, she was beautiful. And funny, and obviously a good person. They were perfect for each other; anyone could see it.

Anyone but them. They sat together and talked, but it was like being under a magnifying glass with everybody in O'Friel's watching. Their conversation felt stilted and awkward, and Anne Marie had that old sinking feeling that the man she was with wasn't interested in her. She called her brother Brian later and told him that she had really liked Mike Scanlan and found him attractive, but felt she'd been brushed off.

She hadn't. Eight days later, they had a real date and got along fine without an audience studying them. And by October, Anne Marie's calendar was full of dates with Mike. Her entry for the fifteenth read, "1st Night w/Mike," and that night marked the end of a long, hurtful relationship and the beginning of one that she had longed for most of her life. Anne Marie didn't mean that they had spent that night together, but this was clearly the beginning of a love match.

The governor could retire undefeated as a matchmaker—he had guessed right. Anne Marie and Mike could not have been better suited. She took him to visit her family and he fit in as if he'd always known them.

Everyone was happy for them. Almost everyone.

Tom Capano had to be the one who chose when to walk away from a relationship. He could not permit anyone to leave him. Debby had never tried; she was too frightened of losing him. Anne Marie had made futile efforts to break up with him, but he knew her trigger points so well that she never succeeded. All he had to do was tap into her guilt, her loyalty, her distress that she might have hurt him, and she was back. She had chafed at the bonds that he began to tighten early in 1995, but usually she exploded only when she caught him tracking her movements.

And then Tom would pull his double-reverse-psychology dialogue, telling her that she deserved so much more than a backstreet romance with a married man, with *him*. "You deserve your *own* Patrick Hosey," he would say, referring to Kathleen's husband, who was, indeed, a wonderful husband to her sister. "You shouldn't waste your time with me."

And it had always worked. It wasn't until Anne Marie met Mike Scanlan that she realized what she did, indeed, deserve. And Mike seemed to be her "own Patrick Hosey." She didn't have to slip out of town to have dinner with a married man. She and Mike could go out in Wilmington and see their friends. She could dream of living in her own house and have children of her own instead of just house-sitting and baby-sitting. She didn't have to tiptoe around Mike's moods; he was even tempered and good natured. He was thirty; Tom was almost forty-seven.

But meeting Mike meant that Anne Marie still had to keep secrets. She knew that Tom mustn't sense how much she liked being with Mike. He had never meant it when he told her to leave him and find someone she deserved. Indeed, she didn't even mention Mike to him for a long time. But even more than that, she dreaded the thought that Mike would ever know just how involved she had been with Tom. Mike was a devout Irish Catholic, and she hated to contemplate what he might think of her if he knew about Tom. Once she met Mike, Anne Marie avoided compromising situations with Tom. She had always been ashamed of being intimate with him, and that was over for good. And now she would have given anything if she could just blink her eyes and make that part of her life go away.

THERE were other women who had tried to make their connection to Tom Capano just go away, only to learn that getting free of him was like trying to escape from quicksand. He had been married when they met him, too, but that hadn't kept him from pursuing them. One of the most frightened of Tom's women was Linda Marandola. She was twenty-five, beautiful in an earthy way, with a cascade of thick dark hair, when Tom first met her in the late seventies. Like Debby and Anne Marie, Linda had found Tom very nice and quite kind, but she had no interest in him as a man. At that time, she was engaged to be married.

Linda was a legal secretary, working for one of Tom's friends, attorney Ted Sprouse.* Sprouse and Tom both lived on West Seventeenth Street and they often socialized, and it had seemed natural enough to occasionally invite Linda to go along with them to lunch when Tom dropped into Sprouse's office.

Tom was five years older than Linda, but he always made an effort to draw her into their conversations and she liked him. When he showed up at Sprouse's office one day and her boss couldn't take time for lunch, Tom smiled and said, "I'll just have to take Linda, then."

That was the beginning of their lunches together, and it was soon apparent that Tom was very attracted to her. If she was honest with herself, Linda would have admitted she felt a spark too—but she *was* engaged, and he was married. He called her office and her home often, urging her to go out with him. He offered her a job at his law firm, and still she declined. But then one night Linda was attending a bachelorette party at Galluccio's Restaurant in Wilmington and she ran into Tom, who was there by himself.

Before the evening was over, Linda and Tom had sex in his car in the parking lot of Galluccio's. She was horrified by what she had done. "I felt so unfaithful," she said a long time later. She never intended to be alone with him again, but Tom began calling her continually, begging her to have an affair with him. He was very persuasive, but Linda planned to be married—and she didn't want an affair with another man.

More than two years later, under remarkably similar circumstances, Linda *did* have intercourse with Tom again, and she had every reason to feel more regret than she had the first time she gave in to him. He showed up at her own bachelorette party, which took place shortly before her wedding. It was 1980, and they were once again at Galluccio's. Somehow Tom had found out where she was. There was a great deal of drinking that night at Galluccio's and Linda left with Tom. He took her to his own home on Seventeenth Street, and they had sex again. Where his wife was, she didn't know—but he assured her there was nothing to worry about.

Linda thought Tom was a really nice guy, particularly when he arranged for her and her bridegroom to move into a large apartment in the Cavalier complex. But she was resolute that she would not have sex with Tom again—not once she was married.

Linda married her fiancé, but her wedding day was blighted when she saw Tom sitting in the church, his face unreadable. At the wedding reception after, Tom cut in on the bridal couple and whirled Linda away from her new husband. He whispered in her ear that his heart was broken, and he wished that she hadn't gone through with her marriage because she was the love of his life. He didn't mention that Kay was pregnant with their first child.

When Linda returned from her honeymoon, Tom wrote and called her, telling her that he loved her and still wanted her. He asked her to get divorced and said he wanted to divorce his wife so they could be together.

Linda had promised herself that she would never tell her husband about Tom Capano. She was horrified that Tom wasn't at all deterred by her status as a married woman. He didn't see any reason why they couldn't continue to meet. Despite her telling him that she wasn't interested, he called and wrote to her many times over the next few years. He still wanted her to come to work for him and he continually proclaimed his love for her.

His letters were bizarre—almost delusional—as he wrote of his belief that they were meant to be together. Yes, there had been two brief physical encounters and Linda was everlastingly sorry for that, but they had never had any kind of permanent commitment. He was still married and Linda knew now that his wife was about to have a baby. She couldn't understand why he continued to stalk her. But he would not stop calling or writing.

When Kay Capano gave birth to their daughter Christy in August of 1980, Linda received a letter from Tom that frightened her. "He said that he wished it had been me who gave birth to his child, not Kay."

Linda refused to see Tom, and she told him that hot summer of 1980 that she didn't want him to call her anymore. That was when he turned vicious. He told Linda that if he couldn't have her, he couldn't stand to be around her. She would be sorry for rejecting him; he didn't want her living or working in the same state with him. He said that he "controlled Delaware" and that she had no choice. She would have to quit her job and move. He set deadlines for when he expected her to do as he ordered.

When she did not, Tom tracked her. She started to get hang-up calls, fifteen or more a day. He phoned her to say he knew where she parked. At night, she had to walk past the law offices of Morris, James, Hitchens & Williams to get to her car and she knew he was watching her. Sometimes she caught a glimpse of Tom staring at her through the window. He was such a moody man, his eyes almost black and the planes of his face all shadowed as he watched her sullenly.

Frustrated and furious, Tom contacted a man he had represented in a landlord-tenant dispute. The man owed him, but Tom offered a barter instead; he had heard that Joe Riley was a wiseguy and he needed something done for him.

Meeting in Tom's office, Riley, who had been convicted of threatening bodily harm to someone almost twenty years earlier, saw a man who looked as if he hadn't slept for a week. Tom said he had "a problem" with a woman. He told Riley that he was "crazy" about a woman who wouldn't have anything to do with him. He confided that he loved her and couldn't live without her. She had told him off and he couldn't eat or sleep thinking about it. He wanted Riley to find someone to knock her over the head or have her run over by a car. "I want her hurt very bad," Tom said. He wanted her punished, physically punished. "Her name is Linda Marandola."

Riley was in his sixties and had seen the other side of the law in his day, but he had never met wiseguy qualifications. His rap sheet was short and he had long since become a police informant. He was getting a little long in the tooth, and he wasn't enthusiastic about breaking some poor woman's legs.

"I don't know why I'm telling you all this," Tom said. "I haven't told anyone about Linda."

"Maybe you feel guilty about what you're thinking of doing," Riley said. He warned Tom that if they ever found out, the Bar Association wouldn't look upon what he wanted to do very favorably.

"I can take care of that," Tom said confidently.

It was September 1980, and Riley found himself a guest at Tom's house, eating dinner with Kay and Marguerite. Kay had given birth to their first daughter only a month before. As far as the women knew, Riley was one of Tom's political acquaintances; he brought a lot of people home to dinner.

Joe Riley didn't say much, but he looked at Tom's pretty young wife, his mother (a widow less than a year), and he asked himself what the hell the guy was thinking of. A few days later, he went to Tom's office. "You got a nice wife, a nice home," he began. "You sure you wanta do this thing?"

Tom said he was sure. He wanted to get even with Linda for rejecting him.

Riley believed he meant it, and he wasn't about to be part of it. He went to a retired FBI agent, whom he had once worked for as an informant, and told him about what Tom Capano wanted. They agreed that Riley would be wired so he could tape Tom's requests. Riley would always claim that he only wanted to knock some sense into the young attorney.

They met again, and as the tape wound, Tom repeated that he wanted "to hurt that bitch."

"You want her killed?" Riley asked.

"No," Tom answered. "I couldn't live with that. Just badly beaten or run over."

They left the matter at that, but first Riley agreed to make some threatening phone calls. Tom asked him to tape the calls so that he could listen to Linda's response to the harassment. Riley was playing both ends against the middle; he apparently had no problem with making a few phone calls. There was money in it, and it wouldn't really hurt the girl.

When Linda refused to quit her job or leave Delaware, Tom had flexed his muscles. Tom had arranged to have Linda and her husband evicted from the Cavalier Apartments. She began to believe that he *did* have great power, and it scared her enough to know that she didn't want to live in "his" state any longer.

In that September of 1980, the young couple moved to Penns Grove, New Jersey, but Linda still refused to give up her job in Wilmington. Despite his threats, Tom did not own Delaware or even close to it. Not then—but he had connections.

It wasn't that hard to find Linda's phone number in New Jersey, and Riley *did* tape his first call to her. When Linda answered, he told her that he was someone who knew all about her trysts with Tom Capano. He was fully prepared to go to her husband and tell him that she had cheated on him, and with whom, if she didn't come up with some money.

There was a long silence and then Linda said firmly, "I don't know what you are talking about, sir," and hung up on him.

That didn't leave much on the tape for Tom to gloat over. But Riley had made many more tapes of Tom talking about the calls he wanted to have placed to Linda. He also had tapes he'd made of Tom's conversation after he had lost track of Linda. (Hounded by Riley, Linda convinced her husband that they had to move again, although she was able to keep the real truth from him. He knew only that she was being harassed by a "former client" of her boss. They moved in with her father-in-law in New Jersey.)

Tom wanted to know every detail of how many times Riley had called Linda at home and at work, or her husband at his DuPont office. He took, apparently, grim satisfaction in knowing that Linda was being driven half crazy by her mysterious caller's threats to expose her two intimate incidents with Tom to her husband.

But Tom didn't know that Joe Riley had gone to the FBI agent–turned–private investigator with his tapes. And one of the private investigator's clients was the Board of Censure of the Delaware Bar Association. It should, perhaps, have been the end of Toms's career, but he received a slap on the wrist instead. A lot of women claimed then—and still claim—that Wilmington was a bastion of good old boys, and that Tom was in the thick of them. Perhaps. His pursuit of Linda Marandola was treated as a man/woman thing, and he walked away from it unscathed. No one thought to let Linda know that it was Tom who had been behind the threatening phone calls. All she knew was that the calls from the stranger had stopped.

It was, perhaps, one of the many times in Tom Capano's life that helped him maintain his belief that he was above the law.

Sometime in 1981, Tom Capano finally lost interest in punishing Linda. Riley didn't know why—but that, of course, was when Tom had fixed his gaze on another woman: Debby MacIntyre. But he didn't forget Linda. Six years later, she was more than startled when he called her office on business and "acted as if we were long-lost friends." It was 1987 and Tom was chief of staff to the mayor of Wilmington. Linda was separated from her husband by then, and at loose ends. She wondered if Tom had really been as mean as he seemed; maybe he really had cared for her, and he had just been desperate when he wrote her bizarre letters and threatened her when she refused to see him.

Linda had no way of knowing, of course, that Tom had tried to have her legs broken and that it was he who had hired the blackmailer to phone her. Given their changed circumstances, Linda gave Tom a second chance and met him in the parking lot of a motel in New Castle. He seemed contrite about scaring her with his passion and she felt he had changed.

A month later, in April, they went to Atlantic City together for her thirty-third birthday. The trip started out well enough. Tom gave her a gold watch that he had had engraved with both their initials, and Linda was touched by the gesture. But their overnight trip turned ugly when Tom began to question her about other men. When Linda told him that she was dating a few men, he reacted with rage. It didn't matter that he had been out of her life for six years and that they had just resumed dating. He seemed to expect her to remain celibate when she wasn't with him. He called her a slut and a whore, and Linda wondered why she had ever thought he had changed. Grateful when she was safely back in Wilmington, she swore she would never have anything to do with Tom again.

In 1987, Tom had a wife and a mistress. And neither Kay nor Debby knew about his liaisons with Linda. If either of them had known about Linda Marandola's ordeal, they might have made different life choices. But of course, they had no idea. Debby knew only what Tom had told her—that some legal secretary had tried to seduce him back in the late seventies.

Anne Marie had even less information. She was fifteen when Tom tried to order a hit on Linda Marandola, and in college when the disastrous trip to Atlantic City took place.

She had no idea how hard it could be for a woman to walk away from Tom Capano. Even in the mid-1990s while Anne Marie was dating Tom, she was unaware that he was pressuring another pretty young woman, Tedra Scopelli,* to let him set her up in an apartment. Tedra had small children and the offer of a free apartment was very tempting. Tom promised to take care of her, pay for her children to go to private school, and even arrange for her to have a job with his brother Louie.

But like Anne Marie, Tedra Scopelli had felt an invisible cage rising around her and declined Tom's offer. But he still called her often enough to make her nervous.

_____ Chapter Fifteen _____

IT WAS OCTOBER 1995, and soon after he and Kay separated, Tom had gone looking for a house to rent. He found one within easy walking distance of the home he had shared with his wife and four daughters. For that matter, the redbrick two-story house at 2302 North Grant Avenue was very close to Debby's house on Delaware Avenue, and only a three-to-five-minute drive from Anne Marie's apartment. It was in a very good neighborhood, across the street from his old boss, former governor Tom Castle.

Tom signed a six-month lease and agreed to pay rent of $2,000 a month for the unfurnished place. The house had been freshly painted a month or so before, and it had a double garage, five bedrooms, and five bathrooms, so that Christy, Katie, Jenny, and Alex could each have her own room. Living all alone may have seemed a little strange to Tom after being married for twenty-three years, but he intended that his daughters would stay over with him at least one night every weekend, and he planned to have visits from both Debby and Anne Marie, although, certainly, on different nights.

He didn't want his daughters to be hurt by the separation, and he figured having them with him on weekends would help them all remain close. Their friends would be welcome, too; Tom thought of himself as a buddy and a counselor to all of the kids. As he liked to say, his daughters came before everything else in his life. "I'm an overprotective father," he often commented.

Now more than ever, he would have to choreograph the comings and goings of his visitors. He couldn't risk having his daughters show up when Anne Marie was there—or when Debby was visiting.

It was all a matter of timing, and Tom had always been methodical about scheduling his life.

As for the family home, Tom dropped into the house on Seventeenth almost every day, walking in unannounced as if he still lived there. Even Debby told him she didn't think that was fair to Kay. "I wouldn't blame her for changing the locks," she said.

"I own that house," Tom answered. "I can go there anytime I want."

IT was October 1995, and the curving roads that snaked by the Grant Avenue house were covered with red and yellow leaves. Most of the surrounding homes were made of stone or brick, and they had the patina of old homes purchased with old money. The ambiance suited Tom. He could not see himself in an apartment, although he could have lived free at the Cavalier complex.

Furnishing such a large house wasn't a problem; Tom furnished it at no cost with stuff from some of the model units at Cavalier; and his brother Joey and his friends Brian Murphy and Keith Brady helped him move everything in. Tom had no knack at all for decorating; the white leather sectional and the entertainment wall with its huge television set took up most of the living room, blocking the fireplace and a doorway. A number of the pictures he hung were of dogs. He had a huge California king-sized bed in his room and another TV and VCR. The furniture in the girls' rooms was a little spotty to start with, although they all had new mattresses and new bedding.

Tom furnished the great room off the kitchen with a couple of reclining chairs and a deep maroon–colored couch with an embossed pineapple pattern. Joey and Keith carried in the beige Berber carpet for that room. The house had lovely hardwood floors, and one condition of his lease was that Tom would cover at least 75 percent of them with rugs or carpeting. He put a low-cost Oriental-type rug in the living room, and planned to use the beige wall-to-wall carpet in the dining room/great room area. Located above the garage, that room was cozier and more convenient than the living room. There too, of course, Tom had a television set and a VCR.

When she first saw the way he had furnished his house, Debby looked at Tom's handiwork and wisely kept her mouth shut. "It was awful," she said. "But that was Tom. He had no taste in clothing, no taste in decorating, and he didn't care. He thought it looked fine."

They were in an interim time, Debby believed. They could move to her house or buy a house when their plans for the future were solidified, but for the moment, the Grant Avenue house was perfect for Tom's needs. He made arrangements to have a cleaning lady come in every other week or so, mostly to vacuum and clean up after the girls.

TOM led both Debby and Anne Marie to believe that he had left his wife to be with them. Debby was happy about it, and Anne Marie was devastated. Even during the time when she was entranced with him, Anne Marie could not cope with the thought that she might break up such a sacred vow as marriage. She had fought against loving Tom because that went entirely against her Catholic beliefs.

But by September 1995, Anne Marie was a long way from being in love with Tom. She had been trying to get away from him for months, and he always seemed to draw her back as if he had an invisible wire that never let her get too far. She hated that. She hated his calling her friends to check on her, and his phone calls, his incessant E-mail, his drop-in visits. Sometimes she saw him driving by on the street below her apartment, probably checking to see if her car was there.

She had been disenchanted with Tom before September, but now Anne Marie had met Mike Scanlan, and she remembered what normal dating could be like. Without realizing what a Pandora's box she was opening, Anne Marie told Tom that she didn't want to see him any longer except on a platonic basis. Tom did not take it well. He would not accept it at first. Then he raged at her that he had broken up his home and left his wife—all for her. And now that he had done it, she was telling him she didn't want him? How could she be so cruel?

It was no use arguing with Tom, or pointing out that she had been fair. Anne Marie had told him he must never consider her when he made any decisions about his marriage, but he hadn't listened.

Anne Marie confided in Kim Horstman once again, telling her that Tom was obsessive about her. He was calling her fifteen to twenty times a day, leaving messages on her answering machine that she *had* to talk with him. Why wasn't she returning his calls? It was vital that they get together to work out their problems. And then there was his E-mail. Whenever she turned on her computer, Tom's E-mail rolled down the screen. He was sending it into the governor's computer system so he couldn't say exactly what he meant, but Anne Marie caught the hidden messages there.

She hadn't told Tom about Mike Scanlan, but with his connections all over New Castle County he had a way of finding out things.

By October, Anne Marie and Mike were dating often. There were nine notations on her calendar: dinners, drinks, parties.

On October 8 the pope came to Baltimore, and Mike took Anne Marie to the Mass he held at the Camden Yards stadium. "I asked her in the beginning of that week," Mike recalled, "and she was kind of surprised—thought I was joking—but she was pretty overwhelmed by it. She has an uncle, a monsignor, and she said several times, 'Oh I wish James [were here]. James would love this!' "

After the pope's visit, Anne Marie had even more dates with Mike. They went to Holidazzle, a fashion show fund-raiser for children with mental disabilities, and to a friend's house for dinner afterward, on October 9. The Faheys usually got together for Sunday dinner, and soon Mike had a standing invitation. "And I usually made it," he said with a grin. Anne Marie's siblings were always vigilant where she was concerned, but Mike walked the Fahey gauntlet and was stamped approved.

Mike had *his* family for dinner the day after Thanksgiving, a tradition for him, and Anne Marie was invited. "I wasn't sure she'd show up," he said. "She knows how tough her family was on me, so I think it was—I thought it might be—'get-back time,' but she came over and had a great time."

The next night, after dinner with his parents, Mike took Anne Marie to *Tosca* at the Grand Opera House. On December 1, the new couple went to Governor Carper's reception, where the marines collected Toys for Tots. And a night later, Mike had a *Caddyshack* party, which was hilarious, with everyone dressed as someone from the Bill Murray movie with its manic golf course antics.

Christmas was approaching but it seemed the oddest season. On December 4, Anne Marie flew to Puerto Rico for a weeklong legislative convention. Along with Tom Carper's press secretary, Sheri Woodruff, she would represent the state of Delaware. But while Anne Marie was in Puerto Rico, she became ill and fainted. Doctors weren't able to diagnose what was wrong with her. It may have been the heat or some bad food. Or it may have been that she was living with such dread that Tom would approach Mike and tell him terrible things about her, she was barely eating.

When she returned from Puerto Rico on the eleventh, Anne Marie plunged into a whirl of activities. There was a Women for Carver dinner, lunch with a friend a day later, and the weekend was filled with parties. Anne Marie always called parties "fiestas" when she noted them on her calendar. On many dates, she jotted down two fiestas on the same night.

As always, her calendar noted birthdays, showers, weddings, and of course, baby-sitting for her siblings' youngsters. She and Mike had a dinner together at the Columbus Inn, a wonderful restaurant in a structure in Wilmington that seemed little changed over centuries. Mike had no idea what she was going through. She didn't want to tell him about Tom and she made excuses about why she had fainted in Puerto Rico, fearful that Mike would find her anorexia disgusting. Finally, because he was so worried about her fainting, she fudged and told him that the doctors couldn't figure out why she was losing weight—that they thought it might be stress or fatigue.

On Sunday, December 18, Anne Marie and Mike went on a Christmas tour to see the lights and decorations in Wilmington. Afterward she helped him decorate his home for Christmas and they trimmed the tree with his brother, Vin. Because Mike was going to Rhode Island for Christmas, they had an early celebration. A photograph from that night shows them together on a love seat next to a miniature Christmas village arranged on drifts of cotton snow.

They *looked* like a couple, with Anne Marie holding their presents in her lap and Mike laughing, his eyes shut against the flash of someone's camera. It was easy to picture them together in Mike's house for many Christmases to come.

Mike left for Rhode Island on the twenty-second and told Anne Marie he'd be back on the thirtieth, in plenty of time to take her to the celebration at Winterthur, Henry Francis du Pont's majestic museum of American arts. Not only did she have a date for New Year's Eve, but it was with the man she truly wanted to be with.

Tom had been working on her, of course, warning her away from Mike. He told her that Mike was a nerd and he was amazed that she would even be interested in him. He hinted that he might have to tell Mike that she wasn't available—that she belonged to him. And if he did so, it would be for her own good, since she apparently didn't have enough sense to know what was best for her.

That sent a chill through Anne Marie. Even imagining a confrontation between Mike and Tom made her sick to her stomach. Tom would make their relationship sound dirty and he would paint her as such a sinner and loose woman—face it, he would make her out to be a slut and a whore (his favorite words for her when he was angry)—that Mike would run for the nearest exit.

It should have been a wonderful time, but Anne Marie was always looking over her shoulder and waiting for the phone to ring. Tom, who had always been so in control, was losing it—or seemed to be. He threatened suicide if Anne Marie didn't come back to him. One night he came up the back stairs to her apartment and burst in when she opened the door. Breathing heavily, he stomped around and collected everything he had ever given her: the television, clothes, records—even a jar of mayonnaise. "I don't want another man watching the TV I gave you," he said, "or seeing you in clothes that I gave you—so I'm taking it all back."

In the end, he relented and returned his gifts, but it was an awful fight. It was only one of many scenes. One night Tom drove her home and refused to let Anne Marie get out of his car until she agreed to talk to him. When she tried to reach for the door, he grabbed her around the neck. He didn't hurt her, and she wasn't afraid of him physically—but it showed that he was out of control. Her life had become a back-and-forth secret tug-of-war.

Another night, Tom drove Anne Marie into the garage at his house on North Grant Avenue and shut the doors behind them. He would not let her go until she agreed to discuss their relationship. *Why?* she wondered desperately. There was nothing to discuss. She had always been claustrophobic, and she felt suffocated in closed-in places. Locked in Tom's garage, she began to panic—but he was obdurate. When he finally opened the doors, she was sick to her stomach.

There would be more scenes like that, and then Tom would send Anne Marie long, almost childlike E-mail, as if everything between them was still all right. The reversal itself was chilling.

Tom used Anne Marie's friends, calling in old favors. Jackie Steinhoff saw him almost every day until mid-October. But when he came into her coffee shop in December, she noticed that he looked terrible. "He began to lose a lot of weight. His cheeks were drawn— he just didn't look good. He looked like a sad person."

Jackie had always seesawed in her opinion of Tom, but she felt really sorry for him as Christmas approached. Anyone would have, she thought.

"What's wrong?" she asked. "You're not eating."

He only shook his head sadly and told her he wasn't sleeping well, either. "He never went into it," she recalled. "He tried to put a smile on, and said, 'Things aren't going good—I'm depressed. We'll talk about it.' " Tom told Jackie he would come down sometime and tell her about his problems, but he never did—not until just before Christmas. "It was the second week of December that he said he wanted to kill himself, that he was suicidal."

Jackie was very worried about Tom and tried to talk to him, but he just turned and walked away. She immediately called Anne Marie, told her that Tom was talking about suicide, and asked her what they could do to help him. But Anne Marie, who was usually the first one to jump in to help someone in trouble, seemed strangely detached.

"He's OK, he's OK, Jackie," she said. "There's nothing wrong with him. He'll be fine."

Jackie wasn't so sure. But Annie knew Tom better than anyone, and if she said he was OK, he was OK.

Tom *was* OK in every way except for his rage at Anne Marie for trying to slip out of his grasp. He knew that she was dating Mike Scanlan and he was furious. It didn't matter that he had promised to marry Debby MacIntyre, or that he had begun dating one of the legal secretaries in his firm in November. Susan Louth was thirty-two, a "great-looking blonde," according to one of Tom's attorney friends, and they were having a rollicking, passionate affair. They had a lot of private jokes, and he often took her to the Villa d' Roma in Philadelphia for dinner. It was the same restaurant that Debby considered "their special place," but the management was very discreet.

Susan knew that Tom dated other women, and he seemed to relish the fact that she dated other men; oddly, he didn't obsess about her. She didn't want a man she could count on—Tom was what she termed "a challenge, and that's what I like in a relationship."

Tom took Susan to his mother's house and introduced her to Marguerite. Thereafter, when his mother referred to Susan, she called her "that slutty little girl," which Tom and Susan found hilarious. When he sent Susan notes, Tom addressed them to "Dear Slutty Little Girl."

Tom was also trying to renew another love affair; he had been looking for Linda Marandola for a long time. He'd heard she was back in town. He appeared to view women as either whores or madonnas. He held less tightly to the former and never quite let go of the latter.

And Tom still walked into his former home whenever he liked. He didn't seem to want Kay, but he would not let her have her own life either. One night, Kay was giving a dinner party when Tom strolled in, uninvited and unannounced. As she sat at the table with her guests, he took his shoes off and plopped his stockinged feet in her lap. He wanted her to massage them. He had embarrassed her in front of her guests, and everyone there, even those who knew that Tom could be imperious with women, was disgusted.

■

In late 1995, Tom was still threatening suicide to Jackie Steinhoff, promising marriage to Debby, jumping into bed with Susan, doing business as usual at Saul, Ewing, and considering new conquests. And he was still trying to *buy* Anne Marie.

Tom's money had always gotten him what he wanted. He told Anne Marie that he had more money than Louie, which was a lie, but his net worth *did* top $5 million. That was more than enough for him to buy whatever he needed. He persuaded Anne Marie to go for a drive and took her to a ten-room house. He offered to buy it for her if she would come back to him. No one who hadn't been without a home could even imagine what pretty houses meant to Anne Marie. She often wrote in her diary about her friends' wonderful houses. A home of her own was the ultimate in security and serenity for her.

Tom also tried to buy her a Lexus, knowing that she had trouble with her Jetta. She looked at him, appalled. He found out that Anne Marie and Kim were hoping to go to Spain together after Christmas. And that was a trip he could approve of. It would get Anne Marie out of Wilmington and away from Mike Scanlan. Mike worried him, and Tom not only cruised by Anne Marie's house to check on her but also started driving by Mike's house, and he was furious when he saw Anne Marie's green Jetta in the driveway late at night. He called to let her know every time he saw her car at Mike's. He was particularly angry that she parked in the driveway and not in the street. He demanded to know if she was having sex with Mike. When she told him she wasn't, that placated him—but only a little.

Back in 1994, Tom had tried to get Anne Marie to go to Spain on his money, and he had managed to make her accept the five $100 bills he gave her, even though she never went to Spain. He knew this was one of her dearest wishes and he could make it come true.

Tom E-mailed Anne Marie and suggested that he give her a plane ticket to Spain for Christmas. Moreover, he would make reservations for her at hotels, arrange everything. She didn't want that. She told Kim about his offer and said that she couldn't get him to accept her no.

November and December had been so turbulent for Anne Marie in her relationship with Tom—or rather, in her attempts to end her relationship with him. Sometimes he would offer her the world—like the plane tickets and the hotels—and then he would turn on her, attacking her insecurities where he knew he could hurt her the most. "She had a problem with her background and the way her childhood was," Kim said. "He would attack her and refer to her as 'white trash,' or [say] she was lucky that he's even going out with her—because of who he is, and where she came from, and what he could buy her."

On December 21, 1995, Tom went ahead and bought Anne Marie a first-class ticket—one way—to Madrid. It cost $1,235.95. He was amazed when she refused to take it. Very reluctantly, he took it back and turned it in to his credit card company for credit.

Tom tried another tack. He told Anne Marie that he had gone to the parish priest at St. Anthony's, where they both attended church, and confessed that he was having an affair with her. "She was humiliated," Kim said. "She felt she could never go back to her church again because the priest knew she had an affair with him. She felt that she had to escape. The obsessiveness of it was weighing very heavily on her shoulders. And sometimes she said, 'I feel like I have to move out of the state to get away from him.'"

But all the while, she knew she couldn't go. She had her family, her job, her friends—and she had Mike Scanlan. She told her friends that for the first time since she had broken up with Paul Columbus, in 1988, she had met someone with whom she felt there was a potential for marriage. And she was scared to death that Tom was going to find some way to ruin that for her.

He was certainly trying. Tom had been working on several fronts to break up Anne Marie's romance with Mike. He now had Jackie Steinhoff convinced that he was terribly depressed, so it was easy to get her to approach Anne Marie for him. "Whenever I did see him, I asked how he was doing, or how he was feeling," Jackie said. "He wanted to take Annie and me out to dinner in Philadelphia—it would just be a good thing to go out and get together."

Although they talked on the phone as much as ever, Jackie hadn't seen Anne Marie purely for socializing for a while. They were both so busy, and Jackie thought it would be fun for the three of them to have dinner.

"I called Annie several times," Jackie said. "She didn't want to go. December was a busy time for her, and she kept saying, 'I have this to do—I have that to do.'"

Tom came into Java Jack's often to see if Jackie had set up their dinner date, but she had to tell him Anne Marie couldn't make it. He urged her to keep calling, and she did. "I said, 'Let's pick a date— pick a date in January.' And she couldn't commit to it. She kind of hemmed and hawed. She never said why. She told me she did not want to go, and said, 'Oh, we'll get together sometime,' but she made it sound more of an effort than anything."

Still, Jackie didn't realize what the problem was. And she thought it would be beneficial for Anne Marie to get out and have dinner with two good friends. Finally, Anne Marie agreed to set a date in mid-January, but Jackie sensed that it was only because she had persuaded her to say yes.

Tom seemed pleased when Jackie told him that she had worked out a date with Anne Marie; the three of them would go to La Famiglia in Philadelphia in mid-January. Despite his tendency to meddle in her business affairs, Jackie was grateful to Tom for all the help he had given her in setting up Java Jack's and, because he seemed so sad, she really wanted to help him.

Anne Marie was sad too—sad that she hadn't known Mike was going to enter her life. Her friend Jennifer Bartels Haughton was in Wilmington for Christmas, and Anne Marie took Jennifer out to dinner at Toscana. Afterward they sat in Anne Marie's car for a long time, talking. Jennifer gave Annie her Christmas gift, and Annie started to cry. She cried for a long time. "She was crying because she said she didn't deserve Mike," Jennifer remembered. "There were so many things about her that she hadn't told him and she was really scared she would lose him if she was honest with him."

PART TWO

Set me as a seal upon thine heart, as a seal upon thine arm: for love is strong as death; jealousy is cruel as the grave.

Song of Solomon 8:6

Chapter Sixteen

DEBBY MACINTYRE WAS EXCITED about New Year's Eve 1995. It was the first time that she and Tom would be together on this holiday. She had promised him a lobster dinner with all the trimmings, and he seemed pleased about that. It was wonderful to be able to have Tom visit when Victoria and Steve were home, and he was so nice to them. Steve particularly admired Tom, and Tom seemed to go out of his way to be, if not a father figure, a grown man willing to take time for a boy. This time, however, neither of her children would be home on New Year's Eve. And Debby worked all day cooking and making sure that everything was perfect for her dinner with Tom. She set a graceful table with the china and silver that she rarely had occasion to use.

But Tom was late, and when he arrived at Debby's house on Delaware Avenue, he was in a foul mood. "He was moody, sulky, and depressed," she would recall. "I asked him what I'd done wrong—and he would only say, 'It's not you.'"

That didn't help her feel any better. This night was to have been a celebration of their new beginning, the start of a year when they could be together all the time. Instead it was a disaster. Tom grudgingly ate the delicious meal Debby had prepared, picking at it indifferently. He didn't brighten up the whole evening and generally acted as if they had nothing to celebrate.

Debby didn't know what was wrong; she wondered if Tom regretted his impending divorce or perhaps felt sad to be away from his daughters on New Year's Eve. But she knew better than to question him too closely.

ANNE MARIE and Mike were also together that night for *their* first New Year's Eve since they'd met. Anne Marie was able to forget for a while the lowering presence of Tom Capano; and she prayed that the year ahead, all the years ahead, would be with Mike. It seemed possible that night. It didn't matter that Mike was fighting off a nasty cold and they couldn't stay out as late as they might have; they enjoyed just being together. They watched Winterthur's fireworks explode into a million cascading colors and then headed for home.

But Anne Marie moved into 1996 apprehensively. Her friends and family knew that she was happy with Mike. Her very *close* friends knew she dreaded that Tom would destroy her new love. They also knew that she was hiding something else from Mike: her eating disorder. She realized that she had to tell him about that soon—but she hoped she would *never* have to admit to Mike that she had slept with Tom.

The physical side of Anne Marie's relationship with Mike was not nearly as intimate as it had been with Tom, and that was OK with her. Mike's restraint was a sign that he cared about her and took his Catholicism seriously. But they kissed and hugged and held hands all the time.

Anne Marie knew Mike was concerned that she was so thin, but unlike Tom, he didn't pressure her to eat. She hoped she could gradually explain more about her eating problems to Mike—about how she sometimes felt as if her life was slipping away from under her and she wasn't able to control anything but her appetite. But that could wait. It wasn't as though she was lying to him; he could see she had lost weight.

MEANWHILE, Tom would not leave her alone, and Anne Marie's way of dealing with him was appeasement. He had been so angry when she refused to accept the ticket to Madrid (although how in the hell was she supposed to come home again with a one-way ticket?). She didn't dare show him the side of her that was angry, too, and desperate to be free of him. By January, she decided that the best way to get away from Tom would be in small increments. If she could slip out of his life without fanfare, it just might work. It was clearly not possible to simply break up with him, but she hoped that she could convince him she loved him as a friend and was appreciative of all he had done for her, and she hoped that gradually, gradually she would become less available to him. She understood that his ego and his feelings were involved. She truly did not want to hurt him.

Even though Tom had become very demanding about wanting to see her, Anne Marie tried to defuse that by having what was basically an E-mail relationship. She became very adept at finding excuses to avoid meeting him in person. Her head was filled with Mike—not Tom.

A few days after New Year's, Mike and Anne Marie ate at the old Charcoal Pit in Brandywine Hundred. Funny—Louie Capano owned it now, and it was still doing great business with both high school kids and people who remembered it from their youth. It had been more than a dozen years since Anne Marie waited tables there, and many good things had happened to her since then. She had a home now and a wonderful job and, she hoped, a future with Mike. They had fun together that night. Being with Mike wasn't anything like the tense and often miserable times with Tom. But then, Mike wasn't trying to keep her on a leash that steadily grew shorter.

DELAWARE was hit by a roaring blizzard on January 8, and Anne Marie and Mike drove a friend of his to Dover, taking the drift-laden back roads in Mike's four-wheel drive. Anne Marie noted it whimsically on her calendar: "Death ride with Mike!"

Tom wanted to see Anne Marie on January 11; she avoided him by staying all night at Kathleen and Patrick's house. She was late to work the next morning because Jackie Steinhoff had, of all things, an attack of gout and was in terrible pain; Anne Marie took her to several clinics before she found one that was open. She contacted Tom as soon as she got to the office to apologize for not being home the night before. What Anne Marie E-mailed to Tom was all true, but she resented having to account for every minute of her time. And like Debby MacIntyre, Anne Marie always seemed to be apologizing to Tom.

Tom's E-mail to Anne Marie was rife with minute instructions on what she must do and references to their old times together. On January 15, he said he was on his way to two of his daughters' basketball games, "so don't worry about calling me until this afternoon after they all leave for Dover. Please call me so we can touch base. . . . Let me know if I can call you on 6636. Te Amo. [I love you, in Spanish.] Oh, forgot to tell you we also had the Olde Bay fries at DiNardo's and we dipped them in barbecue sauce. They were outfuckingstanding."

Tom appeared uninvited at her apartment the next night, and Anne Marie could not shut him out, even though it made her ill when he tried to touch her. Her E-mail to him the next morning was studied and demonstrated her constant conflict about her desire to be free of him and her concern about hurting him.

Good Morning Tommy:
I want to apologize for my "outbreak" last night. I'm sure it must have scared (amongst other feelings) you. Quite honestly, I scared myself last night. Tommy, I had a lot on my mind last night regarding my appointment w/ Gary Johnson. . . . Right now, I need a friend more than anything else. There was a part of me that just wanted to be alone to think things out clearly. So, when I asked you not to rub my stomach, and you responded with how much I hurt you, I couldn't take feeling guilty about that with everything else that I am feeling. It is my fault because I was not communicating with you, and you didn't know how to respond. I am sorry for my behavior. Please try to understand that right now I have some things that I need to "work out" but I'm not sure where or how to start. I know that I am not ready to check into a Clinic, and confront my family, friends and coworkers about my situation. Blah. Blah. Blah. I am not making any sense (as usual) so I am going to sign off. Annie

Sadly, Anne Marie had once again given Tom too much information about herself, and thus, more weapons to use against her. He continued to find ways to draw her back into his life. She had set a date to have dinner with Tom and Jackie as far off in January as she could. Mike was in Bolivia on a business trip toward the end of the month, and if she had to go, that seemed the best time. Anne Marie picked Jackie up and they drove to Tom's house on North Grant. Jackie brought along a pasta maker for Tom—a housewarming gift and a thank-you for all his legal help. Anne Marie asked her not to mention Mike Scanlan during the evening. "They don't get along," she said. "They don't work together well."

Jackie had already mentioned Mike to Tom during a talk at Java Jack's, but she didn't tell Anne Marie; she vowed not to say anything further about Mike during dinner, however.

Tom seemed excited about living on his own and insisted on showing them around the whole house. They dutifully followed him up and down the stairways, admiring the many rooms. He had clearly gone to great pains to have pretty bedrooms for his four daughters. Each of the girls had her own boom box and her own phone. "I want them to feel comfortable here," he explained. "It's their home, too."

The tour ended in the great room at the head of the steps to the garage. Jackie would recall that it was a warm room with a wine-colored couch that faced a television set in the left corner of the room. There was a big stack of oversized pillows that Tom said his daughters liked to hug when they lay on the wall-to-wall carpet to watch television.

They went to La Famiglia for dinner that night and Jackie noted that Anne Marie "wasn't in a great mood," which was strange because she could almost always be counted on to be "real up and real peppy." It had been almost four years since Jackie was so dis-trustful of Tom when he came to their old rental house to visit Annie. And she had long been convinced that he was, indeed, only a good friend. For some reason, Anne Marie had never confided in Jackie about their affair, or even that she was now desperately trying to avoid Tom.

At some point during the evening, Anne Marie excused herself to go to the ladies' room. As soon as she was gone, Tom—who had had several glasses of wine—turned to Jackie and asked desperately, "Why does she hate me, Jackie?"

"What do you mean?" she asked, surprised. "Why would Annie hate you? She doesn't hate you, Tom."

"Oh yes, she hates me, hates me, hates me."

Jackie tried to reason with him, but he had that familiar pitiful look. And Jackie knew that Anne Marie's dates with Mike were be-hind Tom's sad face. Jackie wondered if Tom had loving feelings for Annie after all. If he did, it would be too bad; she knew Annie was really enthusiastic about Mike and Tom didn't stand a chance.

And then Jackie put her foot in it when she tried to change the subject by talking about Anne Marie's surprise thirtieth birthday party that Kathleen Fahey-Hosey was throwing. As soon as the words were out of her mouth, she could tell by the expression on his face that Tom hadn't been invited. "He just seemed shocked," she said. "He said, 'Oh no, I'm not invited,' and I kind of backpedaled and said it was probably just friends, just going to be small."

It was too late; Tom looked stricken.

Later, Jackie would recall that the winter of 1995–96 had seemed such a great time for Anne Marie, now that she had met Mike. "You always kid around," she explained. "Like, 'Annie, is this the guy?' She would be like, 'Yeah, I think so, but I don't want to get too excited because you don't want to jump too far into a relationship.' But she was really happy. She finally met somebody she really cared for and who definitely cared for her."

The awkward dinner at La Famiglia finally wound to a close and Tom drove them home to his house, where Anne Marie had parked her car. He tried to get them to come in and watch a movie with him, but it was after midnight and Anne Marie said they had to get home. Jackie sensed that Anne Marie could hardly wait for the evening to end.

It was evidence of how ashamed Anne Marie was about her affair with Tom that so few of her longtime friends knew about it: only Kim Horstman, Jennifer Haughton—her old friend, who lived near Cape Cod—and possibly Jill Morrison. Others might have suspected, but she never confirmed their suspicions.

IT was such a cold winter that year, with one snowstorm after another sweeping in from the northeast. Wilmington was muffled and chastened by snowdrifts, the whole state blanketed with white upon white for weeks. Gerry Capano bought a snowplow and did a land-office business. But his brothers talked him out of his plan to buy a fleet of snowplows, pointing out that Wilmington had snow-clogging winters only once in a blue moon. What would he do with all his plows during the other years?

Gerry had more toys than any of them, as it was: classic cars, a boat, trucks, guns; he even bought guns for his toddler son, "to save for him." Gerry still spent a lot of time big-game hunting and deep-sea fishing. He was usually one of the top contenders in the shark derby in the Atlantic.

ANNE MARIE'S thirtieth birthday, on January 27, was fast approaching. She had mixed emotions about that. She was still single and still childless, and thirty was a watershed. It didn't matter that, in the nineties, women were marrying later and having children later. If she had to turn thirty, at least she would be doing it with great fanfare.

First, Kathleen was having the "surprise" birthday party for her. It wouldn't be much of a surprise because Anne Marie knew about it, although she didn't let on to Kathleen. In fact, she would be celebrating with her family and friends a night early because her actual birthday fell on the date of one of the biggest events in Wilmington's social season: the Grand Gala Ball. And almost in awe at her luck, Anne Marie had confided to her sister that she would be going with Mike.

The Grand Gala was a wondrous affair that drew the crème de la crème of society—from the du Ponts on down. Even though tickets sold for as much as $500, they weren't easy to come by. That year, the festivities would open with a performance by "The Velvet Fog," Mel Torme. Then there would be a gourmet dinner, followed by dancing in five ballrooms at the Hotel du Pont.

Anne Marie felt like Cinderella. Wearing the perfect dress, she would attend the Grand Gala with the perfect man. It could be the most unforgettable night of her life and a way to bury, at last, the residual memories of that poor, lonely little girl in a cold house, rolled into a ball under a table to avoid the wrath of her drunken father.

Anne Marie had been thrilled when Mike asked her to go to the Grand Gala. She talked to all of her friends and all the other women employees in the governor's office about what she should wear. Even though they were work friends rather than social friends, the governor's executive assistant, Sue Mast, even went with Anne Marie to shop at Morgan's for a suitable—but smashing—gown. She chose a long black dress that showed off her beautiful eyes and complexion. It wasn't a "little black dress," it was a dynamic, sweeping black dress.

Although she knew about her birthday party at Kathleen's house, Anne Marie didn't expect to see Mike there. He had told her he wouldn't be back from Bolivia until the day of the Grand Gala, and he gave her his arrival time so she could pick him up at the Philadelphia airport. In fact, he had arranged to come home a day early so he could be a surprise guest at Kathleen's party.

There was one surprise that Anne Marie dreaded: she did not want Tom at the party. Because she didn't know who had been invited, she called Kim Horstman in a panic. "She was very concerned that there was a possibility that Tom would be invited to the party," Kim said.

Kim had reassured Anne Marie, and then she called Ginny Columbus because Ginny knew who was coming.

"Who's on the guest list?" Kim asked.

Ginny told her and Kim sighed with relief. Tom, of course, wasn't invited.

It turned out to be a wonderful party. Anne Marie did an obligatory whoop of feigned surprise when she walked in to see all of her family and friends, but she was *really* astonished to see Mike grinning at her. She started screaming and ran up to Mike and hugged and kissed him. "She was in a great mood, really happy," Mike recalled. "That was her night."

And so was the next. It seemed that Anne Marie was almost too happy.

The Grand Gala was black tie, and Jill Morrison had been in on the final selection of Anne Marie's dress and shoes. She went by Anne Marie's apartment early on Saturday evening, the twenty-seventh, to wish her happy birthday, and was shocked to find her very upset and angry.

"I wish you wouldn't tell Tom Capano what I'm doing!" she said.

"What are you talking about?"

"He knows I'm going to the Grand Gala with Mike, and he's been calling me all day."

Jill admitted that she had let it slip, maybe even subconsciously, to show Tom that he didn't own Anne Marie. She was sorry that she had. While Jill was in Anne Marie's apartment, the phone rang continually. During that short time, there were six calls from Tom, and Anne Marie told Jill that he said he could find a date and come to the Grand Gala. She was terrified that he would expose their relationship not only to Mike but to the crowd. That would leave her lovely evening, her life itself, in ashes.

"It's the one thing in my life I'm most ashamed of," Anne Marie said hopelessly. All her joy evaporated as she visualized Tom's carrying out his threat.

Eventually, Anne Marie pulled herself together and got dressed. Despite her apprehension, she looked gorgeous. Jill stayed until Mike arrived, reassuring Anne Marie that even Tom wouldn't *really* have the nerve to show up at the Gala and make some kind of public declaration.

Inside, Jill wasn't so sure. After she finished her shopping, she decided to drive by Tom's house to see if his car was there—but she couldn't find the address. She had his phone number, so she called him on her car phone. It was nine-thirty. If he answered, it would mean he wasn't at the ball. When she heard his voice, she hung up, vastly relieved. Annie was safe from his harassment—at least for that night.

The next day, Anne Marie told Jill that it had been the most wonderful night of her life. But not because Tom stayed away. Anne Marie later confided to her therapist that Tom *had* come to the Hotel du Pont. When she left Mike to go to the ladies' room, he was waiting in a small anteroom. He grabbed her arm and pulled her in, but she broke away from him and said she would not allow him to spoil her night. She was back at Mike's side, her heart pounding but her smile steady, before he had time to miss her.

Tom had had no date for the Grand Gala; appearing at the hotel was simply his way of showing Anne Marie that he always knew where she was and who she was with.

Even so, that night at the ball would remain one of her most precious memories. People had teased Mike and asked him where he found the model he was dancing with. And for once, Anne Marie had *believed* she was beautiful. She and Mike agreed that they would date each other exclusively. They weren't engaged, or engaged to be engaged, but they were going steady.

_____ *Chapter Seventeen* _____

As EXHILARATING as her night at the ball had been, Anne Marie worried about how hurt Tom was that she had been with Mike. That was Anne Marie; she had been harassed, tormented, and stalked—but upon reflection, she felt sorry for Tom because of the gloomy picture he had painted of himself during his barrage of phone calls on Saturday. While other women would have been able to tell him where to go in unladylike terms, Anne Marie could not. She was cursed with such an acute empathy for another's pain that she had to apologize—once again—to Tom.

At ten minutes to eight the Monday after the Grand Gala, Anne Marie sent an E-mail to Tom.

First let me start off by saying that I'm sorry for the pain I have caused you over the weekend. I am afraid and I do not know where to begin. I spent a good part of yesterday morning/afternoon at Valley Garden Park thinking about a lot of stuff: Us, Girls, Eating Disorder, my family, etc. I desperately want to talk to you, but I'm too afraid to place the call. I do love you Tommy no matter what happens—I will always love you. Annie

Was it a mixed signal? Yes. Did it mean she wanted to get back with him? No. Anne Marie was still trying to ease out of an untenable relationship without doing any harm. And she was trying to get up her nerve to tell Tom that she wanted to be with Mike, and Mike only. However, Tom would completely ignore that part of her message. And her E-mail was like opening the door to the cage of a fox just an inch so it could breathe more easily.

Tom didn't write back until the next morning—Saul, Ewing's computer had been down—but he responded like a man who was back in the game:

> I desperately want to talk to you, too, and I'll go out of my mind if I don't soon. Please don't be afraid to place the call. I need to hear your voice. I'm leaving now for a meeting. Please call me. Not hearing from you since Saturday afternoon is making me crazy. And you know how much I love you and need you. I'll wait for your call. Te Amo.

The moment she got his answer, Anne Marie realized she had gone too far in her apology. Tom had taken her message to be the exact opposite of what she had intended.

"Hey," she wrote back,

> I am leaving early to meet jointly w/ Johnson and Sullivan @ 4:00 p.m. [Gary Johnson, her therapist, didn't usually work with anorexia and bulimia and had recommended that she meet Dr. Michelle Sullivan, who did.] I then have to pick up the boys and take care of them for the evening. Cass [Kathleen] will not be home until 10:00 tonight. I tell ya, this is hard work. I now have even more appreciation for single Moms. I will try and call before I leave today—I am dealing w/ a difficult Governor today. Annie

She did not want to see Tom. Anne Marie was trying to bind up what she perceived to be his emotional wounds with phone calls and E-mails. Her subsequent messages were filled with excuses about why she could not see him. When he pressed for a Saturday night date, she suggested lunch instead.

But he was so much better at this game than she could ever know. Tom was far from alone, and hardly grief stricken. He and Debby were together often, and there was Susan Louth and a number of other women. And he still walked into Kay's house as if he owned it—which, of course, he did. He was a sultan who wanted his harem to be available to him at all times. Even the women who had managed to elude him occupied his mind. That snowy January, Linda Marandola had received a phone call from Tom, "out of the blue. He said he was just looking through the phone book and he saw my number listed."

Linda had neither seen nor heard from Tom for *nine years*—not since the night in Atlantic City when he had given her the gold watch and then flown into a rage because she admitted she had been seeing other men. Once again, Tom acted as if nothing had ever gone wrong between them. He told Linda that he was separated from his wife, and spoke of how difficult Christmas had been for him because he wasn't with his family. He sounded, in fact, like a whole different person from the jealous, crazy man she remembered.

Things had been difficult for Linda, too; she had not remarried, was laden down with debt, and she was in her mid-forties now, not the ripe Italian beauty she had been in the seventies. Even so, she declined Tom's invitations. Undeterred, he would call her continually from January until Valentine's Day, asking her to have dinner with him. She turned him down, still cautious when she remembered how their meetings had always disintegrated into something frightening.

Tom's E-mail to Anne Marie continued unabated, with one excuse or another for why he needed to consult her. His daughter Katie's friends were throwing a surprise birthday party for her at his house—what should he serve? Would she have dinner with him on Saturday, Sunday? Where had she been when he called at ten P.M.? Could they watch their favorite show—*NYPD Blue*—together, or even over the phone together? Wasn't she tired of doing her laundry at Kathleen's? She could do it at *his* house.

During the first part of February, Anne Marie answered his E-mail very carefully: "I'm not sure what I am doing tonight. I may go out with some friends. If I have to babysit all day tomorrow, I think I will stay clear of Kathleen's house this evening. AMF."

Or: "Sorry I did not call you back last night. I ended up talking to Nigel [an old friend] until 10:30, then wanted to see the last part of NYPD Blue, and of course I fell asleep and woke up at 1:30. Typical Annie . . . and I am supposed to have nachos and beer with my running partners at the gym this Thursday night after we work out."

Tom called in his daughter Katie to warm Anne Marie's heart, and had her send an E-mail. He explained she was learning how to use the computer. Anne Marie responded—but to Katie's message only. She had seen Katie but she didn't know her.

On February 7, Anne Marie ended her E-mail to Tom with what for her would have been agonizing frankness: "Tommy, I meant what I said on Sunday night about right now only being able to offer you my friendship, and if you cannot deal with that then I understand. I'm still very much confused, and I am trying to work out a lot of personal things on my own. . . . Annie."

Their words filled their computer screens, full of nuance, hidden pleas, gently stubborn refusals—and emotional danger for Anne Marie. Tom attempted to draw her into his separation settlement meetings with Kay's attorneys, and still dictated whom she should see, even as friends, and what she should feel about them. Tom answered her early morning communiqué two hours later.

> Good Morning, Annie,
>
> Thank you for the e-mail. Yesterday was very harsh (divorce meeting with attorneys) and I am not sure how to react. I would like to talk to you about it. I'd like to have dinner with you on Saturday night. I need to talk to you about work, and I think you need to talk about Gary Johnson, etc.
>
> I understand that you're confused and want to limit our relationship now to friendship. I love you enough to accept that and ask only that we treat each other kindly and honestly. I don't want to lose you. I also think we shouldn't lose the closeness we've developed. If nothing else, you know you can tell me your fears and hopes and rely on me to support you. I still want to be there for you, which, I guess, is the surest sign that I still love you with all my heart. You cannot do all of this on your own, Annie—no one can. Let me help. Please call me when it's convenient. I'd like to know about Saturday. You look like you could use a good meal! And you have to admit I've always fed you well. Te Amo.

Tom had just pushed most of Anne Marie's buttons. It was not for nothing that he had always been the successful mediator. Cautiously, she answered only his comments about other people. She *did* need a good meal, but pressuring an anorectic was the surest way to make her eat less. She did not respond to his invitation for Saturday night.

ONE night, Anne Marie saw Tom driving by her apartment, slowing down the black Jeep Cherokee and looking up at her windows. It seemed as if he was always somewhere just out of the sweep of her eyes. She was having nightmares about him. He was calling her at all hours, and she let the phone ring and ring until her answering system picked up.

Her tension showed in her E-mail response to him on February 12.

Good Morning Tommy:
    I am not sure if you tried to call me last night or not, my phone is all out of sorts. I called from here this morning, and my machine clicked on, but the sound was very faint. I have a call into the phone company . . . Anyway, enough of that BS. Tommy, you scared me this weekend. Starting with Friday, and all the calls you placed. It really freaks me out when you call every half hour. I truly understand how fragile you are these days, and I feel the same way. But . . . . when you keep calling that way, it makes me turn the other way, and quite frankly shut down.
    . . . I'm sorry that I am nothing but a constant disappointment to you these days; it is not fair to you. I have an idea of what I need to do, I just cannot bring myself to start the process. I apologize for being such a horrible person to you. You are the last person on this earth I want to hurt!!!! Did you have dinner on 17th last night? I thought I saw your jeep parked in front of the white Benz out in front of the house last night when I was coming home from Kevin's. Anyway, I know we have to talk today, but I wanted to start off with this e-mail.

Anne Marie was telling him that she had seen him driving by, but in an oblique way. And she was capitulating about a face-to-face confrontation. It is probable that they did meet that day in February, but it was not noted in their E-mail. Indeed, there would be no electronic messages between them for several weeks. Whatever Anne Marie said to Tom apparently convinced him that she did *not* want to date him for the time being—and probably never.

They had come to a crossroads in their relationship. It was the first freedom Anne Marie had had for a long time from Tom's calls, visits, and messages.

However, he wasn't quite finished. On Wednesday, February 14, Valentine's Day, two men ordered a dozen red roses for Anne Marie Fahey. The first to arrive were from Mike Scanlan and she was delighted to get them. The second floral box was from Tom Capano. She didn't want them. Despite Ginny Columbus's cries of protest, Anne Marie dumped them into her wastebasket.

Valentine's Day wasn't perfect; lately, few of her days were—mostly because of Tom. Anne Marie had gone back and forth about what to wear for her date with Mike that night, worried that if she wore a skirt, he would think that her legs were too fat. Tom had once said that Mike had told someone she looked "great" in a short skirt, and she wondered what he meant by that. Tom also reported that Mike said she had a "shitty apartment." That hurt her.

But then Anne Marie realized that Mike wouldn't say anything like that, and Tom didn't even know Mike, so where was he getting this supposed information? It was just Tom's way of interfering. He had told her often enough that Mike was a nerd and she was a fool to waste her time on him.

That Valentine's Day evening, Anne Marie and Mike had dinner at Vincente's, a restaurant on the Concord Pike near Mike's house. They laughed and had a good time, and for the moment it was easy for Anne Marie to forget Tom. But he was almost always in her thoughts. She was trying, now, simply to avoid him. And all that winter of 1995–96, Anne Marie was growing thinner and thinner, her skin more sallow. She told Jill that Tom tried to be helpful and gave her advice about her eating problems, but there was a hopeless tone in her voice as she said, "Doesn't he *realize* I'm the way I am because of him? I can't control him but I can control what I put in my body."

_____ *Chapter Eighteen* _____

ANN MARIE AND MIKE had so many things they wanted to do together, and her calendar for 1996 was packed with social and family events. Two weeks after Valentine's Day, they went to the Luther Vandross concert at the Valley Forge Music Fair. She and Mike had dinner with her uncle James, the monsignor, at Toscana on February 29, and Mike and James were able to get to know each other.

"In a roundabout way," Mike recalled, "Annie let me know how important her uncle was [to her]—and how important he was in some big decisions in her life—and I took that to mean that dinner and us being alone [him and James] was certainly his chance to get his opinion of me."

They went to the Russian ballet, and to see Tommy Davidson, a black comedian whom Mike admired. He had a strong affinity for African American music and humor, and he wanted to see how Anne Marie would react. She thought Davidson was hilarious. Mike was relieved. "I've designed programs at MBNA around minorities," he explained, "and not everyone is open minded. . . . I couldn't be with someone who wasn't open minded about that. . . . You're dating someone and they're trying to impress you, and you just ask them a blatant question, 'How do you feel about that?'—they're going to give you the answer they think you want to hear. But she had as much fun as I did, so she passed my test there."

Anne Marie was passing a lot of Mike's tests, although he used the word humorously: for compatibility and similar backgrounds, for beauty and grace and kindness, for being a woman who demonstrated a remarkable gift for maintaining her friendships for decades, for their shared values. Still, she lived with the fear that she would fail in Mike's eyes on moral grounds if he knew about Tom. She was a young woman of the nineties, and she had never pretended to be a virgin, but sleeping with a married man was much more of a sin in her own eyes than having sex with someone who was single. She and her friends sometimes discussed the fine points that defined adultery, and Anne Marie was relieved when Jennifer Bartels Haughton pointed out in one of their phone calls, "You have to be *married* to be an adulterer." She knew Jennifer wasn't just being diplomatic; Jennifer didn't know about the affair with Tom.

One of Anne Marie's relatives had broken his marriage vows and it had caused a lot of pain to everyone. Adultery was a sin that Anne Marie detested—and yet she agonized because she had at least contributed to adultery. Her guilt was immense.

She and Mike had talked about marriage—but only as a concept, carefully avoiding a premature commitment. They agreed that they both wanted to marry and have children. Anne Marie brought up the subject of adultery several times, but again as a concept. When she asked Mike what he thought, she usually tried to sound disapproving, often saying, "Why don't they just have the guts to go out of it, tell the other person they don't love them, and go take up with a new person?"

Mike agreed with her and evinced disapproval too, but he didn't realize what she was really talking about. Later, he said somberly, "I'd say, 'Yeah, that's a better way to do it rather than both sides living a lie.' So I reinforced what she was thinking. . . . I had no idea what she was trying to tell me."

Mike did have some idea of Anne Marie's concern about her weight, but she hadn't spelled that out for him, either. She was so afraid of losing him. She had been very thin when they met—it seemed to him that was normal for her.

Since the first of the year Anne Marie had been frightened by her anorexia. She realized that she was *not* truly in charge of her own life and health, but she didn't know how to stop. On many days, she scarcely ate two hundred calories. She didn't vomit, but she spent hours at the Y exercising and took laxatives at night. She and Gary Johnson had agreed that she should see Dr. Michelle Sullivan, whose office was in the Center for Cognitive and Behavior Therapy in Wilmington. She had liked Dr. Sullivan, who was a pretty and petite woman with prematurely gray hair.

Although she enjoyed being thin, Anne Marie was concerned by the way she felt, and she had confessed her need to control her surroundings by excessive dieting and exercise to her brother Robert. He immediately said he would help her pay for therapy.

When Anne Marie and Dr. Sullivan began their work together, on February 28, 1996, she had not communicated with Tom for more than two weeks. She vowed to keep it that way. Still, a part of her may have missed the sense of security she had felt with the gentle, nonpressuring Tom who had always seemed to be around when she was frightened, lonely, or in some kind of distress. When he'd shown her that side of his personality, she began to distrust her own judgment. She had never wanted to hurt him—even during the times she was furious with him. The child inside who had rarely had presents from her father had enjoyed the things Tom gave her, always explaining that it made *him* happy to give her things. That side of Tom was like a very kind father—a role he was accustomed to. And she still hoped that they could have a platonic relationship.

But then there was another side of Tom—a self-pitying, demanding, domineering, controlling side. Anne Marie described his recent behavior to Dr. Sullivan, how he called her fifteen to twenty times in a two-hour period, how he showed up at her apartment and demanded loudly to be let in, until finally she had to relent so her landlady wouldn't hear him. She told Dr. Sullivan that Tom was "haunting" her. Indeed, most of their early sessions dealt with how Anne Marie might find a way to be strong enough to cope with him. She had not heard from him lately. But he never really went away. He was always somewhere in the shadows, it seemed, watching her and keeping track of what she was doing and who she was with.

ST. PATRICK'S DAY rolled round again, and Anne Marie and Jill Morrison had paid $35 apiece for tickets to a breakfast and mass sponsored by the Irish Culture Club.

"The day before," Jill said, "she told me she couldn't go—

didn't want to go because Mr. Capano was on the executive commit-tee and he would be there and she did not want to see him."

They didn't go to the breakfast, but they did go to the Washing-ton, D.C., fund-raiser President Clinton was putting on for Gover-nor Carper's campaign. Jill and Anne Marie got to meet the president personally, and that impressed them. The event went well and a number of people from Wilmington decided to ride back on the train together. All of it was exhilarating.

"But before the train left," Jill recalled, "a bunch of people went out to a bar across the street from the train station and just kind of celebrated the fact that it was a good night, a successful night for the upcoming campaign. Most of the people left on the 10 or 11 [P.M.] train. . . . It was just Anne Marie, me, Joe Farley, Brian Murphy, and Gary Heinz—so we decided to go to another bar. The five of us, when we got home, it was probably about three in the morning."

Tom heard about it; he seemed to know everything Anne Marie was doing, and he called her to tell her that she and Jill ought to be ashamed of themselves, "because we acted like 'whores.' "

Nothing could have been more innocent than a bunch of happy Democrats celebrating, but Tom saw whores and sluts wherever he looked.

MARCH passed without any more calls or messages from Tom. Anne Marie felt cautiously optimistic. She liked Dr. Sullivan and suspected that she was a therapist who would one day make her feel as safe in confiding her secrets as Bob Conner had. There were two issues that she had to deal with, the two things that were the most difficult for her: her anorexia and her past inability to transform her relationship with Tom Capano into one of only friendship.

With Dr. Sullivan's help, Anne Marie began to feel stronger. Ide-ally, in her view, she would be with Mike forever—and Tom would no longer trail her and threaten her. And, perhaps most important to her, he wouldn't feel sad that she no longer loved him.

Easter was approaching, a time of rebirth and renewal. Anne Marie and Mike went to services on Holy Thursday. They would not be together for Easter because Mike was going home to Rhode Is-land. He sent her a card that hardly seemed in the spirit of the sea-son, but it was. It was a picture of a seal, which he explained was an "Easter seal" from the North Pacific.

"I hope your holiday is a good one," he wrote.

I'll be thinking about you. I'm sure everything will be fine. Keep strong. You're doing good. I hope, too, that you get some time for yourself this weekend—a cup of java and the paper, a walk in the park, or sitting alone at home in the dark, one of my favorites. I will look forward to seeing you Sunday evening at the airport. Happy Easter, do be sure to have one of those chocolate or marsh-mallow bunnies for me. Love, Mike

Mike knew that Anne Marie was coping with something and that she was seeing a psychologist, although she had not confided any specifics. She had told him she was working out her feelings about self-confidence and self-esteem and that she had some family problems. Mike knew that her brother Mark was battling alco-holism and that Anne Marie was terribly worried about him—and angry with him at the same time—but he never asked too many questions, sensing that she would tell him all in good time.

Mike knew that Anne Marie had dreams for the future. Her dearest wish was to become a teacher, but she was very loyal to Tom Carper. She wouldn't even consider leaving her job until she had seen him through his upcoming campaign for reelection. "After that time," Mike said, "she had it in her mind that she would move on."

Mike knew nothing at all about Tom Capano, and Anne Marie still hoped devoutly that he never would.

Around Easter in 1996, Anne Marie believed that she was fi-nally free of Tom's influence and was strong enough to fight what-ever battles might come her way. She had confided to her friends that she hoped to marry Mike. She talked about what kind of wed-ding she would like with her friend Jennifer in one of their endless phone calls between Delaware and Massachusetts. Had Mike men-tioned marriage? Jennifer asked. Anne Marie said he hadn't but that they were getting closer all the time.

April was a beautiful month in Wilmington; the dogwood and cherry trees that lined almost every neighborhood street in the city were in bloom. After such a long and bitter winter, everyone was de-lighted to see that spring had come again after all.

On Easter Sunday, April 7, 1996, Anne Marie wrote in the diary she had been keeping for two years (if only in a very sporadic fashion):

Happy Easter! Well . . . another year has passed since my last entry and man o' man has a lot happened. I've been through a lot of emotional battles. I finally have brought closure to Tom Capano. What a controlling, manipulative, insecure, jealous maniac. Now that I look back on that aspect of my life, I realize just how vulnerable I had become. It hurts me when I think about that year. For one whole year, I allowed someone to take control of every decision in my life. Bob Conner's death hurt me / affected me more than anything. . . . My being after Bob's death became the little girl growing up in a chaotic world. I lost all sense of trust. I thought it would be easier that way.

I have been fortunate enough to find another therapist, Michelle Sullivan. No one will ever take the place of Bob—but . . . she's pretty damn close. 5 weeks ago, I was diagnosed w/ Bulimia. My weight is currently 125 pounds. Pretty skinny, but I want more.

Anne Marie was still sick, but her mind was straight and her perceptions were dead on. Once she accepted herself and the fact that a woman five foot ten inches tall was *underweight* at 125 pounds, she could regain her physical health too. She was going to make it.

DEBBY MacINTYRE heard from Tom at least twice a day during the spring of 1996, and they were together in an intimate way several times a week. He had long had a key to her house on Delaware Avenue and the combination to her burglar alarm. Although it always startled her, he would appear in the door to her bedroom late at night, undress in the dark, and crawl into bed with her.

Debby didn't have a key to Tom's house, nor did she ever visit him without calling first. It never occurred to her to ask for a key. She knew that Tom often had his daughters staying there, and beyond that, he had always made the rules in their relationship. "I was very much in love with him," she recalled. "I trusted him and I believed what he told me."

Tom often spent evenings in Philadelphia, explaining to Debby that he had meetings with the main office of Saul, Ewing. Her job also took up a lot of her time. She was in charge of the summer program at Tatnall, along with the before- and after-school programs. Both of her children were on the swim team at Tatnall and her life was very busy. She sometimes fell asleep as she watched the David Letterman show—waiting for Tom—but she never questioned him and she never worried about his fidelity. After all the years she had loved him, they were now a very close couple planning for marriage in the not too distant future. It was all she had ever hoped for.

Debby had never even heard the name Anne Marie Fahey.

Nor had she heard the name Linda Marandola. In April, after six weeks of not hearing from Tom, Linda began to get phone calls again. As she would remember, she finally agreed to have dinner with him on her birthday in April 1996. Tom said he wanted to talk to her about a job as his secretary at Saul, Ewing. She needed a job badly, she was a good legal secretary, and she thought there was no harm in just talking about it.

It was close to Easter when Tom picked her up and drove her to the Ristorante La Veranda in Philadelphia. They had a superb meal, and Tom was attentive and charming; and by the time he paid the $175 tab for their meal, Linda had agreed to apply for the secretarial job at his firm. It would be a lifesaver financially, and for the third time, she began to trust Tom.

When the officer manager at Saul, Ewing began to schedule applicants for the position that would become available at the end of May, Tom gave her Linda's résumé. An interview was set up and Tom and one of the partners talked with Linda. When it was over, Tom advised the office manager that she should hire Linda, who he felt was the best applicant for the job.

Linda *was* hired, due to report for work on May 29. And Tom was back in her life. He had deduced early on that she was having a difficult time paying her bills, and offered to lend her $3,000 until she had a salary again. Hesitant but in a pinch, she accepted. On May 15, Tom wrote her a personal check for $3,000.

ANNE MARIE and Mike were together for all of the bright spring of 1996. They went to weddings, parties, and high school plays, and they spent long evenings with her family. On the first weekend in May, they went to a Kentucky Derby party given by one of Mike's friends. The next day, MBNA was hosting guests at the Point-to-Point steeplechase races on the grounds of Winterthur. The steeplechase had begun as a very posh event to raise money for Winterthur, but after two decades, the Point-to-Point was no longer strictly for the blue bloods of society. The event attracted the common folk, too, along with horse fanciers from all over the world. "This is the only melting-pot event we have," a Wilmington woman said. "It's a great event where everybody can come and just have a good time."

Anne Marie bought a flower-sprinkled cotton dress in a size four to wear to the Point-to-Point. The skirt was long and swirled around her ankles, and she was confident that her "fat legs" were covered. She and Mike watched the races, looked at the vintage cars displayed by collectors, and walked past the entries in the tailgate contest. The Point-to-Point, half reminiscent of Ascot in England, half state fair, was only one of many good times that Anne Marie was having with Mike, days that made her want to pinch herself to see if this was all real, times that did, indeed, have a storybook feel to them.

She didn't agonize that Mike wouldn't call her again. There was a steadiness about him that gave her serenity and trust. They were a couple and their friends expected to see them together. Sometimes Mike sent her flowers for no reason at all, and he included Anne Marie in most of his plans.

AND then, through devices that no one would understand for a long time—perhaps never—Tom Capano reappeared in Anne Marie's life. She had never told anyone what had happened to make her shut him out in February, nor did she immediately explain to her friends why she had let him back in. Indeed, many of them did not know he was back.

The torrent of E-mail between Tom's office and the governor's office began again on April 24, heavily weighted on Tom's end of the line. He initiated these new contacts by telling Anne Marie of a catastrophe in his life. Anne Marie knew that Tom's daughters meant everything to him, and when he called her to say that Katie, his second daughter, was going to have brain surgery, her heart broke for him. She couldn't hang up on him when he was dealing with such terrible news. Tom was very strong, but he could not live if he lost one of his girls to a brain tumor. He told Anne Marie that he needed her—just as a friend—to get through his agony over Katie's illness. He asked her if she would go to the hospital with him to see Katie. And instantly, she was wary.

Perhaps Tom knew what her reaction would be. Anne Marie told him she could not go to the hospital with him. It wasn't her place to be there; it was Kay's place. And she felt angry and manipulated that he would ask her. She reported to Dr. Sullivan that she had been able to say no to Tom about the hospital visit.

"I registered some surprise that she even knew them [his daughters]," Dr. Sullivan recalled. "And she said she had communicated with them. It didn't surprise me because she is extremely friendly with children . . . so her contact with that young person would have made it tougher for her to say no."

She had run into Tom's girls now and again and Tom had always introduced her as an old friend, but she didn't know any of them well enough to visit in the hospital. If Anne Marie had gone to see Katie, however, Tom's lie would have been found out. Katie wasn't having brain surgery. She had only fainted during a basketball game. Of course, Anne Marie didn't know that, but she was suspicious. She wondered if Tom was using a story about his daughter to get to her. She now weighed everything he said to her for some underlying purpose.

Tom had, in fact, experienced something like what he had described to Anne Marie—only not with Katie. Ten years earlier—in 1986—his daughter Alex, who was only fifteen months old at the time, had had a dermoid cyst (a fatty tumor) removed from her head at Children's Hospital in Philadelphia. General anesthesia was required, and Tom and Kay had to wait a few days to find that the tumor was benign. Kay was not as worried as Tom; as a nurse, she was fairly certain it was only a cyst. It clearly had greater impact on Tom. Odd that he would bring up an actual event and transform it to suit his purpose such a long time later.

However, it worked. He and Anne Marie were talking again. And that was what Anne Marie had always hoped for, that she and Tom could be friends. It had been months since they had had a physical relationship. She never intended to have sex with him again; it was hard to believe she ever had.

They were soon exchanging dumb E-mail again with trivia questions. That was safe enough. Some sounded totally innocuous. In their trivia contest, he asked her who made Coach leather and she correctly answered, "Sara Lee." But in reality, he was reminding Anne Marie that he had offered to buy her a Lexus, a very expensive car, outfitted in Coach leather. He cared little for cars, but she was a connoisseur of them. She would have reveled in a Lexus.

It wasn't long before Tom began to call more and more often and to ask questions again, about Anne Marie's health, her financial situation, her friends, her *life*. He knew she was still seeing Mike, and she told him, very cautiously, about some of the places they went.

When she mentioned that a rock had put a crack in her windshield, he was very concerned and warned her that it was dangerous. He insisted she get bids on replacing it. As he had with Jackie, he asked to see her finances, using that as an excuse to drop by her apartment. Jackie had avoided that, but Anne Marie let Tom see her bills. He shook his head and said, "You're getting no place—all you're doing is paying the interest." He chided gently about her clumsiness with money.

When Anne Marie found out that a new windshield would cost $460.55, Tom offered to pay for it. That $460 was a quarter of her monthly take-home pay, but Tom assured her it was nothing to him. He would always say, "Just add that to the running tab," as if he actually enjoyed lending her money. He sent her an envelope by messenger, and when she opened it, a handful of brand-new, crisp bills fluttered to the floor. As the accompanying note suggested, it looked like Monopoly money. She didn't want to keep it, but she finally did after Tom sent her an E-mail the next day: "Regarding the Monopoly money, we'll talk about that in person as you suggest, but remember it's not a gift; it's only a loan with some pretty serious repayment provisions (I didn't go to law school for nothing)."

And indeed, there were serious repayment provisions. Tom rarely spent his own money without a payback in mind. Anne Marie insisted upon paying him back in kind, writing him checks whenever she could.

Money was one of Anne Marie's chief anxieties, and Tom knew it. He assured her over and over that they were only friends now but that he would always be there for her. If she had an argument with Kathleen—a sisterly certainty—he was there to take her side, just as he had always advised Debby that *her* sister did not have her best interests at heart.

Tom prevailed upon Anne Marie to take $500 to pay for part of her therapy, although Robert was making $1,000 and $1,500 payments; she had had some insurance and she was paying as much as she could. She could consider it just another loan.

Then Tom began to contact Kim and Siobhan and some of Anne Marie's other friends to ask about her. She had always hated that; her pride made her furious to think that he was discussing her problems behind her back. It didn't matter to Tom; he was back in Anne Marie's life, and once he got his foot in the door, he was confident that she would see that Mike Scanlan wasn't for her—and that *he* was.

DESPITE his efforts to win Anne Marie back, Tom had never left Debby MacIntyre's life. And she had come to depend on him more than ever. In May, he invited her to go on another trip with him. He had a legal seminar to attend in Washington, D.C., and she went along. They didn't have to slip around now the way they had on the

Montreal trip, and she didn't have to pretend she didn't know him if someone they knew saw them together.

Debby sensed that something was bothering Tom; he was more uptight and moody than ever, but he really didn't want to talk about it. She knew better than to press him.

As hard as Tom was trying to break down Anne Marie's defenses, Dr. Michelle Sullivan was helping her to stand up for herself and be assertive. In their sessions, Dr. Sullivan saw a young woman with a vibrant personality whose humor was so on target that it wasn't easy for even a trained therapist to see the sad little girl peeking out from inside. Laughing at something Anne Marie said, Dr. Sullivan had to bring them both back to why she was there. Anne Marie needed desperately to be assertive.

"If you spent most of your life trying to be compliant so as not to get into trouble," Dr. Sullivan explained, "and when somebody is saying to you, 'Let's work on your assertion,' obviously you are going to start to get panicky that if you *are* assertive, this other person is going to kick you out of their life, or they are going to hate you, or try to manipulate you into trying to go backwards."

In therapy, determined to change the way she had always dealt with her world, Anne Marie was alternately assertive and frightened. She wanted so much to get well, but even as she made progress, she scared herself.

"She had always been compliant," Dr. Sullivan said later. "People who got to know her and really loved her were used to saying, 'Oh you know Anne Marie will go to the show. We will decide and she will just come along.' And as she got firmer and firmer about what she would do and not do, we both knew that some people wouldn't like it—and *that* resulted in increased anxiety."

Moreover, Anne Marie was keeping so many things secret from people she cared about that she must have felt as if she was about to explode. Mike didn't know about Tom, and most of her friends still didn't know that she was back in touch with Tom. They were all relieved believing that she was not.

Anne Marie also thought she was concealing her anorexia, although that was a secret she could not hide. By wearing loose and layered clothing, she could almost disguise her gaunt rib cage, but her image of herself was so distorted that she saw a heavy woman with fat thighs when she looked in a mirror; other people gasped when they saw how thin she had become.

Robert knew, and Tom; and Jill Morrison was worried sick

about her. Anne Marie hadn't seen Kim for a while, and Jennifer was up in New England. Her brother Brian was startled to see how thin she had become when he saw Anne Marie during a get-together at Kathleen's house. "She didn't look good, and I asked her about it," Brian recalled. She admitted to him that she was having some difficulty in that area. "But she was a little cryptic about it because my nephews were around, and there were some other people in the house, so she didn't want to talk about it a lot that day."

Anne Marie assured Brian that she was talking to someone about her problem with food. "She told me that she was getting help for it," he said.

She told her other friends that she thought she was gaining a few pounds. But still, she took the laxatives every night to rid herself of the few calories she had managed to eat during the day. Amazingly, whereas most women on such a starvation diet completely shut down, her menstrual periods continued as always.

Meanwhile, Tom's E-mail to her was written in such a light and witty style that an outsider might never see the control creeping in. Her replies were equally lighthearted and casual.

She was handling Tom well, she thought. She might even be able to have dinner with him and not have to worry that he would misunderstand.

"Hey," Tom E-mailed on May 3. "It's 2:30 and I ain't heard from ya so I was wondering what was up. Please give me a call or e-mail me when you get a chance. Is there a good time to call you? Hope you're having a good day, but my guess is you're not. Think mussels . . . in a white sauce."

MOST of Tom's E-mail had a line or two about menus, restaurants, eating. He would not let up about food, mentioning it so often that Anne Marie almost gagged. He continually asked her to go to dinner with him at one or another of the restaurants where they had once dined. It made her sick to think of it.

Anne Marie tried to convey to Tom what she had learned from Dr. Sullivan. "Please do not worry about me," she E-mailed.

Hey, I'm scared to death that I am killing myself, and that's a very positive thing, because I am forced to do something to make myself better. It's a kind of a bittersweet device. . . . Tommy, I know you want to feed me, but believe it or not, it's not the right answer. I have learned through Michelle and a lot of reading that the more someone tries to get you to eat, the less interested and more deter-

mined you become to do just the opposite. I almost sent myself to St. Francis [hospital] yesterday morning because of how weak I felt. Believe me, Tommy, when I tell you all of this is good for me, because for the first time I am afraid that I am killing myself. . . . I'm ready to tackle this problem I have. I know all you want to do is help, and it's greatly appreciated, but I also need some time alone to work out a lot of stuff. I hope you understand all this mumbo.
Anne Marie

Tom would not give her any time alone. He sent presents. He sent food packages, which she swept into the wastebasket of her office. He made dinner reservations for them for Memorial Day weekend, even after Anne Marie told him she was going away for the holiday. Her replies to Tom's messages were one sentence long and, for her, worded strongly. Dr. Sullivan was helping her to say no and stick to it.

ANNE MARIE finally told Mike a bit more about her anorexia and he was very supportive. They planned to visit Mike's family over the Memorial Day weekend. Anne Marie both welcomed and dreaded the trip. She didn't feel very well and knew that she was growing weaker.

Just before Memorial Day, Tom dropped into Kim Horstman's office at the Smith Barney brokerage firm in Philadelphia, reminding her who he was. She *knew*; she was the one friend Anne Marie had confided everything to. Kim had not seen Tom since she and Anne Marie went to dinner with him at DiLullo's two years earlier. He asked to take her to dinner so they could talk about Anne Marie. "He said he was in town for a partners' meeting and he was very concerned about Annie's health and he wanted to discuss it with me."

Kim called Anne Marie and told her that she was having dinner with Tom, and she laughed and said, "That would be great. He will treat you like a queen, it will be fun—definitely go out with him."

Tom took Kim to the Ritz-Carlton in Philadelphia, and they talked about Anne Marie. "He told me that I was going to be shocked when I saw her because she had gotten so skinny," Kim said, "and that he was very concerned that she was in serious danger."

Kim was frightened when she heard that, and listened carefully as Tom spoke of the possibility of doing an intervention with Anne Marie and committing her to a hospital. Kim suggested that it might be better if they went to Robert and told him how worried they were.

"No," Tom said quickly. "Don't call Robert. Let's think about it some more before we do anything. I've talked to a friend who specializes in eating disorders, and she recommended Michelle. I found Michelle, and I'm paying her."

Tom told Kim that he had given Anne Marie a slip of paper with Dr. Sullivan's name and phone number on it, and that he had told Anne Marie that Dr. Sullivan was very highly thought of. In reality, of course, it had been Gary Johnson who had suggested Dr. Sullivan.

Tom seemed absolutely benign as he described his offer to help Anne Marie pay for the therapy that her insurance didn't cover. He gave Kim the impression that he was paying for all of her sessions, although it was Robert Fahey who was sending the $1,000 checks—not Tom. Tom had prevailed upon Anne Marie only once to accept $500 to give to Dr. Sullivan.

Tom said that Anne Marie had given him a book about eating disorders and he had read it. She had given one to Robert, too, but Tom said Robert hadn't bothered to read it. "I'm the only one who has done anything for her, Kimmie," he said softly. "I buy her groceries—I'm constantly bringing her Gatorade and bananas to build up her electrolytes, and I try to keep her fed, and make sure she's eating correctly." It was all a lie.

"What about her family?" Kim asked, surprised.

"Nothing. I'm paying for everything. I'm in love with her. Why won't she agree to see me again? I have more money than I can spend in a lifetime—I can give Annie anything she wants, the Lexus, the ten-bedroom house. . . . Why is she spending time with that geek when she could be with me?"

Kim knew that Anne Marie was in love with Mike and that he was anything but a geek, but Tom was adamant. "She doesn't take him seriously at all, you know," he said. "It's all just a front to look good in front of her family. She isn't in love with him, and I don't understand why she's wasting her time with him."

Kim simply stared at Tom. She knew Anne Marie and she didn't know him—but he seemed off the wall.

"Am I crazy?" he asked, refilling his wineglass. "Should I back away from her?"

"Yes," Kim said softly. "I think you should—should back away from her."

Kim called Anne Marie the first thing the next morning. She didn't tell her everything Tom had said or repeat his disparagements of Mike. But she did say that Tom Capano seemed to be crazy in love with her and didn't understand why she couldn't love him back.

There was a long silence on the other end of the line.

"Do you love him, Annie?" Kim asked.

"No. No, I don't." Anne Marie's voice was flat, almost dead. She sounded tired and at the end of her rope, as if even discussing it was too much effort.

Tom asked Kim out for dinner again a week later. He said he was in town again for another meeting, and why didn't they get together?

Again, they went to the Ritz-Carlton. They had drinks in the lounge and then moved into the grill to eat. Once more, Tom talked about Anne Marie, warning Kim she would be shocked when she saw her. "He said that when he told Annie he was taking me out to dinner again, she said, 'That's fine—but the next time I want to go with you.' "

Kim wondered if he was flirting with her and thought that couldn't be; he was so crazy about Annie.

Tom ordered the best on the menu and the finest wine. He talked about his family, explaining that his daughters were going to Europe with one of his brothers during summer vacation. "And he mentioned that his daughter had been sick," Kim said. "His one daughter had some kind of brain surgery, and it was a very difficult time for him, but she was doing better. We talked about how his father had been an immigrant and how he made his children all millionaires."

Kim got the impression that Tom was once again presenting himself as a much better suitor for Anne Marie than Mike Scanlan could ever be. He argued that Anne Marie didn't know her own mind. She was jealous of his dating someone else—so that must mean she loved him. "He mentioned he had a date with another woman who worked in Delaware, and Annie said the thought of him being with her made her sick to her stomach."

That didn't sound like the straight story to Kim. Anne Marie had *never* mentioned being jealous of Tom. All she talked about was Mike.

Their meal came to $130, and Tom added a $26 tip. Kim didn't realize that, for him, this was a relatively cheap night out. If it had been $300, it would have been cheap for Tom. He routinely submitted all his bills for dinner with Anne Marie and her friends to Saul, Ewing for reimbursement, marking them as charges connected with the firm's client, the state of Delaware. Anne Marie was employed by the governor of the state of Delaware, but she never knew Tom got his money back for their meals.

Kim called Anne Marie the morning after her dinner with Tom, just as she had the week before. Anne Marie commented that if they decided to go to dinner again, she would like to go with them. Kim knew that Anne Marie wasn't jealous; she felt it was more that she wanted to confront Tom on some of the things he was saying about her—and about the two of them together.

But then Anne Marie E-mailed Tom and vetoed his suggestion that she and "Kimmie" have dinner with him, saying, "I don't feel like sharing." Whenever her friends came along, she knew that Tom tried to enlist them in one of his plans to make her do something. She hated being a specimen to be dissected and discussed. *Poor Annie. Whatever will we do about poor, pathetic Annie?* It was one of Tom's devices.

Chapter Nineteen

TOM WAS HAVING a busy spring. Only a man as organized as he was could have arranged so deftly the many pieces in the mosaic of his life. He told Kim that he considered himself Anne Marie's very best friend, the one human being in the world she could trust. He never let a day go by without some contact with her. Nor did he miss speaking to Debby every day; her problems were a little different from Anne Marie's but she, too, needed him to see what was best for her. He felt that the Tatnall School continued to ask too much of Debby. She was often on the job from very early in the morning until far into the evening.

Tom fully expected Linda Marandola to become his secretary at the end of May 1996. That would, of course, make her privy to knowledge about his phone calls, but he wasn't concerned. However, the week before Linda was scheduled to start, he called her at home and was annoyed to hear that she had left a cutesy message on her answering machine. That was not acceptable.

When Tom got Linda on the phone, he told her to change the message; it was unprofessional and childlike. Linda demurred and Tom said flatly that she could not work for him if she didn't change the message. Again she refused, telling him that what she had on her home machine had nothing whatever to do with her job at Saul, Ewing.

Tom called Linda's machine several times after that and left her messages, repeating that she was immature and childish. As she listened to Tom's angry voice, calling her over and over, Linda realized that she couldn't work for him. What had ever made her think that she could? Nothing had really changed; he was the same man he had always been. She called Saul, Ewing and said that she would not be reporting to work after all. She didn't give a reason.

When Tom's secretary told him that Linda was not going to be taking her place, he nodded grimly and said he would call her and see what her problem was. He explained later that he had had a disagreement with Linda over the weekend and she would not return his phone calls.

Linda still owed Tom $3,000 and that rankled him. He told his secretary that she had shared her financial problems with him and that he had lent her money. "She hasn't paid me back," he said, "and I'm going to fix her ass."

He asked for Linda's personnel file and then had his secretary type up a civil complaint against her. On June 14, Tom filed suit against Linda Marandola, asking for $3,000 plus interest. She didn't even try to answer the suit. There was no point; Linda didn't have any money for an attorney and Tom had so much power in Wilmington. She allowed him to get a default judgment against her.

MIKE and Anne Marie had plans to spend some time in Falmouth, Massachusetts, over the Memorial Day weekend, May 25–27; it would be their first real trip together. Jennifer Bartels Haughton's in-laws had a place on Martha's Vineyard, and Mike and Anne Marie planned to see Jennifer and her husband there. They could take the ferry from the mainland to Martha's Vineyard, and it would be a chance for Jennifer to meet Mike, the man she had heard about in the frequent phone conversations she had with Anne Marie.

But their plans fell through. The house in Falmouth where Anne Marie and Mike planned to stay was full, so after only one day, they headed out to visit Mike's college roommate instead—and he lived too far from Martha's Vineyard. On the way home, they stopped in Rhode Island to see Mike's parents. Although Anne Marie had met them, this was the first time she was in their home. And she was the first girl Mike had brought home since high school. She was touched to see that his mother had placed pictures of Mike as a child in the room where she slept.

Jennifer and Annie missed each other, a circumstance that would sadden Jennifer in a most profound way. And it wasn't the best of trips for Anne Marie. She didn't feel well over Memorial Day weekend. She had come to a point where it was almost impossible for her to eat, and she was getting weaker despite Dr. Sullivan's careful monitoring of her electrolytes. Sullivan knew that Anne Marie was taking as many as fifteen laxatives a day and there was a very real danger that she could have a heart attack.

Anne Marie was under siege. With so many forces attacking her, it was hard for her to fight. She was in love with Mike and afraid of losing him; she was afraid to start eating because she thought she would soon be obese; and she was fearful that she might die because she couldn't eat. But most of all, Tom was haunting her again, despite her many attempts to keep things platonic between them. He had never meant it when he said they would only be friends.

Returning to her job after her trip to Cape Cod, Anne Marie learned from Siobhan Sullivan that Tom had been looking for her over the long weekend. She wasn't really surprised. "He paged me," Siobhan recalled. "When I returned the page, he asked me if I had talked to Anne Marie, and I said no. And he asked me if I knew where Anne Marie was, and I said no."

Siobhan hadn't encouraged any further questioning, but when she told Anne Marie that Tom had paged her and was asking where she was, Anne Marie was very upset. "He's fucking stalking me," she said angrily.

Siobhan tried to calm her down. "Anne Marie, there is a charge. That's a crime, there's a law against that. We can give you protection." She explained that she was, after all, a State Police officer and involved in protecting not only the governor but everyone in his office.

"No." Anne Marie sighed. "I can handle it. I just have to end it with Tom." She confessed to Siobhan that she had been afraid that Tom might have been waiting at her house to confront her and Mike when they got back from New England. She had made the mistake of telling him she was going to Cape Cod for Memorial Day. But she hadn't told him exactly where she was going or with whom. Tom had obviously figured out that she had gone away with Mike.

He had been so insistent that they were going to have dinner at La Famiglia on Thursday night, May 30, that Anne Marie had stopped trying to dissuade him. They met for dinner and she tried to be pleasant, without giving him any signals that she felt more than friendship for him. But the morning after that "date," he was E-mailing her to ask her to come to his house Sunday afternoon to make pasta. Or if she didn't want to do that, they could have dinner at the Villa d' Roma (the restaurant that Debby considered their "special place"). And, oh yes, Tom wanted Anne Marie to start playing golf with him.

It had taken him only weeks to coil himself around her again. She felt the old pressure to report all of her activities to him. It wasn't that she hated Tom—not at all; he was being so damned nice to her. But he didn't seem to realize that he was almost choking the life out of her. She didn't want all the things he was insistent about giving her, but she didn't seem to have the strength to say no.

Anne Marie was faithful in keeping her appointments with Dr. Sullivan, determined to win her fight for her health and her life. Sullivan was a strong ally. "I began speaking with her about her anger that the gifts were manipulative," she recalled. "He might ask her to have some time with him having supper, and what might get added on to that is, 'Oh, let me buy you a dress.' And she found herself angry about that. She had a hard time enough saying no to going out, and she just felt like he kept piling it on and piling it on."

The two of them worked on exercises, using conversational ploys that would help Anne Marie be strong in her resolve.

Tom had been currying favor with Kim and Jackie, and now he told Anne Marie that he had invited her brother Robert and his wife, Susan, along with Kim, to a Cézanne exhibit on June 15 at the Philadelphia Museum of Art. She was invited too, of course. It would be a grand affair, sponsored by Saul, Ewing—his firm had chosen the Cézanne function to celebrate its seventy-fifth anniversary.

Anne Marie didn't go to the Cézanne exhibition, but Robert and Susan did and had a good time. Susan wrote Tom a warm thank-you note. Robert had no idea that Anne Marie and Tom had been anything more than friends. Tom and Robert had known each other slightly for years, and now Tom raved about how much he liked Robert, calling him "my second-favorite Fahey."

Anne Marie was mortified. She didn't want Tom pushing his way into her family. She didn't want her family to know about Tom.

On June 8, Anne Marie and Kim went to a wedding together. Tom had lent Anne Marie his credit card so that she could pay for her gift to the couple: twelve months of floral arrangements. She had repaid him before the wedding; on June 4, she wrote him a check for $122.50 on her Congressional Federal Credit Union account. It was another of the monetary transactions between them, the loans that she berated herself for accepting.

As Tom had predicted, Kim *was* shocked at the wedding to see how thin Anne Marie was. At the same time, she seemed very happy, happier than Kim had ever seen her. Anne Marie told Kim that she was falling in love with Mike.

"Michael was redoing his kitchen," Kim recalled, "and Annie said it was like they were married—because he let Annie pick out the tiles, and Annie was helping him decorate his house. Mike missed the wedding because he was swimming in a marathon the next day, but Anne Marie called to wish him luck and tell him she was thinking about him."

Mike had been training for the long-distance swim in Annapolis since January, and there was no way he could have gone with Anne Marie to the wedding and been able to compete. She understood.

Four days later, on June 12, Anne Marie fainted in her office. She knew why she was so weak and sick, and she didn't want to call Mike to take her back to her apartment. That would mean she would have had to explain how serious her eating problem was. She didn't want him to know; she wanted to be well before she ever admitted all of it to him.

Instead, Anne Marie called Tom and asked if he would drive her home. He was close by and he knew about her problem. He came immediately, scooped her up, and took her to her apartment. For him, it was a triumph, and another beachhead. He told Kim later that he had held Anne Marie in his arms as she lay collapsed on her kitchen floor, and that he had forced Gatorade into her to bring up her electrolytes.

Maybe he did. The Tom who kept track of the insulin in case his friend needed it and the Tom who closed Debby's mother's eyes was good in emergencies. He thrived when he was in charge. It was his forte, and if he was called upon for matters dealing with life and death, so much the better. It was preferable to be the guy with the clear head who deftly took care of business than to be some frantic fool.

Anne Marie insisted on returning to work that afternoon, despite Tom's objections. She had had a moment of true awakening; she realized that she had come close to death as the cramps and nausea of severe potassium loss hit her. More than at any other time, she had chosen to live.

___ *Chapter Twenty* _____

In MID-JUNE, summer drops over Wilmington like a collapsing balloon, humid and hot, with scarcely an interim period for anyone to adjust. On Fridays, all the roads heading south are full of beach traffic. And all the restaurants that can, including Kid

Shelleen's and O'Friel's Irish Pub, open their outdoor decks and patios. The big old city houses seem to trap the day's heat. In the working-class neighborhoods, people in undershirts and halters emerge to sit on their front stoops or drag lawn chairs out in the yard or parking strip to find a spot of cool.

Homemade water-ice stands spring up in Little Italy. The mixture is not a snow cone. It's less than sherbet, more than lemonade, and balm to parched throats. The vendor sloshes a dipper through a washtub full of a slush of shaved ice, lemon, sugar, and water, and then fills a waxed paper cup to overflowing.

The Trolley Square neighborhood lures yuppies to outdoor decks, where they sip Corona and watch the traffic go by. Every hour or so a train crosses the trestle bridge in front of Kid Shelleen's patio, and conversation stops as the cars rumble past. This had been Anne Marie's milieu in recent years, trendy, loud, and fun, but somehow full of the past, too.

Her apartment on Washington Street was close to downtown Wilmington and not nearly as affluent as the Forty Acres and Trolley Square neighborhoods. From her apartment, she could walk up Eighteenth Street, past Salesianum School, Baynard Stadium, the old Wanamaker's department store, and over the Augustine cutoff into Forty Acres and Trolley Square. In June, it was a lovely walk; home owners were sprucing up their yards, watering the grass, planting flowers, pulling weeds. Everything smelled fresh and new.

The June air in Wilmington smelled of honeysuckle and fresh-cut grass; of submarine sandwiches wrapped in waxy off-white butcher paper to keep in the juices of tomatoes, peppers, and onions; of the Delaware River; and of sweat and suntan oil. It was perhaps, of all seasons, the best time for a new beginning.

On June 14, St. Anthony's festival drew its usual crowds. Anne Marie took her nephews during the day and ran into a man she had worked with in the congressional offices down in Washington. "I saw her with her nephews at the carnival," he recalled. "I have to say I was taken aback. I recognized her, but she was not the Anne Marie that I had known—she was always very effervescent, just a happy person, generally. She was still the same happy person at the St. Anthony's festival, but she had lost a lot of weight, and her hair was straight, lightened, and brittle looking." She had in fact reached bottom only two days before, but was rapidly rebounding.

That Friday night, Anne Marie and Mike had fixed Kim up

1

The four Capano brothers posed in the offices of Louis Capano & Sons, Inc., in the late 1980s. The sons of an Italian immigrant carpenter, they turned real estate in Wilmington, Delaware, into a gold mine. Left to right: Tom, Joey, Louie, and Gerry.

Tom Capano, his wife, Kay, and their first baby girl. Tom chose the law over his family's construction business. Rich, ambitious, and politically well connected, he was on his way to the pinnacle of respect and power in Delaware.

2

Even though she was beautiful and the daughter of a socially prominent Wilmington family, Debby MacIntyre, even as a teenager, was lonely and looking for love.

3

Debby, her husband, David Williams, and their baby son. David and Tom Capano worked at the same law firm, and unhappy in her marriage, Debby was attracted by Tom's charm and self-confidence.

Posing in Marguerite Capano's kitchen in the summer of 1980, the wives of the young lawyers at Morris, James, Hitchens & Williams were the best of friends. Third from left: Kay Capano; third from right: Debby MacIntyre Williams, who would soon begin an affair with Kay's husband.

The Capano family at a wedding in 1994. Standing, from left: Tom, Louie, Lauri Merton (Louie's wife), Gerry, his wife, Michelle, and Joey. Seated, left to right: Kay, Marguerite and Joey's wife, Joanne. Only Lee and Marian Capano Ramunno were missing. For the Capanos, family loyalty was everything.

The spacious house in Wilmington once occupied by Catholic bishops became the home where Tom and Kay Capano raised their four daughters.

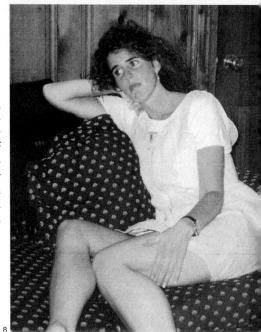

Beautiful, high spirited, and extremely intelligent, Anne Marie Fahey also had moments of deep sadness and self-doubt that left her vulnerable to Tom Capano's kindness and generosity.

8

Anne Marie and her brother Brian, both survivors of a tormented childhood, always looked after each other as adults. All of the Fahey family were extremely close.

9

Anne Marie on a trip to Ireland with Brian in 1994. Very self-conscious about her weight, she thought her legs were too fat and rarely posed in shorts.

Kim Horstman and Anne Marie were so close that they had virtually no secrets. Kim knew that Anne Marie was having an affair with Tom Capano, whom Kim disliked and distrusted.

Anne Marie worked for Tom Carper from 1989 to 1996, first when he was a congressman, then as his scheduling secretary when he was elected governor of Delaware. Carper played Cupid when he introduced her to Michael Scanlan.

Anne Marie and Mike started dating frequently and got to know each other's families. With Mike, Anne Marie believed she had found the right man at last, but she was terrified that he would discover her relationship with Tom Capano.

Anne Marie was living in an apartment on the third floor, right, of the house at 1718 Washington Street in Wilmington when her family and friends discovered that she had completely and mysteriously disappeared.

Investigators could find no trace of Anne Marie at the house on North Grant Avenue that Tom Capano had rented after he separated from his wife. Tom told them that he and Anne Marie had had a dinner date the night of June 27, 1996, and he had seen her safely home.

ATTEMPT TO LOCATE
MISSING PERSON

ANNE MARIE FAHEY
WHITE FEMALE 30, DOB 1/27/66, 5'10", 128 LBS,
RESIDENCE: 1718 WASHINGTON ST., WILMINGTON, DE.

SUBJECT ANNE MARIE FAHEY WAS LAST SEEN ON THURSDAY, JUNE 27, 1996 AT 1718 WASHINGTON STREET, AT APPROXIMATELY 2200 HOURS. SHE HAD DINNER EARLIER BETWEEN 1900-2100 HOURS AT A RESTAURANT IN PHILADELPHIA. HER VEHICLE, WALLET AND CLOTHING WERE FOUND AT THE RESIDENCE. NO CONTACT HAS BEEN MADE WITH ANY MEMBER OF HER FAMILY OR FRIENDS.

IF LOCATED PLEASE CONTACT:

DET.DONOVAN - WILMINGTON POLICE DEPT - (302)571-4512
LT.DANIELS - DELAWARE STATE POLICE - (302)323-4412

This flyer was distributed by the Fahey family, the Wilmington Police Department, and Delaware state police in an attempt to discover Anne Marie's whereabouts. Her family hoped for the best; the police feared the worst.

16

O'Friel's Irish Pub in Wilmington became the unofficial headquarters for the search for Anne Marie. The banner stayed up for almost three years, reminding people that she was still missing.

18

17

One of Wilmington's most important and respected men, Tom Capano seemed above suspicion in Anne Marie's disappearance. Even so, investigators wondered why he had removed a couch and replaced a brand new carpet with this cheap area rug in one room of his house.

FBI agents and Wilmington police searched the backyard of Capano's house on North Grant Avenue on July 31, 1996. He was now the chief suspect in Anne Marie's disappearance and probable murder. But the federal grand jury investigation was kept under wraps for a year and a half.

An FBI search warrant served on Kay Capano on July 31, 1996, included processing the SUV she had recently lent to her estranged husband. Had it been used to transport Anne Marie's body?

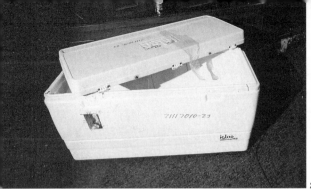

Another piece of potential evidence against Capano was a large Igloo cooler that was found floating in the Atlantic off the Delaware shore.

A final piece of the puzzle was the boat that Gerry Capano often used for shark-fishing competitions in the Atlantic Ocean.

The back of Gerry Capano's house on the Jersey shore, which led to the dock where his boat was moored.

A security camera took a picture of Tom Capano at 8:41 A.M. on June 28, 1996, as he waited for his cash at an ATM in Washington's Trolley Square neighborhood. He needed the money for a chilling mission.

Miller's Gun Center outside Wilmington, where investigators learned that someone close to Tom Capano had purchased a gun for him in May 1996.

The three members of the team that demonstrated they could make a solid case against a man who considered himself above the law. Left to right: Assistant U.S. Attorney Colm Connolly, Detective Robert Donovan of the Wilmington Police, and Delaware's Assistant Attorney General Ferris Wharton.

26

27

Special Agent Eric Alpert of the FBI, the fourth member of the team, was the Bureau's chief investigator in solving the mystery of Anne Marie's fate and bringing her killer to trial.

28

Attorney Tom Bergstrom from Malvern, Pennsylvania, stepped in to represent Debby MacIntyre after she began to doubt Tom Capano.

Attorney David Weiss (with Robert Fahey and Kathleen Fahey-Hosey behind him) represented the Fahey family during Anne Marie's disappearance and in a civil suit against the Capano family. He was elated in January 1999 when Tom Capano was found guilty of Anne Marie's murder.

30

29

Judge William Swain Lee presided over Capano's stormy and widely publicized trial. Sandwiched between his husky bailiffs, the judge left the Daniel Herrmann Courthouse in March 1999 after delivering a withering denunciation of the defendant and passing the stiffest possible sentence.

Defense attorneys Joseph Oteri (center), Eugene Maurer, Charlie Oberly, and Jack O'Donnell (latter two partially hidden) had been unsuccessful in preventing their arrogant client from taking the stand in his own defense.

31

Marguerite Capano was devastated by the verdict against her golden son, Tommy, and a sentence that would shatter her once proud and prosperous family. She grasped the hand of the family's long-time priest, Father Roberto Balducelli, while her son Joey pushed her wheelchair away from the courthouse.

After hearing their father's sentence, Tom Capano's three younger daughters (the first two in short skirts and the girl just emerging from the doorway) were rushed to a waiting car by relatives and friends.

Kathleen Fahey-Hosey and Brian Fahey spoke to the press after sentence was passed on Tom Capano. Still in mourning, they found justice in the verdict, although little consolation for their great loss.

Debby MacIntyre escaped Tom Capano's jealous rage, perhaps only because she had never tried to leave him. After eighteen years in a relationship that ended with another woman's murder, she at last found the confidence to face the future on her own.

A haggard and humbled Tom Capano was led in chains from the Daniel Herrmar Courthouse in Wilmington on March 16, 1999, almost three years after An Marie Fahey's disappearance and murder. He was sentenced to death by leth injection.

with a blind date with Mike's friend Dan, thinking how great it would be if they hit it off, too. They all met at Anne Marie's apartment, and it was apparent to both Dan and Kim that there was no magic, but when they went to the festival, there was so much energy, light, and music that it didn't matter.

Kim and Anne Marie had a chance to talk when the men walked ahead through the crowd. "Oh my God," Anne Marie whispered suddenly.

"*Who?*"

"*Tom*—quick, walk the other way!"

They reversed their steps before Tom saw them. He was with his daughters.

"She said that she had passed out at work," Kim recalled. "She was faint at work, and she called Capano to come pick her up—she reluctantly shared that with me. She was a little sheepish about it to say that she actually called him to pick her up."

The two women managed to hide their concern about the close encounter from Mike and Dan.

Anne Marie had avoided Tom at the St. Anthony's festival, but his E-mail continued. He was still trying to lend her money, buy her things, leave food for her, be *with* her. When she mentioned that her apartment was roasting, he bought her an air conditioner. She was trying hard not to say anything in her cautious E-mail that might give him an idea of something else to buy her.

She had accepted too much from Tom and admitted to herself that it had been nice, back in the days when he "treated her like a princess," to have his presents, his continual concern for giving her what she wanted and needed. No more. And her natural tendency for self-deprecation made her feel that the trap he'd caught her in was her own fault.

IT was June 19, and Anne Marie was having her weekly session with Dr. Sullivan. Sullivan had tried every way she knew to convince Anne Marie that she was a good person, deserving of happiness— and she had begun to succeed. Typical of anorectics, Anne Marie had one part of her body that she hated the most: her legs. They seemed immense and ugly to her.

"Write a letter to your legs," Michelle suggested, and Anne Marie looked at her as if *she* was the one in need of therapy.

It wasn't as silly as it sounded at first; Anne Marie needed to defuse her legs as entities that had power over her. She had begun to come back from her nadir point, she had cut way down on laxatives, was eating more, and now she had to "forgive" her fat thighs. Perhaps only another woman could understand.

Anne Marie grinned gamely and went home to write a letter she had never expected to write.

"I must admit," she wrote,

> that I feel somewhat silly writing a letter to my legs.
>
> I have many insecurities surrounding my life, but the one most prevalent to me is the size of my legs. Below is a list of what goes through my mind on a daily basis:
>
> 1. I cannot wear a skirt because people will see just how big my calves are.
> 2. I struggle through the summer because we wear less, which means more of my body is being exposed.
> 3. Every morning I wake up and talk myself out of wearing a skirt or a dress.
> 4. I have complete anxiety every time Michael sees me in shorts because I think this just might be the last time. I get embarrassed for Michael if we are out in public and I wear shorts.
> 5. I often look in the mirror when I get out of the shower and I yell at my legs.
> 6. If I had thin legs, then perhaps people would classify me as thin.
> 7. I will look at other women and say, "God, if I only had their legs, then maybe I would not be so ashamed of myself."
> 8. A day does not go by that I don't spend some part obsessing over the size of my legs. Blah, blah, blah, blah. AMF

Sullivan's technique had worked; Anne Marie started laughing at herself as her painfully candid letter disintegrated into "blah's." Her calves were well developed after years of playing field hockey, but her legs were really quite good.

On Thursday, June 20, something happened near Philadelphia that frightened Anne Marie. She and her girlfriends talked about it in hushed tones. Aimee Willard, twenty-two, who was a college lacrosse star, left Smokey Joe's, a popular Main Line bar, and headed for her home in Brookhaven. Her car was found on a Blue Route off ramp, its lights on and the engine running—but Aimee was missing. Hours later, her body was discovered in a vacant lot in north Philadelphia. Her skull was crushed and she had been raped and beaten. Aimee's father, Paul Willard, was a Chester County, Pennsylvania, police sergeant, and the case was headlined in both Pennsylvania and Delaware media.

Anne Marie and her friends wondered aloud how Aimee's killer had gotten her to stop her car, and they talked about how they all had traveled the Blue Route often. The dead girl's car had been found close to where Robert Fahey lived and to Katherine McGettigan's old place. The apparent randomness of Aimee Willard's murder disturbed Anne Marie particularly.

On Friday night, June 21, Anne Marie's brother Brian was packing for a trip to Ecuador. His wife, Rebeca, was Ecuadoran and her parents still lived there; he was going to join her for a few weeks. He had to stop by O'Friel's to drop some things off for Jimmy Freel, with whom he coached high school basketball, and he found Anne Marie and Mike there. "They were just hanging around," Brian said. "It looked like they had showed up there after work, and they were sitting at the bar, having a great time. They were holding hands and laughing, and I joked around with them for a little while."

Mike had been in Maine on business all week, and he and Anne Marie were glad to be together again. Anne Marie asked Brian if she could pick him up at the airport when he came home. He told her that of course she could, knowing how much she liked the ritual of picking up returning travelers. "I'll call you with the time of my flight," he promised. "What do you want me to bring you from Ecuador?"

"Jewelry," she said. "Pick out a piece of jewelry for me."

The next day, Saturday, June 22, Anne Marie and Kathleen went shopping together. They stopped at Talbot's and Anne Marie tried on the taupe pantsuit in a size four. It cost almost $300, but it wasn't the cost that made Kathleen gasp—it was the sight of her sister's ribs, stark bones glowing white beneath her skin. She hadn't seen Annie in just a bra and panties for a long time, and she was frightened by Anne Marie's skeletal frame. Kathleen spoke sharply, and because she too was frightened, Anne Marie snapped back. It wasn't a real fight, not even an argument. But it was something Anne Marie mentioned to Mike when she had dinner with him and another couple that night.

She also mentioned it to Tom sometime during the next week, and he acted as if he took it far more seriously than Mike had. He almost seemed pleased when she had tiffs with her sister or her friends. She was sorry she had said anything about it.

On Sunday night, June 23, Anne Marie went to Mike's house for dinner.

On Wednesday, June 26, Kim Horstman and Anne Marie talked

on the phone. They spoke of Aimee Willard's murder, still unsolved, and moved on to happier topics. "Annie sounded great," Kim remembered. "Really great. We talked about her eating disorder and she said that she had gained a couple of pounds, and she was very happy about that. And that she had cut the number of laxatives she was taking in half. So she felt she was getting better. And we talked about her relationship with Michael—and she felt that was going very well, and she was excited about that. It was a very upbeat conversation."

Later that day, Anne Marie met with Michelle Sullivan for her regular session. They spoke about her interaction with Kathleen, the fights they had had after their mother died. They probably touched upon the little argument Anne Marie and Kathleen had had in the dressing room at Talbot's four days earlier, but Dr. Sullivan did not recall that there was any lasting animosity at all. As grown women, the Fahey sisters seemed very close.

Anne Marie presented the letter she had written to her legs and grinned at her doctor. Sullivan warned her not to cut out *all* laxatives at once, while praising her for rebounding. It was a good session, a hopeful session. Things with Anne Marie were suddenly so much better. They were both tired when it was over, but it had been worth it.

That Wednesday night, Anne Marie and Mike talked on the phone. "We were making plans for the dinner with her brother that Saturday evening, the twenty-ninth," he recalled. "So we arranged a time to meet up. She was taking Friday off from work. She was really looking forward to having Friday off. She had some errands planned. The weather was starting to get warm, so she was in kind of that summer mood, and she needed a day to kick back."

When Tom learned that Anne Marie had admired the pantsuit at Talbot's—and that Kathleen had talked her out of it—he called the store branch in Greenville and said he wanted to surprise his wife with the pantsuit. The saleswoman, Kara Sullivan, checked and told him they no longer had it in a size four. But Tom was a very good customer, and she arranged to have it sent over from Talbot's Christiana store.

Tom had made up his mind that he was going to bring Anne Marie back to him. Completely. When she had called him on June 12, *chosen* him to be the man she summoned in a real emergency, he felt sure it was a sign that he had triumphed over Mike Scanlan. Scanlan didn't know what she was struggling with. He didn't know about her financial worries, or that he, Tom, stepped in often to bail her out. He didn't have the history with her that Tom had. Tom wasn't even convinced that Anne Marie had given herself sexually to Scanlan—so he was puzzled about why she still dated him.

But lately, there was so little that Tom could get Anne Marie to accept from him. She would not take the money he offered her; she explained that she had cut up her credit cards and did not want to be in further debt. She even wrote checks to pay back the money he had already given her, although he refused to cash them. She assured him that she was trying very, very hard to get better, and pleaded with him to let her do it in her own way. Her E-mail was more apologetic than ever before, and yet somehow more assertive.

6/26/96: afahey@gov.state.de.us at Internet
Hey Tommy,
    I would like to apologize for being such a downer today. I realize that your day had not been so great either, and I was not much help. I feel like some days I can handle my anorexia and other days I feel overwhelmed by the whole thing. Today has obviously been an overwhelming day. My appointment with Michelle was hard and in depth today, and quite frankly it drained all my energy. I really do appreciate you offering me the Phillies tickets, but right now I am going to focus on trying to get better. Sorry for being such a Doggy Downer today. Take care, Annie.

6/26/96, 6:19 PM Thomas Capano at Sera-Wilmington
Subject Lo Siento Mucho [Spanish: I'm very sorry.]
    I didn't get a chance to read this until after 6:00 and I assume you're gone and won't see this until tomorrow. I hope your sister went easy on you last night. I appreciate the apology but you don't need to worry about it. I just hope you know that all I want to do is help in any way I can. I promise to make you laugh tonight at Panorama, to order calamari and to surprise you with something that will make you smile. Please call when you get a chance.

He must have been picturing Anne Marie's face when he gave her the outfit from Talbot's.

6/27/96, 11:30 AM Thomas Capano at Sera-Wilmington
To: afahey@gov.state.de.us.at Internet
Good Morning,
    Called you at 11:45. Hope your day is better than yesterday. I'm crazy again today, but winding down. I left a message for you so hope to talk to you soon. Please call when you can.

It was a Thursday again—the night that Tom kept trying to designate as their regular night to dine out together. He knew Anne Marie wasn't going to work on Friday; she told him she was taking the day off to be kind to herself. Everyone in her office would be down in Dover, anyway, for the windup of the legislature, up to all hours as state senators and representatives fought to get their bills passed before they all went home until autumn.

If Anne Marie called or E-mailed him back, and if she agreed to go to Philadelphia with him for dinner, Tom vowed he would make it such a perfect night that she would forget all about Michael Scanlan.

PART THREE

And he that does one fault at first,
And lies to hide it, makes it two.

Chapter Twenty-one

As THE OFFICERS from the Wilmington Police Department and the Delaware State Police looked around Anne Marie's tiny apartment in the wee hours of Sunday, June 30, they had only the information they could glean from her sister, her boyfriend, and her other friends. Except for the hang-up on the fourteenth call on her answering machine, the messages there were all from her family and very close friends.

Any investigation into Anne Marie's disappearance was in the most embryonic state. It might not even be necessary to go further with it. She could be home by morning. Still, cops tend initially to accept the darkest explanations. Mark Daniels, Steve Montague, and Bob Donovan weren't about to wait until Monday to look for her.

They were hampered, however, by the absence of some vital details. If she had planned to accept Tom's E-mailed dinner invitation, Anne Marie had told no one. Tom had told Debby that he had a meeting in Philadelphia on the evening of Thursday, June 27, and that he would probably drop by her house around 9:30 P.M.

And yet it was clear that sometime between Thursday afternoon when she walked away from the Carvel building and Saturday night when Mike and her family went to her apartment and checked on her, Anne Marie had disappeared. If she had been scheduling secretary for an insurance executive or someone in management at the Hotel du Pont, there would have been concern, of course—but not something akin to panic. Anne Marie was the person responsible for organizing the details of the life of the governor of Delaware. If she was truly missing, it might be because of something that involved the state of Delaware. This was not a missing persons report that would routinely be put on hold until the missing adult had been gone forty-eight hours. This might very well be something else entirely, something that could impact the security of the top office in the state.

After they had listened to Anne Marie's phone messages, the state and local investigators looked through the rooms of her small third-floor apartment, nodding as the people who had called them explained which things were the way they should be and which were atypical of Anne Marie Fahey.

They talked to the landlady. They looked at the green 1995 Volkswagen Jetta parked across the street where Anne Marie usually left it. They paced the sidewalk in front of the white house that was now broken into separate apartments, the night brightened a little by streetlights.

"Maybe she *walked* away," Donovan said.

Kathleen shook her head. "No. She was very conscious of her safety in this neighborhood; she wouldn't walk alone outside, especially at night."

Brian Short, a tenant in the apartment house next door, spoke to the police. He hadn't seen Anne Marie for a few days, he said, but he remembered seeing her sometime in the past few weeks, leaving with a middle-aged man. The man's car had been a black "Broncotype" vehicle.

It was nearly 3 A.M. before Jill Morrison and Ginny Columbus almost reluctantly handed Mark Daniels several sheets of what appeared to be a law firm's stationery. His eyes scanned down the pages, and then he handed them silently to Bob Donovan.

Both men recognized the name on the law firm's letterhead. Tom Capano. *Tom Capano*. He had once been Donovan's boss's boss. For that matter, he had also been Daniels' boss's legal adviser. City, county, state: everyone knew him. He was a straight shooter, a longtime and well-respected public servant. But these letters were obviously very personal. Anne Marie Fahey might as well have been saving intimate letters from the governor himself. They wouldn't have been any more surprised.

However, the letters substantiated what they had found in the missing woman's diary. They had a dictatorial tone to them, and had apparently been sent along with cash or checks.

The first letter had no date, but was probably several months old, as it mentioned Christmas.

Dearest Annie,

Please consider the enclosed an early—and only partial—Christmas gift. I want you to be able to join Kathleen and Patrick at the Saloon on Saturday night. When we talked about it before, it seemed to me that you wanted to go but had decided against it because of the cost. Now you can afford to do what you wanted to do. Also, since Robert has apparently changed his dinner plans to Sunday, you can be part of the celebration. Should Robert decide to have you for dinner on Saturday instead, then please use this to buy dinner (no drinks!) next week for Sherry and your hostess. Of course, you could tell Robert you're busy on Saturday and would like to see him on Sunday. I know that by doing this I am encouraging you to go to Robert's on Sunday. That means you will not be free to have dinner with me either at home or at the Villa d' Roma. As much as I want to be with you on Sunday, I want you to be able to go to the Saloon because I think it will make you happy to share an evening with your family. Annie, I will miss you next week more than you can imagine. It would help a lot if we could be together on Sunday night after Robert's. I promise to get you out of the house as early as you like on Monday morning. Please consider it. And please accept this gift in the spirit in which it is given. All I want is to make you happy and be with you. I love you . . .

Kathleen told them she had taken her husband, Pat, out for dinner at the Saloon during the first week of December 1995. Anne Marie hadn't gone with them.

Another, dated May 2, 1996, read:

Annie, this is not a gift; it is a loan to replace your windshield. You can repay half of it when you get a check from your insurance company. The balance can be repaid at the rate of five dollars per week. Of course, if you default, there is a penalty. You will have to scrub my toilets and iron my boxers.

Please accept this. The windshield stresses you and it's dangerous. I could do more if you would let me (like replace the Jetta with a Lexus 300 ES Coach Edition). Maybe some day.

Tom

P.S. Don't these bills look like Monopoly money? But I got them from a bank. Honest.

A third letter was dated only five days earlier—June 25:

Annie, just add this to the balance. Consider it a consolidation loan (that's a joke). Kidding aside, you should not be penniless for several days in case of an emergency (like an overpowering yearning for a latte).

I'd have sent more but I know you'll have a hard time accepting even this. Please accept it in the spirit in which it's given and don't spend it on Jill.

Tom

The letters were directives; Capano sounded like a border collie herding sheep, heading off objections and alternatives before Anne Marie could think of them. Either the missing woman was his mistress or he *wanted* her to be his mistress or he was the most generous guy in Wilmington.

The investigators couldn't ask Anne Marie what the letters meant or what her connection to Tom Capano was. She was missing. The first thing they needed to do, then, after they checked out her apartment thoroughly, was to try to contact him.

At this point they had no idea what they were dealing with; Anne Marie's disappearance could have been the result of a lovers' quarrel, she might have gone away on her own, or she might be dead. Detectives learn to consider the worst-case scenario. For them a body must be considered the result, first, of a homicide; second, of an accident; third, of a suicide—and only when those possibilities have been ruled out may they decide that death came of natural causes. But of course, there was no body.

If something *had* happened to Anne Marie Fahey, and if it had happened in her apartment, the detectives were late going in: She had been missing for almost three days. Worse, her apartment was certainly contaminated—in terms of evidence—by the comings and goings of the family and friends who were looking for her. Doorknobs, drawer pulls, and flat surfaces had been touched, and the toilet had probably been flushed. Most people don't think the way a detective does, and quite naturally, those who were worried about Anne Marie weren't thinking about disturbing physical evidence as they looked for clues to her whereabouts.

What was done was done. And there was certainly no overt sign that anything violent had taken place in Anne Marie's third-floor apartment. Except for the food on the counter and a few garments that had not been hung up, everything seemed to be in order.

There was no point now in telling anyone not to touch things. Probably it wouldn't matter anyway. Chances were that Anne Marie was with someone she knew and trusted, that she had just grabbed her keys and left on a momentary whim.

And the chances were just as good—better, maybe—that she wasn't.

BOB DONOVAN, thirty-three, would have had a hard time working as an undercover detective. He was big, square, and his short crew cut only accentuated his strong features. He looked for all the world like an Irish cop from a long line of Irish cops. He was Irish, but he was the first police officer in his family. It was something he had wanted to do for as long as he could remember. In June 1996, he had been a Wilmington Police officer for nine years, with the first seven and a half on the road in Patrol. He had been in Detectives only a year. Detectives worked all major crimes, but the homicide rate in Wilmington wasn't very high. (Nineteen ninety-six would show the highest number in years—twenty-two homicides; ten was average, with most of them drug or gang related.)

Bob and his wife, Karen, had two small children, ages five and one. He was home asleep at 12:30 A.M. when he was rousted out of bed by the watch commander for the Wilmington Police Department's third watch. As one of two detectives on call for the weekend, Donovan had been available for call-out from 4 P.M. Friday and would be until 8 A.M. Monday morning. All he was told was that he was to respond to 1718 Washington Street in reference to a missing person. That was fairly unusual—missing persons complaints didn't generally elicit night call-outs—but he didn't ask questions. He had arrived at Anne Marie Fahey's apartment fifteen minutes later.

There were an awful lot of cops there for a missing persons report: Donovan's supervisor, Sergeant Elmer Harris, and two uniformed officers from the Wilmington PD, Sergeant John Snyder and Officer Paul McDannell. Surprisingly, there were also two Delaware State Police officers, Lieutenant Mark Daniels and Sergeant Steve Montague.

Donovan, whose kindness has been extolled by any number of people caught in the face of tragedy, could display a somewhat watchful attitude at first meeting, and watch he did; he seldom missed a thing. A long time later, when he was asked what he found at Anne Marie Fahey's apartment, he said quietly, "A room full of people."

Kathleen told the detectives that Anne Marie had been seeing a therapist—Dr. Michelle Sullivan. Perhaps she might know something that would help. Used to late-night emergency calls, Sullivan answered on the second ring. When she heard Anne Marie was missing, she didn't hesitate. "I'm coming right over," she said. She was worried, too.

Dr. Sullivan told them that she knew Anne Marie well. She had not seen her, however, on Thursday; their session had been on *Wednesday* evening. Anne Marie was to have seen Dr. Neil Kaye, the psychiatrist who monitored her prescriptions, on Thursday afternoon. Asked if Anne Marie knew Tom Capano, Sullivan confirmed that she did—and without violating her doctor-patient ethics, told them that Anne Marie had an ongoing relationship with him.

Bob Donovan knew who Tom Capano was, although he doubted if Capano knew him. As chief of staff to the mayor, Capano had overseen the Wilmington Police Department for some time, and he was friendly with a lot of the top brass, both working and retired. He was an important figure in Wilmington.

By 3:30 A.M., Bob Donovan, Elmer Harris, Mark Daniels, and Steve Montague were driving through the dark, winding streets of the Kentmere Park neighborhood looking for Tom's house. It was Sunday morning, and the affluent residents along North Grant Avenue all seemed to be asleep. Like its neighbors, the windows of the redbrick house at 2302 North Grant were dark.

The quartet of detectives knocked on the door. And waited. They knocked again and heard sounds from inside the house; someone was coming to the door.

Tom Capano, wearing a robe, opened the door and stared at them. He appeared to have been asleep, and smoothed his hair with a quick hand. He didn't seem particularly startled to see them, or particularly welcoming.

They identified themselves and he looked at them sleepily, then asked them to step inside. Capano led the detectives through the foyer to a living room beyond and gestured for them to sit down on the white leather couch that dominated the room.

"Are you aware about why we want to talk with you?" Mark Daniels asked.

"Yes. I am aware." Tom nodded. "I've spoken to one of Anne Marie's friends and I understand that you're looking for her."

"Do you know where she is?"

Tom shook his head. "I don't—I haven't seen her since, ah, either Wednesday—maybe Thursday night. We had dinner at a restaurant in Philadelphia."

"That was . . . ?"

"The Panorama. And we left there and came back to Wilmington—to my house, this house."

Tom was very open with the detectives, answering Daniels's questions and others that Donovan interjected—expanding on his memory of what he now believed had been Thursday night. He said he had picked Anne Marie up in front of her apartment sometime between six-fifteen and six-thirty that night. She had been wearing a light-colored floral print dress, as he recalled. They had driven to Philadelphia in his Jeep Grand Cherokee, eaten a pleasant dinner of, he thought, fish of some sort. He said he had paid with a credit card and that, as usual, Anne Marie calculated the tip for him and signed the check. Afterward, they had come back to his house—but only briefly.

"I went inside to get some things for her—food: rice, bananas, spinach, soup—and I had a gift for her. I can't remember now if I'd left it in the house or if it was in my car."

Tom said he had then driven Anne Marie to her apartment, but he recalled that, when they pulled up, she had gone ahead. "I had forgotten something in the Jeep and had to go back and get it. She opened the gift—but I don't think she took it completely out of the box."

He remembered carrying the food upstairs for her and putting it on her kitchen counter. "Oh, and she asked me to check her air conditioner. I did—and it was working fine," he said. "I think I used the bathroom too."

He explained that he had stayed only a few minutes and then had left for home. "I was back here by about ten."

"Did you stop anywhere on the way?" Donovan asked.

"I think I stopped at the Getty gas station on Lovering to get a pack of cigarettes."

"Have you talked to Miss Fahey since then?" Daniels asked.

"No," Tom said. "I haven't."

"Do you have any idea where she might be?"

"Anne Marie is very airheaded, unpredictable," he said, half smiling. "I think she's probably just run off someplace and she'll be back to work on Monday. She'll come walking in right on time."

"If she ran off, where do you think she might have gone?" Daniels asked.

"The beach, probably. I really thought she was down at the ocean with her friend Kimmie—Kim Horstman—until I talked to Kimmie earlier tonight."

It was apparent that Tom Capano knew Anne Marie Fahey quite well. He was aware that she had planned to take Friday off from her job in the governor's office. Everyone else was going down to Dover for the end of the legislative session and would probably be staying up all night. "She didn't want to go," he said, and told the investigators that she had problems at work and hated going down to Dover for the twenty-four-hour sessions that marked the virtual end of the political year.

Tom also told them that Anne Marie had had a "big fight" with her sister earlier in the week, speculating that an airheaded girl with so many problems had almost certainly simply decided to run away from her life for a few days.

Asked to describe his relationship with Anne Marie, Tom was frank. He told the detectives that he and Anne Marie had once been involved sexually but that they now had only a very close friendship.

"We haven't done anything sexual for the past six months," he explained. "She has psychological problems, she's been on medication, just having a hard time dealing with it all. I've spent a lot of time helping her with her psychological problems."

Asked if he thought Anne Marie might be suicidal, Tom sighed. That concerned him because he felt she was definitely suicidal. He told the detectives that she had talked a lot about committing suicide with pills in the past. The medicine she was taking currently was making her sick. "She wakes up at night with insomnia," he added. Tom said he knew Michelle Sullivan. In fact, he was the one who arranged for her and Anne Marie to meet.

"You give Miss Fahey a lot of gifts?" Donovan asked.

Tom nodded. He gave lots of people gifts, and that included Anne Marie. "Lately, I've regularly been giving her food. I've given her money, and I recently gave her some Cézanne prints."

"Mr. Capano," Mark Daniels asked suddenly, "can you tell us whether or not Anne Marie is in this house at the moment?"

"No," he said. "She is not."

"If you knew where she was, and if she had just gone away, and she told you she didn't want anyone to know where she was, would you tell us?"

"No, I'd respect her confidence."

When Donovan and Daniels explained that Anne Marie was officially a missing person whose family was terribly concerned, and no one knew if she was in danger or needed help or what might have happened to her, Tom changed his mind.

"Well, under those circumstances, I would tell you. But I don't know where she is, and so I can't tell you."

They had been talking in a very polite, if edgy, fashion for half an hour. Now the detectives asked if they might take a look around the house, and Tom shook his head. "My daughters are asleep upstairs," he said. "This isn't a good time." He explained that he didn't want to frighten his four girls with strange men clomping through the house, aiming flashlights at them. They acquiesced but said they would be back the next morning—actually, later the same morning.

Tom Capano had been cooperative—up to a point. They hadn't seen his daughters, but they took his word that the girls were in the house, sleeping upstairs. They didn't have a search warrant or any probable cause to get a search warrant. Moreover, they didn't know Anne Marie Fahey and they couldn't form an opinion on whether she was the kind of young woman who would go away for the weekend without telling anyone because she was stressed out or because, as Tom Capano said, she was an airhead given to such behavior.

They did know that Tom Capano had a solid reputation in Wilmington and that there had never been a breath of scandal about him. His brothers, yes. But not Tom. Tom was the "good Capano," and he certainly appeared to be going about his life as he normally did. He didn't look like a man who was about to rabbit on them.

"We'll be back later today," Daniels said. "We'd like to talk with you more then."

Tom nodded and walked them to the door. The lights were out in the house before they had turned the corner and headed back downtown.

IT was a warm Sunday morning at ten when the Wilmington and State Police investigators returned to the Grant Avenue house. This time, their knocks on the front door went unanswered. They went back several times over the next few hours and found no one home. Puzzled, and a little annoyed that Tom Capano seemed to be deliberately avoiding them, they went looking for him, driving past the huge old houses in the neighborhood, the Delaware Art Museum, along the Bancroft Parkway, and past the big white stucco house on the corner of Greenhill and Seventeenth where Tom's estranged wife and children lived. They knew he drove a 1993 black Jeep Grand Cherokee and they watched for it.

In the meantime, they went back to Anne Marie's apartment

house. Mark Daniels talked with her landlady, Theresa Oliver. She explained that she kept the apartments secure from the street. "To get to the second or third floor," she said, "you have to go through that clear storm door first, and it has a dead-bolt lock. Anyone would need a key."

Mrs. Oliver told Daniels that a woman named Connie Blake lived in the apartment directly below Anne Marie's. "But she's at the shore—and won't be home until tonight."

As the investigators passed Kay Capano's house for the sixth or seventh time, Bob Donovan spotted Tom coming out of the garage area. They walked up to him, and this time, Tom was far more agitated than he had been the night before. He responded to their questions in short sentences, telling them that he was upset with himself for having said so much when they had wakened him hours before. He felt that he had betrayed Anne Marie's privacy by telling the police about their affair, but he had been groggy from taking several Excedrin PMs, and now he was sorry.

They asked to see his house and Tom agreed—but not happily. He followed them as they drove to his house. It was not a formal search; it was only a walk-through, but he seemed to resent the idea of detectives peering into his rooms and wouldn't give them permission to open drawers or look into his closets. It was, perhaps, an indication that they hadn't believed what he had told them earlier in the morning, and Tom was not accustomed to having his words questioned, particularly not when it came to police matters.

Tom's house was immaculate. "It was very clean, very orderly. We were looking for Anne Marie Fahey," Bob Donovan recalled. "But she wasn't there."

Nor was there any sign that she had been there. Tom led the detectives through the house and into the double garage beneath the dining room–great room area. They saw the pretty bedrooms he had decorated for his daughters, the lavish master bedroom, the kitchen, dining area, living room. All the furnishings were apparently brand new. But there was no indication that Anne Marie Fahey had even been in any of these rooms or that anything untoward might have happened here.

It was still Sunday, June 30—a day that seemed to be forty-eight hours long. Tomorrow, Anne Marie might walk into the governor's office at 7:30 A.M., rested, relaxed, and with a new sprinkling of freckles across the bridge of her nose from a weekend in the sun. That was Tom Capano's prediction.

The detectives hoped that he was right, but like all good cops, Bob Donovan had a feeling in his gut that told him otherwise.

_____ *Chapter Twenty-two* _____

KATHLEEN FAHEY-HOSEY had gone home to check on her babies, but she was back at Anne Marie's apartment at seven-thirty that Sunday morning. Neither she nor Mike Scanlan had slept during the wee hours after the detectives had left to go to Tom Capano's house. She met Mike now on the front porch of 1718 Washington Street. Besides her worry about her sister, Kathleen had another burden on her mind. Mike hadn't seen the letters from Tom, and Kathleen knew she had to tell him what she had found. If she didn't, somebody else was going to bring it up. There was no other way; Anne Marie would just have to straighten things out with Mike when she came home.

"Mike," Kathleen said, "we need to talk."

She told him about the letters and warned him that it appeared that Anne Marie had been somehow involved with Tom Capano— and it seemed to have been more than just a friendship. Her words hung suspended in the air between them for a long moment as Mike tried to assimilate what they might mean. Finally, he tapped Kathleen on the arm and said, "Let's go up."

If her relationship with Tom Capano was too much to take in, the most important thing, still, was to find Anne Marie. Shafts of early morning sun sliced through the windows now, but nothing had changed in her apartment. They had hoped against hope that there might at least be a message on her answering machine—some clue to where she might be.

For many years now, the orphaned Fahey siblings had formed a tight circle. If one of them was in trouble or in danger, they all were. Already they were mobilizing, prepared to do whatever they had to do to find their sister and bring her home safely. Early on, they decided that one of them would try to be in her apartment at all times. If she called, or if someone called *about* her, there would always be someone to answer the phone; there would always be someone waiting to welcome her back. And if someone had hurt her, he—or she— would have to answer to the family.

The Faheys dealt with what they had to. They all had long experience in working through trouble and tragedy. Frightened as they were, they didn't panic. Robert recalled how disturbed his wife, Susan, was when there was no word from Anne Marie. "Susan had had no experience with chaos; she was raised in upper-middle-class America," he said. "For us, chaos and turmoil were not intimidating; we had long since been forced to develop skills to cope."

They clung together that Sunday morning, all except Brian, who got the news of his sister's disappearance when he was thousands of miles from home. When he'd left for Ecuador, he had told a friend not to give his phone number out to anyone, "unless someone in my family dies." Brian's in-laws didn't speak a word of English, and if a call from the States came in while he and his wife were away, they wouldn't be able to understand.

When the phone rang in Ecuador on Sunday, Brian heard his wife answer it and say, "Hi, Kathleen," and his breath slowed. "I knew it was bad news."

ON Monday morning, everyone in the governor's office waited nervously. Anne Marie was almost always the first to get to work, but she wasn't there at seven. Or seven-thirty. Or eight. They didn't really expect her to be, as much as they hoped they were wrong. Now, Anne Marie gazed from the front page of the *Wilmington News-Journal,* her photograph visible through the window of every newspaper vending machine along the downtown streets, a beautiful girl with huge eyes and soft lips.

One of the Faheys' earliest decisions was to get word out to the public so that everyone would look for Anne Marie. They were in complete agreement with the authorities to release information to local newspapers as soon as possible. Sheri Woodruff, Governor Carper's spokeswoman, helped the Faheys understand the workings of the media. Mark Daniels had taken the picture of Anne Marie to the *News-Journal* and asked for coverage that might elicit tips from the public. The short article about her was to be the first eight inches in what would become many miles of newsprint. *Carper Staffer Is Sought,* read the headline. "Anne Marie Fahey . . . was reported missing by family members at 12:15 a.m. Sunday. . . . Fahey, who works in Carper's Wilmington Office, left without her wallet or vehicle. . . . Police have checked hospitals and with family and friends without success."

Because she was the governor's secretary and because she was beautiful, wire services picked up the story of Anne Marie's disappearance. Some reporters commented on the fact that Anne Marie had disappeared exactly one week after Aimee Willard; it had become the practice of the media to link vanishings and murders, particularly when the women involved were young and lovely and lost from the same general area. But Aimee's body, sadly, had been found within hours, and Anne Marie had been gone, according to news reports, for more than eighty.

It took Brian until Monday morning to get as far as Miami, and it was afternoon before he landed in Philadelphia. Father James, his uncle, picked him up and took him to where he'd parked his car at the Friends School. Brian then drove straight to Anne Marie's apartment, where he and his sister and three brothers pored over Annie's address book, dividing up the pages. "We all got on a telephone somewhere," Brian said, "and started to call all of her friends, and then tried to come up with a list of people who *weren't* in the book that might have known her whereabouts."

Anne Marie had so many friends and acquaintances, and it helped to keep busy. They even called the family she had lived with in Spain on the faint possibility that she might have made plans to go back to the country she loved so much.

They continued to find reasons, however far-fetched, to believe that Anne Marie was OK. Maybe she hadn't read a paper or listened to the radio or watched television. Maybe she was really getting away from it all and she didn't know that everyone was looking for her. Their explanations began to stretch so thin that they could see one another's eyes through the gaps in their logic. And what they were thinking was chilling.

The police had already done a door-to-door canvass of the houses around Anne Marie's apartment and searched the park across the street, even though it had so few trees along the greensward that they doubted she could have been hidden there. It seemed more likely that she had left her apartment in a vehicle, but they could not be sure. They didn't even know *when* she had vanished.

Perhaps the last to see her on the governor's staff was Diane Hastings, the office manager. She told the investigators that she had ridden down in the elevator with Anne Marie at about 4:30 P.M. on Thursday. "I was going home and she was going home."

"What was she wearing?" she was asked.

"Jeans and a white scoop-neck T-shirt. She was happy that she had the next day off, and she was going to read a book in the park and have a manicure, a pedicure."

Since several of her friends recalled that Anne Marie had

planned to spend Friday getting a pedicure and other beauty treatments at the Michael Christopher Designs salon, and then go to Valley Garden Park with a good book, it was possible she had spent Thursday night in her apartment, gone to the salon, and then encountered someone in the park the next day.

But a check with the staff at the salon brought the information that Anne Marie had not shown up for her appointment—nor had she called in to cancel.

Valley Garden Park was on the Hoopes Reservoir, northwest of Wilmington, and old-timers on the police force remembered the beautiful park's ghosts of murder. In 1956, ten years before Anne Marie Fahey was even born, Alberta Cousins, twenty-two, also made it a habit to take books to Valley Garden Park. On August 23, almost nine months pregnant, she sat in the park reading, shoes off in deference to the stifling heat. As police reconstructed what happened next, a bullet had whizzed by her head, startling her. She apparently got to her feet and had made it part of the way to her car when a second bullet slammed into her right side and pierced her heart. A police officer found her hours later, much too late to save her unborn child.

The murder of Alberta Cousins launched the most massive State Police investigation Delaware had ever seen. A shell casing was found 135 feet from her body, and indentations there showed where her killer had sat as he took a bead on her, but the police had no way to find her killer—not until twenty-five years later, when a woman with a niggling conscience came forward to describe a man she had observed close to the park that day. Using a computer-generated composite image, the police found that it matched almost exactly the photograph of a man imprisoned in Florida. The man had confessed to his cell mate, saying, "I shot a woman in Delaware once." But he had mental problems and no one had ever taken him seriously until the composite matched. By the time that happened, the convict was long dead.

FOUR decades after the massive search for Alberta Cousins's killer, another search began in the Valley Garden Park, searchers and dogs below, helicopters above. Sweeping wider and wider, the searchers beat the bushes and looked along the open ground with little hope. Anne Marie's car was still parked on Washington Street, and the park was much too far to walk to. She would have to have had a ride to reach it. And there was no reason at all to think that she had.

Bob Donovan entered Anne Marie's name and description and

the details of her disappearance into the DELJIS-NCIC systems at 10 A.M. on Monday morning. She was in the computer, a routine investigative tack but one that was often effective. The National Crime Information Center's computers in Quantico, Virginia, could connect missing people with incidents outside their usual environments.

Michelle Sullivan talked to the police again and told them that she feared Anne Marie had been abducted. She recalled a remark Anne Marie had made once during a session. It had seemed out of context, but now she wished she had pursued it further. Anne Marie had said that she was afraid that someone might kidnap her.

"She came into the office and mentioned that [a friend] said that somebody could kidnap her," Sullivan told police. "I said, 'Well, talk to me more about this,' and she said, 'Oh, I don't know—somebody could just take me away or something.' "

Sullivan had asked her, "Who would do this?"

"Probably a third party."

"What do you mean—that somebody would *hire* a third party?"

"Yeah."

"Who would do that?"

"Tom Capano."

Even before this conversation, Anne Marie had told Sullivan about Capano's stalking behavior and his incessant phone calls. Michelle Sullivan had been trying to get her to contact the Attorney General's Office or go to the police. But Anne Marie had been adamant that she couldn't do that; it would be too embarrassing, especially because she worked in the governor's office. She feared the press might find out. But she told Sullivan that she had gone so far as to contact an acquaintance in the Attorney General's Office and pretended she was asking for advice for a friend.

"Anne Marie asked her friend, 'Somebody I know is being harassed. What would you tell her to keep herself safe?' And then she wrote down the answers," Sullivan told the police.

It was apparent to the detectives who were looking for her that Anne Marie had been worried about a number of things, and most of them could be linked to Tom Capano. *But why would she think he would have her kidnapped?*

And had he? They couldn't ask him at the moment. Since Sunday afternoon, he had made himself unavailable to them.

ON July 1, Mark Daniels had driven to the Ristorante Panorama in Philadelphia and asked to speak to the waiters who had been on duty on June 27. It was fairly easy to establish from a credit card receipt that Tom Capano and a companion had eaten at the Panorama that night. Jacqueline Dansak's initials were on the check, designating her as their server.

Daniels soon found that Dansak had an excellent memory. She said she remembered the couple well; they were distinctive in several ways. "They were unusually dressed for the atmosphere," she explained. "And this couple—especially the female—she was wearing a flower-printed dress. Most of our clientele are from the Main Line . . . very fashionably dressed, bedazzled and bedecked and whatnot. Most women [who come in] wear black or something a little more jet-setty looking."

Jacqueline Dansak had always liked to figure out couples' relationships to each other, but she had been at a loss with this pair. They gave her so little to go on. They didn't seem like a dating couple, nor did they look married. They clearly weren't there on business. The man was considerably older than the woman, but not quite old enough to be her father. And there was virtually no interaction between them; it was as if they were trapped in the same elevator together, staring glumly ahead.

"They didn't speak to each other at all," Dansak said. "This man—the gentleman—ordered everything for the woman without even consulting her. They started off with cocktails. They had a three-course meal. I sold the special to the woman—she had swordfish. The gentleman had veal or chicken."

Looking at the check, which had come to a total of $154, she could tell that the man had ordered a Myers's rum and tonic for himself and a Sea Breeze (vodka and cranberry juice) for the woman.

Aside from their not speaking, Dansak noted that the woman was very quiet—"somber. She looked haggard and gaunt. Her hair was unkempt. She was very thin."

They had barely touched their food, she reported. "They picked at it. I had to wrap it up. I asked the woman if she wanted something else—because she wasn't eating it."

But the woman had only shaken her head. She hadn't seemed angry—or frightened, for that matter. She had seemed more depressed or sad, as if she wasn't at all happy to be there.

Dansak explained the Visa receipt to Lieutenant Daniels. It indicated that Thomas J. Capano had begun to run a tab at 7:10 P.M., and the final amount was run through the credit card machine at 9:12. There was a generous tip included in the receipt.

"The gentleman pushed the check and the credit card receipt toward the woman," Dansak recalled, also an unusual circumstance. The woman had apparently figured up the check and added the proper tip. The receipt was signed "Thomas J. Capano."

The couple would have left shortly after nine-fifteen, although Dansak said she hadn't actually seen them go. But she had remembered them even after they left because their demeanor was so odd; the woman looked so unhappy, and the man seemed so bossy to her. The waitress could not tell Mark Daniels what they talked about during the two hours they were in the Panorama, or even *if* they had talked. The woman had tried to smile at her when she approached the table, but it seemed an effort.

The man? She could remember nothing special about him more than his glasses, which had a tint to them that virtually hid his eyes. Daniels showed Jacqueline Dansak a photograph of Anne Marie; he didn't have a picture of Tom. She said that she recognized her as the woman who had eaten there Thursday night.

So far, Tom Capano's story of that Thursday evening seemed to be completely accurate. The doggie bags in Anne Marie's refrigerator were from the Ristorante Panorama, and one had contained a scarcely touched portion of swordfish. The cotton dress with flowers on it sounded like the dress the detectives had seen in her apartment. Everything indicated that she had come home from Philadelphia, gone up to her apartment with Tom, who had carried the doggie bags and the gift from Talbot's upstairs for her, and then left. She had taken her dress off, but had half folded it and tossed it over a settee instead of hanging it up as she routinely did.

It didn't sound as if the evening had been a happy one, however. Even a waitress who didn't know them had wondered why Anne Marie and Tom had seemed glum and had only picked at their meals. She was quite sure, though, that they weren't having an argument; they just seemed to be at an impasse, bored, or even silently angry. But that evening was becoming more and more important to investigate, since Jacqueline Dansak appeared to be the last person— other than Capano—to have seen Anne Marie before she vanished.

On Tuesday morning, July 2, with Anne Marie still missing, the Wilmington paper noted that she had last been seen in an unidentified Philadelphia restaurant on Thursday night and added quotes from her brothers. "This is very odd . . . very confusing for everybody," Robert told reporters. "It's so unlike her to be out of touch for more than an afternoon, let alone a whole weekend. She's your normal, 30-year-old single girl with a lot of local friends and family."

Kathleen, Robert, Kevin, Mark, and Brian were spending most of their time at Anne Marie's apartment. Mark moved in so that someone would be there constantly. He was the brother she had agonized over, loving him so much that she wept for him. Now, she was gone—and Mark would have done anything to get Annie back. They all would.

The police asked Kathleen to inventory everything in Anne Marie's apartment to see what might be missing. She did, and the only things she could be sure of were Anne Marie's keys, her Walkman, and the blue topaz ring that Paul Columbus had given her. Anne Marie had worn that ring with the cotton dress they'd found flung over her settee; it matched the little blue flowers in the pattern. But now it was missing, along with Anne Marie. And by the end of the day, rumors were already circulating that she had last been seen dining with a "prominent Wilmington attorney" in Philadelphia just before she vanished.

DEBBY MACINTYRE was only peripherally aware that a woman was missing in Wilmington. In retrospect, she remembered that she had seen the picture of a pretty woman on the front page of the paper and read the headline. It didn't seem to touch her world, and she rarely read crime news. She had heard the rumor but thought nothing of it. Wilmington was filled with attorneys, many of whom could be described as prominent.

Sometime on that Tuesday, Debby got a phone call at work from Tom. "I have something very shocking to tell you," he began. "You'd better sit down."

Automatically, Debby sank to her chair, ready for what must surely be bad news.

"Do you recall reading about a woman who is missing who had gone to dinner with a prominent attorney?"

"I think I saw something in the paper . . ."

"You heard that she was last seen having dinner with a prominent attorney?"

Debby waited, her heart suddenly thudding.

"That was me."

"Oh, no," she breathed.

"I'm a suspect in her disappearance," Tom said. "I've hired Charlie Oberly to represent me. I wanted to call you now because I'm going down to Stone Harbor a day early for the Fourth."

"Who is this woman?" Debby asked, puzzled.

"Her name's Anne Marie Fahey. I'll call you later tonight and we'll talk about it."

Debby was stunned. What had Tom been doing with a woman who had disappeared? For that matter, what had he been doing having dinner with another woman without even mentioning it to her? It was as if the earth had opened up beneath her feet and everything in Debby's world had begun to slide in. She would have bet money that Tom had no secrets from her—not about women. She had bet her life on him for fourteen years.

Tom was still talking. He said that Charlie wanted to speak to her on the phone and asked her when he could call her.

"Five-thirty, I guess," she said. "At my house."

Charlie Oberly was a respected attorney in Wilmington and had once been the Delaware State Attorney General. He was a good friend of Tom's. Debby didn't mind talking to him. Actually, she wanted to find out more about what was going on. She stayed at work for another hour, blindly doing what she needed to do to clear her desk. But she couldn't focus or concentrate as she tried to figure out what on earth Tom was involved in.

When Charlie Oberly called Debby, he asked her if she had spoken with Tom on the previous Thursday night and during the day on Friday. That was simple enough to answer. Tom had said he had a meeting with his law firm in Philadelphia on Thursday night and she had spoken to him on the phone a couple of times after ten—the first time, she thought, was during *ER,* and again later. She had seen Tom early Friday morning and talked to him on the phone a few times during the day, and he had spent Friday night with her.

Oberly listened to her timetable but he didn't give her much information. She needed to talk to Tom.

At nine-thirty Tuesday evening, Tom called her from his mother's house in Stone Harbor. By this time, Debby had had too many hours to think and she was very upset. As soon as she heard Tom's voice, she said, "Who *is* this Anne Marie Fahey?"

"I've been seeing her."

"*When?*"

"Up until September of last year, but it's over."

"Are you in love with her?"

"I did fall in love with her," Tom said, "but it's over, Debby."

She could scarcely believe that Tom had been that involved with another woman and never once mentioned it to her. On the rare occasions when she dated anyone else, she had always told him. And now it seemed that Tom had hidden what was apparently a love affair from her, even as he kept telling her how very much he loved her.

"How can you tell me you love me?" she asked.

"I do."

"I know she's a lot younger," Debby said. "I can't compete with someone who's thirty years old."

"She had so many problems," he said. "I was so good to her—I was helpful and I was interested—but then I couldn't get rid of her. She was so mentally ill, Debby, and she attached herself to me, and I knew I had to unload her."

"How long, Tom?" Debby asked. "How long did you see her?"

"About three years."

"Three years?"

Tom kept insisting that she had nothing to feel bad about now, since he was no longer in love with Anne Marie Fahey. He didn't seem to understand why she was so emotional, but Debby was so distraught that, for once, she couldn't hide her real feelings. She felt betrayed, and she felt a fool for never once suspecting him.

Tom said he was sorry that he'd ever had to tell her about Anne Marie, but since it was probably going to hit the news any minute, he wanted her to know the truth first. Of course, he had no idea what had happened to Anne Marie, who was such a ditsy girl that he never could tell what she might do next. She could be any of a dozen places.

"Are there others?" Debby asked when he had finished telling her about Anne Marie, a woman she had never even *heard* of until the day before.

"*One* other," he replied quietly. And then he said that he had been seeing Susan Louth since November.

"Why didn't you tell me?" Debby cried. "How could you let me believe that I was the only woman in your life?"

"I didn't want to hurt your feelings."

"My *feelings?*" Debby felt as though she had no breath left in her body. "Don't you know that lying to me is worse than that?"

Debby wasn't even thinking she could be making Tom so angry that he might leave her. She spoke her mind without thought of the consequences. She was absolutely devastated, but she didn't think of leaving *him*. Her mind scurried around, trying to mend the damage, albeit unconsciously. Her future had been with Tom for so long that she couldn't imagine life without him. It wasn't that she believed even for a second that he could have done anything to the girl; Tom wouldn't hurt anyone. Debby's pain came from his cheating on her and telling her lies.

Finally she told him that she could take anything as long as they were truthful with each other. "No more lies, please," she said. "OK? Let's put it all out on the table, here. You said you wouldn't tell me because you didn't want to hurt my feelings. You've hurt me more than you know by *not* being up front with me. Please, from now on. Please promise. Please don't lie to me anymore. If there is somebody else, please tell me. I'd rather know than have it this way."

Tom promised. "So I thought everything was fine and wonderful," Debby recalled. "From that point on, I never knew there was anyone else. I believed him."

Tom had been anxious to get away from Wilmington for the Fourth of July holiday because he didn't particularly want to talk to any more detectives until he and Charlie Oberly established some ground rules. Although he had evinced interest in helping them find out what had happened to Anne Marie, he was not about to have them declare open season on his personal affairs. There were aspects of his life and his family's life that were none of their business.

His whole family would be at the shore for the long holiday weekend, and he suggested to Debby that she might want to get away for a while too. The press was going to have a field day with this thing. He had to tell Kay, too. He wanted her to round up the girls and head for the shore as soon as possible. Otherwise they would probably have reporters *and* police making their lives miserable.

Tom's name did hit the papers on July 3, although the coverage was more subdued than it might have been:

> Anne Marie Fahey . . . was last seen by Wilmington attorney and political insider Thomas J. Capano when the two had dinner Thursday night in Philadelphia, according to friends and sources close to the investigation. . . . Police said they do not consider Fahey's dinner companion, whom they did not identify, to be a suspect and said he had been cooperative with investigators.

It was the first breath of scandal ever to touch Tom, and everyone who knew him was surprised. But he was separated from his wife, and there was no indication in the article of what his relationship with Anne Marie might have been. It wasn't a crime to take a pretty woman out to dinner.

Back at Anne Marie's apartment, which her family had set up as a headquarters in the search for her, Brian didn't comment to the press on Capano's possible involvement in the case. "Her disappearance is so seamless," he said quietly. "It's not that the trail's run out. There *is* no trail."

On Wednesday, July 3, the Faheys began passing out hundreds of flyers bearing Anne Marie's picture to businesses that promptly taped them up in prominent spots or in their front windows. They were offering a $10,000 reward for information that would lead to finding Anne Marie. She had been missing six days now, and her face was rapidly becoming familiar around Wilmington. Soon the flyers would cross the Pennsylvania and New Jersey state lines. Newspaper articles and television and radio coverage of her disappearance were growing exponentially, and lots of tips and suggestions were coming in to the investigators—but as in most high-profile cases, virtually all of them were useless. Because people wanted to help, they tended to imagine that the young women they saw alone in bus stations, grocery stores, and airports were Anne Marie. But none of them was.

At noon on that first Wednesday, a mass was held for Anne Marie at St. Joseph's. Three dozen of her friends and family prayed for her safe return, and then her brothers and sister took up their quiet vigil on the broad white porch of the house where she had lived. They still hoped that she might come back to them, although their spirits sank lower with every passing day. But they were positive of one thing: if she was able, Anne Marie would either call them or find a way home. And when she did not, they had to accept that she could not. That left a number of possibilities—all of them bleak: she was being held somewhere against her will; she had amnesia; she was ill or injured; or she was dead. That last possibility was too terrible to contemplate, and yet their minds sometimes went there, in thoughts that skittered like mice over a gravestone.

The next day was the Fourth of July. It was to have been a day of celebration for the Fahey family, who had planned a barbecue. Instead, they would spend the day in a massive search for their sister. Anne Marie's family and friends asked for help from the public to search Wilmington's Brandywine Park and canvass her neighborhood for any possible clues to her disappearance. Volunteers were asked to come to the Baynard Stadium at 8 A.M.

Three hundred people—friends and strangers—showed up. With police assistance, they were split into search groups, working in assigned areas so that the same places wouldn't be searched twice and others missed. They spread out, only an arm's length apart in the park itself, looking under trees and bushes and along the banks of Brandywine Creek. On the city streets and alleys of Wilmington, they looked into garbage cans, empty garages, anyplace where a person, a body, a weapon, clothing, or some other physical evidence might be hidden.

Police helicopters equipped with infrared devices had scoped out the huge park earlier in the week. With infrared film, freshly turned dirt and decomposing bodies of humans and animals glow red, something that cannot be detected by the human eye. Nothing had shown up. But now, one of the search teams found a small area of fresh dirt that was hidden from the air. Grimly, the police began to dig with shovels. There was nothing buried there. Some women's clothing turned up; it wasn't Anne Marie's size or recognizable as anything she had ever worn.

The Faheys continued to make themselves available to reporters and used the vast resources of the media to help find Anne Marie. They knew when they made that decision that they would lose any vestige of their privacy and be subjected to endless interviews and speculation. But it was a very pragmatic choice. "We knew we could speak out well," Robert recalled, "and we were fairly photogenic. It was the best way we knew to find our sister."

The long day ended and still there was not even a trace of Anne Marie. If she was dead, the police investigators didn't know where she had died. The putative crime scene would be the last place she was said to have been—her apartment—but they had found no sign of a struggle there. The last person she was known to be with—Tom Capano—had been questioned and his house briefly examined. Nothing there seemed out of the ordinary. In order to get a search warrant, the investigators would have to establish a probable cause to indicate that a crime had been committed and that there might be evidence in a house, a yard, or a vehicle. They did not yet have that probable cause.

_____ Chapter Twenty-three _____

WHILE THE OFFICIAL INVESTIGATION of Anne Marie's disappearance was hampered by a complete lack of evidence of foul play, one of her friends was able to contribute a few more provocative details. Kim Horstman told Bob Donovan that she had spoken to Anne Marie on Wednesday night, the night before she vanished, and it had been a very upbeat conversation. Kim had been one of the first of Annie's friends to learn that she was missing. Susan Fahey, who had gone to high school with Kim, called her at her brother's house shortly after Anne Marie had failed to show up for dinner on Saturday night.

"She asked me if I knew where Annie was," Kim said, "and I didn't know where she was." But her first thought was that Annie might be with Tom. She wasn't going to give that deep secret away to Susan, so Kim decided to call Tom herself. She got two numbers from information. When she dialed the first number, a young girl answered, so Kim hung up, believing it was Tom's family's house. But when she called the second number, Kay answered. She hung up again. But Kay, suspicious, pressed *69 and called her back.

Kim didn't say anything. If Annie was OK, she didn't want to make things worse. To be on the safe side, Kim had her brother call Tom's house this time and ask for him.

When Tom came on the line, Kim asked, "Where is Annie?"

"What do you mean?" he asked.

"Where is Annie? She is missing. Do you know where she is?"

Tom seemed confused and upset at the news that Anne Marie was missing. "Where are you?" he asked Kim.

"I'm at my brother Michael's house," she said.

"I thought you were supposed to be at the shore this weekend," Tom said with surprise in his voice. "I thought Annie was with you at the shore."

Kim explained that their lease at the shore had ended on that very day, but Tom kept asking her where she was, until she finally made him understand that she was at her brother's.

"She was going to the shore with you this weekend, Kimmie," Tom insisted.

"That was never the case."

Tom sounded genuinely stunned and told Kim that she had "blown his mind" because he was sure Annie was with her. He seemed very agitated and asked her over and over where she was calling from. He finally took her number and said he would call her back.

Kim dialed Anne Marie's apartment next but she got only the answering machine. By this time it was eleven on Saturday night. At midnight, Tom *did* call Kim at her brother's house. In a twenty-minute conversation, he said he had had time to think and decided that Anne Marie must have just gone away for the weekend—that she'd had a rough week. He told Kim about what he called "Annie's big fight" with Kathleen and said he'd had dinner with Anne Marie on Thursday night.

"He said he was confident that she would be back to work on Monday," Kim recalled, "and that this whole mess would be cleared up."

Then Kim told Tom that she'd heard Kathleen was going to file a missing persons report with the Wilmington Police.

"I wonder if they'll be looking for me," he said in what seemed to be a non sequitur.

Calls went back and forth during the wee hours of Sunday. Kathleen called Kim and put her on the spot. She asked Kim if she knew who Tom Capano was and what connection he had to Annie.

"I said I knew of him—I had heard Annie speak of him," Kim said, and recalled that she had lied to Kathleen to protect Annie. "She asked if I thought they were involved—because she had found some disturbing letters at Annie's apartment. I said no—I didn't have any knowledge of that. I was sure that Annie was going to be to work on Monday, and I didn't want to betray her confidence."

Tom's explanation had soothed Kim's fears. At that point, she really believed that everything would be all right, and the last thing Anne Marie would want was for Kim to reveal her secrets.

But then Tom called Kim again, just before eight on Sunday morning, complaining that the police had, indeed, come pounding on his door around 3 A.M. He told her he'd been very groggy because he'd taken five or six Excedrin PMs so he could sleep. He now believed that Anne Marie had probably gone away for the weekend with Jackie—that he'd been confused before when he thought it was Kim. Tom spoke to her for thirty-eight minutes, and most of his conversation was his calm reassurance that Anne Marie was perfectly fine and there was no reason for anyone to be worried.

Tom spoke to Kim again on Sunday night and made an odd request. He was calling to *ask* if he could call her later. He said he was at Kay's house and couldn't talk. She heard him yelling to someone in the house, "Let Uncle Louie in! Uncle Louie's at the door!" Then Tom hung up hurriedly, promising to call her back later that night—but he didn't. And of course, Annie had not come to work on Monday.

Kim shared all of this information and her worries with Bob Donovan. She told him that Tom Capano was a control freak and that Anne Marie had been trying, with little success, to break away from him since the previous summer.

Kim also talked to Robert Fahey several times during the first terrible week of Annie's disappearance, and once his name hit the papers, Kim was anxious to speak with Tom again. At Robert's suggestion she kept a pad and pencil near the phone. She planned to write down everything Tom said to her so that she would remember it all precisely. However, it would be a while before she heard from him again.

LIEUTENANT Mark Daniels gleaned a similar assessment of Tom Capano from yet another source. On July 2, he got a phone call from Lisa D'Amico, who worked at Michael Christopher Designs. D'Amico told him that she was the one who always cut Anne Marie's hair. The two had become confidantes and Anne Marie had shared intimate secrets with her. While she hadn't shown up for her appointment on June 28, D'Amico remembered their conversation during Anne Marie's last appointment, in May. She had been happy and excited about being with Mike Scanlan. "But she said that Tom Capano was crazy and that he scared her," D'Amico told Daniels. "She wanted to stop seeing him, and they were always getting into arguments about it. He kept giving her stuff. He'd wait for her outside her apartment and she wouldn't let him in."

Anne Marie had told D'Amico that Capano had "gone crazy" and grabbed her, accusing her of ruining his life. She said that she was going to tell him that they no longer had any relationship, even though she was frightened that he might harm her.

TOM had had an appointment for some dental surgery for weeks. He kept that appointment on Tuesday morning, July 2, and then left for the shore. He was under a lot of stress, and he probably felt more secure in the comparative privacy of his mother's huge brown house at Stone Harbor. Two fake owls were anchored on the deck off the second story to scare away the seabirds before they left their droppings. Standing beside them, all you could hear was the roar of the sea, perhaps a comforting sound in Tom's mind compared to the detective's questions in Wilmington.

FEW people in Wilmington knew Charles Freel by his given name; he was Bud Freel to everyone. Bud, of course, was one of the owners of O'Friel's Irish Pub, former owner of Buddy's Bar, and more important, a Wilmington city councilman and director of the Office of External Affairs for the Delaware State Department of Transportation. Bud had been Tom Capano's good friend for over twenty years; they had worked closely together on many Democratic campaigns. Bud was also very close to the Faheys. Anne Marie was like a little sister to him.

Bud had been in Dover at the Legislative Hall when his brother Ed called him on Sunday afternoon with the news that Anne Marie was missing. Ten hours later, in the early hours of July 1, the legislature closed up shop for the summer. And just before dawn, Ed told Bud that he had learned that Tom Capano was the last person to have seen Anne Marie before her disappearance.

With no motive beyond friendship, Bud had called Tom's house and left him a message of concern. "I knew he had been friends with Anne Marie," he said, "and I told Tom I was thinking about him and I felt bad. If there was anything I could do, to let me know."

Tom called Bud back Monday evening. "It was a very brief call," Bud recalled. "He just said that I was going to hear a lot of shit about him in the next couple of months—and not to believe it. And that he was going to need my support. And he basically hung up."

Bud Freel was equally concerned about the Fahey family. On Wednesday morning, July 3, he went to Anne Marie's apartment to talk with her brothers and sister, hoping he would find them there without the crowds of people who were coming by out of compassion or curiosity. "They were asking me questions," Bud recalled, "and I basically couldn't answer. So while I was there, I offered to talk to Tom."

Bud was caught between two sides of a mystery involving people he cared about, a situation that wasn't likely to happen anywhere but Wilmington, where everyone was somehow connected. Anne Marie's family was searching desperately for any nugget of information they could find about her disappearance, and a dark cloud was forming rapidly over Tom's heretofore impeccable reputation. They weren't talking to one another; Bud was the natural link. He decided to drive to Stone Harbor and talk to Tom. "My hope," Bud recalled, "was that he would come back and cooperate with the police and do whatever he could to help."

Back in Wilmington, flyers with Anne Marie's pictures had just begun to blossom in store windows. The search for her was omnipresent there, but the Atlantic Ocean made all of it seem very far away. It was July 3 when Bud pulled up at Marguerite Capano's house on the beach and walked in through the sliding glass doors on the ocean side. One of Tom's daughters was sitting on the couch with a friend, and Bud asked where her father was. She pointed to the den in the back of the house. He found Tom talking on the phone. Bud Freel was an imposing man, standing well over six feet, with a physique that was reminiscent of a professional wrestler's; no fat, just substance. He could fill a doorway. Tom looked a little startled when he saw Bud looming over him, but he only raised his eyebrows in a silent question.

Bud waited until Tom was off the phone. Not a man to edge his way in, he started with the hard questions. "I asked him if he had any information or knew anything about the whereabouts of Anne Marie," he recalled, "and he said he didn't."

Bud suggested that Tom might talk to the police anyway and Tom replied that he already had—twice. "I answered their questions," Tom said. "I let them search my car. I don't know what else I can do."

The two men talked for three hours, going over scenarios of what might possibly have happened to Anne Marie. But first, Tom tried to convey to Bud how good he had been to her. He said he had always thought only of what was best for Annie. But he was not as reluctant as Kim was to reveal the private secrets of their relationship. He told Bud they had once been lovers, but now they were only very good friends—he had become Anne Marie's best friend.

"All the police were interested in," Tom complained, "were all the dirty little details—how often we had sex, and where we had sex, and they wanted to know all the intimate things she told me. Bud," he said in an anguished voice, "I can't violate her trust like that."

"Tommy," Bud said earnestly, out of his own concern for what might have happened to Anne Marie, "just go back and sit down with them. You answer their questions—and the ones you don't want to answer, you tell them you're not going to. This thing is going to steamroll—it's an interesting story for the media, her being the scheduling secretary for the governor. This isn't going to stop, and before you know it, we'll have *Hard Copy* here in Wilmington, Delaware."

Tom sat in an overstuffed chair, his legs crossed, as they talked. He smoked a number of cigarettes, but he seemed calm as he explained to Bud that he too was "pretty upset." Still, he didn't think letting the police have at him was the answer. He turned their conversation back to the reasons why Annie might have left. Maybe she'd just gone to the beach for a whole week. Maybe she'd just wanted to get away by herself. Maybe she'd decided to go to the eating disorder clinic he'd told her about.

"We would explore each one of them," Bud Freel recalled, "and in the case of the first two—why would you go away and not take your money and your credit cards? And in the last one, I said—even though those places have rules of confidentiality, if they saw her picture in the paper, wouldn't they have contacted a family member?"

Tom would then agree that Bud was probably right. But they were going round and round about his coming back and cooperating with the investigators. When Bud finally left to drive back to Wilmington, he didn't feel that he'd accomplished what he'd set out to do.

Tom called the next morning—July 4—and asked Bud what was going on. Bud told him what was in the *News-Journal*, about the massive search of Brandywine Park with all of the people who had turned out to help.

Then Tom got around to the main reason for his call. He said that Charlie Oberly was not happy with him for talking to Bud. His lawyer was upset.

"Why would he be upset if you're talking to *me?*" Bud asked, perplexed. They were old friends, searching for a way to find another friend.

"He wants me to ask you if you were wired," Tom said.

Bud erupted, insulted that Tom would even think of such a thing. "I did a lot of shouting and cussing," he admitted. "I summarized everything I told him the day before. He was hurting himself, hurting his kids, his family, if he didn't get his butt back to Wilmington and talk to the police."

Bud finally calmed down and asked Tom what he could do to help him. "It was at that point," Bud would recall, "that he asked me if I would talk to the Faheys about talking to him. It was important, he said, for them to know how good he had been to their sister."

Tom wanted to talk to Robert Fahey, but he asked Bud to act as an intermediary. And Bud did, calling Robert on July 5. Robert told Bud that he did not want to meet with Tom, but he would take a phone call from him. He said he would be home from five to five-thirty that night, waiting for Tom's call.

It never came. After three calls to Tom in one day, Bud finally heard from him at 9 P.M. "I'm not going to call Robert at this time," Tom said, "because I'm going to come back on Monday and talk with the police."

Bud believed him. He spoke with Tom again sometime over the long Fourth of July weekend. For some reason, Tom hadn't gone out to buy a Wilmington paper, but instead asked Bud to tell him what was being written.

Deputy state attorney general Ferris Wharton had commented

on the missing persons case, but not officially. He was speaking as the chief prosecutor in New Castle County—although there certainly was no case as yet that would necessitate prosecution. Wharton, who had an impressive record of convictions in high-profile homicide cases, was native born and familiar to most Wilmington residents. Tall and lanky with straight brown hair that was forever flopping over his forehead, he seemed almost shy outside a courtroom, but he was a powerful force in front of a jury. Fortyish, Wharton was still an athlete; he worked out at the Y, played basketball, and every summer spent his vacations riding in a bicycle convoy across Iowa—which he found was not nearly as flat as everyone thought.

Wharton had the look of a Gary Cooper or a Jimmy Stewart. He was the kind of an attorney whose easy, quiet presence made people feel somehow calmer, a nice guy with a keen mind—unless they happened to be the subjects of his cross-examination. Then his questions could lure them into snares they never saw coming. Wharton sometimes watched basketball tournaments from a bar stool at O'Friel's. Like Bud Freel, he knew both the Faheys and the Capanos, if not as well, and like everyone else, he wondered what could have happened to Anne Marie.

"Each day, you become more and more pessimistic about the outcome," he told a *News-Journal* reporter, phrasing his statements cautiously. He was still talking about a missing persons case, but everyone was growing edgy. The whole town seemed to know that Anne Marie had been seeing both Tom Capano and Mike Scanlan, and Wharton was not about to comment on that. "Everybody who had contact with her, in a very broad sense," he said, "is a suspect. . . . The complete spectrum of options is out there. She's missing."

MONDAY was the eighth of July. It was the day Tom had promised Bud Freel that he would come back to Wilmington to talk to the police. Anne Marie had been missing for eleven days. Tom called Bud to say that he was meeting with his attorneys in the morning and would probably talk to the police that afternoon.

But he didn't. Instead, he called Bud in the evening and repeated his tirade about the police and their sick, prurient interest in his sex life. He could not bring himself to sit still for that. The police were trying to set him up, and he wasn't going to go in and let them do it.

Bud was exasperated. "You know, Tom," he began, "I just don't get it. Anne Marie's been missing now for more than a week. They just want to sit down and ask you some questions in hopes there might be something that you know, and you might not even realize you can be helpful to them. If you're not willing to do that, I have nothing else to say to you."

It was their last conversation.

WHEN Tom finally came back to Wilmington, he turned to his good friend, Brian Murphy, for companionship. Tom and Brian had been friends for twenty years, ever since they played on the Wilmington Rugby Club team with Dan Frawley. Later, Murphy became the city's public information officer and reported to Tom when he was Mayor Frawley's top aide. Tom had lent Murphy $15,000 to pay his daughter's tuition at Ursuline Academy. He was a generous creditor who rarely called in his loans to male friends.

Tom and Brian Murphy ate dinner together in Little Italy and Tom confided that he was very frightened. He showed Murphy some threatening letters he had received, letters that accused him of hurting Anne Marie. They were unsigned. Tom told Murphy that he had no idea what had happened to her. It was obvious that Tom didn't want to be alone in his house on Grant Avenue, so Murphy went home with him. They sat in the two La-Z-Boy recliners in the great room and watched late-night television with the lights off so no one driving by could see them. They sipped Sambuca until it grew light outside. Murphy suggested that Tom make a public statement telling everyone what he had told him. An innocent man shouldn't have to worry about anonymous threats.

JULY 8 was a very important day in the investigation of the disappearance of Anne Marie Fahey; although the public was not yet aware of it, the federal government moved quietly into the picture. Although the media said President Clinton had given that directive, that wasn't true. Clinton *had* called to talk with Governor Carper, but not to offer federal aid in the probe. It was a call about a friend. Whenever the White House wanted to talk to Carper, it was Anne Marie who was contacted to schedule conferences. The president—who had shaken Anne Marie's hand only three months earlier—phoned Carper to offer his sympathy to the Fahey family. And his promise of federal aid in the search for Anne Marie was couched in politically savvy terms. He had added the phrase "should that [federal aid] be necessary or appropriate."

It wasn't really up to the president. In truth, the federal government routinely assists state and local law enforcement agencies in a variety of ways. And the reverse is also true. It isn't necessary to have a presidential proclamation to bring federal law enforcement into the picture—but Clinton's offer made a great news lead for the media that were following the case avidly.

Still, when he read the news about Clinton's call to Carper, Tom was unnerved. He didn't know Robert Donovan, but Donovan was at least a Wilmington Police detective. And Mark Daniels was a longtime State Police detective. Tom knew Ferris Wharton to speak to, and they sometimes made small talk when they met in checkout lines. The men who were investigating Anne Marie's disappearance were all known entities to Tom, part of the fabric of Wilmington, where he felt comfortable.

In fact, Tom rarely left Wilmington, except to go to Philadelphia. A circle drawn on a map would show the remarkably small confines in which he operated. Occasionally he made a trip for law seminars, or went down to Boca Raton for vacations—but Wilmington was a place he had always been able to count on, a city with no unsettling surprises. With tact, diplomacy, and mediation, Tom had worked out all manner of problems to his satisfaction. He could not understand the need for the federal government to enter into what was, at heart, a local concern.

As it was, anyone living outside Delaware would be easily confused by the interweaving of state and local government. The state Attorney General's office is in Wilmington, and since there are only three counties in all of Delaware, the senior deputy attorneys general act as county prosecutors would in most states, but they reported to Delaware attorney general Jane Brady. Ferris Wharton, for instance, had prosecuted cases all over Delaware.

For a while, word that the feds were coming into the case was only a rumor. On July 8, it became a reality, but it was still a secret. And they would have come in on any baffling case where local authorities asked for help. The fact that Anne Marie was the governor's secretary made headlines, yes, but for the FBI and the U.S. Attorney's office, all that mattered was that a young woman was missing and her family was in agony. It would have been the same if she had been a secretary at DuPont or a waitress at Galluccio's.

AT forty-three, Eric Alpert had been an FBI special agent for fourteen years. He had earned his law degree from the Cumberland School in Birmingham, Alabama, and had served in New York City, Buffalo, Baltimore, and Washington, D.C., before being assigned to the Wilmington office. In February 1996, Alpert had been honored at the Philadelphia City Hall for his work as the coordinator of the

Violent Crime Fugitive Task Force; his team had been successful in bringing in cop killers. That operation had meant long hours away from his wife, Lisa, and their children (who were five and two), and he wasn't particularly anxious to jump into another high-pressure investigation. Still, as he read about Anne Marie's disappearance in the papers, Alpert thought it sounded like an interstate kidnapping. Wherever she was currently, she had obviously been in Pennsylvania early in the evening of June 27 and had been taken back to Delaware.

On Tuesday, July 2, Alpert had called Bob Donovan at Wilmington Police headquarters and asked, "Is there anything we can do to help?"

There was. Donovan said the police were hoping to get pen registers on phone lines of people closely connected to Anne Marie Fahey. The devices note the time, date, and numbers called from designated phones. To obtain pen registers, the U.S. Attorney's office would have to participate.

Another man who worked for the federal government had offered assistance to the local investigators. He was to become the prime mover in solving the seemingly impenetrable puzzle of Anne Marie's disappearance, but he came on board with little fanfare. Assistant U.S. Attorney Colm Connolly was only thirty-two when he was tapped by his boss, U.S. Attorney Greg Sleet, to investigate what would become the biggest case of his career. He had already prosecuted more than a hundred defendants for a whole spectrum of offenses ranging from embezzlement and arson to extortion and tax evasion. One of the myriad convictions he had won involved a fraud conspiracy and money-laundering case with fourteen hundred victims; another involved a case of armed bank robbery, conspiracy, and weapons violations. Connolly had commendations from FBI director Louis Freeh and the Nuclear Regulatory Commission, and he was the first Delaware recipient of the Director's Award for Superior Performance, an award given to fewer than 3 percent of all assistant U.S. attorneys. Still, when he was assigned to investigate the mysterious disappearance of Anne Marie Fahey, he had yet to work a kidnapping or homicide case. Indeed, when he came into the case, no one knew what—if any—charges might be brought against a suspect.

Compactly built, Colm had black hair and intense brown eyes, and his roots reached back to Ireland just as deeply as the Faheys'. Like Tom Capano, Colm had been president of his class at Archmere (twice). He was much younger than Tom, but he and Tom's brother

Gerry had attended the Catholic prep school at the same time and played on the junior varsity soccer team together. Connolly was remembered at Archmere for both his popularity and his brilliance. He had a B.A. degree from Notre Dame and an M.A. from the London School of Economics; his law degree was from Duke—with honors.

Where Tom had never ventured far from Wilmington, Connolly—a native of Hockessin, Delaware, just northwest of Wilmington—had lived in the Philippines, China, and England. He had wanted to be an attorney since he was seven or eight. Appointed to be an assistant U.S. attorney when he was in his mid-twenties, the youngest of Sleet's twelve prosecutors, Colm brought a remarkable combination of intellect and intuitive skill to the job. Although he would deny it, he had the heart of a crusader and unshakable ethics. He detested prejudice, cruelty, and con games that ripped off the innocent.

It was clear he had the tenacity and talent for deductive reasoning to work a kidnapping or a homicide case. Connolly had never been hesitant about joining detectives at the most unsavory and gritty crime scenes. He was a hands-on prosecutor, part of every probe from the very beginning.

Connolly and his wife, Anne, met in law school. She was a corporate attorney for the firm of Skadden, Arps, the largest law firm in the world, working at the Philadelphia branch. She had always been someone he could talk to and bounce things off, and he could count on her for sound advice and opinions.

Colm and Anne had met Bob Donovan for the first time on a bitterly cold evening in 1992 when Colm went to pick up Anne—and their across-the-hall neighbor in the apartment house where they were living—at the train station. It was not an auspicious meeting.

That night, when Anne got off the train and hurried through the chill air to Colm's car, she had her hair tucked into her coat collar and wore a hat that almost obscured her face. She and the neighbor ducked into Colm's car, and he pulled out heading for home. But it wasn't long before he saw the Wilmington Police car that was "about six inches" behind his car, making every turn he did—and then the blue lights began to whirl.

Colm was furious, and he bailed out of the driver's door and headed back to demand to know why he had been stopped. Bob Donovan and his patrol partner, Liam Sullivan, rushed by him and went up to his car to check out the occupants.

"At that point," Colm said, "I looked up and saw three members of the DEA [Drug Enforcement Administration] task force standing behind their cars and some trees. I'd had a meeting with them the week before, but I couldn't remember their names."

Connolly had been in the Wilmington office of the U.S. Attorney's office for only a month, and he was notoriously bad with names. Now, he hoped they remembered *his* name. Luckily, they recognized him.

What had happened was that a DEA agent had misidentified the occupants of Connolly's car as drug runners getting off the train from New York, carrying contraband into Wilmington. Bob Donovan and his partner had been called to assist the DEA in an arrest. Still fuming, Connolly went down to the Wilmington Police Department later that night and gave Donovan a piece of his mind.

"He wasn't happy," Donovan recalled laconically.

"Monday," Connolly laughed, "I got a call from ATF [Alcohol, Tobacco and Firearms] and they said they wanted to talk to me on a case. I go over—and who's sitting there? Bob Donovan. They wanted me to prosecute some guy he'd pulled out of the train station—with drugs on him."

This time, Donovan had the real drug runners. Connolly did prosecute the case, and he and Donovan were friends from then on.

Now Connolly and Donovan, along with Eric Alpert, were entering into an investigation that would consume them, not for weeks or months but for years. It wasn't going to be easy, and they had an idea going in that it might take a while, but they were determined to find out where Anne Marie had gone.

Connolly had never operated as a boss, which was particularly important when a number of agencies were involved in a case. In this probe, Alpert would represent the FBI and Donovan the Wilmington Police. "I think it's important to lead by consensus," Connolly would explain later. "There was never a situation where I came in and said, 'We're doing this—and that's it.' We all made suggestions, and it never got to a place where I had to make the final call."

Connolly and Donovan would talk to each other every single day, and on many days with Alpert as well. Their personalities and styles were completely different but they complemented one another perfectly.

The pen registers would be their first strategy. To protect the privacy of citizens, the U.S. Attorney's office has to participate in deciding if it is imperative to attach a pen register to a phone. At Alpert's request, Connolly filed papers with the U.S. District Court outlining why his office believed there was reason to monitor Tom

Capano's phones. There was good reason to think that Anne Marie might have been taken across a state line against her will. Her psychologist, Michelle Sullivan, and some of her friends believed she might well have been kidnapped. Both of these actions were federal transgressions.

It was enough. Pen registers were connected to Tom Capano's phones. Connolly also asked for a toll back edit—which would allow the government investigators to scan back to see whom Tom Capano might have called for the last fifteen days—during the vital time period between June 27 and June 30 and thereafter. Pen registers would show both local and long distance calls.

Still, at this point there wasn't a full-scale federal investigation. Connolly and Alpert discussed whether it might not be helpful to the Fahey case if they were to look into financial records—credit card billings, gas receipts, and other records that would reveal the comings and goings of Tom Capano. Obtaining such documents was routine in federal investigations, but they would need subpoenas. And if they found enough in Capano's financial records to warrant it, Connolly could ask for a federal grand jury investigation.

But once such a probe began, federal law would forbid them from sharing what they found with anyone but each other and the Wilmington Police Department. That would mean that Ferris Wharton would be out of the loop, and so would the Fahey family and Anne Marie's friends. As much as they might want to discuss the case, Connolly and Alpert—and Donovan, who would be the point man from the Wilmington Police Department—could not.

ON July 9, 1996, with Tom's input, Brian Murphy drafted a statement meant to be published in the papers and read on television and radio:

> The disappearance of Anne Marie Fahey remains as much a mystery to me as it does to her family and friends. I can only say I share the gut-wrenching emotions of Anne Marie's family and pray for her safe return.
>
> While I can do nothing to end the speculation of the public and press, I can state for the record the pertinent facts of my last meeting with Anne Marie.
>
> I did have dinner with Anne Marie in Philadelphia on the evening of Thursday, June 27th. We returned to Wilmington. We drove to her apartment at approximately 10 pm. I walked Anne

Marie into her apartment, stayed a few moments, said good night and left. I noticed nothing unusual as I left. That was the last time I saw or spoke to Anne Marie. I then drove home where I remained until I left for the office the next morning.

While Anne Marie had some problems, there was nothing out of the ordinary in either her conversation or behavior that would lead me to believe anything was amiss. I am at a complete loss to explain what caused her disappearance.

It is difficult to respond as to how others may characterize our relationship. Frankly, the nature of our relationship is and will remain a matter between Anne Marie and myself. What is relevant and important is that Anne Marie and I are good friends and parted company good friends that evening.

I was informed of Anne Marie's potential disappearance by phone late on the evening of Saturday, June 29th, by a mutual friend. While I was concerned, I was also aware that Anne Marie had taken Friday off from work and concluded she had probably gone off with friends for the weekend. At that time, there was nothing to lead me to believe she would not be at work on Monday morning, July 1st. At approximately 3 am on the morning of Sunday, June 30th, I was awakened by four police officers at my home. Since then, I have and will continue to fully cooperate with investigators. As much as anyone else, I want to know Anne Marie's whereabouts.

I will not be granting interviews or making further statements. I want to thank my friends who have offered their many kind words of support and encouragement and ask all concerned to pray for Ann Marie's safe return.

Tom read it over and nodded. He told Brian that it "looked pretty good," and he would run it by his attorneys and get back to Murphy that afternoon. But he never did. That statement would not be released for two and a half years.

Tom did make a statement that day, a much more private one. He called Robert Fahey and left a message on his answering machine, his words stumbling over one another, separated by "ummm's" and "ahhhh's."

"Robert," he said, "this is Tom Capano.

"It's Tuesday. It's 12:39 on July ninth. I think you know from Bud that I really want to speak to you and anybody else in your family who cares to. Bud tells me you're maybe not really interested in speaking to me and I guess I can understand that. Robert, I don't know what to say . . . I really do want to talk to you."

Tom explained that he wanted to see Robert "face-to-face" because "I have some things I want to show you. I have some things I
want to tell you.

"I care for Anne Marie a great deal, Robert. Apparently, from
what Buddy's telling me, that hasn't come through and I don't understand that. And I know I'm babbling because I'm out of my
freaking mind with, uh, everything. . . . There's one thing I want you
to know. I have talked to the police twice. I have told the police I
will talk to them as many times as they want. But I am not gonna
talk about ancient history.

"Anne Marie has a right to privacy and I have a right to privacy
and I am not going to tell them details of things we did a year ago or
eight months ago or all this incredibly personal stuff they want to
know from me. OK? . . . I will talk to them about Thursday night. I
will talk to them about anything, but I am not going to talk about
ancient history. . . . Maybe you can't understand that. . . . I mean,
do you and Kathleen want to read stuff in the newspaper? 'Cause
you know it's going to leak. It's personal. I know I'm rambling but I
desperately would like to talk to you. . . . I wanted to come see you
all at that apartment but I know that Kathleen would just frankly
gouge my eyes out. Ahhh, I'll stop. Please call me, Robert."

Robert did not call him. He didn't believe that Tom would tell
him what he needed to know and he wasn't about to play games.

If Tom's affair with Anne Marie was now public knowledge, his relationship with Debby MacIntyre remained a secret. Moreover, on
his instructions, she was out of town visiting one of her brothers.
But Tom had always chosen women as his confidantes, and on July
15 and 19, he called Kim Horstman, talking to her as if they were
longtime trusted friends. He brought her up to speed on what had
happened to him, beginning with his surprise when Bud Freel came
to his mother's home. Bud's visit and his later calls alarmed Tom.
"He said Bud told him that he was there on behalf of Annie's family," Kim recalled, "and that he said, 'If you have her, could you
please return her?' "

Tom told Kim he was shocked. *"Have her?"* he had asked, and
reported that Bud said that the family thought Tom had kidnapped
her. "He said he just looked at Bud," Kim recalled, "and he said he
asked him, 'Do you really think I would do anything like that?' and
Bud said, 'No,' but Tom should come home to Delaware."

Tom also explored any number of theories about Anne Marie's
disappearance with Kim, confiding that there was a big turf war

going on between the State Police and the other agencies, and they were all "screwing up the investigation."

Kim was writing it all down, and her notes were precise. "He told me the first possible scenario was that Annie comes home. The second is that Annie is found—we find her body—and that the evidence around the body will lead the police in the right direction. And three, she's never found, and come Labor Day, the police are going to be getting a lot of pressure from the governor's office to indict somebody."

At that point, Tom said that he would be "the fall guy."

Tom wanted to know exactly whom Kim might have spoken to. The police? Mike Scanlan? He wanted to be sure the police knew the two of them had had dinner to discuss an intervention "to help Annie."

Tom told Kim there were rumors flying around, and one was that Anne Marie had had an affair with Governor Carper when they were in Washington, D.C. He wondered if perhaps that was true. Kim was amazed. She knew nothing of the kind had ever happened. Tom also told her about a state trooper who had harassed Annie, and a neighbor who had been paying attention to her. He mentioned a man Annie had worked with five years before.

Kim sensed that he was reading from some kind of script as he made certain points over and over. Indeed, he called her back four days later and asked to review their last conversation. Tom stressed that he had been so good to Annie, helping her with money, being sure that he ordered extra food at restaurants so she would have doggie bags at home. And when he steered the conversation for the umpteenth time to the night of June 27, Kim felt as though he was drilling her on the sequence of events.

Tom told Kim that he'd talked to Anne Marie every single day without fail. "Did you talk to her Friday?" she asked. "The day after she disappeared, did you talk to her?"

She held her breath, waiting for his answer.

"Friday? No. Oh, no, no, no, no. I was going to call her on Friday, but I went out for my morning walk, and by the time I got back, I never got around to calling her."

On July 19, Tom called Kim just as she was leaving work at the brokerage firm. "He felt that the two of us knew Annie the best," she said, "and if we put our heads together, we could come up with something . . . to explain where she was."

Tom asked Kim what she was doing for the weekend, and when she told him she was going to the shore, he said, "That's funny. I was going to invite you to spend the weekend at the shore with me."

Kim didn't know what to say. And then she hurriedly explained she was busy both days.

"Why don't you go into work late on Monday?" he suggested. "And come here Monday morning and we will put our heads together and try to come up with where she is."

"All right," she lied. "I'll call you when I get to the shore."

She didn't call him. There was something frightening about him. But Tom called Kim again several days later.

"The last thing I remember Tom saying to me," she recalled, "is that the thing that upset him so much is that not only did he lose Annie, he was going to lose me as well, which I thought was an odd statement. It wasn't like we were close."

Tom had been adamant that he could not talk with the police without sacrificing Anne Marie's—and his own—privacy. But he assured Kim that he had never hurt her. "You don't think I would hurt a hair on her head, do you?" he pressed.

"At the time," Kim said, "I was very skeptical. But I was afraid to say anything."

Kim was Annie's closest friend. She had known about her affair with Tom Capano and had seen it change from warmth and trust to possession and anxiety. Now she was certain of one thing. She didn't want to spend a minute alone with Tom Capano.

_____ Chapter Twenty-four _____

TOM APPARENTLY had no real comprehension of the forces that were gathering to investigate his relationship with Anne Marie. When he should have been looking over his shoulder at the U.S. Attorney's office and the FBI, he was still planning how he would deal with the Wilmington Police. Unless he could make the ground rules, he was extraordinarily reluctant to get into an interrogation session with local investigators—partly because he knew it wouldn't be just with city police; it would also be with the Delaware State Police and the Executive Security Unit.

A lot of people seemed to be poking their noses into his private life, which made him uncomfortable, an alien feeling for Tom. How ironic that he, the man to whom the Wilmington Police chief once reported every morning, the man from whom the governor himself sought advice, should now be in such an untenable position. The search for Anne Marie had spread, it seemed, over half the Eastern seaboard, and as Bud Freel had predicted, the national media were hovering already. *Inside Edition, Unsolved Mysteries,* and the *New York Times* had contacted one principal or another in the case and asked for interviews.

Although Tom would insist he had tremendous respect for the Wilmington Police Department, the way every federal law enforcement agency in the country seemed to be jumping in bothered him. In reality, those who knew him said that Tom counted on the Wilmington Police to bungle the investigation. He figured that everything would die down by the end of summer and he could get on with his life.

Tom spoke with Harry Manelski, who was a retired Wilmington chief of police. "We talked in general terms about the case," Tom said later, "and we talked about what was clear to both of us— about the massive political ramifications of the case; and what with the federal government and State Police and the governor's security task force, just something didn't smell right. I said, 'Harry, you know, I'd like to get this cleared up. I've even tried to reach out to the family, but I don't know what to do.' "

Manelski suggested that Tom talk to Lieutenant Mike Maggitti, who was head of the Wilmington Detective Division, and he offered to arrange a meeting. That meeting never took place. Tom was still adamant that he would not talk to the police about his family or his personal life. *He* would set the conditions of any police interview. Meanwhile, Anne Marie was still missing and the Wilmington Police were at an impasse. It was obvious that Tom was never going to submit willingly to questions about her disappearance.

Anne Marie's siblings kept their lonely vigil at her apartment, often sitting on the front porch, as if watching to see who came up and down Washington Street and might help them find their sister. Someone had wound yellow ribbons around the porch's thick white columns. Everyone in town knew that Annie was gone, and her family members were approached with all manner of words of sympathy and concern, suggestions, and theories. The case was like gold to psychics and would-be psychics, who called or wrote with their otherworldly messages about where Anne Marie might be found. A missing persons case with so much publicity attracted pseudoscientists, the definitely peculiar, and the just plain crazies. And still, the Faheys were polite to them all, always hoping that someone might provide the shred of information that would lead them to their sister.

Through Robert's connections, Revere Outdoor Advertising offered to donate a billboard along Interstate 95 at the Delaware 141 interchange, with an 800 number that anyone with information could call. Now, forty thousand motorists a day read, HELP US FIND ANNE MARIE FAHEY: 1-800-TIP-3333, as they drove the interstate.

It was so hard for any of the Faheys to sleep at night. Their days took on a grim routine, a marathon of hope, anxiety, and mourning. By mid-July, Kathleen, Kevin, Mark, Robert, and Brian probably knew in their hearts that Annie wasn't coming back. If she was alive, she would not have stayed away for more than a month; she would have found some way to come home or to get word to them.

If Anne Marie had left of her own accord, as Tom Capano suggested, how was she surviving? None of her clothing was gone; she didn't have her purse or her wallet. The only things missing were her keys and her favorite ring, and maybe her Walkman. She didn't have her car, and there had been no activity on her credit cards, no checks written or withdrawals from her bank account.

And so her family was still caught in that no-man's-land of not knowing. They could not, however, accept that she was gone forever; in the best of moments—which were fewer and fewer—they believed that she would come home. They had to believe that; they did not even have the bleak cleanness of knowing she was dead, or the closure of a funeral mass and a grave to visit. And so they were caught on a seesaw of hope and despair.

Mike Scanlan was officially on vacation, but he was really looking for Anne Marie. He was with her family every day, and they all took some comfort from one another. Wakeful, Mike sometimes wandered out into his garden at dawn and pulled weeds. The images that kept popping unbidden into all of their minds could sometimes be blotted out with physical activity.

None of them knew that the federal government was investigating Anne Marie's disappearance. It might have made her family and friends feel more hopeful, but it was vital at the moment to keep the participation of the U.S. Attorney's office under wraps.

Tom didn't know either. And until an actual federal grand jury investigation might begin, Ferris Wharton knew only that it was a possibility. As interested as he was in working on the baffling case, he was willing to step out of it completely if it meant that all the power of the federal government could be channeled toward finding Anne Marie. He finally told the press that Tom Capano and his attorneys would not submit to any further talks with the police. "We can't talk to Capano unless he agrees to talk," Wharton said.

Like almost everyone else along the Eastern seaboard, Governor

Tom Carper wondered if Anne Marie was still alive. In his office, her desk sat empty, and as the month of July inched by, one hot, humid day after another with no word at all, he commented that he usually saw a glass as half full, "but we're being realistic," he said. "We realize the glass is half empty."

The rumor mills, always active, worked overtime. One persistent thread of gossip held that Anne Marie was dead and her body buried under the new Home Depot store. Nearly finished, the sprawling home supply store was being built under the supervision of Joey Capano and the commercial division of Capano & Sons. Wilmington detectives came out to the site, asked questions, and looked around. If Anne Marie's body was buried somewhere under the concrete of the huge store, they realized, they might never find her. They didn't have any evidence to get a court order to jackhammer the whole floor. And such a project would have cost millions of dollars.

The Home Depot went into advertising and publicity overdrive to avoid tremendous revenue loss, as Wilmingtonians shivered with the thought that Anne Marie might lie buried beneath the aisles where they shopped.

The Wilmington investigators traveled to FBI headquarters in Washington, D.C., to confer with special agents expert in solving missing persons and homicide cases.

"There's not going to be any miracle revelation, no divining rod to say where she is," Ferris Wharton said. "But they might say, 'Have you considered this?' or, 'From our experience, you might want to look over here.' "

On July 18, Colm Connolly and Eric Alpert, representing the U.S. Attorney's Office and the FBI, invited the Wilmington Police to join them in a grand jury investigation of Anne Marie's disappearance. Once the Wilmington Police signed letters signifying that they wanted to participate, the police were no longer allowed to share information with *anyone*. The letters were signed, and now the police had, indeed, made a "federal case" out of it.

On July 19, Eric Alpert and Bob Donovan traveled to the inner sanctum of the FBI's Behavioral Science Unit in Quantico, Virginia. There they sat down with a half dozen agents skilled in studying the patterns of a vast array of antisocial killers. The profilers of the Behavioral Science Unit are not as all-knowing as they are sometimes portrayed in movies or on television—no human could be—but they have an intuitive sense, honed by scores of interviews with murderers and by studying hundreds of cases. Given descriptions of a group of suspects in a particular case, they can usually point investigators in the right direction by identifying the most likely suspect.

Alpert and Donovan didn't have a handful of suspects in the disappearance of Anne Marie; they had only one—and that was Tom Capano. They laid the circumstances of the case out for the profilers, and together they explored many scenarios and possibilities. No one at Quantico suggested they were on the wrong path.

On July 24, Robert Fahey wrote a letter to Tom and had it hand delivered to Saul, Ewing. The Faheys had had no contact with Tom, save for the one message he left on Robert's answering machine earlier— that disjointed explanation of why he could not speak with the police.

"Dear Mr. Capano," Robert wrote.

> We are writing to request your assistance in locating our sister, Anne Marie Fahey. Four weeks have passed since she was last seen alive. She was with you the last time her whereabouts can be independently verified. As the last person to be seen with Anne Marie, one would hope that you would do the right thing, come forward and share all you know about Anne Marie's disappearance.
>
> The authorities have invested significant effort into interviewing anyone thought to have any information which may help our cause. Everyone in the community has been very helpful and forthcoming with information. Other than two brief conversations with the police in your home immediately following Anne Marie's disappearance, you have been unwilling to submit to an unrestricted police interview. Your team of lawyers has been very effective at communicating for you but very ineffective at helping us find our sister. Do what your father, Louis, would expect of one of his sons. Come forward and share all you know about Anne Marie's disappearance.
>
> Imagine, if you will, that this case involved one of your four daughters, not our sister. We know you would expect the last person to be seen with your children to come forward and be helpful. You would want that person to do the right thing and provide assistance. It has been four weeks and you have yet to come forward to assist the authorities without conditions.
>
> We urge you to put our interests in finding our sister ahead of all other personal concerns. We are talking about someone's life. Please help us today.
>
> The Fahey Family.

Tom did not respond.

_____ *Chapter Twenty-five* _____

ON JULY 25, Connolly, Donovan, and Alpert had not one particle of physical evidence. But they suspected it was not a kidnapping case but a murder case they were striving to build against Tom Capano. They believed they had a motive, the oldest motive in the world: jealousy, possessiveness, maybe revenge. But they had no body. They had no eyewitnesses. They had no blood. They had no weapon. They had no crime scene. They didn't even have signs of a struggle. Indeed, they were faced with an almost impossible task. Suspicion and innuendo and all the gut feelings in the world were not enough to get an arrest warrant—much less a conviction.

The three investigators had little money and less manpower; they were *it*. And they were motivated by the picture of a young woman whose absence had broken a lot of hearts and the challenge presented by an arrogant and powerful suspect who was thumbing his nose in the face of the law.

A searingly invasive look into Tom Capano's private life was about to accelerate. The last week of July was very busy for the investigators—but they were discreetly busy. Donovan and Alpert continued their interviews with Anne Marie's friends and associates. They were hearing the same elements over and over, although each person they interviewed remembered different anecdotes that illustrated the growing schism between Anne Marie and Tom.

Bob Donovan talked again to Lisa D'Amico, who told him that Tom Capano had once grabbed Anne Marie by the neck and called her a "slut" and a "bitch." He interviewed Jill Morrison and heard the horrific details of Anne Marie's struggle to escape from Tom over a period of almost a year, leading up to the night she vanished. The government team learned that Anne Marie had been desperate, frightened—but resolute—about extricating herself from Tom's grip. And what they were hearing in their interviews sounded nothing at all like the relationship that Tom had described to them. *Was* Anne Marie as ditsy and spacey as he maintained, or was he only painting a picture he wanted them to believe?

Al Franke, whom Anne Marie had once dated and who had become a good friend, told Donovan about the time—only six to eight weeks before she vanished—when Tom climbed up the fire escape to Anne Marie's building and made a forced entry into her apartment. At that time, she told Franke, he had been in a towering, bellowing rage, and once more he had started taking back various gifts he had given her.

On July 26, Connolly and Alpert were poring over copies of Tom's credit card bills when one in particular caught their attention. On June 29, two days after Anne Marie disappeared, Tom had made a purchase totaling $308.99 at the Wallpaper Warehouse. That struck them as a little odd. Why would a man who was only renting a house buy wallpaper? They asked a few questions and learned that the Wallpaper Warehouse also did business as Air Base Carpets.

Alpert drove to the warehouse on Route 13 in New Castle County and talked to Michael Longwill, the general manager. When asked to check his records, Longwill found that Tom Capano was a repeat customer. On September 30, 1995, he had used his Master-Card to buy several Oriental rugs and a room-sized remnant. The bill at that time had come to $2,349.92. Longwill could determine the type of carpets by codes noted on the bill, and he told Alpert that the large remnant Tom had purchased was a looped-weave beige Berber carpet. It was all that was left on a roll sold three months earlier. Longwill was even able to give Alpert the name of the man who had purchased most of that roll.

"Now, on June 29, 1996," Alpert asked, "did Mr. Capano buy another carpet from your store?"

"Yes," Longwill said. "I sold him an Oriental rug and pad. He came in—let's see—at 1:36 in the afternoon."

It was not an expensive rug, more of a knockoff of the real thing, dark green with various colors in the design. Longwill said there had been nothing unusual about Capano's manner. He had carried the pad, and an employee carried the rug to his car.

Alpert contained his enthusiasm, although later he and Connolly would agree that this was the first break they had in trying to solve the puzzle of Anne Marie's disappearance.

Bob Donovan contacted the man who had purchased the bulk of the roll of carpet that Tom had bought the previous September. That would have been at the time he moved into the North Grant Avenue house. The other buyer, the owner of a bed-and-breakfast, showed Donovan the thick-looped beige carpeting that covered most of the downstairs of his house. Longwill had assured Alpert that this carpet was *exactly* the same as the carpet Tom had purchased. Same lot number. Same color. Same roll.

"You have any extra?" Donovan asked.

"Sure," the innkeeper said. "You can take a hunk of what's left over."

Whether the fibers in that beige carpet would be needed for comparison, no one knew, but it was bagged into evidence, just in case.

They were getting a little lucky. They were now able to put two pieces of their investigative puzzle side by side. Donovan had also spoken with Ruth Boylan, the woman who cleaned Tom's house every other Monday.

"When did you clean his house last?" Donovan asked.

"July twenty-second," she said.

"And before that?"

"June twenty-fourth," she replied. "You see, I was supposed to clean it on July eighth next—but Mr. Capano called me on maybe the fifth or sixth, and he said I didn't need to clean it because they'd all been away for the Fourth of July, so it was still clean."

She knew the whole house well, but she told Donovan that she was concerned about something that seemed a little peculiar. She said she'd let herself in as usual on the twenty-second and begun to clean. But when she moved into the great room off the kitchen, she was surprised. The room was changed.

"How?" Donovan asked.

"Well, for one thing, the sofa was missing—and the carpet had been taken up and there was an area rug there."

This had puzzled her because the carpet was practically brand new and in perfect condition. So was the sofa. It had been sitting right there four weeks ago, kind of crosswise in the room, facing the TV set, and now it was gone.

"What color was that sofa?"

"Kind of a deep rose, with a pineapple print or motif, all the same color."

Mrs. Boylan said she had stood looking at the room, shaking her head. Neither the couch nor the rug had had a worn spot or a stain on them. Now, she said, the room was rearranged, with the TV flat against one wall and two reclining chairs facing it. The rug didn't cover nearly what the carpet had. She wondered whose idea it was to change the room, because it had been nicer the way it was before.

The three-man investigative team had a feeling that something had happened in that room off Tom's kitchen that he wanted to conceal. The couch that had been there was gone, and he had replaced the carpet with a cheap rug. Why?

Alpert talked once more with Michelle Sullivan, Anne Marie's counselor, who told him she could not imagine that Anne Marie would have gone willingly to Tom's house on the night of June 27. "The *only* reason I can think of that Anne Marie even went to dinner with him that night would have been to break off their relationship."

On July 29, FBI special agents Kevin Shannon, Gordon Cobb, and Kathy Canning again interviewed Jacqueline Dansak, the waitress at the Panorama. Shannon showed her a lay-down of photographs and she chose those of Anne Marie Fahey and Tom Capano. That, in itself, wasn't startling—their pictures had been in the Philadelphia papers—but Dansak's recall of the couple was. She said that the woman in the picture was healthier looking than the woman she had served. "It was the Fahey girl, all right—but she was very frail, sallow, sad," the waitress said. "She appeared disheveled and uncomfortable."

Dansak told Agent Shannon that she got the impression that Capano had wanted her to leave them alone. After she served cocktails, he had ordered a bottle of wine and said he would pour it himself. He had ordered chicken or veal, and Anne Marie Fahey had ordered fish. But neither of them ate their entrées.

When she was told about the waitress's description of Anne Marie's glum demeanor during her meal with Tom at the Panorama, Michelle Sullivan nodded sadly. It all fit. During their last session, just the night before she disappeared, they had been working toward giving Anne Marie enough confidence to cut Tom completely out of her life. And Anne Marie was frightened of Tom, so frightened that Sullivan had encouraged her more strongly this time to report his behavior toward her to the Delaware Attorney General's Office.

She still didn't want to do that—not yet. But she had been making great progress toward standing up for what she wanted out of life. "And she was *not* suicidal," Sullivan said. "Not at all."

There had been no physical evidence in Anne Marie's Washington Street apartment that would remotely indicate that she had been injured or killed there. Connie Blake had told the investigators that the glass door that closed off the stairs to her second-floor apartment and Anne Marie's third-floor dwelling was always locked, although the two women often left the doors to their own apartments unlocked until they went to bed. They felt secure because no one could reach the stairway without a key to the door off the foyer.

Oddly, the combination had been reversed on Thursday night when Blake came home. The dead bolt on the glass door was unlocked, something that rarely happened. And of course, Anne Marie's door was locked, with the dead bolt thrown, which Theresa Oliver had opened with her key the following Saturday night.

Connie Blake (who had once been Mayor Dan Frawley's secretary) and Anne Marie were friends. In fact, she had once lived in Anne Marie's apartment. When she moved downstairs, she had told Annie about the vacancy. Blake knew both Mike Scanlan and Tom Capano, and from time to time had seen each of them picking Anne Marie up. She had seen Anne Marie for the last time at about 6 P.M. on the Thursday night she had dinner with Tom. "I was in my living room and she pulled up across the street and parked her car. She was wearing a white blouse—that's all I noticed."

Blake did not see Anne Marie later, although she was home all evening, packing for a weekend at the shore. She watched a Pay-Per-View movie, something about an American president, as she packed. She was used to hearing sounds from Anne Marie's apartment—someone walking, water running, the low tones of a phone conversation, occasionally a loud television program. The layout of their apartments was almost the same. "You enter the living room first," she explained, "and walk through the dining area, with the kitchen on the right. Anne Marie's bedroom was on the back on the left, with the bathroom on the right. I have two more rooms—a den and a dressing room."

Blake told the investigators that the movie was almost over when she heard the sound of footsteps coming from Anne Marie's apartment. "They weren't high heels—just muffled walking. Someone walking through to the bedroom. It wasn't very distinctive."

The time? As closely as she could judge, it would have been somewhere between a quarter to and eight minutes to ten. It sounded as though there was only one person in the rooms above. Connie said she'd turned off her TV at ten and had gone to bed at eleven. She had heard nothing at all from upstairs during the night, nor did she hear Anne Marie moving about in the morning. They went to work at the same time and often chatted on their way out, but not on Friday. When she came home at noon, Blake saw that Anne Marie's car was still parked where it had been the evening before.

ON July 30, Anne Marie's continued absence was cast in a more sinister light. The public had no knowledge of the gears that had begun to mesh. Nor did the Fahey family. But suddenly the news media were reporting that her disappearance was now being considered a criminal case and that Tom Capano had been named a suspect. No one was saying what he was suspected of. But Anne Marie was still missing, and if any evidence had been found to indicate what had happened to her, the investigators were not revealing it.

Ferris Wharton's official comments were more inscrutable than ever. "In a broad sense, sure, Tom Capano is a suspect," he said. "So are other people the police are curious about. Certainly, in any circumstance, the last person seen with her is a suspect. . . . As more and more time goes by, the possibility of a benign explanation diminishes, given her close ties to her family and her job. You have to conclude foul play came into the picture. It's just sort of an evolutionary thing. I think most people would now say it's likely that she's a victim of a crime."

Charlie Oberly sprang to Tom's defense, saying that his friend and client had been made a "scapegoat," and a sacrifice to political pressure. "You've got everyone from the president of the United States on down wanting it to be solved. But they've been able to come up with nothing. They are branding this person without a shred of evidence, and that is terrible."

Marian Capano's husband, Lee Ramunno, spoke up for his brother-in-law: "Tom is a wonderful person. Honest. Decent. He has the respect of the community. It's ludicrous that someone would suspect him. . . . He was at the restaurant with her, and when they left, he brought her home. They've established that the person living in the apartment underneath did not hear any struggle or noise. After that, who knows?"

The investigative team had been convinced for weeks that whatever had happened to Anne Marie, it had not occurred in her apartment. Except for the food left out and the jumble of shoes, everything there was as it always had been. And Connie Blake would almost certainly have heard any sounds of a struggle. But they had needed something to put on an affidavit to show cause why a search warrant should be granted for Tom's house. Now they had that. The first crack in the seemingly impervious wall that Tom and his attorneys had thrown up was the credit card charge at Air Base Carpets. That, along with the missing carpet and sofa, and the statements of Anne Marie's friends and her psychologist, gave them their probable cause.

They didn't doubt that Anne Marie had been scared to death of Tom Capano and of what he might do next; none of the three men who had taken on the quest of finding her believed that she had gone willingly to Tom's house. But they *did* believe that she had gone there.

Although Tom's rented house was surrounded by other houses, the lots were large and the homes had thick, solid walls. In an earlier canvass of North Grant Avenue and neighboring Kentmere Place, the detectives hadn't talked to anyone who remembered hearing a scream or an argument on the night of June 27. But memory and checks with the weather bureau verified that it had been beastly hot that night; everyone had their air conditioners turned on high. A scream or an argument would not have been heard inside the houses nearby. If Tom had, for some reason, become enraged at Anne Marie inside the house where he lived alone, no one else would have heard any sound at all above the hum of air conditioners.

IF Tom would not come to the investigators, then they would go to him—or rather, to the house where he lived. Eric Alpert drew up an affidavit listing the reasons for a federal search warrant that would allow the FBI team and Wilmington police to thoroughly search the brick house on North Grant Avenue. Once they had the search warrant in hand, Tom could not refuse them entrance.

Federal magistrate Mary Pat Trostle approved the warrant, which was immediately sealed.

The FBI trains special teams to carry out searches, teams skilled in retrieving and preserving evidence. They were authorized to search both the Grant Avenue house and Kay Capano's Chevrolet Suburban (the vehicle that Kay told the investigators Tom had borrowed early on June 28, saying it was because he would have the girls with him for the weekend). An evidence response team from the Baltimore FBI office was on hand at eight-fifteen in the morning of July 31, 1996. Two evidence vans parked in the driveway at Tom's house. At least two dozen expert searchers were ready to check every room, corner, and closet. Tom was present to accept the search warrant, but he soon left.

For the moment, they had all avoided the media, which was getting precious little information from official sources. If reporters found out that something interesting was happening at Capano's house, they would descend in droves.

Special Agents David Roden, John Rosato, and Chris Allen went first to Kay's house to process her vehicle. It had been five weeks since anyone had seen Anne Marie. The Suburban almost certainly had been cleaned since then—but they knew that valuable evidence can sometimes be so infinitesimal that the human eye fails to see it.

When vehicles are processed, they are divided into sections and then vacuumed thoroughly. Filters are attached to the end of the hose so that whatever is retrieved from a particular section can be isolated and bagged into evidence. Often, evidence teams also take carpet samplings.

When the three special agents began work on Kay's Suburban, they found two plaid blankets in the rear compartment. These were taken into evidence, along with sweepings from the floor and seats. All of it would be hand carried to the evidence lab so that the chain of evidence would be unbroken. When they were finished, the searchers didn't know if they had hit the jackpot or not—but they had gleaned dozens of hairs and fibers.

Back at Grant Avenue, the FBI searchers, Wilmington Police officers, and Delaware state troopers swarmed over Tom's rental house and his 1993 Jeep Cherokee. Kathleen Jennings and Bartholomew J. Dalton, two of the attorneys on the growing staff of lawyers who represented Tom, stood by to observe the search.

Timothy Munson, the Supervising Resident Agent of the Wilmington FBI office, was there. So were Eric Alpert, Colm Connolly, and Bob Donovan. Before the sun set, they intended to search every inch of the house and property.

Agents and police moved over the somewhat ragged yard. There were no flowers there beyond a few perennials that had come up without nurturing. They dug nine holes, prodded the lawn with metal poles in spots that seemed too high or too low, and moved a metal detector slowly over the grass. Two black Labradors, necrosearch dogs, had been brought up from Milford, Delaware, and their handlers led them around the property.

The dogs, trained to detect the odor of decomposition, showed no interest. The human searchers found nothing.

The day promised to be hot and sultry—and crowded. By ten-thirty, word of the search had gone out to radio, television, and newspaper reporters. Neither the FBI searchers nor the reporters planned to give in to the sun beating down. Kentmere Park was not a neighborhood used to police activity, and the rows of official cars and those with logos of television and radio stations looked alien along the pretty curving street. Some of the residents kept their drapes closed; others passed out iced tea and lemonade.

It was an awkward search, with reporters peering at the officers and agents over the backyard fence. If they found some sign of Anne Marie, virtually the whole world would know about it within fifteen minutes. The FBI searchers tried to ignore their audience, shaking their heads as one reporter or another called out a question. A television station's helicopter circled overhead, its rotors making a thrub-thrub-thrubity sound that seemed to bounce off the three-story houses along the street.

Special Agent Kenneth Dougal, with twenty-eight years in the

FBI, was the evidence response team leader. He entered the house first for a walk-through to see what was there. Then he assigned specific personnel to designated areas. Everything seemed very neat, but they had expected that; Ruth Boylan had cleaned the house the week before. But they weren't looking for surface cleaning. They were looking for something minute, something that she—or anyone else who might have wiped away stains—would not have seen.

Eric Alpert had indicated in his affidavit that the investigative team would be looking for weapons, tools, and "body parts," which could be taken literally or could mean blood. They didn't expect to find a pool of blood or a large stain; if such a thing had ever been in Tom's house, it was long gone. What the searchers hoped for was a speck so small that it might have been missed. They could not risk spraying with Luminol or leuco-malachite green or other chemicals that might reveal where large areas of blood had been cleaned up; it might also destroy the blood for DNA testing.

Special Agent Linda Harrison, a sixteen-year veteran with the FBI, was responsible for searching the great room off the kitchen. Ruth Boylan had said that Tom had recently changed the furnishings in that room. Squinting, Harrison used her own eyes to sweep the room for blood spots. She found them. Or thought she had. Tiny, isolated, dark brown flecks. The one on the baseboard was only two millimeters wide, but large enough to do a presumptive test that showed it was blood from *some* source. She found another tiny speck on the metal cover at the bottom of the radiator on the wall where the TV stood, but she dared not use any of it for testing. With cotton swabs moistened with sterile water, she lifted the dried blood, and then allowed the swabs to air-dry before she packaged them in brown envelopes and gave them to Dougal, who was photographing the room and the brown spots. Only after photographs of the specks were enlarged would other microscopic dots show up in a faint spray pattern around the ones that could be seen with the naked eye. The paint on the walls looked fresh; in case the room had been painted since June 27, the agents sawed out squares of wallboard for testing in the lab.

If this *was* blood, would it match Anne Marie's DNA? At the moment it was a moot question. They had yet to find anything that they could use to determine her DNA profile. Her own passion for cleanliness had defeated them every time. There had been no blood in her apartment, and nothing from which they could extract DNA. Her toothbrush was free of her saliva; her hairbrush had no hairs wound around the bristles. Most people fail to clean the U-joints in their sinks until they are clogged with hair—but when the plumbing was dismantled, it had no hairs. Even the inside of her hats had no strands of her beautiful hair caught there. If they had found hairs with tags (roots), the criminalists might have had a chance to isolate her DNA. But Anal Annie had been true to form in her neatness.

Now the FBI search team had found what they knew in their guts was human blood. Somehow the investigators would have to find Anne Marie's DNA. There had to be a way, even though the samplers they had wouldn't be enough to attempt a familial match with her siblings.

They also found blood flecks in Tom's laundry room and on the door there. And there was something else that might or might not be vital to the investigation. There were many, many cleaning compounds and bleaching agents, far more than in most households, especially a bachelor's household. Several could be used to remove bloodstains. One, Carbona, was specifically meant for that purpose. That might be significant, but lots of people had Carbona cleaners in their cupboards.

A murmur went through the wilting reporters who waited stoically in the afternoon sun. The FBI team was carrying out a toilet. What could that mean? The search team hoped to find evidence caught in the trap. Obviously, this was not going to be a slam-dunk case, where everything came together like clockwork. At the end of the day, none of the searchers knew if the bits of hair and fiber, the minuscule dark brown speckles, the vacuum cleaners, the blood spot removers, the mops, the small ax with fibers attached, the broken fireplace poker, or any of the other items they carried away in the two vans were going to make any difference at all in an investigation already five weeks old.

Time and the FBI crime lab would tell.

ON August 1, the *News-Journal* had long articles about the search of Tom Capano's house. But there was more. Somehow the Wilmington paper had gotten access to Anne Marie's diary and printed sections of it all over the front page. For a woman who guarded her privacy so carefully, it was, perhaps, a final cruelty. If Anne Marie was out there alive somewhere, she would be destroyed to see all her secret thoughts revealed for readers to digest along with their morning coffee and rolls. Very soon, other area papers picked up the story. Everything she had written about Tom—and about Mike—was no longer secret, all of her hopes and dreams and disappointments, her essence, corroded by printer's ink.

It was galling for the three men building a case; Colm Connolly hadn't released anything about the investigation. But people were talking to insistent reporters, and so, much that the investigators had tried to keep hidden for the good of the probe was coming from other sources.

Ironically, Tom came off better than one might have expected. A cry went up from his defenders. Joe Hurley, perhaps *the* top Delaware criminal defense attorney and an old friend, said, "It's unimaginable! I sent [Tom] a note myself—in sympathy more than anything else. This will haunt him to his grave and hurt his career—which has been exemplary."

Charlie Oberly told the *News-Journal* that his client had only been trying to help Anne Marie with her problems by bringing her food and tempting her with dinners at her favorite restaurants. Far from being estranged from Tom, Oberly said, she only recently had sent him messages full of affection. "Tom was trying to boost her spirits," he said.

Tom himself refused to be interviewed for the long article in the *News Journal,* but he did give reporter Valerie Helmbreck a quote, his first: "I've personally been devastated by this."

FERRIS WHARTON was about to step out of the investigation—at least for the time being. Far from being resentful that the federal government was treading on state turf, he welcomed the assistance of the U.S. Attorney's office and the FBI. "They have greater resources," Wharton told the *News-Journal* reporter Cris Barrish. "They have the manpower, technical expertise, people with forensic expertise. The purpose is to find out what happened to her [Anne Marie] and to the extent that the FBI can resolve that situation, we're very thankful that they can step in to help."

But Wilmington and all of Delaware is insular and self-contained. The idea of the government coming in and pressuring one of their own rankled some people, and indeed, the *News-Journal's* headline on August 3 read: *FBI Uses Typical Tactics With Capano.*

Charlie Oberly, who had served as Delaware's attorney general for three terms, was outraged for the Capanos, characterizing the FBI search of Kay's car as "Gestapo tactics," and calling Tom "a scapegoat." Indeed, Tom had a groundswell of support from highly placed people who could not imagine him as either Anne Marie's stalker or her killer.

Anne Marie's sister, Kathleen, felt differently. "I've known Thomas Capano for probably 15 years," she told a *Philadelphia In-*

quirer reporter. "Up until six weeks ago, I thought he was a nice man. Now, I probably know more about Thomas Capano than his wife even does. And what I know of him now—he's not a nice man. Now, looking around the apartment, I realize there are a lot of things that he gave her—things that Annie didn't have the money for. Expensive cappuccino makers. . . . There's this big TV in her living room. I asked her where she got it. She said she won it. I was like, 'Oh—that's good luck!' Now, things make sense."

None of her siblings were angry with Anne Marie because she hadn't told them everything about her life; they would not have judged her. They would have helped her get free of Tom. Now, it might be far too late. But still, they paid the rent on her little apartment, and one or another of them waited there for her to return. If they let her apartment go, it was like saying she was never coming home at all.

_____ *Chapter Twenty-six* _____

DEBBY MACINTYRE'S reaction to what was happening to Tom was predictable for a woman who had been programmed to be submissive for almost two decades. She figuratively put her hands over her ears and eyes to shut out what she could not deal with. And Tom had told her not to read the newspapers, assuring her, "They're full of lies. And they'll just upset you." As always, she had obeyed.

Early on the morning of August 1, when the stories about Anne Marie's diary and the search of Tom's house hit the headlines, Debby was already on her way to the Philadelphia airport. "I left for Nantucket that morning," she recalled. "I was gone for nine days."

Certainly she had her head in the sand. She was in full-fledged denial. She didn't *want* to read the newspapers or watch television news that not only gave intimate details about her lover's affair with another woman but also suggested he might be a kidnapper and a murderer. Debby needed to believe Tom's reassurances that nothing had changed, that he was still there for her, and that all the things people were saying about him were ridiculous falsehoods. She had never been much of a news buff, and when she returned home from Nantucket it was not that hard for her to ignore the newspapers and keep her TV turned off.

If she had allowed herself to follow the unfolding story, the investigation and the ensuing publicity would have been a nightmare for Debby. To come so close to a happy ending with Tom and to see it destroyed by his connection to a woman she never knew existed would be almost more than she could bear. Debby believed blindly in Tom. Her vision was so focused on what he told her to think that she saw nothing to the left or right of it.

Tom had admitted lying to her about seeing Anne Marie—and Susan Louth, too—but he had promised he would never lie again. They were still together, and she knew he would protect her—as she would protect him. If doubts about Tom ever began to creep into her mind, Debby blocked them. Tom hadn't stalked Anne Marie; that was totally unlike him. He was a good man who was being hounded, and she, for one, believed in him. "I believed everything he told me," she recalled. "And it was really only coincidence, but every time something really major happened in the case, I happened to be away from Wilmington."

As Tom had told her so often, hadn't he always been there for her? Hadn't he been the one who shut her mother's eyes? How could she *not* believe in him? How could she ever leave him?

THE crack in Tom Capano's armor gradually opened wider. Little by little the federal investigation was gaining momentum. Tips were coming in, and one of the initially most promising came from an employee of the Capano & Sons construction company.

On July 1, Shaw Taylor had been puzzled by a message from a fellow employee telling him to have the Dumpsters emptied at the family firm at 105 Foulk Road. Taylor remarked to Louie's son, Louis Capano III, that it wasn't the regular day for emptying the Dumpsters—they were still half empty. The younger Capano called his father on his cell phone to ask him why. Louie told him to get off the cell phone at once and not to discuss the matter over the phone.

Their curiosity aroused, the two young men peered into the Dumpsters, but they saw nothing but trash there. Two of the Dumpsters held ordinary garbage and two others had construction materials from a building that Capano & Sons was gutting so that it could be tenant-fitted-out for a new renter—a bank. All the bins were barely half full. Still, in line with Louie's orders, calls were made to Harvey & Harvey, a Wilmington waste disposal company, and the Dumpsters were emptied. The ordinary garbage went to the Cherry Island dump on the eastern edge of Wilmington, close by the Delaware River; the construction debris had to be taken to the Delaware recyclable-products landfill off U.S. 13, south of the city.

When word of their premature removal trickled down to the investigation team, their first thought was that Anne Marie's body might have been in one of those Dumpsters. If not her body, then there was the matter of the missing couch and carpet from the great room at Tom's house.

Cops often joke about their profession, saying, "It's a dirty job, but somebody's got to do it." The investigative team's next search was *truly* a dirty job. For five days—from August 12 through 16—Bob Donovan, Eric Alpert, FBI evidence teams, and Wilmington Police officers spent their days at the dumps and landfill. Colm Connolly joined them when he could. They were all garbed in the white coveralls that they wore on evidence searches, which were soon less than pristine.

"We held our noses," Alpert recalled. "I guess you didn't really need training to do that search. At Cherry Island, the garbage was spread out, and then these huge 'dozers with metal treads went back and forth over it, crushing it before it was buried. It was all the same brownish color when they finished."

"You couldn't recognize that couch if you saw it," Bob Donovan added. "Everything was broken down into small pieces."

Then it rained and things got worse. "We sank in mud to our knees," Alpert said, "and our boots came off. We stank. We began to feel like, What's the use?"

It was a little better at the other site, where the construction debris had been dumped. At least it didn't smell. But nothing looked as it once had, and in the end, the investigators had to agree that any further searching was useless. In their hearts they didn't believe that Anne Marie's body was there. They hoped it wasn't. But they were quite sure that there had been something in those Dumpsters that caused Louie to order them emptied when they were half full. Was Louie somehow involved in Anne Marie's disappearance? They didn't know. But they believed *something* connected with the case had been taken to the dump before it was reduced to indistinguishable rubble.

Nobody was calling it murder, not officially. Officially, the FBI was calling Anne Marie's disappearance "interstate kidnapping."

THE toll back edits on Anne Marie's and Tom's phones had been completed, and all the calls Tom was currently dialing out were being printed on the pen register. Connolly began to chart a time line.

Only one call had initiated from Anne Marie's phone on the evening of Thursday, June 27. At 11:52 P.M., someone had hit *69 to see who the most recent caller had been. That call was from Mike Scanlan, who had phoned from a friend's house to invite Anne Marie to join him at Kid Shelleen's. Phone records and her answering system showed that Mike's call had been at 9:45. Who was in Anne Marie's apartment at 11:52?

Tom had made numerous calls on that vital night and the day after. At 12:05, he had checked his voice mail at Saul, Ewing. He had made two calls to Debby MacIntyre, one a *69. On Friday, he had called Debby several times, beginning early in the morning. He had called her from Stone Harbor later in the morning.

Tom didn't stay another night in the brick house on North Grant Avenue. He told his friends and family that he couldn't live there anymore, not with the memories of cops and FBI agents overrunning the place. If there were other memories there that disturbed him, he didn't speak of them. He vacated the premises as of September 30, 1996, but, in reality, he moved in with Louie the night the search warrant was executed, and later, he moved in with his mother. There was plenty of room in the big house on Weldin Road, where he'd grown up, and Marguerite was glad to have him. He was seeing Debby several times a week and he continued to assure her that everything was fine, despite the occasional intrusion of cops and agents, who were more bothersome than dangerous.

The search warrants, however, kept coming. On August 23, eight weeks after Anne Marie Fahey had vanished, Tom was forced to submit to a search warrant that asked for samplers of his blood and his body hair. With one of his attorneys, Bart Dalton, he appeared at Riverside Hospital, where an FBI technician waited. Drawing the vial of blood was easier than taking the hair samples. Hair must be plucked—from the head, the genital area, and possibly other body sites. To be useful in DNA testing, the tag (or root) has to be present, so the hair cannot be cut. Pubic hair has characteristics different from head hair.

It was an ignominious event for Tom, one in a series. He was not accustomed to such invasions of his home, his cars, his person, and he was growing annoyed with the stubborn investigative team. But it was only the beginning. And maddeningly, the media seemed to have a line into his run-ins with the authorities. Tom had never sought publicity—even when he was a public figure. He certainly didn't care to see his personal business on the front pages of the Wilmington and Philadelphia newspapers.

In fact, Tom had no idea how much of his personal business

Colm Connolly, Bob Donovan, and Eric Alpert already knew. His credit card statements and his bank statements revealed a great deal about him, as they would for anyone: patterns of spending, personal preferences, available income. Unusual and one-time purchases stood out, too.

In checking Tom's banking transactions, Connolly saw that Tom had cashed checks on two consecutive days for $8,000 and $9,000. It appeared that Tom might be "structuring," a tactic drug dealers—or anyone who wanted to hide money from the IRS—often used. Any withdrawal of over $10,000 required that a CTR—a currency transaction report—be filed.

Connolly called Ron Poplos of the Internal Revenue Service and asked him for some help in following Tom Capano's money trail. Either Tom had been preparing to launder money by deliberately structuring or he had reason to stockpile it. Poplos was game and he was a veteran of the Whitewater investigation, expert on tracking where money came from and where it went. Why would Tom have needed $17,000 in cash when he already had a cushy bank account?

Tom obviously liked to dine out often and well. It was rare for him to spend less than $100 for dinner, and not at all unusual for the bill to top $300. In one month, on one of his credit cards, he had dined at the Dilworthtown Inn, the Victor Cafe, Toscana, the Ristorante La Veranda, Panorama, Pan Tai, Kid Shelleen's, Madeline's, the Shipley Grill, and DiNardo's Famous Crabs. His Visa and MasterCard statements averaged between $2,000 and $5,000 a month. He often purchased designer women's clothing at Talbot's, but he also bought more prosaic items, shopping at the Happy Harry's drugstore in Trolley Square or the Sports Authority.

Tom had shopped at Happy Harry's on Sunday, June 30. What he had purchased was not stipulated, but Alpert and Donovan showed a clerk the bill, and he described a man who sounded like Tom: he had been looking for a cleaner that would remove bloodstains. The clerk said he had recommended one of the Carbona cleaners and the customer bought it.

But Tom might have had a perfectly innocent reason to buy a cleaner that removed blood. He had four teenage daughters who visited him, and his colitis was so severe that he often bled from the rectum, staining his underwear.

The FBI lab had determined that the dark brown specks on the baseboard in the great room in the Grant Avenue house *were* human blood, and there was enough of it for a sampler to compare with a known DNA profile—but the investigators had been unable to find any of Anne Marie's blood. It was desperately important to find a sample. The blood used for the tests of her potassium levels that Michelle Sullivan had ordered had been disposed of.

But then, looking over her day-planner, Eric Alpert saw something that had so far escaped notice. Anne Marie had jotted down "Blood bank." Her family said that she had been a regular blood donor, and a search of her E-mail confirmed that she had given blood in April.

"Blood banks usually extract and save plasma," Alpert said, "and plasma won't work for DNA testing. But sometimes the plasma isn't as pure as it might be. We figured if we could trace that plasma, we might be able to use it for comparison purposes."

It was better than wading through the city dump for almost a week, but it was almost as frustrating. The Blood Bank of Delaware's records did verify that Anne Marie had donated blood. Chris Hancock, a donor advocate, told the investigators that careful histories of donors were taken, including their social security numbers. After Anne Marie had passed her medical interview, a unit number—unique to her—was assigned to her that would stay with her blood or plasma. It was an FDA requirement. Anne Marie's unit number for her last donation was 0387029.

But where was that blood now? Alpert found that the red cells had been shipped to a hospital. The rest of it had been used for fresh-frozen plasma, but the plasma wasn't even in the country. It was on its way to the Swiss Red Cross, somewhere on a ship in the Atlantic Ocean. At the government's request, Chris Hancock arranged to retrieve Anne Marie's plasma, and it came back, still frozen: 0387029. Now it was up to the FBI lab to see if it matched the spots found in the great room in Tom Capano's house.

Special Agent Allan Giusti was a DNA analyst in the FBI laboratory. "DNA," he explained, "is an abbreviation for 'deoxyribonucleic acid,' the blueprint every living organism is made of, which is found in the form of a twisted ladder that is called a double helix."

Body fluid stains larger than a quarter are fairly easy to match to known samplers. But minuscule amounts of body fluid and tissue can be tested too. One test, termed the PCR test, is used when the sampler is minute. It actually amplifies substances like saliva on the back of a stamp or a tiny stain of semen or blood. Starting with one DNA molecule, Giusti could chemically multiply it. "If you do that approximately thirty times, you're increasing the starting amount of DNA by about a billion," he explained.

The resultant pattern of dots could be matched with dots from a known donor.

Tom Capano had been forced to give blood, but he had refused to allow his daughters to give samples, indignant that the federal investigators should even ask. In August 1996, as he began his tests on the unknown blood specks retrieved on July 31, Giusti had Tom's and Anne Marie's blood, as well as other samples: Ruth Boylan's, Susan Louth's, and Debby MacIntyre's—all people who had been in Tom's house.

Tom, Debby, Ruth Boylan, and Susan Louth were all excluded absolutely as the source of the blood in the great room. But Giusti found that there was only one chance in eleven thousand that anyone *other* than Anne Marie Fahey had lost that blood. "So we had that blood match in late August 1996," Connolly said. "But we didn't announce it. We waited six months to make it public."

There had not been enough blood, certainly, to prove that Anne Marie was dead. How much might have been on the missing carpet and couch, no one would ever know. But the FBI lab had found another match—not blood but fibers. The carpet samples that Bob Donovan had retrieved from the bed-and-breakfast owner matched beige carpet fibers vacuumed from Kay Capano's Suburban. Under a scanning electron microscope that enlarged the samples exponentially, it was apparent that they had come from the same source. Someone had used Kay's SUV to transport the missing carpet.

Although they still had a long way to go, Colm Connolly was confident that he had enough evidence to move forward. He sent Tom's lawyers a letter on August 5, notifying them that their client was under investigation by a federal grand jury.

GRAND jury investigations are different from actual trials. What takes place there is secret, and witnesses may not have their attorneys with them, although they may leave the room after each question they are asked to consult with them. In Delaware, grand juries may sit for up to eighteen months. There are twenty-three jurors in all, and at least sixteen must be present at a session; twelve must agree in order to hand down an indictment. Grand juries start and stop, assembling whenever the prosecutor needs to elicit testimony. Unlike a regular jury, grand jurors are rarely required to be present day after day until a verdict is reached. Reporters can only watch the people who go in and out of the grand jury room, and speculate on why they were summoned.

On August 29, 1996, Colm Connolly was the prosecutor in the

first grand jury session in the Capano case, questioning a number of reluctant witnesses, who would appear only under a subpoena. The first six witnesses summoned included Louis Capano Jr.; his son, Louis Capano III; and employees of the family construction company. Louie stayed in the grand jury room for an hour and a half and left without making any comment to reporters.

Even though they were compelled to testify, the witnesses had various ways to balk. They were able to invoke the Fifth Amendment, and their attorneys could demand to know if the witness has ever been intercepted by electronic communication. (Ironically, although the government wasn't taping them, some of the principals had been taping one another.) This session marked only the beginning of what would seem like endless grand jury testimony.

COLM CONNOLLY had grown up in Delaware, but he didn't really know the Capano family. He remembered Gerry vaguely from his days at Archmere, and before this case, he had heard Tom's name mentioned—but only once—when he was working on a political corruption case. He didn't know the man. They were from different generations.

Connolly encountered Tom for the first time on September 10, 1996, after he subpoenaed his sixteen-year-old daughter, Christy, to appear before the grand jury. Tom had been telling friends that the blood spots found in the great room could be traced to either Christy or his daughter Katie, but he was infuriated that Connolly had called Christy as a witness. For a moment, the two men faced each other in the hall, Connolly's face bland and Tom's suffused with rage. "He got about a foot and a half away from me," Connolly recalled, "looked me in the eye, and said, 'I hope you can sleep at night.'"

Connolly said nothing. He walked away—but the gauntlet had been thrown down. Tom Capano was a father prepared to fight fiercely to protect his daughter. Or was he protecting himself?

When she took the stand, Christy Capano refused to answer Connolly's questions and now faced contempt of court charges.

_____ Chapter Twenty-seven _____

DEBBY MACINTYRE had been seeing Tom clandestinely for fourteen and a half years and openly for one. Tom suggested that it would be prudent for them to say that their romantic relationship had begun *after* he separated from Kay. That would protect Kay's feelings, and besides, the feds were already poking around in his private life enough; there was no need to give in to their salacious curiosity.

As always, Debby did what Tom requested. She had no desire for everyone to know that she and Tom had been intimate since 1981. Except for lies of omission and her one blatant lie to her family when she joined Tom in Montreal, she had always told the truth. Indeed, when Bob Donovan interviewed her on July 23, she told him what she remembered—save for the fact that she classified Tom as only a very good friend whom she had known for twenty years.

"I talk with Tom every day," she said, "and see him once or twice a week."

"Has he ever talked about a relationship with Anne Marie Fahey?" Donovan asked.

"Never."

In a way, that was true. He had never mentioned Anne Marie until after she disappeared. Asked to recall whether she had talked to Tom on Thursday night, June 27, Debby said she had. "I called him sometime between ten and eleven," she said. "I know it was in the middle of *ER*. He called me back at about eleven-thirty. I called him at twelve-fifteen, but he didn't answer and I hung up. He called me back within five or ten minutes."

That call had come in with an odd ring, the extended shrill that indicated that the calling party had hit *69 to return the last call made to his number.

"How about on Friday—the next day?"

"I saw Tom Friday morning between eight and eight-thirty at the Tower Hill track," Debby said. "He was walking. He called me around ten-thirty to say he was playing golf that day at the Wilmington Country Club."

Donovan jotted down his notes in short sentences, and they continued in a staccato fashion:

"Spoke with Tom later on Friday at approx 1730.

"Tuesday, July 2. He called her at work around 1500 and told her that he had been out to dinner with Anne Marie Fahey.

"Did not know that Tom was having any relationships."

Debby didn't know where Tom had been for most of the day on Friday, the twenty-eighth. He might have called her several times during the day but she wasn't sure. She said she had spoken with him on Saturday, and he had stopped by on Sunday twice. The second time, he had told her that the cops were at his house and they had searched it. "He was very upset," Debby told Donovan. "He felt he was being set up, but he didn't discuss what was going on."

It seemed strange that she hadn't pressed him for details. Debby appeared to be so confident that no one realized that Tom ran the show and that she would never dream of insisting that he tell her what was wrong.

As he had done for years, Tom had suggested a script for Debby to follow, and she stayed with it; it was what he wanted. They were together and everything was going to be fine. If she remembered things that frightened her, the memory never even got up to the surface of her mind before she buried it. One of the memories that would loom large with the investigating team when they discovered it was a favor Debby had done for Tom. She had buried that recollection deeper than all the rest.

"I honestly never thought about the gun," she would recall. "I never connected buying the gun for Tom with Anne Marie Fahey until a long time later."

Sometime very early in the spring of 1996, Tom had phoned to ask Debby to do something very special for him, something very "important." He wouldn't tell her what it was, so she hadn't said either yes or no. But in April, Tom asked her again and this time specified what the task was; he wanted her to buy a gun for him.

"Why?" she asked, mystified.

"Somebody is trying to extort me," he'd explained. "I'm not going to *use* it. I just want to threaten this person. I'll give it back to you."

She told him she didn't want a gun in the house. But Tom said that he was concerned about her—a single mother living alone. He pointed out that crime rates were up and that it would be wise for her to have a gun handy—just in case.

"I told him I didn't want to do it," Debby recalled. But Tom begged her, telling her he *really* needed her to buy the gun. He didn't say why he couldn't buy it himself, or anything about who was extorting him, beyond saying it was a man. "I won't use it," Tom said. "You know I'm afraid of guns—but I need it to scare this guy off."

At length, Debby had agreed to do it, and as he always did, Tom gave her detailed instructions. "He told me to go to the Sports Authority," she said, "and go to the hunting section. I was supposed to walk in the front door and turn to the left."

She did that, but when she asked for a gun, Debby made the mistake of saying she was buying it for a friend. The salesman told her that was against the law. She could not transfer a firearm to someone else. Embarrassed, she left the store. Surprisingly, Tom wasn't angry. "He just said, 'Fine. Don't worry about it.' "

A month or so later, Tom took Debby to Washington, D.C., for a lawyers' conference, and they had a wonderful time. It was only the third trip he had ever taken her on, so each one was memorable. Then shortly after they came home, he asked her again to purchase a gun for him. "I'm afraid to do that, Tom," she said. "I can't transfer a firearm to somebody else. It's against the law."

"Don't be ridiculous," he said. "People do it all the time. It's nothing you should worry about."

He was so good at making her feel foolish, and he pooh-poohed her reservations until she finally said yes. The next day, May 13, Tom picked Debby up in front of Tatnall School and drove her to a little gun store—Miller's—out on Route 13. He waited in the car while she went in.

She was very nervous, but this time she knew what to say. She asked to see a small weapon suitable for self-defense. The salesman showed her a few guns, and she chose a Beretta .22 caliber revolver. She paid $180 for it and, at the salesman's suggestion, purchased a box of bullets. He cautioned her about transferring the gun, and she signed a form saying that she would not. That worried her—but Tom's displeasure worried her more.

"I was afraid Tom would get mad if I didn't do what he wanted me to," she recalled a long time later. "I was always afraid he would get so angry that he would leave me."

Back in Tom's Jeep Cherokee, Debby told him how concerned she was about breaking the law. Again he laughed and told her not to be "ridiculous."

Tom put the gun and the bullets behind the backseat of his Cherokee and took Debby to a nearby restaurant for a BLT and a glass of iced tea. It was all so normal. He drove her back to Tatnall in time for the afternoon session, thanked her profusely for helping him out, and drove away.

Debby had never seen that gun again. For a long time, she worried because she had broken the law, but then she had put it out of her mind—just as she put so many things that worried her out of her mind, back in recesses she seldom visited.

ON September 6, 1996, Debby MacIntyre took another step that would entangle her in a morass of deception and distortion. At eleven that morning, Bob Donovan, Colm Connolly, and Eric Alpert came to her house on Delaware Avenue to interview her in preparation for her grand jury testimony. Now she enlarged upon what she had told Donovan in their first interview, but she still did not tell them that she and Tom had been lovers for many, many years.

Debby remembered Thursday, June 27, mostly because it had affected Tom's life so severely and made him confess his unfaithfulness to her. In the morning, she and Tom had had their usual phone conversation sometime between nine-thirty and ten-thirty. She didn't hear from him again until shortly before five, when he told her he had a business meeting in Philadelphia.

Debby explained to the investigators that she was in charge of Tatnall's swim team and that both of her children had a swim meet that night. She had called Tom about ten-thirty, but he wasn't home yet, so she left a message. "Tom called me back between eleven-thirty and twelve-thirty," she said. "He sounded like he always did, except very tired."

Debby recalled that Tom had berated her over something about Tatnall, growing so angry that he hung up on her. When she tried to call him back, there was no answer—and she didn't leave a message. Within a few minutes, he had *69'd, calling back to ask her why she had hung up on him. Of course, she hadn't. "Then we both calmed down and said good night," she said.

Debby described the events of the next day, June 28, pretty much as she had told Bob Donovan, but she added a few details. She'd seen Tom walking at the track early and didn't see him again until he showed up unexpectedly at eleven that night. He had come to bed with her and stayed at her home until about noon the next day. "I think he went to do some errands, then," Debby said, "because he was going to have his kids that night—Saturday."

On Sunday? Tom had come to her house at one in the afternoon, upset because the police had wakened him in the middle of the night. He had been so disturbed, in fact, that he had put his hands on his head and she could see him trembling. But she had not questioned him. She never questioned him.

At five that afternoon, Debby said, Tom came back to her house—in even worse shape—because the police had actually come into his house and searched through it. She had no idea what for. She didn't dare ask.

Debby told the three investigators that she hadn't known Tom had had dinner with the girl who was missing until the following Tuesday—when Tom told her. They could see that she was very supportive of Tom and that they were lovers, but Debby said firmly that

she was sure he had had nothing whatever to do with the girl's disappearance. Could she really be so in the dark about his life when he
was away from her?

"When you visit Tom," Connolly asked, "do you go in the front
door?"

"No," Debby said. "He leaves the garage door open for me and
I drive in and go up the stairs—or rather I did, before he moved to
his mother's." He had always known she was coming, she said, but
he had never given her a key to his house.

"Do you know why he got a new rug in the den—that room off
the kitchen?"

"Oh, he spilled wine," Debby said. "I asked him about it—
probably sometime in July. He told me that he'd spilled wine on the
carpet, and on the sofa, too."

She also mentioned seeing a hole in the wall, where Tom said a
picture had fallen down. The investigators already knew about the
hole in the great room wall. They'd examined it during the July 31
search and found nothing revealing. It was just a hole in the wall behind a picture. Beneath the plaster, the bricks had no nicks in them,
no tool marks. No gun barrel debris.

At this stage in the investigation, Connolly, Donovan, and
Alpert were inclined to think that Tom Capano had erupted into a
sudden and violent rage when Anne Marie tried to break up with
him. The most likely weapon would have been his hands; she had
probably succumbed to being beaten or strangled. She had undoubt-
edly bled a great deal, enough to leave such visible stains on Tom's
carpet and couch that he'd been forced to get rid of them. But no
one really knew what had happened.

Debby MacIntyre testified before the federal grand jury on September 10, giving the same information she gave Connolly, Donovan, and Alpert. No one asked her about a gun, and she certainly
didn't mention one. On a conscious level, Debby had still not connected the gun she purchased to the disappearance of Anne Marie.
She still believed Tom's characterization of the Fahey girl as an unpredictable airhead who was as likely to leave town without an explanation as anyone he'd ever known.

Debby had managed to slip into the grand jury room without
the media seeing her. No one in Wilmington linked her to the proceedings—which was a great relief for her. A few weeks later, she left
for several weeks on a guided tour of the Italian and French Riviera
with her church group from St. Ann's. She had always loved to

travel; it was a respite from her job and her life. The problems in Wilmington were, quite literally, half a world away.

Back in Wilmington, the investigative team still wasn't sure what to make of her. Was Debby part of what had happened to Anne Marie, or was she a woman deluded by love?

_____ Chapter Twenty-eight _____

AUTUMN CAME to Delaware as swiftly as every season does, without any warning; the sweet pungent smell of burning leaves filled the chill air, and summer was only a memory. Anne Marie, who had disappeared during the first week of summer, was still missing. Kathleen had finally packed up everything in her apartment and her brothers moved it into storage.

Tom's rental house sat empty. The new tenants weren't moving in until December 1 and the owners of the house gave Anne Marie's family permission to visit the house that they believed was the last place their sister had been alive. They had never had a chance to say good-bye. They moved quietly through the empty rooms, saying little, their faces solemn.

THAT fall, as more secret grand jury sessions were held, Wilmington and Philadelphia newspapers sued to have the affidavits for search warrants in the Fahey case unsealed. With a more pressing need, the Fahey family begged to know what was happening in the probe.

On November 11, Colm Connolly appeared to be giving in to media pressure when he agreed that there was no longer any need to keep the affidavits sealed. After all, Tom Capano's attorneys already knew many details of the investigation and who the witnesses were. It was almost impossible to keep a secret in Wilmington. In actuality, Connolly had caught the defense off guard; he was unperturbed about having the public learn of the growing evidence and information that painted Capano as something less than the beleaguered innocent he purported to be.

The Fahey family had hired attorney David Weiss to represent their interests. Weiss, himself a former assistant U.S. attorney, had explained to them that much of the information unearthed by a grand jury investigation could not be disclosed. Still, it was so hard for the Faheys to wait and wonder. They retained a private detective to do a parallel investigation. Nobody on the federal investigative team resented that. It was very difficult for them not to be able to talk with Anne Marie's sister and brothers about what they were doing, but federal law forbade it. At least, with the unsealing of the affidavits, the family could see that progress was being made. Whether the rest of the public had a right or need to know the intimate details of the probe was questionable. It was unlikely that anyone was in imminent danger from the prime suspect, but people were fiercely curious. Seldom had there been a case on the Eastern seaboard that sparked so much speculation.

The only faction truly upset when Judge Trostle unsealed the affidavits was Tom Capano and his attorneys. They, too, had argued to see the documents—but *privately.* The last thing Tom wanted was to have the whole world know what cause the government had had to invade his privacy and his home. His attorneys filed to block their release, delaying the Faheys' chance to see them.

While the tug-of-war over unsealing the affidavits went on, the grand jury continued to meet; Connolly, Alpert, and Donovan were relentless in their search for the truth, the intensity of which Tom Capano could never have imagined. If he was innocent of harming Anne Marie Fahey, that would come out as the people in their lives marched into the grand jury room in the federal building and answered Connolly's questions. If he had destroyed her, that would come out, too.

There were those, like Tom's sister, Marian, and her husband, Lee Ramunno, who stood by Tom without flinching. But there were others, like Kim Horstman, Jill Morrison, Ginny Columbus, and Jackie Steinhoff, who remembered a friend they had cherished, a friend caught in a net not of her own making.

Although there were no hurrahs from the three men who were quietly tracking Tom Capano, things were beginning to happen behind their wall of silence. Not everyone in Wilmington found Tom the "good Capano." An informant had come forward, an informant who could never be identified. Indeed, the manner in which the investigators found a remarkable document could never be revealed, and even the assumption that it was one individual who came to them might not be true. When any of the three was asked how they found the timeline pages, a shadow fell over his eyes.

"I can't tell you that," one said. "I can only say that none of the names mentioned in connection with that discovery is correct."

But suddenly, in November 1996, Eric Alpert asked for a search warrant for the office of one of Tom Capano's law partners. The attorney himself had no idea of what was hidden there between the volumes on one of his bookshelves. He got a telephone call from the U.S. Attorney's office to say that federal officers were on their way over, instructing him to disturb nothing. He had no inclination to do so, anyway. How the papers got to their hiding place would remain as cryptic as the way the investigative team found out they were there. Special Agent Kevin Shannon reached deftly into the bookcase and extracted ten sheets of paper.

There was no date on the pages, but the times jotted down in Tom Capano's handwriting were obviously a day in his life—a significant day.

6:30—Gerry
7:00—Kay
7:15—track
7:45—DM
8:00—Louis?
8:30—calls
8:45—Louis
?—MAC Machine
9:15–10:30—drive to SH
10:30–11:00—wait for Gerry
11:00–12:00—Marian's
12:00–12:30—Mom's
12:30+—Gerry
12:30–1:30—lunch w/ Gerry
1:30–3:00—view property, discuss price and CI sale
3:00—Gerry leaves
3:30—Tom leaves
5:00—dump loveseat
5:30—17th St.—dinner
11:00—leave kids

Back in Connolly's office in the Chase Manhattan building, all three of the investigators studied the timeline. It covered sixteen and a half hours of a day, and it didn't look like a shopping list or a simple roster of errands to do. Surely they could identify the date through the process of elimination. It probably wouldn't be before June 27, and it didn't match what Debby had told them about Thursday. Friday, the twenty-eighth, was a better bet. She had seen Tom on the twenty-eighth at the track and then not again until after eleven that night. The most galvanizing item on the list was "dump loveseat."

They'd already established that Louie Capano had ordered the Dumpsters at his construction company emptied on July 1, when they were half full. And Tom had bought the new rug on June 29. That wasn't on this list. No, the most obvious date was Friday, June 28, and Tom had clearly kept this list as a reminder to himself about where he was supposed to be on that day—right down to half-hour segments. He must have known his house would be searched and probably expected a search of his office as well. So he had hidden his crib sheet in someone else's office.

On the second sheet of paper, Tom had made notes to refresh his memory. It seemed very important that he be able to recall whom he had spoken to on June 28 and what their knowledge of his private life was.

He had called someone (whom they later determined was attorney David McBride) to decline a golf date that afternoon.

He had called Deputy Attorney General Keith Brady "to make plans to meet for happy hour that evening so had pleasant conversation with Laura Kobosko and asked her to convey message to Keith."

Under the Brady notes, Tom wrote, "knew of relationship with Anne Marie; knew I had concluded she was a 'head case.' " He also noted that Brady had helped him move carpets into his house "in October."

The rest of the notes Tom had hidden were chilling remembrances of Anne Marie. His reminders to himself focused on several elements: her instability, her incompetence at handling money, her family problems, and how she told him her innermost thoughts. It was clear he also wanted to have an explanation ready if her blood was ever found in his house.

"On Tuesday, June 18," Tom wrote,

> called for AMF and Ginny said she had gone home because of a "problem" . . . AMF later same day advised that trip home was necessitated by blood stains on clothing from heavy menstrual flow.
>
> AMF came to my house for dinner—got salmon from Toscana: irrational; fear of pregnancy; sexual contact.
>
> Dinner at Dilworthtown Inn on 6/20; lobster tail . . . discussed second job (waitress at fine dining establishment); showed me check register (writes on every line; take home pay of $844;) returned to Grant Avenue.

There were more pages, details of dates, discussions, and phone calls with Anne Marie. Tom had obviously been totally obsessed with her and all the minutiae of her life. But he denigrated her and her family. His perception was that her siblings were not treating her well. Indeed, he jotted down negative comments about how almost *everyone* in Anne Marie's life was treating her badly and "driving her crazy."

Everyone but Tom.

For June 27, Tom had written: "Appointment with Dr.; don't like him; expensive ($55 for 20 minutes.); offer ticket to Hare event (I had 12) *She* chooses Panorama instead; reservation for 7:00; call at 6:25 from office to advise on way; *very* depressed."

From Jacqueline Dansak's description of the unhappy woman she waited on, Anne Marie hadn't wanted to be at the Panorama with Tom. She hadn't eaten anything and had seemed miserable. *When* had she told him she no longer wanted to see him, not as a lover and not even as a friend? In his Jeep Cherokee going home? At her own apartment? Or during what the three investigators believed were the very last moments of her life, in the great room off Tom's kitchen?

Some kind providence had given them a timeline. All they had to do was follow it back, decipher what Tom's abbreviations meant, and find the evidence that might be connected to the entries he had hidden so carefully. They had worked long hours of overtime and they had been lucky. Would fortune continue to smile upon them?

Life and work didn't stop for any of them. They all had other cases to work, in between their investigations of Anne Marie's case. When it began, Connolly had a one-year-old son. (He would have two more sons before it was over.) Donovan and Alpert both had very young children at home, but there wasn't much family time. "Christmas came and went for two years," Alpert would recall, "and we hardly knew it."

THE Christmas season of 1996–97 was the second holiday season Debby had spent with Tom, and things seemed to *her,* at least, to be normal. They were talking about marriage and the future. For the most part, Tom was very good with her children, and her son, Steve, idolized him. A year ago, Tom had been so moody, but she understood that. It was his first Christmas away from his daughters.

Victoria was not as fond of Tom. He humiliated her as she came downstairs to meet her date for the Holiday Dance. She looked beautiful in a little black, sleeveless dress, and she was so excited; her date and all of their friends were watching her entrance.

"You look like a slut," Tom said, but he was smiling, "just like a little slut."

Victoria burst into tears, sobbing in front of her friends. When Debby looked at him, horrified, he was surprised. "What? *What?*" he asked. "I didn't mean that as an insult. I say that to my girls all the time. They think it's funny."

"I never liked him after that night," Victoria would recall, although Tom left an apology on her answering machine and he assured Debby he hadn't meant anything negative.

They smoothed it over, but Victoria viewed Tom cautiously after that. But her mother was going to marry him and she was so happy. In all the years before, Debby had waited at the edge of Tom's holidays. She had helped him choose presents for his girls, and one year she had even gone with him downstate to pick up the puppy he was giving them. Kay never knew that the dog she loved so much had ridden home from the kennel cuddled in Debby's arms.

Tom had never bought Debby sentimental or impractical presents, and again he ran true to form. For Christmas 1996, he gave her a cobalt blue KitchenAid mixer. It had all the bells and whistles, cost over $300, and was something she had wanted, but it wasn't exactly what a man in love might pick out.

Tom sensed that Debby was disappointed. "He asked me, 'What would you really like?' " she recalled, "and I said, 'You've never bought me anything nice—any jewelry.' So two days later, he came walking into my house with this 'guilt' gift, a solid gold necklace. I told him I'd wear it all the time, and I did—for a long time. I still believed I was the only one in his life."

She was very touched. It wasn't an engagement ring, but the chunky solid gold necklace felt warm around her neck, reminding her that Tom loved her. Debby was forty-seven years old and she had never believed that anyone had truly loved her. Now she did.

_____ Chapter Twenty-nine _____

ON JANUARY 3, 1997, the affidavit that Eric Alpert had prepared five months before as he sought a search warrant for Tom's house was released to the public. Dozens of facts and theories filled the *News-Journal*'s pages, and few of them burnished Tom's reputation as a devoted family man and a kind and concerned friend. Nor did the headline, *Evidence Points to Capano*.

As, of course, the evidence did. The explicit coverage caught Tom's attorneys off guard and they asked for time to respond. U.S. Attorney Greg Sleet, Connolly's boss, refused to comment on one of the few aspects of the case that the public didn't know: the test results on the blood spots found in Tom's house. The investigators had known for months that they matched Anne Marie's DNA, but that information wasn't in the affidavit and they were under no obligation to reveal it.

"I think Tom realized for the first time," Connolly said, "that he was playing out of his league. He had expected all along that he would be dealing with the Wilmington Police Department. It wasn't that we had loads and loads of money. This was basically an investigation run by three people—Donovan, Eric, and myself—who, on occasion, would bring in others like Ron Poplos.

"I believe that the shorter the loop, the better," he continued. "We didn't talk to anyone, except for Greg Sleet. No one really knew what was happening on the case."

Now, for the first time, Debby MacIntyre's name appeared in conjunction with Tom's. It was only a two-sentence notation, almost hidden in the column after column of details: "On June 28, 1996, at 12:30 a.m., *69 was also dialed from Capano's phone. This retrieved a call from 47-year-old Debby MacIntyre, a Tatnall School director and Capano friend who lives on Delaware Avenue."

Tom had assured Debby that there was nothing to worry about, that things were almost back to normal. But in fact, the investigation was just beginning to move into high gear. And the *News-Journal*'s January 3 coverage of the Fahey-Capano case rekindled public interest.

Like most law enforcement professionals, all three of the men who were investigating the case had private telephone listings. But at 3 A.M. the next morning, Colm Connolly's phone rang. When he answered it, there was no voice on the other end of the line.

At 3 A.M. the morning after that, Eric Alpert's phone rang. When *he* answered, there was only silence.

At 3 A.M. on Saturday morning, Bob Donovan's phone rang. When he answered, it was the same.

While they could not be certain, they had little doubt who was making the calls. If it was a silent threat telling them to back off, it didn't work. They had all known going in that their investigation

would be unpopular with any number of people. And there was no
way to be anonymous in Wilmington. The Connollys had bought
their home from a good friend of Tom Capano. One of their sons
was scheduled to be in a preschool class taught by a woman who
supported Tom loyally; they were asked to withdraw their child.
Indeed, Kay Capano was the Connollys' pediatrician's nurse-
practitioner. Although they knew she was excellent at her job, it
would be awkward. They arranged to see the pediatrician alone.

It seemed that all the lives involved in this complicated case
were woven together in some bizarre cross-stitched tapestry. Initially
there were as many people who backed Tom loyally as there were
those who grieved for Anne Marie and her family. In Wilmington,
seventy thousand people were like two thousand—all of whom
knew one another in some capacity. And everyone had an opinion.

For Kathleen, Robert, Kevin, Mark, and Brian Fahey, the release of the affidavit brought no good news. They understood now
the whys of the July search of Tom's house, but it confirmed their
fears that Anne Marie was dead. When Charlie Oberly denounced
the FBI as running an investigation "fueled by innuendo and rumor"
and said that the Capano family's right to privacy had been "totally
destroyed," the Faheys were angry. Their sister had lost her privacy—and so much more—months ago.

Tom's attorneys released four notes that further obliterated
Anne Marie's confidentiality. Written on the governor's stationery in
May and June of 1996, they were short notes to "Tommy." To someone who didn't understand how hard she had struggled to leave Tom
without setting off an emotional explosion, they sounded friendly.

"Tommy," said one of the notes,

> Hola Amigo! I wanted to drop you a wee note to let you know
> how much I appreciate all you have done and continue to do for
> me. You're a very genuine person.
> We've been through a lot the past couple of years, and have
> managed (through hard work, determination and perhaps a bit of
> stubborn Irishness and Italian tempers!) to prevail. You'll always
> own a special piece of my heart.
> Love you—
>
> Annie (Me)

The note was a prime example of Anne Marie's gentle way of
saying good-bye. Tom could have a piece of her heart, but he could
no longer own all of her. Connolly, Alpert, and Donovan under-

stood too well what Anne Marie was saying in her deliberately cheerful notes; they knew that her blood had stained Tom's walls. They also knew they were still a long way from building an airtight case against him.

When Charlie Oberly said that Tom hoped that Anne Marie would be found safe, David Weiss spoke to the press on behalf of the Faheys. "My clients' initial reaction is that if Mr. Capano cared for Anne Marie—as the notes offered by his attorney are intended to suggest—we ask him to come in and talk to the authorities."

Tom did not.

Robert Fahey found Oberly's statements "beyond reckless" and deplored his comparing Tom Capano to Richard Jewell, the security guard who was falsely accused of planting a bomb at the Atlanta Olympics, only to be vindicated later. For the moment, headlines about the case were built on rhetoric rather than fact.

"The Faheys were an amazing family," Connolly recalled. "When we got frustrated during the investigation, we'd meet with them, and we couldn't tell them anything—and then *they'd* get frustrated. You could see the *pain* on their faces, and yet they were so eloquent and so classy. That gave us more motivation than anything to keep on going."

TOM CAPANO hired a second high-profile attorney. Joseph A. Hurley had recently made news in another sensational case. He represented eighteen-year-old Brian Peterson, the wealthy teenager who, with his girlfriend, Amy Grossberg, pleaded guilty in Wilmington to killing their newborn son and disposing of his body in a Comfort Inn motel Dumpster in Newark, Delaware. Joe Hurley was of the Melvin Belli–Gerry Spence school of lawyers, whose confidence knew no bounds. At his first press conference on the Fahey-Capano case, he announced, "I have arrived!" Despite his penchant for dramatic moments, Hurley was an excellent criminal defense attorney.

THE grand jury probe continued, and the investigation swept in wider and wider circles. Caught in the dust churned up were the private thoughts and deeds of people who had never known Anne Marie. On January 11, 1997, sixteen-year-old Christy Capano was found in contempt of court for her September refusal to answer questions about her father. The Third District U.S. Circuit Court of Appeals opinion was a landmark decision, which decreed that, unlike spouses, children and parents could be forced to testify against each other in criminal proceedings.

Louie Capano's marriage to champion golfer Lauri Merton had occasionally hit rocky shoals; like the other Capano brothers, Louie was said to have a roving eye. But were it not for Tom's grand jury investigation, Louie and Lauri's problems would probably have gone unnoticed by everyone but their close friends. However, Lauri had become suspicious of what her husband might be up to when she was away, and she had bugged Louie's phone. Now the investigators wanted to know what conversations between Tom and Louie she might have inadvertently recorded. She refused to surrender the tapes, citing the marital privilege, and was held in contempt of court.

On March 26, Lauri's attorneys asked to have her citation overturned. On April 24, the Third District Court of Appeals declared that Lauri did not have to give the grand jury her tapes but said she would remain in contempt until she testified. What Lauri testified to, if anything, could not be revealed. There was no privacy for anyone involved with Tom; reporters noted that Louie's blond friend, Kristi Pepper, drove away from the hearings in a car that was registered to him.

Tom's health deteriorated as the grand jury investigation lumbered on. He had a cervical laminectomy to stabilize the vertebrae in his neck in January 1997, but he complained of residual pain. And the stress of the investigation aggravated his colitis. He had been seeing Dr. Joseph Bryer, a psychiatrist, for a feeling of impending disaster since August and was prescribed various antianxiety medications—Wellbutrin, Paxil, and Xanax—in an effort to calm his nerves.

PROVING the crime of murder when there is no body is probably the toughest assignment a prosecution team can take on. It was essential that Colm Connolly build a seamless case. He could not cave in to public pressure to make an arrest. If he should go into court prematurely and a defendant was acquitted, double jeopardy would attach and he could never be tried again. Any defense attorney worth his salt would suggest to a jury that Anne Marie could well be alive. Two flecks of blood that matched her DNA profile would not prove beyond the shadow of a doubt that she was dead. And although Tom Capano might be a complete tyrant who treated women like objects, that didn't prove he was a killer.

There were still myriad elements of Anne Marie's disappearance that the investigators didn't know. Her body might be buried somewhere and could be retrieved and an autopsy performed. There might even be eyewitnesses to what had happened to her. There almost certainly were people who knew more than they were saying. Thus, the probe continued, its pace sometimes maddeningly slow to those who waited for some watershed moment. It had to be that way.

IN early September 1997, Eric Alpert filed another affidavit. Included in the information set forth was the story of Tom's obsessive revenge against Linda Marandola, which had been reported to the FBI by an informant in 1980. Now the public knew that Anne Marie Fahey was not the first woman Tom had stalked. Members of the Delaware Supreme Court's Censure Committee hastened to say that they had never been informed of the Marandola matter. But one member *had* been, and he happened to have been one of Tom's bosses at Morris, James, Hitchens & Williams at the time of the complaint. Seventeen years later, he had no comment about the matter.

The FBI seized Tom's E-mail. In doing so the investigators talked to the woman in charge of the computers at Saul, Ewing and learned that Tom had asked her a few days after Anne Marie vanished if his E-mail had been destroyed. He had been somewhat dismayed, according to the witness, to learn that it had not.

The balance of public opinion in Wilmington was tipping. Tom resigned from Saul, Ewing without giving a reason.

WHATEVER Tom had done during the day after Anne Marie vanished, he apparently spent much of it with Gerry. In their strategy sessions, Connolly, Donovan, and Alpert had come to believe that the missing components of the case probably rested deep in the bosom of the Capano family. They had learned the Capano credo: *Family was family.* Louie, Joey, and Gerry had good reason to revere their older brother—none more than Gerry; Tom had bailed them all out of trouble, and now, perhaps, it had been their turn.

Gerry Capano's name had stood out in the time line Tom wrote for Friday, June 28, 1996. His name appeared opposite five items: *6:30, 10:30–11:00, 12:30+, 12:30–1:30,* and *3:00.* And for *9:15–10:30,* Tom had written, "drive to SH." "SH" had to be Stone Harbor. Gerry had a house and a boat there. Of all the Capano family, he was the one who spent the most time at Stone Harbor.

Gerry still had the cherubic features that had once made him such a cute little kid, but his avocations were all so macho that one wondered if he was still trying to prove himself to his older brothers. When he wasn't hunting grizzly bears and moose in the great Northwest in the winter, he competed in shark-fishing derbies in the Atlantic Ocean off Stone Harbor. He had neither his brothers' business acumen nor their cleverness.

Joey wasn't mentioned in Tom's notes. But the trio of investigators suspected that Gerry and Louie might well have fallen on their swords to protect Tom—as long as their swords weren't too sharp. Both of them had a great deal to lose and they were vulnerable, Gerry perhaps more than Louie.

With the first-year anniversary of Anne Marie's disappearance near at hand, it was obvious that some pressure had to be exerted on Gerry and Louie. They were clearly not willing to talk without some incentive. Of course, there wouldn't be any way to lean on either of them unless they had Achilles' heels when it came to the law.

Louie had had trouble in the past with illegal campaign contributions and bribery of public officials, and his financial dealings were very intricate when it came to the IRS. A multimillionaire, he was a brilliant real estate and construction entrepreneur but he had been known to grease wheels when it came to zoning and building permits. Tom's diplomacy and connections had allowed Louie to walk away with few repercussions, but he probably had been left with some anxiety about the government's interest in his business dealings.

Louie was called back before the grand jury and asked countless questions. Both his business and his personal life were suffering. All unwittingly, his wife and his son, his only child, had become involved in the aftermath of Anne Marie's disappearance. If Louie was stonewalling the government to protect Tom, he was also putting his immediate family at risk.

Gerry Capano's activities were even more suspect. His drug use was common knowledge, some of his close friends had prison records, and Gerry collected weapons the way some men accumulate baseball cards. Any one of these preferences could put him and those around him in jeopardy with the law. Intelligence said that Gerry was still the spoiled kid in the Capano family, the bad little boy. In his cups, he had ruined many a holiday and reduced his mother to tears. When he wasn't drinking or drugging, Gerry was likable, but he wasn't smooth and he wasn't brilliant. His judgment had never been very good, and he had the Capano instinct to look after his own.

Gerry looked like the weakest link in the chain the family had erected to protect Tom. Maybe Tom had drawn Gerry into his own dark plan because he knew that more than anyone else his little brother was malleable.

Given Gerry's proclivities, Connolly and Alpert contacted the ATF (Alcohol, Tobacco and Firearms) agency. Diane Iardella, an ATF agent and her husband, Doug, a Wilmington police detective, joined the investigation. Both of the agencies they worked for had had reason to look suspiciously at Gerry's activities. Now, because Tom Capano was under suspicion, the rest of his family were drawn into the probe. The "feds" would watch Gerry's activities and apply pressure if he broke any laws. The Iardellas added much to the team.

When they weren't at their half-million-dollar beach house in Stone Harbor, Gerry and his wife, Michelle, lived in a beautiful home on Emma Court in Brandywine Hundred. On the night of Wednesday, October 8, 1997, there was a loud knocking at their door. A federal search warrant was about to be executed; the warrant specified that authorities had reason to suspect they would find evidence of three crimes: possession of cocaine, distribution of cocaine or possession with intent to distribute, and possession of a firearm by a drug user. The ATF agents did not come away empty handed. In an unlocked gun safe in one of the children's bedrooms, they found ten shotguns, four rifles, four revolvers, and eight "illegal explosive devices."

They located two more revolvers and another shotgun in the dining room. They also verified Gerry's possession of drugs. Field testing established that there was cocaine in his truck and a Baggie with cocaine in the laundry room cupboard (along with a rolled-up dollar bill and a credit card with powder residue on the washing machine). There was marijuana in the laundry room and in a tool chest in the garage. A guest—Gerry's business partner—had both cocaine and marijuana on his person.

Carrying out the search warrant verified that Gerry had broken the law that forbids a drug user to possess guns. He couldn't have looked more guilty of the crimes they suspected unless he had had white powder clinging to his nose and a bandolier around his chest. Even so, Gerry could find legal arguments that would tend to cut down the sentence he would receive. He could claim, at least half truthfully, that he used the weapons for lawful hunting and sporting, and that he collected them as a hobby. A conviction on such a gun charge could bring him about six months in jail. And in point of fact, the raid had not unearthed much weight in the illegal drugs found.

A week later, however, the federal agents raided Ed Del Collo's house and found another gun. Del Collo was Gerry's best friend, but he was also a convicted felon. And convicted felons are not permitted to own guns. A check of the serial numbers showed that Gerry had purchased the gun for Ed. He had broken another federal law; he had not only transferred guns, he had purchased them for a convicted felon. Furthermore, he could not argue that all the guns he'd ever possessed were for lawful hunting and sporting purposes.

Now Gerry was looking at three years or more in prison.

A week later, the Division of Family Services began an investigation of Gerry and Michelle's suitability as parents. Authorities were concerned that their children, both toddlers, were living surrounded by guns and drugs.

Some time earlier, Tom had stepped in to help Gerry and said he should consult an attorney, even telling his little brother whom to call. Gerry did, and his lawyers suggested that the federal agents were raiding his home solely to force him to implicate his brother in a murder investigation.

Interestingly, Joe Hurley, Tom's attorney, distanced his client from the raid. He didn't want Tom's image soiled by the mention of drugs and an arsenal of weapons. Hurley told reporters that he wasn't surprised that Colm Connolly had been involved in the gun and drug investigation. "That is a small office over there," Hurley said, thus dismissing the Delaware U.S. Attorney's office as pretty small potatoes.

Connolly had no comment.

Gerry's attorney called Connolly often now, asking if Gerry should come in for questioning. "We kept saying, 'We're not ready for him yet.' We acted as if we weren't that anxious to talk to him," Connolly said. "We said, we're not going to bring him in—to borrow a line from *The Godfather*—until we had an offer he couldn't refuse."

They would let Gerry sweat until he would have no choice but to tell them the truth. If their hunch was right, Gerry was the most vulnerable in the Capano dynasty and quite possibly the one who had the information they needed to move in on Tom.

_____ *Chapter Thirty* _____

THANKSGIVING WAS APPROACHING and the Faheys faced another holiday season without knowing what had become of their sister. The flyers with Anne Marie's picture on them were still out there, but they were weathered now, faded by the summer sun and winter storms. It didn't seem possible that a person who was loved so much could simply disappear off the face of the earth and never be found. But Anne Marie had.

And then, like the first pebbles of a massive rock slide, it began. All of the digging at the underpinnings of the Capanos had weakened the family loyalty that heretofore had overridden everything. Loyalty, usually an admirable trait, is not always a good thing—not when it is blind and when the object of that loyalty is undeserving.

On Saturday, November 8, 1997, and by agreement, a perspiring and nervous Gerry Capano appeared at the IRS office building with his attorney Dan Lyons. Because reporters were watching Connolly's office and the Wilmington Police Department, Ron Poplos had offered the use of his office. The IRS building was off the beaten path, north of Wilmington. The government probers hoped they could interview Gerry without having it turned into a media event.

Colm Connolly, Eric Alpert, and Bob Donovan had waited a long time to hear what Gerry had to say. Along with Poplos and the Iardellas, they were basically the entire investigative team and they had worked on a shoestring budget for seventeen months to solve a case that many said was unsolvable. This interview could turn out to be what they had been waiting for.

As they questioned Gerry, they had some idea of what they were about to hear. They had come to believe that Tom had been with Gerry on the day after Anne Marie Fahey vanished. One neighbor they talked to in Stone Harbor thought he had recognized Tom and seen Kay's Suburban parked around the corner for several hours in the middle of the day.

They believed that Gerry might know where Anne Marie's body was—and if they were lucky, he might even be able to shed some light on what had driven Tom to commit murder. But they were unprepared for the whole story, a story that revealed the modus operandi of a man as cold as death itself.

It was four in the afternoon. Shadows fell across the barren boughs of the trees in Rodney Square, where people huddled together waiting for buses to take them home. It was hard to believe that two years before, Anne Marie's November calendar had been full of happy times with Mike. So much had changed.

Gerry had not come forward with an open heart; before he agreed to have his formal statement taped, he had signed a plea bargain with the government that would save him from prison. But he also asked for protection from prosecution for his sister, Marian, and her husband, Lee Ramunno, and his mother. He wasn't sure how many people in his family might be holding back information from the government.

For the record, Connolly began by discussing the terms of the plea bargain. "You understand," he said, "you are agreeing to plead guilty to misprision of a felony—the felony being kidnapping—and in return, the government is entering a plea agreement with you, which has a stipulated sentence of three years' probation? And you understand that any statement you make has got to be the truth, the whole truth, and nothing but the truth, correct?"

Gerry said yes to all the stipulations. He gave Tom's address—which was Marguerite's Weldin Road home—and his own on Emma Court. He was ready now to tell them of how Tom had come to him in trouble long before Anne Marie Fahey disappeared, about how he was worried for Tom and his family.

"Now," Connolly said, "isn't it true that sometime around February of 1996, your brother, Thomas Capano, asked you to borrow some money?"

"Yes, he did . . . $8,000."

"Did he tell you why he needed to borrow that money?"

"Yes, he said that two people were extorting him . . . a girl and a guy."

"OK. And the girl—did he say that he had had a relationship with her?"

"No."

"Did he describe her as crazy or anything?"

"Yes."

"Did he have any subsequent conversation with you in which he told you what this woman and her boyfriend were attempting to do to him?"

"To ruin his career."

Gerry explained that he had lent Tom the $8,000, and that sometime between February and June, Tom had asked to borrow a gun. Gerry had first offered him a shotgun. "He told me he was afraid for his life," Gerry said; "that he was afraid he was gonna get beaten up by this girl's boyfriend if he didn't pay them the money."

"Did he take a gun from you?"

"Yes . . ."

"What kind of gun?"

"It was a ten-millimeter."

Gerry said he had shown Tom how to use the handgun, which he had given to him unloaded. But when Tom gave it back to him sometime later, it hadn't been fired. It was in the same condition it had been when he'd taken it.

"Now," Connolly asked, "during this conversation when he asked you to borrow a gun, isn't it true that he also asked you if you knew a person that could 'help him out'? Didn't he ask you if you knew anybody who could break somebody's legs?"

"Yes . . . I told him yes, that I might. I talked to a friend of mine and nothing ever came out of it."

"Now, isn't it also true that sometime between February 1996 and June 28, 1996, your brother Thomas told you that if this woman—this woman he had spoken about—hurt his kids, he was going to kill her?"

"Yes, because she had threatened him several times about hurting the kids at the bus stop or doing something else to them."

"Isn't it also true that during this time frame he made a request to you about using your boat?"

"He said that if this girl or this guy hurt his kids, and he killed them, could he use the boat? And I didn't—I just blew it off 'cause I didn't think he was serious. I just thought he was blowing off steam."

"And that's why you never went to law enforcement authorities?"

"That's right."

Asked to recall the circumstances at 6 A.M. on June 28, Gerry said he had walked out of his house on Emma Court that morning to find his brother's black Jeep parked in his driveway. Surprised, he had walked up to the passenger-side window and peered in. Tom was sitting there, reading the morning paper.

"What did your brother say to you?"

"He said, 'Can you get hold of the boat?' "

"And what did you say?"

"I said, 'Did you do it?' "

"And by that, what did you mean?"

"He'd either killed the girl or the guy who was threatening to hurt his kids."

"And what did your brother Thomas say in response?"

"He nodded."

"Did he ask if you could help him?"

"Yes he did . . . I told him I didn't want to get involved, that I had a beautiful wife and kids and a great life and I didn't want to ruin my life."

"What did he say?"

"He said, 'Don't leave me cold—don't leave me flat. I need you, bro.' Stuff like that."

Tom had suggested that he could use Gerry's boat by himself, but Gerry said he'd refused. Tom didn't know anything about boats. "No way" did he have the experience to do that. So Gerry had agreed to help Tom get rid of the body of the "extortionist" he had killed. They agreed to meet at Tom's house on North Grant Avenue.

"When you went into the garage at Grant Avenue, what did you see?"

"I saw a cooler and a rolled-up rug."

The rug had been long, Gerry recalled, about three-quarters the size of the garage, and the cooler was big. "It looked to be about four feet long by two feet wide," Gerry said.

"Was there anything unusual about the cooler?"

"There was a chain wrapped around the cooler." Gerry added that the chain looked new and had a lock on it.

Gerry said that he and Tom had taken the cooler to his house in Stone Harbor, and from there onto his fishing boat, *Summer Wind.* He remembered that it was very heavy and he heard ice rattling inside it. A Styrofoam cooler wouldn't have attracted much attention at the shore; many fishermen used such coolers to keep fish on ice.

And then Gerry said he had steered the boat out into the Atlantic Ocean.

"About how far out?" Connolly asked.

"I would say about seventy miles. Somewhere between sixty and seventy-five miles. I would have to look at the chart."

"How deep was the water there?"

"Hundred and ninety-eight feet."

"What did your brother do?"

"Lifted the cooler up and put it in the water."

"Did the cooler sink?"

"No."

"What did you do with it—because it wouldn't sink?"

"Took my shark gun out and shot it once with a deer slug, and it still wouldn't sink."

"What did your brother do then?"

"I maneuvered the boat back to where the cooler was floating."

"Did you help your brother move it next to the boat?"

Gerry firmly said no. He had turned the boat's motor off and told Tom he was on his own. Then he had walked to the front of the boat, given Tom two anchors, and turned his back on what was happening so that he didn't have to watch.

"I was telling him this was really wrong," Gerry offered.

"But were you able to determine what he was doing by the sounds?" Connolly asked.

"Yes . . . seems to me like he was opening up the cooler, fighting with the rope [chain] and the tide—and throwing up—and tying the anchors to something."

"Did you eventually turn around?"

"When I asked him if he was finished."

"And then you turned around and what did you see?"

"I saw a foot sinking into the deep."

"And it was a human foot?"

"Yes."

"Did you see anything besides the foot?"

"Only a little bit, a little bit of calf."

"Did you see any blood?"

"A little blood coming out of the cooler."

"Did you know what was in the cooler?"

"I assumed what was in it."

"What did you assume?"

"I assumed it was one of these persons who had threatened to hurt his kids."

Everyone in the room, including Gerry Capano, knew now who had been in that cooler, but no one said it aloud.

Gerry said that he and Tom had taken the cooler apart while they were out in the ocean. They had thrown the top and bottom into the sea separately as they cruised back to Stone Harbor, and then drove back to Wilmington.

There, Tom had asked Gerry to help him move a sofa, a dark maroon sofa that was in the great room.

"Was there blood on the sofa?"

"There was a stain—he [Tom] said he had cleaned it. I said, 'You better cut a piece out of it before you throw the sofa away.' "

Then they broke an arm off the sofa so it would look damaged enough to be discarded. They could see there was blood on the foam beneath, but they found very little had penetrated.

"Where was the blood on the couch?"

"On the top right-hand side, [about where somebody's] shoulder would be."

And then they had put the damaged sofa in Kay's Suburban and taken it to the Dumpster at Capano & Sons. All that remained at Tom's house of whatever had happened was the rolled-up carpet in the garage. Gerry had seen only the outside of that; he couldn't tell them what color it was or if there were bloodstains on it.

Gerry said Tom had given him a story to tell if he was ever questioned. Once he left Tom, he wrote it down on a Post-it and stuck it in his wallet so he would remember, but in the end, he hadn't used it. He was telling the truth.

THE moment that Gerry Capano confessed that Tom had dumped a cooler in the Atlantic Ocean, Eric Alpert and Bob Donovan remembered an item on Tom's credit card bill. They had seen it when they were poring over the bills looking for charges that might be relevant. But it didn't seem particularly important that Tom had bought a Styrofoam cooler at the Sports Authority on Saturday afternoon, April 20, at 3:15, using his MasterCard. It was an Igloo 162-quart marine cooler and it cost $194.84 with tax. At the time, they knew Tom had no boat.

"I think it didn't mean too much then," Alpert recalled, "because we were looking for items around June twenty-seventh—and this was pretty remote in time." But now the fact that Tom had bought a huge cooler no longer seemed remote or irrelevant.

They had broken the back of the case, but there was little jubilation for Connolly, Donovan, Poplos, and Alpert. The woman they had come to know better, perhaps, than anyone they had known in life had been carried out to sea and dumped in Mako Alley, where the sharks prowled. It was a horrible thought. They still didn't know *how* Anne Marie had died. But now it looked as if Tom Capano had not simply lost it in a burst of jealous rage. He had been carrying out a well-organized plan. He had apparently set up a scenario about extortionists way back in February, a good four months before Anne Marie vanished. *All those months . . .*

Had Tom known what day he would kill her? Or had he kept his dark strategy in abeyance to use as a contingency plan? Would it have come into play at any point when he became convinced that he could no longer bend Anne Marie to his will and make her come back to him? For some reason, June 27 appeared to have been Tom Capano's day of decision. Bolstered with newfound confidence that she had the right to choose whom she would love, Anne Marie had, all unaware, finally convinced Tom she didn't want to be with him.

The cooler was gone in the Atlantic Ocean, the couch was buried beneath hundreds of layers of garbage. Only the cruel game plan remained, something Tom had surely never expected would be revealed. Only two people had ever balked at the role he had cast them in; one was Linda Marandola and the other was Anne Marie Fahey.

THE house that Lou Capano had built so proudly was crumbling. Two days after Gerry's confession—on Monday, November 10— Louie Capano appeared at the IRS building with his attorney Catherine Recker. He too signed a plea agreement. Admitting that he had lied to the grand jury out of his allegiance to Tom and his belief in his brother's innocence, Louie agreed to tell everything he knew about the death of Anne Marie Fahey and plead guilty to tampering with a witness in exchange for a sentence of one year's probation.

Louie said he had no knowledge of what had happened until Tom called him on Sunday morning, June 30, 1996, and asked him to come over. When he arrived at North Grant Avenue, Tom told him that the police had shown up in the middle of the night and that he was very upset.

"He told me that he had had a relationship with Anne Marie Fahey," Louie said. "And that she was anorectic and bulimic and a troubled person—that he had stopped seeing her and he didn't want his wife, Kay, to find out about their relationship. He also told me that after he had dinner with her that evening [June 27], they went back to his house. While he was upstairs using the bathroom—when he came down—she had slit her wrists and had gotten blood, a superficial amount of blood, on the sofa."

Tom had explained that he and Gerry had gotten rid of the sofa in the company's Dumpster on Foulk Road, and asked Louie to have it dumped. "After the conversation with my brother," Louie said, "I went up to the job. We had men working, and I was curious and looked in the Dumpster behind the building. I saw what looked to be like a sofa, turned upside down, and I saw the legs."

He meant the *sofa's* legs; he said he hadn't seen any sign of a body. He'd made a mental note to have the Dumpster emptied, but it slipped his mind.

It had not slipped Tom's mind. Louie said he had called on Monday morning to ask if it had been dumped yet. "I told him no," Louie said, "but that I would have them dumped."

"Did he tell you what had caused him some concern on Monday morning?"

"Anne Marie Fahey had not shown up for work," Louie said.

"He was concerned that the police might start looking around and could get the Dumpsters."

At that point, Louie said he believed Tom to be innocent of any crime against Anne Marie Fahey. Tom had done a good job of convincing him she was a very disturbed and impetuous young woman who would show up in her own good time.

Louie said that sometime later he had asked Tom why the carpet in his great room was gone. Was that bloody too? "He told me he had disposed of some carpet at the Holiday Inn over in New Jersey. It was cut up and put into plastic bags."

The Capanos happened to own that particular Holiday Inn, and Tom told Louie he had asked the manager to have their Dumpsters emptied early, too.

"Did Tom tell you he had put other items besides a sofa in your Dumpsters at 105 Foulk Road?"

"Yes. He told me that he put [in] some of Anne Marie Fahey's personal belongings and a gun."

They might have known. Tom had been punctilious about erasing every sign that Anne Marie had ever been to his home, much less died there. He wouldn't have risked keeping a gun around. They had no idea what kind of gun it was; he had given the ten-millimeter back to Gerry. But a check of gun sale records might turn up someone close to Tom—or even Tom himself—who had purchased a gun around the time Anne Marie disappeared. It would be a tedious process, but if someone had given his real name when he purchased a gun, they could find it.

Louie recalled a conversation he had had with Tom prior to his own grand jury testimony on August 29, 1996. Tom had been living at Louie's Greenville mansion after he moved out of the blighted North Grant Avenue house.

"I was just getting out of the shower—it was the morning of my testimony—and he came in and basically asked me to provide him an alibi for Friday morning—[to say] that he had come to visit me on Friday, June twenty-eighth."

Tom had suggested a script for Louie to follow, even though he would be committing perjury. "I would say that he just put personal belongings in there [the Dumpster] because he didn't want his wife, Kay, to know he was having a relationship with Anne Marie Fahey."

"Did he say anything about the sofa?" Connolly asked.

"He told me not to say it was in there."

As Louie's testimony continued, it became apparent that all

three of Tom's brothers had some knowledge of what had happened to Anne Marie, and that they had covered up for him.

"Do you recall a conversation you had with your brother Joseph Capano in the winter of 1997?" Connolly asked.

"It was a very brief conversation in Florida—at the pool. I just asked him if he had taken care of the anchor. And he told me that he had—meaning that he had replaced one of the anchors that was on my brother Gerry's boat."

"And how did you know anything about an anchor to ask this question of Joe?"

"My brother Gerry told me that my brother Tom used an anchor on his boat to get rid of the cooler."

Louie remembered walking in the street in front of Gerry's house on Emma Court sometime in November 1996. Gerry had been unable to keep the ugly secret any longer, and he had confessed to Louie that Tom had come to him looking for a gun, and "anybody who could break somebody's bones."

Louie continued haltingly. "And . . . he told me that he took my brother Tom out on a boat in Stone Harbor and disposed of Anne Marie Fahey's body."

"And did Gerry also tell you about a conversation that he and Tom had before June twenty-eighth—that Tom had made a request of him?"

"Yeah. Tom had said to him that he had been blackmailed by this woman, et cetera, and—if he killed her, could he just go for a boat ride with Gerry . . . Gerry didn't believe Tommy was serious."

THE government team warned both Gerry and Louie not to tell anyone that they had made statements about Anne Marie's murder. If Tom knew that his world was about to come down around him, there was no telling what he might do. He was a man with so many masks that even those closest to him seemed not to know him. He had threatened to commit suicide in the past. He certainly had the wherewithal to leave the country if he chose to run.

The FBI put a twenty-four-hour-a-day surveillance on Tom on November 10, 1997. Eric Alpert carried a radio tuned to the surveillance team's frequency with him all the time. Early on Wednesday morning, November 12, his radio crackled. "Capano's at his brother Joey's house," the agent told him. "They're loading suitcases into his Jeep."

Connolly was in the grand jury room, where Gerry and Louie

were repeating the information they had already given, and Alpert paged him urgently. When Connolly was in the hallway, he told him that it looked as though Tom was going to make a run for it. He was in a car, heading toward Philadelphia.

They agreed the time had come for an arrest. Connolly said it was important to stop Tom's vehicle before he crossed the Delaware state line into Pennsylvania. If he was arrested there, he would be taken before a magistrate and the whole process delayed. Alpert told the agents following Tom's Jeep Cherokee along I-95 to move in. He was apparently oblivious to the government cars that were tracking him. Tom was signaled over, and FBI agents surrounded his car and told him he was under arrest for the murder of Anne Marie.

"I heard the sirens over the radio," Alpert recalled. "I knew they had him."

And Tom was still in Delaware. The arresting agents reported that he had not resisted as they cuffed his hands in front of him. He appeared to be resigned, as if he was expecting to be arrested.

Ironically, Tom hadn't been going anywhere. Casually dressed in a navy blue jogging suit, he was only driving Joey and his wife, Joanne, to the airport, where they could catch a plane to Fort Lauderdale. He had planned to turn around and head home. He had promised Debby that he would cook a steak dinner for her that night. "He said we'd have a really romantic evening," she remembered, "because I was leaving for Italy the next morning." Instead, she heard the news that Tom had been arrested.

Tom was driven to the U.S. Attorney's office on the eleventh floor of the Chase Manhattan building, in custody before word flashed like a forest fire over the media's network. Almost immediately, reporters took up vantage points as close as they could get to the U.S. Attorney's office.

Tom had aged in triple time over the seventeen months since Anne Marie had vanished. The skin beneath his eyes was mottled and purple. But head held high, he seemed to ignore the cuffs on his wrists as if they had nothing to do with him. As he was led into the conference room, Tom's heart may have skipped a few beats; a 162-quart Igloo cooler sat there. It wasn't the real cooler, but Connolly had had Bob Donovan shoot into it in the spot Gerry specified in his affidavit. An anchor and a lock and chain rested near the cooler. No one mentioned the items as Tom walked by.

Colm Connolly hadn't really spoken to Tom since that day in September when they had first met in the hall outside the grand jury room. Now he remembered what Tom had hissed at him that day.

"The day Tom was arrested," Connolly recalled, "he was brought in here to a conference room and an agent sat with him. I went in to tell him that his attorneys would be coming shortly. I started to shut the door, and then I opened it back up and I said, 'By the way, Mr. Capano, I sleep very well at night.' "

Tom let out a deep breath and put his head in his arms. For the moment, the arrogance that was such a central part of him had vanished. It had felt good to say that, but a half hour later, thinking better of his remark, Connolly came back and softened his words. Tom was sitting with his attorneys as Connolly said, "I don't want you to think this is a personal thing. Because it isn't."

It was and it wasn't. Connolly, along with Bob Donovan and Eric Alpert, had kept their promises to Anne Marie's family to find her killer. And they believed they had done that. Starting out, they had had no way of knowing who he—or she—was. Tom Capano had never cooperated with the investigation. And they were a long way, still, from proving his guilt in a court of law. Facts rather than personal feelings were all that mattered.

With his lawyers beside him, Tom had regained his composure. He looked at the man who had pursued him almost a year and a half and spoke to him as if they were old friends, as if he had done nothing wrong.

"But Colm," he said softly, "it was my *daughters.*"

What did he mean? Was he referring to the story about extortionists threatening his four girls—or was he simply explaining that he had struck out at Connolly because he'd subpoenaed Christy to testify before a grand jury?

Bob Donovan was in that conference room and so was Eric Alpert. Tom was told that the government had statements taken from his brothers Louie and Gerry that described the way he had disposed of a body.

"You *believe* them?" Tom said to no one in particular, incredulity in his voice.

In answer, Connolly played the tapes of his brothers' statements for Tom. He listened, stone faced.

"We know," Connolly said, "that Mr. Capano purchased a 162-quart marine cooler on April 20, 1996. And we know he is neither a hunter nor a fisherman."

"Yeah," Tom said knowingly, "but my brothers are."

STROBES flashed as Tom was led, still in handcuffs, to a van to be taken to Gander Hill, the prison over which he had once had authority, the prison he had helped build when he worked for Governor Castle. But now he would be only another inmate in a white uniform. He would spend his first night in the infirmary—standard for new prisoners.

Tom would have to be in lockdown for his personal safety. Former cops, prosecutors, and public officials are never popular in prison. Alone in his cell, he would have fewer privileges than the inmates in the general population. But his jailers wondered if perhaps there were some among the seventeen hundred prisoners who remembered the billboards and the flyers with the picture of a pretty Irish girl—the young woman who the papers had said had wanted only to be free of the man who was now one of them.

Charlie Oberly and Joe Hurley told reporters that, of course, Tom would plead not guilty. They managed to suggest that it was utterly ridiculous that he had been arrested. But for the moment, the man who loved luxury and fine dining was nobody special. The cuisine on his first long day of captivity was hardly Villa d' Roma or Toscana fare: cereal and chipped beef for breakfast, Texas hash for lunch, and liver and onions for dinner.

At O'Friel's Irish Pub, there was a subdued gathering, marked more by tears than laughter. Someone asked Kevin Freel if he was going to take down the massive yellow ribbons tied there for Anne Marie, and he said slowly, "I haven't even thought about that, yet."

Already there were rumors that Annie had been dumped in the sea and would never have a proper burial beside her mother and her father, close to Kate McGettigan. For a Catholic, that was a terrible thing. For anyone, that was a terrible thing.

Kevin kept remembering the sight of her, snowflakes caught in her hair, beautiful Annie with her feet planted on the worn wooden floor, grinning mischievously at him as she roared "KEV-EEEE!"

It was too hard to know that she would never come again.

PART FOUR

And much of Madness, and more of Sin,
And Horror the soul of the plot.

EDGAR ALLAN POE

_____ *Chapter Thirty-one* _____

WITH HIS ARREST, Tom not only lost much of his own personal luster—he severely smudged the image that his father had fought so hard to maintain: *Louis Capano & Sons,* honest, hard-working, united. Now there were many in Wilmington who were glad that Lou had not lived to see what his family had come to. Some of the Capanos might rise again, but would they ever be rid of the shame, the innuendo, and the rumors? And it had all just begun. Tom's murder trial lay ahead.

Louie hadn't lost his cool when he was questioned by the government investigators, but Gerry was a basket case, in tears much of the time because he had betrayed Tom. Louie's attorneys prepared a press release that appeared in most area papers on November 12, 1997, hard on the heels of Tom's arrest:

Louis Capano, Jr. voluntarily contacted federal authorities and provided information and cooperation which has led, in part, to the arrest of his brother, Thomas Capano. . . . Louis Capano had no direct knowledge of his brother's actions, but rather has provided information regarding events following the disappearance of Anne Marie Fahey. . . . Louis Capano did certain things during the course of the investigation which he now regrets. . . . Louis admits he misled the authorities but did so motivated by belief in his brother's innocence. . . . The picture of Thomas Capano portrayed by these charges and evidence is completely foreign to the brother Louis thought he knew.

Tom's whole family would be caught by the ubiquitous cameras and by reporters who dragged their personal lives into the public domain. If Tom's arrest did nothing else, it seemed to strengthen his brothers' marriages. Joanne, Lauri, and Michelle stood solidly behind Joey, Louie, and Gerry. Marian and Lee had always presented a strong front to the world. But the family itself broke into pieces. Marguerite could not forgive Louie and Gerry for what they had done to Tommy. She did not understand how they could have betrayed their brother. In his mother's eyes, Tommy had been through so much, and now his own flesh and blood had turned on him. Father Balducelli was concerned about Marguerite; she had a bad heart and other health problems, and seeing her favorite son in chains just might kill her.

Although Marguerite had always looked askance at Debby MacIntyre, they were in accord now; neither woman would accept that Tom was guilty of murder. It was unthinkable. On vacation in Rome, Debby was saved from the worst of the media hoopla. There, for the moment, she could almost forget the way things were steadily growing worse at home. But she would have to come back to Wilmington and see the man she loved, the man who had pledged to marry her, diminished and locked away from her. She didn't think she could bear it.

JUST as there are said to be no atheists in foxholes, there are few professionals in law enforcement who will deny that they sometimes receive help from invisible allies, perhaps angels sent to earth to avenge the cruelest crimes. Only a day after Tom Capano was arrested, the Wilmington investigators would receive a piece of physical evidence that no law of probability could have predicted.

"I think we worked awfully hard, yes," Colm Connolly said, "but there were a lot of *lucky* things—or maybe divine things—that happened. At some point, you have to wonder . . ."

On November 13, the media was filled with the details of Tom's arrest and Gerry's statement. Bob Donovan and Eric Alpert were sitting in Alpert's office when a secretary told him there was someone calling about a cooler.

"I watched Alpert pick up the phone," Donovan recalled, "and all of a sudden his face changed, and he was frantically scribbling down notes."

"There was this guy on the phone," Alpert elaborated. "I wasn't too enthused when he said his friend had found a cooler in the ocean more than a year earlier. But then I asked him if there was anything distinctive about it. And he said that it didn't have a lid when the guy found it. I motioned Donovan over at that point. And then the guy said, 'Well, it has a bullet hole in it.' That was all it took—Bob and I were out of the office and on our way."

If it was *the* cooler, it would be a miracle. After a year and a half, the cooler they needed for trial should have been in Cuba; given the tides, the wind, and a dozen different variables, there was simply no way that a cooler discarded 60 miles out into the Atlantic Ocean could ever have drifted to within a few miles of the Delaware shore. Alpert and Donovan didn't really believe that it could be the same cooler. Even so, they nudged the speed limit as they headed south toward Smyrna, where the caller, Ron Smith, lived. Smith told the investigators that he had been reading newspaper coverage of Tom Capano's arrest when something struck a chord in his memory. He said that a fellow fisherman named Ken Chubb, whom he knew from his summer place down on the Delaware Coast, had found something in the ocean.

"I was working on my boat the day Chubb pulled in," Smith continued. "He said, 'Hey, take a look at this!' and I said, 'Take a look at *what?*' and he shows me this cooler he found."

Alpert and Donovan held their breaths when Smith said the cooler had no lid. And he and Chubb had agreed about the source of the holes that marred the back. "I said, 'Yeah, they were bullet holes,'" Smith told them. "I hunt deer. I do target practice. I know what bullet holes look like. As a matter of fact, I stuck my finger in one. It was made by a twelve-gauge shotgun."

"When did this happen?" Alpert asked.

Smith had perfect recall. But more important, he could validate times and dates. He had already called Chubb to ask when he'd found the cooler and learned it was during the Fourth of July weekend of 1996. By checking his own gas receipts, he was able to confirm the date when he'd first seen the cooler. That weekend was seven to ten days from the time Tom Capano had reportedly dumped Anne Marie's body and the cooler far out at sea. The information about the bullet holes and the missing lid had never been in the newspapers. Smith drew Alpert and Donovan a map to Ken

Chubb's beach house. "The cooler's there in his shed, behind his trailer. He knows you're coming."

Ken Chubb had been fishing off Rehoboth Bay for ten years, and he told Alpert and Donovan he thought he'd made a lucky find a year and a half earlier when his son said, "I see something floating over there, Dad!"

When he eased his boat over the white object, they found it was a cooler—missing a handle and its lid. "It had two bullet holes in it," Chubb recalled. "And it sort of amazed us all. We were questioning, wondering why anybody would shoot it. Looked like a brand-new cooler."

"Did you notice anything on the inside of the cooler?" Alpert asked.

"It had a stain on it."

"What kind of stain?"

"Sort of a pinkish-looking stain on the bottom. It's not unusual for a fish cooler, you know, because fish bleed."

Chubb said it was the same size as the battered cooler he had been using. "I thought, well, I can take the top off of mine and the handle, and I'll convert this one, patch them two holes, and I can make myself a nice cooler."

And he had done that, using two of the rusted screws from his old cooler and two new ones still in the hinge of the cooler he'd found. He filled the bullet holes with fiberglass. "I've used it ever since to hold the fish I catch," Chubb said, and he'd been surprised when Ron Smith called and told him that the police were looking for the cooler.

Alpert and Donovan carried their unexpected treasure back to the evidence lab. It looked like any large Styrofoam cooler, but it wasn't. Like almost everything else manufactured, it had marks of identification. When they checked with the Igloo company in Houston, Texas, they learned that it was a somewhat limited production item. In 1997, the company had made 7,797 of them, and a similar number in 1996. All large coolers had a bar code that meant something to the company and the stores that sold them. The number 034223 signified it was an Igloo product. And 08162 showed it was the 162-quart model. Moreover, there was a date code stamped into the bottom of the cooler, a little clock face with arrows pointing to the month and year. This cooler had come off the assembly line in May 1993.

But more important, the bar codes on the coolers identified the stores where they were purchased. When the bar code for this cooler was entered into the computer of the Sports Authority store on the Rocky Run Parkway across from the Concord Mall in Wilmington, it matched the store's code for a 162-quart Igloo cooler.

The investigators already knew that Tom had purchased an Igloo cooler there on April 20, two months before Anne Marie vanished. Short of saying this was the *exact* cooler, it was a match. But how that cooler made its way almost to the Delaware shore from far out in the ocean was something no one could explain.

FOR a year and a half, the case against Tom Capano had seemed to go forward with agonizing slowness. Now it accelerated. On November 14, Delaware attorney general Jane Brady assigned Ferris Wharton to prosecute the case. Colm Connolly was cross-designated not only as an assistant U.S. attorney but as co-counsel with Wharton in the Delaware State prosecution. They were nothing at all alike, but they were naturals together. Alpert and Donovan would stay on as investigators.

Of the four of them, three were native-born Wilmingtonians. Only Alpert was an "outsider," having been raised in Alabama. Wharton had left Delaware long enough to get his degree from the University of Illinois College of Law, and of course, Connolly had traveled half the world before returning.

Wharton had served as a deputy attorney general since 1980; he was the chief prosecutor in New Castle County until 1997 and became a state prosecutor thereafter. He had vast experience with murder cases, and it was somewhat ironic that he had had to be completely shut out of the investigation during the federal grand jury process. During his eighteen years with the Attorney General's Office, Wharton had been in charge of the Trial Unit, the Drug Unit, and the Rape Response Unit of Delaware's highest legal office. He was voted the best criminal prosecutor in the state by *Delaware Today* magazine's lawyers' poll in 1996.

Wharton's roster of murder trials was extraordinary and included the dismemberment murder of a Baltimore city police officer by his wife, herself a former police officer; the murder of Marie Kisner by David Dawson, an escaped prisoner; the double murder of Joseph and Beverly Gibson and the abduction of their infant son by Joyce Lynch; the murder of a north Wilmington couple in their home after they had tried to protect their daughter from Lonnie Williams, who unsuccessfully blamed his crimes on his multiple personality disorder; the rape/murder of an eight-year-old girl by Keith Thompson, who had kidnapped her from her grandmother's home and abandoned her body at a construction dump site; and the death of four-year-old Bryan Martin, forced by his mother, Carol Albanese, to drink the mouthwash that killed him. Of the eighteen people waiting on death row in Delaware, five of them were Wharton's.

But he had remained outside the investigation of Anne Marie's disappearance for almost a year and a half. "I only knew what I read in the paper," he said. "Just what anyone in Delaware might know—until the arrest was made."

If Tom had two of the best criminal defense attorneys in the region—and he did—the prosecution team was also top flight. There would never be any dissension among them, none of the resentment that often occurs when local, state, and federal branches of the law work the same case. The four men worked together as a smoothly orchestrated team, with one goal in mind.

MOST people never think of what kind of trail they leave behind as they go about their daily lives. Unless we are someplace we should not be or with someone we should not be with, we are unconcerned about who might have seen us at one place or another, what receipts we have signed, or what roads we have driven. Gasoline and restaurant receipts matter only as items to be tossed in our income tax files.

But sometimes it is vitally important *not* to be seen or remembered, to leave no records behind. Gerry Capano had outlined a grisly round-trip mission that took almost eleven hours, crossed two states, and involved a number of transactions. From the first hour after his arrest, Tom had sneered at Gerry's version of what happened on June 28. To try to confirm it, the investigators fanned out once more to follow Tom's trail from Grant Avenue to Emma Court to Stone Harbor to the open sea and back to Grant Avenue. The more backup they could find to substantiate the state's case, the better.

Jeffrey Stape, who lived next door to Gerry on Emma Court, told the investigators that he had seen Tom Capano's car in Gerry's driveway very early in the morning of June 28. "I went out to get my paper at 5:45 A.M.," Stape said. "My house faces Gerry's garage. Tom was parked in the driveway with the motor running. He saw me and turned away."

Stape knew Tom's car—a black Grand Cherokee. And he knew Tom by sight.

And although the public wasn't aware of it, FBI agents had already been to Stone Harbor a year earlier—when Tom's timeline notes were discovered in 1996. They had quietly done a land-and-sea search at the New Jersey shore. They had even asked Gerry's neighbors if they had seen anything large enough to be a body being carried to or from a boat. But no one had. In retrospect, who was going to look twice at a cooler?

Still, they hoped they might find witnesses as alert as Ron Smith and Ken Chubb. Tom had been either very discreet or very lucky in conducting a series of long-term affairs without being discovered. They suspected his luck might, at last, have run out.

Perhaps not. According to Gerry, he and Tom had driven down to Stone Harbor on the morning of June 28 after Tom got some money from the ATM of the Wilmington Savings Fund Society at Trolley Square. Tom had noted that, too, on his timeline pages. Now, a security officer of the bank pulled the frames from the automatic video camera at the ATM for the FBI. Tom's face was there at 8:41 A.M., the date and time clearly stamped on the photo.

Assuming that he and Gerry left Wilmington shortly thereafter, they could not have made it to Gerry's beach house much before 11 A.M. Had they arrived any earlier, a number of people might have seen them. Gerry spent little time at his own lawn care business back in Wilmington and he didn't like gardening; he employed a local firm to take care of his house in Stone Harbor.

Gary Barber, who was a schoolteacher, worked summers for his family's lawn care business. Shortly before nine-thirty on the morning of June 28, he went to Gerry's house to replace an automatic sprinkler head. In order to set the time clock on the revised system, Barber had to enter the house itself. That was no problem because he had a key. However, he was mortified when he heard the burglar alarm sound and realized he didn't know the code to turn it off.

The alarm had sounded for almost twenty minutes as four calls were automatically dialed into the monitoring service. It was close to 10 A.M. when a Stone Harbor police officer drove up in front. The alarm was turned off, Gerry's house was secured, and everything was back to normal when Gerry and Tom arrived with the cooler. A half hour or so earlier and they would have driven up and seen a police car parked at the house.

One of Gerry's Stone Harbor neighbors remembered now that he had seen Kay Capano's Suburban parked down the street late in June 1996. He had been curious enough to ask Gerry what Tom was doing down at the beach, but couldn't remember what Gerry said.

■

ANNE MARIE's brothers and sister held the almost impossible hope that her remains might still be found so that they could have a funeral and a burial. But she had been gone now for seventeen months, and if her earthly remains sank where Gerry said they did, it was where the two-hundred-feet-deep continental shelf ended abruptly and the waters plunged to a depth of fifteen hundred feet. As strong as her spirit still was in the hearts of those who loved her, her body was where the sharks swam.

Fortunately, Matthew Pleasant, a criminal investigator for the U.S. Coast Guard who was stationed in Cape May, New Jersey, had called the Delaware State Police and offered to help in the search for Anne Marie. Pleasant told the investigators that he had worked in navigating search-and-rescue operations for the coast guard. The nineteen-year veteran had spent a dozen of those years as an electronics and sonar technician. Sonar senses underwater objects and is often used to search beneath the sea after plane crashes. There was a faint chance that it might help locate Anne Marie.

It was worth a try. The cost of a coast guard sonar hunt was estimated at well over $250,000. That would, of course, have been far more than the investigators' budget, but it was possible that a sonar-equipped submarine might be in the area for other tests.

They found one. First, Pleasant interviewed Gerry Capano and wrote down what he recalled about his journey out to sea on June 28, 1996. Gerry said he had headed for Hereford's Inlet from Stone Harbor with the sun over the bow of his boat. It had taken him and Tom two to two and a half hours to reach the spot where he cut the motor, and he was certain the water depth had been 198 feet. He wasn't as sure of his compass headings.

At the time, Gerry had already sold that boat, *Summer Wind*. On June 23, 1996, he had signed a sales agreement to buy a more powerful one—a twenty-nine-foot Black Fin—for $101,000. When he and Tom left Stone Harbor with their tragic cargo five days later, it had been one of his last ventures in his old boat. At the state's instruction, Gerry arranged to buy *Summer Wind* back. Pleasant, Gerry, and Petty Officer Davis headed out to sea in the Hydra-Sport 2,500 cc craft on a day when the weather mimicked that of June 28, 1996. Davis had a GPS receiver with him (a global positioning system that pilots and seamen use to mark their locations anywhere in the world). They had the way points stored in Gerry's LORAN (a system that indicates a boat's location), calculations from the coast guard navigator and from Meridian Science (a company that locates lost ships), and an estimated speed of twenty-nine knots. They determined that Gerry was probably telling them the truth as he remembered his course, but that he was not very good with navigational charts and was more a seat-of-the-pants sailor.

Anne Marie's body could be anywhere along a ten-mile stretch. Nevertheless, the coast guard and the navy carried out a sonar search from the coast guard cutter *Hornbeam*. They were looking for the two anchors Gerry said he had given Tom to weigh down Anne Marie's body. The floor of the sea was smooth, except for the rake marks left by commercial fishing vessels. At one point, the searchers thought they had found something, but they discovered it was only some commercial fishing gear, a chained bag used to drag the ocean bottom for scallops.

The crew eventually located eleven objects—all of them oceanic junk.

It was a nearly impossible mission. Currents and storms had changed the sea bottom and buried objects with churning sand. But in June 1998, a last-ditch effort was made to find Anne Marie's remains on the floor of the Atlantic. Unlike the timing of the search for the occupants of John F. Kennedy Jr.'s downed plane—which was begun almost at once after it vanished over Atlantic waters, much closer to the shore—it had now been two years to the day since Anne Marie's body disappeared in the water sixty miles out to sea. A miniature submarine sidled along the ocean floor near Stone Harbor, feeling for objects with its mechanized claw. The searchers did find a chain and an anchor, but they were the wrong size and in no way matched the description of those that Gerry Capano told the investigators about.

In the end, they had to give Anne Marie up to the sea. There would be no more searches. "Our hope was that they would find Anne Marie's remains," Robert Fahey said later, "and we would have some semblance of a burial. Now we were denied that forever." Anne Marie Fahey was declared legally dead.

In the spring of 1998, New Jersey high school students who were cleaning up the Brigantine beach area—which is some thirty miles north of Stone Harbor on the Atlantic Ocean—had found a four-by-four-inch piece of a human skull. The Atlantic County medical examiner determined it had been in the ocean a year or more. Tests showed it was not Anne Marie's.

_____*Chapter Thirty-two*_____

IT WAS TWO WEEKS BEFORE THANKSGIVING 1997. After being evaluated in the prison infirmary, Tom would be assigned to a cell, probably in the protective custody unit. He was, after all, a former prosecuting attorney—a species almost more unpopular in prison than ex-cops. And he was infamous; for days, his name and picture had been in every paper not only in Delaware, but also in Maryland, Pennsylvania, New Jersey, and New York.

Dr. Carol Tavani, a neuropsychiatrist employed by the Delaware Prison Health Department to see prisoner patients fifteen hours a week, evaluated Tom on November 14. Tavani's discipline looked far more to pharmacological treatment than Freud to treat patients. She took Tom's medical history and found nothing of much importance beyond his colitis and a spell of hypertension some years earlier. Even in his present circumstance, the psychiatrist found her patient "most pleasant. He was cooperative with me . . . cognitively, intellectually intact. Very upset . . . that his brother—or brothers— would have turned on him."

Tom confided that he wished he had had a fatal heart attack, but denied that he had suicidal thoughts. Dr. Tavani extracted a promise from him that he would not try to kill himself. It seemed to her that he was very anxious, terribly depressed, and worried about his daughters.

And indeed he must have been; those were completely appropriate emotional responses for someone who has just been charged with murder and locked away from the life he knew. Tom's world had plunged from the opulent surroundings of his mother's estate on Weldin Road to the bare essentials of life in a crowded prison.

After a few days in the infirmary, Tom was moved to solitary confinement in Cell 1 in the 1-F pod at Gander Hill Prison; 1-F was the area that held prisoners who for one reason or another had to be designated "administrative segs." Inmates who feared for their safety, those who had been threatened, and those who were being disciplined were placed in segregation there.

Like the other nine single cells in the pod, Tom's was approximately six by ten feet and faced the guards' bubblelike modular unit. There was no privacy. There was a bunk with a thin foam pad, a small table bolted to the floor, a pale fluorescent light, a toilet and sink, a narrow window looking out on the prison yard, and vents on the opposite side of the common wall shared with Cell 2.

Tom would be locked in twenty-three hours a day. His one hour of "rec" would be used for exercising, showering, cleaning his cell, and making phone calls. But the calls would be limited and often cut off in midsentence. And Tom would have his rec hour by himself, although some of the prisoners on the 1-F pod were permitted to mingle. He was a man alone; other prisoners weren't allowed past the red line painted in front of his cell.

For a man who had always had whatever he wanted, imprisonment was a shock. For a man who had a television and a VCR in most of the rooms of his house, the lack of TV or even a radio left him with endless empty days. Even the number of books he could have was curtailed; Tom was permitted only six a month.

Always fastidious, he wrote to Debby that he was living in filth. He shuddered to think of where his sheets and blankets had been before he got them. Even the number of pairs of socks and shorts he could have was specified, so he said he had to wash his underwear in his toilet when he ran out.

Tom could have visitors, but not nearly as many as he wanted, and the visits were over too soon. His attorneys tried to come by every Wednesday—if not more often. He was sullenly outraged that he had come to such an existence.

But he had. On November 22, 1997, the New Castle County grand jury made it absolutely official when Tom Capano was indicted on state charges for the first-degree murder of Anne Marie Fahey. He continued to be held without bail, and a bail hearing wasn't even likely to be set until after the holidays.

Two days before Christmas, Judge William Swain Lee of the Superior Court was appointed to the Capano case. Lee was much admired for his experience, brilliance, and common sense. Attorneys on both sides of the case were heartened. If anyone could maintain a sense of order and dignity in what would be the trial of the century in Delaware, it would be William Swain Lee.

ALONE in his cell almost constantly, Tom evaluated his chances to get out on bail. He could count on his mother (although he worried that she would be a "crybaby and make a scene"), on his daughters, and to some extent on Kay—except that she was going ahead with the divorce. And he knew that Debby's love for him was steadfast and completely dependable; as always, she would do whatever he directed. Debby's testimony would never hurt him; she would say exactly what he told her to say. His sister, Marian, and her husband, Lee, were there for him, and his brother Joey. Louie and Gerry, of course, had betrayed him. But Tom had the best attorneys in the business. And he had a handful of male friends who would stand by him; he had been generous in helping some of them pay for houses or their kids' education. There were other women, too, that he thought would come through in a pinch—Susan Louth, for one.

Tom didn't expect to be in Gander Hill for very long; they couldn't hold him without bail endlessly. Delaware statute said that the prosecutors would have to hold a proof positive hearing to prove to a judge that they had a good case to take into court. Tom figured if they were basing it on Gerry's babblings and what Louie knew, they might as well forget it.

As for the state proving that he had stalked Anne Marie, there were dozens of E-mails, notes, and records that showed she had been his friend to the end. His attorneys would make short shrift of anyone who said otherwise.

Tom was intelligent and he was great with people, *any* people who happened to move through his life—except, perhaps, for prison guards. He had always made his own rules, and now he railed against the rules at Gander Hill. He was not an easy prisoner to deal with.

Among the prisoners who came to the 1-F pod was a man with far more experience as an inmate than Tom. Nicholas Perillo, forty-five, had a potent on-and-off addiction to both drugs and alcohol and a rap sheet that went back almost two decades. He was silver haired and very handsome, spoke in a gruff voice that sounded remarkably like Sylvester Stallone's, and had a mother whose heart he had broken often and a brother who was a successful television actor, appearing on such shows as *ER*. Perillo was always looking for an angle. He was an admitted burglar, forger, and thief, but even so, he was exceedingly likable and he always *meant* to do better. Perillo was smart and he was con wise—but he wasn't violent.

By rights, Perillo probably should have long ago received the "big bitch"—thirty-four years and ninety days in prison as a habitual offender. But he had slipped out of that when a young woman attorney went to bat for him. While he was in prison in 1989, he married the attorney who had made the plea bargain for him and, because she had so much faith in him, vowed to mend his ways. It could have been a made-for-a-miniseries marriage, but when he was released in 1992, Nick slid back into the seductive world of drugs and alcohol. His marriage foundered, and he shattered any romantic illusions his wife might still have had when he burglarized her house.

Perillo had been arrested often enough that Gander Hill was familiar to him. On his last sojourn, the prison was full to bursting and he had to sleep on a pallet on the floor of Booking and Receiving for three months. When he was charged with third-degree burglary after being found drunk and asleep in a vacant house next door to his mother's in the fall of 1997, he knew he was going back to Gander Hill. But he had no intention of sleeping on the floor again.

"When the officer told me to go get a mattress out of the corner and pointed me to a particular cell, there were six people laying on the floor," he said later. "So I walked up to the desk and told them I had a codefendant currently incarcerated at Gander Hill and I was afraid for my life and wanted protective custody. I knew they would give me a cell and a bed and I wouldn't have to sleep on the floor."

Unlike Tom, Perillo was delighted to get his own cell in the 1-F pod. He drew Cell 2, identical to Tom's and right next to it.

Perillo read the papers; he knew who Tom Capano was, but he didn't realize that Tom was in the 1-F pod until he heard the other prisoners yelling at him when he was taking his hour of rec. Curious, he went to the doorway of his cell and saw Tom in the hall.

Even though the prisoners in segregation were discouraged from talking to one another, there were ways. During meals, the flaps at the bottom of their cell doors were opened and they could hunker down on the floor and talk back and forth. Men who were out for rec could slide notes under cell doors and receive notes the same way. If the guards had stepped away from the bubble, they could even cross the painted red lines.

There is no place that challenges its residents to beat the system more than a jail or a prison; rules there cry out to be broken. And all humans need to communicate. Perillo and Tom were both Italian and of an age. They became acquainted despite the restrictive environment, trading life stories and books. Nick could match Tom for charm anyday, and for intelligence. After the two men got to know each other, he told Tom he would get his brother's autograph for Tom's girls.

Perillo had pretty much run out of people on the outside who trusted him, so he didn't use all of his telephone time. And he was down to his last twenty cents in his commissary account. In his real life, Tom had used the phone continually, checking on his daughters and his lovers several times a day. Now the fact that he was permitted only a certain number of calls rankled him. He desperately needed to find a way to circumvent the phone system.

All phone calls from Gander Hill had to be collect, of course, and the inmates got access to the outgoing phone lines by punching in their prisoner identification number (SBI) first, and then dialing numbers from an approved list. Tom's list was soon full, but other prisoners, like Nick Perillo—and Harry Fusco, a man waiting trial on sex offenses—had phone time they never used. Perillo explained the ways that he and other prisoners could make calls for Tom. Tom had family, friends, *and* money; many of his pod mates had neither.

Tom rapidly got himself into a position where he had more control over his life, and also the lives of people on the outside whom he felt needed direction. If he wanted more phone calls, he now had a way to make them. He could have Kay send checks to the commissary accounts of some of his new friends.

IRONICALLY, Debby MacIntyre felt that she and Tom had had their best times together in the months just before his arrest. "We saw each other practically every day," she recalled. "He would come over to the house—just stop in—almost every night. Maybe one evening or two he wouldn't come because he was doing something with his office friends."

Debby had been serene in the knowledge that they would be married before another year passed. She was scarcely aware that the investigation into Anne Marie Fahey's murder was continuing and was still focused on Tom. "I knew he didn't do it," she said. "Later, they [the investigators] asked me, 'Didn't you even think that he was a suspect and she's disappeared?' and I said, 'No.' Because I believed that she had gone off—as Tom told me—that she'd gone off the deep end and joined some cult in Colorado or someplace. He told me that he had ended his relationship with Anne Marie in September of 1995 when we decided we would get married one day. It wasn't any part of our life. We never talked about it."

There was no proof, Tom had told her a long time back, that Anne Marie was even dead. If she was, no one knew where or how, he pointed out, and none of it had anything to do with him.

But when Debby came home from Rome in late November, Tom was in jail. Even so, he convinced her that he would be out within a matter of weeks and that they would go on as they always had. Even from Gander Hill, Tom could control her life.

Debby continued to suffer from an emotional reaction that many women share. Talk shows call it the "disease to please," and those who suffer from it never feel good enough about themselves to protect and defend their own needs, or to set boundaries. Any confrontation makes them physically ill, and many who seek therapy actually *apologize* to the therapist for talking about themselves; above all, it is essential not to make anyone else uncomfortable or angry.

With Tom in prison, Debby did her best to please him, to keep up his spirits. She couldn't visit him because visits were reserved for his daughters and his family, but Tom called her almost every evening and she curtailed her activities so she would be there when he called. They wrote each other daily letters.

In those phone calls, "We really talked more about emotions," Debby recalled. "How he was feeling, how he was faring, what I was doing. We rarely talked about the case. He said a couple of times that he didn't want to talk about the case because he didn't know how safe the phones were—the phone he was calling from."

At one point, however, Debby brought up something that had begun to eat at her. Now that Tom was charged with Anne Marie's murder, it was almost impossible for her *not* to think about it. She asked Tom what had become of the gun she bought for him.

His response was immediate and stern. "Please don't mention that on the phone. I don't want to discuss anything like that on the phone or about the case." He seemed so agitated that she instantly regretted mentioning the gun.

With Tom's warnings ringing in her ears, Debby didn't care much for the men who had brought him down—Colm Connolly, Eric Alpert, and Ferris Wharton, particularly. Bob Donovan seemed somehow nicer to her. He didn't say much, and he didn't seem to be bearing down on her as hard as the others. But still, she knew they wanted her to help them convict Tom and she wasn't going to do it.

Debby was getting another kind of pressure from Tom himself. Although she was perfectly content to wait for him until he got out of jail after his bail hearing, Tom kept urging her to see other men and have sex with them. He still found that thought as arousing as ever—perhaps more so because he no longer could make love to her himself.

In fact, Tom had always been almost obsessively curious about the bodily functions and responses of the women he was intimate with. Unlike most men, he seemed fascinated with their menstrual cycles and demanded to know all of their secrets. Nothing was too personal for him to ask or write. Either he was convinced that his mail was private or he didn't care. His long letters to Debby were full of pornographic descriptions and sexual innuendo, declarations of his love, complaints about his unbearable living conditions, and his hope that it would all be over soon. But most of all, they told her what to do.

Christmas 1997 was yet another holiday for the Fahey family without Anne Marie. Yet there was the hope that when Tom Capano went to trial, they would finally have some kind of closure. Tom fully expected to get out on bail and to prepare for trial in the comfort of civilized surroundings. Debby just wanted to have him back with her.

_____ Chapter Thirty-three _____

THERE WAS NO WAY for the men building the case against Tom to know for certain how Anne Marie had died. The utensils and tools taken from Tom's house had tested negative for human blood, refuting their original suspicions that, in a blind rage, he had beaten her to death. Gerry Capano said the ten-millimeter handgun he'd given to Tom in February 1996 had been returned unused. And a tedious search through receipts of gun sales in the state of Delaware for the first six months of 1996 had turned up no record of a firearm being sold to Tom Capano.

However, there was a record of a gun sale to someone close to Tom. The investigators learned that Debby MacIntyre had bought a .22 caliber Beretta handgun on May 13—forty-five days before Anne Marie vanished. That purchase certainly interested them.

Whatever had happened to Anne Marie, now Connolly, Wharton, Alpert, and Donovan were convinced that her fate had been plotted out carefully for a long time before she disappeared. Tom had borrowed money from Gerry way back in February 1996— $8,000, allegedly to pay off an extortionist. If there really had been an extortionist, why didn't Tom simply go to his bank and take money out of his own account? He had had a balance of over $153,000 at the time. Indeed, he'd paid Gerry back the very next day. No, it was obvious that Tom had borrowed the money from Gerry to make sure that his little brother would have the extortionist story firmly in his mind. And then, whenever Tom might need to get rid of a body, Gerry wouldn't ask questions.

And he hadn't. Gerry wasn't happy about dumping a body at sea—but he had gone along with Tom's pleas. He'd kept his back turned while Tom removed the body from the cooler and weighted it down before dropping it overboard.

Now it seemed that Tom had drawn Debby into his crime, persuading her to be the goat who bought a weapon for him, but not just before he intended to kill Anne Marie—forty-five days in advance. It was one more indication that Anne Marie's murder was premeditated.

The investigators looked again at Tom's E-mail from May through June 1996 and found it full of his dogged insistence that Anne Marie have dinner with him—that she keep him informed of her plans. "Hey," Tom E-mailed her on May 3. "It's 2:30 and I ain't heard from ya so I was wondering what was up. Please give me a call or e-mail me when you get a chance. Is there a good time to call you? Hope you're having a good day, but my guess is you're not. Think mussels . . . in a white sauce." There were many like that, apparent attempts to lure Anne Marie into a meeting that might be their last.

They looked at the statement from Siobhan Sullivan, Anne Marie's state trooper friend. Anne Marie had told her that Tom was "a fucking stalker" in May 1996. Anne Marie was afraid of Tom, but the prosecution team realized that she had had no idea of how dangerous he might be; she never knew that he had asked another woman to buy a gun for him—that he had made plans to get rid of a body. And none of them believed for a moment that Debby MacIntyre had bought that gun for herself.

But where was it now?

On January 8, 1998, Tom Capano pleaded not guilty to charges of first-degree murder. His bail hearing—the proof positive hearing— was set to begin in the first week of February. He and his lawyers concurred that Debby MacIntyre would be one of the best witnesses they could present. Tom knew she was scared to death to testify for him; he also knew she would do it. She would do anything for him.

On January 28, Tom wrote a letter to the woman he purportedly loved and planned to marry. In earlier letters, he had persuaded her to accept a date with another man, urging her to have sex with him, which she could not do. Now he wrote a letter that would haunt her, although it was clearly a picture of who *he* was, rather than a portrait of her.

Dear Deb,

It's 11:57 p.m. and with any luck, you're naked right now on all fours with your dinner date making you come like crazy, doggy

style. Actually, you say something in your Monday night letter—
which arrived tonight—about having your period. Okay, so maybe
you're naked anyway, so he can admire your magnificent body on
your knees with his dick in your mouth while he sits in a living
room chair—giving him the best blow job he's ever had. The
thought of these things made me have two relaxation sessions since
I found out about your date . . . and one of them was in the middle
of the day today while I was standing up in a corner of my cell!

Tom's pornographic musings about Debby's date took him a
page and a half, and then he told her he had bad news. His three attorneys—Charlie Oberly, Joe Hurley, and the new addition, Gene
Maurer—felt that it was essential that she testify at his bail hearing.

Please forgive me, but I agree with them, as I will explain, and I
freely admit that it's purely selfish. . . . [He allegedly quotes his attorneys:] "Debby MacIntyre is an important witness for us, but
maybe more importantly, she's an impressive witness. We want
Judge Lee to see and hear this very credible and honest woman because she will make a very positive impression. . . . She comes
across not just as honest, but also as level-headed and mature."

Since Tom referred continually in his letters to "dumb" mistakes that Debby had made, this was a new approach for him. He
pleaded with her to overcome her fear of publicity and reminded her
that she would surely have to testify when his case came to trial, so
she might as well testify at the proof positive.

He warned her that Bob Donovan would be on the stand reading both roles in interviews she had given and it would be so much
better if she spoke for herself. "[My team says:] 'She will help our
case,' " Tom wrote. " 'And Judge Lee will observe her demeanor and
listen to her tell her own story in her own words with inflection, an-
imation and emotion. . . .' Deb, darling, they are right and I have to
agree with them. I know how important your privacy is to you. I
don't want you to have cameras surrounding you either."

And then Tom added some information that he wanted her to
impart to the judge. "The [newspaper] reports will be done even if
it's just Donovan giving his version of what you said. (And leaving
out the parts that do me the most good. For example, about the
pulls in the carpet and the dislike I always felt for it.)"

Tom had names for Connolly and Wharton. Connolly was his
least favorite and had earned three epithets: "the Nazi," "the
snake," and "the weasel." Wharton was "the hangman."

"I'm pissed," Tom wrote, "that the Nazi got to interview you today, but I understand how it happened."

Tom ended his letter by appealing to Debby's sympathy, something that had always worked. He told her that Lee Ramunno wasn't being allowed to visit him as his lawyer, because he was considered only a family member by the state, that Marian was hesitant to "talk trash" about Gerry in court, that he hadn't had time to ask his mother to testify for him (something that Marian was against, too), that his daughters were depressed, his wife had fought with him, and his showers were ice cold. He signed the letter, "I love you, Tom."

BY the time she got Tom's ingeniously crafted letter, Debby had something else on her mind. On the date he wrote—January 28, 1998—she had a meeting with the prosecution team and it hadn't gone well. Tom had told her what she must say about buying the gun—about her fear of the "crime wave" in Wilmington and being alone with children, and how he had frowned on her having a gun. It was all a lie, but she had agreed to do it to protect him.

With the attorney that Tom had recommended beside her, Debby waited nervously for Connolly to ask her questions. She was not a practiced liar; even an amateur interrogator could have seen her telegraphing which answers weren't true. But she began with the truth, correcting the lie she had told the grand jury. "My relationship with Tom Capano extends many more years than September 1995," she admitted. "We did not become romantically involved until that time, but over a period of years prior to that, we did have sexual encounters."

Debby was also truthful when she said she was completely unaware of Anne Marie Fahey's existence until Tom told her on July 2, 1996, about his relationship with her.

"Has he ever said anything to you about whether the government located Anne Marie Fahey's blood in his Grant Avenue home?" Connolly asked.

"Yes. Something about DNA. That's all I can tell you."

"Has he ever told you an explanation as to why government agents would have found Anne Marie Fahey's blood in his house?"

"No, no—he said it was a small, pinprick size. . . . We never talked about Anne Marie Fahey and what his involvement was with her. We never did."

She was believable. Some women might have screamed at their lovers and nagged them for more details about another woman in their lives. Not this woman.

When asked about the Carbona milk and bloodstain remover, Debby recalled giving Tom a bottle many months before June 27. She denied seeing guns or ammunition in Tom's house or knives—beyond the block of kitchen knives she had given him as a housewarming present. She said she didn't know if Tom's close friends owned guns.

"Do you own any hunting knives?"

"I do not."

"Do you own any handguns?"

"I did." Debby tried to appear casual, but every nerve was quivering. Her short answers suddenly became long, stuttering explanations. She admitted buying a gun, but she said it was in the winter or spring of 1994 or 1995. And she offered the explanation that Tom had scripted for her, her fear of being burglarized or having a break-in. She was all alone with two teenagers.

Debby added that a coworker at Tatnall who taught a course in gun safety had offered to teach her how to use a firearm. She said she had never used the gun at all; her words tumbled out all wrong. "I remember coming home on the very last day of school in June," she lied. "My son was in my room. It [the gun] was locked in a suitcase, but I was really nervous about him finding it—so I got rid of it. And I updated my alarm system instead."

Connolly had a way of asking, "Are you certain?" about the dates she gave and the things she said about the gun. She stumbled over whether it had been January or June, or 1994, 1995 . . . 1996.

"I got rid of it June—say the tenth—because that was the last day of school," she said through numb lips. "And I took it apart. There's a piece that comes out of the bottom of it and I took it apart and I put them [the two pieces] in separate bags. Trash bags."

Debby said she'd thrown the gun parts and the bullets into the garbage can on Friday, June 10. (That would have been two and a half weeks before Anne Marie vanished.) She didn't know what kind of gun it was, but she told Connolly about the gun store out on Route 13. "I just asked for a small gun that would be easy and comfortable and not intimidating."

With every lie she told, Connolly came back with another question that she couldn't really answer. "When you bought the gun," he asked, "had you ever discussed your intention to buy a gun?"

"I had talked about it with Tom."

"Was he with—"

"He thought it was a bad idea," she said quickly.

She said she couldn't remember what color the gun was—

maybe silver, maybe black—or how much it cost, how she'd paid for it, or exactly how long she'd had it.

"How long do you think you owned this gun?" Connolly pressed.

"Three to five months."

"When you bought it, what season was it?"

"Winter . . . spring . . ."

"You're very certain [you got rid of it] on the second Friday in June?"

Debby got in deeper and deeper. No, Tom had never seen the gun. He didn't know she'd thrown it away in the garbage. Not until the next day, "Say Sunday," she said.

"And what was his reaction?"

" 'Good. Update your security system.' "

"Did you ever lend him the gun?"

"No."

At that point, Eric Alpert quietly set a .22 caliber Beretta on the table in front of Debby, and she froze. *Had they found her gun someplace?*

"Was that the type of gun?"

"Uhhhh . . . I don't think it was that big."

Now Connolly showed her a copy of the receipt for the gun she'd purchased. "Does this help refresh your recollection of when you bought the gun?"

Debby could see the date. "In May," she said, her own voice echoing in her head. "I thought I bought it well before that."

Connolly wanted to know the time of day and the day of the week that she had bought the gun. And she kept remembering Tom taking her to the gun shop—even as she lied to protect him, and didn't know why. Tom was innocent. *She knew he was innocent . . .*

"And you're certain the only person with whom you discussed your intention to buy the gun, prior to the date you purchased it, was Tom Capano?" Connolly had a way of asking the same question three different ways.

"Yes . . . yes."

"But you're also certain that Tom Capano never touched the gun?"

"To the best of my knowledge."

"Well, if the gun was in your exclusive custody from the date you purchased it up to the day you got rid of it, how could Tom Capano touch the gun?"

"I put it in the trash." *Why had she said it that way?*

"So he didn't," Connolly said. "So if his fingerprints are on the gun with the serial number that you purchased . . . how would you account for that?"

Connolly hadn't said Tom's prints *were* on the gun. He had said *if,* but Debby was floundering.

"He took it out of the trash?" she asked.

"So, did he know ahead of time when you were throwing it out?"

"No, I told him after I put it in the trash."

"Well, how soon after?"

"Saturday or Sunday. The trash is picked up on Tuesday."

"Are you certain of that?"

Debby wondered if they thought *she* had done something to Anne Marie. Her head was spinning with all the questions about the gun. Connolly kept asking her if she was *certain* about when she had put the gun parts and the bullets in the trash. And she wasn't because it was all a lie. She had seen that gun for only five minutes after she bought it. Then she had given it to Tom.

"So you could have told him before the trash was picked up by the city?"

"Yes . . . *yes.*"

Apparently satisfied, Connolly then asked her if Tom had ever told her about somebody who was trying to extort money from him.

"Yes . . . He told me that somebody was trying to get money from him. That's it. I can't even tell you the guy's name."

"Has he ever discussed with you anything about someone trying to extort money from him after Anne Marie Fahey's disappearance?"

"No."

"Has he told you whether or not he's ever given money to somebody who tried to extort money from him?"

"No."

"Have you ever had any conversation with Tom Capano since June 27, 1996, about the gun you purchased on May 13, 1996?"

"No," Debby said. And then she reversed her answer. "That's probably not true. I probably alluded to the fact that 'I got it and I don't know what I was thinking—I'm glad I got this new security system or I'm getting this new security system . . .' "

The interview was over. Of course, the .22 caliber Beretta they showed Debby wasn't the gun she had purchased. Nobody knew where that gun was. But Debby had the impression that they knew more about the gun than she did, and that Tom knew a lot more than he was telling her.

■

"THE volcano erupted on January twenty-eighth," Debby said. "There was a flash in my head halfway through that interview. That's the only way I can describe how I felt. The Tom that I knew wasn't this man who could kill this woman. But once I betrayed him or rejected him—so to speak—I woke up and I realized the position I was in because I loved him and believed him and trusted him. I was compromising myself, my safety, and that of my children. It *was* like a volcano erupting."

Adam Balick, Debby's attorney, wasted no time in calling Charlie Oberly to tell him what had happened. When Tom heard about it, he immediately attempted damage control in a letter to Debby. First, he pointed out how incredibly stupid she had been to suggest he might have taken the gun out of her trash can. How could she have said such a thing? He criticized the lawyer he'd chosen for her for not telling Colm Connolly to "go to hell," and said Balick should have filed a motion to quash.

"I keep saying they cannot be trusted," Tom wrote, as he virtually spelled out what Debby should have said. Too late now. He wrote as if he hoped a prison censor would read the letter and report to the state.

> And, unfortunately, I'm always right. I told Charlie that I knew you had bought it, why you got rid of it—because of Steve and his friends. Hey, that's not the first time nor will it be the last time you made an impulsive purchase—just remember the house fiasco last year—and then [you] realized it was a mistake. Apparently, you used your credit card so it's not like you were trying to hide anything. And, as for having the actual gun—which we doubt—so what? They've got to connect it somehow and Charlie doesn't think—and I agree—they can't, even if it does have my print on it someplace. So what if I touched it when you showed it to me?

It was clear that Tom wasn't going to admit in writing that he was the one who had insisted that she buy the gun for him. He was putting it all in Debby's ballpark. The gun was her problem.

Tom was even more intent on Debby's testimony for the defense in his upcoming bail hearing. He reminded her that she was *not* under his "spell." And he was emphatic that she search her memory about a cooler. "As for that damn cooler, you couldn't have forgotten it," he wrote forcefully. "It was in the crawl space behind the mirrored, louvered doors and we opened them to look for screens in late April. Or right after I bought it, you came over and couldn't pull all the way in the garage because it took up too much room and the garage was tight anyway. Maybe you didn't pay attention, but when you said, 'What the hell is that?' I told you what it was—a fish cooler for Gerry's new boat."

Debby had absolutely no recollection of seeing a fish cooler either in Tom's garage or in the crawl space. But she knew he expected her to repeat what he'd told her about it in the proof positive hearing.

Tom also set down a blueprint of exactly what she was to do on that day in court. First of all, he wanted her to march in with her head held high, with her attorney on one side of her and Stan, a male friend from Tatnall, on the other. He warned her that she would be overwhelmed if she didn't have two strong men to cling to. She was not to drive herself to the courthouse; she would be too nervous.

"Be sure you swim the day you testify," Tom ordered. "You will wait in an airport-like line to go through a metal detector. Adam will decide whether you will wait just outside the courtroom or go to the witness room."

Tom described the courtroom to Debby, cautioning her that it would be intimidating because it was so big. "Yes, I will be there at the table with my guys," he wrote. "A bailiff will escort you to the witness box where you will be sworn in. The Judge will be next to you. Whichever side calls you asks questions first; then the other side gets to ask questions. When the questioning is over, Judge Lee will tell you you're excused."

And then, fearing he hadn't been explicit enough, Tom gave Debby a short course in courtroom law. She might have been ten years old from the way he lectured her. "My guys will certainly be nice to you," he promised.

Try to answer most questions either "yes" or "no," but sometimes you'll have to explain things. Connolly will try to put words in your mouth, so don't let him.

You will run into the cameras and reporters as soon as you leave. Let Adam just keep saying "no comment" as the three of you push your way through them. They won't follow you to Adam's office. Once there, relax and then leave with Stan to get a drink at Pala's. I'm serious. If you don't go back to Adam's office, just walk into the lobby with him, say goodbye, and go through the lobby and out onto Shipley Street and to the garage. Walk briskly to the garage while holding Stan's arm. You must not drive out of the garage at Pala's. Do go to Baltimore later and do not work the next day. I still think you should take the rest of the week off and go to Boston.

It was Tom's usual puppeteer routine, only more so. Debby's testimony at his bail hearing meant so much to him that he wanted to be sure she didn't goof it up. As an afterthought, he told her not to wear her glasses when she testified. That way, she wouldn't be able to see anyone in the courtroom—especially the Faheys. They would surely be there, and he didn't want her looking them in the eye and getting confused.

Tom needed her at the hearing to reflect well on him. What was important was how she came across to Judge Lee. She was going to be his ticket out of Gander Hill.

Tom continued to go to a great deal of effort to make sure Debby knew exactly what to do, just as he had done with Anne Marie, trying to orchestrate her life to suit him. He wrote to Debby on January 29, January 30, February 1, and February 2, repeating his instructions over and over, always reminding her how stupid she had been with her whim to buy a house and then backing out. That was his way of telling her how to explain her silly idea about buying a gun, only to throw it in the garbage.

He might have saved himself the trouble.

Debby had hit the wall. She could deny only so much and then she began to doubt. It was not that she had stopped loving Tom. "I wanted so much to believe him," she recalled, "but there were things I had to question."

Debby dismissed her attorney, and with her ex-husband advising her, she approached another attorney about representing her. Perhaps for the very first time, Debby was taking charge of her life. In a rush of pain, she had moments of wondering if Tom might be throwing her to the wolves. He wanted her to lie, but he would not tell her the truth. She had suppressed that realization again and again, only to have doubts sneak back in.

Wednesday, February 4, 1998, came and went, and Debby was not at the bail hearing to testify for Tom. He was thunderstruck. He had been so certain that he would get out of jail that he had packed his clothes before leaving his cell. "I'll send someone to pick that up," he told the jailers.

Indeed, he had heard rumors from his family that Debby wasn't going to testify for him, and he had laughed at them. When his attorneys broke the news to him, he looked at them in disbelief and

told them they were wrong. Belatedly, he got the note Debby wrote
to him, telling him she couldn't do it.

Judge Lee's decision at the end of the proof positive hearing on
February 6 went against Tom. He would continue to be held without
bail, awaiting trial, which was tentatively set to start in October 1998.
In Ferris Wharton's considerable experience, most proof positive
hearings took only a few hours. Tom Capano's had taken five days.

"It was a mini trial," Connolly commented. So much information had been presented: the records from Tom's phones, the picture
of him at the ATM machine on the morning of June 28, receipts for
the fishing cooler and for gasoline bought by two boaters in Stone
Harbor on June 28, the receipt for the Beretta, all the interviews
with Anne Marie's friends and coworkers. It seemed that there
could be no secrets about Anne Marie Fahey or Tom Capano left.

But there were secrets still. And Debby, like many others,
dreaded October 6 and what promised to be endless weeks of trial.
Tom returned to his cell and unpacked his belongings, fuming that
Debby's failure to testify for him had cost him his freedom.

BUT he didn't give up. Within days, Tom began to bombard Debby
with letters that would fill an entire book, letters designed to evoke
guilt, love, despair.

> Dear Deb,
>   So. I did open the envelope and I read it because I did not be-
> lieve what I had been told. I am beyond shocked. The one thing I
> always thought, believed, loved, was that I could always rely on
> you and your unconditional love. To have that yanked away from
> me this week is almost too much to bear. And it was done coldly
> and with finality. I guess I always knew that this day would come
> but knowledge has not dulled the pain. I am, quite literally, numb
> with that sinking feeling in my stomach. I've been abandoned in
> my time of need by most of the people I cared about and who I
> thought cared about me. I would have bet my life on your unlim-
> ited devotion and loyalty. Perhaps that's exactly what I have
> done—at least my freedom—and find that I have lost.

And that was only the first paragraph in a letter that went on
for many more pages. Tom wrote again the next day to chastise
Debby about her gun statements to Colm Connolly. He said that she
had missed her chance to vindicate herself in the media when she refused to testify at his bail hearing. "It was crucial Judge Lee heard

and saw you instead of allowing Connolly to paint you as a liar and an adulteress. You chose not to allow that to happen. We will both have to live with the consequences. Good luck. I wish you happiness. Perhaps I'll see you in October, but I doubt it."

Tom had controlled Debby for seventeen years. Now he used every manipulative trick he knew to bring her back to his side and his defense. With his written words, he pulled her closer, berated her, pushed her away, and then attempted to reel her back in. It was a hellish thing because she had loved him for a very long time, and she still did.

Beyond making her feel guilty for betraying him, Tom set out to frighten her.

> They can still charge you with conspiracy or whatever if they really believe you are involved—which, of course, you are not. If they believe they have a weapon used to commit murder and can prove that, *and* they can also *prove* you bought the weapon to help me commit murder, then they will charge you with a crime. . . . Because Connolly is ruthless, he will threaten you with charges at some point to get you to change your story and testify against me at trial. He's bluffing. Let's suppose for the sake of argument they can prove the gun they showed you at the interview was the one you bought and has my fingerprints on it. Juicy, yes. But how can he prove it was used to commit murder? They don't have a body to examine for gunshot wounds.

Tom was aghast that Connolly would suggest that he controlled Debby. "The irony of Connolly thinking you are under my spell is rich because you generally do the exact opposite of what I suggest. Do you think I don't consider these things before I offer advice?"

He was furious with Debby, and almost every letter ended with a last farewell of some sort. But he kept writing—because he needed her testimony. Or perhaps because he was afraid of what she might say as a witness against him.

_____ Chapter Thirty-four _____

ON FEBRUARY 10, 1998, Debby retained a new attorney, Tom Bergstrom, who had a one-man law office in Malvern, Pennsylvania, a suburb of Philadelphia. A very tall, solid man with a good Midwestern face, who had practiced law for thirty years, he'd graduated from the University of Iowa and gone right into the marine corps for a four-year tour of duty in Southeast Asia. After he left the marines, he worked for the Department of Justice in its organized crime and racketeering section. Like Connolly, Bergstrom had worked as an assistant U.S. attorney; from 1975 he had run his own solo practice as a criminal trial attorney. His only assistant was his wife, Dee, a striking woman with white-blond hair, who not only served as a paralegal but was a shrewd judge of human nature.

In January 1996 Bergstrom had defended John E. du Pont against the murder charges resulting from the shooting of Olympic wrestler David Schultz. *Philadelphia Magazine* named Bergstrom one of the top criminal defense attorneys in Pennsylvania.

Bergstrom was probably the *last* attorney Tom would have wanted for Debby. When he learned somewhat belatedly that she had retained him, he was appalled—and he characterized her new lawyer as "loathsome," calling him "the Malvern malefactor" and "pond scum." The fact that another of his least favorite people— Debby's ex-husband, Dave—had recommended Bergstrom made Tom even angrier.

But there was more than rage behind Tom's attacks on Bergstrom. Bergstrom was smart and skilled and he would protect his client against anyone, and that included Tom. Tom needed Debby in his camp no matter what, and Bergstrom was a major threat.

Tom was convinced that if he forgave Debby for failing to support him at the bail hearing, she would come back to him as loyal as always. But he had to do some backtracking because he had sent her a final, final farewell letter on February 9, telling her he would no longer read her letters and ending with, "I wish you peace and happiness from the bottom of my heart and apologize for everything, especially for the invasion of your privacy. Keep swimming, take care of yourself, move on, find contentment."

But he was not quite as bereft as he sounded. Now that Debby had defected, Tom contacted another of his mistresses who might be a good witness for him. He was corresponding with Susan Louth, the blond legal secretary Marguerite Capano called "that slutty little girl." Susan was living in the Virgin Islands, but their relationship in Wilmington dated back to 1995 and 1996. There were holes in Tom's case he felt Susan could fill.

But not like Debby. On reflection, Tom realized Debby was still a loose cannon and started courting her again with phone calls and letters on February 24. He knew she would be in a terribly vulnerable emotional state; because of her involvement with him, she had just been fired from her job at Tatnall School. Tatnall had been Debby's life for a dozen years, and she had worked early and late without complaining, doing double duty. That had always annoyed Tom.

There was no question at all about Debby's competency in her job, but a prestigious private school apparently dared not risk the scandal that she had been plunged into. Tearfully, Debby gathered her staff together and said good-bye before she cleared out her office. Then she left on an already scheduled trip to New England.

On a Sunday in late February, there was an article in the paper about Debby's dismissal, and Tom tried to call her that evening. He knew she would be embarrassed and heartsick. He got only her answering machine. When he lost his phone privileges a day later for breaking yet another rule at Gander Hill, he asked one of his attorneys to call Debby and express his concern, and to urge her to fight Tatnall's decision.

Tom followed that with a letter he gave to one of his attorneys' legal aides to deliver personally. He wanted Debby to know that his good friend Nick Perillo would be calling her to convey how worried he was about her.

The first two pages of his letter were full of concern for Debby. He didn't begin to berate her until the third. She had returned one of his long letters with only a short note and he was concerned that she might be accepting the advice of her new attorney and rejecting his.

"I loved you with every fiber of my being," Tom wrote. "We planned the rest of our lives together." He reminded her of all the people who did not love her and who had failed her, and then went on,

> I wasn't perfect. I don't want credit. You don't owe me. But I loved you, from rubbing your aching hip—to helping you clean out your garage attic—to taking you to Villa d' Roma, sharing Montreal with you, listening to your problems as a sounding board. I thought you were my best friend. I thought I was your best friend . . . I would never have abandoned you when you needed me, despite my own fears. I say before God and swear upon the lives of my children that I would have stood by you regardless of the cost. I would have trusted you. I would have fought for you. I would not have listened to an obvious incompetent, written a "Dear John" *note* (not even a letter,) and then run out of town so I wasn't even available to comfort you in your most desperate hours.

Tom had told Kim Horstman, of course, that he and Anne Marie were best friends. One could only suspect that he had also been "best friends" with Susan Louth, Linda Marandola, and the other women he saw regularly. But, wisely, he mentioned none of those women in his fourteen-page reconciliation letter to Debby.

"Do not forget," he wrote, "that no one has ever loved you as I have, despite my many failures. Do not think that those who come after me will ever approach the depth of love bordering on adoration that I have given you." And after four more pages of similar sentiments, "I beg you to do me the kindness of writing at least one more time and explaining why you did what you did and are doing, as well as [not] responding to these letters from my heart . . . I do love you and I always will and I can't give it up . . . Adoringly, Tom."

Tom wrote Debby three letters on February 26, as passionate as the hero of a romance novel, as pitiful as a dying man's last request. He was concerned that neither he nor Nick Perillo could get her on the phone. But a deeper worry gripped him when he *did* get her on the phone. Debby told him that Bergstrom had asked to see his letters. Tom was horrified. He had just ordered her to get another attorney when the prison phone line went dead.

"He must have thought I'd hung up," Debby recalled. "But I didn't. His phone time was over and they would cut off conversations in the middle."

"Why would he want my letters?" Tom wrote minutes later, even though he knew it might take days for Debby to get this letter. "More importantly, why would you consider giving them to him, regardless of what he says? Now there's *him* to contend with?"

There was, indeed. And Tom had good reason to be worried. On February 26, he filled eight pages with his small, precise handwriting as he told Debby what she must do. "There is only one way now," he wrote, "for you to prove your love clearly, completely, and unequivocally and also to demonstrate that your act [of] abandoning me when I most needed you was not something you will ever do again. This is my ultimatum and this is your choice: me or your lawyer. You cannot straddle the fence. You must choose between us.

"Lawyers are a dime a dozen," he wrote. "True love is rare. . . . To prove that this is no momentary flash of a broken heart, I make the same offer to prove my love for you. I will fire Charlie, Joe, and Gene . . . who are all my friends . . . [even though] I am imprisoned and will soon go on trial for my life."

Reading his bizarre ultimatum, Debby finally saw what she had to do. "Sometimes," she recalled, "I didn't even read all of those endless letters he sent. And I would just agree with what he told me to do on the phone—because he wouldn't stop talking until I did. But I got the message in this letter, and I knew I wasn't going to fire Tom Bergstrom. I never believed he would fire his attorneys."

Debby liked the Bergstroms and felt protected for the first time in many long years. They were no-nonsense people who were demonstrating that they cared about what happened to her. Dee, particularly, was intuitive about Debby's feelings. Women *know* how other women feel, although it is almost impossible to explain this to a man.

"Still," Debby said softly, "and I don't know if anyone can understand this—I still loved Tom and I still wanted to believe in him. Even at that low point, I couldn't hear the things in his voice that I heard later."

On February 27, Debby and Tom Bergstrom met Wharton, Connolly, Alpert, and Donovan in Wharton's office in the Carvel building. With Bergstrom's approval, Debby agreed to cooperate with the prosecution team. She would answer their questions truthfully. Although she hated the thought, Debby also agreed to have a recording device attached to her phone, and henceforward Tom's letters suggesting that she lie about evidentiary matters would be read not only by her attorney, but also by Connolly, Wharton, Alpert, and Donovan.

In addition, *all* of Tom's mail would be copied—in and out— and would be saved, without being read, until such time as that might become necessary.

Dee Bergstrom understood Debby's anguish and explained to her husband and the all-male prosecuting team that very few women would be able to turn off overnight a love that had lasted two decades. Often to their own detriment, she said, women cling to memories of how they perceived their relationship. For the moment, Debby was fragile, but she was doing her best to break free of Tom.

"We don't wake up one morning," Dee told them, "and just say, 'I don't love him anymore.'"

USING ANOTHER PRISONER'S SBI number, Nick Perillo had to try five times before he managed to get through to Debby. He was completely unaware that calls from Gander Hill to her home were now being recorded. "I'm right next to Tom," he told her. "He wanted me to call you to see what your schedule was—and [to tell you] that he misses you. Well, of course, he misses you."

"Ah, God. Doesn't he know it's past that for me?"

"OK."

"You can tell him that for me . . . I'm past missing him."

Perillo's words were mixed up and he sounded unsure. He told Debby that Tom had given him a letter with a number of questions to ask her, but the guards had caught him as he crossed the red line and taken it. He was doing this from memory. "He wants to know if the rumor is true?" he said. "I don't know what that means."

"I don't know," Debby said carefully.

Perillo asked her if what was in the paper that day—about Tom asking her to get the gun—was true, and she said it was. He hemmed and hawed and hung up without really saying anything, and then called back to ask if she'd gotten "the delivery." She said she had. He was talking about Tom's letter insisting that she fire her attorney.

The very fact that Tom was worried enough to have another inmate—a stranger with a rough voice—call to nudge her only confirmed what she had decided.

Debby had agreed to tape Tom's calls, although she hated doing it. "I couldn't do it for long," she recalled. "It was too difficult for me to take the calls and not be truthful, and when I told them I couldn't stand it any longer, they took the device off. I really wanted the phone blocked. It was torturous to hear it ring and not pick it up."

Wharton arranged for her phone to be blocked to all calls from Gander Hill. It was easier for her. But from about February 27 to March 3, Debby did record Tom's calls. Although he was somewhat out of the loop—or rather, late in the loop—he knew now that Debby had caved in about the gun and admitted that she had bought it at his request.

His voice, questioning, jabbing, accusing, incredulous, and ugly, filled up most of the tapes. He wanted to know everything she had told Connolly and the other prosecutors. He kept asking why she had told them she bought the gun.

"I told them the truth," she said. "I told them I bought it and gave it to you. You wanted it and I gave it to you."

"Why did you *say* such a thing?"

"Because you did."

She kept repeating that she had only told the truth.

"Don't say that. Just tell me what you said."

There was such loathing in his voice that when Debby listened to the tapes a long time later, she had to ask Bob Donovan again and again to turn them off. "They made me ill," she said. "I heard things in his voice then that I'd never noticed before."

"Do you know what you've done to us?" Tom hissed.

She leaned her head against the wall, knowing now that it was not *she* who had destroyed their relationship. Impossible as it seemed, impossible to explain, she still loved the man she remembered. It was as if there were *two* men: the Tom she had loved for seventeen years and the Tom in Gander Hill.

From that point on, Debby didn't read his letters. "Bob Donovan came and picked them up," she remembered. "He was very kind, very understanding. He took them away, unopened. It was easier for me not to have to read them."

Although Debby didn't send Tom any more letters, she wrote them. It was only an exercise in trying to understand her own feelings. She typed her letters to Tom on her computer, letters with no place to go. Sometimes she hoped it would all turn out to be a terrible mistake. But she knew better.

NICK PERILLO had received $25 for making his call to Debby; following Tom's orders and without asking why, Kay Capano had deposited the money into Nick's commissary account. He accepted it, but Nick had made another move the day before. He'd written a letter to Ferris Wharton. In it, he explained that Tom Capano had asked him to phone a person called Debby, who was going to blow the case wide open if she didn't stop talking to the prosecutors. "He asked me to call Debby to remind her to fight the hypocritic bastards and not change her story about where she disposed of the gun in the trash can."

Four days later, Perillo told his attorney, Tom Foley, about what Tom Capano was planning, and Foley agreed to talk with the prosecutors about it. Perillo confided to Wharton that Tom had told him he always got involved "with head cases like Fahey" and that he had called Debby a "stupid dumb bitch."

While Perillo was not averse to being rewarded for information, he was also uneasy about what Tom seemed capable of doing. Perillo was a con man and an admitted drug addict, but he would no more have plotted to hurt someone physically than the guards in the bubble would. He told Wharton that Tom was very angry at Debby. "Very angry."

Perillo had been in the system a long time and he knew that information could be traded for a possible reduction in sentence. Wharton took him up on his offer to provide information about Tom, albeit without making any promises. Perillo also had a private backup plan he didn't share with the prosecutors. This was a big story, and he thought he might just contact *Inside Edition* or one of the other tabloid shows and see if he could sell some information. Nobody accepted his collect calls.

On March 4, Perillo had some fairly startling news for the prosecutors and got a message out to them via a guard. Tom had asked him if he knew anyone who might want to burglarize Debby's house. "He told me it would be easy picking. He has the key and will give the alarm code to me—to send her a message." Perillo said that he did know people who could commit a burglary for him, although it would take some time to find them.

Tom had finally realized that Debby was not only unwilling to lie on the witness stand for him, she was going to stay with that "loathsome lawyer" Tom Bergstrom. As an attorney himself, he knew any lawyer worth his salt would advise her to look after herself, and that might lead her to cooperate with the "the Nazi" and "the hangman."

Debby had told Tom she would be leaving on St. Patrick's Day for Sanibel Island in Florida for her children's spring vacation trip and would be gone until March 28. In the second week of March, pursuing his burglary plans, Tom told Perillo that Debby's home was full of valuable possessions, in both a monetary and a sentimental sense. He wanted her to be so afraid and, at the same time, so aware of who was behind the burglary that she would never even think of cooperating with the prosecutors.

Tom's plan to have Perillo find a burglar to send Debby a very frightening message was not a momentary aberrance. He had a perfect visual memory, an ability that many people don't possess. He could close his eyes and picture every room in Debby's house, and in those rooms, the places where she kept jewelry, art, antiques, silver, china, stereos, television sets, VCRs—all those things that burglars delight in.

With utmost care, he drew five maps: of Delaware Avenue and the side streets near the little white house, of the three floors of Debby's house, and of an exterior view showing entrances and the direction doors opened.

For each room, Tom noted the valuables to be found there and pointed out hiding places. He had meticulous orders for the second floor, where Debby's bedroom and office were. He wanted to be sure she knew who had sent the men who ravaged her home. "Must remove plastic bag with sex toys and videos," he instructed. "In either: • office closet; • closet opposite Master Bath on right side; • Built-in cabinets in Master Bedroom outside wall; • Inside luggage in either closet." He added that the floor-to-ceiling mirror in the bedroom

MUST BE SHATTERED, and that all the artwork must be removed from Debby's bedroom or slashed to ribbons.

Other than Debby herself, there was only one person who knew what the mirror meant or where the sex toys were—her lover, Tom Capano. It would be like writing his name on her bedroom wall; she would get the message loud and clear.

To be sure that the burglars Perillo contacted would be well prepared, Tom added a sixth page with thirteen instructions. Giving orders was almost a fetish with him, and this mission had to be accomplished perfectly.

MARCH 18–MARCH 28

EARLIER IS BETTER

1. SHOULD ENTER AND EXIT BACK DOOR.
2. ALARM PANEL ON SHORT WALL TO LEFT GOING FROM KITCHEN INTO DEN.
3. UPON ENTRY ALARM WILL EMIT QUIET, STEADY TONE. 60 SECOND DELAY TO ENTER CODE. MUST FLIP DOWN COVER ON PANEL. RED LIGHT—ARMED AND GREEN LIGHT—DISARMED. ENTER 43391.
4. HOUSE IS HEAVILY SHRUBBED ON THREE SIDES. NO OBSTRUCTED VIEW FOR/FROM HOUSE BEHIND GARAGE SO ONLY VIEW. PARK ON STREET.
5. RESET ALARM WHEN LEAVING. (ALL DOORS MUST BE SHUT TO RESET). ENTER 43392.
6. NO MOTION DETECTORS ANYWHERE SO COULD ENTER THROUGH SLIDERS GLASS.
7. DIAGRAMS FAIRLY ACCURATE AND IDENTIFY POTENTIAL VALUABLES.
8. CAR KEYS SHOULD BE ON RACK IN KITCHEN OR IN PANTRY CLOSET WITH OPENER.
9. TOTAL OF 5 TVS. BEST ONE IN MASTER BEDROOM.
10. MUST SHATTER FLOOR TO CEILING MIRROR ON WALL IN MASTER BEDROOM. ABSOLUTELY REQUIRED.
11. MUST LOCATE AND REMOVE PLASTIC BAG WITH SEX TOYS AND VIDEOS IN A CLOSET IN MASTER BEDROOM SUITE OR UNDER BED.
12. ALL ART IS VALUABLE. MUST REMOVE ALL OR SLASH AND DESTROY.
13. JEWELRY IN TOP DRAWERS OF FURNITURE IN DRESSING ROOM OF M.B.R. BUT MAY BE HIDDEN IN CLOSETS OR BUILT-INS.

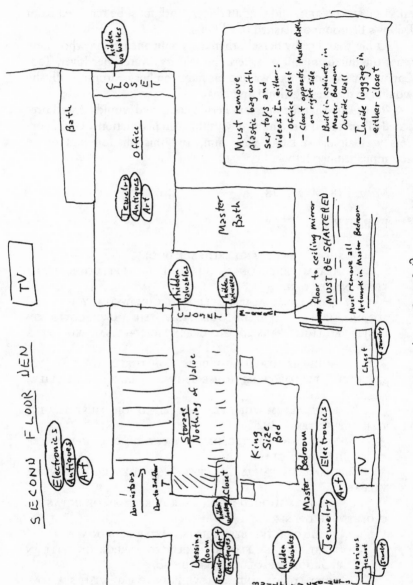

Only ten days earlier, Tom had written Debby a stack of love letters. "Never ever forget that I love you now and forever," he said. "My silly fantasy was to believe your promise that you'd be waiting for me whenever I got out and we'd have the rest of our lives together." Maybe it was a silly fantasy; or maybe it was a fatally misguided smugness that Debby would believe anything he told her.

At this point, Tom didn't insist that Debby be physically hurt; he wanted Perillo to find burglars who would destroy those possessions she loved the most and that were reminders of their lovemaking. And he wanted her to be so frightened that she would never consider giving the slightest degree of comfort or information to the enemy camp.

Perillo turned Tom's maps and instructions over to the prosecutors.

On March 13, Debby and Tom Bergstrom met with the state's team in Ron Poplos's office in the IRS building. Poplos was helping them investigate the Capano brothers' tax records. The media seemed to know whenever something momentous was about to happen in the Capano case, and the prosecutors were now taking special pains to avoid reporters. One thing that seemed to work was to vary their meeting spots from Connolly's office to Wharton's to Poplos's.

They had to tell Debby about the diagrams that showed every room of her house and Tom's plan to find someone to burglarize it. As Connolly set down the pages in front of her, she stared at them uncomprehendingly at first, and then felt a sense of chilling recognition. "Everything was there," she recalled. "I could not have told you where the words and the numbers were on my alarm system, but Tom had remembered them all. It was obvious he had worked for a long time on those drawings. And I knew that I couldn't stay in the house that meant so much to me. I would never feel safe there again."

Every interview with the prosecuting team peeled away another layer that had been private for Debby. Sitting in a room full of men, she admitted that Tom was a voyeur who frequently urged her to date other men and tell him about any sexual encounters that might occur. She told them of the night she had gone to her twentieth high-school reunion, where she had met an old boyfriend and they talked about how they had never consummated their relationship when they were teenagers. They were both single now. Tom had been excited about the prospect that that might happen. "He called when he knew we were home," she said with embarrassment. "He watched us through the windows."

She told them then about Keith Brady and what had happened the day Tom brought him to her house. That could prove to be sticky; Brady was Ferris Wharton's boss in the Delaware Attorney General's office. It seemed that Tom Capano's excesses were going to bring down half the state before the investigation was over.

If it had to be, it had to be. What mattered was bringing some justice to Anne Marie Fahey, the girl who had written about Tom in her diary four years earlier, "We have built an everlasting friendship. I feel free around him, and like he says, he 'makes my heart smile'! He deserves some happiness in his life, and it makes me feel good to know that I can provide him with such happiness."

It was obvious now to all of the men who were about to prosecute Tom that he had always sought happiness for himself and never worried how he degraded other people in his headlong pursuit of pleasure.

When asked about Tom's sexual practices, Debby said, "He was never rough during sex. He was very gentle—loving."

But denied sexual satisfaction and complete control over the women in his life, Tom appeared capable of extreme violence. If that trait had been part of his lovemaking, his prosecutors would have recognized the man they were dealing with sooner.

_____Chapter Thirty-five_____

TOM DIDN'T REALLY KNOW why nothing came of his plan to have Debby's house burglarized. Perillo wasn't in the cell next to him any longer, and Tom could talk to him only if Perillo was out in the yard for a smoke during his rec hour and came close enough to Tom's window, or if Perillo sidled over the red line on the floor when the guards weren't looking.

When the burglary didn't happen, Tom began a number of other plans on many fronts. And oddly—or perhaps not oddly—he continued to look to the women in his life to provide alibis for him.

Susan Louth had written back to him and seemed to be totally in his corner. In his reply to her letter, he said that his cousin Loretta Farkas had been surprisingly supportive. "She also told me," he wrote, "that she saw Debby MacIntyre's picture in the paper and that she looks like a shrew and a backstabber. Pretty perceptive."

Tom added a paragraph of ugly descriptions of Debby's sexual proclivities. And then he asked Susan to drum up some "word of mouth support" for him, suggesting that she start rumors about Debby that would reach his "jury pool."

But he had a more specific request. In thinking about his case, he had realized that it would be necessary to show that he didn't have the physical strength to carry a cooler with a body in it down the back stairs at the North Grant Avenue house and lift it into the back of the Suburban. Gerry had already told prosecutors that he hadn't helped Tom do that, so he needed a witness who would testify that he wasn't a strong man.

Toward that end, he suggested a "memory" to Susan about the day he had lent her a dining room table and chairs. He reminded her that she had to help him carry the table because he was too weak to handle it alone.

"I do remember how heavy the dining room table was," she wrote back. "I remember coming to your house and helping you move the table and chairs. . . . I was sore for a week."

Tom's letters to Susan were rife with sexual references, reminding her of how intimate their relationship had been. For the moment, she was a member of his team.

There were Tom's daughters, too. They adored their father, and he told everyone what a hard time they were having with him locked up. He had tried to claim that the blood found in his house had come from them—and then raged when the prosecutors attempted to get blood samples. Some closely tied to the case believed that Tom might call his girls as alibi witnesses if he had to.

Indeed, Tom, who often bragged about what an overprotective father he was, had given his daughters' address and phone number to a fellow inmate. Harry Fusco didn't have anyone to call and he had traded his phone time to Tom for commissary money and certain favors. Harry, a sex offender, called the girls with messages from Tom, wrote to them, and treasured the letters they wrote back. He had pictures of some of the beautiful teenagers in his cell.

EVEN as he seethed over Debby's defection, Tom suspected that he might never be acquitted of murder without her. And he still could not believe that there wasn't some way to summon her back. He had cajoled, promised, threatened, and groveled, but Debby hadn't responded as he fully expected she would. He had always believed that he fulfilled her sexual needs completely. He suspected that she might be suffering from a kind of sexual starvation. If he could provide a solution—albeit once removed—she might be more pliable.

Tom considered his choices of a surrogate lover and thought of Tom Shopa. A longtime friend, Shopa was tall and handsome, and he was divorced. The two Toms had gone to school together at Archmere. Shopa was a C.P.A., and he had written to him soon after he was arrested, a kind and concerned letter. On the last Sunday in March, Shopa and another old friend accompanied Tom's daughter Katie to Gander Hill for visiting hours.

Tom knew that Shopa lived only a few houses down Delaware Avenue from Debby, and he asked him to intercede with her. "He wanted me to find out if she still loved him, and why she wasn't writing to him," Shopa would recall. "And if she wasn't going to continue writing to him, would she return the letters that he sent her?"

Following Tom's instructions, Shopa called Debby and asked her if she still loved Tom. "She said, 'I love him very much,' and used the word 'soulmate' in describing their relationship," Shopa recounted.

Shopa reported that information in another visit to Tom, and explained that Debby could not write to him because of an addendum to an agreement with the state. Nor could she return his letters, because they had been turned over to the state as evidence.

Tom said that he was concerned about Debby—she needed a shoulder to cry on, and he wasn't able to be there for her. And then he asked his old friend for a bizarre favor. "He felt," Shopa said with embarrassment, "that she was *needy,* and he wanted me to take care of her, to kind of be there to help her, to be strong for her . . . and—and—also to have—a physical relationship with her, to sleep with her."

Shopa was shocked. Never in a million years had he expected his old friend to suggest something like that. He was too appalled, in fact, to say much at the time. But the idea was upsetting and inappropriate. Why would Tom ask him to do such a thing?

Tom apparently didn't hear the shock in Shopa's voice. Two days later, on March 31, he reached out from his cell with his pen once more. This time his target was, perhaps, the most vulnerable of all. He wrote an eight-page letter to fifteen-year-old Steve Williams, Debby's son.

Ever since September 1995, Steve had come to think a lot of Tom. Tom had been a great pal. His arrest and the publicity surrounding it had been hard for Steve. Tom's letter to him was written in a warm, man-to-man style and it was totally confusing, designed to open barely healed emotional wounds. Tom assured Steve he would be out of prison by Thanksgiving, "for sure," and that he planned to take Debby to Provence and Tuscany for a month or two. He spoke of his daughters, Christy, Katie, Jenny, and Alex, mentioned the boys they were dating and the trips they were taking—to Jamaica, Boca Raton, and Disney World.

And then Tom moved smoothly into what his life in Gander Hill was like. "Besides the pain of being separated from my kids," he wrote, "I suffer from being held in solitary confinement—supposedly for my own protection, although I know that's bullshit and it's part of a plan to break me."

From there, Tom went on to an intimate discussion of his long affair with Steve's mother. "I should have listened to your mother many years ago when she urged me to follow my heart and not hide our relationship or limit it to certain times. . . . At the very least, I would not now be in this predicament."

Writing, still, to a fifteen-year-old boy, Tom held back little. "Your Mom has made nothing but bad decisions since January 28th which have hurt me more than anything I've ever experienced. I'll let her tell you if you want to know and she wants to tell you. Despite the tragic choices she has made—which I mostly blame on others—I cannot stop loving her."

Tom told Steve he blamed his father and his mother's "unethical lawyer" for frightening and confusing Debby. He assured Steve that he loved him like a son, and had since he was a baby for a "special reason."

(Tom was *not* Steve's father, it that's what he was implying, and there was absolute scientific proof of that fact, but perhaps he thought such a suggestion would strengthen his hold over Debby.)

He asked the boy to be stronger than his mother had been and to keep his letter private. And then Tom got around to what probably was the main reason for the letter.

First, give your mom a long, hard hug, tell her it's from me and that I love her, miss her, and need her very much. Second, tell her I am 1000% certain *your* phones are not tapped unless she gave them permission, and that I'd still like to call on *your* line. I need the number. Third, tell her to be extremely nice to Tom Shopa because he has what she needs and can be trusted to be very private and is definitely interested in helping her take care of it but is too shy to ask—so she'll have to ask him.

Tom ended his letter to Steve by wishing him a true love and soul mate, "as I found your mom."

Fortunately, Steve didn't read the letter, beyond scanning it and seeing that it looked very long and complicated. Nor did Debby. It ended up in the growing stack of Tom's correspondence in the prosecutors' file.

FOR all of his fascination, obsession, and fixation on the psychology of women, Tom saw their world through weirdly slanted lenses. He loved to talk about the private parts of their lives and their bodies; he remembered the details of their menstrual cycles, their problems with PMS and even their ovulation patterns in a way that was faintly creepy. And yet he had not a clue about how a woman's mind worked. But how could he have thought that supplying Debby with a surrogate sexual partner—a man with whom she had no emotional connection beyond friendship—would make her contented and serene, and grateful to him? His bland assumptions had horrified Shopa, but Capano had taken his silence for assent.

And thus encouraged, he had written to a teenage boy about his mother in unmistakably suggestive terms and had asked him, in effect, to be a pimp for her, telling his mother to be "extremely nice" to Shopa.

Before Debby stopped writing to him, Tom had asked her for Steve's telephone number often. And he had been particularly insistent about wanting her daughter, Victoria's, phone number and address at college. "What if there was an emergency?" he asked Debby. "What if I couldn't get in touch with you?"

"I never wanted him to have Victoria's address or phone number," Debby recalled. "I couldn't imagine any emergency where he'd need that. Later, I was awfully glad he didn't have it."

WHEN his crude ploy to win Debby back with surrogate seduction failed, Tom set out on another scheme. If he could not be sure that she was part of his team, then he would have to make certain that she didn't play for the opposition.

Tom's new neighbor in Cell 2 was a cocaine dealer, Wilfredo "Tito" Rosa. Rosa's operation in the Wilmington area had been extensive, and he was looking at thirty years in prison for his part in a ring that had sold seventy pounds of the addictive white powder in two years.

The month after Tom was jailed, Rosa had been moved into the cell next to Tom's. Thus, their "friendship" extended further back than Tom's and Nick Perillo's. Rosa wrote to Colm Connolly and said that he and Tom had once managed to talk to each other three or four hours a day by using the slots at the bottom of their cell doors or the window-yard technique.

In December of 1997, Rosa told the prosecutors that Tom had been seething over his brother Gerry's betrayal. They whiled away the hours in the 1-F pod kidding about what Tom could arrange to have done to his enemies. Rosa told Connolly that *he* was the first on Tom's hit list. Tom wanted Connolly " 'taken care of.' I told him no way," Rosa confided. "No federal prosecutors!

"We were kidding about having Gerry whacked," Rosa said. "But then it got serious. He wanted me to look into what the cost and what the details were about having Gerry killed."

Surely, he couldn't have been serious. A brother was a brother. But according to Tito Rosa, Tom *was* serious. Through their talks, he learned that Rosa was worried about how he was going to pay off the mortgage on his house down in Townsend while he was in prison in Smyrna, only a few miles away. He had $95,000 owing on it, and his wife and baby wouldn't have any place to live if he lost it. If Rosa helped him kill Gerry, Tom assured him, he would pay off his mortgage as well as any expenses connected with a hit man.

Rosa told Connolly that he never intended making good on the hit on Gerry, but he planned to take the money. Then he was going to snitch on Tom to the state and hope for a reduced sentence. But Rosa didn't go down to Smyrna; at the end of December, he was sent instead to the federal penitentiary in Fairton, New Jersey.

Nevertheless, Rosa said he had managed to stay in touch with Tom through his wife, Lilia.* Tom wrote to Lilia and she forwarded his letters to her husband. And it worked in reverse, too. Reportedly, Rosa sent Tom a picture of Lilia and their baby. Rosa said he'd done other errands for Tom; he was only one of many inmates whose phone privileges Tom had taken over. After he was moved out of Gander Hill, Rosa said, he'd called Tom's relatives to check on him around the time of the bail hearing, and everything seemed fine.

And then he heard that Tom had been denied bail and was still sitting in prison. In March 1998, Rosa was moved back to Gander Hill on another matter and into the 1-F pod. And although he was housed several cells away from Tom, they had managed to communicate fifteen or twenty minutes a day by standing near each other's windows during yard time.

By March, Tom's rage at his little brother was no longer uppermost in his mind. Connolly already knew about the burglary plot he'd set up with Nick Perillo—but now Rosa told Connolly that Tom was willing to go further than that to punish Debby. "He was afraid that she was gonna break," Rosa said, "because the federal government was poking around, asking her questions."

When Rosa was moved into the cell next to Tom's, they resumed their hours-long discussions of what could be done to be sure that Debby didn't cooperate any further with the prosecutors. It galled Tom to think that the woman he had once controlled completely should now be in a position to pose such a threat to him.

There was no solution, really, but to have her killed. When Rosa seemed receptive, Tom slipped him some pictures of Debby and gave him her address on Delaware Avenue. He explained—as he had to Perillo—that her house was almost invisible behind tall hedges and that a fence separated it from the neighbors on either side.

"There was a good possibility," Rosa told Connolly, "that someone could just walk up to her door like a flower delivery guy and just whack her."

It seemed not to have occurred to Tom that he was dealing with men who were exceptionally con-wise. He was vastly underrating Colm Connolly and Ferris Wharton; he was barely aware of Bob Donovan and Eric Alpert. And he was certainly unaware that his jailhouse confidants were talking to his prosecutors.

Tom listened with interest when Rosa told him that he believed his brother-in-law Jorge would be willing to murder Debby if the price was right. They decided it would be safer to talk in code. Debby would be referred to as "tuna," and instead of saying "kill" or "murder," they would say "black."

Writing in Spanish, Rosa actually sent a letter to Jorge using the code words. He told his brother-in-law to ask no questions, but simply to rewrite the contents in his own handwriting so Tom wouldn't recognize the real author, mail it to Lilia to send on to Tom. Then in order to assure Tom that the conspiracy to murder was moving ahead, Jorge was to go take photographs of Debby's house, which were to be sent to Rosa at Gander Hill.

All in good time, Rosa showed Tom the photos of the house that had been so familiar to him for many years. He was apparently convinced that it was only a matter of time before the hit on Debby was accomplished.

Rosa's letter to Jorge had mentioned a "blackened tuna," in Spanish. "Does that mean a dead Deborah MacIntyre?" Connolly asked him.

"Right." He nodded. "[The lady] being dead."

The investigators found Jorge, who turned over a copy of the letter that discussed a murder and the photographs of Debby's house. They told Rosa to limit his conversations with Tom to the discussion of the plot to kill his ex-lover. But Tom wasn't satisfied with that; he evidently felt the plan was going so smoothly that he told Rosa he wanted to add a hit on Gerry to the contract.

On June 9, 1998, Debby and Tom Bergstrom had a meeting with the prosecution team. Every time she thought she had absorbed the worst pain their revelations brought, she was wrong. But these men whom she had resented deeply because she thought they were persecuting the man she loved had now become friends. The scales had fallen from her eyes, and like it or not, she had long since realized that Tom didn't love her and had, perhaps, never loved her. But this day brought such ugly revelations that her conscious mind quite literally refused to listen to them.

Just as she and Tom Bergstrom were about to leave the June meeting, Connolly said something to her about a murder plot. "I heard it," Debby remembered, "but I didn't hear it. It went over my head. In the middle of the night, his words came back and I started to think about it and thought that couldn't be what he'd said."

She called Bergstrom the next day, and when he returned her call, he told her that it was apparently true. Tom had been trying to have her killed.

"Oh, my God," Debby gasped. The only thing she thought about was her children, Steve and Victoria. Moreover, the press had found out about Tom's murder plot and it would probably be all over Wilmington soon. She had to get to them and tell them before they read about it in the papers. "I got in the car and went looking for them," she said. "Victoria was working a block from the federal building and she would have to walk by the reporters. I found them both in time—and I guess it's funny now, but they saw the look on my face and each of them blurted, 'What's the matter? Did I do something wrong?' "

She just hugged them.

On August 31, 1998, Tom was indicted on three counts of criminal solicitation (for the two murder plots—against Debby and Gerry—and the plot to burglarize Debby's house). These three charges, if proven in a court of law, could result in a sentence of thirteen years in prison. But you can pour only so much water into a vase, and if Tom was convicted of murder, the charges might be moot.

Tom's defense team was taking one hit after another. They denied vociferously that there had ever been real murder plots, and hinted that the state had deliberately put prison snitches next to Tom to entice him into wrongdoing. Tom Bergstrom characterized Capano's plots as those of a man "acting in total desperation and arrogance."

The Fahey family looked on with weary understanding. It had been so long now, and they resented anyone who tried to slow down Anne Marie's day in court. They were understandably angry at the defense team. "How can [they] come out and feed this stuff to people and expect us to believe it?" Kevin asked.

"He just seems to be a desperate person who is trying to control MacIntyre the way he controlled Annie," Kathleen commented.

The women in Tom's life, from mistresses to daughters, had been offered up to burglars, alleged hit men, and sex offenders. It was not a question of their safety but of his; it was a matter of priority. (It took until June 13, 1998, before Tom conceded that his daughters were not the source of the blood spots found in his house. When he stipulated to that, he saved them from giving blood samples or from having to testify about their menstrual periods.)

Even so, there were those who said privately that Tom was prepared to ask his daughters to lie for him if need be. They clearly adored him. As a last-ditch effort, would he suggest they testify that they had been in his house on June 27 and therefore he could not possibly be the one who killed Anne Marie? One of Tom's defense attorneys had left the team unexpectedly the first week of April. Joe Hurley resigned without any public explanation, although it was alleged that he was unwilling to go along with Capano's proposed game plan. Hurley made his exit as splashily as he made his entrance, vowing he would never reveal his reasons in this lifetime.

Headed for trial, Tom still had four attorneys representing him: Charlie Oberly, Gene Maurer, his old friend Jack O'Donnell, and a new member of his team, whose flamboyance made up for the loss of Joe Hurley—Joe Oteri of Boston. Many people said Oteri was the top criminal defense attorney on the East Coast.

The state didn't have nearly as much weight in terms of sheer numbers—only two prosecutors—but they were arguably the two men whom Tom hated and feared the most: Colm Connolly and Ferris Wharton, the "Nazi/snake/weasel" and "the hangman." Neither was a showboater; both were workhorses, and although there were witnesses that each would give his right arm to cross-examine, there was no lead prosecutor. They would be co-prosecutors in every sense of the word.

PART FIVE

. . . nor shall any person be subject for the same offense
to be twice put in jeopardy of life or limb;
nor shall be compelled in any criminal case to be a
witness against himself, nor be deprived of life, liberty,
or property, without due process of law. . . .

Fifth Amendment,
Constitution of the United States

IT HAD BEEN A LONG TIME COMING, but finally, on October 6, 1998, the trial would begin—first with jury selection, and then in earnest. In retrospect, it was autumn that seemed to have marked critical turning points in Anne Marie Fahey's life and death. In earlier autumns, she had returned to Wilmington to work for Governor Carper, tried to break up with Tom, and met Mike Scanlan. In the Capano family, Tom, Louie, and Joey all had October birthdays. Debby had divorced her husband in October. In later autumns, Tom had left Kay, proposed to Debby, and been arrested for murder. Thanksgiving had long since ceased to be a time of celebration for all of the principals in this case. But after a long sultry summer, perhaps it was fitting that Tom's murder trial should begin in the bright coolness of October.

The Daniel J. Herrmann Courthouse hunkered over an entire block of downtown Wilmington, only grudgingly giving up enough space on each front corner for two tall holly trees. Huge, gray stoned, with massive colonnades across the front, the courthouse looked as if it would last a century, although Wilmingtonians were already suggesting it was obsolete. The Wilmington library was kitty-corner across the street, the Hotel du Pont was straight across on the other side of Rodney Square. In October, the trees in the square still had leaves, but they changed color a little more with each chilly night.

This trial above all trials attracted the curious like a magnet. The sidewalk and the wide steps in front of the courthouse drew passersby who all seemed to have an opinion, many speaking conspiratorially to anyone who would listen. "Thomas is a good man—he could not have done what they say." "Ahh, the old man must be spinning in his grave today. His sons killed him, you know—to get at his money." "It's those women—they made him do it." "That poor mother. To see it all come to *this.*"

When asked if they actually *knew* the principals, most of the rumor carriers shook their heads. But they felt qualified to judge—from what they'd read in the papers, or seen on television, or even heard in the neighborhood.

Those who made it into the courtroom were extremely determined, or lucky—or privileged: family members of the victim and defendant, of course; the press; and those willing to rise before the sun and drive through the hazy dawn to wait in a serpentine line. Everyone had to pass through metal detectors before they could even move into the courthouse. The winding marble stairs to the third-floor courtroom, number 302, were smoothed and worn in the center of each step, testimony to the hundreds of thousands who had climbed there. Between the second and third floors, traffic would halt as people up ahead were checked for contraband.

The rotunda at the top of the stairs was high and splendid. Bronze banisters kept the crowd back from the well that channeled upward through the two flights of curving stairs; the floor was marble. Three courtrooms with ornate portals reaching to the ceiling of the rotunda opened off the waiting area. It was a grand, if not economical, use of space.

Kathi Carlozzi, a pretty woman in middle age and a secretary from the Superior Court, had been chosen to make the decisions about who would get in and who would not. The organizing of the press and the gallery in the Capano trial would be meticulous. Court employees had already been through a baptism of fire with the high-profile cases of Amy Grossberg and Brian Peterson. Kathi would also keep track of the forbidden items: cell phones, cameras, recorders, and laptop computers. Regulars pasted their names on the phones and other gear; eventually, when court recesses ended too quickly, even half-empty cans of pop were labeled and left on the battered table in the rotunda area.

The last step before access to the courtroom itself was granted was to hand over purses and briefcases before passing through another metal detector. Kathi was unfailingly pleasant, but immovable when she had to be.

Courtroom 302 had an octagonal theme that was translated in its windows, wood trim, five hanging lamps, and wainscoting. The high ceiling was golden, molded in bas relief. Majestic as it was, the room's acoustics were lousy, especially when the nine wooden benches on each side were packed with avid spectators whose whispers and murmurs bounced off the lofty walls. The courtroom was so long and narrow that those in the backseats seemed a football field away from the witnesses.

Each day Kathi Carlozzi would usher the Faheys and Capanos in first, and, two warring families, they were separated by both an invisible boundary and a true one, the center aisle. The Capanos took up several of the forward rows on the left, and the Faheys sat on the right. Neither side acknowledged the other, except at the times the push of the crowd jostled them together in the aisle or doorway. Then, they were civil.

Members of the working press quickly chose their seats, and only then was the public allowed in. Many of them had never been in a courtroom before. They rushed in to find a good seat. The massive courtroom was actually designed to hold only 122 people, although there would be many times in the weeks ahead when spectators would make room for as many bodies as the long benches could possibly hold.

There was an air of expectation when Tom's trial began, even though nothing much was going to happen until a jury was picked—and that could take a long time. With the proliferation of pretrial publicity, it might not be easy to find prospective jurors who had no opinion about the innocence or guilt of Thomas Capano.

The cast of characters who took the stand would change continually; the prosecution expected to call more than a hundred witnesses, and the defense team hinted that it had almost as many. The constants would be Judge William Swain Lee, who looked more than a little like Robert Redford; Ferris Wharton, Colm Connolly, Bob Donovan, and Eric Alpert, the prosecutors and investigators; and for the defense, lead defense attorney Joe Oteri, Charlie Oberly, Gene Maurer, and Jack O'Donnell.

They were all top criminal defense attorneys, but very different from one another. Oberly was avuncular and quiet spoken, solidly versed in the law and a detail man; "the bookkeeper," some called him. Gene Maurer was slender and intense, with a Beatleish haircut, and often wore a worried look. Tall with gray curly hair, Jack O'Donnell was an old friend of Tom's who usually practiced law in Florida. It was O'Donnell who would frequently hug Tom's daughters or pat Marguerite's shoulder during breaks. He smiled easily. O'Donnell had bailed Gerry out of trouble years before. And when Joe Oteri signed on to defend Capano, wags called Tom's four attorneys the "dream team." And they were a million dollars'—or more—worth of lawyers.

At sixty-seven, Oteri had proved that a poor boy from south Boston could one day be a highly successful attorney. The ex-marine was living on borrowed time, however, and not from scrapes in the Korean War. When he was in his twenties and still handling divorce cases, he encountered a Boston police officer who had just lost a child support case to his estranged wife, whom Oteri, to his regret, represented. The enraged cop shot his wife and then wounded Oteri in the knees, back, and head. Scrambling under a car, he realized dully that the shooter was coming to finish the job. But at that moment the injured wife made a noise and the maddened man turned back to shoot her in the head. Forgetting Oteri, he swallowed his gun and fell dead beside her.

Emerging alive from beneath the car, Oteri decided that being a divorce lawyer was far too risky, and his practice through the years since had become heavily weighted with safer clients—defendants who had drug or murder charges hanging over their heads. He was good at winning acquittals and was not the favorite attorney of the DEA. Handsome in a dangerous way and dapper with his snow white hair, mustache, and beard, and his dark eyes, Oteri had graduated from Boston College and Boston College Law School, just as Tom had. In fact, Tom had attended his lectures, and he selected Oteri from a roster of high-profile criminal defense attorneys.

Joe Oteri had a sense of humor, a lightning-quick intelligence, and didn't mind the media at all, cheerfully wading through reporters. He was a showman and a scrapper. His failings were his tendency to shout at a jury to emphasize his points and his condescension to witnesses who were obviously a few steps down the social ladder from himself or elderly. These elements of his style were annoying but apparently unconscious on his part.

No one yet knew what Tom Capano's defense would be. In the summer just past, his attorneys had filed more than two dozen motions asking for the obvious—to disqualify Gerry, Louie, and Debby as witnesses and to ask for a change of venue—or the ridiculous: They wanted Judge Lee to forbid the Fahey family and their friends from sitting in view of the jury or showing emotion in the courtroom. They asked to have Connolly removed as a prosecutor, claiming his federal grand jury investigation was tainted, and they maintained that the evidence seized in the search of Tom's house was "fruit of the poisoned tree," obtained with an illegal search warrant.

Judge Lee had denied all their motions, save for granting permission for the Department of Correction to release Tom's medical records. Were his attorneys considering a not-guilty-by-reason-of-insanity plea? Since Lee would not throw out the possibility of a death penalty verdict, finding Tom criminally insane might well save his life. But it was doubtful that a man of his ego would agree to such a plea.

As had been expected, jury selection took a very long time—almost three weeks. Each side had twenty peremptory challenges and could dismiss that many potential jurors without giving a reason. They could also be dismissed for cause. It was Monday, October 26, before the actual trial began. Twelve jurors and six alternates had finally been seated. It promised to be a prolonged trial, and extra alternates would guarantee there would be at least twelve sitting jurors. None of their names were released to the media.

The litigants sat at three long tables on the left side of the courtroom, one behind the other: the court staff closest to Judge Lee, then the prosecutors, and finally the defense. Whoever addressed the jury would move to a lectern on the right side of the room.

Tom was sandwiched between his attorneys and kept under the watchful eye of court deputies. Those who knew him were surprised to see that he seemed to have shrunk. His skin, like that of all longtime prisoners, displayed the yellow-white pallor of jail and his features were pinched. Even so, he still carried himself with a familiar confidence. He often turned to the gallery to mouth messages to his mother, his daughters, his sister. He virtually ignored his guards, managing somehow to look as though he were a member of the defense team, and not the defendant.

FERRIS WHARTON made the opening statement for the state. He began with Anne Marie's own voice. Who better could tell the jury of the struggle she had put up to free herself from the man who now sat at the defense table?

"I finally have brought closure to Tom Capano. What a controlling, manipulative, insecure, jealous maniac. . . ."

With a conscientious juxtaposition of facts and time, Wharton told the jury that less than two weeks after that entry in Anne

Marie's diary, Tom had bought a huge cooler. "It wasn't the kind of cooler you might throw some sodas and some beers in," he pointed out. "It was a 162-quart cooler. Huge. It was the kind of cooler you might take on a boat when you go fishing. . . . But it was a curious purchase for the defendant because although he could well afford it, he didn't have a boat and he had no interest in fishing."

Moving on, Wharton described Tom's next step. "On May 13, he made another curious purchase, through a woman by the name of Debby MacIntyre," he said, and told the jury about the little gun store out on Route 13. The gun she had bought had disappeared, but the cooler would end up as "Anne Marie Fahey's coffin. You see," he said, "that person—Thomas Capano—had determined that if he could not manipulate Anne Marie Fahey into being with him, she would be with no one—*forever.*"

Connolly and Wharton had agreed going in that they would not over-try this case; the facts were there, the witnesses were present who would corroborate the facts. And there were vital pieces of physical evidence waiting. Thus, in a very short time Wharton encapsulated the case against Tom: a jealous man, a woman who resisted, a gun, and a cooler. And now he proposed to introduce to the jury everyone who was involved with the case, beginning with Judge Lee and moving on to the prosecution and the defense teams, a gesture a surprised Joe Oteri did not appreciate. "If Your Honor please," he objected, "I'll introduce myself and the group to the jury!"

"Your Honor," Wharton countered with exaggerated innocence, "I think I'm entitled to do that."

"You're entitled to do that," Judge Lee said with a hint of a smile. "I'm sure you'll get a second chance, Mr. Oteri."

Judge Lee set the tone of the trial in a courtroom so filled with emotion that it would be a continual balancing act. His sidebar conferences, out of the jury's hearing, would keep both sides defused, and his sotto voce comments were often hilarious. Lee had six attorneys (seven if you counted the defendant) with completely different personalities and, of course, different goals. He wanted everything on the record and he demanded order, but he understood that this marathon trial must never be allowed to veer out of control. Lee understood too well that the defendant had within him the capacity to turn the proceedings into a circus.

Ferris Wharton, even with a laid-back style and his easy connection to the jury, had an awesome task in front of him. For twenty-eight months now, federal and state investigators had been uncovering evidence and witnesses to knit hundreds of details into a net that was about to drop over Tom Capano. The jury must be made to understand the evidence and, so very essential, the sequence of events. Information that had become second nature to the investigators had to be explained to twelve jurors who had come to this courtroom with open minds.

To help him track Tom through his alleged preparations for murder and the cover-up, Wharton had a huge chart prepared. The Middle Atlantic Great Lakes Organized Crime Law Enforcement Network, a government-funded organization that provided support and an information-sharing nexus to police and prosecutors and often built demonstration aids for trials, had constructed this chart. There were photographs of the houses and the buildings involved, of the vehicles and boats, and all of the receipts of credit-card transactions. As Wharton spoke, the jurors could follow the deadly time line themselves.

"We went to them with a vertical arrangement," he recalled, "and they showed us it would be easier to follow if it was spread out horizontally—starting in Gerry Capano's driveway at 5:45 A.M. on Friday morning, June twenty-eighth."

Rising to present his opening statement to the jury and using the huge chart to illustrate his remarks, Wharton began to explain what had happened the morning after Anne Marie died. Gerry Capano's neighbor had seen Tom parked outside Gerry's house, and then watched as Gerry walked up to the passenger window.

"His brother asks him if he can take a boat ride," Wharton said. "And that must have sent chills through Gerry Capano's body because he knew what that meant, because months before that date, his brother had talked to him about the need to use that boat to dispose of a body or bodies."

Tom had borrowed money and a gun from Gerry back in February 1996—Wharton continued—to set up the story that he might have to kill blackmailers and extortionists who were threatening his children. "Tom Capano played the brother card hard," Wharton said. When Tom came to his house and asked to use the boat, Gerry knew why. "So they agreed to meet later at Tom Capano's house, but Gerry had to do some things first. He had to pick up somebody and take him to work before he could leave. Now, they had a routine; Gerry would call as he's approaching Thomas Pitts's apartment to make sure he's out of bed and ready to be picked up. This is a bill from Gerry's phone which shows the call, 6:35 A.M., to Thomas Pitts. He picks him up and takes him to work.

"Ultimately, he rendezvoused with the defendant, but—before that happens—Tom Capano has some things to do, too. Seven o'clock or so, he goes to his wife's house. . . . Kay has a Chevy Suburban. It's a bigger car, more space. He switches cars. . . . And then he goes up to Tower Hill at 7:45 . . . and walks around the track for a while. He's got some time before Gerry will get back to his house. And he sees Debby MacIntyre—a chance encounter—as she's going to work at Tatnall School, and they say hello."

Most mornings, Tom exercised at the track. There was a body waiting for him back at his house that morning but he had still taken pains to maintain his usual schedule.

"Then he goes home," Wharton said, pointing to a picture, on the chart, of the Grant Avenue house, "and Gerry arrives. . . . Tom has got a cooler in the garage, a large cooler. He's got chains. He's got a lock. And Gerry helps him with the cooler to get that in the car."

But Gerry didn't want to leave his truck at Tom's house—so the two brothers drove to the Acme supermarket's parking lot at Trolley Square. "There's also a MAC [ATM machine] at Trolley Square. And at 8:41 A.M., the defendant withdraws $200 from the MAC machine."

What was Tom thinking as he heard all of the details, verifiable details, of what he had been confident was a completely secret day? Receipts, phone bills, minutiae had caught him as accurately as if a candid camera had literally been following him around.

"They head off to Stone Harbor. Nine-twenty-seven A.M., they're en route," Wharton continued. "The bill for Tom's portable phone reflects a call from outside of Delaware. And somewhere around 10:25 A.M., they arrive at Gerry's house in Stone Harbor."

The jurors, who had just seen Gerry's huge house in Wilmington, blinked slightly as Wharton pointed to the photo of another half-million-dollar house, at the shore.

"One of the first things the defendant does when they get to Stone Harbor is get on Gerry's phone," Wharton said. "He calls Debby MacIntyre on her line at Tatnall School at 10:31. It's only a minute conversation. He also calls Kay Capano's house at virtually the same time."

Tom and Gerry bought gas at a marina in Stone Harbor from a young woman who recognized Gerry. They paid $138.86 cash. Because it was cash there was no receipt with a time on it, but the next charge on that Friday morning was at 11:33. "So about this time is when Tom and Gerry head out to sea on Gerry's boat." Wharton tapped on the picture of a boat, the *Summer Wind*, which had carried Anne Marie's body in the cooler. "Gerry Capano follows the sun. And he heads out sixty miles or so and he notices that the depth gauge is about 190 feet. And they throw Anne Marie Fahey in her coffin off the boat. But it doesn't sink. Even wrapped in chains, it doesn't sink.

"So to get that cooler to sink, Gerry takes out a shotgun that he keeps on the boat, which he uses for sharks, puts a slug in it—not buckshot, but a slug—and shoots the cooler. It let water come in so that it will sink.

"Still doesn't sink."

Anne Marie's brothers and sister knew what had happened to her, but the retelling was agonizing for them. And the jurors' faces mirrored—what? Shock? Horror?

"Gerry brings the boat around," Wharton continued, "to the side of the cooler, and they bring it in to the side. And Gerry's had enough at this point. This is wrong. This is *wrong,* and he goes to the front of the boat and looks away as his brother wrestles with the cooler, wrestles with the chains. He gives him an anchor—two anchors—and the defendant wraps the chains and the anchors around the body of Anne Marie Fahey, which is now taken out of the cooler, and Gerry turns around to see a foot, a part of a calf, sinking into the ocean."

Wharton then told the jury of how the cooler had been disassembled, the lid thrown into the ocean one way and the main portion, marred now with two holes from the slug, another.

The two men were back in Stone Harbor by 3:30 P.M., when Tom made another call, Wharton told the jury.

Then they returned to the Grant Avenue house, where the two brothers dismantled the couch in the great room, with its "basketball-sized" bloodstain at shoulder height on the right side. Pointing again to his timeline chart, Wharton said, "This location is 105 Foulke Road. There's a project being conducted there. Louis Capano's business was renovating some of the buildings there. And they had these large Dumpsters—they're almost the size of railroad cars. They throw the couch into one of those Dumpsters and Gerry leaves.

"But Tom Capano's not done yet," Wharton said. "He still has Kay's car. A little after six-eleven, he fills it up with gas at Deerhurst Exxon—$54.85 worth. Returns to Kay's, spends some time with his kids, goes home—goes to Debby MacIntyre's house and basically crashes at eleven o'clock. But he's not done yet. He's not done cleaning up. He's not done covering up what he had done on June twenty-seventh, because on June twenty-ninth—the next day after the trip to Stone Harbor to dispose of Anne Marie Fahey—he buys a new carpet at Air Base Carpet. And the day after that, he buys stain remover at Happy Harry's."

Wharton now had a more difficult task. He had to try to tell the jury who Anne Marie Fahey had been. To sum up a life in half an hour, to explain why a beautiful young woman had fallen in love with a married man seventeen years older, wouldn't be easy. He could only give the jurors the facts and impressions he had gleaned, to describe her transcendent beauty and her vast capacity for love. If he had been able to bring her back just for a moment to stand before the jury, he would have. But Anne Marie wasn't in the courtroom, at least not in the sense that anyone could see or hear. She could be portrayed only in words, photographs, and videotape.

Wharton moved on to the last night of Anne Marie's life. He described the strange evening at the Ristorante Panorama, where Tom and Anne Marie sat through a three-course dinner and barely ate— or even spoke. The timetable was extraordinarily important here. "So they leave the restaurant sometime around nine-twelve," Wharton explained. "That's when the receipt is printed. It's a little unclear what happens next. It depends on who you believe."

Did they return to Tom's house, or did he take Anne Marie home? Wharton told the jurors that someone was in her apartment between 9:45 and 10 P.M., according to Connie Blake, who lived beneath it, and not someone in high heels. Someone was also there at 11:52—someone who dialed *69 on her phone to determine who her last caller had been.

"And at 12:05 A.M.," Wharton said, "for some reason, Tom Capano decides it's necessary to call the Saul, Ewing answering service to get his voice mail . . . what that does, if you think about it, is place him in his house at that time."

Less than six hours later, Tom was waiting in his brother Gerry's driveway for help with a "problem."

Wharton touched on the carpet, the blood evidence, the cooler, the gun, and the bloody couch. He let the jury know that Gerry, Louie, and Debby had initially held back the facts of their participation in the case and had been allowed to plea-bargain in exchange for telling the truth. (If something is likely to come back and bite him, the prudent lawyer brings it up himself before the other side can spring it.)

"The state has the burden of proving the defendant's guilt beyond a reasonable doubt," Wharton told the jurors. "The evidence will show you that before Anne Marie Fahey stepped out of the Ristorante Panorama on June the twenty-seventh, she had a life, she had a family. She loved people and people loved her. She had friends. She had confidants. You will see and hear from many of them. Before Anne Marie Fahey stepped out of the Ristorante Panorama with Tom Capano, she had a job. She had responsibilities. The governor of the state depended upon her to make sure his schedule was set. After Anne Marie Fahey stepped out of the Ristorante Panorama with Tom Capano on June the twenty-seventh, no one—not her family, not her boyfriend, Mike Scanlan, not her many friends, not a single one of them, no one from work, not her employer, not the governor, not anybody—has had any contact at all with her.

"Ladies and gentlemen," Wharton concluded, "a person like Anne Marie Fahey, someone who loved so much and is loved by so many, just doesn't disappear. Someone like Anne Marie Fahey who is responsible just doesn't disappear without a trace unless something is terribly, terribly wrong. Something did happen which was terribly, terribly wrong to Anne Marie Fahey. The evidence will show you, ladies and gentlemen, that the man she described as 'a controlling, manipulative, insecure, jealous maniac,' the man who would not even allow her to decide what she had for dinner on June 27, 1996, would not allow her to decide with whom she was going to spend the rest of her life. The evidence will show you, ladies and gentlemen, that Tom Capano murdered Anne Marie Fahey."

Tom Capano looked straight ahead. People in the gallery had no clue about what he was thinking; they could see only the back of his expensive suit.

JOE OTERI began his opening remarks by promising the jury he would not talk for an hour and a half, and he pointedly reintroduced his team. Then he explained that in Boston attorneys called other attorneys "brother." "My brother, Mr. Wharton," he said, "pointed out to you that Tom Capano was a controlling freak because he ordered a meal for Anne Marie Fahey at the Panorama. You will hear that Tom Capano considers himself a gentleman. You will hear there's an E-mail between Anne Marie Fahey and a girl named Kim Horstman where she tells her, 'Go to dinner with Tom—he's a perfect gentleman.' A gentleman who is a host at dinner orders dinner for his guest."

Oteri started out magnanimously, dealing with the easier questions about the case. He said he didn't want to cast shadows over Anne Marie, and then he proceeded to do just that, moving swiftly to chip away at her character. "We have no intention of besmirching this girl's background or reputation," he said, "but we must talk about reality also. Anne Marie Fahey was not an eighteen-year-old high school kid. She was a thirty-year-old woman in 1996. She had been with Tom Capano off and on for two or three years, so she wasn't a kid starting out with some older guy. She had lived in Spain. She had lived in Washington, D.C.—that cesspool—and she had been down there working. [She] came back here and was involved in politics. One grows up mighty quickly in politics even in a state as small as Delaware. Anne Marie Fahey knew what was happening."

Oteri listed the things Tom had bought or given her: the new windshield, the air conditioner, the $500 for her therapist, $30 by messenger when she was broke. "She was onto a good thing," he said with a slight sneer in his voice. "And she used it, and more power to her."

It might have been a tactical error to denigrate Anne Marie, the victim. But who could read the impassive faces of the jurors?

As for Gerry Capano's testimony against his brother, Oteri dismissed Gerry as having a "brain like a fried egg. He has used drugs for years. He's also a boozer. He's a typical screwed-up rich kid who never had to earn anything in his life. You will hear that he's a poster boy for the 'me generation.' "

The lawyer from Boston was fully aware that he didn't have to prove anything; the burden of proof was on the prosecution. Oteri's remarks touched upon nothing that was absolute and everything that vilified the victim and the state's witnesses. He maintained that Tom Capano had done his best to help the investigation into Anne Marie's disappearance. He had finally given up only because he was afraid.

"Tom Capano tried to arrange to speak to Wilmington Police officers," Oteri said, "but subsequently, his house was searched by the FBI, and he stopped that because he could no longer trust anyone. He tried to arrange a meeting with the government early on— on the condition that he would only talk about the night in question, not any other night, and Mr. Wharton refused it. He came back with an offer—another offer—saying they would speak about any aspect of his relationship with Anne Marie Fahey, but he would not talk about other people or other events. Again, it was refused."

Oteri told the jurors that Tom had been "terrified" by the "massive police presence" and felt no one would believe him. "Based on his prior experience as a lawyer and a political operative," Oteri said, Tom was "convinced he could not get a fair hearing from the feds. If he spoke to them, they would only twist his words and hang him up. You will hear that Tom Capano was a wealthy lawyer, had a big house, four beautiful daughters. You will hear he was a managing partner of a fancy law firm. He was socially active, belonged to prestigious clubs. All at once—if Tom Capano talks to people—this is all gone, because no one's going to believe him, because the feds have picked him as a target of this investigation from the beginning."

Joe Oteri was an old hand at fighting "the feds" and he made the government sound evil and predatory. He stressed that even President Clinton and Governor Carper had inserted themselves into the search for Anne Marie, bringing federal investigators in as early as July 8. "He knew that the FBI and Mr. Connolly and the United States Attorney's Office and all their massive resources would be directed toward this one case," Oteri said. "There's a massive use of power, there's massive amounts of money and people and resources that can be brought to bear, and all the gloves come off and it's bare-knuckle fighting."

It was true that the investigation had focused on Tom Capano early on. The last person to be seen with a murder victim is always the first suspect. But would mentioning Tom's wealth, prestige, and his beautiful daughters endear him to this far from wealthy jury?

"Tom Capano is a bright guy," Oteri continued in his streets-of-Boston accent. "If Tom Capano is buying a coffin with this big cooler, would he go to a store a couple of miles from his house? Would he buy it with his credit card? Would he leave it with the bar code on it that puts it right to that store? That's insanity. He wouldn't do a thing like that. Wouldn't he arrange to dump it someplace? He never goes out on boats. You will hear evidence that Tom talked to his brother Joe about doing something for Gerry—the kid brother—who was very good to Tom's kids by taking them out on his boat. You will hear that Gerry had just bought a new $125,000 boat and Tom wanted to get him something. Joe suggested a cooler."

Oteri dismissed the $8,000 loan from Gerry. He could explain that. He would explain the borrowed gun. But most of all, he would explain through testimony that Tom Capano had not murdered Anne Marie. "Anne Marie Fahey died as a result of an outrageous, horrible, tragic accident, that only one other person—who was there—knows everything that happened that night."

A buzz started in the courtroom. This was the first time that anyone suggested that Anne Marie had died in an accident. What accident? Where? Was Tom there? And who was the other person who had been present?

"Tom Capano and his brother Gerry," Oteri continued in a startling admission that Tom had been involved in a death, and its subsequent cover-up, "disposed of Anne Marie Fahey's body by placing it in a cooler and taking it to sea and sinking it. You're going to hear that Tom Capano is not the least bit proud of that. You will hear that it was motivated by fear for himself, by a desire to protect himself, by a desire to protect others. You will hear what happened to Anne Marie Fahey's body. This is the difficult thing you're going to have to do. You hear about what happened to Anne Marie Fahey. You are revolted. You want revenge. You want to strangle the person that did it. But you can't—because you're jurors. You're twelve people. You have to decide—never mind what happened after she died. *How* did she die? Was it murder, or was it not? Was it an accident? Was it something?"

Joe Oteri had just pulled a sensational rabbit out of his hat. The question was, could he make it hop? He ended his opening remarks with a patriotic paragraph about America and the "presumption of innocence" that ruled its courts. "What that means is any one of us—me, you, this lady, Wharton—no matter what we're accused of, no matter what we're charged with, we stand here in this jury room before you, sir, and you, ma'am, and everybody else, presumed innocent. And we will remain innocent, wrapped in a cloak of innocence, until that prosecution can rip that cloak from you by proof beyond, and to the exclusion of, all reasonable doubt.

"And until that's done, Tom Capano is innocent."

THE opening statements in a trial give the jury an overview of the entire case. Both the state and the defense attorneys tell the jurors what happened and how they will prove it. Their conclusions are, of course, dissimilar. Now, each had to produce compelling witnesses and physical and circumstantial evidence to validate their rhetoric.

The first morning of the trial had come to an end and with economical use of time; both sides had finished their opening statements. The suggestion that Anne Marie had died in an accident had everyone guessing. It could not have been an automobile accident; there had been no damage to any of the cars involved in the case. Had she fallen down Tom's stairs or drowned in his bathtub? One reporter thought Oteri was suggesting that some kind of kinky sex had gone wrong.

Outside the courthouse, reporters crowded around Oteri. He

seemed comfortable when he said, "Yes, Anne Marie did die at Tom's house."

"Why did he take her out on the boat if it was an accident?" someone asked.

"Because you can't keep it at home," he shot back in jest. But it was a sick joke and drew only nervous laughter.

Oteri was already walking away as someone asked him, "But why didn't he call 911?"

_____ *Chapter Thirty-seven* _____

ONE PART of the long journey toward the truth was over; the witnesses and the evidence came next. Now, Colm Connolly and Ferris Wharton would present their case to the jurors. Often, one of them began with the direct examination of a witness and the other did the redirect. Each had a mind geared to details, but Connolly was the more intense of the pair, while Wharton often began his questioning with an easier style, homing in later. Tom's "dream team" watched carefully for any weak spots that might provide an opportunity to jump in on cross and lessen the impact of the testimony.

No one in the courtroom heard what went on in the sidebar conferences at Judge Lee's bench. On the opening day of the trial, there was a discussion of something as simple as the problem of the Capanos' bringing bags of candy to pass around to lawyers and paralegals. Judge Lee commented dryly that he would not allow the attorneys to speak with candy in their mouths. More important was Lee's disapproval of Tom's demeanor.

"Tom's turning around and talking to his family all the time," Lee said, "and they've [Department of Correction guards] asked him to stop, and he's told them he's not going to stop. This trial is not a visiting period with his family."

Brian Fahey was the first witness for the prosecution. Anne Marie's family had waited for twenty-eight months to tell her story, but it must have been difficult for him, her closest sibling in age, to remember the good and the bad times. As one reporter said, "Brian had his heart in his eyes. Looking at him, you felt that he had known Anne Marie so well and generally understood people on a spiritual level—as if he somehow knew things without having to ask."

Brian answered Wharton's questions carefully and without

emotion. He recalled the day they all lost their mother and Anne Marie's struggle to grow up amidst chaos. She had, indeed, grown up, working hard for her education as they all had. He remembered the last time he had seen her, sitting in O'Friel's and holding Mike Scanlan's hand.

"She asked if she could pick me up at the airport [when he came back from Ecuador]. I said yes, and then I told her I would call her and give the time and flight and all that."

But when he came back, Anne Marie was not there. He had never seen her again.

Joe Oteri's cross-examination continued his attempt to disparage Anne Marie. Brian would not go along with Oteri's characterization of his dead sister as having an "Irish temper." When Oteri tried to paint her as neurotic and promiscuous, it fell flat; Brian simply gazed at him with a calm but resolute expression.

Yes, it was true that the Fahey family had filed a civil suit against Tom Capano and members of his family. Yes, they had hired an attorney, David Weiss. Once Oteri had brought the matter up, Wharton asked Brian on redirect why he and his siblings had filed such a suit.

"Basically, we believed that Tom Capano had murdered my sister," he replied. "We believed that he got his brothers to help him cover it up. And so we decided that we needed to do something—to take action."

"Why?" Wharton asked.

"We were very mad and believed that they were responsible for causing my family a great deal of pain, for killing my sister, and being perfectly content to [let us] live out the rest of our lives without ever knowing what happened to our sister. And I didn't think that they should be able to get away with that without us putting up some kind of fight."

The animosity between the Fahey and Capano families was palpable and dramatic. The Capano side of the gallery stared stonily at Brian. But there was more drama in the courtroom than most people there realized. At 2 P.M., Judge Lee received a phone call that said, "Capano is going down in an hour."

Lee called a sidebar conference to inform the attorneys about the death threat against the defendant. Joe Oteri's witty response was, "May Mr. Capano be moved up to the prosecution table, please?"

Wharton smiled. "Well, if you trust him up there with us."

Lee pointed out the extra guards he had stationed in the courtroom and the consensus was that it was a crackpot call. An hour passed and nothing happened. The trial went on, and no one—not even the media—knew about the death threat.

The next day, Colm Connolly began questioning Kathleen Fahey-Hosey. She was very pretty and looked a little like the pictures of Anne Marie, but she was blond, more petite, and wore glasses. Kathleen recalled her dread when her sister had not been home waiting for Mike Scanlan to take her to Robert and Susan's house for dinner on the night of June 29. Connolly showed her a picture of the small settee in Anne Marie's apartment. "Do you recognize any of the clothing on this couch as being there when you went to the apartment on June twenty-ninth?"

"Yes. The robe and the blue-and-white striped shirt and blue pants."

"How about this item right here?"

"That's a floral dress that Anne Marie bought to wear to the Point-to-Point with Mike Scanlan."

"Were there any noticeable stains or tears in the dress when you saw it?"

"No."

How the floral dress, in perfect condition, got to Anne Marie's apartment was a big question. She had only one floral dress and she had been wearing it when she had dinner with Tom in Philadelphia on that last Thursday night. Had she changed into something else after she arrived home—if she *had* arrived home? Or had Tom brought it back to her apartment deliberately, just as he may have brought the box from Talbot's and the food found on the counter?

Kathleen believed that Tom had done just that, but there was no way to prove it. She told the jurors about that frightening Saturday night when they realized Anne Marie was missing, and about finding the letters from Tom Capano. Then she began to read the letters aloud, her sister's secret letters. Her clear voice was the only sound in the courtroom as she read Tom Capano's directives to her sister, coaxing Anne Marie to accept money and gifts from him.

"Now," Connolly asked, "as of June 29, 1996, did you have any knowledge that there had been a relationship between your sister and Tom Capano?"

"No, I did not."

"Did you know they knew each other?"

"I did know they knew each other. Wilmington's so small and Annie working for the governor and Capano doing bond work, she would mention he might be in now and then because she had known I knew him from before."

"Had you ever asked Anne Marie whether there was anything between her and Tom Capano?"

"No, I did not."

"Did you find any birth control pills in the apartment that night?"

"I found a box of birth control pills. To me, it looked like a sample pack. There may have been like five months' worth. They were unopened."

"Was Anne Marie's toothbrush in the apartment?"

"Yes."

"Did you at some point inventory everything that was in the apartment?"

"Yes. I was ordered by the court to inventory everything."

"Was anything missing that you recognized?"

"Anne Marie's keys were missing and her Walkman and her blue topaz ring."

The keys were the important item; someone had needed those keys to get into her apartment the night Connie Blake heard footsteps overhead.

When the trial resumed after a lunch break, Kathleen read her sister's diary aloud. If she heard a familiar, lost voice echoing in her words, still, in order to convict the man she believed was Annie's killer, Kathleen had no choice but to reveal Anne Marie's deepest secrets in a crowded courtroom. The diary had been published, but never before spoken aloud to strangers.

Connolly asked Kathleen if Anne Marie had had plans for the future. Yes, she had savings bonds tucked away. She had had hopes for marriage and babies.

"Anne Marie had plans to vacation with you in the summer of '96?"

"I think it was the third week in July," Kathleen said. "She was coming to the shore with my husband [and me] and two other couples for a week in Avalon. She gave my husband a check for four hundred dollars."

"Do you have any reason to suspect that Anne Marie would have run off?"

"No, I do not."

"Did she ever run off before?"

"No, she hasn't."

"Do you have any reason to suspect she would have committed suicide?"

"Absolutely not."

"Had you ever seen her manifest signs of violence toward anybody?"

"Anne was very gentle and sweet. She was not violent at all."

"Are you aware that she had told others that she had . . . exhibited violent behavior toward your father?" Connolly pressed.

"If I remember correctly," Kathleen answered, "my father used to take Anne Marie's change and she got tired of it, and chased him around the house with a field hockey stick."

"How old was she?"

"Probably junior high."

THERE was a break before Gene Maurer began cross-examining Kathleen. In the hallway, reporter Donna Renae from WHYY-TV murmured to Kathleen, "You're very brave."

"I always said this was Anne Marie's last fight," she replied quietly, "and I am going to finish it for her."

Most of the press and gallery were out in the hallway, phoning in stories, so that few saw that the Fahey family's priest gave Kathleen a quick blessing as she knelt in the aisle of the courtroom before she took the stand again.

Maurer questioned Kathleen intensely about when she had seen the twenty-seven-inch television set; whether the box from Talbot's had been opened; and whether she had seen some Cézanne prints Tom had given Anne Marie. "And there was, I guess," the defense attorney said, "continuing discussions . . . concerns on your part, maybe some friction between the two of you, that you felt Anne Marie did not manage her money well?"

"Yes."

"Anne Marie told you she had won the TV?"

"Yes. She told me Mrs. Columbus bought a chance for her and she won."

"Your characterization of Anne Marie's response when you would talk about this money issue was that she was 'snippy.' Is that right?"

"It was a source of contention."

The thrust of Maurer's questioning was clear; he wanted to suggest that Anne Marie and Kathleen were not really close, that Anne Marie had lied to her big sister and been snippy. Anyone who ever had a sister knew that was often the way even loving sisters interacted.

Maurer brought up a red herring when he asked, "Did Anne Marie have a red-and-white striped shirt?"

"I don't know. I don't remember seeing it in her laundry basket."

"Now, when you did your inventory of her apartment," he persisted, "did you find a red-and-white striped shirt?"

"No."

"Nowhere?"

"No."

"How many pairs of sneaks did she have?"

"I may be off by a pair or two, but she had a number of pairs of sneakers."

"I take it she also had more than one jogging outfit?"

"I know of a purple one. She may have had a blue one, too."

"Do you know if she had a black one?"

"I'd have to look at my list."

If Maurer could establish that some of Anne Marie's clothes were missing from her apartment, the defense might be able to bolster its scenario. He questioned Kathleen exhaustively on every detail of what she had found in Anne Marie's apartment, and she admitted that the shoes that Annie usually wore with the blue floral dress were there. How this line of questioning meshed with the accident theory remained to be seen.

And now Maurer put Kathleen through an ordeal. She had felt guilty enough about reading her sister's diary for the prosecution. Maurer asked her to read the rest, the sections written in the beginning of her relationship with Tom—when Anne Marie had been besotted with him.

On Friday, February 24, 1995, Anne Marie had written,

> I have shared my soul with T. I gave him my whole world, body and love. What I have not shared with T. is my fear of abandonment. I will withhold thoughts, info, etc., about myself if I think it may steer someone away from me. If I ever have the opportunity to speak to T. again, I will share everything, even my soul, and let him know exactly the way I feel. If I am rejected, at least I know that I told him about me, and let him into my world.
>   I love you T.

There were other entries, written by a young woman who seemed virtually defenseless in dealing with a man she thought she knew—a man whom she perceived to be gentle, kind, and as vulnerable and sad and lonely as she was. In those entries, Anne Marie seemed nothing at all like the savvy, opportunistic woman Joe Oteri had described. She sounded as gullible as any eighteen-year-old. In asking Kathleen to read the diary, it was possible that Maurer had given the prosecution a two-edged sword.

On re-cross, Connolly asked, "All of the diary entries you just read with Mr. Maurer were from the year 1994 and before March 1995?"

"That's correct."

At last, Kathleen could step down. All the while she had testified, Tom had glared at her with unmistakable hatred, "as if daring me to say what I needed to say." Now, as she walked between the lectern and the defense table, he hissed, "You fucking bitch."

Remembering it months later, Kathleen said, "I used to like Tom Capano, just like everyone else did. He actually said that to me when I stepped down from the witness stand. And the jurors heard him."

THAT was the way this long-awaited legal contest would continue. And between tearful memories and complicated testimony on police procedure and forensic evidence, there would be occasional smiles. But there would also be—despite all of the pretrial media coverage—startling revelations.

Tom Capano had long suffered from colitis, his particular response to stress. On the second day of trial, Oteri signaled Judge Lee urgently. Tom was having an attack of colitis, and he was rushed from the courtroom, something that would happen more than once. Medicine was prescribed for him but it had to be taken with food. Judge Lee then had to explain to the jurors why the defendant often ate bagels and sipped water as the trial progressed.

Dr. Neil Kaye, the psychiatrist who monitored her prescriptions and saw Anne Marie on the last afternoon of her life, testified that she had made the decision to rid herself of the man who was "freaking her out" by calling her every half hour and sending her endless E-mail. But Kaye admitted she had never told him the man's name.

Curiously, Dr. Kaye wore a wooden hat to court. It was very expensive, and meticulously carved from a single block of wood, so that it appeared to be an actual half fedora, half cowboy hat. He set it carefully on his knee as he testified. When Oteri asked him about his hat, he acknowledged that it was somewhat unwieldy and hot, but said he collected wooden hats and a trial was as good a place as any to display them. Dr. Michelle Sullivan knew the name of the man Anne Marie feared. It was Tom Capano. And she told the jury about her patient's determined struggle to break off with him.

∎

IN sidebar conferences, the defense attorneys fought to keep out of the jury's hearing statements Anne Marie had made to her friends about Tom. They submitted to Judge Lee that much of what Jill Morrison, Siobhan Sullivan, Jennifer Haughton, Jackie Steinhoff, Ginny Columbus, and Kim Horstman might say would be hearsay or even triple hearsay. They claimed it would show "prior bad acts" of their client. The prosecution maintained that her friends' testimony would validate Capano's stalking behavior.

Judge Lee finally decided to let their testimony in because it would show Anne Marie's state of mind. There was no other way to do that. "I think her state of mind becomes important," Lee said, "for a number of reasons because somehow we now know that she died in his house—the defense has indicated that in its opening argument. . . . And we are told that this was a very tragic, ill-defined accident. . . . In order for the state to approach the concept of there being some intentional homicide—because they are not interested in proving an accident occurred in the house—they have to show a change in their [Anne Marie and Tom's] relationship that made it more toxic. And that this pattern of calling her under circumstances that were inconsistent with the E-mails, inconsistent with the portrait of domestic tranquillity . . . is important in balancing the emotional condition of their relationship at this time."

Judge Lee ruled, however, that Jill Morrison could not tell about the time Tom made Anne Marie tear up all the pictures of her old boyfriends while standing over her as she tearfully complied. Nor could Jill testify about how he flew into a rage if Anne Marie spoke to anyone in the office when she was on the phone with him. "He'd tell her she was to talk to him and no one else," Jill had told Wharton. But the defense objected to testimony about these incidents because Jill was unable to pinpoint the time they had occurred.

Allowed now to speak for Anne Marie, her friends followed one another to the witness stand. They spoke to the jury of the hovering, smothering presence Tom had become in their friend's life. They recalled his incessant phone calls, his unexpected visits, his continual E-mail, and his rage when Anne Marie began to date Mike Scanlan. Jill Morrison testified about her friend's anguish when Tom drove his Jeep Cherokee slowly by Mike's house, and his inevitable calls to Anne Marie later to tell her the exact times he'd seen her car there.

The prosecuting attorneys moved through their witnesses, some talkative and some speaking haltingly because of stage fright or emotion. The presentation flowed effortlessly. Now that all the components of the case were assembled, no one listening could ever have known how hard they had worked to put them together.

The gallery and the media waited eagerly for particular witnesses. Everyone wondered if Tom's brothers would actually take the stand and repeat the information that had led to Tom's arrest. Could Gerry and Louie look Tom in the eye and say the words that might bring him the death penalty?

Joe Oteri had claimed to be looking forward to cross-examining Gerry. "Gerry and I will have some good times," he said, smiling and almost licking his lips.

GERRY was the soft spot in the strong Capano front. He had idolized Tom from the time he could talk and he was reportedly agonizing about testifying against him. He was thirty-five years old, but Gerry had never really grown up. Whatever their faults, the three older Capano brothers were hard workers. Gerry still played most of the time, fueled by cocaine and alcohol. He hung out at drag strips with his customized Corvettes and, of course, hunted and fished for dangerous prey. Probably none of them really needed to work, but all but Gerry had the work ethic bred into them. Gerry knew he didn't even have to show up at his landscaping business; the money kept flowing in from the firm that his long-dead father had built.

On the morning of November 9, the time had come for Gerry to testify. His golden curls had long since given way to incipient baldness, but he still had his round baby face. He wore a very expensive suit and a tie that had probably cost $100, but he also had two gold earrings in his left ear. He was clearly nervous as a cat as he took the stand. Now he could look directly at Tom and, beyond Tom, into the faces of his extended family, who filled the benches on the left side of the courtroom.

His eyes already glistening, Gerry waited nervously for Colm Connolly's first question. After Gerry verified that the statements he had given to the grand jury a year earlier were true, Connolly began with February 8, 1996, when Tom asked Gerry for a loan of $8,000. "I wrote a check and went to the bank," Gerry said.

"Why didn't you give him a check?"

"He wanted cash."

"Did he pay you back?"

"Within a week or so."

Connolly showed Gerry the deposit slip from his own bank

when he returned the $8,000. It was dated February 13, 1996. Tom's check for repayment was number 1666.

Gerry testified that Tom had been frightened by someone who was threatening him. "He said he was scared that the guy was going to hurt him. He was afraid the guy was going to beat him up or hurt him—come to his house and hurt him."

"What did you tell him?"

"I originally told him, 'You should call the police.' "

But when Tom didn't want to do that, Gerry had offered him a shotgun "because it was better home protection."

"Is a shotgun easier," Connolly asked, "for somebody who is not familiar with guns in terms of hitting their target?"

"Yes—he didn't want it. He wanted a handgun." Gerry had then given Tom the ten-millimeter Colt, and he had returned it sometime before Gerry moved to Stone Harbor in mid-May.

"What did you do with this gun?"

"I gave it to a guide friend of mine that I went hunting with," Gerry said, "as a tip—I've gone grizzly-bear hunting with him and moose hunting."

Gerry could not remember exactly when Tom had told him that someone was threatening to hurt his children, but he did recall Tom's words. "He said that if either one of these persons that was threatening to hurt his kids were to hurt one of the kids and he had to do something to them, could he use the boat?"

And that day had come. Gerry had good recall of the Friday morning that Tom showed up in his driveway. Three hours later, he was helping his brother load the huge cooler into the back of Kay Capano's Suburban. Gerry said the cooler was heavy enough so that it took two men to lift it.

"Were there any noises coming from the cooler?" Connolly asked. Several people in the gallery gasped.

"Sounded like ice was inside the cooler," Gerry replied. Apparently, Tom had prepared for any eventuality; he had packed cubes from his refrigerator's ice maker around the body in the cooler. If there was an unforeseen delay, the contents of the cooler would not begin to decay.

Connolly asked Gerry to describe what happened after he and Tom drove to Stone Harbor.

"He backed up in the driveway and I believe we both went inside," Gerry said. "And I think I went to the bathroom first and he used the phone." Tom glowered at Gerry as he testified. "And then I got a couple of fishing rods and put them in the boat and started it up. We both carried the cooler down to the boat and then put the chain and the lock in a plastic bag and carried it down to the boat."

"Now, why did you take fishing rods with you in the boat?"

"So it would look like we were going fishing."

"Were you worried that this cooler looked unusual on a boat?"

Gerry shook his head. "No—it's your typical fishing cooler."

Hours later, they were far out in the ocean. Gerry said his LORAN was in its depth-finder mode, and it registered 198 feet when he cut the motor and told Tom he was on his own. The sea was choppy and he heard Tom throwing up repeatedly as he wrestled with the cooler.

"How did the cooler get into the water?" Connolly asked.

"I'm unclear on whether or not I helped him pick it up and put it in the water and then walked to the front of the boat—or if he did it himself."

"Did the cooler sink?"

"No."

"How do you know?"

Gerry looked sweaty and queasy as he recalled shooting into the white Styrofoam and seeing something reddish pink flow from the bullet hole. (The dead don't bleed, but melting ice inside would have been tinged by the blood that had trickled from whatever wounds Anne Marie had sustained. The longer she had lived, the greater the quantity of blood. But this had been far too pale to be fresh blood.) Gerry gulped as he described the gush of pinkish fluid he had seen.

"When the cooler didn't sink," Connolly asked, "what did you do?"

"We pulled the boat up next to it," Gerry said, "and then I shut the boat off and went back up to the front."

"So, now," Connolly pressed, "the first time you helped him [lift the cooler over the side of the boat]; the second time you [only] pulled alongside the cooler?"

"Right. That's when I told him he was on his own—and I went to the front of the boat."

"Why did your boat have two anchors?"

"I always carry two anchors," Gerry said. "If you anchor up the front of the boat and the back of the boat, it stays still."

Gerry testified he had leaned against the bow rails and looked straight ahead, with his back to Tom. "I was telling him," he testified, "this was not right—this was wrong."

He had heard Tom rustling around with the chains and anchors, gagging from his grisly task. "I asked him," Gerry said, " 'Are you done? Are you done?' and he finally answered yes, and I turned around." Gerry's face was pale green with the memory of it as he answered Connolly's questions. "I saw a foot going down."

"A human foot?" Connolly asked.

"Yes."

"Were you able to determine what gender this human foot was?"

"No," Gerry answered with agitation. "No . . . No." He had seen enough to know that there had been a human body in the cooler, but he had had no idea who it was or if it was male or female.

"Where was the cooler?" Connolly asked.

"The cooler was floating. I believe we jockeyed the boat around again to pick the cooler up, and then we dipped it in the water to clear out everything that was in there—ice or whatever—and then we pulled it into the boat and we headed for home."

"What happened to the bag with the chain and the lock in it?"

"It got thrown in. I didn't see the lock and the chain get thrown in," Gerry said. "I saw the keys to the lock get thrown in."

As for the cooler, Gerry said he'd used a Phillips head screwdriver to unscrew the hinges that held the top on. "Tom was driving slowly when I did that," he testified. "And then about five minutes later, we just threw the cooler in too, and we just kept heading home."

"Now, when you headed back to the shore, did you pursue a certain course?"

"Yeah. I turned around and headed 310—310 degrees." He said he used only the compass to get his bearings.

"On the way back to Stone Harbor," Connolly asked, "what did your brother say to you?"

Gerry had kept his eyes down for most of his testimony, staring at his hands or the floor, and he continually grabbed tissues from a box as if to stanch the tears that welled up in his eyes. He looked for all the world like a naughty schoolboy confessing that he had done something bad. Now he looked up and Tom caught his eyes. Gerry appeared desperately apologetic.

"We didn't talk very much," Gerry said. "He just said it was going to be all right—that he would never let anything happen to me. Because I was telling him, 'This is wrong!' and I was scared."

In his panic, Gerry had almost missed the New Jersey coast. They were south of Cape May. He turned the wheel hard right and headed up along the coastline.

"Now when you were out on the ocean," Connolly asked, "did you see any other boats?"

"I did—I saw a small boat out in the same area we were in, with a dive flag."

"Did you see any people?"

"No."

"About how far away was this other boat?"

"Quarter mile."

"Weren't you afraid if you fired a shotgun you might draw attention to yourself?"

"No—people are always firing guns out there trying to kill sharks, catch a big shark," Gerry said. "You have to kill it before you can bring it in the boat."

It was clearly a different world sixty-five miles out in the Atlantic Ocean, a world where Anne Marie Fahey never belonged. In the early afternoon of Friday, June 28, 1996, at the hour when Tom Capano was weighting her body down and lowering it into the choppy sea, she had planned to be sitting in the cool green of Valley Garden Park reading a book.

As gruesome as it was, Gerry's testimony was not really a surprise. Joe Oteri had already conceded that Tom had dumped Anne Marie's body in the ocean, but no one knew what had happened late on the night she died. There had been no further mention of the "accident" that killed her.

GERRY CAPANO had just begun his ordeal on the witness stand.

"Who drove home [to Wilmington]?" Connolly asked him.

"Tommy did."

"And on the way, did he ask you anything?"

"He told me what to say if I was ever questioned."

"What did he tell you to say?" Connolly pressed.

"That he had met me in the morning at my house to talk about a property my mother was giving him and myself, and that I left and went to the beach. And then that he left and went over to my brother Louie's house to talk to Louis about the property, and then he met me down to the beach later and we had lunch down at the beach. And then I think it was—we went and walked a new piece of property that I was buying down there—or had already bought—and he either said he was going over to my sister's in Stone Harbor or my mother's in Stone Harbor. But, you know, I left first."

In fact, the two men returned to Wilmington, and in response to Connolly's questions, Gerry described to the jury how he had helped Tom get rid of the bloodstained couch. "It had a stain on it," Gerry recalled. "On the right, if you were sitting on it, on the right side about shoulder height. It was about the size of a basketball."

"What did you do with the couch?"

"We carried it out the double doors of that room and down the steps, which would be in the front of the house, and around to the garage. And at that point, I cut the stained piece out of it and tried to break the couch up so it looked like it was just an old broken couch, and we threw it in the Dumpster."

Gerry testified that he couldn't see the color of the stain on the maroon upholstery, but when he cut into the couch with his pocketknife, he saw "something red" on the foam underneath.

WHEN it became apparent that Tom was under suspicion in Anne Marie's disappearance, Gerry had met with Dan Lyons, an attorney that Tom had recommended. It was two months after Anne Marie vanished. Gerry testified that Tom had instructed him to tell Lyons the "same thing we talked about in the car coming home."

"Did you make a record of what he told you?" Connolly asked.

"I did."

"What did you write it on?"

"A yellow postee [Post-it]."

"What did you do with the yellow Post-it?"

"Stuck it in my checkbook and it stayed there."

"Now, Mr. Capano," Connolly asked, "would you read what you wrote down in your note as a result of the conversation with your brother, please?"

"We were at my house at 5:45. Wanted to talk about Capano investments. I went to work. Then met you at your house about seven-thirty, eight. We talked. I left for the beach. Did my thing, saw you around elevenish. We talked again because you saw Louie. Then I left. You stayed. I met you at your house around five to help move a love seat. It looked old. That's all. Helped you throw it in the Dumpster. Then I left. That's what I'm telling Dan Lyons on Friday."

Gerry said he'd lied to his own attorney at first and only later told him the truth.

"When did you tell him the last part of the story—about your brother asking you, if he hurt somebody, could he use the boat?"

"Before I went and took the lie detector test—"

Gerry realized instantly that he had said the one thing he had been warned not to say. Neither side wanted him to mention the polygraph test. His face crumpled and he buried it in his hands, muttering, "I'm sorry—I'm sorry."

Oteri turned white and Tom clenched his jaw.

Case law in Delaware Superior Court provides that testimony about polygraphs must not be referred to without a proper foundation. Gerry had been warned and he had forgotten.

Oteri asked to approach the bench. Maurer requested a mistrial and Oteri backed him up.

They had been in trial for almost five weeks. And now they might have to start all over.

_____ *Chapter Thirty-eight* _____

MOST OF THE GALLERY and the jury had no warning that the trial might be over, and they ate their lunches unaware of any problems. When they returned at two-thirty that Monday afternoon, Judge Lee had decided that the trial would proceed. He instructed the jurors to disregard Gerry's last answer.

Colm Connolly was almost finished with Gerry, and Joe Oteri waited for his turn. Connolly asked Gerry about his boats and the replacement anchor that his brother Joey had found for him.

"Why did that become necessary?"

"Because of the newspaper articles that said I sold the boat without an anchor." Gerry testified that he had given the anchor to Joe Hurley, who was then one of Tom's attorneys. He had no idea why Hurley wanted it.

After Connolly played the tape of the statement Gerry had given a year earlier to the grand jury, Gerry agreed that he had signed a plea agreement at that time, "so that I didn't go to jail."

"What did you plead guilty to?" Connolly asked.

"Misprision of a felony," Gerry said, "which means that somebody did wrong and [I] didn't tell [the authorities]."

Gerry had asked for immunity from prosecution for more than himself. He wanted Joey protected and Marian, too—just in case—and he asked that his best friend not be prosecuted for being a felon who owned guns. He knew that Louie was making his own plea bargain. From the tortured look on Gerry's face, it was obvious that if it were possible, he would have begged for Tom's freedom, too.

Now Connolly elicited the information that Gerry was a long-time substance abuser, who had consumed a gram or two of cocaine a week before June 28, 1996. After that ghastly day out in the Atlantic Ocean, he had doubled the grams.

"Do you know whether you were high on cocaine or any other substance on June 28, 1996?" Connolly asked.

"When? When I went on the boat ride?"

"Yes."

"No sir," he said convincingly. "I was not."

Gerry had been unable to keep Tom's secret to himself. It hadn't been long before he realized that it was Anne Marie Fahey's foot he saw sinking in the ocean. He had told Louie what happened sometime during the holiday season of 1996, and later, of course, he had confided in his attorney Dan Lyons.

"The conversation you had with your brother Louie—you can't recall when it occurred?" Connolly asked.

"No—not the exact date. We were walking up and down Emma Court."

"Do you have any recollection of what Louie was wearing?"

"Yes." Gerry shut his eyes, concentrating. "He was wearing a red Mickey Mouse jacket with black leather sleeves."

JOE OTERI got to cross-examine Gerry late that same afternoon. The crisp shirt Gerry had begun the day with was rumpled and soaked with sweat. He eyed Oteri warily.

Oteri began with a patronizing approach. "My name is Joe Oteri. I come from Boston, I tend to speak a little fast, and I have an accent. If you have any problem understanding me, please—time-out—and I'll stop. OK? May I call you Gerry?"

"OK."

"Call me Joe. OK? Now, Gerry, do you remember the first time you used cocaine?

"No sir."

"Any idea when it was?"

"Years and years ago."

Oteri, of course, wanted the jury to believe that Gerry was so steeped in alcohol and illicit drugs that it was a wonder he remembered his own name, much less any boat ride on the Atlantic Ocean two and a half years ago. He led Gerry skillfully into a discussion of the merits of so many drugs that Judge Lee blinked from time to time: cocaine, marijuana, crank (speed), psilocybin mushrooms, crack, barbiturates (which Gerry said he had no experience with), Valium, Xanax, Placidyl, quaaludes, Percodan, LSD, mescaline, ecstasy.

Gerry made no attempt to downplay his addictions. The question was whether Oteri had convinced the jury that his brain had long since been reduced to mush.

But he wasn't finished with Tom's little brother. Gerry had another day on the witness stand and Oteri figuratively mopped up the floor with him. It wasn't difficult; Gerry had no sterling qualities or past good deeds to balance his admissions that he had spent most of his life playing with bigger and bigger toys. He liked to hang out with "tough guys," many of whom had police records. He liked to shoot at living creatures and he rarely worked. He was at times a surly drunk, and was now being ostracized by many members of his own family.

Oteri drove the shaft home as he quoted from phone calls that Gerry, in his cups, had made to his mother. As Tom's lead attorney read the contents of the calls aloud, Marguerite Capano, white haired and frail, sat there in the courtroom in a wheelchair, fussed over by solicitous relatives. Her eyes were full of tears.

"Now, Gerry," Oteri asked, "do you remember making a phone call and leaving this message on February 9, 1998, to your mother? 'Mom, this is your son Gerry. I called you but Katie hung up on me. Then I called again and her little asshole boyfriend hung up on me. You have ten minutes to call me back. If you don't, you can go fuck yourself.' "

"I was drinking that day," Gerry said. "And I remember apologizing afterwards. . . . It's not nice to talk to your mother like that. I was drinking and very upset."

"How about the second call, Gerry?" Oteri asked. "Do you remember saying this? 'Mom, this is your son Gerry. You better fucking call me. I'm tired of being the bad guy. If you don't fucking call me, you'll never fucking see me or my wife or my kids again. What? Are you pissed because I told the truth? Because Joe fucking Hurley couldn't break me down? As far as I'm concerned, you have three sons. One is a murderer in jail for fucking life, one you hate—and that's Louie—and Joey. Like I said, you can go fuck yourself. Did you really think that I would go to jail for twelve fucking years? If you thought I was bad on the stand [the proof positive hearing], God fucking help you if this goes to trial. I'll think up even more shit to keep my ass out of fucking jail. And I'll make up fucking shit as I go along to keep Tommy in there for fucking life. I hate him. You got ten fucking minutes to call me back or you'll never see my kids again. I'm not threatening you, but if you don't call me back in ten minutes, you can go fuck yourself . . .' "

Gerry was clearly not a prosecutor's dream witness. And he was no gentleman. It was obvious his rage had been torched by his mother's blind devotion to "her Tommy," but had he been lying to protect himself and get even with his brother? The state believed that Gerry was telling the truth about June 28, 1996; every bit of their investigation validated his memory of the day Anne Marie was thrown away in the sea. And, though Oteri hinted that he had a tape of Gerry's messages, there was no tape. And the jurors remembered that omission.

THIS was not a good day in court. When Judge Lee called for the noon break, Tom attempted to move toward his mother, and his guards wrestled him into the hall. He was consistently imperious with them and they resented it. Judge Lee stepped into the hallway as the scuffle continued. This was what he had feared. Sitting in the courtroom as if he was, indeed, a member of the dream team for the defense, Tom was apparently convinced that he was in charge.

Lee called the attorneys to a sidebar. Ferris Wharton said Tom had threatened to hit one of the guards "upside the head. That was what occasioned Lieutenant Meadwell to get him out of the courtroom. It appears to be a test of wills here."

"I don't really know what I'm going to be able to do about this," Judge Lee began. "I certainly don't want him mistreated. I certainly don't want him to leave the courtroom. On the other hand . . . he continues to act like a practicing member of the bar here, chatting. . . . He's never taken seriously the admonitions that he can't talk with members of the gallery, members of the family, and with the paralegals, with whom he is continuing to conduct business."

Even Tom's own attorneys were at a loss about how to control him. He had peppered them with notes telling them what questions to ask, and to keen observers, they appeared to be growing disenchanted with his suggestions. Charlie Oberly asked Judge Lee to warn Tom that his behavior was out of line.

Lee sighed. "I've had dialogues with him in the past and I realize the frustration he feels. I realize there's a certain therapeutic value to him to be able to chew out the judge, but I'm really past that stage of the proceeding."

Hesitantly, Oteri repeated a request that Tom had made. "Your Honor allegedly shows facial motion to indicate displeasure, disbelief, or some things at certain parts of the testimony . . . the interpretation is that you are showing disbelief or incredulity . . . at my questions. This is the complaint."

"Of who?" Lee asked in surprise.

"Of my client."

"I hope that's not the case," Lee said. "But I'm not someone who's inanimate."

No one but Tom felt that Judge Lee was making faces. He was not at all happy with the way his trial was going.

COLM CONNOLLY made no heroic attempts to rehabilitate his witness when he asked questions of Gerry in redirect. He let Gerry explain that Marguerite had turned her back on him, and Kay had asked him to stay away from her and Tom's daughters. The moment he went to the federal prosecutors and told them what Tom had done, Gerry was treated like a leper by much of his family.

Had Gerry told the truth? He was a broken man on the witness stand, and it was apparent how much he had lost by talking to the investigators. If it wasn't the truth, why would he have turned on the brother he idolized?

TOM'S estranged wife was in the process of reassuming her maiden name, but she was still Kay Capano when she took the stand. The gallery was curious; Kay had managed to stay out of the strobe lights that followed Tom. She still worked at the pediatric clinic and made a home for her four daughters. She was very thin and the circles beneath her eyes were darker than ever. But she held her head up.

When Ferris Wharton asked her about her marriage to Tom, she told him that officially they had been married twenty-six years, although they had been separated for more than three.

"Do you have any children?" he asked, if only for the jury's sake. Almost everyone else in the courtroom knew about their four girls.

"Christine is eighteen," Kay said. "Katie is sixteen, Jenny will be fifteen next week, and Alex is thirteen." She explained that Christine was in her freshman year in college in New York.

Wharton moved quickly over their separation and Tom's stay at Louie's estate before he found the North Grant Avenue house.

"Have you been to the house on Grant Avenue?"

"Just a couple of times."

"Did you go inside, or—"

"I went inside, yes."

"Did you have any particular arrangement as far as visitation with your children?"

"We didn't have anything formalized," Kay said. "It was essentially that he would see them on the weekend or he would drop by frequently to see them. On the weekends, they would stay at his residence—usually just one night on the weekend."

"I want to talk to you about some events on June twenty-seventh and June twenty-eighth of 1996," Wharton continued. "You appreciate the significance of those dates in this case?"

"Yes."

"Do you know where you were on the evening of the twenty-seventh?"

"I was home on the twenty-seventh."

"Do you know where your children were on the evening of the twenty-seventh?"

"They were home also. One of my daughters had just returned from camp. That's how I remember the date . . . They may have gone out at some point during the evening, but they spent the night at the house."

Kay described for Wharton the two cars she and Tom owned— the large blue Suburban and the smaller black Jeep Cherokee.

"Did you see the defendant on the twenty-seventh of June?"

"No, I did not."

"Did you see him on the twenty-eighth of June—Friday morning?"

"Friday morning? Yes, I did. It was a little bit after seven o'clock. [I was] outside in the backyard hosing off my dog. I had just jogged."

"Where did you see him?"

"You know, I don't remember what direction he came from. I just remember hosing off the dog and he was right there."

"How long did he spend at your house, approximately?"

"Oh," Kay said, "ten or fifteen minutes."

"Do you recall how he was dressed?"

"Casually." Kay could not describe exactly how Tom was dressed, but he hadn't worn a suit and tie.

"Did you observe any scratches or marks or injuries to him?"

"No—nothing."

"What kind of facial hair did he have?"

"He had a beard."

Since Kay remembered nothing unusual about Tom's physical appearance, Wharton asked, "Was there anything about his demeanor that struck you as being out of the ordinary?"

Tom's lawyers objected and Judge Lee overruled them. They

needn't have worried. Kay testified that Tom had been as he always was. But when he left, he took the Suburban, leaving the Jeep for her. She didn't know why.

"I guess what I'm asking you," Wharton said, "is did the defendant take your daughters for the weekend on Friday?"

"No, not on Friday."

Kay said she saw Tom on Saturday between five and six, and the girls spent the night with him. Tom had come to pick them up and had kept the Suburban until Sunday night or Monday morning.

"Now, when he picked the girls up on the twenty-ninth [Saturday], was there any difference in his demeanor—his behavior?"

"He seemed a little agitated."

Wharton then jumped ahead eighteen months. "Since he has been arrested, have you sent any money orders to people at the Gander Hill correctional facility?"

"Yes, I did. Twenty-five dollars, and there were a couple of fifties."

"Do you know how many you sent?"

". . . six or ten . . . I never kept a record of it."

"Did you send money orders to anyone other than the defendant?"

Kay nodded. "All of them [were] . . . I can remember three different names."

"What names do you remember?"

"Tito. And Nick Perillo, and then there was someone else, but I don't remember his name."

"Fusco?"

"You know, I think I did, but I don't remember. I know that name."

Wharton didn't stress the names to the jury. Who and what they were would come out later in the trial. Kay had simply done what Tom asked. Like the other women in his life, she had long since grown used to his directives.

Wharton had one more question. "In 1995 to 1996, did any of your four daughters have brain surgery?"

Kay looked at him, slightly puzzled. "No."

It was a quarter of five on a long November afternoon, but Kay had only to face Jack O'Donnell on cross and then she could go home. She knew O'Donnell and didn't fear him. He had been very good to the girls when they insisted on coming to court, giving them hugs and trying to ease their pain.

"How are you?" O'Donnell asked.

"Swell," Kay said flatly. It was obvious she would rather have been anywhere but where she was.

"I'll get you in and out of here soon," O'Donnell promised. All he wanted to do was emphasize that Tom often took the Suburban when he was driving their daughters, that he was a devoted father at their sports events, and that the Capano house was a magnet for their girls' friends.

"Tom would stop by frequently," he asked, "either on the way to work or after work—just to see the girls for a few minutes here and there?"

"Yes."

"And these would be among the times when he would just stop by unannounced that you were talking about?"

"That's right."

There were no fireworks while Kay was on the stand. She seemed only to be a tired, worn woman whose marriage had been a sham for a quarter century, a woman who was trying desperately to protect her daughters from the scandal surrounding the father they idolized. Through it all, she retained her dignity.

Somehow the reporters, who seemed to live at the courthouse, knew everything that was going to happen. If Kay had disappointed them, the word was out that Louie would be testifying very soon. More titillating than that were the rumors in the media underground that Debby MacIntyre would appear soon after. Short of Tom himself explaining their affair, Debby was the witness everyone wanted to hear.

_____ Chapter Thirty-nine _____

LOUIE CAPANO'S TURN to testify against his brother came on Friday, the thirteenth of November. The witnesses the media sought most avidly entered the courtroom through a side door to avoid the throng of reporters at the top of the stairs, and left the courthouse itself through the back door. Gerry had done that, and now Louie too appeared suddenly at the front of the courtroom. Where Gerry had been anguished, Louie was polished and suave, obviously a man who was not easily flustered. However, he did appear curious about the room in which he found himself. He looked at the gallery and stared up at the high ceiling as if he had never been in a courtroom before. And perhaps he hadn't; Tom had always taken care of Louie's legal problems before they reached the courtroom stage. "For a minute there," reporter Donna Renae commented, "Louie looked around as if he were a child lost in a mall."

But the richest Capano soon settled comfortably into the witness chair, and Louie answered Ferris Wharton's questions easily, often flashing a winning smile. Gerry's face had been a mask of torment; Louie's was animated as he agreed that he had testified three times before the federal grand jury, lied twice, and had subsequently pleaded guilty to tampering with a witness.

"Is there a sentence which the federal government is going to recommend that you receive as a result of entering that guilty plea?" Wharton asked.

"One year probation."

"Do you have any obligations yourself under that plea agreement?"

"Just to tell the truth." Louie said he understood that, should he lie, he could be prosecuted for a number of crimes. He was quite prepared to tell the jurors what Tom had told him on Sunday, June 30, 1996.

"Tom and I went back to the enclosed porch on the back of the house," Louie said. "And he then told me about his relationship with Anne Marie Fahey."

"You were aware of his marital status at that time?"

"I knew he was separated from his wife, Kay, but I wasn't aware of any extramarital affairs at all."

Louie said he knew Debby MacIntyre because his son, Louis III, had attended the Tatnall School, but he had no idea that Tom had been having an affair with her for years. It seemed incredible that Tom had been able to keep his liaisons with women secret even from his own brother, but Louie had no reason to lie about that now. He testified that Tom told him he was trying to reconcile with Kay and that they were seeing a psychiatrist together in the hope that they could mend their marriage. That was the reason he had had to remove every trace of Anne Marie Fahey from his house, Tom said. He had assured his brother that Anne Marie was a neurotic mess he had simply been trying to help, but then she'd slit her wrists and bled all over his sofa. He told Louie that he and Gerry had disposed of the ruined couch in the Dumpster outside Louie's office building and asked him if he would have it taken to the refuse station as soon as possible. Louie had believed Tom, and understood his concerns about Kay's finding out.

"Now, as of Sunday," Wharton asked, "Tom told you that the police told him Anne Marie Fahey was missing?"

"Yes," Louie said. "He told me that he had given her money and she was planning to take Friday off and that he suspected she was just away for the weekend at the beach and that she would show up on Monday."

Louie said he had forgotten all about having the Dumpsters pulled until Tom called urgently Monday morning to remind him. "I said, 'Sure,'" Louie testified, "and I did. I called Chris Nolan, who works for me, and he called Karen Feeney, and Karen called Shaw Taylor, and Shaw Taylor told Dick Armstrong, and Dick told my son, Louis III."

Wharton asked Louie if Tom had ever mentioned throwing anything besides the bloody couch in the Dumpsters.

"Well," Louie said, "when they were searching the dump, he told me that he had thrown a gun in the Dumpster and that he hoped they found it in the dump because it would prove it had never been shot."

Wharton asked Louie why he had lied—twice—to the grand jury.

"I did that," Louie said, "because I believed in my brother's innocence, and anybody who would know my brother, know his reputation, would know that he couldn't be involved in anything like this. And I love him and try to protect him."

But there came a time when Louie had had to decide which of his brothers needed the most help. He testified that sometime in November 1996—after his second grand jury appearance—his kid brother, Gerry, seemed to be in terrible shape. "He cried and told me he took Tom out on the boat," Louie began. "I was pressing Gerry because I just knew something was going on that I didn't know about. And Gerry began crying and telling me he had been having nightmares and that he took Tom out on a boat."

That was the day that Louie, wearing his Mickey Mouse jacket, had walked up and down Emma Court with Gerry in front of his house. And Gerry had spilled his guts, sobbing as he told Louie about how Tom had disposed of Anne Marie's body in the ocean. From that point on, Louie said, Gerry had become more and more desperate, ridden with panic and guilt.

"Did you talk to your brother Thomas," Wharton asked, "about whether or not you would go in to the police and tell them what you knew . . . or Gerry should?"

"Yes, in the early summer of 1997, at the Imperial Deli in the

Fairfax Shopping Center, I told him we should go in and talk to the police . . . It was affecting Gerry tremendously and our entire family."

"What did he say to you?"

"He told me that we shouldn't go to the police," Louie said, staring down at Tom. "He told me that they didn't have enough evidence. And he didn't want to ruin his life or his daughters' lives."

Louie testified that he had attempted one more time to get Tom to talk to the police. He, Gerry, and Tom had met alone in a conference room in Charlie Oberly's office. "I told Tom sternly that Gerry and I were going to go to the authorities."

"Well, did you go to the authorities then?"

"No," Louie answered, "we did not."

"Why didn't you?" Wharton asked.

"Tom convinced us not to," Louie said, "and told me that if the situation was reversed, that he would do the same for me—that he didn't want to, that it wasn't time. And he talked about his children, et cetera, and convinced us not to go in."

"Did he say anything about what would happen to either you or Gerry if you guys got in trouble withholding this information?"

"He told us that he would protect us," Louie said, "and tell the authorities everything."

Tom had also told Gerry to grow up and be a man, intimating that only a cowardly kid would turn in his own brother.

"When did you become aware," Wharton continued, "that the authorities had executed a search warrant on Gerry's residence?"

"I was at Rehoboth Beach playing in a golf tournament and apparently they had raided Gerry's house the night before. Tom called me and asked if I had heard the news."

"What did he tell you about that raid?"

"He told me he wasn't going to accept responsibility for Gerry using drugs and for getting raided and busted."

"Gerry was on his own?"

"Gerry was on his own," Louie agreed, at least as far as Tom was concerned.

From that point on, whenever Gerry told Tom that he couldn't stand it any longer and he had to tell the police about what had happened to Anne Marie Fahey, Tom had upbraided him for being immature, urging him again to "be a man."

LOUIE's turn on the hot seat of cross-examination was coming. Gene Maurer questioned him unmercifully about the lies he had told to the grand jury, suggesting that no one should believe him now. He submitted that Louie had lied to protect himself just as much as to protect Tom. And then Maurer brought up the dicey subject of Kristi Pepper. Tom was not the only Capano brother whose extramarital affairs became uncomfortable in the last week of June 1996.

Louie admitted that he had entertained Kristi at his house on June 27 and 28 while his wife, Lauri, was playing in a golf tournament at the shore.

"Did you have any fear of her coming home that night?" Maurer asked.

"Yes, I did."

"About how many times," Maurer asked, "did you phone down to the shore?"

"Lots," Louie said. "Lots. Probably a dozen. Maybe more."

"So you're calling down to the shore to make sure that she's still down there so she doesn't come up and come upon you and Kristi Pepper and her kids hanging out at your mansion in Greenville?"

"That's correct," Louie said.

"And you got the other people out of there in time for her to come the next night—June twenty-ninth?"

"That is correct."

Maurer submitted that Kristi Pepper had taped Louie's phone calls. If that was true, *two* women had taped Louie's calls to keep track of what he was up to. "You were trying to persuade her," Maurer suggested, "that what she remembered she didn't really remember?"

"That's correct."

Louie admitted that he had been concerned about what Kristi was saying to the government investigators and that he had put pressure on her to change the information she was passing on to them.

"You learned at a later time, did you not," Maurer asked, "that many of those phone calls that you and she were having, in which the pressure was being imposed, had been taped by her with the consent and understanding of the government? Is that right?"

"That's correct."

It was rumored around Wilmington that Louie's wife, Lauri, had been so enraged when *her* tapes of Louie's phone calls turned up conversations with Kristi that she had taken a golf club to his new BMW. Maurer asked Louie if it was true that he had lied to his insurance company about how his car was damaged.

"I wasn't untruthful . . . I didn't tell the insurance company anything."

"Did you later have a conversation with Kristi Pepper about that subject matter?"

"Yes."

"Weren't you, in fact, upset and angry with Kristi Pepper because Kristi Pepper had told Detective Donovan what you had told her about how the accident occurred?"

"That's correct . . . [but] I don't recall exactly what I told Kristi Pepper—"

"There was somebody there that wasn't told the truth, right?"

"That's true."

"Either Kristi Pepper wasn't told the truth . . . or the insurance company?"

Louie was chafing just a bit under Maurer's relentless questions, and the jurors looked confused. They had heard the name Kristi Pepper two dozen times and knew that she had been the paramour of the married witness, but no one could figure out what had happened to Louie's BMW by listening to the obscure questions—or what they had to do with the case against Tom. Louie kept talking about a "different interpretation" of the cause of the accident.

"Well," Maurer said, "there were two ways the accident could have happened. Right, Louie? It happened because your then wife, Lauri Merton, grabbed the wheel of the car while you're going over the St. George's Bridge and the car rammed the guardrail?"

"That is correct."

"Now, another story gets out there, doesn't it—where your wife is involved in a one-car accident?"

"It *was* a one-car accident."

"Without you in the car, though?"

"I never heard the story that she was by herself."

The jurors looked even more confused. Louie explained that he and his wife were insured by the same policy, so that it made no difference. Neither he nor Maurer ever explained what had happened to his BMW, but several people in the gallery who thought they knew grinned. Louie's prize BMW had looked as if it had been through a tornado. Louie was emphatic that he was still married to Lauri Merton despite his friendship with Kristi Pepper.

Louie was on the stand most of the day. Maurer had perhaps succeeded in showing him as something less than a faithful husband or a straitlaced citizen (and even a liar), but Louie had been convincing when he described Tom's attempts to cover his own tracks at the expense of Gerry—and of Louie himself.

And yet, they were still brothers. During his testimony, Louie had searched his memory for some detail about a friend's occupation and, as he had done his entire life, looked down at Tom for help. For a moment, it was as if nothing had changed between them, but Tom only stared back at him coldly as if looking at a complete stranger. Finally, Louie had shrugged his shoulders. For the first time in their lives, they weren't on the same side.

The Capano section of the gallery that Friday, the thirteenth, seemed to support Tom rather than Louie. There had never been much love lost between Louie and Lee Ramunno, Marian's husband, who continued to champion Tom. During a break on the marble stairway outside the courtroom, Lee had encountered Louie, who put his hand on Lee's shoulder and muttered, "You're the world's biggest asshole." Lee walked by him without replying.

Finished with his testimony now, Louie walked toward the family benches, but as he attempted to step into a row and take a seat, Lee put his leg up on the bench in front of him, blocking Louie. Marian turned around and whispered, *"Lee! Let him in!"* After the next break, Louie hurried in and deliberately took Lee's seat.

TOM continued to eat bagels at the defense table when he took his pills, and a courtroom artist drew cartoons of him—full of bagels and with a forked tail—much to the hilarity of the media. The heat in the courtroom rose higher and higher; many of the Capanos were barely speaking to one another; and Tom's own attorneys looked with more and more distaste at the barrage of suggestions he passed down the table to them. Judge Lee watched his courtroom warily, alert for any smoldering embers that could erupt suddenly into flames.

Thanksgiving was less than two weeks away and there promised to be a decimated group around Marguerite's table. But although Anne Marie was gone, her brothers and sister were closer than ever. "That was the gift that Anne Marie left us," Kathleen would recall. "Losing her brought the rest of us together, stronger even than before."

ON Wednesday, November 18, there was, perhaps, the most provocative lineup of witnesses in the six-week-old trial. The state was going to call Debby MacIntyre. Somehow, court watchers knew it, and the lines of people determined to get into Courtroom 302 curled around and around the stairwell. Debby had never talked to the press and no one knew what she might say about Tom Capano. Did she still love him? Or did she hate him now?

Before the prosecutors called Debby to the stand, however, they had to make a difficult decision. Keith Brady had been the chief deputy attorney general of Delaware for three years. He was Ferris Wharton's superior and his friend. He was a good man, married, with a family, but the information that Tom had induced Brady to participate in a ménage à trois with himself and Debby was going to come out; there was no way to stop it. Connolly and Wharton understood now what absolute control Tom had maintained over Debby—but it was a concept that would be difficult to impart to a jury. By calling Keith Brady, they could show that Tom had offered Debby up to Brady in what he hoped would turn into a sexual orgy. And even then, Debby had followed his directions without question. They had seen it themselves; Debby had been so blindly devoted to making Tom happy that she never questioned him about *any* orders he gave her. She always believed what he told her.

If the prosecutors called Brady to the stand first, their direct examination would be as sensitive as they could phrase it. They couldn't just pretend that Tom hadn't brought Brady to Debby's house that night, now years in the past. But even as Connolly and Wharton understood that Brady's career, his marriage, and his place in the community would be in peril, they had no choice but to call him as a witness against Tom Capano.

Keith Brady, who reported directly to Jane Brady, the attorney general of Delaware (no relation), took the stand. He was pale but resolute and his answers came with an economy of words and without emotion. He kept his eyes on Colm Connolly and didn't glance around the courtroom. He knew that Connolly had no alternative but to question him.

Brady explained that he had once been Tom's assistant when they both worked for Governor Castle as his legal advisers. When Tom left, Brady had taken his place as chief counsel. Tom had, he said, confided in him about Anne Marie. "He initially had indicated to me that he found her to be a very attractive woman," Brady testified, "and over a period of time, he eventually told me that they were involved in a relationship."

"Do you recall," Connolly asked, "if he said anything about whether or not this relationship needed to be kept confidential?"

"Yes," Brady answered. "I recall one incident in which he said that, because she worked in the governor's office and his law firm was doing a significant amount of legal work for the state, that it was important that the relationship be kept confidential."

Brady said that Tom had told him about his trip to the Homestead with Anne Marie. He wanted to have a long time alone with her and was unhappy when she ended their relationship. Tom had called his office on Friday morning, June 28, to ask him to play golf, but Brady said he was attending a CLE (Continuing Legal Education) seminar that day.

"When did you learn that Anne Marie Fahey was missing?" Connolly asked.

"I was in my office working on Sunday, June thirtieth, and I received a call from Ferris Wharton," Brady said. Wharton had told him that Tom Capano was the last person known to have been seen with her.

After that, Brady said, he and Tom had played phone tag on Monday and Tuesday, leaving messages. Because Brady was a prosecutor, he took notes of the conversations they finally had. "He said he was blown away by what was happening," Brady testified, "spooked by the way the cops were treating him."

Tom told Brady essentially the same things about the night of June 27 that he had told the police, his brother Louie, and Debby. Brady was not only Tom's old friend; he was also the second-highest-ranking law enforcement official in Delaware. He had turned his notes over to the law enforcement officers who were investigating the case.

He himself had been recused from the case. "That means," Brady said, "I was not participating in it or informed of any of the events, details, or substance of the investigation."

And now, Connolly asked Keith Brady if Tom had ever confided in him about Deborah MacIntyre.

"Yes—he first mentioned her when we worked together in the governor's office in the early nineties," Brady said. "He told me she was a wonderful person that he cared very much about."

"Did he tell you what the nature of his relationship with her was?"

"My recollection is that he told me they had a long-term relationship."

"Did you ever have a sexual encounter yourself with Deborah MacIntyre?"

"Yes."

An audible gasp rose from the gallery—save for the press rows. The line of questioning had turned on a dime and shocked everyone else in the courtroom. "Who arranged that sexual encounter?" Connolly said, moving ahead swiftly.

"Tom did."

"Was this while he was having a relationship with her?"

"Yes it was," Brady answered. "My understanding of his interest in my having a sexual encounter with her was that that would be in the context of his relationship with Deborah MacIntyre."

"No more questions, Your Honor."

But Joe Oteri, for the defense, would have many questions. He had been briefed by Tom, who knew Keith Brady's secrets. But first, Oteri suggested that Brady, five years Tom's junior, had long been jealous and resentful of his client.

"In other words," Oteri said, "you really didn't like the guy?"

"That's not true."

"You liked him?"

"Yes."

And now Oteri had his opening. "And because you liked him, you confided in him and he confided in you. Correct?"

"Yes sir."

"And you confided in him the fact that you had adulterous relationships. Correct?"

"I confided in him that I had committed adultery."

"On numerous occasions," Oteri said, "with three different women at least."

"No."

"How many women have you committed adultery with?"

"More than one."

"More than two?"

"I have committed adultery," Brady said evenly, "with three women, not including Deborah MacIntyre."

Oteri labored the area of questioning, asking for the length of Brady's adulterous incidents, and Connolly objected.

Judge Lee sustained the objection and Oteri moved on to the night at Debby's house. In answer to his probing questions, Brady testified that he had been unable to achieve an erection when Tom instructed Debby to perform fellatio upon him.

He was a man in pain. Mercifully, Oteri changed the subject, asking about the carpets that Brady had helped Tom carry into the Grant Avenue house when he first moved in.

Then, returning to the subject that fascinated the gallery, Oteri asked, "You had a second encounter with Deborah MacIntyre?"

"I had a drink with her."

"She propositioned you?"

"That's not my recollection."

Before he was finished with Brady, Oteri returned once more to the night in Debby's house after his golf game with Tom. Although it was true he was trying to save Tom Capano's life, his questions struck many in the gallery as crude and irrelevant. "Let me ask you a question now, sir. You were thirty-nine, forty years old at the time. You didn't want to be there. You're butt naked or half dressed, you got your clothes off, you're in a bedroom with a guy and a woman who are naked and doing the nasty, and you didn't want to *be* there? Somebody holding a gun on you to keep you there?"

"No one was holding a gun to me."

"Did Debby MacIntyre grab you and say you can't leave?"

"No, she did not."

"In other words, you were there because you wanted to be there, because you wanted some action."

"No."

"No? Never mind." Oteri turned away with mock disgust.

"I'm *ashamed* that I was there."

"Ashamed of the other relationships you had, too?"

"Yes."

"I have no further questions."

IN his pursuit of pleasure and self-gratification, Tom Capano had left a number of victims behind. It was Connolly's intention to prove that Debby had been one of them. And the man on the witness stand might well have been another. Connolly moved to ask a redirect question. "You've testified that you were involved in a sexual encounter with the defendant and Deborah MacIntyre and about your participation in some adulterous affairs. What are the repercussions of your testimony about that?"

Brady gazed at him. "It has been a profoundly agonizing experience for my family. I am dealing with it with God's help as well as I can. My family is dealing with it. They have been devastated by it, obviously. I am extremely remorseful for the anguish I have caused my wife and my children and my parents."

TOM barely glanced at the man he had once considered a good friend. Brady was leaving the courtroom—but Tom knew who was going to take the witness stand next. Debby. Not long ago he had told Debby what an asset she would be in a trial and how well she would reflect on the side she supported. But now she wouldn't be testifying for him. She was going to be on the side of "the Nazi" and "the hangman."

Aware that she no longer even read his letters, Tom had tried a more subtle tack to bring Debby back to his side. He had arranged to have books sent to her. "One was called *Marguerite*," Debby would later recall, "some kind of romance and not the sort of book I ever read. The other was about Canadian provincial history. I knew what he was trying to convey. He was saying, 'Think of my mother—and remember the wonderful time we had in Montreal.' But it was too late for that."

_____Chapter Forty_____

IT WAS SHORTLY AFTER ELEVEN on the morning of November 18 when Debby MacIntyre entered the side door of the courtroom, took the witness stand, and raised her hand to be sworn. She was familiar to many Wilmingtonians, but those in the gallery who didn't know her were surprised to see that she looked nothing like a sultry femme fatale. She was petite, her face was clean of makeup as always, and she didn't look anywhere near her age, which was forty-eight. She wore a powder blue skirt and vest, a tailored white blouse.

Inside, Debby was frightened, and yet there was relief in finally being able to tell her whole story. Even though she had friends who had supported her in the year since Tom's arrest, there had been so many things she wasn't allowed to talk about. "There were legalities," she said, "that I had to keep secret until the trial."

She looked down now on Wharton, Connolly, Alpert, and Donovan—the men who had once annoyed her and whom she now trusted completely. And she looked Tom in the eye. He was scowling at her, and yet his displeasure no longer had any effect on her. He no longer had any power over her. *He was just a man.*

Ferris Wharton would conduct Debby's direct examination. He had warned her she might be on the stand all day—and quite possibly for several days. She had to be prepared to bare her personal life for all the world to see and to have Tom's attorneys ask impertinent and insulting questions. They would have to—Debby was probably the prosecution witness most dangerous for Tom.

For the first hour of her testimony, Wharton led her through her own life. It was odd; after almost two decades of hiding her affair with Tom, she now told the jurors and the gallery all of the details of their relationship. Asked about buying a gun for Tom, Debby related that he had asked her several times to do him that favor. And finally, when he again asked her on Mother's Day—May 12, 1996—after they had returned from a romantic trip to Washington, D.C., she told him she would do it. Tom had made it easy by picking her up at Tatnall and driving her to Miller's gun shop.

"Do you recognize what that is?" Wharton asked her, holding up a form.

"It's a receipt for the gun and the bullets that I purchased."

He held up another form. "That is the form," Debby said, "that I filled out that said it was against the law to transfer firearms."

"It bears your signature?"

"Yes."

Debby identified a whole series of forms that she had signed and then immediately violated by turning the little Beretta over to Tom. It had cost her "around $180."

"Did he ever pay you back for the gun?"

"No."

For most of the evening and early morning hours of June 27–28, 1996, only Debby and Anne Marie had been in touch with Tom. Now Wharton asked Debby to reconstruct her activities during that vital time period and, in doing so, place Tom in certain locations.

"Let me ask you about the date, June twenty-seventh of 1996," Wharton said. "Do you recall speaking to the defendant that day?"

"The first time [was] in the morning, about nine-thirty to ten-thirty . . . I was at work."

"When was the second time?"

"About five . . . He told me he had to go to Philadelphia for a meeting and wouldn't be too late and would call to say good night when he got home about nine."

"What were you doing that evening?"

"I was going to a swimming meet at the Arden Swim Club. I was director of the summer program at the time, and Tatnall's swimming team was swimming against Arden. I often went to the swimming meets as support, [and] both of my children were swimming in the meet."

Debby explained that her son, Steve, didn't drive but that Victoria had driven in her own car and joined them at the meet. Afterward, she gave her children money to pick up take-out food at T.G.I. Friday's. They all ate together in the kitchen at home.

"What did you do for the remainder of the evening?"

"I was sitting in the kitchen reading the paper, finishing a glass of wine—by myself—and my children had gone to other parts of the house." Debby said she had cleaned the kitchen, locked the doors, checked on her children in their rooms, and then gone to her own room on the second floor, at about ten-thirty.

"Did you make any telephone calls that evening?" Wharton asked.

". . . at approximately ten-thirty, I called Tom Capano . . . at his house at Grant Avenue."

"Did you speak to him?"

"No."

"Did you leave a message?"

"Just saying I was home and, 'If you don't get in too late, I'd love to hear from you. If not, I'll talk to you tomorrow. Good night.' "

Debby said she got ready for bed then, and was in bed watching *ER*. "I was watching it as I left the message and recall seeing a close-up shot of the black doctor on the show—I think his name is Eriq La Salle."

"*ER* is on from when to when?"

"Ten to eleven."

Debby said she had dozed off with the television on when she was awakened by a phone call from Tom. She glanced at the screen and saw David Letterman, who seemed to be in the middle of his opening monologue.

"What was the nature of that call?" Wharton asked. "What happened in that phone conversation?"

"I said, 'Hello,' " Debby replied, "and he said, 'Don't you *ever* leave a message on my voice mail.' I was puzzled because I had done that many times before. I didn't understand why I couldn't leave a message on his machine. . . . He was very irritated."

"Tell us about the rest of his conversation."

"I talked about what I had done and the swimming meet, and he asked me if I could help him do something tomorrow morning . . . I told him that I had to go to Tatnall. The next day was payday, and that I had to distribute the paychecks."

"What was his reaction to that?" Wharton asked.

"He got angry. Tatnall School is kind of a hot button with us. At the time I was working these two jobs that required more than enough of my time, and he felt very clearly that I was being taken advantage of by the school, and so whenever we talked about Tatnall, he would get very agitated."

Debby testified that the call had ended badly. "I was upset by the tone of the conversation. He wanted to cut the call off and I didn't want to hang up when I was upset. [The conversation ended] rather abruptly."

Disturbed, Debby had tried to go to sleep but had only tossed and turned for about forty-five minutes. She called Tom back but the phone rang four times with no answer. She didn't want to leave a message and make him angrier, so she hung up.

"What happened then?" Wharton asked.

"Very shortly—within a minute—the phone rang back one long ring [the ring of a *69 callback] and I picked up the phone and said, 'Hello,' and heard nothing. Then it rang within seconds—a normal ring—and I picked up the phone and said, 'Hello,' and he said, 'Hello.' He said, 'I *69'd you. Why did you hang up on me?' "

This conversation with Tom was much friendlier than the last. It was past midnight. The longtime lovers chatted easily, and Tom asked Debby again for her help the next day. She said she would go in to Tatnall very early and try to get the paychecks handed out so that she could help him. She had no idea what he wanted her to do.

FERRIS WHARTON believed that in all likelihood, Tom had just killed Anne Marie, or perhaps was in the process of doing so when Debby left the message on his voice mail at ten-thirty. The shrill ring of the phone would have frightened him. At that point, Tom couldn't have known that Gerry would help him dispose of her body. Was it possible he expected Debby to do that? Was that why he needed her help?

Debby testified that when she called Tom at 6:45 the next morning, he told her he no longer needed her help. And of course, he didn't; by that time he had Gerry lined up with his boat.

For Debby, that Friday had been an ordinary day; she had no idea her world was beginning to crash. She saw Tom at the track and he told her he planned to play golf later in the day. Then he called her at work sometime after ten. She didn't know he was calling from Stone Harbor; he sounded relaxed as he said, "I'm still trying to get a golf game together," and promised to be with her by nine that evening.

Wharton produced a copy of Debby's day-planner for June 28, 1996. "What did you have planned that day?" he asked.

"Well," she said, "I got the paychecks out in the morning." She had gone in at six, an hour early, because she thought that Tom needed her. "At eleven I had a meeting with the parent of a pre-camper, a little boy three or four years old."

"What's at 3:45?"

"I took my son to the dermatologist."

"Do you recall what else you did that day?"

"I probably took prescriptions from the dermatologist to the drugstore—Happy Harry's."

Debby testified she had stayed home that Friday evening, waiting for Tom—but he wasn't on time and she went to bed.

"Did he arrive?"

"About eleven, anywhere from eleven to eleven-thirty. He walked upstairs to my room."

"Did he have a key to your house?"

"Yes, he did."

Tom had also known the combination to the alarm system, something the state was now fully aware of. His eyes never left Debby's face as she testified.

"What happened when he came up to your bedroom?"

"He just said, 'I'm sorry I'm late—fell asleep in front of the TV with the kids. Can I stay?' "

"What did you say?"

"I said yes."

Debby recalled that Tom had fallen asleep immediately after he crawled into her bed. He was still there Saturday morning and she noted that, for some reason, he had been driving Kay's blue Suburban. It was parked in her driveway.

Tom had left to do some errands Saturday afternoon, she said, and she didn't see him until about one on Sunday afternoon. "He just came over unannounced and walked into my house and was very upset, with his head in his hands," Debby said. "I could see he was visibly shaken. He said, 'I feel like I've been set up; somebody has set me up.' "

"Did you ask him what he was talking about?"

"He said, 'I can't tell you—not yet.' "

Tom was sitting in the wing chair in her living room while she knelt in front of him in concern. He would tell her only that the police had come to his house at three in the morning. In five minutes, he was gone.

But Tom had come back shortly and called her out to his car. "He gave me a bag with three adult movies in it," she testified. "He said, 'Hang on to these; it would be embarrassing if somebody found these.' "

"How long was he there that time?" Wharton asked.

"Sixty seconds."

And, Debby testified, Tom had come over for a third time on Sunday afternoon—but only for five minutes. "He said that the police had come back to his house again and that he had to pack up his children and take them back to their house and then go back to the Grand Avenue house, and they searched it again."

"Do you know whether he made any phone calls from your house at that time?"

"Yes," Debby said. "He asked to use the phone."

Wharton entered Debby's phone bill for June 1996 into evidence. It showed that someone had made three phone calls to New Jersey that afternoon and evening—one to the Holiday Inn in Penns Grove, the motel the Capanos owned, and the others to the motel manager's home.

"Did you make those phone calls?"

"No."

Debby had been pleasantly surprised when Tom asked her to spend that Sunday night with him at his house. He had her drive into the garage and walk up the stairs to the great room. Although she had been worried about him, he told her nothing about why the police had come to his house twice. Indeed, it wasn't until Tom had called her on Tuesday, she said, that she knew he was the last person to have been seen with a woman whose name she had never heard: Anne Marie Fahey.

Debby told the jury that she had been shaken to realize that Tom had apparently been seeing Anne Marie for "about three years."

"During that time," Wharton asked, "in 1993 and 1994 and 1995, were you still seeing Tom Capano?"

"Yes, I was."

"What was he telling you about how he felt about you during that time period?"

"He was telling me that he loved me very much."

"Had you had some arrangement whereby you would be sort of exclusively seeing one another?"

"We were not exclusive, no," Debby said softly. She had been so upset "because he hadn't told me about her, and I had always told him when I was going out on a date with somebody, or who I was seeing, and he hid this from me."

Before Judge Lee called the lunch break, Debby testified about the mysterious changes in Tom's great room—the new rug, the missing couch—and his explanation that he had spilled red wine on both the original carpet and the maroon love seat.

Bob Donovan had been sitting in a spot at the prosecutors' table where he believed Debby could look at him as she testified. Indeed, for most of the morning he thought they had held eye contact. He knew how vulnerable she was and how Tom had controlled her for so many years. At some point, Donovan realized with a sinking sensation that Debby wasn't looking at him; she was staring into Tom's eyes. During a break, he walked over to Debby and said, "You're not looking at *him,* are you?"

"I am, Bob," Debby said.

"Don't do it, Debby," Donovan pleaded. "He's trying to get into your heart."

"It's OK," she said. "My heart is closed to him."

Debby would later recall that moment. "And it was true," she said. "My heart *was* closed to Tom. But I intended to keep on looking at him as I testified. I wanted him to realize what all his lies had done and to know that I was no longer fooled by him."

Whether she was as strong as she felt at that moment remained to be seen. Debby's marathon testimony had just begun, and so far she had to deal only with Ferris Wharton, whom she liked and who was not going to spring any surprises. Even so, for the rest of that first day, Debby answered questions about her seventeen-year affair with Tom—five hours on the witness stand as every shred of her private life became fodder for the media. Through it all, she stared at Tom and he glared back at her, sometimes shaking his head from side to side as if to say, Debby, how *could* you do this?

He had once been so sure that she didn't have the common sense to know how to behave at the proof positive hearing that he sent her tedious letters of instruction. Now she was here on her own, and at Wharton's urging, she read those endless letters aloud for the jury. He'd told her what to say about the gun, about the cooler, about their relationship.

At 4:55 on that long afternoon, Judge Lee called a halt to the proceedings. But not to Debby's testimony; she knew that she might be on the stand all week. Yet, in a way, she had an absurd sense of freedom. She had slipped out of Tom's control, and the earth hadn't opened up and swallowed her after all.

As Tom was led away from the courtroom in chains, he turned toward the reporters who waited for a word from him. His face a forlorn study, he said, "She broke my heart."

FOR much of Thursday, November 19, Debby again read from the letters Tom had sent her from Gander Hill. She also read her own letters to him, letters written only eight months earlier. Clearly, she had still been conflicted—even after she agreed to tape his phone calls to her home. But then, she had never denied that she still loved Tom at that time.

"Today, I received a letter from you," she read from one of her letters to him,

> that was written from the heart and it made me cry for both of us who can't hold on to each other. You think I have betrayed you. I have not. I have told the truth and we must both live with the truth.
>
> I know completely without a doubt that you love me. I never doubted your love. Some letters were horrible and I could not read them. But some of it was true. I had been walked over most of my life and by you for sure. I guess I let the men of my life walk over me more than anyone else.
>
> You can build me up and point out my strengths better than anyone . . . but you can trash me like no other as well. I'd like to think that I know you better than anyone, but maybe I don't. Yes, we were one—soulmates. . . . There is no way that can be taken away, regardless.

"Often I wonder," Debby read in the hushed courtroom, "why all this tragedy had to happen. What happened and why are you involved? Will you ever be able to tell me? I think not, and that will always keep us apart."

Ferris Wharton asked Debby if it was true that the day after she wrote the letter she had just read, she came in to speak to him and Colm Connolly and told them about buying the gun.

"Yes, I did."

And still, she had written to Tom, trying to explain to him why she was not changing lawyers, despite his insistence that she fire Tom Bergstrom. "For me," Debby read aloud,

> changing lawyers is not proving to you that I love you. . . . I could not mentally or physically make another change without compromising my health. I am tapped out and can take little more. Besides, I like him and believe in him. . . . If you love me, you will support me for the choices I have made. . . .
>
> I want to believe more than anything that we will go to our eventual destinies in the future knowing that both of us have been loved and have loved completely.

Debby put her last letter to Tom in her lap as Wharton offered the next exhibit for identification. It was the floor plan of her home that Tom had drawn with all of the things she treasured marked for the attention of a burglar. She had seen it before, of course, but she had tried to bury the memory of Tom's meticulous scheme intended to intimidate and terrify her.

Wharton then peppered Debby with short questions about her home and the mirror in her bedroom. "What was the significance [of that mirror] as related to Tom Capano?"

Her voice was hushed. "We could watch ourselves having sex in the mirror."

The jurors would have a chance to review the diagrams of Debby's house at their leisure, but now, alert, they craned their necks to see what Tom had drawn.

"During the period of time roughly from March eighteenth to March twenty-eighth of 1998, did you have any travel plans?"

"Yes—to go to Sanibel Island in Florida."

"You had a lengthy relationship with the defendant, did you not?"

"Yes, I did."

"Did you fall in love with him? Did you tell him that?"

"Yes, I did."

"Did he ever tell you that he was in love with you?"

"Yes, he did."

"Did he ever tell you that you were soul mates?"

"Yes."

"Did he ever tell you that he would give his life for you?"

"Yes, he did."

"Did he ever tell you about dumping Anne Marie Fahey's body in the Atlantic Ocean?"

"No, he did not."

"Did he ever tell you that she died as a result of an accident?"

"No, he did not."

"No other questions."

FERRIS WHARTON turned away, but Debby still sat in the witness chair, waiting. Now it was Gene Maurer's turn to question her, and she knew he had ample ammunition. She had lied to the federal investigators and to the grand jury. It was all documented. She had stonewalled them to protect Tom, because he had asked her to. In the beginning, she had detested Colm Connolly for trying to hurt Tom.

Now it was obvious what Maurer intended to do. His questions demanded answers that seemed to show Debby as a faithless friend to Kay Capano, a tempting seductress who almost forced Tom to have sex with her back in 1981, and the initiator of the idea to bring Keith Brady to her house.

Quoting letters Debby had written to Tom shortly after his arrest—letters written when she shared his view that Connolly and the other investigators were trying to trap him—Maurer read: " 'And I can't think of why they think I would hurt your case. Maybe he [Connolly] thinks I've had a change of mind since your arrest, but I don't know how an obsessed mind works.' "

Debby's blind devotion to Tom had come back to haunt her. Again and again, Maurer quoted her own words. She had truly believed what Tom told her about the federal investigators and she had distrusted them. She had lied to them then to protect Tom. Might not she be lying now to protect herself?

At last, that day was over. The trial would not resume until Monday. But there would be headlines and endless television and radio coverage about her testimony. If being the other woman was a sin, Debby was paying the price. And Connolly and Wharton had warned her that it might get even worse.

_____ *Chapter Forty-one* _____

ON MONDAY, Maurer hammered Debby with questions about purchasing the Beretta, pointing out that she had had six separate meetings with investigators—including the grand jury—and still continued to lie about buying the gun for Tom. She didn't deny it. It was true. He had told her that he would die for her. It was really the other way around; at the time Maurer referred to, not only would Debby have given her life for Tom, she had surrendered her free will and the control of her mind. She had believed everything he told her about his innocence and the conspiracy against him. Could *anyone* understand that?

Once more, Maurer asked Debby about the encounters with Keith Brady and with her high school boyfriend. It had been Tom who was the voyeur but his attorney painted Debby as the harlot. "Now, these particular incidents that we just talked about relating to sexual activity that were brought up on direct examination are things that you say Tom basically made you do?"

"He asked me to do them, yes."

"Not because that was an interest that you had, sexually, or things that you were interested in doing?"

"We had talked about it—"

"Does that mean it was something you were interested in doing too?" Maurer asked with a trace of sarcasm in his voice, "or only because he asked you to do it?"

"I agreed to do it because he wanted me to do it," Debby said quietly. "And I agreed because I was afraid not to."

Finally, Maurer moved away from questions about sex and began to question Debby's testimony about the time period from June 26 through June 30. It was a strong defense technique: repeating what she had said earlier but with a hint of doubt in his voice as if he saw deception there.

"Gene Maurer is one of the best criminal defense attorneys in Delaware," Debby said a long time later, "and I was prepared for an onslaught of questions—but in the end, Tom didn't allow him to do his job. There were long pauses between questions while Maurer read the notes that Tom kept handing him. It was obvious that Tom was in charge. And that helped me, because the pauses gave me time to gather my wits."

"Basically," Maurer asked, changing directions again, "you say you learned on July second that the man that you'd waited for for all those years and who you wanted to marry was involved with a younger, attractive woman?"

"I don't know if those were my words, but—"

"But you learned that?"

"I learned that."

"How upset were you?"

"I was upset."

"Angry?"

"I was upset."

"*Extremely* upset, weren't you?"

"Yes, I was."

But then Maurer's words shocked Debby, just as Connolly and Wharton had warned her. "Didn't you, in fact, find out about Anne Marie Fahey—not on July second—but on *June twenty-seventh and June twenty-eighth?*"

"No, Mr. Maurer, I never heard of Anne Marie Fahey until July second."

"Didn't you go to 2302 Grant Avenue on June twenty-seventh or June twenty-eighth with a firearm to visit Tom?"

"Mr. Maurer," Debby said, her voice loud in her own ears, "I never left my property from the time I returned home from the Arden Swim Club until the next morning when I went to the Tatnall School."

"Very strenuous about that, aren't you?"

"I am."

"Didn't you have your firearm at Tom Capano's house on June twenty-eighth of 1996, where you first learned about him and Anne Marie Fahey?"

"No, I did not."

"You deny that you discharged the firearm?"

Debby looked at Maurer as if he had gone mad. She saw Tom's face was a smug mask. "I deny that I discharged that—"

"Are you absolutely certain about that?"

"I'm *absolutely* certain."

"And you deny that *your* firearm discharged that night in that house, striking her?"

"I don't know what happened with that firearm. I gave that firearm to Tom Capano on May thirteenth."

The courtroom hush broke into scattered gasps and murmurs. The defense was apparently accusing Debby of Anne Marie's murder. Debby looked down at Tom, her chin set. He would not meet her eyes. She realized then that he was quite willing to throw her away to save his own skin. "I remember looking at him," Debby said, "and he finally looked up at me and he knew what I was thinking: It's come to this, Tom, and here we are."

Her day on the stand was far from over, but it wasn't Debby who broke; it was Tom. In midafternoon, Jack O'Donnell reported to Judge Lee that Tom was lying on a bench in the holding cell. "He claims he's having a very bad colitis attack—that this is the worst it's been." Tom felt he was too weak to continue and wanted the judge to recess court for the day.

They were so close to the end of Debby's testimony. She had been on the stand for three days and it seemed cruel to ask her to come back another day for the ten to fifteen minutes that Connolly estimated it would take to finish his redirect.

In the end, Judge Lee decided to continue with Debby's testimony. Tom would have to ride in the bus back to Gander Hill anyway, and in court or on the bus, the time would be the same. "I'm sure that's going to be unpleasant for him but so's the ride back going to be unpleasant for him," Lee said. "And without dealing with the issue too much, I'm not inclined to let him tell me when I can hold court—and I think there is a certain element of that involved in this."

No one in the courtroom could miss the way Tom sought to control his own attorneys, the guards—and now even the judge. His notes to Oteri and Maurer had become more frequent and intricate. And he still turned to chat with his family whenever he felt like it. Even as an attorney who knew what the protocol should be, he continued to try to make his own rules.

For another forty-five minutes, Maurer continued to ask Debby questions that implied that she was somehow involved in Anne Marie's death. She was exhausted; the gallery was exhausted. But she knew she hadn't been anywhere near Tom's house on the night Anne Marie died, and there was no way on earth anyone could prove that she had been.

It was almost six when it was finally over and Debby was allowed to step down from the witness stand. Tom, still gripped by intestinal spasms, shuffled out of the courtroom and onto the bus bound for Gander Hill.

THANKSGIVING was only two days away when Nicholas Perillo took the witness stand. Handsome and glib, he was an instant hit with the women in the gallery. Perillo told the jurors of Tom's plans to have Debby's house burglarized and how Tom had ordered that special attention be given to the destruction of items that would remind her of their love affair. Perillo spoke with easy familiarity about Kay Capano and Christy, Katie, Jenny, and Alex, Tom's daughters. Apparently, Tom hadn't been at all concerned about having his fellow prisoners contact them. Of course, Perillo was a prime target for the defense, but he cheerfully admitted his failings in his deep, tough-guy voice.

Jack O'Donnell suggested that Perillo had deliberately ingratiated himself with Tom. Yes, Perillo agreed, he had asked his brother, the *ER* actor, to send Tom's daughters an autographed picture.

"You were earning Tom's trust, weren't you?"

"I was making a fifteen-year-old tickled to death that she had a picture of some actor—I thought it would be a nice thing to do, given the situation the poor kids were in."

"You had no ulterior motives?"

"Absolutely not."

"It never occurred to you, if you set Tom Capano up, you might have Christmas dinner outside of the institution this year?"

"That's absolutely ridiculous!" Perillo's face was a study of imperious outrage.

"Well, you're going to have Christmas dinner outside the institution, aren't you?" O'Donnell pressed.

"That has absolutely nothing to do with my participation in his case," Perillo said. "I'm here to tell the truth to this jury, this courtroom, and it has absolutely nothing to do with why I'm in prison—*absolutely nothing.*"

"You're here to tell the truth as a law-abiding citizen for what—the first time in your life?"

"Got to start somewhere."

". . . You've agreed you are a liar, haven't you?"

"Sure."

"You've lied, stolen, and cheated nearly your entire adult life? Agreed?"

"Agreed."

There was something refreshing about Nick Perillo. But most compelling, more than anything he said, were the scrupulously drawn floor plans of Debby's house that he had delivered to Ferris Wharton. No one but Tom could have drawn them. No one but Tom knew Debby's security code or where she hid her jewelry, her valuables, and her secret things. And he had given those drawings to the man on the witness stand, apparently in the belief that he was ordering a burglary of the home of the woman who loved and trusted him.

Such an action was not that far removed from betraying another woman who had loved and trusted him; only, in Anne Marie's case, the state believed he had carefully planned to murder her. That was why Jack O'Donnell fought hard to destroy Nick Perillo's credibility. He succeeded in showing Perillo as a prison snitch, a devout con artist, and a sometime liar, but few in the gallery perceived him as a man comfortable about blatant cruelty to women.

THANKSGIVING was over and suddenly it was winter. The trial was heading into December like a juggernaut. The state presented a number of witnesses who had talked with Debby throughout the day on Friday, June 28—at the Tatnall School and at the bank where she cashed a petty cash check. They all described her as having been completely normal in demeanor. Furthermore, their testimony proved she could not have been with Tom and Gerry in Stone Harbor that day. But the tiny tracks Tom had left behind were beginning to entrap him. By now the jurors had seen his false timeline, the notes designed to hide his real activities on June 28.

There was more in that packet of paper that Special Agent

Kevin Shannon had found hidden in Tom's law partner's bookcase on November 6, 1996. Ten pages of notes described Tom's recall of his contacts with Anne Marie in the last two months of her life—or more likely, they described the way he intended to characterize their relationship to the authorities if that should become necessary. He seemed a man obsessed with keeping notes as if he might lose control of himself if he didn't have something to stabilize him.

> I was in Stone Harbor Easter Weekend! . . . Thursday, 5/23/ came to deliver book re: anorexia, retrieved from Robert previous evening . . . [She] cried in my arms. Shoulders so thin.
>   . . . High maintenance? Materialistic? Showed me freckle on belly needing attention. Pulled up jumper. No modesty. Described trip to Cape to visit Jen, and spend weekend alone on Vineyard. Wanted time to think.

Day by day, Tom had written notes about Anne Marie, right up until the last day of her life. As Kevin Shannon read them aloud, there was the sense of a massively smothering presence. "Same weekend as trip to Wildwood with Kathleen. Gave her a 'care package' and videos. Didn't want to watch videos with Kathleen because she wouldn't 'get it.' Disappointed that sister had detailed agenda because wanted no plans because of aversion to rigid schedule."

What must it have been like for Anne Marie to have this man monitoring virtually every breath she took, every thought she had, and then recording them? He was, indeed, a man obsessed.

"6/27." It was the last day of her life, and Tom had written, of that day, "Reservation for 7:00. Call at 6:25 from office to advise on way. *Very* depressed."

Was he speaking about Anne Marie—or about himself?

BOB DONOVAN, who gave testimony often in this seemingly endless trial, took the stand once more to say that a call had initiated from Tom's cell phone near Miller's gun shop on the day Debby bought the Beretta. Tom's assertion that he had been nowhere near the gun shop was another lie revealed. Just as he hadn't bought cigarettes the night Anne Marie died—Donovan had found that Getty's wasn't even open at that time. Tom's little lies were like bits of string wound into a ball that became larger and larger until it threatened to roll over him.

NOW another of the women Tom had counted on to do his bidding shocked him. Susan Louth, whom Jack O'Donnell described as "a great-looking blonde," told the jurors that Tom had written her from Gander Hill and asked her to lie about his physical strength. And so she had written the letter confirming his contention that she had had to help him move the dining room table he lent her.

"Is that true?" Connolly asked.

"No."

"So, why did you write this?"

"Because I knew that's what he wanted to hear and I didn't have the heart to say 'You know, I see what you're trying to get me to do here.' I didn't want to go that way because I still really cared about him. And I wanted to be able to write and stay close to him."

The woman Tom called "slutty little girl" read the letters that had passed between them. Here too, his manipulation dominated the words. Susan's assignment had been to spread rumors about Debby MacIntyre.

Of all of Tom's women who had testified thus far, Susan Louth, the paralegal who had moved from Delaware to the Virgin Islands, seemed the least damaged; even though she admitted she had fallen in love with him, she had viewed their affair as a temporary fling.

The FBI evidence gatherers, the criminalists, and the scientists testified next. Painstakingly, Wharton and Connolly elicited the explanations about how the flecks of blood found in Tom's great room had been matched to Anne Marie Fahey's plasma. How carpet fibers found in Kay's Suburban matched the carpet Tom had removed from the great room. The cooler . . .

THERE had been a large white Styrofoam cooler near the prosecution table for the entire trial. It wasn't *the* cooler. Connolly and Wharton had planned all along to end the state's case with the introduction of the cooler during Ken Chubb's testimony. On December 2, the actual cooler that had been found floating so close to the Delaware coast sat, finally, under the evidence table. Connolly asked questions of Ron Smith, the man who had called Eric Alpert to tell him about the cooler his friend had found over the Fourth of July weekend. Smith was a perfect witness and things were going well.

Next, Wharton questioned an FBI firearms and tool-mark expert, Michael Ennis, about the two holes that were blasted in the Igloo cooler. Although the holes had been filled with an epoxy material, Ennis said he had been able to detect the presence of lead particles. "Anytime you have the bullet fired from a firearm, you also get any debris that might be in the barrel. . . . The chemical test [on the cooler] was positive for lead behind the hole number 1 on the back

side of the piece of plastic and also on the piece of insulation between hole numbers 1 and 2 and hole numbers 3 and 4."

Connolly, sitting at the prosecution table, heard whispering
from the defense attorneys. He followed their eyes and saw they
were looking at the Igloo cooler—the *real* cooler. They were planning to find a way to bring the cooler out on cross-examination so
they could lower its impact on the jury.

When Wharton finished his questioning of Ennis, he turned
back, as always, to Connolly, asking the judge, "May I have a moment?" It was the way all the attorneys made sure they hadn't
missed something before they dismissed a witness. "I told him what
I'd heard," Connolly recalled. "We had no choice—we had to introduce the cooler with the witness on the stand. Ennis wasn't expecting it but he could deal with the surprise."

In one of the most dramatic moments of the trial, albeit previ-
ously unplanned, Connolly and Wharton reached under the evidence
table and picked up the cooler that had borne Anne Marie to her
ocean grave. The courtroom was silent as they carried it—like pall-
bearers—to a spot in front of the jury box. As they set it down, the
wooden handles snapped and vibrated, raising goose pimples on the
arms of the watchers in the gallery.

As big as it was, everyone wondered how in God's name Tom
Capano could have forced Anne Marie's five-foot ten-inch body into
its confines. Someone whispered in a voice that carried down the
row, "He must have broken her feet to put her in there."

"Mr. Ennis," Wharton asked his startled witness, "state's exhibit 235—is that the Q79 cooler which you examined?"

"Yes sir, it is."

"The one in which you found the lead in the holes?"

"That's correct."

After Kenneth Chubb testified that he and his son had found
the cooler with blood still inside, the state rested its case. Charlie
Oberly rose to assert that the state had failed to prove how Anne
Marie Fahey had died and asked Judge Lee for a directed verdict of
acquittal.

Lee refused, saying that was for the jury to decide. Court ad-
journed at 2:40 P.M. on Wednesday, December 2. The defense would
present its case beginning Monday, December 7.

In his opening statement, Joe Oteri had claimed that Anne
Marie died as the result of a horrible accident and hinted broadly
that he would produce a surprise witness. Perhaps on Monday he
would say what that accident was and explain why Tom had not

called for help from the police and paramedics instead of attempting to cover up all traces of Anne Marie's death.

As the courtroom emptied of spectators, Anne Marie's brothers and sister stepped quietly to the area beyond the rail and stood near the cooler. For all its fragile, eggshell-like construction, it had been their sister's coffin, the last place she was known to have been. Understanding how important it was for them, Connolly and Wharton turned away to allow the Faheys their moment of prayer and meditation.

It might well be that that battered cooler was the piece of evidence that would convict Anne Marie's killer.

_____ Chapter Forty-two _____

THINGS WERE NOT GOOD in the defense camp. As Tom's dream team of attorneys prepared to begin their case, he notified them on Thursday, December 3, that he felt they were not responsive to his strategies. He had always opted for the "chain saw approach" to his defense—believing it was prudent to present *everything* that might possibly be of help to his case. Nothing would be too much, he felt, because you could never tell which witness or bit of information would swing the jury in his direction. His attorneys blanched at the idea.

Tom was furious that Oteri, Maurer, O'Donnell, and Oberly seemed to be ignoring his advice, the questions he wanted them to ask and his game plan. He said he intended to fire them. They thought he might change his mind when he considered what it would mean to do that at this delicate point in his trial, but he was resolute. He gave them strict orders not to notify Judge Lee of his decision, but they felt they had to tell him what Tom was about to do. On Monday, December 7, Tom was prepared to make a motion to dismiss his legal staff and proceed *pro se*—to speak for himself.

Judge Lee, Tom's four attorneys, and Connolly and Wharton discussed the implications of having the defendant serve as his own attorney in what might turn out to be a death penalty case. A psychiatrist had examined Tom and found that his competency was not an issue.

"He wants to get to that jury," Judge Lee said. "I have no

doubt about that. He's always felt he could create a bond with that jury."

OUT of the presence of the jury, but with Tom in the courtroom, Joe Oteri rose. "If Your Honor please, at this time we would move to be allowed to withdraw as counsel, collectively—myself, Mr. Maurer, Mr. O'Donnell, and Mr. Oberly. . . . We have a serious strategic difference with the defendant as to how the case is to be tried. . . . The defendant is committed to a course of conduct, as far as the presentation of evidence and the rest of it goes."

Tom rose to explain his decision to Judge Lee. "If I were a soldier in a foxhole and I had ten grenades available, I'd use all ten of them if I was surrounded by the enemy. . . . My counsel collectively believes that—in Joe's words—he prefers to proceed with a 'scalpel.' His approach is that 'less is more.' I do not want to sit in jail three years from now for something I didn't do and be saying to myself, If only they had known *this* or if only they had known *that*."

Tom told Judge Lee that Jack, Gene, and Charlie were friends of over twenty years. And even though he had known Joe only since May, he was "almost like a father to him. But I've got to face myself and I owe it to my kids."

Letting his attorneys go was yet another thing that caused Tom to say, "It breaks my heart."

But finally he submitted a compromise, a "hybrid. . . . Let them present the defenses they think are needed . . . and allow me to present those *I* think are necessary."

Judge Lee asked Tom if he realized how his plan might sit with the jury and that it might "be consistent with the position the state is trying to present in this case."

Interestingly, Tom spoke of the state as one man—Colm Connolly. "I absolutely know how he's going to try and twist it," he said. "I'll just have to deal with that as best I can. Everything has been twisted already." Tom clearly hated Connolly.

His own attorneys could not agree with his hybrid concept of defense. And Judge Lee reminded Tom that, were he hiring an attorney, he would not hire someone who had tried his last criminal case twenty-two years ago (which Tom had), and of the best-known adage in law: that a lawyer who represents himself has a fool for a client. Tom's four lawyers feared for him; they knew he wanted to call witnesses who would surely do him damage: another woman in his life, for instance. And Tom was shocked to learn that, should he proceed alone, he would not be allowed to explain to the jury why he no longer had attorneys with him.

In the end, Judge Lee gave Tom another day to decide if he really wanted to represent himself. And after almost twenty-four hours of discussion, he decided that he would stick with his original attorneys. Whether they would have chosen to represent him in the first place had they known what a minefield they were entering was a moot question. In the days ahead, they would often be reduced to the status of paralegals, running errands for Tom. And despite the fact that they had been invited to stay on his team, court watchers could not help but notice the body language at the defense table. Joe Oteri kept widening the gap between himself and Tom, and often turned his back on his client. Tom's notes were passed to his lawyers in a flurry of white. They barely glanced at them before they shook their heads slightly.

The defense witnesses were weak—character witnesses, some of whom affirmed that Anne Marie had often called Tom at his office, one who had seen him out at dinner once with a woman "who had a very full head of hair," some who apparently had been called to dispute the depth of Anne Marie's affection for Mike Scanlan. The E-mail was trotted out again, full of banter, trivia, and menus. Bob Donovan was called for an exhaustive examination that might ferret out conflicting statements made to him by Debby MacIntyre.

In a case that had become more and more convoluted, the defense called an unlikely ally: Squeaky Saunders—the man whom Tom had prosecuted in the days when he was a young criminal attorney. When Ferris Wharton pulled the Saunders case file to prepare for cross-examination, he was fascinated to read that Squeaky, who was still incarcerated, had been convicted of shooting his victim in the head and attempting to dispose of the body in the Delaware River, where it was soon discovered. Judging from the placement of the blood on the missing sofa from Tom's great room, it was likely that Anne Marie had also been shot in the head. It was almost as if Tom had refined the MO of the Saunders case, correcting, he thought, Squeaky's mistake by disposing of Anne Marie's body far out in the ocean.

Squeaky's testimony, however, dealt not with murder but with his assessment of Nick Perillo as an untruthful prison snitch who was not to be believed. In a trial rife with interesting headgear, Squeaky held his own; he wore a towering turban.

In his cross-examination, Wharton suggested that Squeaky was testifying for Tom because he hoped his murder conviction might be overturned if he could prove prosecutorial misconduct—something he had been claiming for two decades. If he helped Tom now, Wharton suggested, it was possible that Tom might admit errors in the 1975 trial in which he had been one of the prosecutors.

Joe Oteri was furious and jumped to his feet to object. "That's totally unethical of Mr. Wharton!"

Wharton, usually slow to anger, responded, "If he's going to accuse me of something unethical, I demand an apology in open court."

It was a frustrating trial, made more so by the rising heat in the courtroom and the spectators packed into every spare corner of space. Judge Lee knew that tempers were bound to flare and he watched the combatants carefully. Usually he was able to defuse situations with his wry humor before the court and in sidebar conferences. But ever since Tom had attempted to fire his attorneys en masse, morale was low. Joe Oteri told a reporter that some mornings he felt like pulling the covers over his head instead of going to court.

Joey Capano was scheduled to appear next in Tom's defense. Although he looked as handsome and tanned as ever, Joey confided to reporters that his health was not good; he feared he had inherited Louis Sr.'s heart trouble. In what seemed like one long run-on sentence, he described his heart attacks and his sixteen cardiac surgeries. He said his wife, Joanne, had once inadvertently saved his life as she reached for the phone to call 911 in the middle of the night. "I wasn't breathing," he said. "She thought I was dead, but she leaned on my chest when she grabbed the phone and revived me."

As he took the witness stand, Joey had five weeks to go before yet another surgical procedure on his heart. Marguerite had so many worries about her boys. Unlike Louie, Joey was a very casual dresser, his former-wrestler's body straining at the seams of his jacket. As he gestured, reporters saw that he had lost a fingertip on one of his hands (he had caught it between two boats).

Joey testified that Tom had come to him in March of 1996 for advice on what to buy Gerry to show how grateful he was because Gerry had been so nice to Tom's daughters. "I suggested that he purchase something such as a cooler," he said. "I said Gerry could always use one of those." There had been nothing at all ominous about that purchase, he insisted.

Joey said that Gerry's memory was not all it could be because his drinking clouded it. "He tends to get things twisted," he testified. Oteri nodded. Joey's testimony boosted Oteri's contention that Gerry was given to confabulation—to mixing up fact and fiction to fill the

"Swiss cheese holes" in his memory. To win an acquittal for Tom, it was absolutely vital that Gerry appear to be demented by drugs and alcohol. The Capano family was split right down the middle; Louie had spoken for Gerry, and now Joey was standing behind Tom.

JOE OTERI had gotten his "Swiss cheese" theory from Dr. Carol Tavani, the psychiatrist who examined Tom just after he was arrested in November 1997. Dr. Tavani testified to the depression that had gripped Tom in March 1998—a period that coincided with Debby's defection to the state investigators. On direct, Tavani testified to her concern for her patient and how she had tried numerous combinations of antidepression and antianxiety medications to bring him some relief.

On the witness stand, Tavani also diagnosed Gerry Capano for Oteri, and said she had found that he was a "confabulator," with "Swiss cheese holes" in his memory. She even analyzed many of Anne Marie's writings and suggested that, in her opinion, they showed she had had a very pleasant and friendly relationship with Tom Capano.

Upon cross-examination, Ferris Wharton queried Tom's psychiatrist about the best way for physicians who deal with mental health to evaluate patients. Tavani agreed that it was vital to meet the patient and do face-to-face screenings before beginning treatment. There were so many factors to consider: body language, general demeanor, rapidity of response, the state of nourishment, eye contact . . .

"In fact," Dr. Tavani offered, "most of our communication is nonverbal. Eighty-five percent of our communication—from those who have studied this sort of thing—is actually nonverbal."

Wharton had deftly led the psychiatrist into a trap; Dr. Tavani had never met either Gerry Capano or Anne Marie Fahey. She had not even watched as Gerry testified. By her own definition, she had no access to the essential 85 percent of nonverbal communication she needed to properly assess a patient. Tavani, who appeared squarely behind Tom, lost much of her credibility the moment she began to diagnose "patients" who were not and never had been under her care. Moreover, she agreed that she and Tom had built up so much rapport that he had refused to speak with any other prison mental health professionals.

More defense witnesses appeared, many to speak of rumor, not fact, and it soon became obvious that the crux of the defense case would be the testimony of Tom Capano himself. As Judge Lee had noted, Tom did, indeed, want to get to the jury. He had been a popular, well-liked man for all of his adult life. Apparently he felt that his most compelling evidence was his own personality and his ability to explain to the jurors the reality of what had happened on the night of June 27, 1996.

DEFENSE attorneys in homicide trials fight to keep their clients off the witness stand. Once the defendant finishes with the friendly questions of his own lawyers, he will face cross-examination. Any legal expert would have warned Tom not to testify, and his four attorneys did just that. Judge Lee certainly went over the pitfalls with him. But those who knew Tom would have bet money that he was going to do it. He had backed off reluctantly from handling his own defense, but a week later, on December 16, 1998, Tom rose from the defense table to take the witness stand. The jury was taken off guard; the mouths of three jurors actually dropped open. The Faheys looked alert and suspicious.

Tom placed his hand on the Bible to be sworn in, but as he sat down, his arm hit it, knocking the Bible from its place. He tried to grab it as it fell to the floor, but failed. It was a jarring moment. Someone far back whispered low enough so only her neighbors could hear, "So much for God's truth."

In a navy blue suit and red tie, with his floppy pompadour neatly combed, Tom was ready to explain everything in his own words. He seemed self-contained and happy to have his time in the spotlight. His cheering section was packed with relatives—his mother in her wheelchair with his cousin Loretta, his daughters, his extended family (but not Kay), all of them smiling tensely at him. Anne Marie's family was there, too, to hear, for the first time, what Tom might say about their sister's disappearance. There were new faces in the gallery, and some who had been there every day without fail. Emily Hensel and Kurt Zaller were the most constant court watchers—they had been first in line every morning since the first day.

THE court transcripts of Tom Capano talking about himself and blaming others for the crimes he was accused of would fill nine transcript books—books whose type had been reduced so that four pages could be printed on one. In person, he was a natural talker, very competent and in control. He had a wonderful voice, soft and reassuring, a voice that might have belonged to a movie star, a preacher, or a politician. He spoke directly to the jurors, giving them more of his attention than he gave to Joe Oteri, who conducted the direct examination.

Tom gave his life's history, sparing no good deed he had done and emphasizing that he was not as wealthy as his brothers. In a sidebar, the state objected to an endless recitation of Tom's benevolence and Oberly said it was only traditional character evidence. Connolly reminded the defense attorneys that if they "wanted to get in all the good stuff, we have to get in all the bad stuff."

At this point Judge Lee sided with the defense attorneys, but warned them, "At some stage before you canonize him, understand that there will come a time and place when the other side of Tom becomes an issue."

After he had finished telling about his work with the church, the poor, the elderly, and small children, Tom answered questions about his brother Gerry, pointing out that he was "an overgrown kid" who had been nice to Tom's daughters. And it was perfectly natural that he had purchased a large cooler to say thank you to Gerry. He had put the cooler in the crawl space under his house, however, waiting for the family Fourth of July party to give it to him.

There was nothing new in Tom's testimony; he stuck close to the scenario already presented by the defense, although he often wandered off into long, ponderous explanations. When he did that, he asked Oteri, "Am I rambling?" and explained that his medications had not kicked in or, conversely, had kicked in too much.

When Tom spoke of Debby, it was to describe her as a woman who had virtually forced herself on him. "I wasn't particularly interested in fooling around with somebody who—that if I did—could easily result in the loss of my job."

He was far from gallant. There was an audible *whoosh* from the gallery when he said, "Secondly, Debby was by far *not* the most attractive female of the group. . . . And, third, one of the things you learn playing high school football is there's a phrase beginning with *B F.* [Buddy fucking.] You never do that," Tom told the jury. "Her husband, Dave, wasn't a friend of mine, but we worked together— you just never fool around with a friend's lady."

But of course, he had.

Tom's testimony continued day after day, morning to late afternoon. After he had pointed out how duplicitous Debby MacIntyre was and that she was not to be believed, he began on Anne Marie Fahey. Tom made it a point to refer to Anne Marie, her family, and her friends by their first names, as if to show that he was intimately acquainted with all of them. And in a sense, he was; he had insinuated himself into her life, demanding to meet her friends and family, to know everything about them—just as he had made it a point to know everything about Anne Marie.

It was four days before Christmas when Tom half smiled as he told the jury how well he had known Anne Marie and how much she had trusted him. "She told me all the deep dark secrets of the Fahey family. I know them all," he confided. "Again—assuming she was telling me the truth. And one of my vanities is that I'm pretty good at keeping confidences. I don't intend to talk about them. I didn't intend to talk about them then and I don't intend to talk about them now."

Almost immediately, Tom set about smearing Anne Marie's image. "She was absolutely insistent [about telling of her personal background]. She told me she had a very wild period in her life when she was, in her own words, promiscuous. . . . She felt compelled to tell me that she had been so wild that she had been tested for AIDS. I was expecting some deep dark secret." Tom chuckled.

He continued to expose a dead girl to a list of smirking surmises about her transgressions. She had once dated a man of another race, she had had a "nervous breakdown," and she had anorexia. Still saying how good he was in keeping confidences, Tom wrinkled his forehead trying to think of more of Anne Marie's alleged secrets to tell the jury. "There are probably other confidences she shared with me," he apologized, "but I don't remember right now."

To anyone listening, Tom's testimony about Anne Marie was a brutal exposure of her life as *he* wanted the world to see it. There was no way of knowing if what he was saying was true. In his recitation, Tom was always the kindly friend who gave her good advice on friends, relatives, and financial matters. He had been unfailingly generous. He had bought most of her clothes and made sure that she had enough to eat. He alone had known what really went on in her heart.

At one point, Tom told the jurors that Anne Marie hadn't even been a very good Catholic. "Anne Marie was not a devout Catholic just as I'm not a devout Catholic. . . . We were both what are referred to as 'cafeteria Catholics.' Those things we liked, we did—and those things we didn't like, we ignored."

No one doubted that Tom was directing his own case now. The life seemed to have gone out of Joe Oteri. He would ask a short question and his client took off from there. Tom was a race car out of control, talking about whatever he wanted and apparently convinced that he was making a good impression as he described Anne Marie's failings and his efforts to look after her.

From time to time, he reminded the jurors: "I've tried very hard not to trash people."

On December 21, Joe Oteri had finally moved through Tom's tedious asides and comments to the evening of June 27. Tom confirmed that he and Anne Marie had gone to the Ristorante Panorama. They had gone there, he said, to discuss her problem with anorexia—over dinner. "And so we weren't yucking it up," Tom explained. "The atmosphere was serious but not any worse than that."

Then he went on to say that "something serious" had occurred regarding the menu, however. "Panorama has two types of calamari on the menu; one is breaded and deep fried and the other is not—it's sautéed in a garlic sauce and it's terrific," Tom told the jurors. "Well, she brought us the wrong calamari dish. And Anne Marie was quite upset—she had worked so many years in restaurants that she had no patience for people who make mistakes like that. . . . She had the idea most of the day in her head she was going to eat one of her favorite dishes that night and the waitress screws it up . . . so she was very upset about that."

Otherwise, Tom said, their meal had been pleasant. They had drinks and wine, and they had discussed leaving more than a 20 percent tip even though "the waitress was a klutz."

They had left Panorama about nine-fifteen. "We talked mostly about the Olympics on the way home." Tom said he'd told Anne Marie he could get tickets for her, "and she got all animated . . . and said, 'You lie!' She was quite excited."

He thought it had taken them about half an hour to get to Wilmington, driving down I-95 and exiting at 202 southbound. They had gone to Anne Marie's apartment first. "We had talked about if she was awake enough—[so] we decided to watch ER together . . . at my house because my house was cool and her house was hot as blazes. . . . So she ran upstairs, took the doggie bag from the restaurant with her—I want to mention that. She said she was probably going to change. She was used to me every week giving her her food supply, the things I learned she would eat. And so I think I had a little Acme bag with some soups and grains and things like that that she brought up as well."

Tom added that the perishables he had for her were in his refrigerator on Grant Avenue. "The apartment was so hot she came right back down again." ER was about to start, he said, and she kept clothes at his house she could change into; he had T-shirts and small-size men's gym shorts there.

"Did she turn on the air conditioner in her apartment?" Oteri asked.

"I don't believe she did." She hadn't been up there more than ten minutes, Tom said.

"What time did you arrive back at your house on Grant Avenue?"

"*ER* had started—but just barely."

"So that would place it at shortly after ten o'clock?"

"That is correct."

"Where did you park your car?"

"In the garage—and on that point," Tom added, "my garage was so narrow that if I pulled in, it was impossible for somebody on the passenger seat to get out, so Anne Marie would get out. . . . I pulled in and she walked in after me."

Tom recalled that it was very cool in the great room because his air conditioner had been on all day. "We watched *ER.*"

"Did anyone change their clothing—?" Oteri began to ask.

"Actually, Anne Marie took off her panty hose just for the sake of being more comfortable. . . . She did not bother changing into any other clothes. . . . I just took off my suit coat and tie. We both took off our shoes."

"Where were you situated while you were watching *ER?* Who was where?"

The courtroom was hushed, waiting to hear what would come next. Tom's answers were growing more lengthy and complex, and it took a careful ear to extract the kernel of an answer to the question that Oteri had asked from all the words, words, words.

"I typically would sit in the daddy chair—the recliner. And Annie would stretch out as best she could on the love seat. It was a love seat—it was not a sofa. It was not a sleeper couch as some people have said. It was not—it was big enough for her to lie down on but only with her knees pulled up. . . . Now, during the course of the TV show, at one point I went off and sat on the couch with her and she might lay her head on my shoulder or something like that. And we definitely did do that. It was pretty much how it was going at the end of the show."

"And you watched the entire show with her?"

"Yes. Although Anne Marie—as Anne Marie always did—well, most of the time did—Anne Marie often falls asleep in front of the television and never sees the end of an eleven o'clock show because she wakes up so early in the morning. At one point Anne Marie fell asleep and I didn't wake her up. So I saw the entire show and she did not. I did wake her up for the end."

Tom's words flew together, but haltingly and repetitiously. It almost seemed as if he was viewing another scene in his head, one he was hesitant to describe.

"Could you move without waking her up? Could you get up or down without waking her?" Oteri asked.

"Yes. Yes."

"The show ends at eleven o'clock. After the show ends, what did you do?"

"Well, I heard the phone ringing sometime during the show. I didn't bother answering. I suspected it was Debby because I had told Debby I would probably see her later that evening. And it was not at all unusual for Debby to come over, say eleven o'clock at night, and spend the night, especially during the summer, when her kids were out of school. I remember how the show ended but at the end of the show, I got up to use the powder room, so I checked my voice mail, and sure enough, there was a message from Debby."

"Were you concerned she would come over?" Oteri asked.

"No. Because I think—I mean, what I figured was that, you know, Anne Marie and I might, you know, hang out to the end of the news. Then I might take her home. Sometimes we would both fall asleep. There were literally times when she would wake up at one-thirty, two o'clock in the morning, and we were both sound asleep, and she would come over and kick me and say, 'Come on, Capano, you got to drive me home.' Sometimes she did spend the night." Tom blinked at Oteri and asked, "Where was I?"

"Talking about the phone call. You went into—"

"As I suspected, it was a call from Debby, and I did call her back from the study." Tom seemed back on track now. "And we had a brief and pleasant conversation. She started on her normal Tatnall subject, which was always a red flag before my eyes. And she said, 'Can I come over now?' And I said, 'Not right now, you know. I've got company. It will have to be later,' or something like that. And I just hung up."

Tom said it was about eleven then. He said he'd gone back to the great room to be sure that Anne Marie hadn't fallen asleep again. "We had both sort of stretched out on the love seat, talking. . . . I knew we both had the next day off . . . and she really did tell me she might be going to the beach with Kim or going to the outlets and [we were] talking about my potential golf game. I figured I'd be taking her home—probably by the end of the news, or she might decide to stay as long as the beginning of Letterman. We were winding down the evening."

Tom went on for some time about the golf game he had hoped to play on Friday and some in the gallery sighed. What did that have to do with anything?

"You said you stretched out on the love seat?" Oteri asked, bringing Tom back to the vital night.

"No. Well, we didn't lie down next to each other. I don't mean to give that impression. We were sitting right next to each other . . . our legs were stretched out straight." He explained that Anne Marie was to his left, and "adjacent to my body."

"Any parts of her body touch your body?"

"Pretty much her entire right side."

"Were you engaged in any form of—"

"No, no."

"—kissing or anything?"

"No. No. Not that way." There was, at times, a certain prissiness about Tom; it was hard to picture him as the man who had bragged about having so many mistresses. When he was disturbed with a question, he bubbled out a string of "No, no, no, no, no, no, no's," as if he were truly shocked.

"All right," Oteri said, "what happened next, sir?"

"Well, the next thing I knew," Tom answered in a rush, "Debby MacIntyre was in the room. She must have entered the front door. She had a key to my house and I had a key to her house. I even had a garage door opener for her house. And she was pretty ballistic at the time."

The courtroom buzzed. Although Gene Maurer had hinted at it when he cross-examined Debby, this was the first outright testimony that put her in Tom's house on the last night Anne Marie was seen.

Tom testified that Debby had used her key to come through his front door. She would have to have entered at his front door, walked down a few steps, turned left through a narrow hallway to the kitchen. A few steps more and she was in the great room.

"We didn't hear her come in because of the noise of the air conditioner," Tom said. "And Debby also has a very soft tread. She's a very small lady, and we didn't realize she was there until she started yelling. I heard her before I saw her. She was yelling as she got closer to the love seat. And then I saw her standing more or less at the end of the love seat. And yelling."

Tom said Debby had been on the right side of the love seat, a woman furious. "She was yelling, 'Who's this? What is this all about? Is this why you couldn't see me?' "

And suddenly, Tom detoured to editorialize on Debby's work pressures, his "red flags" when the Tatnall School was mentioned. He wanted the jurors to know that it was not strange that Debby had snapped.

"As far as she was concerned, basically I was spending all my romantic time with her. So all of this is sort of coming out and I'm trying to say, 'Relax. Let's slow down. I mean, Anne Marie and I are friends—' "

Oteri interrupted to ask what Debby had been wearing.

"I know she had on a T-shirt and some kind of shorts and carrying a little something—"

"Was that 'something' a purse—or do you know what it was?"

"Something a woman might carry around in the summertime for personal stuff."

Tom testified that he had been caught between two angry women. "I was listening to Anne Marie saying, 'Capano, what the hell is this?' And I was turning to Anne Marie to try to explain, to say, you know, 'Hold up,' " Tom said, speaking faster with remembered emotion. "And I got up. I stood up to face Debby. And Anne Marie is in the background muttering, 'I don't want to put up with garbage like this.' And she actually had gotten her panty hose from wherever she had thrown them or put them on the table, and she said, 'I want to go and I want to go now.'

"And she started to put—I was glancing back and forth between Anne Marie and Debby. And Annie was in the process of pulling her panty hose up and getting her shoes—"

"You were standing?" Oteri rushed to say.

"Yes."

"And Annie was—"

Colm Connolly objected to the leading question. Oteri was trying desperately to help Tom get his story out in a way that made some kind of sense. Judge Lee sustained the objection.

"I was standing."

"Where was Anne Marie in relation to you?"

". . . to my right, and Debby was more or less in front of me. As I said, Anne Marie was pulling on her panty hose, and you know, she wasn't screaming at me but she was making it quite clear whatever was going on here was ridiculous and [she] wanted no part of it and she wanted to go home immediately."

"What was Debby doing?"

"Debby was off the wall," Tom said, his face expressing shock. "Debby—I had known Debby a long time. Debby was completely snapped. She was all red from the neck up. She was not coherent. I'm trying to explain to her that 'This is not what you're trying to make it out to be. Anne Marie and I are friends. You know, I have female friends.' "

Tom testified that Debby wasn't even listening to him. "She was starting to cry and she was saying, 'All these years I've waited for you,' and things that just didn't need to be said."

"How long did this incident take?"

"Which incident?" Tom had been so caught up in his own words. "I mean, what part of the incident?"

"From the time she came in until the time you're telling us about—the hollering, and . . ."

Tom could not give an estimate.

"All right," Oteri said evenly. "Did something happen after you stood up?"

"Yes."

"Tell the jury what happened."

"Debby shot Anne Marie," Tom said flatly. "And it was absolutely, positively, and certainly accidental."

So there it was. The terrible accident. Tom stared ahead and stopped in the middle of his long explanation, seemingly unable to pick up the thread of his thoughts.

"Tell the jury what happened, Tom," Oteri urged.

"She had bought this gun," Tom said, now incorporating a number of elements that touched on previous testimony, "which she claims she gave to me, but she had bought this gun in May for self-protection. And she particularly made a point of having it with her if she went anyplace at night. Debby frightens very easily. And so she must have had the damned thing in her little carry thing, and the next thing I know I see the gun in her left hand—Debby is left-handed.

"And Anne Marie even saw it and said, 'Oh, my God,' like making fun of it. I couldn't even take it seriously. She never threatened me; she never threatened Anne Marie. She basically said things that were suicidal. You know, 'After all this time, if I can't have you and if you want somebody younger and prettier,' and all that sort of stuff. She said, 'I have nothing to live for. I might as well shoot myself.' This is all the talk of somebody who had lost it," Tom said confidently. "So—"

"Where was the gun while she was doing this?" Oteri asked.

But Tom's testimony had become a virtual monologue; he seemed to have forgotten his lead defense attorney completely.

Finally, he answered, "The gun was in her left hand, which was down. I didn't think it was in any kind of threatening position."

"Not pointed at you or Anne Marie?"

"No . . . and I, again, I looked in Anne Marie's direction to see how far she was getting, and when I looked back to Debby, the left arm was coming up and I thought, Oh my God, she's going to shoot herself! And so I reached out with my right hand to grab her left hand to pull the gun away from herself. And as I did that, a shot went off. I couldn't believe it. And she couldn't believe it either."

Tom said that even though Debby had "snapped," she was able to tell him later that she didn't have the clip in the gun. But a bullet had somehow come out.

The Faheys sat rigid. Whether they believed Tom or not, it was the first time they had heard about their sister's last moments. They listened for some information that might let them know she hadn't suffered. That was the dread they had lived with.

"I didn't hear anything from Anne Marie," Tom continued, scarcely taking a breath. "So I looked back to Anne Marie and she was motionless on the sofa. And I said, 'No, this can't be possible,' and I checked her, and sure enough, she had a head wound on the right side of her head near her ear. And then I became a wreck. Debby became a wreck, too."

Tom said that he had pulled Anne Marie off the sofa and tried CPR, after Anne Marie didn't respond to "little smacks to her face."

"I even got Debby involved in the CPR efforts." He said he had put a pillow under Anne Marie's head and looked for a flashlight to see if her eyes were dilated. "Or," he asked himself aloud, "were they the opposite of 'dilate'? No. *Dilate*. And they didn't."

They had both worked over Anne Marie for a long time, Tom said, as long as there seemed to be any chance she was alive. Tom described his state of shock, and Debby's. "So you got two people in a state of shock—and one dead," he said, drawing a breath.

"Did you call nine-one-one or anybody else?" Oteri asked.

"No," Tom said with regret in his voice. "Most cowardly, horrible thing I've ever done in my life. It was like my whole life flashed before me."

What was a man to do? Tom looked at the jury imploringly. Debby was sobbing and hysterical, his life was flashing before his eyes. "I always thought I was a guy with some guts, and I wasn't.

And I'm just being selfish, too, to protect myself and also to protect Debby. And so, since I knew the paramedics could not do anything—I knew Anne Marie was dead—I chose not to call the paramedics or the police but to protect myself and, to the extent I could, to protect Debby."

Oteri asked Tom what he had done then—at eleven-thirty at night, with Anne Marie dead on the floor before him.

He had tried to comfort Debby first, he said, telling her it had been an accident and not her fault. "If I had been honest with her and told her I was seeing Anne Marie and on what basis, she would not have had reason to snap."

Then Tom said he had put Debby in her car and sent her home. He would take care of what had to be done.

"After Debby has left. What do you do?" Oteri asked quietly.

"I break down," Tom recalled. "I fell apart and I cried and I screamed at myself and I punched the wall, and after about five minutes of that, I did something I'm capable of doing. I compartmentalized. And then I just said, I have to do something. What am I going to do? *What am I going to do?* And the first thing I have to do is take care of Anne Marie's body."

And then Tom said he'd remembered that he had some things downstairs that he had a choice of using. He had a brand-new garbage can—"I couldn't bring myself to think that we're talking about a corpse." He couldn't put her in a garbage can, he said, not even a brand-new one. So that left the cooler.

"I brought the cooler upstairs," he said. "I put Anne Marie in the cooler and I wrapped her in one of the cotton blankets from the guest room."

"What was she wearing?" Oteri asked.

"The same outfit she had worn to dinner. And she and her shoes were in there, and eventually I put the gun in there."

If Anne Marie was wearing her flowered dress, then where had the flowered dress come from that ended up back on the settee in her apartment? People in the gallery had read about that and looked confused.

Tom testified that he had eventually left his house on Grand Avenue that evening. And he remembered that—for some insane reason—he still had the gun with him. "I put the gun underneath the front seat of my car."

And then he remembered that he had forgotten to mention something that he wanted the jury to know. "Despite what was said from the witness stand," Tom testified, "Anne Marie had seen the gift from Talbot's. Once she saw the box, she knew exactly what it was. She was very happy. And she opened it up and she didn't break the gold seal. She *never* broke the gold seal. She looked and confirmed what it was and just gave me a very big smile. Showed she was very happy. And I imposed one condition on her . . ."

His voice trailed off. "But I guess I'm beyond that . . ."

Oteri asked Tom to speak up and he explained he had been on automatic pilot by then. "I felt as though I had to go to her apartment and bring over the gift and bring over the perishables that were in my refrigerator—like strawberries and bananas. Anyway, I had something else that I thought to bring over with me." He could not remember what it had been.

Now, Tom admitted a number of things he had done, all on "automatic pilot."

"I did make that star-six-nine call. I wanted to find out if I was the last one she had spoken to. And I heard a man's voice answer that I didn't recognize, so I realized I was not the last one. . . .

"I did go to her room. I did turn her air conditioner on. I did not touch her bed. I did not go through her closet."

Tom offered his guess that it had been Anne Marie herself who had left a jumble of shoes and a mess in her closet because she had been in such a hurry to take a shower and change before going to dinner with him.

____ *Chapter Forty-three* _____

AFTER THREE DAYS OF LISTENING to Tom, everyone in the courtroom wondered how long it would take him to finish his seemingly interminable explanations. He had yet to give his version of the long ride to Stone Harbor and the trip on Gerry's boat to Mako Alley. Perhaps he thought that if he was able to convince the jurors that Anne Marie's death was an accident, he could go home again and pick up his life. Even Debby MacIntyre would have nothing hanging over her head but a tragic accidental shooting. Tom had admitted he was a coward—but apparently he could live with that. He seemed more anxious to show the jury that he was a gentleman who always treated his women well.

On Tuesday, December 22, Tom was on the stand again, explaining how he had "compartmentalized" and done what he had to do. Gallantly, he had sent Debby home so that she wouldn't be involved. On the same trip to the basement when he chose the cooler over the garbage can as a body receptacle, he found a bottle of Clorox bleach. He estimated that he had spent only ten to fifteen minutes putting Anne Marie's body in the cooler. He wasn't sure just when he had used the bleach—before or after he went to Anne Marie's apartment. It was only a three-to-five-minute drive. He had let himself in with her keys.

"I've only done this [compartmentalizing] one other time in my life—when my father died," Tom told the jury. "And yet I didn't have enough sense not to pour Clorox straight onto a dark maroon love seat, and it left a very large discoloration."

Tom insisted that Gerry could not have seen as much blood on the couch as he had described because the Clorox had turned the maroon upholstery yellow. "I also tried to clean up [the floor]; there were some fairly light bloodstains on the carpet," he said. "And then I just sat down and tried to think of what I was going to do at this point—what I could possibly do."

Oteri had seen the effect that Tom's matter-of-fact explanations were having on the jurors and tried to soften his image. "Now," he asked, "are you normally an emotional person?"

"Yes," Tom said.

"You're not being emotional today," Oteri offered.

"No—well, first of all, I'm drugged, and secondly, I'm compartmentalizing again." Tom said that Dr. Tavani had increased his dosage of Xanax (for anxiety) and added another drug whose name he'd forgotten.

"Does that, in your opinion, account for your semi-zombielike state?" Oteri led.

Connolly objected, but was overruled. Judge Lee let Tom testify about the effects of his prescription drugs. If Lee was erring at all during this trial, it was always on the side of fairness to the defendant. He allowed Tom to go even further and explain how his father's death had made him "put his feelings in the attic."

Once more, as his testimony continued, Tom drew Debby into his accidental-death scenario, incriminating her even further. Regarding the toll back edit of calls from his phone, he testified that all of them had been placed, but not for the reasons Debby stated. Yes, he had called his office answering system to establish he was home at 12:05 A.M. And he and Debby had called back and forth about what they should do to get rid of Anne Marie's body. He had to get the cooler and the carpet out of the great room, and she had known he was far too weak to do it alone. He said Debby had volunteered to come back and help him. "She was certainly at my house no later than one," Tom said.

"When she arrived," Oteri asked, "what did you do, the two of you?"

Tom said they had carried the cooler down the steep narrow back steps to the laundry area and the garage beyond. "It was something I could never, ever have done myself," he stressed. "And she helped me. And then we moved furniture around and we rolled up the rug. It was almost wall-to-wall, with rubber padding underneath. Very heavy. It took two people to lay it when it was first brought in."

According to Tom, Debby stayed with him for a while and he reassured her over and over that Anne Marie's death had been only a horrible accident. He said he himself would bear the guilt because he had not been honest with her about Anne Marie.

Tom's avowed concern for others carried over into his testimony about Gerry's part in disposing of Anne Marie's body. He told the jury he had tried desperately not to involve his little brother, but Gerry had been adamant about not giving Tom the keys to his boat. As for Gerry's testimony that Tom had once told him he might have to kill an extortionist, Tom appeared baffled.

All he could think of by way of explanation was that Gerry was a "wiseguy wannabe. He's the one," Tom said, "showing off in his drunken state [about] his acquaintances from the strip joint in Philadelphia—the Doll House. [They] once mentioned to him that they might ask him to make use of the boat. Actually, I think he said it in front of Joey, as well. We, of course, thought it meant in connection with a drug transaction."

Tom was horrified at the suggestion that he would have involved Gerry in any murder plan. "I never, never—I wouldn't do that to my brother!"

Debby had called him early Friday morning, Tom said, asking him what he was going to do about Anne Marie's body. "I told her I wasn't certain," he testified. "Again, I wanted to shield her from knowledge in the case." But he had agreed to meet her at the Tower Hill track.

The state's case against Tom was so confining that, to show he was telling the truth, he would have to wedge into his scenario dozens of times and other details to fit. He couldn't ignore the evidence of his phone calls, his use of Kay's Suburban, the picture at the ATM, or many other inflexible elements of the case against him. He said he happened to have a chain around his house left over from the snowy winter of 1996. He had the padlock because his locker at the Wilmington Country Club had been broken into. At one point, he said, he had slipped the Beretta into the cooler and sealed it with the chain. Once again, Tom testified that he was much too weak to lift it—so Gerry had helped him put it in the back of Kay's Suburban. Their tasks accomplished in Wilmington, Tom said, he and Gerry had headed for Stone Harbor with Tom at the wheel, driving at his customary fast clip.

Throughout his testimony, Tom had chided Joe Oteri for calling him "sir," and now, in the midst of statements that were chilling even in that stifling hot courtroom, he smiled boyishly at Oteri when asked, "Would you say, sir, that you were disorganized and panicky?"

"If you call me 'Tom,' I will."

"Tom," Oteri said through gritted teeth, "would you say that you were disorganized and panicky?"

Seeming to luxuriate in his own words, Tom said, "I was disorganized trying to be organized. I'm not sure 'panicky' was the right word at that point. I was trying to focus, and as I said, trying to compartmentalize and just concentrate on the immediate task at hand and not let myself think or feel."

To protect his brother, Tom said, he had refused to tell Gerry anything, despite his "newsy" questions on the hour-and-a-half trip to the Jersey shore. Tom's testimony regarding the disposal of Anne Marie's body scarcely differed from Gerry's, although he said he didn't believe Gerry could have seen an ankle disappearing into the water. Tom spoke of how seasick he had been. The trip out on the rough sea had been tough on him. But he had persevered throughout the day. And it was a very long day, which included disposing of the couch in a Dumpster at one of Louie's construction sites. The last thing he'd had to do to cover up Anne Marie's death was cut up the bloodied carpet, stuff the pieces into garbage bags, and dispose of them in a Dumpster outside the Capanos' Holiday Inn, just across the bridge in New Jersey. (Later, of course, Tom had had to remind both Louie and the motel manager to have their Dumpsters emptied early.)

With all that accomplished, Tom said, he had gone to Kay's house to spend the evening with his girls. "I saw them twice every day," he said fondly. "The kids wanted pizza and to have me watch a video with them." He couldn't remember what movie they had seen because he fell asleep.

Whenever Tom spoke of his children, he smiled expansively, and he seemed never to miss an opportunity to explain what a perfect father he was, how much his daughters adored him, and how he cherished them. This was, perhaps, not an act; Tom appeared to see himself as the ideal family man. And yet he felt no compunction—and never had, apparently—about betraying his wife. Tom testified he had left his girls that Friday night to drive the few blocks to Debby's house. Twenty hours after Anne Marie had died of a bullet wound in her head and he had disposed of her body, he slipped into a dreamless sleep in the bed of the woman he claimed had shot her.

In an aside, Tom testified that he had told both Gerry and Debby he would protect them. "I would assume the burden. Legal protection—emotional, mental protection," he said, half smiling at the jurors. "I didn't want them to have to live with the same horrible feelings that I live with."

Continuing his testimony, Tom said that on Saturday morning, he and Debby had slept late and "made love," and then he had gone off to Air Base Carpets to buy a new rug for the great room. "I told her I was going to buy a new rug that would not go under the kitchen table so it would [not] get food stains on it."

Colm Connolly sat at the prosecution table, listening, jotting down notes. He would remember every single word Tom was saying. It seemed odd to him that Tom would say he told Debby a lie about the replacement rug. If, as Tom insisted, Debby had been the one who shot Anne Marie and helped him give CPR to her bloodied corpse, would she not have *known* why it was necessary to buy a new rug?

Tom testified about the weekend and how annoying it had been to have investigators shadowing him, "hiding outside my children's home," searching his house. It had been a terribly busy weekend for him. His girls were with him on Saturday night—and he spoke at length about that. Then on Sunday, June 30, Tom said, he had had to reassure Debby often, speak to Louie and "Kimmie," and have dinner with Kay. And several jurors blinked slightly when he added that he had also been "due to see a young lady."

"I told her I was running late," Tom said, "and then I went to where she was living. She was not in particularly good shape [due to an ankle injury]. I mean, she was barely mobile, a very stubborn type of person: 'I don't need help—I can take care of myself.' And I stayed with her for a couple of hours and, you know, tried to get her something to eat . . . she was on the first floor when I arrived, and I got her upstairs in bed and I left . . ." Tom saw Oteri's look and trailed off, ". . . and I'll stop."

So far the jury and the gallery had heard about Susan Louth, Debby, Anne Marie, and Tom's estranged wife, Kay, and now he had mentioned a mystery woman. And Connolly and Wharton were still looking for a way to bring in Linda Marandola, yet another woman, to testify. The man was apparently indefatigable.

Tom spoke of his anxiety when he realized the federal government had inserted itself into the investigation. Not only had he been concerned about coming forward at that point with all the force of the feds against him, but he had agonized over discussing Anne Marie's personal affairs.

"Directing your attention to early February 1996," Oteri asked, "did you have occasion to acquire cash?" [Oteri had to find a way to explain IRS agent Ron Poplos's discovery that Tom had withdrawn $25,000 in cash in three segments around Valentine's Day 1996.]

Tom explained that he had. He had cashed checks on two consecutive days for $8,000 and $9,000. "It just seemed kind of showy," he said, "to go back a third time—so that's why I asked Gerry if he could loan me the $8,000 in cash."

Tom said he needed $25,000 near Valentine's Day in 1996—to help Anne Marie. He said he'd begged her to let him pay for inpatient care for her in a clinic for eating disorders. He wanted her to see how serious he was about wanting to help her by showing her the actual cash. But she had thrown it back in his face.

THIS would be the last day in court before Christmas. Joe Oteri had a mountain of inflammatory testimony to neutralize before Colm Connolly cross-examined Tom, and he plodded gamely ahead. "In February 1998, you learned that Deborah MacIntyre did something, is that correct?"

"I learned that she had agreed to become a witness for the government."

"Subsequent to learning that, did you go to anyone and tell them the story you've told here?"

"No one who wasn't privileged."

"Is there a reason—tell the jury the reason," Oteri urged, "why you didn't tell anyone this story prior to trial."

"Well, I'm kind of a confidential person," Tom began. "You know, it would just sound like sour grapes at the time. I mean, she— not she, but the slickster from Philadelphia [Tom Bergstrom,

Debby's lawyer], who outwitted us. . . . And I never—to this day—I still can't believe that Debby would lie so much. I mean, that's not really Debby who came in here. So—"

"But, sir," Oteri said, managing to interrupt Tom's aimless flow of words, "you've just been *betrayed* by a woman you've been protecting for two years—"

"A woman I'm in love with," Tom declared.

"Would you not, at that point," Oteri persisted, "go on a rooftop and scream, 'I'm taking the fall for something she did'?"

". . . I was basically out of my mind for a couple of weeks and not thinking rationally," Tom explained. "There were issues with changing attorneys and my mental status and condition. That's when they really had to jack the drugs up. . . . I was just going to be looking to put together a final legal team and follow the advice of the four chiefs."

"Which was to trust the jury?" Oteri added quickly.

Tom explained that he had gone out of his mind in Gander Hill after he learned that Debby had betrayed him. He had become suicidal. "I was operating on about half my cylinders. I was confused. I was not thinking clearly. Solitary confinement has a significant effect on people. I learned," he said bleakly, "that the woman I loved and had been protecting had turned on me and stabbed me in the back, betraying me."

Tom's expression was pitiful as he said he had never betrayed Debby; he had torn *her* letters to bits and flushed them down the toilet to protect her. He was "crushed" when he learned of her betrayal, full of various medications, vulnerable, and he had allowed himself to listen to Nick Perillo when he "suggested that I do something to get revenge.

"He brought it up," Tom told the jury. "He played on the anger phase of it and told me that his profession was burglary and that I should allow him to either burglarize it himself or arrange a burglary of her house. And my brain was like mush then. . . ."

"And what happened after he made this suggestion?"

"It preyed on my mind," Tom said. "He kept bringing it up. At first, I was totally nonresponsive, and at one point I did succumb to it. I let my anger and frustration and hurt get the best of me and I agreed with him to do it."

Tom said that Perillo had asked for directions and an outline of the house. He admitted drawing the plans but he said they had taken him no more than twenty minutes to scribble down. Because he was so hurt by Debby's betrayal, he had added the two very personal requests about the mirror and sex toys in her bedroom.

Tom insisted he had changed his mind a few days later and asked Perillo to give the diagrams back. But he never saw them again—not until they appeared in this courtroom. He said that Perillo had agreed with him when he decided against the burglary. "He said, 'This is something you should not do,'" Tom recalled. "But he never gave them back to me because he told me he had seen someone he thought was an investigator enter my cell and he panicked and tore them up and flushed them down the toilet."

JUDGE LEE closed court at 4 P.M. on December 23. "Merry Christmas," he said. "We will be back here next Tuesday."

AND when court reconvened, the jurors, who had been sitting with inscrutable faces, would have to make at least two major decisions. Was Tom Capano innocent, or guilty, of killing Anne Marie Fahey? And if they should find him guilty, should they recommend to Judge Lee that he receive the death penalty?

Outside the thick stone walls of the old courthouse, there were Christmas lights in the trees of Rodney Square and streaks of snow. But there was no sign of Christmas in Courtroom 302.

_____ *Chapter Forty-four* _____

TOM HAD A STUBBLY BEARD on December 29—and not by choice; he explained to Joe Oteri that Gander Hill had run out of razors.

That day, Oteri finished up the last of his direct examination with a question that demanded an explicit answer. "Tom, did you kill Anne Marie Fahey?"

"No!" Tom said dramatically. "A thousand times, *no.*"

"Thank you," Oteri said. "Nothing further."

"I loved Anne Marie Fahey," Tom called after him.

"Nothing further."

ALTHOUGH Ferris Wharton would have leapt at the opportunity to cross-examine Tom Capano, there had been no question about who should do it. Wharton willingly stepped aside because it had to be Colm Connolly. Tom had despised the assistant U.S. attorney going into the trial, and Connolly had done nothing to endear himself to the defendant. Each day when he greeted Judge Lee, the jury, and the defense attorneys, Connolly never once acknowledged Tom. It maddened Tom further to be so completely ignored, and Connolly knew it.

Tom had no inkling of how dangerous Connolly might be to him. They had many things in common. Both had gone to Archmere Academy, where they were immensely popular and respected, and they were both attorneys. But there the similarities ended. Tom had long polished his own image as a clever attorney by surrounding himself with sycophants. His wealth, his charisma, and his connections had landed him a number of prestigious jobs, but the word in Wilmington's legal community was that he wasn't nearly as intelligent as he thought he was. On the other hand, Connolly was positively brilliant. He knew Tom's Achilles' heel and he was prepared to strike at it again and again to bring him down.

Courtroom 302 was jammed with spectators. Family members from every side were there, and a number of attorneys had come to watch the duel. The thermostat read eighty-five degrees, and it was so hot that Judge Lee dimmed the lights to give at least the illusion of coolness. The water had long since been drained from the air-conditioning system and they couldn't open the doors. They had already lost a couple of jurors to illness, and one after her arrest for possession of marijuana. As they neared the finish line, Lee didn't want to have to resort to any more alternates.

Tom's demeanor was entirely different now. He had obviously attempted to forge a bond with the jurors and had spoken directly to them when Oteri was questioning him. But as he turned toward Connolly, his smile was gone. He no longer looked friendly, and his stare was icy. His pinched expression showed his irritation.

Connolly and Wharton had planned this encounter with exactitude, jubilant when they learned that Tom was going to testify and they would be able to cross-examine him. Connolly's first questions hit Tom with the force of a boxer who jabbed, jabbed, and jabbed again before his opponent saw his fist coming. It was instantly apparent that Tom's control of the proceedings was over.

"Since June 28, 1996," Connolly asked, "how many crimes have you committed?"

Tom repeated the question, buying time. "Whatever I did," he answered finally, "—I have been charged based on the Perillo testimony, but that's a false charge. Somebody said something in here about the way I withdrew money from the bank apparently violates a federal law—which was unknown to me [the structuring violation]. I asked my brother Louis to lie before the grand jury."

"So you suborned perjury?"

"Whatever that is."

"You asked him to lie. You are a lawyer. You know what perjury is?"

"Yes."

"So you suborned perjury?"

"If that's the name of the crime."

"So you obstructed a federal investigation when you asked him to lie before a grand jury?"

"Well, I don't know if that constitutes both crimes."

"Objection, Your Honor," Oteri said. "That is not a crime. It's an attempt to obstruct."

"So you *attempted* to obstruct justice?"

"Well," Tom said with a withering look, "if that's what it is, that's what it is. I thought I was asking him to commit perjury. I don't know much about federal criminal law."

"You wanted Deborah MacIntyre to testify falsely at your bail hearing?"

"Yes, that's true."

"Any other crimes you committed after June twenty-eighth . . . ?"

"None that I know of."

"Desecration of a corpse?"

"I *said* what I did on June twenty-eighth—I already mentioned that."

"So, that's three crimes?"

"No," Tom said, and then proceeded to correct Connolly, precisely as he and Wharton had hoped he would do. "I asked my brother to lie before the grand jury. I did want Debby to lie to protect myself and also herself. And I said, generically to the first question, that whatever the crimes are that I committed on June twenty-eighth in the fact of my disposal of Anne Marie's body or anything related to that, yes, I'm guilty of them too, and I'm sure I will be charged with them."

"How many lies have you told related to the disappearance of Anne Marie Fahey . . . ?"

"Well," Tom said, annoyed, "I certainly don't have a number, but I know I never told anyone the truth. I just said I lied to everyone. I said I took her home at ten o'clock and that's the last I saw of her."

Apparently certain he had convinced the jury that Debby had killed Anne Marie, Tom was imperious with Connolly. He had given his version of Anne Marie's fatal shooting to Oteri. But now, Connolly began to question him about *everything*, beginning with his appearance in Gerry's driveway on June 28.

"It's five forty-five and you're sitting in this driveway and reading the sports page?"

"Trying to."

"You're reading the sports pages seven hours after Anne Marie Fahey died in your great room at Grant Avenue, correct?"

"I was attempting to distract myself," Tom said stiffly, "since I had already tried very hard to bury my emotions."

"This is seven hours after Debby MacIntyre, so you say, threatened to kill herself in your great room on Grant Avenue?"

"Yes—which I knew was not going to happen."

"Oh, you knew when she put that gun to her head she wasn't going to kill herself?"

"I never said she put the gun to her head," Tom said. "I said I *thought* she was going to put the gun to her head, and I also knew that Debby wouldn't do that."

"And yet you reached out to stop her?"

"Well, just in case . . . The Debby I knew I did not think [would kill herself] but I wasn't going to take any chances."

Tom had begun to differentiate between "the Debby I knew" and a kind of half woman, half she-devil he felt Debby had become under the control of the federal government and her attorney, Tom Bergstrom.

Connolly asked questions about every moment of Friday, June 28, and predictably perhaps, Tom became confused. He could not remember how many times he had seen Kay. But he was sure he had had a "pleasant" conversation with Keith Brady's secretary when he tried to arrange a golf game with Brady. It was "normal," he said.

"And this 'normal' conversation took place less than ten hours after the woman you deeply loved, as you say, was—"

"No, no, no, no, no, no." The more agitated and annoyed Tom became, the more "no's" he strung together.

"—was contemplating suicide?"

Tom had misunderstood the reference. "No, no, no, no, no, no. I'll play your game," he sniffed. "I *did* deeply love Anne Marie Fahey. You never even knew her."

"This conversation you characterized as normal occurred less than ten hours after Debby MacIntyre, a woman you have testified you deeply loved, was talking about suicide, correct?"

"Yes."

"This normal conversation is less than nine and a half hours after Anne Marie Fahey, a woman you testified you deeply loved, died in the great room?"

"Yes."

Connolly asked Tom where he had purchased the chain and lock he'd mentioned. He thought it was at the Brosius-Eliason store, but would not say definitely. Too bad. Ron Poplos had checked and found that Tom hadn't bought either one at Brosius-Eliason.

The questions hit Tom like so many rubber-tipped darts, cumulatively annoying. But Connolly led him into a minefield when he asked for specifics about the last moments of Anne Marie's life. How had they been sitting? Were their legs pointed straight out from the love seat when Debby surprised them?

"At one point we were," Tom said carefully. "I'm trying to get my timing straight. At one point she had pulled her legs up onto the love seat and sort of bent them."

Tom said neither of them had jumped up when Debby came screaming through the kitchen.

"It was such a surprise that somebody was yelling in another room in your house that you both stayed on the couch?" Connolly asked.

Tom stuck by his story that he and Anne Marie had remained seated until Debby was right next to the love seat.

"How long transpired before she entered the great room and put a gun in her left hand?"

"I can't answer that," Tom said. "Seconds seemed like minutes; minutes seemed like hours. I was all just—this whole nightmarish scene just happened so quickly."

But he was sure that Anne Marie had been angry and started to put on her panty hose because she wanted to leave. "She wants out. She wants to leave. She wants me to take her home."

Women in the courtroom looked at one another. Panty hose are not easy to put on, particularly on a hot, sticky night. Why would Anne Marie have bothered? She could have left them behind and made a run for it.

"Do you recall testifying that Anne Marie saw the gun and was making fun of it?"

"Making fun of it might not have been the right word. She was just, you know . . . 'Nonsense.' "

Tom was gradually backing down from his direct testimony; he didn't recall some of the statements he had made. But he insisted that Anne Marie hadn't been afraid of the wild woman waving a gun.

Connolly began to ask questions about where the gun was when Debby allegedly began to lift it. Its position, its angle? Where was it pointed?

Tom struggled to keep up with Connolly's questions. "The gun started to move," he said, "and as I said, my belief was that if the movement had been allowed to continue, it would have gone to her head in this fashion—" He gestured.

"So you reached out with your right arm to stop this?"

"Yes."

"What did you grab?"

"I grabbed her wrist so that I could keep it from going any further."

"How high was the gun?"

"Probably hip high, what somebody might call shooting position."

For every answer Tom gave, Connolly had three or four more questions. Tom said he had pushed the gun down toward the floor.

"So how far away are you from Anne Marie Fahey at this point?"

"Almost touching. I'm at the end of the love seat and Annie is still sitting there. I guess she had finished putting her panty hose on—which is something she *absolutely* would have done anytime. And at that point, I believe she was putting her shoes on."

"What color shoes were these?" Connolly asked and unwittingly opened up a rambling monologue from Tom about the green shoes he had bought Anne Marie in Philadelphia. But his babble was only diversionary. To those familiar with trajectory, it was unlikely that a gun pointed down at the floor could have been fired diagonally up, fatally wounding Anne Marie in the head and leaving a bloody circle on the top of the love seat.

Perhaps realizing this, Tom hastened to say that Anne Marie had not bent over to put on her shoes. He said she had her feet on the floor and was sliding them into her shoes, using only one finger. But after several more questions, he was not able to recall just how Anne Marie had managed this contortionistic feat.

Connolly tried again. "Could you describe what you saw in terms of her putting her shoes on?"

"I saw her sitting on the love seat," Tom began. "The shoes were in front of her. You've asked me if I remember her bending over. This is not something I thought of before. She certainly was not bent over in a very extreme position."

"OK," Connolly said finally. "Can you tell us where her head was positioned as she put her shoes on?"

"Straight up."

"Straight up above the top of the couch?"

"No. Maybe just the very top of her head was above the head of the love seat."

Anne Marie was five foot ten inches tall, and yet Tom said her head had been below the back of the love seat.

Tom described once more his recall of the moment Anne Marie died. After the shot sounded, he said, "the first thing I did was look at Debby in a state of complete shock and bewilderment. Debby looked at me the same way. And I know we exchanged a few words and then all of a sudden: shock. I mean, I turned to see because Anne Marie wasn't saying anything. She wasn't yelling or screaming—so I turned around and . . . I saw she had been hit."

"OK," Connolly said quietly. "Where had she been hit?"

"As I said before, the right side of her head, behind the ear."

"How close was it to her ear?"

"I can't tell."

"How many inches?"

"I don't know."

"You can't give us an estimate of how many inches away from her ear?"

Tom paused for a long time. "I didn't measure it, Mr. Connolly."

"How many inches down from the top of her head . . . ?"

"I don't know."

"Could you estimate?"

"I'm not allowed to do that."

"Was it three inches from the top of her head?"

"It may have been."

Connolly realized full well that this testimony about wounds and blood was painful for Anne Marie's family, but he also knew they wanted to get at the truth about their sister's death. More important, he was aware that as a former prosecutor, Tom knew all about bullet wounds.

Tom hedged continually now, refusing to give Connolly any specifics. He would not say how much blood there had been, citing the low light in the room. There had been some blood in Anne Marie's hair, on the carpet, on the love seat. Not a lot. He couldn't begin to estimate how much. He said Anne Marie's eyes had been open and her mouth closed as he began to give her CPR. He had shone a flashlight in her eyes to see if she was dead.

"I could tell the flashlight did not cause her eyes to be dilated," he said.

"It's your testimony that during the entire twenty minutes [you worked on her], the rigidity of her body did not change, correct?"

"Didn't seem so to me," Tom said. "I was mostly concentrating on trying to get air into her lungs and making sure her airway was not blocked."

The jurors had already heard Tom's version of the sequence of events that followed that night, but Connolly went through all of it again, questioning Tom's answers. Tom seemed more at ease now that he didn't have to discuss the position of the gun, Debby's hand, and Anne Marie on the love seat. Now that he didn't have to speak of wounds and blood.

Tom denied that he had taken the groceries and the box from Talbot's to Anne Marie's apartment to make it look as if he had left her at home at ten. It had just been a "ridiculous" thing to do, to go driving wildly through the streets of Wilmington with the gun beneath the seat of his car. Tom admitted to making the *69 phone call from her apartment. He said he had felt relieved to know that he could not be singled out as the last man to call her.

CONNOLLY had a pattern of taking Tom to the edge of an abyss and then deliberately changing direction, only to return later to the same spot with renewed intensity. Tom testified that forensic evidence would have had no importance in explaining Anne Marie's death. "My statement would be more important—what I was prepared to tell the Wilmington Police" in July 1996.

Wharton and Connolly had pored over the transcript of the complicated murder case Tom himself had prosecuted in the mid-seventies and now Connolly wound Tom's own words around him. "You knew because of your involvement in the Squeaky Saunders case," he said, "that forensic evidence is critical to determining the cause of death. Is that right?"

"Actually no, you're not right," Tom corrected once again. "That case turned entirely on the testimony of people who said they were with him at the time of the murder."

"Well, do you recall [your] actually telling the jury in that case how important forensic evidence was because the victim was shot three times?"

"I don't remember." Tom watched Connolly as if he really were the snake he had so often called him.

"Shot three times by three different people—do you remember that?"

"Now I do, yes."

"And it was critical to your argument," Connolly said, "to establish that Squeaky Saunders fired the first shot, the lethal shot?" Did Tom recall that?

"No, I don't," Tom said. "But I take your word for it. You've obviously studied it."

". . . and do you recall testimony that established the trajectory of bullets critical to deciding who fired the first shot?"

"I don't remember that." Tom looked uncomfortable. "It's 1976. I don't remember."

"The victim in that case was shot from behind by Squeaky Saunders?" Connolly pressed.

"I'm not going to talk about it."

". . . shot in the head—one lethal shot about five inches from the top of the head? Correct?"

"I'm not talking about it."

"Did you get the idea to dump the cooler in the ocean from your participation in the Squeaky Saunders case?"

Tom clamped his mouth shut for a long time, then finally said, "I most certainly did not."

"Do you remember the significance of the sluice gates in the Squeaky Saunders case?"

"Not a clue." Tom tried to sound bored, but it wasn't convincing.

"Do you remember that *you* said to the jury: 'If you're going to dump a body into a creek—especially if you're in the area of Delaware City—that creek leads out to the Delaware River and then into the ocean. Therefore, that body is going to disappear'?"

"No, I don't remember saying that."

"And then you said," Connolly continued, " 'Well, the state suggests that the people involved in dumping that body did not know that the area was controlled by sluice gates, did not expect that body to surface as soon as it did, and would be found as quickly as it was, and I think that's important.' "

Tom said he had no memory at all of that statement.

"Do you remember telling the jury in the closing argument that the gun was broken apart and was disposed of? You said, 'There's some disagreement as to who exactly had what parts of the gun . . . but the important point is that the gun was disposed of. We don't have the gun. If we had the gun, it would be a lot easier case.' "

Tom was clearly unnerved that Connolly had come up with a case he'd prosecuted twenty-two years earlier. "Perhaps I can end this nonsense," he said, fixing the prosecutor in his steely gaze, "by telling you that I remember next to nothing about this case, and it certainly has no connection whatsoever to this case or to the events of June twenty-seventh."

That was for the jurors to decide.

Connolly asked Tom about the $8,000 and $9,000 checks he had cashed in February—and then the $8,000 he had borrowed from Gerry to make a total of $25,000. "This was the twenty-five thousand dollars you wanted to give to Anne Marie Fahey?"

"That's absolutely correct and the truth."

"You had a hundred fifty-six thousand dollars in your checking account on February 8, 1996, didn't you?" Connolly asked.

"I find that difficult to believe."

"Let me show you your bank statement," Connolly said, moving toward Tom. It was obvious that Tom particularly hated having Connolly come close to him to hand him documents; his loathing was palpable. And it was just as apparent that Connolly deliberately invaded some invisible personal space of Tom's when he approached him.

"And you said you needed twenty-five thousand to shock Anne Marie?"

"Yes, I was using it for that purpose."

Tom said he had been distressed when Joe Oteri mentioned the money on direct examination. "I did want it to be confidential," he said. "I figured showing Anne Marie a check for twenty-five thousand dollars—I just figured the hospital is so many bucks a day, but I thought it would, you know, shock her and let her know how serious it was."

"So you testified twelve days ago a check would shock her?"

"I misspoke," Tom said. "A check would not have shocked her—it's a simple piece of paper. Dumping twenty-five thousand dollars on her kitchen table would at least get her attention, if not her agreement or her gratitude."

But Tom said that Anne Marie had been angry at his gesture, so he had taken the money back and put it in his bedroom closet. However, the prosecution and those who were following the case closely wondered why Tom had *really* wanted that much money in cash.

Had he offered it to Anne Marie—who made only $30,000 a year—in a grand gesture to coax her to come back to him? Perhaps she had never seen that money at all. Had he stockpiled it to hire someone who would punish or destroy her for rejecting him? Or, as he testified, had he only wanted her to get well and been so unselfishly concerned for her that he was willing to pay $25,000 to a clinic?

WHEN Tom resumed his testimony the next day, two days from 1999, the courtroom heated up along with Connolly's cross-examination. It was apparent to everyone that Tom's life had been consumed with women. He spoke freely about Anne Marie's life, letters, fears, hopes, and menstrual problems, and Connolly reminded him about Debby's belief that she and Tom would marry one day. Tom was also voluble about Debby's life, letters, fears, and, especially, her stupid mistakes.

"You believed Debby wasn't very intelligent?" Connolly asked.

"Debby was not very academic," Tom replied. "She was intelligent in some ways. In book learning, she was not."

More of Tom's letters to and about Debby were read into the record. Where Tom was concerned, she had been "submissive." He used the word often, reminding her that she had no backbone and that everyone pushed her around. Connolly asked Tom about the "buttons" he pushed to manipulate Debby. His letters proved that he had known exactly what to say to her to achieve a desired response. He had known all the things she held dear as well as those that upset her: the gold necklace he gave her for Christmas 1996 (his very first gift of jewelry), her father, her children, *his* children, her home, her sister, Tatnall, the memory of Montreal.

The jurors had heard Debby testify and knew she wasn't stupid; she had been a woman in love who was trying to believe in Tom. Even locked up, he had obviously pushed buttons and pulled strings.

Tom had a hot button, too, and Connolly knew just how incendiary it would be to mention Tom's daughters. In their very first meeting, Tom had lashed out at Connolly because one of his daughters had been called before the grand jury. Now, when Connolly quoted a passage from a letter to Debby that mentioned the four girls, Tom was instantly furious. "Do not ask me questions about my children," he spat out.

Connolly ignored the order and continued to read from Tom's letter, in which he wrote how much his daughters missed him and how unfair it was that they should be upset. "Now this idea of invoking your kids," Connolly said, "is the same thing you did with Anne Marie Fahey, right?"

"You're way out of line here."

Tom had exaggerated his daughter Katie's illness to elicit Anne Marie's sympathy and get her to resume their exchange of E-mail. "And with Debby MacIntyre," Connolly continued, aware that Tom was seething, "when things got really bad and you needed her to co-operate, you would reference your kids?"

"Don't go there."

Connolly moved on to the other people in Tom's life who had trusted him, believed in him, depended on him—and whom he had betrayed. The list was a long one: his psychiatrist, Dr. Joseph Bryer, who had once been prepared to testify that Tom was telling the truth; Tom Shopa; Debby's son, Steven; Adam Balick, the attorney he chose for Debby. Connolly had only to read Tom's own words in the endless letters he wrote, so perfectly crafted to manipulate and control. He had used his words like so many staples to pin the people in his life precisely in the position that would satisfy his needs.

_____ *Chapter Forty-five* _____

ON MONDAY, JANUARY 4, 1999, Tom was back on the witness stand, still under cross-examination. He made no attempt at all to hide the hatred in his eyes whenever he looked at Connolly.

Tom admitted that he had learned on March 17, 1998, that Debby knew about the burglary plan and had seen the maps he had drawn of her house. "At which time," Connolly said, "you wrote her a letter. You explained your version of the Perillo incident, correct?"

"I attempted to, yes."

"OK, and here again you hit on the theme of your adoration for Debby. You write: 'I wept then and I'm weeping now and trying to do it silently. Oh, God, Debby, how could you leave me like this and hurt me so? . . . Oh God, why can't I stop loving you?' That's your writing?"

"Absolutely," Tom said.

"OK," Connolly said. "Now, let's look at the letter you wrote to Susan Louth on the same day, March seventeenth: 'Dear Slutty Little Girl, My oldest cousin on my mom's side has been writing me. . . . She told me she believes I'm guilty of only two things—extreme stupidity and taking my pants down too often. . . . She also told me

. . . she thinks Debby looks like a shrew and a backstabber. Pretty perceptive. Do you think I should tell her that she swallows and loves it?'

"So on the same day you're writing how much you totally love Debby MacIntyre, you're describing to Susan Louth she's a shrew and backstabber, she swallows and she loves it. Right?"

"I was a mess during the entire month of March and my emotions went the whole gamut," Tom said. "I mean, I was depressed, I was sad, I was angry, I was vindictive. I was funny."

It was Tom's fallback position. Whenever he was faced with his dichotomous ploys, he explained that his brain had turned to "mush." And yet, he seemed completely in control of his faculties now. He fenced with Connolly, bristling whenever his daughters were mentioned. He was enraged that the police had involved them by coming to their house on Greenhill Avenue.

"Children were involved? Did they stop your children?" Connolly asked.

"No, they were obviously waiting right outside. . . . They can interview me, but they can do it in a proper manner—how did they know I wasn't coming out of the garage with a car full of kids?"

Tom's daughters had often been in the courtroom, listening to the testimony, hearing the most intimate details of their father's other life. Kay hated to have them go to court, but Tom encouraged them to be there, cheering him on.

Connolly submitted that Tom had lied to his own attorney Charlie Oberly and provided him with an anchor—one that he knew was a red herring. "You knew that Mr. Oberly spoke with members of the press, went on national TV in May of 1997—and showed the anchor to make people believe that Gerry's boat was not missing an anchor?"

"Yes, I did."

"You hadn't even told your attorneys that Debby MacIntyre was involved in the death of Anne Marie Fahey?"

"I'm not answering that."

"You hadn't told your attorneys as of January 4, 1997, that Anne Marie Fahey had been killed?"

"I'm not going to break the attorney-client privilege."

Connolly suggested that there were even more people Tom had used to protect himself: his sister, Marian, his mother, Kim Horstman. And then he marched again into the inflammatory subject of Tom's daughters, although he could not have estimated how hot his rage might burn. "Now, notwithstanding what you've told us about your deep love for your daughters, you used your daughters in this investigation, did you not?"

"*Do you really want to get into this?*" Tom's eyes warned the prosecutor not to go further.

"Did you use your daughters to impede the investigation?" Connolly persisted.

"You tormented my daughters," Tom said. "You tormented my mother."

"All right. Let's talk about your daughters."

"No," Tom said. "No, we're not."

"You were given an opportunity to make it so that your daughters would not have to be interviewed by the government," Connolly said. "All you had to do was agree to submit to an interview yourself. You didn't do that, did you?"

"That's not a choice."

"You had a choice."

"No, no, and you, as this unethical—"

The attorneys headed toward Judge Lee even as Tom started to rave at Connolly. Joe Oteri asked for a mistrial. Connolly reminded Judge Lee that the state had offered not to talk to Tom's two younger daughters. If he had signed an affidavit that he would not call them as alibi witnesses, Tom himself wouldn't even have had to talk to the investigators. But he wouldn't do that. For all of his posturing about being the perfect father, the state believed Tom's daughters were his ace in the hole and he was not above asking them to lie for him. For a long time, Tom, of course, had blocked even the taking of blood samples from his daughters to eliminate them as sources of the blood specks in the great room.

Judge Lee denied the motion for mistrial and allowed Connolly to continue questioning Tom about his daughters.

"Now," Connolly began again, "you had the opportunity to prevent your daughters from undergoing any trauma associated with an interview, correct?"

Tom rose up in his chair in such towering rage that everyone in the courtroom felt his fury. Robert Fahey and David Weiss watched the transformation from their bench with horror. Neither had ever seen a human being so angry. Capano had "steam from his ears, snakes from his eyes," Robert recalled. "His eyes were bulging. He had bulging veins in his face where people don't even have veins. At that moment, he was pure evil."

"Absolutely INCORRECT!" Tom roared at Connolly. "You heartless, gutless, soulless disgrace for a human being!"

Connolly paused, his arms folded across his chest, watching a man completely out of control. Even he hadn't expected an explosion like this.

The jury stared at Tom Capano with shocked fascination. Whenever they were confused by something in the courtroom, they had looked to Judge Lee for guidance, and they looked at him now, obviously wondering what they should do. Lee took a long deep breath. He was angry, too—but at the defendant.

Connolly started to resume his line of questioning. "You not only had the opportunity by agreeing—"

"Why don't you explain what you did to my mother?" Tom shouted, smacking the microphone in front of him.

"OK, Your Honor," Connolly said, "we did nothing to his mother—"

"You did nothing to my mother?" Tom screamed. "That's a lie right there in front of the Court!"

Judge Lee turned to the guards. "Please take Mr. Capano out of the courtroom."

As Tom was wrestled out of the courtroom, he pulled away from his guards and turned to the jury. "He's a liar!"

Robert Fahey wished he'd had a camera to record the moment as the man he felt was the real Tom Capano emerged from behind his charismatic shell, but then he felt a chill. "That was probably what my sister saw just before she died," he said. "The last face Annie saw."

THE trial was not over, nor was the cross-examination, but for all intents and purposes they had come to a stopping point. A somewhat chastened defendant took the witness stand the next morning, January 5, but no one who had seen his awesome temper would ever forget it. Judge Lee made sure that it would not happen again in his courtroom, adding his instructions to the advice Tom's own legal team had given him.

"There will be no apologies to the Court and the jury for yesterday's outburst," Lee warned. "You are simply to answer the questions directed to you by Mr. Connolly. He will be permitted to ask questions on cross-examination subject *only* to your attorneys' right to object. You will answer all questions put by Mr. Connolly. Failure to do so will result in appropriate admonitions. . . . If you refuse to accept the responsibilities of responding to cross-examination, there are Draconian sanctions which can be imposed and they will be considered."

Lee evinced such a stern presence that even a man as mercurial as Tom saw he meant business. But he still answered Connolly's questions sullenly. Finally, near the end of his cross-examination, Connolly asked Tom, "Until the first day of trial, they [the Faheys] had not heard one iota of explanation from you or anybody representing you to account for the whereabouts of their sister, correct?"

"Not from me, they hadn't," Tom agreed.

"And unless Gerry told the authorities what happened to Anne Marie Fahey, the Fahey family *still* would not know?"

"Oh no, oh no, oh no," Tom disagreed. "If Robert had called me back, if Robert had responded to me when I asked for Bud Freel, when I asked for Kim Horstman, if Kim had come to my mother's home in Stone Harbor when I asked her, it would have made a world of difference."

Tom complained because the Faheys were suing his family for "some thirty million dollars or whatever the hell the number they're throwing around is."

"Well," Connolly said, *"you've* actually talked about a book or a movie deal for this case, haven't you?"

Tom shrugged. "In jest," he said. "I have no intention of writing a book."

Connolly held out a letter Tom had written to Debby on January 29, 1998, a year earlier. "On page nine of this letter, twelve lines down, the sentence begins with 'Tonight—' "

"Yes."

"You write, 'I will focus on the book and movie stuff after the hearing next week,' right?"

"That's what it says."

"No further questions, Your Honor."

Later, on re-cross, Connolly asked Tom about why he had been so insistent that Anne Marie's best friend, Kim Horstman, join him at the shore and about why he had lied to her.

"By getting her to meet with me in person," Tom explained, "or trying to get Robert to meet with me in person, we could begin to undo everything . . . and by the way, what is the lie?"

"Well," Connolly explained, "you told her to come to Stone Harbor so you could put your heads together so you could figure out where Anne Marie might be."

"Yeah, that part," Tom said, still failing to see a lie.

"You knew where Anne Marie was."

"That part, yes," Tom admitted. "But I figured that was the

only way I could get her to attend in order to, again, move against the greater evil."

"The greater evil being?"

"What had happened to Anne Marie."

THE jury had now seen two sides of Tom Capano. Either he was the weak and vulnerable—but charming—gentleman the defense wanted them to see, or he was the self-absorbed, conscienceless sociopath the state had described, a complete and utter narcissist.

Morale was low in the defense camp. Gene Maurer was away from the courtroom doing paralegal work much of the time. Tom and his attorneys had little connection to one another; their disagreements were reflected in the way they rarely conferred anymore. He still wanted them to pull out all the stops and use his "chainsaw" approach, and they continued to try to dissuade him, even though it was like shouting into the wind.

There was a flurry of interest when the defense called a surprise witness. Kim Johnson was an attorney's wife who lived with her family across the street from Debby. In the past week, she had contacted the defense attorneys to say she had information about the case. On the stand, she testified that she had seen Debby MacIntyre drive into her driveway late in the evening sometime in June 1996. "I heard her kind of issue a terrible kind of an anguished sob as she kind of fell out of the car, and then she quickly ran to the side door of her house."

Johnson said she had mentioned what she had seen and heard to her husband. She could not be sure of the date, however, but tried on the witness stand to reconstruct it by remembering when her children had left for summer camp, almost three years earlier. She thought it had been close to July 4, and after the eleven o'clock news, on a weekday. Johnson admitted that she had never told the authorities about hearing Debby sob.

Ferris Wharton cross-examined her. He asked Johnson about pear trees that had been trimmed in the interim, and taller trees whose leafy branches had hung over Debby's driveway in June 1996, which would have obscured much of her view. She testified that she had been able to see and hear someone 205 feet away—a distance more than the length of three courtrooms. More important, Wharton asked the witness about what kind of light fixture there had been over Debby's garage door. Johnson told him the fixture had two bright bulbs in it, allowing her to see quite well. And she spoke of seeing a "flash of blond hair" as the sobbing woman passed beneath them.

Wharton knew that on the night Anne Marie died the light fixture on Debby's garage had not been the double-bulb motion-detector setup it was at present; until January 1997, it had been an old-fashioned porcelain socket with a single low-watt bulb. Moreover, Johnson admitted that, only the night before her testimony, she had refused to let the four investigators look out her window to determine what they could see from that viewpoint.

"I said I would really prefer that you not do that because my sons are in the next room," she said.

"Your husband suggested that maybe only one person go up?"

"Um-hmm."

"And you still declined?"

"I believe I did because I was concerned for my sons, who knew nothing of this."

Johnson's testimony was rendered virtually useless. No one would ever know what she might have been able to see or hear from her window, far from Debby's driveway. Both Debby and her daughter, Victoria, had blond hair, and Kim Johnson said she hadn't seen a face. She had no good reason for not coming forward sooner. Her husband listened in the back of the courtroom while she testified that he didn't remember her telling him about any incident that involved Debby MacIntyre sobbing in the night.

Tom's sister, Marian, and brother-in-law, Lee Ramunno, testified next, principally to undermine Gerry's credibility. Ramunno was garrulous and Marian obviously torn as she denigrated one brother in her efforts to save another.

Tom had been insistent that his attorneys call his mother to the witness stand to further vilify her youngest son, but they would not. Beyond compassionate regard for a woman whose heart condition made her health tenuous, Joe Oteri told Judge Lee, "We're not going to call her, for reasons of strategy permitted to all of us, not permitted to Mr. Capano. I want the record to indicate we're not calling her. It's something the four of us are in total agreement on, and Mr. Capano can do what he wants later."

The last defense witness was Angel Payne, a physical education teacher at Ursuline Academy. She testified that Katie Capano had, indeed, "fainted or fallen down" during a basketball game in the spring of 1996, when she was in the eighth grade.

"Do you recall whether Mr. Capano responded to the school when it happened," Gene Maurer asked, "and what his reaction was?"

"Not specifically," Payne said, offering a vague answer. "I know that I've talked to him about his daughters, and anything that would happen, I would call him."

"And his reaction would be?"

"He would be very upset and probably start to panic as most parents would."

Ferris Wharton had no questions to ask of the young teacher.

Wharton and Connolly then called a number of rebuttal witnesses to answer questions raised during the defense's case, among them Tom Bergstrom, Debby's attorney. Since Tom had described Bergstrom repeatedly as "the Malvern misanthrope," "the slickster," and "loathsome pond scum," the prosecutors thought the jurors might like to see the real man. Bergstrom came across as what he was: a kind man who was concerned about and involved in the case solely to protect his client. (Although he didn't advertise it, Bergstrom had not billed Debby for all the hours he spent on her case.)

Kim Horstman came back on rebuttal to testify that Tom had, indeed, told her in late May 1996 that his daughter Katie had undergone surgery to remove a brain tumor a few months earlier.

"And did he indicate anything about her recovery from surgery?" Connolly asked.

"Yes," Kim answered, "he said that she was doing much better and was going to be able to go to Europe with her uncle Lou that summer."

Now IRS agent Ron Poplos testified. Poplos had helped the investigators as they traced Tom's expenditures, deposits, and withdrawals, but he had also volunteered for a lot of the tiresome legwork. He said he had talked to the managers of a number of hardware stores, looking for the origin of the chain and padlock used on the cooler, and had never been able to trace them—particularly not to Brosius-Eliason. And it was Poplos who had spoken, however briefly, to Tom's mother, Marguerite. Since Tom had shouted at the jurors telling them to check on how badly his aging mother had been treated, Connolly asked Poplos about that.

"Did you serve a subpoena in August of 1997 on Marguerite Capano?"

"Yes, I did—It was on August twelfth," Poplos said. He had gone to her beach house in Stone Harbor.

"What were you wearing?"

"Blue jeans and a sweatshirt."

"And did you see Mrs. Capano?"

"Yes, I did," Poplos said. "I went around to the back of the house. I didn't see a door at the front—you know how beach houses are; they face the beach side. There was a glass-enclosed area open— a glass sliding door. And I knocked on the door. And she came to the door and I asked if she was Mrs. Capano. She said, 'Yes.' "

Poplos handed her the subpoena, she looked at it and shook her head, and then she closed the door. Poplos said he had been polite to her and that he had never even shown her his badge. And that was the extent of the harassment of Marguerite Capano by the federal investigators.

IN the thirteen weeks of this seemingly endless trial, the state had presented more than a hundred witnesses and was nearing the end of its long list when Bud Freel recalled for the jury the day in July when he had driven to Stone Harbor to see his friend of twenty years, Tom Capano. Bud and Kathleen had dated for six years, the Faheys were like family, and Tom was an old friend. It had seemed possible at the time that Freel could help them all by persuading Tom to talk with the police. But despite his promises, Tom never had. Thereafter, Bud had had nothing to do with him. When he left the witness stand, he walked past the defense table, never glancing at Tom.

Tall and dignified, Robert Fahey, Anne Marie's big brother, was the last witness in the prosecution's rebuttal. He read the letter he and Brian had composed and hand-delivered to Tom on July 24, 1996. They had begged him to give them the consideration that he would want if one of his own daughters was missing.

When Joe Oteri asked him if a person should always do what his lawyer told him, Robert said, "No."

"You think a person should hire a lawyer, pay him money, and then not *listen?*" Oteri asked, perplexed.

"I believe that happens," Robert said. Smothered laughter rippled in the courtroom; of late, Oteri's client had scarcely been listening to him.

Oteri suggested that Tom had only been protecting someone else. "The only thing you wanted was what *you* wanted," he said to Robert Fahey, returning to the subject of his letter to Tom, "and not what he might be doing to help someone else?"

"The only thing I wanted was my sister back, sir."

■

On Wednesday, January 13, 1999, Colm Connolly would speak to the jurors for the last time before they retired to debate the guilt or innocence of Tom Capano. Final arguments reflect the attorney who makes them. Some are emotional and some are cerebral. Connolly was—at least in court—the latter. Although he had empathized as much as he could with the agony of Anne Marie's family, he felt that the best way to bring her justice was to present the facts, the inconsistencies, the obvious lies, the sad truths about her death, to this jury of six men and six women, and to ask them to use their own common sense as they made their decision.

All the details of this case were in his head, although he occasionally glanced at a thick binder that he and Wharton had prepared so he could make reference to certain letters and E-mail printouts. Connolly had lived and breathed the investigation for more than two and a half years, not from a desk in the U.S. Attorney's office but in the field, alongside Bob Donovan, Eric Alpert, and Ron Poplos. Two of his children had been born during that time, and the son who was a baby when he started was a boy now. Sometimes, for all of them, it seemed as if their lives *were* the investigation. As Alpert had said once, Christmases came and went and they had scarcely noticed.

There was deep emotion in Connolly's heart as he began to talk. Despite his studied indifference to Tom's histrionics and rages, Connolly knew his subject well. He viewed the defendant as a cruel and dangerous man. He reviewed all of the evidence that pointed to Tom's guilt. And out of the thousands of details, he asked the jurors to concentrate on five vital categories. "The most important piece of evidence is Gerry's testimony," he said. "The second area of evidence concerns the cooler, the lock and chain. The third area concerns Deborah MacIntyre's testimony about purchasing the gun. The fourth area, I suggest to you, is the defendant's demeanor on June twenty-eighth" (the day after the murder).

"The final area of evidence," Connolly submitted, "is the defendant's testimony itself. It is not credible. His demeanor on the stand is consistent with the person Anne Marie Fahey described to her psychologist and friends. It is consistent with the person who wanted to control every aspect of Debby MacIntyre, and it is consistent with the person who would not lie still as Anne Marie Fahey embraced Michael Scanlan."

For three hours and forty-seven minutes, Connolly presented to the jurors every stitch of the net that he and the other investigators had woven to drop, finally, over Tom Capano. And the cumulative facts and Connolly's ability to link those facts together brilliantly produced the devastating profile of a man for whom the truth was only relative as it suited him. Connolly reminded the jurors that Tom himself had admitted that he had told more lies than even he could count. He was a man who was quite probably a complete narcissist—and a murderer.

Connolly played for the jury tapes of Tom's degrading and scathing phone calls to Debby after she had told the truth about the gun. She was no longer submissive to him, and hate dripped from Tom's words on these tapes. He had been frustrated in his attempts to use her. He would use *anyone*—even his precious daughters—to further his own interests.

"The defendant wanted Anne Marie Fahey to play by his rules," Connolly said as he concluded. "He is a man who does not believe he should be subjected to the same rules as everybody else. . . . He refuses to answer questions; he refuses to abide by the rules of the court. . . . He is extremely resentful when the police want to interview him. . . .

"Well, there are rules we all have to play by. Those are rules of law. Mr. Capano has received due process of law at this trial, and now it is time for you to do justice. And justice demands that you return a verdict that is consistent with all the evidence that we have presented. And the only verdict consistent with the evidence is a verdict of guilty. . . . Thank you."

EVEN in the dead of winter, it was suffocatingly hot in the courtroom. Jack O'Donnell had a strep throat, and Joe Oteri had a pounding headache when he rose to make his final arguments for the defense. Oteri was a street fighter, an attorney whose style was to raise his voice along with his arguments. Still trying to run the show, Tom had disapproved of his lawyer's footwear, annoyed when Oteri showed up that day in his lucky cowboy boots. He had warned Oteri that Wilmington was much too conservative for cowboy boots. Oteri wore them anyway.

And it was questionable whether Tom was happy with Oteri's line of argument; he suggested that Tom's actions after Anne Marie died had been too stupid to be part of any plan. No, it had all been the same grotesque accident that he had told the jurors about in his opening statement.

Oteri allowed that this trial had all the ingredients of a fictional television courtroom drama: the "kinky sex," dumping the body, lying to the victim's family and the police. "But my client is not charged with those things," he shouted. "You can't vote guilty because you don't like Tom Capano or what he did."

Tom was not, Oteri insisted, "some kind of evil genius," plotting the perfect murder. "But *this* is the gang that couldn't shoot straight." He described Tom as an incompetent bumbler who should have known he wasn't strong enough to carry a body down the basement stairs and that a Styrofoam cooler wouldn't sink. Likening Tom to the "village idiot," Oteri asked the jury, "What kind of moron would kill her in his *own* house?"

And then, Oteri said, Tom had compounded his clumsiness in a way that didn't match his intelligence. He had driven eighty miles an hour to Stone Harbor with a body in the car. "If Tom Capano wanted to plan and do this crime," Oteri said, "do you believe for one minute he couldn't have pulled it off in a less *stupid* way? It's a horror show—Tom was in a panic, running around like a maniac, hysterical."

There was no clever Tom Capano orchestrating a murder. No, Tom had been devastated by the sudden death of a woman he truly cared about, according to Oteri. It had all come about because of a jealous woman. He pointed out that Deborah MacIntyre was the shooter—the person who had fired, however accidentally, the bullet that killed Anne Marie Fahey. Oteri asked the jury to hold the gun and prove to themselves what happens when someone tries to knock the gun hand down. "See if they don't instinctively pull the trigger."

But even given the fact that the fatal shooting of Anne Marie Fahey had been accidental, Oteri was scathing in his denunciation of Debby MacIntyre. "She is a devil of deceit, that woman is," he shouted.

At a break, Oteri asked reporter Donna Renae for aspirin and she produced some from the bottom of her purse. "For a moment," she remembered, "I felt guilty. I didn't want to do anything to help him convince the jury that Tom Capano was innocent."

All told, Oteri spoke for three hours and forty-one minutes, questioning repeatedly why anyone could possibly believe the "false witnesses" that, he said, the state had based its case on: Gerry, Louie, and Debby. He reminded the jurors that they had all made deals with the prosecutors. In conclusion, he told the jurors that whatever their verdict was, the United States always won because liberty was preserved whether an innocent man was set free or a guilty man was convicted.

When Oteri returned to the defense table, Tom jumped up suddenly and held out his hand, spooking his guards, who were understandably a little jumpy now about his sudden movements. The two men, defendant and attorney, embraced awkwardly and unconvincingly.

In his closing argument, Connolly had pointed out hundreds of aspects of the defense that made no sense at all in the light of reason. In his close, Oteri had been pure emotion, reinforced with a number of epithets. The jurors had listened attentively to them both. And the media had begun to lay odds.

When Ferris Wharton began to address the jury, it was late on Wednesday afternoon and Courtroom 302 was still stifling. But no one moved. "Something happens when you crank up the volume," Wharton began, referring to Oteri's top-of-the-lungs delivery. "You get distortion." He suggested to the jury that arguments delivered in a shout didn't become any more logical. "Thomas Capano's actions speak louder than Mr. Oteri's words."

With his easy sense of humor, Wharton said he would not repeat Oteri's reading of the entire E-mail correspondence between Anne Marie and Tom. "I won't read them," he said, "not because they're not important but because you might come out of the jury box and come at me."

And well they might have; this was one of the first trials in America in which E-mail was a major evidentiary factor—but by now the jurors must surely have memorized much of the correspondence between the victim and the defendant. They already knew about Anne Marie's sad attempts to keep Tom at bay by responding to his torrent of E-mail.

For Tom Capano, Wharton pointed out, gifts meant guilt; it was his way of keeping Anne Marie in his debt, and so he had continually urged her to accept presents from him. He was a man who gave only because he wanted to get, however. "Sometimes," Wharton said, "you hug your wife because you love her—not because you expect something."

The dinner hour had come and gone, but Judge Lee had decided they would continue. This would be the last day of trial. And to help moderate the ninety-degree temperature, when the rest of the courthouse offices closed, Judge Lee had the doors to the courtroom propped open.

Anne Marie herself had written the words that best captured Tom Capano—at least in the state's estimation. Wharton read from the Easter 1996 entry in her diary: "controlling . . . manipulative . . . insecure . . . jealous . . . maniac." He looked at the jurors. "Which one of those terms *doesn't* fit Thomas Capano?"

After an hour and a half, Wharton stepped away from the lectern. It was over now, save for Judge Lee's instructions to the jury. This is usually the driest part of any trial, but no one left the gallery as Lee spoke. He explained they had only one decision to make—guilty or not guilty of first-degree murder. At one point, Lee showed his own exhaustion—and humor—as he glanced at a page and then tossed it over his shoulder, saying, "I think we've covered that."

At 9:50 P.M. on Wednesday, January 13, 1999, it was time for the jurors to retire to begin their deliberations—although surely they would get a good night's sleep first. They were taken to the Hilton in Christiana, but no one would know where they were until it was all over. It was a young jury—average age thirty-eight—and they had come from all walks of life. Tom Capano's fate was in their hands.

THE icy air outside the courthouse was a shock to both the participants and the onlookers. They had been in another world for days, weeks—months. It seemed impossible that the trial was finally over. If Tom Capano should be acquitted of Anne Marie Fahey's murder, this trial would truly be over. But before he could walk away from Gander Hill, Tom would have to post bail on the charges that he had contracted to have his brother Gerry and Deborah MacIntyre killed. And there was no question that he could come up with the money.

But if he should be found guilty, there would be another kind of trial. The jury would have to agree on a recommendation to Judge Lee about Tom's sentence: life in prison—or death by lethal injection.

Nobody expected a swift verdict; the jurors had mountains of evidence to go through, statements, tapes, letters. The cooler held a peculiar fascination. A reporter had bought an identical cooler and found that he could fit into it by lying in a fetal position. Reportedly, one of the thinner jurors accomplished the same thing, although both of them were unable to tuck their feet completely in. In order to close the lid on the Styrofoam coffin, Tom had almost certainly broken Anne Marie's legs and feet. It was a disturbing thought.

The rule of thumb with jurors is that the longer they deliberate, the more likely they are to acquit. Thursday passed. And Friday. By Saturday, the crowds on the wide courthouse steps and across the street in Rodney Square had grown bigger. Wilmingtonians were edgy, aware that many hours had passed without a verdict. Television vans lined the curb and reporters stood ready. Feelings were running so high that a phalanx of uniformed Wilmington Police officers was ready to line the path into the courthouse.

It didn't matter anymore if those who waited—either in person or in front of their televisions—had actually known Anne Marie Fahey. She had become so familiar to Delawareans that she seemed a part of their families. The wave of public sentiment seemed to be overwhelmingly against Tom Capano.

But that was the public. The vast majority of people who took an interest in the case had never been in the courtroom and knew only what the media had told them about the evidence against Tom. And for some, the thirty-one months that had elapsed since Anne Marie Fahey disappeared had softened the reality of her tragedy. The case seemed more like a soap opera now than something that had happened to a real person. But everyone had an opinion.

It was Saturday night when the word came. The jury had reached a verdict. However, it would take until Sunday morning for everyone involved to reassemble on the third floor of the Daniel J. Herrmann Courthouse. All that night, the principals waited to hear Tom Capano's fate. There would be fourteen hours between the jurors' unanimous decision and the moment they could announce what it was.

ALTHOUGH the crowd had gathered earlier, the people they wanted to see began arriving at the courthouse at 9 A.M.—Judge Lee, coatless but with a tartan scarf around his neck, Ferris Wharton, the Fahey family. Although the onlookers, unsure of the proper protocol, clapped for Lee, they were hushed as Anne Marie's siblings walked by. A relative pushed Marguerite in her wheelchair; her remarks to reporters were angry. As if she already knew what the verdict would be, she announced that her son was innocent, and was scathing about the woman—surely Debby MacIntyre—who was ruining his life. Colm Connolly and Bob Donovan were the last to jog briskly up the steps and disappear beyond the double doors.

And then the crowd pushed in toward the metal detectors just inside those doors. A hundred and fifty people squeezed into the courtroom, more packed the winding stairwell, and more than three hundred reporters and photographers stood poised on the street below.

Tom, wearing his dark blue suit, walked in surrounded by guards, but he still managed his usual smile and greeting for his mother, his daughters, his sister. On this morning, even Kay was there, all of them waiting for the words that would change *their* lives, too.

At 10:01 A.M. on January 17, as Judge Lee asked the jury foreman to read the verdict, Kathi Carlozzi stood at the doors of the courtroom, one hand protruding into the rotunda area. If the verdict was to acquit, she would put her thumb down; to convict, her thumb would be up. With that signal, word would pass down the winding stairway and out to the packed street.

Until this moment, the jurors had avoided Tom's eyes—not a good sign for any defendant. But now the jury foreman, a pipe fitter for General Motors, looked directly at Tom as he read the verdict. "Guilty as charged." The six armed guards behind Tom braced for his reaction, but he showed no emotion at all. He neither flinched nor turned to look at the jurors.

Kathi's thumb went up. Thomas J. Capano had just been found guilty of first-degree murder and a muffled roar of approval sounded from the crowds outside. The man who had been a leader among leaders in Wilmington was a pariah now. But there were those who still loved him, and they were the very people he had accused the investigators of hurting: his mother, his daughters, his sister. Marian Ramunno put her arms around her sobbing mother, and then Marguerite struggled from her wheelchair to go to Tom's daughters, who wept in shock. They had believed their father when he told them he would soon be free to come home to them. Nothing any outside force could have done came close to the despair Tom had brought to them.

And across the aisle, Anne Marie's family cried, too. They had found justice, but their sister was never coming back.

Outside, in the streets of Wilmington, there was a celebration, with cheers and whoops and clapping whenever one of the "heroes" emerged from the courthouse and walked through the honor guard of Wilmington policemen. The courthouse steps became the perfect site for press conferences, and the Faheys, David Weiss, Colm Connolly, Ferris Wharton, Joe Oteri, Jack O'Donnell, Charlie Oberly, and Gene Maurer all agreed to be interviewed by the clamoring press. The atmosphere was more like a festival than the aftermath of a murder trial.

But Colm Connolly told the crowd that this should not be a celebration. "Tom Capano put a lot of people through a lot of distress, suffering, and pain," he said. "My heart goes out to the Fahey family. . . . We don't have Anne Marie Fahey here. That's a loss that the Fahey family and all of Anne Marie's friends will never be compensated for."

Notified at home, Debby MacIntyre came down to the courthouse, walking through the crowd that parted in surprise to see her.

Tom had always told her she couldn't appear in public without his direction, but she wasn't afraid anymore. The jury had obviously believed her, and that made up for a lot of anguish and embarrassment. She told reporters that she was happy for the Faheys, and intended to go on with her life, a life in which Tom Capano would have no part.

The whole of downtown Wilmington, usually as quiet on a Sunday as a cemetery, was filled with people. Down at O'Friel's Irish Pub, Kevin Freel opened the doors early and his patrons, many of whom had known and loved Annie, lifted a beer in her memory and in triumph.

THE penalty phase of Tom's trial began on January 20, 1999, and it was fraught with pitfalls for him. The prosecutors had not been allowed to present evidence of "prior bad acts" that he might have participated in. But now, in the penalty phase, they were able to call Linda Marandola, the woman Tom had stalked and threatened over the years. His obsession with her was eerily like his fixation on Anne Marie. As they pondered what their recommendation would be—a life sentence or death—the jurors studied the woman on the witness stand. She was in her forties now, and she was no longer beautiful.

Linda Marandola testified about the phone calls, the threats, and Tom's insistence that he owned the state of Delaware and the city of Wilmington. If he could not have her, then she could not live in his city or his state. The gallery murmured when Marandola recalled that Tom had come after her many times—the last time only four months before Anne Marie Fahey died.

Ferris Wharton commented that if Tom had been chastised by the bar when his harassment of the witness first became known, all of the rest of the awful, vindictive tumbling down might not have happened. But to "the everlasting shame" of the lawyers who chose to look the other way, he had continued to feel that *he* didn't have to answer to the laws of ordinary men.

Anne Marie Fahey's birthday was approaching as the penalty phase neared its close. Had she lived, she would have been thirty-three on January 27. The defense wanted very much not to have that coincide with the jury's deliberations on Tom's sentence.

His family pleaded for him; Gerry and Louie, the brothers who he felt had ultimately betrayed him, wept on the witness stand as they begged for Tom's life. Kay Ryan (no longer Capano), the wife Tom had betrayed, spoke first to the Faheys. "I can't imagine losing one of my siblings, and I'm sorry. I'm sorry for your loss. And I'm so sorry that Tom was somehow involved in this."

Kay looked as if she hadn't slept for days. No longer a part of the close-knit family she had always hoped for, she now had to bring her four daughters to court to plead for their father's life. And only for their sake, she too was going to try to save him. "Well," she began what was clearly a distasteful task for her, "I'm not here to stand by my man. I'm here for my daughters. I've been as repulsed by his vile actions and behaviors as most of you here in the courtroom have been. I will say—for everything that he's done—he has been a loving father and there has been a very close relationship he's maintained with his daughters. . . . I've said to the girls when they started learning about all these things that went on in his life that no matter what he's ever done . . . their father loved them very much.

"I think," Kay said, "for Tom to receive the death penalty would just have horrific effects on my daughters. In time, they may determine that the relationship with their father might lessen—but they should be the ones to interrupt the relationship, not by lethal injection, not by Gerry, not by the judge, not by the government. . . . If you can't do it for Tom, do it for the girls. They need him in their life."

And then Tom's daughters, tremulous teenagers, slender and lovely in their tiny skirts or tight pants, accentuating their long coltish legs, their long dark hair shining, their beautiful eyes softened by unshed tears, took turns on the stand. Alex, thirteen, Katie, a week away from her seventeenth birthday, Christy, eighteen, and Jenny, fifteen, described a man the court watchers scarcely recognized. He had taught them to drive, gone to their sports events, joked with their friends, and been a counselor to many of them. The girls were wonderful young women; that was apparent. But it was just as apparent that their father had failed them in so many ways.

And now, Tom summoned all of those whom his attorneys had refused to call earlier. His mother, Marguerite, in her wheelchair, pleaded for his life as Joe Oteri gently questioned her. She didn't understand the rules of law that said his guilt had already been established and that she was allowed only to ask that he live. Judge Lee had to remind her she could not tell the jury that her son was not guilty of murder.

Father Roberto Balducelli, his face a study of compassion and kindness, could barely hear the questions Oteri put to him, but the old priest dutifully recalled all of Tom's good works for the church.

Tom himself had the right to allocution, the right to speak on his own behalf. He could no longer argue his innocence; if he took the stand, he must stay within strict guidelines and beg for mercy. It was, of course, not in him to beg, but he took out the notes he had prepared.

"I hope you can appreciate," he began somewhat petulantly, "that it is pretty difficult for me to speak to people who have already rejected me. . . . What's the use? You've made your decision and I'd be less than honest if I didn't tell you we're still reeling from it."

He turned his face away from the jurors, rejecting *them*. And Tom began a rambling monologue in which he referred to himself in the third person. "The Tom Capano that used to exist was someone people trusted, sometimes with their lives . . . people liked me. A friend of mine who served in Vietnam once said that if Tom Capano is your friend, he'll take a bullet for you. One of my cousins tells me I'm loyal as a dog."

Tom quoted the Beatles song "Yesterday," which summed him up, he said; he was, indeed, "half the man I used to be." A "hundred-watt lightbulb back, say, in 1995, and what am I today? Twenty-five-watt lightbulb? Maybe a seven-and-a-half-watt nightlight."

Tom blamed his situation on the "duplicity of friends," of people he had helped who had deserted him. His words were a paean of self-pity. "My proudest accomplishment by far are my four daughters. . . . The argument will be made that I'm somewhat of a monster because I allowed them to communicate with Harry Fusco [the convicted sex offender in jail with Tom]. I'm not allowed to talk about the evidence but I can tell you this. I'm proud of my girls. A lonely, deserted individual, and they were willing to give their time [to Harry]. . . . If you think I'm perverted, I can't help that."

Then Tom wandered to the edge of the guidelines for allocution and fell off as he began to harangue the prosecutors. "My kids were harassed. They were lied to and—"

"We're done." Judge Lee rose up from the bench, sick to death of Tom's arrogance. "Please take Mr. Capano out of the courtroom."

"I take it back," Tom cried out, and Lee allowed him to stay. Tom then continued to tell the jury and those gathered in the courtroom what a valuable person he was. He would not beg for his life, he said, but asked to be allowed to live for the sake of his mother and daughters. He did not admit that he had killed Anne Marie, and his remarks only reaffirmed that he was a human being whose main concern was himself—his image, his wants, his needs. Despite all the cogent arguments, all the rhetoric, from a half dozen excellent attorneys, it was Tom himself who left that negative picture in the minds of the jurors.

In order to return with a recommendation that Tom Capano be sentenced to death, the jurors would have to agree by a majority vote that the *aggravating* factors of his crime and his capability for violence outweighed the *mitigating* factors of his past good works, his family's need for him, and the possibility that he might be a useful person, even behind bars, in helping others. But whatever they decided, the onus would not be on them but on Judge Lee when it came to the final decision. They would only recommend a sentence for the convicted man.

Colm Connolly reminded the jury that the state had already proven beyond a reasonable doubt that Anne Marie's murder was committed as the result of substantial planning and premeditation. These were two powerful aggravating factors. Gerry's testimony had shown that as early as February 1996 Tom had begun to plan not only a murder but also the disposal of the body of his victim.

"We talked about the defendant's behavior on June 28," Connolly reminded the jury. "How calm he was. Think about the presence of mind to hit star six-nine from Anne Marie's apartment to place her in that apartment. Think about the planning that had to go into hitting the eight-hundred number thirteen minutes later back at the defendant's home to create a false alibi. And then, think again, the final category I spoke [about] how ludicrous the defendant's story was—how it defies common sense. . . . There's no rational explanation to account for all the mounds and pieces of evidence that we gave you except for the idea that the defendant planned and premeditated this crime."

Connolly remarked that Oteri's "village idiot" theory didn't make sense. "The issue he raised was that you'd never commit a murder in your own house. But you *would*. Because if you take somebody in a car, you run the risk that somebody else might be there. You take them out to the woods, you don't know who's going to be around. The *only* environment Tom Capano controlled absolutely on June 27, 1996, was the environment at 2302 Grant Avenue."

He reminded the jurors that had it not been for a "pin drop size blood stain," Tom had come close to getting away with murder. Tom had believed that he had a good plan, Connolly said, and he had believed he controlled local law enforcement. "Remember, Henry Herndon was the managing partner of the defendant's law firm when that tape that you heard—that tape that had to do with Linda Marandola—was played for Herndon and *nothing happened.* Now, you heard that tape. How could anybody listen to that tape and not think something horrible was going on?"

Connolly pointed out that the tapes that showed Tom ordering physical injury and harassment of Linda Marandola, a woman he could not have, had been played for Mayor Dan Frawley long before Tom became his right-hand man. "He [Tom] had a track record of getting away with things," Connolly said. "He thought he could control Wilmington police. He had his contacts. . . ."

Without retrying the case, Connolly reminded the jurors of the crime and the cover-up, of Tom's absolute self-interest as he used other people to buy the gun, to help him get rid of the body. And the cover-up. How cruel to let the victim's family suffer. "He could have saved a lot of people from a lot of pain and a lot of suffering," Connolly said. "He didn't. Think about the callousness of stuffing Anne Marie Fahey's body in the cooler. What kind of a person do you have to be to be capable of that? What kind of person do you have to be to be reading the sports pages the next morning while you're sitting in your brother's driveway and a person you claim you 'deeply love' had been stuffed into a cooler by you less than a half day before? What kind of a person do you have to be to dump the body sixty miles out in the ocean? . . . You need to think about that."

Tom, Connolly pointed out, had done nothing in prison thus far to suggest he would ever obey the rules, much less help other prisoners learn to read. And his daughters? When, really, had Tom thought about his daughters? "When he says to her [Linda Marandola] 'I wish you could have been the mother of my first born'?" Connolly continued. "When he went to Gerry . . . about loaning him the boat and the gun? When he bought the cooler? . . . Was he thinking about his daughters on June 27th, 1996? No, he was thinking of himself."

Perhaps the most devastating example of what Tom, the man who claimed to be a protective father, had done was caught in the letter Connolly now read to the jury. It was written to Tom from Harry Fusco in September 1998. " 'Tom, thank you for letting me talk to the kids. I love them very much as I know they love me very much. They are like me—like my own—and Katie has said I am like "Dad." . . . The girls sent me a picture of all of them, and to protect them, you, and myself, I tell everyone they are my kids . . .'

"He did know Harry Fusco was in communication with his daughters," Connolly told the jury. "And if he really loved his daughters, he would not have put them in communication with Harry Fusco. Having your daughters send pictures to a convicted child molester is not loving your daughters."

Finally, Connolly submitted to the jury that there was no argument at all for keeping Tom Capano alive. He had had every privilege, but he had wasted his heritage and used the people who loved him most. "Evil is the absence of good," Connolly said, quoting a Catholic teaching that evil is not an existence in and of itself. "Like a vacuum. That's what the defendant is; he's a black hole. He's a vacuum of evilness, and he sucked in all those different people into the black hole. He's ruined their lives—from Gerry to Louie, to his daughters, his ex-wife, his mother, the Faheys, Keith Brady, [Debby MacIntyre], Susan Louth . . . Anne Marie Fahey . . ."

Jack O'Donnell, Tom's longtime friend, rose to address the jurors about the mitigating factors that argued Tom should live. He said that Tom could not have planned to murder Anne Marie. "We already know from the evidence presented," he said, "that Tom had purchased tickets and planned to take Anne Marie Fahey to a Jackson Browne concert on August 5th."

O'Donnell said that Tom could not have known that Gerry would be available on Friday, June 28. The cooler? Merely a Fourth of July gift to thank Gerry for being so nice to Tom's daughters. And Tom's demeanor, according to witnesses, had been very calm and normal the night of Anne Marie's death. Could a man planning a murder have been so calm?

Trying to save Tom's life, O'Donnell argued that he was not an entirely rational man, and had demonstrated he was given to rash and impulsive acts. "I suggest to you that when you consider all that evidence, it suggests a lack of premeditation or substantial plan."

Linda Marandola? O'Donnell said that Tom had been young, and set up by Joe Riley who had done most of the talking on the tapes to deliberately incriminate him. What had happened to Linda, O'Donnell said, was merely "phone harassment." And the very fact that she dated Tom again was proof she wasn't really afraid of him. "The watch he purchased for her in Atlantic City, she kept all those years. . . ."

O'Donnell praised Tom for his good works for the church and for the aged and infirm. "So Tom did some good things," he said, "I don't think the government disputes that." Then he painted the bleak picture of Tom's world if the jurors chose to sentence him to life in prison. "Probably more onerous punishment for him if you think about it," he said. "This is a man who could go to lunch at the finest restaurants who will be eating baloney and cheese for the rest of his life. This is a man who could travel the world who will be shuffling in leg irons at best . . . who will be confined to a nine by twelve or less cell . . . who will never hug his daughters again . . . or attend their graduations . . . or weddings . . . or other festive occasions."

O'Donnell said he felt that once Tom was transferred to a prison facility, he would have the opportunity to help other inmates. Perhaps teach them to read. "But most of all," O'Donnell concluded in a surprising fashion, "I ask you to consider the effect of your recommendations on his brothers, Louie and Gerry. . . . Gerry is a mess. If you can't find it in your hearts to recommend life for Tom because of Tom . . . do it for his mother . . . for his daughters . . . for his ex-wife . . . , please find it in your hearts to do it for Louie and especially for Gerry."

Ferris Wharton gave the last argument of the trial. He decried O'Donnell's contention that the murder of Anne Marie had been rash and impulsive, or that Linda Marandola had not been afraid of Tom. "The rekindling of Linda Marandola's relationship," he said, "is also more of a testament to the defendant's relentlessness and persistence than anything else. You've heard how he can be. You've heard how he was on the phone with Debby MacIntyre. . . . He can be charming. But above all, he was *relentless*. . . ."

How many mitigating factors were there left in Tom Capano's makeup? "Perhaps there was good in him," Wharton acknowledged. "Fifteen years ago. Ten years ago. But there was also evil in him. There was substantial evil in him. . . . Perhaps at one point, there was this duality . . . a battle going on, if you will, for his soul. But that battle has been lost. What you see now is the Tom Capano that you have to recommend a sentence for."

Wharton doubted that putting Tom in the general population of a prison for the rest of his life would be a wise idea. "There are people there to relate to," he pointed out. "There are people to control . . . to manipulate. There are people to do things for, do things to. There are the Harry Fuscos in prison. There are the Nick Perillos in prison. There are rules to be broken. There are ways to get over . . . inmates to be influenced."

Wharton noted that Tom had never once mentioned tutoring prisoners or helping them with their education during his allocution. No, he had thought, as always, of himself. And now the jurors would have to decide if the aggravating factors outweighed the mitigating factors as they looked back over Tom Capano's life and Anne Marie's death.

"And when you answer those questions," Wharton said, "you will have an opportunity to do more than simply confine the evil that Tom Capano has become. Because that type of evil is relentless and will not be confined. You will have the opportunity to end its presence in your lives, ladies and gentlemen, because that type of evil must be ended."

WHEN the jurors returned for the second time with a decision, the city of Wilmington held its breath. Tom was led into the courtroom to hear his fate, and he seemed as insouciant as always. He looked toward his mother, who sat tearfully in the courtroom, and mouthed, as he often did, "I'll be OK," or, less likely, "It'll be OK."

It was late on Thursday afternoon, January 28, 1999. The jurors recommended by a vote of ten to two that Tom Capano be put to death by lethal injection. Only once in Delaware history had a judge gone against a jury's recommendation of the death penalty.

Outside, horns blared, people clapped and cheered.

Now it was up to Judge William Swain Lee.

Chapter Forty-six

JUDGE LEE HAD MANY THINGS to consider as he decided what Tom Capano's sentence should be. The jurors' recommendation would certainly have tremendous weight, but there was one haunting voice, a voice that spoke for the whole family. It was Robert's, as he sat on the witness stand during the penalty phase, on January 21, and remembered his sister and the pain of losing her.

For sixty days, the Faheys had kept a vigil at Anne Marie's apartment and then entered a lost place, where they still were. "And the best description I can give anybody is that it is a black hole without boundaries," Robert said, "and it is as black as it gets. There is no light."

Robert talked of their search for someplace where they could feel Anne Marie's presence so they could say good-bye to her. They had been to the Grant Avenue house. "If you had a sibling or a spouse or a child or someone that you deeply cared about, and they were killed in a car accident, and that car was towed away to a junk-yard, I would argue that everybody in this courtroom would go to that junkyard and look at that car, especially if the body had never been recovered. And that was our way of trying to see where Anne Marie's last resting place was. . . . We knew in our hearts she had died in that room. And we had to go and see it and touch it and say a prayer for Anne Marie . . . by going to the place where she was brutally murdered."

Robert spoke of never having been able to have a funeral for his sister. "You think about how important a funeral is, because there are rituals, and some of the rituals I never appreciated the benefit of because they had always been there. And when they're not there, you don't have the opportunity to grieve.

"You don't have a viewing. Rather than a piece of plastic with a bullet hole in it, you generally have a wooden coffin. And you go to the funeral home, and you can say your prayers and hug everybody collectively that's there to support you. So instead of a funeral, we have a cooler for a coffin and we have images that are just very, very painful."

As pitiful a substitute as it was, they *had* all gathered around the cooler and prayed for their sister. Now, as Robert spoke, people began to cry; even reporters who *never* let their emotions show in public had tears running down their faces. Anne Marie had been with them all along, but as part of a legal puzzle, and it had been easier to look away from the real woman. But as her brother talked about her, the sounds of sniffling and nose-blowing grew stronger.

"Rather than Anne Marie being buried in a family plot next to her grandmother and her mother," Robert said, "instead of being surrounded by her family when she died, Anne Marie was surrounded by her killer and her killer's brother.

"And she was thrown over the side of a boat, wrapped in chains and anchors and rope, rather than in her finest dress. And rather than being in a coffin—whether it was a hundred thousand dollars or ten thousand—she was in an Igloo cooler.

"And rather than being buried next to her mother, she was thrown into a piece of water that's known as Mako Alley. So instead of my mother, she had sharks."

Robert remembered how his family and grandmother had gone to the shore for a week every summer. He said he and his siblings would continue to do that for their children, but it would never again be the same. "I can't go anywhere near the Atlantic Ocean, because I know my sister is out there, probably in a million pieces, and it's not a real pleasant thought."

They would never know, any of her brothers and her sister, if Anne Marie had been beaten or tormented before she died. And even though their religious beliefs told them she was safe with God, their minds would go back forever to that night when she died and wonder about that.

Kathleen would say, "I hope he shot her from behind and she never had to be afraid. I cannot bear to think that she was afraid."

AND now, Judge Lee thought of all those things as he struggled to make the most awesome decision any man can make, and one few would seek to make.

On March 16, 1999, he was finally prepared to sentence Tom Capano. The day before St. Patrick's Day was cold, much colder than the two days in January when crowds had gathered to hear the decisions the jurors had made. Spring seemed months away, the sky was leaden, mounds of dirty snow covered the curbs in front of the Daniel J. Herrmann Courthouse, and spectators bundled up against the wind. With each increment of this seemingly endless legal procedure, the crowds had grown. Now there was no room to walk; reporters, cameramen, families, friends, bystanders, and the curious filled every spare inch of the sidewalk and the wide apron of steps. People even began to climb onto the concrete walls around the steps. Some watched with binoculars from Rodney Square across the street. The television trucks weren't just from Wilmington and Philadelphia; there were network news trucks, too.

Would Tom Capano get the death penalty? Most said no. They couldn't see how the man could fall any lower than he already had. Others said he was "gonna fry," even though the death penalty in Delaware is accomplished by lethal injection.

"I feel so sad for his mother," a woman said to her friend. "Look at her there in her wheelchair with all the cameras poking in her face—they shouldn't treat an old woman like that." But, of course, they did. Running backward, photographers aimed their cameras directly into the faces of Marguerite and Tom's daughters.

Above the clamor of people talking and the sounds of traffic on the busy corner opposite the Wilmington Public Library, a crazy, cacophonous noise penetrated the air sporadically. Two men in a long 1950s Cadillac convertible drove repeatedly around the block, apparently so they could show off their horn. They laughed and waved but the crowd only stared at them. Whichever side they were on, none of the people who had gathered here found anything remotely funny about this landmark day.

The Faheys and the Capanos had arrived and gone up to the courtroom. Kay Ryan had come downtown with her daughters but she could not bear to walk past the cameras again. Her daughters entered the courthouse while she waited down the street in a friend's car. She didn't really want to hear what the judge would say.

Marguerite's wheelchair sat in the aisle near the railing on the right side of the courtroom in which Tom's sentence would be pronounced. For some reason, now that it was almost over, the Capanos and the Faheys had reversed sides of the courtroom—but then, it wasn't even the same courtroom. Another hearing was being held in Courtroom 302.

Father Balducelli held Marguerite's hand and her family crowded around. It had been one thing after another for her; Joey had undergone heart surgery and survived, again. Now she trembled as she waited to hear if her Tommy would survive.

The room was packed, and for once, Judge Lee allowed people who could not find seats to stand along the walls. Tom walked in and looked toward his mother—toward his daughters. And once more, he mouthed, "It will be all right . . . It will be all right."

Judge Lee looked at the gallery, the attorneys, and the convicted man. No one knew what he might have been thinking during all the months of Tom's trial; judges rarely betray their feelings. He had been unfailingly gracious and in control of his courtroom, but he had never once commented on the proceedings in any personal way.

Now, he began to read the statement he had prepared.

"This is the time established for the sentencing of Thomas J. Capano, who has been found guilty of murder in the first degree by a jury which also found the existence of an aggravating statutory circumstance by a vote of eleven to one, and recommended the sentence of death by a vote of ten to two. . . .

"The Court is required to give great weight to the jury's recommendation. I have completed that process."

But Judge Lee said he had found the law itself inadequate to describe what had happened during the trial just held, and he had decided to supplement his decision with further remarks.

"The gradual revelation of the personality and character of the defendant," he began, "clearly was a factor in both the verdict of the jury and its recommendation concerning appropriate sentence. It is a significant factor in my sentencing decision today.

"Thomas J. Capano entered this courtroom on trial for his life, a man presumed innocent, and almost immediately embarked on a course of conduct to rebut that presumption. Intelligent, educated, affluent, accomplished, and charming by reputation, he proceeded to negate all of the advantages his life had provided during the harsh confrontation with reality which is a criminal trial, and eventually revealed an angry, sinister, controlling, and malignant force which dominated the courtroom for months.

"From the beginning, he systematically and contemptuously degraded all of those who participated in the proceedings: the prosecutors, the witnesses, prison personnel, the Court, and his own attorneys.

"From direct insults to prosecutors to withering stares at witnesses, continuous claims of privilege from correction officers, constant violation of the rules of the Department of Correction and the limitations established by the Court, and suborning perjury, to the constant undermining of the efforts of the excellent team of lawyers he assembled to represent him, Thomas Capano needed to show everyone that he was in charge and that he held all those who he viewed as adversaries with contempt.

"In spite of imposing his will on his attorneys in matters where, by law, the decision was rightfully theirs, the possibility remained that he would be acquitted, until he insisted they adopt his unsupported theory of the case in the defense opening statement, which all but required his testimony once a promised credible witness failed to materialize.

"*Again* against the unanimous advice of his counsel, the defendant insisted on testifying and solidifying the remaining area of weakness in the state's case by presenting a story of Anne Marie Fahey's death which the jury found incredible.

"Having sealed his fate on the question of guilt or innocence, he displayed the malevolence of his nature, which became crucial in determining sentence."

Judge Lee continued to read, each sentence blasting the man who had made a mockery of his courtroom for well over three months. "The defendant," he said forcefully, "insisted on a 'chainsaw' approach, attacking, maiming, and destroying the character and lives of lovers, friends, and family who had, in his eyes, been disloyal to him in his time of need. . . .

"The defendant fully expected to get away with murder and, were it not for his own arrogance and controlling nature, he might well have succeeded. . . .

"If the virtuous Tom Capano ever existed, he no longer did at that time. He chose to use his family as a shield, make his brothers and his mistress accomplices, use his friends and attorneys for disinformation, attack the character of the prosecutor, make his mother and daughters part of a spectacle in an effort to gain sympathy, chide his brother [Gerry] to 'be a man' when the weight of the investigation fell upon him, rely on character assassination when that brother is compelled to testify, and insist that the family ostracize him for telling the truth. . . .

"He even bullied, berated, and undermined the efforts of his own lawyers, who believed they could gain his acquittal. The defendant has no one to blame for the circumstances he finds himself in today except himself. . . .

"The selfishness, arrogance, and manipulativeness of Thomas Capano," Judge Lee continued, "destroyed his own family as well as the Fahey family. He did not hesitate to use his family to commit or suborn perjury or to ask for the mercy he specifically refused to ask for himself. His only remorse is for himself. . . .

"Tom Capano does not face judgment today because his friends and family failed him. He faces judgment because he is a ruthless murderer who feels compassion for no one, and remorse only for the circumstances he finds himself in.

"He is a malignant force from whom no one he deems disloyal or adversarial can be secure, even if he is incarcerated for the rest of his life.

"No one except the defendant will ever know exactly how or why Anne Marie Fahey died. What *is* certain is that it was not a crime of passion but, rather, a crime of control. By all accounts, she had ceased to be the defendant's lover but had never escaped his sphere of influence, control, and manipulation. Anne Marie Fahey could not be permitted to end the relationship unless he said so. She could not be allowed to reject him.

"The defendant's premeditation and planning was a contingency that perhaps he hoped would never happen—but did—on the evening of June 27, 1996. He chose to destroy a possession rather than lose it; *to execute an escaping human chattel.*

"Considering and weighing all the evidence, the verdict and the recommendation of the jury was just. Mr. Capano, would you rise for sentencing, please."

And there, in that hushed courtroom, Judge William Swain Lee sentenced Tom Capano to die by lethal injection in the presence of ten witnesses. His execution date was to be June 28, 1999, three years to the day from the time he threw Anne Marie's body into the Atlantic Ocean.

THERE was an automatic appeal, and Tom Capano did not die on June 28. He is in "max max," in prison in Smyrna, Delaware. Tom was in every sense of the phrase a man who had everything. But he wanted more than that. He wanted everything *his* way. And when he took a young woman's life because she would not submit to his will, he destroyed them both.

Afterword

WHEN I RETURNED to Wilmington it was full summer, 1999, the kind of weather that always colors my memories of living in the Philadelphia-Wilmington area when I was a teenager. All the wind, snow, and rain that seemed part of Tom Capano's trial had evaporated in the drought of 1999. Only the heartiest plants kept their heads up when the city forbade watering lawns and gardens, but the honeysuckle perfumed the night as it probably has since the first settlers arrived in New Castle.

After three years of an investigation and trial that seem to have touched almost everyone in the city with sorrow for a promising life lost too soon and for families blighted with dissension and shame, I somehow expected to find that at least some of the people involved had moved away from Wilmington to start over. But no one has. The years ahead may change their decisions; more likely, they may only soften the edges of raw pain and bright memory. It is not a city one leaves; family structures reach too deeply into the earth there, and for everything that is ugly, three or four beautiful new things appear. More and more of the old row houses are being renovated, and there are traditions all around Wilmington that newer cities cannot duplicate. Joe Oteri might have figuratively waved the American flag a bit too much in his arguments to defend Tom Capano, but if he did, he picked the right city, a city integral to all our histories no matter where we live in this country.

TOM CAPANO went out of his way to refer to the Faheys as "white trash" and to suggest that Anne Marie had told him deep, dark secrets about them. But that characterization was only one of the many cruelties he practiced. Because the Faheys committed themselves to using the media to find out what happened to Anne Marie, their tough, early years—unlike those of most families—were exposed for the world to see. And that still hurts. In actual fact, the Faheys are a family of professionals now, with very comfortable lives. Kathleen believes—as they all do—that the loss of Anne Marie strengthened the bonds of their family—and they remain strong.

Kathleen and Patrick Fahey-Hosey had two sons before Anne Marie died, and they have since had a little girl. "My daughter fills an empty place in my heart," Kathleen said. "She's even got curly hair." But she sighs as she reflects on the fact that her sister never got to be a mother herself. "Anne Marie was pure sweetness," she said. "She would have been married by now. But I was lucky to have had my sister for as long as I did." Kathleen, who got her B.A. from Newman College, is now working toward her master's degree in education there.

Robert and Susan Fahey, Kevin and Linda Fahey, Brian and Rebeca Fahey all have growing families. They have worked hard to protect their children from any further publicity and they have been fairly successful. What is harder to explain, when their children ask, is what happened to their aunt.

On July 7, 1999, the Faheys at last had a memorial service for Anne Marie. "It took us," Robert said, "as long to get over the weeks of trial as it lasted—and then we had Anne Marie's funeral service."

"The service was more for the other people who loved Anne Marie," Kathleen said, "people who hadn't been through the whole process of the trial. For me, at least, the trial did bring some closure."

The Fahey family *is* suing the Capano family in a civil case. The amount of the suit—a minimum of $100,000—doesn't matter to them. "No one in the Capano family ever apologized or said they were sorry to us," Robert said. "Tom's lawyers never apologized to us or acknowledged us." The Faheys are very resentful of those Capanos who knew where Anne Marie was and "sat there for a year and a half and said not one word."

The suit against Capano Management Company, Louis Capano and Associates, Inc., Brandywine Plaza III Associates L.P., and Landmark Motels charges the four Capano brothers individually with myriad offenses ranging from conspiracy to murder. It was delayed pending the outcome of Tom's criminal trial.

Kathleen and Brian have become active in supporting the rights of crime victims. The two spoke at the twelfth annual Crime Victims' Rights Week seminar in Atlantic City, New Jersey, in April.

Kim Horstman is married and gave birth to a daughter in the summer of 1998. The baby girl's name is Anne Marie.

Ferris Wharton spent his summer vacation riding his bike across Iowa, which was just as hot as Wilmington. He awaits the inevitable, another murder case to prosecute.

Colm Connolly surprised those who expected him to stay with the U.S. Attorney's office by resigning in late March. He has since joined the Wilmington law firm of Morris, Nichols, Arsht & Tunnell as partner. The firm's clients include U.S. Steel, J. P. Morgan, and Coca-Cola. He admitted that it was a pragmatic decision. He and his wife, Anne, had their first daughter, "Maggie," on September 3, 1999. A man with four children under five has finally had to leave public service for the better salary available in the private sector. At least for now.

Bob Donovan is still with the Wilmington Police Department.

Eric Alpert is assigned currently to FBI headquarters in Washington, D.C.

Colm, Ferris, Eric, Bob, and Ron Poplos traveled to New York to see the Yankees play in July; it was the closest thing to a celebration they had after Tom Capano's conviction.

Tom's "dream team" of lawyers, whose advice he ignored, will not represent him as he appeals his death sentence from the maximum security unit at the Delaware Correctional Center in Smyrna. Oteri and O'Donnell have gone back to their practices in Boston and Florida, and Maurer and Oberly have other work to handle. Lee Ramunno—Tom's sister, Marian's, husband—will handle the appeal. The appeal process can be tortuous and lengthy, and it is unlikely that Tom will actually face death for several years. However, since the U.S. Supreme Court allowed states to bring back the death penalty, Delaware's Board of Pardons has never recommended that any death penalty sentence be reversed.

But even at this late date, Tom Capano could conceivably avoid the death penalty. It would mean letting go of his arrogance and his pride. If he were to admit to killing Anne Marie and disposing of her body to avoid the detection of his crime, and if he signed an agreement that he would not appeal a reduced sentence, some attorneys close to the case think he might live to spend his life in prison.

For his daughters, whom he professes to love above all else, would he surrender his pride?

In what could one day become a convoluted legal question, Judge William Swain Lee is seriously considering running for the governorship of Delaware. If he should win the election and be the sitting governor when Tom Capano reaches the end of the appeal process to avoid execution—save for a pardon by the top executive in Delaware—what would "Governor William Swain Lee" do? Could he step aside? And if he did, would the decision be made by another elected official who wasn't somehow connected to Tom in his earlier incarnation as a politician popular with both Democrats and Republicans in Delaware?

Keith Brady still works for the Delaware State Attorney General's office, but he has been transferred to the civil division.

Gerry and Louie Capano were sentenced on the charges they agreed to when they finally told the federal investigators what they knew about Anne Marie's death.

Gerry had to spend an hour in a jail cell in the federal courthouse before he came to the courtroom, handcuffed, for sentencing. A U.S. district judge, Sue L. Robinson, accepted his guilty plea to illegal possession of firearms by a drug user, and sentenced him to time served and three years of supervised release. He was prohibited from leaving Delaware for sixty days, and to own or possess weapons. Earlier, Gerry had forfeited his gun collection—most of it to the government—and his brand-new $35,000 truck.

Gerry and his wife, Michelle, were arrested in Stone Harbor, New Jersey, at 1:30 A.M. Sunday, August 15, 1999, and charged with disorderly conduct for shouting obscenities at each other on a local street. Stone Harbor police chief Steven O'Connor said that they also pelted the arresting officers with obscenities. They were charged and released, but, for Gerry, it might be more serious; he was still on probation.

For pleading guilty to interfering with a witness (Kristi Pepper), Louie was sentenced to one year's probation. He was also ordered to undergo urinalysis within fifteen days and take two follow-up tests. He was forbidden to own or possess guns. And fined $25.

Louie was also required to remain in Delaware for sixty days, but he begged for relief from that restriction, citing his need to travel on a moment's notice for business and to caddy for his wife at golf tournaments. A few days later, the judge lifted Louie's captivity in Delaware.

Debby MacIntyre never again felt safe in her house on Delaware Avenue—not after Tom drew diagrams of every room and described the things most precious to her to a man he believed was a burglar. Frightened, she sold the little white house and bought a semidetached home. It reminded her of better days in her childhood, and she showed me the spot where her father had taught her to roller-skate.

It was obvious that the one thing Debby always wanted and never really had was a happy family. She is a talented photographer, and the walls of her home are filled with pictures she has taken of her relatives. The best of all is a poster-sized picture of her father whirling his three-year-old granddaughter Victoria.

Things that Debby used to weep over no longer concern her. When the Wilmington Country Club told her that they were revoking her membership permanently, she laughed. After what she had been through, it didn't matter. And at almost fifty, Debby is starting out on a new career and a new life. It seems impossible to her now that she spent almost two decades trying to please Tom Capano. With counseling, she now sees her choices in life more clearly and she is certain that she will never again allow herself to be manipulated by any man. Her daughter and son have stood solidly beside her and she is very proud of them.

Debby's daughter, Victoria, and Tom's daughter Christy were longtime friends, and they bumped into each other over the 1998 Christmas holidays. They have done something that their mothers have not been able to do—and may never be able to do. They are friends again.

Debby thought she had seen and heard the last of Tom Capano, but she got a note from Father Balducelli in July of 1999. He asked that she come to his office at the rectory. "The first thing I thought," she said, "was that he was going to tell me they didn't want me on the church trip to Europe. I told him I would come right over."

The eighty-six-year-old priest, who had been Debby's priest for more than twenty years, told her that he had something for her—something he had held on to since mid-June. At the time Father Balducelli was very busy with St. Anthony's of the Hills, the camp he started for children. But now he was going away for a while and felt he had to give Debby the envelope someone had given to him.

"It was a letter from Tom," Debby said. "I had always wondered how I would feel if Tom ever wrote to me again. And the truth is that I felt nothing. I had forgiven him, I guess, a long time ago. I don't hate him—but we had nothing in common any longer. Our lives aren't connected in any way." She could see that Father Roberto wanted her to read the letter from Tom, if only so he could report back that he had delivered it. He hadn't read it, of course; he'd read only the cover letter Tom had given to him.

Tom's letter began as if nothing had ever happened, as if the past three years had only been a nightmare. "He said, 'Please sit down and write to me, Debby, privately and sincerely,' " Debby quoted. "And he said I had hurt his feelings when I testified that he meant nothing to me any longer.

"I'd hurt his feelings!" Debby laughed despite herself. "The problem was that there were three very important items missing from his letter. He didn't apologize for setting me up to be robbed. He didn't apologize for hiring somebody to kill me. And most of all," she said, serious again, "he never apologized for saying I killed Anne Marie."

Looking at his letter, which was not unlike dozens of letters he had sent her, she could, at last, see the emptiness and the narcissism of the man she had once loved. She thought, she said, of Anne Marie Fahey, who had seen through Tom a lot sooner than she herself had. "He didn't even admit he had killed Anne Marie. He just breezed forward as he always had. He thought the past didn't matter, and all he had to do was write another letter."

Debby told me that she knew she was OK. She had no reason, ever, to write to Tom Capano again. But she worried about Father Roberto and she leaned across the table to be sure that he could hear her words despite his profound deafness.

"Father, be careful," Debby said. "Tom's hurt everyone who's ever tried to help him. I don't want him to hurt you."

And looking into the old priest's eyes, Debby saw that his years had brought wisdom. He had pleaded for Tom's life, but he knew who and what Tom Capano was.

WHEN I GO BACK to Wilmington, I see all the places where Anne Marie Fahey lived and worked. And even though I never knew her, her essence seems to linger in the city where she belonged. At O'Friel's, where her banner still hangs, it seems almost possible that, if I only turn around fast enough, I can catch a glimpse of the young woman so many people loved.

_____Acknowledgments_____

WRITING THE STORY of Anne Marie Fahey's disappearance was, in many ways, the most difficult task of my career. Not only was it a tragic story; it was also complicated and convoluted, and it involved dozens of people with widely divergent opinions. While the actual writing is my task, I have been blessed with more help than I could have ever hoped for as I researched the facts. Since I am not "Jessica Fletcher" of the television series _Murder, She Wrote,_ I don't solve murders; I look for the best detectives and prosecutors in America and chronicle the way _they_ solved them and brought justice to the victims. Even though they were probably tired of talking about it, Colm Connolly, Bob Donovan, Eric Alpert, Ron Poplos, and Ferris Wharton shared their memories of this remarkable marathon investigation with me. And I could see that it had meant far more to them than merely doing their jobs.

To tell Anne Marie's story, it was necessary to write about her family, too. My admiration for the Faheys knows no bounds and I want to thank Robert Fahey and Kathleen Fahey-Hosey particularly for their contributions to my book. I will never forget your sister.

The personnel in the Daniel J. Herrmann Courthouse went out of their way to be nice to me. Thanks to Kathi Carlozzi, Dolores Bledsoe, Kathleen Feldman, Julie Chapin, Christine Mason, John White, Jeanne Cahill, Maureen McCaffery, Jean Preston, Frances White, Alexis Finlan, and Patrick O'Hare.

Thanks to Kevin Freel and the gang at O'Friel's Irish Pub, where everyone in Wilmington shows up sooner or later.

Ever since I began to gather information on this case in 1996 I have counted on my East Coast correspondents. Of them all, Eleanor Repole was the most insistent that there would one day be an answer to the continuing mystery of what happened to Anne Marie Fahey and that _I_ would write a book. You were right, Eleanor! The rest of the Delaware-Maryland–Pennsylvania–New Jersey contributors are: Mary Kemp, Valarie Metzelaar, Suzi Douglass, Dov O'Nuanain, Emily Hensel, Kurt Zaller, Laurene Eckbold, Kim Sawchuk, Terri Carpe, Loretta Lawrence, Jo Ellen Brackin, Michele Hamilton, Jane Sylvester Cox, Loretta Walsh, Peggy Carter, and Jo Ann Kirk. Some of you took photographs and some helped me understand the ambiance of the area while others helped me find my way around Wilmington, Newark, New Castle, Stone Harbor, and Cape May.

When I wrote to Debby MacIntyre, I really didn't expect her to agree to talk with me. But she did, and I do thank her for sharing her thoughts and memories about a very painful time in her life. Debby, I wish you happier days ahead.

Thanks to Tom and Dee Bergstrom, Pete Letang, Doug Most, David Weiss, Jack and Gemma Buckley, and Maria Avon.

Special thank yous go to Maureen and Phil Milford, who may know more about Wilmington than anyone and who shared that knowledge and read my manuscript to be sure I had done my research accurately. And to Donna Renae, an outstanding reporter—late of Wilmington, now of Seattle—who was able to answer every question I threw at her about the long, long trial of Tom Capano. (And to her husband, Joe de Groot, for his ribs and iced tea!) To my daughter, Leslie Rule-Wagner, for her skill at photography. Even though she spent much of her time in Delaware taking "pictures" of regional ghosts for *her* new book, she captured every image I needed for *my* book.

All books are team efforts; *this* book was more than that. Working with editors is a little like learning to dance with a new partner, and I am lucky that this is the fifth book I have written with Fred Hills and Burton Beals. We have long since learned to get along and understand each other almost intuitively. The rest of the team, all of whom worked overtime, are Leslie Ellen, Jennifer Love, Priscilla Holmes, Tracey Guest, Felice Javit, Chuck Antony, Andy Goldwasser, Edith Fowler, and the folks at Dix Type. Thanks to David Rosenthal, Annik LaFarge, and Carolyn Reidy for believing in this project.

As always, I thank my first reader, Gerry Brittingham Hay, and my lifetime literary agents, Joan and Joe Foley of the Foley Agency, and my theatrical agent, Ron Bernstein of the Gersh Agency.

This book reminded me that the bonds of family mean more than anything. I thank the family that stands behind me: Laura, Rebecca, and Matt Harris; Leslie and Kevin Wagner; Andy Rule; Mike Rule; Marni Campbell; Bruce, Machell, and O-Jazz Sherles; and Luke, Nancy, and Lucas Fiorante. To Freda and Bernie Grunwald, Donna and Stuart Basom, and cousins Chris McKenney, Sara Plushnik, Jim Sampson, Karen Hudson, Bruce Basom, Jan Schubert, Christa Hansen, Terry Hansen, Sherman Stackhouse, David Stackhouse, Lucetta May Bartley, and Glenna Jean Longwell and all their progeny.

Most of all, I thank you, my readers, for your loyalty, your letters, and your input. I can be reached through my Web page at www.annrules.com. If you wish to contribute to the friends of Anne Marie Fahey, please go to http://links4you.com/AMF/

Photo Credits